The Flower Adornment Sutra

An Annotated Translation of the Avataṃsaka Sutra

With a Commentarial Synopsis Of the Flower Adornment Sutra

Volume Six

Chapter 39 (cont'd)

Kalavinka Press
8603 39th Ave SW / Seattle, WA 98136 USA
(www.kalavinkapress.org)

Kalavinka Press is associated with the Kalavinka Dharma Association, a non-profit organized exclusively for religious educational purposes as allowed within the meaning of section 501(c)3 of the Internal RevenueCode. Kalavinka Dharma Association was founded in 1990 and gained formal approval in 2004 by the United States Internal Revenue Service as a 501(c)3 non-profit organization to which all donations are tax deductible.

To refrain from doing any manner of evil,
to respectfully perform all varieties of good,
and to purify one's own mind—
This is the teaching of all buddhas.

The Ekottara Āgama Sūtra (T02 n.125 p.551a 13–14)

A Note on the Proper Care of Dharma Materials

Traditional Buddhist cultures treat books on Dharma as sacred. Hence it is considered disrespectful to place them in a low position, to read them when lying down, or to place them where they might be damaged by food or drink.

Kalavinka Press books are printed on acid-free paper.
Cover and interior designed by Bhikshu Dharmamitra.
Printed in the United States of America

The Flower Adornment Sutra

The Great Expansive
Buddha's Flower Adornment Sutra

An Annotated English Translation of the Avataṃsaka Sutra
By Bhikshu Dharmamitra

With a Commentarial Synopsis
Of the Flower Adornment Sutra

Volume Six

Kalavinka Press
Seattle, Washington
www.kalavinkapress.org

Edition: HY-SA-1025-1.0 / Kalavinka Buddhist Classics Book 15a
The Six-Volume Set ISBN (paperback): 978-1-935413-47-9
This Volume Six ISBN: 978-1-935413-53-0
Vol. 1 ISBN: 978-1-935413-48-6
Vol. 2 ISBN: 978-1-935413-49-3
Vol. 3 ISBN: 978-1-935413-50-9
Vol. 4 ISBN: 978-1-935413-51-6
Vol. 5 ISBN: 978-1-935413-52-3
The Six-Volume Set ISBN (Adobe PDF): 978-1-935413-54-7
Library of Congress Control Number: 2025947392

Publisher's Cataloging-in-Publication Data

Names: Dharmamitra, Bhikshu, 1948, translator. | Śikṣānanda, 652 CE, translator. | Prajñā, 734 CE, translator.

Title: The Flower Adornment Sutra. An Annotated Translation of the Avataṃsaka Sutra. With a Commentarial Synopsis of the Flower Adornment Sutra.

Other titles: *Mahāvaipulya Buddha Avataṃsaka Sūtra.* English

Description: HY-SA-1025-1.0-chinese/english. | Seattle, Washington : Kalavinka Press, 2025. | Series: Kalavinka Buddhist Classics, Book 15a | Includes bibliographical references. | English and Chinese. | Summary: "The Flower Adornment Sutra is Bhikshu Dharmamitra's extensively annotated original translation of the Mahāvaipulya Buddha Avataṃsaka Sūtra or "The Great Expansive Buddha's Flower Adornment Sutra" which he has rendered from Tripiṭaka Master Śikṣānanda's circa 699 ce Sanskrit-to-Chinese 80-fascicle translation as Da Fangguang Fo Huayan Jing (Taisho Vol. 10, no. 279). Appended here as the conclusion to Chapter 39 is Dharmamitra's English translation of Tripiṭaka Master Prajñā's translation into Chinese of "The Conduct and Vows of Samantabhadra" which is traditionally included as the conclusion of Chinese language editions of this sutra. Altogether, this sutra consists of 39 chapters that introduce an interpenetrating, infinitely expansive, and majestically grand multiverse of countless buddha worlds while explaining in great detail the cultivation of the bodhisattva path to buddhahood, most notably the ten highest levels of bodhisattva practice known as "the ten bodhisattva grounds." To date, this is the first and only complete English translation of the Avataṃsaka Sutra. This special bilingual edition (English / Chinese) includes the facing-page simplified and traditional Chinese scripts to facilitate close study by academic buddhologists, students in Buddhist universities, and Buddhists in Taiwan, Hong Kong, Mainland China, and the West."-- Provided by publisher.

Identifiers: LCCN 2025947392 | ISBN 9781935413479 (paperback) | ISBN 9781935413547 (adobe pdf)

Subjects: LCSH: Tripiṭaka. Sūtrapiṭaka. Avataṃsakasūtra. | Bodhisattva stages (Mahayana Buddhism)

LC record available at https://lccn.loc.gov/2025947392

Volume Six Table of Contents

Chapter 39 – Entering the Dharma Realm (cont'd) 3919
- 38 – Sarvajagadrakṣāpraṇidhānavīryaprabhā 3919
- 39 – Sutejomaṇḍalaratiśrī 3971
- 40 – Gopā 4009
- 41 – Māyā 4085
- 42 – Surendrābhā 4121
- 43 – Viśvāmitra 4127
- 44 – Śilpābhijña 4127
- 45 – Bhadrottamā 4137
- 46 – Muktisāra 4139
- 47 – Sucandra 4141
- 48 – Ajitasena 4143
- 49 – Śivarāgra 4145
- 50 – Śrīsambhava and Śrīmati 4147
- 51 – Maitreya 4177
- 52 – Mañjuśrī 4335
- 53 – Samantabhadra 4337

Chapter 39 Conclusion: The Conduct and Vows of Samantabhadra 4391

Volume Six Endnotes 4429

Variant Readings from Other Chinese Editions 4439

Bibliography 4485

Glossary 4487

About the Translator 4523

A Commentarial Synopsis of The Flower Adornment Sutra 4525

Kalavinka Buddhist Classics Fall, 2025 Title List 4673

The Flower Adornment Sutra

Volume Six

The Great Expansive
Buddha's Flower Adornment Sutra

The Mahāvaipulya Buddha Avataṃsaka Sūtra

(Taisho T10, no. 279)

Translated under Imperial Auspices by
Tripiṭaka Master Śikṣānanda from the State of Khotan

English Translation by Bhikshu Dharmamitra

正體字

396b09 ‖ [4]大方廣佛華嚴經卷[5]第七十三
396b12 ‖ [9]入法界品第三十九之十四
396b13 ‖ 爾時善財童子。往大願精進力救護一切眾
396b14 ‖ 生夜神所。見彼夜神在大眾中。坐普現一切
396b15 ‖ 宮殿摩尼王藏師子之座。普現法界國土摩尼
396b16 ‖ 寶網。彌覆其上。現日月星宿影像身。[10]現隨
396b17 ‖ 眾生心普令得見身。現等一切眾生形相身。
396b18 ‖ 現無邊廣大色相海身。現普現一切威儀身。
396b19 ‖ 現普於十方示現身。現普調一切眾生身。現
396b20 ‖ 廣運速疾神通身。現利益眾生不絕身。現常
396b21 ‖ 遊虛空利益身。現一切佛所頂禮身。現修習
396b22 ‖ 一切善根身。現受持佛法不忘身。現成滿菩
396b23 ‖ 薩大願身。現光明充滿十方身。

简体字

大方广佛华严经卷第七十三

入法界品第三十九之十四

尔时，善财童子往大愿精进力救护一切众生夜神所，见彼夜神在大众中，坐普现一切宫殿摩尼王藏师子之座，普现法界国土摩尼宝网弥覆其上，现日、月、星宿影像身，现随众生心普令得见身，现等一切众生形相身，现无边广大色相海身，现普现一切威仪身，现普于十方示现身，现普调一切众生身，现广运速疾神通身，现利益众生不绝身，现常游虚空利益身，现一切佛所顶礼身，现修习一切善根身，现受持佛法不忘身，现成满菩萨大愿身，现光明充满十方身，

Chapter 39

Entering the Dharma Realm (cont'd)

38 – Sarvajagadrakṣāpraṇidhānavīryaprabhā

At that time, Sudhana the Youth went to the Night Spirit, Sarvajagadr akṣāpraṇidhānavīryaprabhā, or "Power of Vigor in the Great Vows to Rescue and Protect all Beings." He saw that night spirit in the midst of that immense congregation, sitting on a lion throne made of a trove of sovereign *maṇi* jewels displaying images of all palaces everywhere. She was sheltered by a jeweled net stretched overhead that was made of *maṇi* jewels displaying images of the lands everywhere throughout the Dharma realm. Reflected in her body:

There appeared bodies with the appearance of the sun, moon, stars, and constellations;

There appeared bodies that adapted to beings' minds and allowed them all to see her;

There appeared bodies matching the forms and appearances of all beings;

There appeared bodies taking on a boundlessly vast ocean of forms and appearances;

There appeared bodies everywhere displaying all forms of deportment;

There appeared bodies manifesting everywhere throughout the ten directions;

There appeared bodies everywhere training all beings;

There appeared bodies carrying out vast and swift implementations of the spiritual superknowledges;

There appeared bodies incessantly benefiting beings;

There appeared bodies always roaming throughout space, benefiting others;

There appeared bodies bowing down in reverence before all buddhas;

There appeared bodies cultivating all roots of goodness;

There appeared bodies receiving, preserving, and never forgetting the Dharma of the Buddha;

There appeared bodies completely fulfilling the bodhisattva's great vows;

There appeared bodies emanating light that completely filled the ten directions;

正體字

現法燈普滅
396b24‖ 世暗身。現了法如幻淨智身。現遠離塵暗法
396b25‖ 性身。現普智照法明了身。現究竟無患無熱
396b26‖ 身。現不可沮壞堅固身。現無所住佛力身。現
396b27‖ 無分別離染身。現本清淨法性身。時善財童
396b28‖ 子。見如是等佛剎微塵數差別身。一心頂禮。
396b29‖ 舉體投地。良久乃起。合掌瞻仰。於善知識。生
396c01‖ 十種心。何等為十。所謂於善知識生同[已>己]心。
396c02‖ 令我精勤[11]辦一切智助道法故。於善知識生
396c03‖ 清淨自業果心。親近供養生善根故。於善知
396c04‖ 識生莊嚴菩薩行心。令我速能莊嚴一切菩
396c05‖ 薩行故。[12]於善知識生成就一切佛法心。誘誨
396c06‖ 於我令修道故。於善知識生能生心。能生
396c07‖ 於我無上法故。於善知識生出離心。令我修
396c08‖ 行普賢菩薩所有行願而出離故。

简体字

现法灯普灭世暗身，现了法如幻净智身，现远离尘暗法性身，现普智照法明了身，现究竟无患无热身，现不可沮坏坚固身，现无所住佛力身，现无分别离染身，现本清净法性身。

时，善财童子见如是等佛刹微尘数差别身，一心顶礼，举体投地，良久乃起，合掌瞻仰，于善知识生十种心。何等为十？所谓：于善知识生同己心，令我精勤办一切智助道法故；于善知识生清净自业果心，亲近供养生善根故；于善知识生庄严菩萨行心，令我速能庄严一切菩萨行故；于善知识生成就一切佛法心，诱诲于我令修道故；于善知识生能生心，能生于我无上法故；于善知识生出离心，令我修行普贤菩萨所有行愿而出离故；

- There appeared bodies serving as Dharma lamps everywhere dispelling the world's darkness;
- There appeared bodies that, with pure wisdom, completely understood dharmas as like mere conjured illusions;
- There appeared Dharma nature bodies that renounced the darkness of attachment to the objects of the senses;
- There appeared bodies that, possessed of universal wisdom, illuminated dharmas with complete clarity;
- There appeared bodies that were invulnerable to all misfortunes and the fever of the afflictions;
- There appeared bodies that were invincibly solid;
- There appeared bodies possessed of the Buddha's power of having no place in which they abide;
- There appeared bodies that were free of discriminations and that had abandoned the defilements; and
- There appeared bodies possessed of the fundamental purity of the nature of dharmas.

After seeing her different bodies such as these that were as numerous as the atoms in a buddha *kṣetra,* Sudhana the Youth bowed down in single-minded reverence before that night spirit, prostrating his entire body there on that spot of earth, only rising after a goodly while, whereupon he respectfully pressed his palms together, gazed up at her in admiration, and had ten kinds of thoughts with regard to the good spiritual guides. What were those ten? They were as follows:

- He conceived of the good spiritual guides as sharing the same mind as he possessed, "for they enable me to become intensely diligent in acquiring the dharmas that are the provisions for the path to all-knowledge";
- He conceived of the good spiritual guides as producing purity in his own karmic fruits, "for I develop roots of goodness by drawing near and making offerings to them";
- He conceived of the good spiritual guides as producing his adornments of the bodhisattva practices, "for they enable me to swiftly adorn the bodhisattva practices";
- He conceived of the good spiritual guides as producing his successful development of all the dharmas of a buddha, "for they persuade and instruct me, thereby enabling me to cultivate the path";
- He conceived of the good spiritual guides as having the ability to bring about birth, "for they are able to produce the unexcelled dharmas in me";
- He conceived of the good spiritual guides as instigating emancipation, "for they enable me to achieve emancipation by cultivating all the practices and vows of Samantabhadra Bodhisattva";

正體字

於善知識
396c09‖ 生具一切福智海心。令我積集諸白法故。於
396c10‖ 善知識生增長心。令我增長一切智故。於善
396c11‖ 知識生具一切善根心。令我志願得圓滿故。
396c12‖ 於善知識生能成[*]辦大利益心。令我自在安
396c13‖ 住一切菩薩法故。成一切智道故。得一切佛
396c14‖ 法故。是為十。發是心已。得彼夜神與諸菩
396c15‖ 薩佛剎微塵數同行。所謂同念。心常憶念十
396c16‖ 方三世一切佛故。同慧。分別決了一切法海
396c17‖ 差別門故。同趣。能轉一切諸佛如來妙法輪
396c18‖ 故。同覺。以等空智普入一切三世[13]間故。同
396c19‖ 根。成就菩薩清淨光明智慧根故。同心。善
396c20‖ 能修習無礙功德。莊嚴一切菩薩道故。同境。
396c21‖ 普照諸佛所行境故。同證。得一切智照實相
396c22‖ 海淨光明故。同義。能以智慧了一切法真實
396c23‖ 性故。同勇猛。能壞一切障礙山故。同色身。隨
396c24‖ 眾生心示現身故。同力。求一切智不退轉故。

简体字

于善知识生具一切福智海心，令我积集诸白法故；于善知识生增长心，令我增长一切智故；于善知识生具一切善根心，令我志愿得圆满故；于善知识生能成办大利益心，令我自在安住一切菩萨法故，成一切智道故，得一切佛法故。是为十。

发是心已，得彼夜神与诸菩萨佛刹微尘数同行，所谓：同念，心常忆念十方三世一切佛故；同慧，分别决了一切法海差别门故；同趣，能转一切诸佛如来妙法轮故；同觉，以等空智普入一切三世间故；同根，成就菩萨清净光明智慧根故；同心，善能修习无碍功德，庄严一切菩萨道故；同境，普照诸佛所行境故；同证，得一切智照实相海净光明故；同义，能以智慧了一切法真实性故；同勇猛，能坏一切障碍山故；同色身，随众生心示现身故；同力，求一切智不退转故；

He conceived of the good spiritual guides as completely possessing the ocean of all merit and wisdom, "for they enable me to accumulate all the white dharmas of pristine purity";

He conceived of the good spiritual guides as producing growth, "for they enable me to grow [in my progress toward] all-knowledge";

He conceived of the good spiritual guides as completely possessing all roots of goodness, "for they enable my vows to reach complete fulfillment"; and

He conceived of the good spiritual guides as able to accomplish great benefit, "for they enable me to achieve sovereign mastery in becoming established in all bodhisattva dharmas, in succeeding in the path to all-knowledge, and in acquiring all the dharmas of the Buddha."

These were those ten. After he had these thoughts, he acquired [aspects of] practice that were of the same sort as those of the night spirit and all bodhisattvas, [aspects of] practice that were as numerous as the atoms in a buddha *kṣetra,* namely:

Comparable power of mindfulness by which the mind always recalls all buddhas of the ten directions and three periods of time;

Comparable intelligence by which one distinguishes and decisively understands all the different gateways into the ocean of dharmas;

Comparable destiny by which one is able to turn the wheel of the wondrous Dharma of all buddhas, the *tathāgatas;*

Comparable enlightenment by which one uses space-like wisdom to everywhere enter all three periods of time;

Comparable faculties by which one perfects the bodhisattva's faculty of pure and radiant wisdom;

Comparable resolve by which one is well able to cultivate the unimpeded meritorious qualities with which one adorns the path of all bodhisattvas;

Comparable sphere of action by which one everywhere illuminates the sphere of action in which all buddhas act;

Comparable realizations by which one acquires the pure light with which all-knowledge illuminates the ocean of all phenomena's true character;

Comparable meaning by which one is able to use wisdom to completely understand the true nature of all dharmas;

Comparable courageousness by which one is able to destroy the mountain of all obstacles;

Comparable physical bodies by which one adapts to beings' minds in manifesting bodies;

Comparable powers by which one becomes irreversible in one's quest to attain all-knowledge;

正體字

396c25‖ 同無畏。其心清淨如虛空故。同精進。於無
396c26‖ 量劫行菩薩行無懈倦故。同辯才。得法無礙
396c27‖ 智光明故。同無等。身相清淨超世間故。同愛
396c28‖ 語。令一切眾生皆歡喜故。同妙音。普演一
396c29‖ 切法門海故。同滿音。一切眾生隨類解故。同
397a01‖ 淨德。修習如來淨功德故。同智地。一切佛所
397a02‖ 受法輪故。同梵行。安住一切佛境界故。同大
397a03‖ 慈。念念普覆一切國土眾生海故。同大悲。普
397a04‖ 雨法雨潤澤一切諸眾生故。同身業。以方便
397a05‖ 行教化一切諸眾生故。同語業。以隨類音演
397a06‖ 說一切諸法門故。同意業。普攝眾生置一切
397a07‖ 智境界中故。同莊嚴。嚴淨一切諸佛剎故。同
397a08‖ 親近。有佛出世皆親近故。同勸請。請一切
397a09‖ 佛轉法輪故。同供養。常樂供養一切佛故。同
397a10‖ 教化。調伏一切諸眾生故。同光明。照了一
397a11‖ 切諸法門故。同三昧。普知一切眾生心故。

简体字

同无畏，其心清净如虚空故；同精进，于无量劫行菩萨行无懈倦故；同辩才，得法无碍智光明故；同无等，身相清净超世间故；同爱语，令一切众生皆欢喜故；同妙音，普演一切法门海故；同满音，一切众生随类解故；同净德，修习如来净功德故；同智地，一切佛所受法轮故；同梵行，安住一切佛境界故；同大慈，念念普覆一切国土众生海故；同大悲，普雨法雨润泽一切诸众生故；同身业，以方便行教化一切诸众生故；同语业，以随类音演说一切诸法门故；同意业，普摄众生置一切智境界中故；同庄严，严净一切诸佛刹故；同亲近，有佛出世皆亲近故；同劝请，请一切佛转法轮故；同供养，常乐供养一切佛故；同教化，调伏一切诸众生故；同光明，照了一切诸法门故；同三昧，普知一切众生心故；

Comparable fearlessness by which one's mind becomes as pure as space;
Comparable vigor by which one tirelessly practices the bodhisattva practices for countless kalpas;
Comparable eloquence by which one acquires the light of the unimpeded knowledge of dharmas;
Comparable peerlessness by which one possesses purity in the physical marks surpassing that of everyone in the world;
Comparable pleasing words by which one causes all beings to be filled with joyous delight;
Comparable marvelousness of voice by which one everywhere expounds on the ocean of all Dharma gateways;
Comparable fullness of voice by which beings each understand whatever is said in accordance with their individual type;
Comparable purity of meritorious qualities by which one cultivates the pure meritorious qualities of the Tathāgata;
Comparable wisdom grounds by which one receives the wheel of Dharma in the presence of all buddhas;
Comparable *brahmacarya* by which one becomes established in the sphere of all buddhas;
Comparable great kindness by which, in every moment, one extends loving-kindness to include the ocean of beings in all lands;
Comparable great compassion by which one rains down the Dharma rain to benefit all beings;
Comparable physical actions by which one uses the practice of skillful means in teaching all beings;
Comparable verbal actions by which one uses voices matching those of each type of being in expounding on all Dharma gateways;
Comparable mental actions by which one everywhere gathers in all beings and places them in the realm of all-knowledge;
Comparable adornments by which one purifies all buddha *kṣetras;*
Comparable personal proximity by which, whenever buddhas appear in the world, one always draws near to them;
Comparable entreaties by which one requests all buddhas to turn the wheel of Dharma;
Comparable offerings by which one always delights in making offerings to all buddhas;
Comparable teaching by which one trains all beings;
Comparable radiance by which one completely illuminates all Dharma gateways;
Comparable samādhi by which one everywhere knows the minds of all beings;

正體字

同
397a12‖ 充遍。以自在力充滿一切諸佛剎海修諸行
397a13‖ 故。同[1]住處。住諸菩薩大神通故。同眷屬。一
397a14‖ 切菩薩共止住故。同入處。普入世界微細處
397a15‖ 故。同心慮。普知一切諸佛剎故。同往詣。普入
397a16‖ 一切佛剎海故。同方便。悉現一切諸佛剎故。
397a17‖ 同超勝。於諸佛剎皆無比故。同不退。普入
397a18‖ 十方無障礙故。同破闇。得一切佛成菩提智
397a19‖ 大光明故。同無生忍。入一切佛眾會海故。同
397a20‖ 遍一切諸佛剎網。恭敬供養不可說剎諸如
397a21‖ 來故。同智證。了知彼彼法門海故。同修行。順
397a22‖ 行一切諸法門故。同希求。於清淨法深樂欲
397a23‖ 故。同清淨。集佛功德而以莊嚴身口意故。同
397a24‖ 妙意。於一切法智明了故。同精進。普集一切
397a25‖ 諸善根故。同淨行。成滿一切菩薩行故。同無
397a26‖ 礙。了一切法皆無相故。

简体字

同充遍，以自在力充满一切诸佛刹海修诸行故；同住处，住诸菩萨大神通故；同眷属，一切菩萨共止住故；同入处，普入世界微细处故；同心虑，普知一切诸佛刹故；同往诣，普入一切佛刹海故；同方便，悉现一切诸佛刹故；同超胜，于诸佛刹皆无比故；同不退，普入十方无障碍故；同破暗，得一切佛成菩提智大光明故；同无生忍，入一切佛众会海故；同遍一切诸佛刹网，恭敬供养不可说刹诸如来故；同智证，了知彼彼法门海故；同修行，顺行一切诸法门故；同希求，于清净法深乐欲故；同清净，集佛功德而以庄严身、口、意故；同妙意，于一切法智明了故；同精进，普集一切诸善根故；同净行，成满一切菩萨行故；同无碍，了一切法皆无相故；

Comparable complete pervasion by which one uses one's power of transformation to fill the ocean of all buddha *kṣetras* and cultivate all the practices;

Comparable abodes by which one abides in the great spiritual superknowledges of all bodhisattvas;

Comparable retinues by which one dwells together in the company of all bodhisattvas;

Comparable points of entry by which one everywhere enters even the most subtle places in the world;

Comparable mental deliberation by which one knows the *kṣetras* of all buddhas everywhere;

Comparable visitation to pay one's respects by which one everywhere enters the ocean of all buddhas' *kṣetras;*

Comparable skillful means by which one manifests in all buddha *kṣetras;*

Comparable supremacy by which one becomes unmatched in all buddha *kṣetras;*

Comparable irreversibility by which one is unimpeded in everywhere entering the ten directions;

Comparable dispelling of darkness by which one acquires the great wisdom light acquired by all buddhas when they attained bodhi;

Comparable unproduced-dharmas patience by which one enters the ocean of all buddhas' congregations;

Comparable pervasion of the web of all buddha *kśetras* by which one respectfully makes offerings to all *tathāgatas* in an ineffable number of *kṣetras;*

Comparable realization of wisdom by which one completely knows the ocean of every Dharma gateway;

Comparable cultivation by which one compliantly practices all Dharma gateways;

Comparable aspiration by which one maintains intense zeal for the pure Dharma;

Comparable purity by which one accumulates the buddha's meritorious qualities as adornments of one's body, mouth, and mind;

Comparable subtlety of mind by which one possesses wisdom that completely understands all dharmas;

Comparable vigor by which one everywhere accumulates all roots of goodness;

Comparable pure practice by which one completely fulfills all the bodhisattva practices;

Comparable freedom from obstacles by which one completely understands all dharmas as signless;

正體字

同善巧。於諸法中智
397a27║ 自在故。同隨樂。隨眾生心現境界故。同方便。
397a28║ 善習一切所應習故。同護念。得一切佛所護
397a29║ 念故。同入地。得入一切菩薩地故。同所住。安
397b01║ 住一切菩薩位故。同記別。一切諸佛授其記
397b02║ 故。同三昧。一剎那中普入一切三昧門故。同
397b03║ 建立。示現種種諸佛事故。同正念。正念一切
397b04║ 境界門故。同修行。盡未來劫修行一切菩薩
397b05║ 行故。同淨信。於諸如來無量智慧極欣樂故。
397b06║ 同捨離。滅除一切諸障礙故。同不退智。與
397b07║ 諸如來智慧等故。同受生。應現成熟諸眾生
397b08║ 故。同所住。住一切智方便門故。同境界。於法
397b09║ 界境得自在故。同無依。永斷一切所依心故。
397b10║ 同說法。已入諸法平等智故。同勤修。常蒙
397b11║ 諸佛所護念故。同神通。開悟眾生令修一切
397b12║ 菩薩行故。同神力。能入十方世界海故。

简体字

同善巧，于诸法中智自在故；同随乐，随众生心现境界故；同方便，善习一切所应习故；同护念，得一切佛所护念故；同入地，得入一切菩萨地故；同所住，安住一切菩萨位故；同记别，一切诸佛授其记故；同三昧，一刹那中普入一切三昧门故；同建立，示现种种诸佛事故；同正念，正念一切境界门故；同修行，尽未来劫修行一切菩萨行故；同净信，于诸如来无量智慧极欣乐故；同舍离，灭除一切诸障碍故；同不退智，与诸如来智慧等故；同受生，应现成熟诸众生故；同所住，住一切智方便门故；同境界，于法界境得自在故；同无依，永断一切所依心故；同说法，已入诸法平等智故；同勤修，常蒙诸佛所护念故；同神通，开悟众生令修一切菩萨行故；同神力，能入十方世界海故；

Comparable skillfulness by which one has sovereign mastery of wisdom with respect to all dharmas;

Comparable delight in adaptation by which one manifests spheres adapted to beings' minds;

Comparable skillful means by which one skillfully practices all that should be practiced;

Comparable protection by which one receives the protection of all buddhas;

Comparable entry of the grounds by which one is able to enter all the bodhisattva grounds;

Comparable foundations by which one becomes securely established in all bodhisattva stations;

Comparable predictions by which all buddhas bestow one's prediction [of future buddhahood];

Comparable samādhis by which, in but a single *kṣaṇa,* one everywhere enters all samādhi gateways;

Comparable establishment by which one manifests the many different works of all buddhas;

Comparable right mindfulness by which one abides in right mindfulness of the gateways of the sense realms;

Comparable cultivation by which one cultivates all the bodhisattva practices to the very end of all future kalpas;

Comparable pure faith by which one abides in the most ultimately joyous devotion to the measureless wisdom of all *tathāgatas;*

Comparable renunciation by which one extinguishes all obstacles;

Comparable irreversibility of wisdom by which one develops wisdom equivalent to that of all *tathāgatas;*

Comparable rebirths by which one manifests for the purpose of ripening beings;

Comparable abodes by which one abides in skillful methods leading to all-knowledge;

Comparable objective spheres by which acquires sovereign mastery over the objective spheres throughout the Dharma realm;

Comparable independence by which one forever cuts off all reliance upon any states of mind;

Comparable discourse on Dharma by which one has already entered the wisdom that realizes the uniform equality of all dharmas;

Comparable diligent cultivation by which one always receives the protection of the buddhas;

Comparable spiritual superknowledges by which one awakens beings and induces them to cultivate all bodhisattva practices;

Comparable spiritual powers by which one is able to enter the ocean of the worlds of the ten directions;

正體字

同陀
397b13‖ 羅尼。普照一切總持海故。同祕密法。了知一
397b14‖ 切修多羅中妙法門故。同甚深法。解一切法
397b15‖ 如虛空故。同光明。普照一切諸世界故。同欣
397b16‖ 樂。隨眾生心而為開示令歡喜故。同[2]震動。
397b17‖ 為諸眾生現神通力普動十方一切剎故。同
397b18‖ 不虛。見聞憶念皆悉令其心調伏故。同出離。
397b19‖ 滿足一切諸大願海。成就如來十力智故。時
397b20‖ 善財童子。觀察大願精進力救護一切眾生
397b21‖ 夜神。起十種清淨心。獲如是等佛剎微塵數
397b22‖ 同菩薩行。既獲此已。心轉清淨。偏袒右肩。頂
397b23‖ 禮其足。一心合掌。以偈讚曰
397b24‖ 我發堅固意　志求無上覺
397b25‖ 今於善知識　而起自己心
397b26‖ 以見善知識　集無盡白法
397b27‖ 滅除眾罪垢　成就菩提果
397b28‖ 我見善知識　功德莊嚴心
397b29‖ 盡未來剎劫　勤修所行道
397c01‖ [3]　我念善知識　攝受饒益我
397c02‖ 為我悉示現　正教真實法

简体字

同陀罗尼，普照一切总持海故；同秘密法，了知一切修多罗中妙法门故；同甚深法，解一切法如虚空故；同光明，普照一切诸世界故；同欣乐，随众生心而为开示令欢喜故；同震动，为诸众生现神通力普动十方一切刹故；同不虚，见闻忆念皆悉令其心调伏故；同出离，满足一切诸大愿海，成就如来十力智故。

时，善财童子观察大愿精进力救护一切众生夜神，起十种清净心，获如是等佛刹微尘数同菩萨行；既获此已，心转清净，偏袒右肩，顶礼其足，一心合掌，以偈赞曰：

“我发坚固意，志求无上觉；
今于善知识，而起自己心。
以见善知识，集无尽白法，
灭除众罪垢，成就菩提果。
我见善知识，功德庄严心，
尽未来刹劫，勤修所行道。
我念善知识，摄受饶益我，
为我悉示现，正教真实法，

Comparable *dhāraṇīs* by which one everywhere illuminates the ocean of all the complete-retention *dhāraṇīs;*

Comparable esoteric dharmas by which one completely knows the sublime Dharma gateways in all sutras;

Comparable extremely profound dharmas by which one understands all dharmas as like empty space;

Comparable radiance by which one everywhere illuminates all worlds;

Comparable delight by which one instructs and delights beings in ways adapted to their mental dispositions;

Comparable quaking and movement by which one manifests the power of the spiritual superknowledges for beings and everywhere shakes all *kṣetras* throughout the ten directions;

Comparable non-futility by which one trains the minds of all beings who see one, hear one, or recollect one; and

Comparable emancipation by which one completely fulfills the ocean of all great vows and develops the wisdom of the Tathāgata's ten powers.

So it was that, having contemplated the Night Spirit, Sarvajagadrakṣā praṇidhānavīryaprabhā, Sudhana the Youth produced these ten pure mind states and acquired comparable bodhisattva practices such as these that were as numerous as the atoms in a buddha *kṣetra*. Having acquired these, his mind became even more purified, whereupon he bared his right shoulder and bowed down in reverence at her feet. He then single-mindedly pressed his palms together and spoke these praise verses:

I have made the solid resolve
determined to seek the unexcelled enlightenment.
Now, I think of the good spiritual guides,
as being the same as me in this.

It is due to seeing the good spiritual guides,
that I accumulate endless pure dharmas,
extinguish the defilement of the many offenses,
and perfect the fruit of bodhi.

Because I have seen the good spiritual guides,
meritorious qualities adorn my mind, and,
to the very end of all future *kṣetras* and kalpas,
I will diligently cultivate the path they have practiced.

I recall the good spiritual guides
drew me in and benefited me,
and, for my sake, fully revealed
the right teaching's genuine Dharma.

正體字

397c03 ‖ 關閉諸惡趣　顯示人天路
397c04 ‖ 亦示諸如來　成一切智道
397c05 ‖ 我念善知識　是佛功德藏
397c06 ‖ 念念能出生　虛空功德海
397c07 ‖ 與我波羅蜜　增我難思福
397c08 ‖ 長我淨功德　令我冠佛繒
397c09 ‖ 我念善知識　能滿佛智道
397c10 ‖ 誓願常依止　圓滿白淨法
397c11 ‖ 我以此等故　功德悉具足
397c12 ‖ 普為諸眾生　說一切智道
397c13 ‖ 聖者為我師　與我無上法
397c14 ‖ 無量無數劫　不能報其恩
397c15 ‖ 爾時善財。說此偈已。白言大聖。願為我說此
397c16 ‖ 解脫門。名為何等。發心已來。為幾時耶。久如
397c17 ‖ 當得阿耨多羅三藐三菩提。夜神告言。善男
397c18 ‖ 子。此解脫門。名教化眾生令生善根。我以成
397c19 ‖ 就此解脫故。悟一切法自性平等。入於諸法
397c20 ‖ 真實之性。[4]證無依法。捨離世間。悉知諸法
397c21 ‖ 色相差別。亦能了達青黃赤白性皆不實。無
397c22 ‖ 有差別。而恒示現無量色身。所謂種種色身。
397c23 ‖ 非一色身。

简体字

关闭诸恶趣，显示人天路，
亦示诸如来，成一切智道。
我念善知识，是佛功德藏，
念念能出生，虚空功德海。
与我波罗蜜，增我难思福，
长我净功德，令我冠佛缯。
我念善知识，能满佛智道；
誓愿常依止，圆满白净法。
我以此等故，功德悉具足，
普为诸众生，说一切智道。
圣者为我师，与我无上法，
无量无数劫，不能报其恩。”

尔时，善财说此偈已，白言：“大圣，愿为我说，此解脱门名为何等？发心已来为几时耶？久如当得阿耨多罗三藐三菩提？”

夜神告言：“善男子，此解脱门，名教化众生令生善根。我以成就此解脱故，悟一切法自性平等，入于诸法真实之性，证无依法，舍离世间，悉知诸法色相差别，亦能了达青、黄、赤、白，性皆不实，无有差别，而恒示现无量色身。所谓：种种色身、非一色身、

You closed off the gates leading into the wretched destinies,
revealed the road to the destinies of humans and devas,
and also revealed all *tathāgatas'*
path to the realization of all-knowledge.

I recall that the good spiritual guides
are treasuries of the Buddha's meritorious qualities
who are able in every mind-moment to produce
an ocean of meritorious qualities as vast as space.

Please bestow on me the *pāramitās,*
bring about the increase in me of an inconceivable amount of merit,
instigate the growth of my pure meritorious qualities,
and enable me to be crowned with buddhahood's silken headband.

I recall that the good spiritual guides
are able to fulfill the path to the Buddha's wisdom,
I vow to always rely upon them
to reach complete fulfillment of the pure dharmas.

It is because of [guides] such as these
that my meritorious qualities may all become perfected
and that I will teach the path to all-knowledge
in order to everywhere benefit all beings.

The Āryā has served as my teacher
who has bestowed on me the unexcelled Dharma.
Even in measurelessly and numberlessly many kalpas,
I would still be unable to repay your kindness.

Then, having spoken these verses, Sudhana the Youth addressed the Night Spirit, saying, "O Great Āryā, please teach me this gateway to liberation and what it is called. Also, how long has it been now since you resolved to attain bodhi and how much longer will it take to attain *anuttara-samyak-saṃbodhi*?"

The Night Spirit then told him:

Son of Good Family, this gateway to liberation is known as "teaching beings to produce roots of goodness." Due to perfecting this liberation, I have awakened to the uniformly equal nature of all dharmas, have penetrated the true nature of all dharmas, have realized the dharma of non-dependence, have left the world behind, have fully known the differences in all dharmas' forms and features while also being able to comprehend that the nature of blue, yellow, red, and white is unreal and devoid of any difference, and I have become able to constantly manifest countless form bodies, namely:

Many different kinds of form bodies;
Non-singular form bodies;

正體字

無邊色身。清淨色身。一切莊嚴色
397c24‖ 身。普見色身。等一切眾生色身。普現一切眾
397c25‖ 生前色身。光明普照色身。見無厭足色身。相
397c26‖ 好清淨色身。離眾惡光明色身。示現大勇猛
397c27‖ 色身。甚難得色身。一切世間無能映蔽色身。
397c28‖ 一切世間共稱歎無盡色身。念念常觀察色
397c29‖ 身。示現種種雲色身。種種形顯色色身。現無
398a01‖ 量自在力色身。妙光明色身。一切淨妙莊嚴
398a02‖ 色身。隨順成熟一切眾生色身。隨其心樂現
398a03‖ 前調伏色身。無障礙普光明色身。清淨無濁
398a04‖ 穢色身。具足莊嚴不可壞色身。不思議法方
398a05‖ 便光明色身。無能[1]奪。奪一切色身。無諸闇破
398a06‖ 一切闇色身。集一切白淨法色身。大勢力功
398a07‖ 德海色身。從過去恭敬因所生色身。如虛空
398a08‖ 清淨心所生色身。最勝廣大色身。無斷無盡
398a09‖ 色身。

简体字

无边色身、清净色身、一切庄严色身、普见色身、等一切众生色身、普现一切众生前色身、光明普照色身、见无厌足色身、相好清净色身、离众恶光明色身、示现大勇猛色身、甚难得色身、一切世间无能映蔽色身、一切世间共称叹无尽色身、念念常观察色身、示现种种云色身、种种形显色色身、现无量自在力色身、妙光明色身、一切净妙庄严色身、随顺成熟一切众生色身、随其心乐现前调伏色身、无障碍普光明色身、清净无浊秽色身、具足庄严不可坏色身、不思议法方便光明色身、无能映夺一切色身、无诸暗破一切暗色身、集一切白净法色身、大势力功德海色身、从过去恭敬因所生色身、如虚空清净心所生色身、最胜广大色身、无断无尽色身、

Boundless form bodies;
Pure form bodies;
Form bodies having all kinds of adornments;
Form bodies that are seen everywhere;
Form bodies equal in number to all beings;
Form bodies appearing everywhere before all beings;
Form bodies emanating pervasively illuminating light;
Form bodies that the observer never grows weary of seeing;
Form bodies possessed of the pure major marks and secondary signs;
Form bodies with radiance that causes separation from the many kinds of evil;
Form bodies manifesting great courage;
Form bodies that can only rarely be encountered;
Form bodies that cannot be outshone by any others in the entire world;
Form bodies endlessly praised by the entire world;
Form bodies always immersed in contemplations in every mind-moment;
Form bodies manifesting many different kinds of clouds;
Form bodies of many different shapes and colors;
Form bodies manifesting countless miraculous powers;
Form bodies emanating marvelous radiance;
Form bodies with all kinds of pure and marvelous adornments;
Form bodies adapting to and ripening all beings;
Form bodies training beings by adapting to their inclinations as they appear before them;
Form bodies with unimpeded and universally shining light;
Form bodies that are pure and free of defilements;
Form bodies that are fully adorned and indestructible;
Form bodies that are radiant with inconceivable dharma methods;
Form bodies that cannot be outshone by anyone and outshine all others;
Form bodies that, free of all darkness, dispel all darkness;
Form bodies that have accumulated all the pure dharmas;
Form bodies possessed of great strength and an ocean of meritorious qualities;
Form bodies born because of past expressions of reverence;
Form bodies born from a mind as pure as space;
Form bodies that are supremely vast;
Form bodies that are indestructible and inexhaustible;

正體字

光明海色身。於一切世間無所依平等
398a10‖ 色身。遍十方無所礙色身。念念現種種色相
398a11‖ 海色身。增長一切眾生歡喜心色身。攝取一
398a12‖ 切眾生海色身。一一毛孔中說一切佛功德海
398a13‖ 色身。淨一切眾生欲解海色身。決了一切法
398a14‖ 義色身。無障礙普照[2]耀色身。等虛空淨光明
398a15‖ 色身。放廣大淨光明色身。照現無垢法色身。
398a16‖ 無比色身。差別莊嚴色身。普照十方色身。隨
398a17‖ 時示現應眾生色身。寂靜色身。滅一切煩惱
398a18‖ 色身。一切眾生福田色身。一切眾生見不虛
398a19‖ 色身。大智慧勇猛力色身。無障礙普周遍色
398a20‖ 身。妙身雲普現世間皆蒙益色身。具足大慈
398a21‖ 海色身。大福德寶山王色身。放光明普照世
398a22‖ 間一切趣色身。大智慧清淨色身。生眾生正
398a23‖ 念心色身。一切寶光明色身。普光藏色身。現
398a24‖ 世間種種清淨相色身。求一切智處色身。

简体字

光明海色身、于一切世间无所依平等色身、遍十方无所碍色身、念念现种种色相海色身、增长一切众生欢喜心色身、摄取一切众生海色身、一一毛孔中说一切佛功德海色身、净一切众生欲解海色身、决了一切法义色身、无障碍普照耀色身、等虚空净光明色身、放广大净光明色身、照现无垢法色身、无比色身、差别庄严色身、普照十方色身、随时示现应众生色身、寂静色身、灭一切烦恼色身、一切众生福田色身、一切众生见不虚色身、大智慧勇猛力色身、无障碍普周遍色身、妙身云普现世间皆蒙益色身、具足大慈海色身、大福德宝山王色身、放光明普照世间一切趣色身、大智慧清净色身、生众生正念心色身、一切宝光明色身、普光藏色身、现世间种种清净相色身、求一切智处色身、

Form bodies appearing as oceans of radiance;
Form bodies that are equally independent of anything in the world;
Form bodies that unimpededly pervade the ten directions;
Form bodies that, in every mind-moment, manifest an ocean of many different forms and appearances;
Form bodies that increase the happiness of all beings' minds;
Form bodies that draw forth an ocean of all beings;
Form bodies that in every pore are expounding on the ocean of all buddhas' meritorious qualities;
Form bodies that purify the ocean of all beings' inclinations and dispositions;
Form bodies that decisively determine the meaning of all dharmas;
Form bodies with unimpeded pervasively brilliant illumination;
Form bodies emanating pure light as vast as space;
Form bodies emanating vast pure radiance;
Form bodies that illuminate and reveal the undefiled dharmas;
Form bodies that are incomparable;
Form bodies with different kinds of adornments;
Form bodies that everywhere illuminate the ten directions;
Form bodies manifested at the right time in response to beings;
Form bodies abiding in quiescence;
Form bodies that extinguish all afflictions;
Form bodies that serve as a field of merit for all beings;
Form bodies that, when seen by any being, are not seen in vain;
Form bodies possessing the power of great wisdom and courage;
Form bodies that are unimpeded in being present everywhere;
Form bodies manifesting everywhere throughout the world as clouds of marvelous bodies that benefit everyone;
Form bodies possessed of an ocean of great kindness;
Form bodies that are kings of the jeweled mountains of immense merit;
Form bodies that emanate radiance everywhere illuminating all of the world's rebirth destinies;
Form bodies possessed of great wisdom and purity;
Form bodies that produce right mindfulness in beings;
Form bodies emanating the light of all jewels;
Form bodies that are treasuries of universally pervasive radiance;
Form bodies revealing the world's many different signs of purity;
Form bodies that seek the bases of all-knowledge;

正體字

現
398a25‖ 微笑令眾生生淨信色身。一切寶莊嚴光明色
398a26‖ 身。不取不捨一切眾生色身。無決定無究竟
398a27‖ 色身。現自在加持力色身。現一切神通變化
398a28‖ 色身。生如來家色身。遠離眾惡遍法界海色
398a29‖ 身。普現一切如來道場眾會色身。具種種眾
398b01‖ 色海色身。從善行所流色身。隨所應化示現
398b02‖ 色身。一切世間見無厭足色身。種種淨光明
398b03‖ 色身。現一切三世海色身。放一切光明海色
398b04‖ 身。現無量差別光明海色身。超諸世間一切
398b05‖ 香光明色身。現不可說日輪雲色身。現廣大
398b06‖ 月輪雲色身。放無量須彌山妙華雲色身。出
398b07‖ 種種鬘雲色身。現一切寶蓮華雲色身。興一
398b08‖ 切燒香雲遍法界色身。散一切末香藏雲色
398b09‖ 身。現一切如來大願身色身。

简体字

现微笑令众生生净信色身、一切宝庄严光明色身、不取不舍一切众生色身、无决定无究竟色身、现自在加持力色身、现一切神通变化色身、生如来家色身、远离众恶遍法界海色身、普现一切如来道场众会色身、具种种众色海色身、从善行所流色身、随所应化示现色身、一切世间见无厌足色身、种种净光明色身、现一切三世海色身、放一切光明海色身、现无量差别光明海色身、超诸世间一切香光明色身、现不可说日轮云色身、现广大月轮云色身、放无量须弥山妙华云色身、出种种鬘云色身、现一切宝莲华云色身、兴一切烧香云遍法界色身、散一切末香藏云色身、现一切如来大愿身色身、

Form bodies that, by merely manifesting a subtle smile, cause beings to develop pure faith;
Form bodies emanating light adorned with all kinds of jewels;
Form bodies that neither seize on nor forsake any being;
Form bodies that are not at any definite or ultimate stage;
Form bodies manifesting the power of miraculous empowerments;
Form bodies manifesting all the spiritual superknowledges and spiritual transformations;
Form bodies born into the clan of the Tathāgatas;
Form bodies that renounce the many forms of evil and appear everywhere throughout the ocean of the Dharma realm;
Form bodies that everywhere appear in the congregations of all *tathāgatas*;
Form bodies possessed of the ocean of many different forms;
Form bodies that flow forth from good conduct;
Form bodies manifesting appearances adapted to those who should be taught;
Form bodies that no one in the world ever wearies of seeing;
Form bodies emanating many different kinds of pure light;
Form bodies manifesting the ocean of all three periods of time;
Form bodies emanating an ocean of all the kinds of light;
Form bodies manifesting an ocean of the countless different kinds of light;
Form bodies surpassing any in the entire world in their fragrance and radiance;
Form bodies manifesting an ineffable number of solar orb clouds;
Form bodies manifesting vast lunar orb clouds;
Form bodies emanating countless clouds of Mount Sumeru's marvelous flowers;
Form bodies sending forth clouds of the many different kinds of garlands;
Form bodies manifesting clouds of lotus flowers adorned with all kinds of precious jewels;
Form bodies producing clouds of all kinds of burning incense that pervade the Dharma realm;
Form bodies scattering clouds filled with all kinds of powdered incense;
Form bodies manifesting embodiments of the great vows of all *tathāgatas*;

正體字

現一切語言音
398b10‖ 聲演法海色身。現普賢菩薩像色身。念念中
398b11‖ 現如是等色相身。充滿十方。令諸眾生。或
398b12‖ 見或念。或聞說法。或因親近。或得開悟。或見
398b13‖ 神通。或覩變化。悉隨心樂。應時調伏。捨不善
398b14‖ 業。住於善行。善男子。當知此由大願力故。一
398b15‖ 切智力故。菩薩解脫力故。大悲力故。大慈力
398b16‖ 故。作如是事。善男子。我入此解脫。了知法
398b17‖ 性。無有差別。而能示現無量色身。[3]一一身。
398b18‖ 現無量色相海。一一相。放無量光明雲。一一
398b19‖ 光。現無量佛國土。一一土。現無量佛興世。一
398b20‖ 一佛。現無量神通力。開發眾生宿世善根。未
398b21‖ 種者令種。已種者令增長。已增長者令成熟。
398b22‖ 念念中。令無量眾生。於阿耨多羅三藐三菩
398b23‖ 提。得不退轉。善男子。如汝所問。從幾時來。
398b24‖ 發菩提心。修菩薩行。如是之義。承佛神力。當
398b25‖ 為[4]汝說。善男子。菩薩智輪。遠離一切分別
398b26‖ 境界。不可以生死中。長短染淨。廣狹多少。如
398b27‖ 是諸劫。分別顯示。何以故。菩薩智輪。本性清
398b28‖ 淨。離一切分別網。超一切障礙山。隨所應
398b29‖ 化而普照故。

简体字

现一切语言音声演法海色身、现普贤菩萨像色身。

“念念中，现如是等色相身充满十方，令诸众生或见、或念、或闻说法、或因亲近、或得开悟、或见神通、或睹变化，悉随心乐，应时调伏，舍不善业，住于善行。善男子，当知此由大愿力故，一切智力故，菩萨解脱力故，大悲力故，大慈力故，作如是事。

“善男子，我入此解脱，了知法性无有差别，而能示现无量色身，一一身现无量色相海，一一相放无量光明云，一一光现无量佛国土，一一土现无量佛兴世，一一佛现无量神通力，开发众生宿世善根，未种者令种，已种者令增长，已增长者令成熟；念念中，令无量众生，于阿耨多罗三藐三菩提得不退转。

“善男子，如汝所问：‘从几时来，发菩提心，修菩萨行？’如是之义，承佛神力，当为汝说。

“善男子，菩萨智轮远离一切分别境界，不可以生死中长短、染净、广狭、多少，如是诸劫分别显示。何以故？菩萨智轮本性清净，离一切分别网，超一切障碍山，随所应化而普照故。

Form bodies manifesting the sounds of all voices and languages expounding on the ocean of dharmas; and

Form bodies manifesting images of Samantabhadra Bodhisattva;

In every mind-moment, I manifest bodies with forms and appearances such as these that fill the ten directions and induce beings to see them or bear them in mind or hear them teaching the Dharma which may cause them to draw near because of this, which may allow them to awaken, or which may enable them to witness the spiritual superknowledges or see spiritual transformations. Adapting to all of their mental dispositions, they accord with the right time in training them to relinquish unwholesome actions and abide in wholesome practices.

Son of Good Family, you should understand that it is due to the power of great vows, due to the power of all-knowledge, due to the power of the bodhisattva liberations, due to the power of great compassion, and due to the power of great kindness, that one engages in endeavors such as these.

Son of Good Family, having entered this liberation, I completely understand the nature of dharmas as undifferentiated and thus I am able to manifest countless form bodies, every one of which appears with an ocean of countless forms and characteristics. Each of those characteristics emanates countless light clouds. Each of those light rays reveals countless buddha lands. In each of those lands, countless buddhas are shown arising in the world. And each of those buddhas manifests countless powers of spiritual superknowledges that activate beings' roots of goodness from previous lives, cause those who have never planted them to plant them, cause those who have already planted them to increase them, and cause those roots that have already increased to ripen. So it is that, in every mind-moment, countless beings are enabled to become irreversible in progressing toward *anuttara-samyak-saṃbodhi.*

Son of Good Family, as for your question about how long it has been since I resolved to attain bodhi and began to cultivate the bodhisattva practices, with the aid of the Buddha's spiritual powers, I will be able to describe such matters for you.

Son of Good Family, the bodhisattva's sphere of wisdom leaves far behind all realms of discrimination and it cannot be distinguished or revealed by resort to any of *saṃsāra*'s designations of kalpa duration such as long, short, defiled, immaculate, vast, or narrow. And why is this so? This is because the bodhisattva's sphere of wisdom is by nature fundamentally pure, apart from the web of all discriminations, and beyond the mountain of all obstacles, for it illuminates everywhere by adapting to those who should be taught.

正體字

善男子。譬如日輪無有晝夜。但
398c01║ 出時名晝沒時名夜。菩薩智輪亦復如是。無
398c02║ 有分別。[5]亦無三世。但隨心現。教化眾生。言
398c03║ 其止住前劫後劫。善男子。譬如日輪住閻浮
398c04║ 空。其影悉現一切寶物及以河海諸淨水中。
398c05║ 一切眾生。莫不目見。而彼淨日。不來至此。菩
398c06║ 薩智輪。亦復如是。出諸有海。住佛實法寂靜
398c07║ 空中。無有所依。為欲化度諸眾生故。而於
398c08║ 諸趣隨類受生。實不生死。無所染著。無長
398c09║ 短劫[6]諸想分別。何以故。菩薩究竟。離心想
398c10║ 見一切顛倒。得真實見。見法實性。知一切世
398c11║ 間。如夢如幻。無有眾生。但以大悲大願力故。
398c12║ 現眾生前。教化調伏。佛子。譬如船師常以大
398c13║ 船。於河流中。不依此岸。不著彼岸。不住中
398c14║ 流。而度眾生。無有休息。菩薩摩訶薩。亦復如
398c15║ 是。以波羅蜜船。於生死流中。不依此岸。不著
398c16║ 彼岸。不住中流。而度眾生。無有休息。雖無量
398c17║ 劫修菩薩行。

简体字

“善男子，譬如日轮，无有昼夜；但出时名昼，没时名夜。菩萨智轮亦复如是，无有分别，亦无三世；但随心现，教化众生，言其止住前劫、后劫。

“善男子，譬如日轮，住阎浮空，其影悉现一切宝物及以河海诸净水中，一切众生莫不目见，而彼净日不来至此。菩萨智轮亦复如是，出诸有海，住佛实法，寂静空中无有所依，为欲化度诸众生故，而于诸趣随类受生；实不生死，无所染著，无长短劫诸想分别。何以故？菩萨究竟离心想，见一切颠倒，得真实见，见法实性，知一切世间如梦、如幻；无有众生，但以大悲大愿力故，现众生前教化调伏。

“佛子，譬如船师，常以大船，于河流中不依此岸、不著彼岸、不住中流，而度众生无有休息。菩萨摩诃萨亦复如是，以波罗蜜船，于生死流中不依此岸、不著彼岸、不住中流，而度众生无有休息；虽无量劫修菩萨行，

Son of Good Family, this is analogous to the orb of the sun for which there is no "day" or "night." It is only with reference to its time of rising that one refers to "daytime" and with reference to its time of setting that one refers to "nighttime."

So too it is with the bodhisattva's sphere of wisdom. It has no such distinctions at all and, what is more, it does not have any "three periods of time." Rather, it is simply in accordance with the manifestations of the mind in the transformative teaching of beings that one speaks of it as occurring in an earlier kalpa or a later kalpa.

Son of Good Family, this is just as when the orb of the sun hangs in the sky over this continent of Jambudvīpa. Its reflection appears in everything adorned with jewels and in the still waters of the rivers and the ocean, doing so in such a way that no being fails to see it reflected in these places with his own eyes, yet that clearly shining sun does not itself descend to any of these places. So too it is with the bodhisattva's sphere of wisdom when it rises over the ocean of all realms of existence and dwells in the quiescent emptiness of the Buddha's genuine Dharma. There it is not dependent on anything at all, but still, out of a wish to teach all beings, he takes on births in the rebirth destinies in ways adapted to the various types of beings dwelling there.

As he does this, he does not actually take birth or die, he remains free of any defiling attachments, and he has no conceptual discriminations with regard to any kalpas, whether long or short. And why is this so? This is because the bodhisattva has ultimately abandoned all inverted conceptions, perceptions, and views and has acquired perception accordant with reality by which he perceives the true nature of dharmas. He realizes that the entire world is like a dream and like a conjured illusion in which there are no beings at all. It is solely due to the power of his great compassion and great vows that he appears before beings to teach and train them.

Son of the Buddha, this is just as it is with a ship captain who is always sailing an immense ship through the currents of a river and in doing so, does not rely on this near shore, does not become attached to that far shore, and does not stay in the middle of the river's currents as he ferries beings across without ever resting.

So too it is with the bodhisattva-mahāsattva who, using the ship of the *pāramitās*, navigates the currents of *saṃsāra* without relying on this near shore, without becoming attached to that far shore, and without staying in the middle of the currents as he ferries beings across without ever resting. In this, although he passes through countless kalpas cultivating the bodhisattva practices, he still never

正體字

未曾分別劫數長短。佛子。如
398c18 [7]大虛空。一切世界於中成壞。而無分別。本
398c19 性清淨。無染無亂。無礙無厭。非長非短。盡未
398c20 來劫。持一切剎。菩薩摩訶薩。亦復如是。以等
398c21 虛空界。廣大深心。起大願風輪。攝諸眾生。令
398c22 離惡道。生諸善趣。悉令安住一切智地。滅諸
398c23 煩惱生死苦縛。而無憂喜疲厭之心。[8]善男
398c24 子。如幻化人。[9]肢體雖具。而無入息及以出
398c25 息。寒熱飢渴憂喜生死十種之事。菩薩摩訶
398c26 薩。亦復如是。以如幻智平等法身。現眾色
398c27 相。於諸有趣。住無量劫。教化眾生。於生死中
398c28 一切境界。無欣無厭。無愛無恚。無苦無樂。無
398c29 取無捨。無安無怖。佛子。菩薩智慧。雖復如是
399a01 甚深難測。我當承佛威神之力。為汝解說。令
399a02 未來世諸菩薩等。滿足大願。成就諸力。佛子。
399a03 乃往古世。過世界海微塵數劫。有劫名善光。
399a04 世界名寶光。於其劫中。有一萬佛。出興于世。
399a05 其最初佛。號法輪音虛空燈王如來應正等
399a06 覺。十號圓滿。彼閻浮提。有一王都名寶莊嚴。
399a07 其東不遠。有一大林

简体字

未曾分别劫数长短。

“佛子，如太虚空，一切世界于中成坏而无分别，本性清净，无染无乱，无碍无厌，非长非短，尽未来劫持一切刹。菩萨摩诃萨亦复如是，以等虚空界广大深心，起大愿风轮，摄诸众生，令离恶道，生诸善趣，悉令安住一切智地，灭诸烦恼生死苦缚，而无忧喜、疲厌之心。

“善男子，如幻化人，肢体虽具，而无入息及以出息、寒、热、饥、渴、忧、喜、生、死十种之事。菩萨摩诃萨亦复如是，以如幻智平等法身现众色相，于诸有趣住无量劫教化众生，于生死中一切境界，无欣无厌，无爱无恚，无苦无乐，无取无舍，无安无怖。

“佛子，菩萨智慧虽复如是甚深难测，我当承佛威神之力为汝解说，令未来世诸菩萨等满足大愿、成就诸力。

“佛子，乃往古世，过世界海微尘数劫，有劫名善光，世界名宝光。于其劫中，有一万佛出兴于世。其最初佛，号：法轮音虚空灯王如来、应、正等觉，十号圆满。彼阎浮提，有一王都，名宝庄严；其东不远，有一大林，

distinguishes any particular number of kalpas, whether long or short.

Son of the Buddha, this is like the great empty space in which all worlds are created and destroyed even as it is free of any discriminations in this regard. Its fundamental nature is pure, free of defilement, free of any disorder, free of any impediments, free of any weariness, and neither long nor short. It persists throughout all future kalpas, continuing to hold all those *kṣetras*.

So too it is with the bodhisattva-mahāsattva. Using his vast and deep resolve that is as vast as the realm of empty space, he produces the whirlwind of his great vows that draws in all beings and induces them to leave behind the wretched destinies and take birth in the good rebirth destinies and then enables them all to establish themselves on the ground of all-knowledge. Thus he extinguishes all their afflictions and the sufferings and bonds of *saṃsāra* while still remaining free of any thoughts of sorrow, joy, or weariness.

Son of the Buddha, just as a magically conjured person, though complete with limbs and body, still does not have any of ten things, namely inhalation, exhalation, cold, heat, hunger, thirst, sorrow, joy, birth, or death, so too it is with the bodhisattva-mahāsattva. Using his wisdom cognizing the illusory nature of phenomena and the uniform equality of the Dharma body, he manifests many kinds of physical forms and features and abides for countless kalpas, teaching beings in all the rebirth destinies within the realms of existence. With respect to all the spheres of experience encountered in *saṃsāra*, he has no delight, no weariness, no love, no hatred, no suffering, no bliss, no grasping, no relinquishing, no peace, and no fear.

Son of the Buddha, although the bodhisattva's wisdom is so very deep and difficult to fathom as this, receiving the aid of the Buddha's awesome spiritual powers, I shall explain it for you to enable bodhisattvas in future ages to completely fulfill the great vows and completely develop all the powers.

Son of the Buddha, long ago, in the ancient past, back beyond kalpas as numerous as the atoms in an ocean of worlds, there was a kalpa named Fine Radiance in which there was a world named Jewel Radiance. During that kalpa there were ten thousand buddhas who appeared in the world. The very first of those buddhas was named King Illumining Space with the Voice of the Dharma Wheel, the Tathāgata, the Arhat, the One of Right and Universal Enlightenment. He was referred to by all ten of the buddhas' titles.

On that continent of Jambudvīpa, there was a royal capital known as Jewel Adornment. Not far to the east of it was a great forest known

正體字

名曰妙光。中有道場名
399a08‖ 為寶華。彼道場中。有普光明摩尼蓮華藏師
399a09‖ 子之座。時彼如來於此座上。成阿耨多羅三
399a10‖ 藐三菩提。滿一百年坐於道場。為諸菩薩諸
399a11‖ 天世人。及閻浮提宿植善根已成熟者。演說
399a12‖ 正法。是時國王名曰勝光。時世人民壽一萬
399a13‖ 歲。其中多有殺盜婬佚。妄[1]語綺語。兩舌惡
399a14‖ 口。貪瞋邪見。不孝父母。不敬沙門。婆羅門
399a15‖ 等。時王為欲調伏彼故。造立囹圄。枷鎖禁
399a16‖ 閉。無量眾生於中受苦。王有太子名為善伏。
399a17‖ 端正殊特。人所喜見。具二十八大人之相。在
399a18‖ 宮殿中。遙聞獄囚楚毒音聲。心懷傷愍。從宮
399a19‖ 殿出入牢獄中。見諸罪人杻械枷鎖。遞相連
399a20‖ 繫。置幽闇處。或以火炙。或以煙熏。或被榜
399a21‖ 笞。或遭臏割。裸形亂髮。飢渴羸瘦。筋斷骨
399a22‖ 現。號叫苦劇。太子見已心生悲愍。以無畏聲。
399a23‖ 安慰之言。汝莫憂惱。汝勿愁怖。我當令汝悉
399a24‖ 得解脫。便詣王所而白王言。獄中罪人苦毒
399a25‖ 難處。願垂寬宥施以無畏。

简体字

名曰妙光；中有道场，名为宝华。彼道场中，有普光明摩尼莲华藏师子之座。时，彼如来于此座上，成阿耨多罗三藐三菩提，满一百年坐于道场，为诸菩萨、诸天、世人及阎浮提宿植善根已成熟者演说正法。

“是时，国王名曰胜光。时世人民寿一万岁，其中多有杀、盗、淫佚、妄言、绮语、两舌、恶口、贪、瞋、邪见，不孝父母，不敬沙门、婆罗门等。时，王为欲调伏彼故，造立囹圄，枷锁禁闭，无量众生于中受苦。

“王有太子，名为善伏，端正殊特，人所喜见，具二十八大人之相。在宫殿中，遥闻狱囚楚毒音声，心怀伤愍。从宫殿出，入牢狱中，见诸罪人杻械、枷锁递相连系，置幽暗处，或以火炙，或以烟熏，或被榜笞，或遭膑割，裸形乱发，饥渴羸瘦，筋断骨现，号叫苦剧。太子见已，心生悲愍，以无畏声安慰之言：‘汝莫忧恼！汝勿愁怖！我当令汝悉得解脱。’便诣王所而白王言：‘狱中罪人苦毒难处，愿垂宽宥，施以无畏。’

as Marvelous Radiance in which there was an enlightenment site known as Bejeweled Blossoms. Within that enlightenment site there was a lotus flower dais lion throne adorned with universal-radiance *maṇi* jewels.

At that time, that *tathāgata* attained *anuttara-samyak-saṃbodhi* on this very throne and then continued for a full hundred years to sit at that enlightenment site, expounding on right Dharma for bodhisattvas, devas, the people of the world, and everyone else in Jambudvīpa whose roots of goodness from previous lives had become adequately ripened.

At this time, the king of the country was named Light of Victory. The life span of that world's population was a full ten thousand years. Among them there were many who engaged in killing, stealing, sexual misconduct, false speech, lewd and frivolous speech, divisive speech, abusive speech, covetousness, hatred, and wrong views, who failed to show filial reverence toward their parents, and who also failed to show any respect for *śramaṇas,* brahmans, or other such persons.

At that time, wishing to discipline those individuals, the king built a prison in which he confined countless beings in fetters and shackles and compelled them to undergo sufferings there.

The king had a son, a prince named Fine Conqueror, one who was extraordinarily handsome, one who people delighted in seeing, one who possessed twenty-eight of the auspicious marks of a great man. From within the palace, he heard from afar the sound of the prisoners' screams as they were being tortured. Feeling sadness and sympathy for them, he left the palace, went into the prison, and saw the criminals there in manacles, fetters, and shackles, tied together and confined in dark places where they were burned, confined in smoke-filled rooms, beaten with cudgels or canes, or had their kneecaps sliced off. Naked, with disheveled hair, hungry, thirsty, wasted, with ligaments cut and bones showing, they screamed as they were subjected to the pain of such excruciating cruelties.

Having witnessed this, the prince's mind was filled with compassionate sympathy. With a voice that allayed their fears and with comforting words, he said, "You must not feel such distress and torment. Do not be worried or frightened, for I shall see to it that you will all be released."

He then went to the king and addressed the king, saying, "The excruciating cruelties inflicted on the criminals in the prison are difficult to abide. Please forgive them, pardon them, and bestow the gift of fearlessness on them.

正體字

時王即集五百大
399a26 臣而問之言。是事云何。諸臣答言。彼罪人者
399a27 私竊官物。謀奪王位。盜入宮闈。罪應刑戮。有
399a28 哀救者罪亦至死。時彼太子。悲心轉切。語大
399a29 臣言。如汝所說但放此人。隨其所應可以治
399b01 我。我為彼故。一切苦事悉皆能受。粉身沒命。
399b02 無所顧惜。要令罪人皆得免苦。何以故。我若
399b03 不救此眾生者。云何能救三界牢獄諸苦眾
399b04 生。一切眾生在三界中。貪愛所縛。愚癡所
399b05 蔽。貧無功德。墮諸惡趣。身形鄙陋諸根放逸。
399b06 其心迷惑不求出道。失智慧光樂著三有。斷
399b07 諸福德滅諸智慧。種種煩惱濁亂其心。住苦
399b08 牢獄入魔罥網。生老病死憂悲惱害。如是諸
399b09 苦常所逼迫。

简体字

"时，王即集五百大臣而问之言：'是事云何？'诸臣答言：'彼罪人者，私窃官物，谋夺王位，盗入宫闱，罪应刑戮。有哀救者，罪亦至死。'

"时，彼太子悲心转切，语大臣言：'如汝所说，但放此人；随其所应，可以治我。我为彼故，一切苦事悉皆能受，粉身殁命，无所顾惜，要令罪人皆得免苦。何以故？我若不救此众生者，云何能救三界牢狱诸苦众生？一切众生在三界中，贪爱所缚，愚痴所蔽，贫无功德，堕诸恶趣，身形鄙陋，诸根放逸，其心迷惑，不求出道，失智慧光，乐著三有，断诸福德，灭诸智慧，种种烦恼浊乱其心，住苦牢狱，入魔罥网，生老病死忧悲恼害，如是诸苦常所逼迫。

The king then assembled his five hundred great officials and asked them, "What should be done about this?"

The officials replied, "Those criminals have stolen state property for their own use, have usurped the powers of the royal office, and have burglarized the palace grounds, thereby committing offenses for which they should be executed. Anyone who would take pity on them and seek to rescue them would commit a crime for which he too would be executed."

That prince's thoughts of compassion then became even stronger, whereupon he told those great officials:

> According to what you have just said, if you simply release these men, then you can instead subject me to the punishments that would have been appropriate for them. For the sake of those criminals, I can endure all those painful punishments. Even if you pulverize my body and I thus lose my life, I shall not have any concerns on this account. It is only necessary that these criminals be allowed to avoid undergoing these punishments.
>
> And why do I propose this? If I do not rescue these beings, how might I ever be able to rescue all suffering beings in the prison of the three realms of existence? By this I mean all beings in the three realms of existence:
>
> Who are held in the bondage of craving;
> Who are blanketed with delusion;
> Who are destitute of meritorious qualities;
> Who have fallen down into the wretched rebirth destinies and taken on forms that are ugly;
> Who have become heedless in the way they use their faculties;
> Whose minds have become confused and hence do not seek the path of emancipation;
> Who have lost the light of wisdom;
> Who have become happily attached to the three realms of existence;
> Who have cut off all their merit;
> Who have destroyed all their wisdom;
> Whose minds are made turbid and confused by the many different kinds of afflictions;
> Who dwell in the prison of suffering;
> Who have entered the net of Māra;
> Who are tormented and injured by birth, aging, sickness, death, sorrow, and lamentation; and
> Who are forever oppressed by all kinds of sufferings such as these.

正體字

我當云何。令彼解脫。應捨身命
399b10║ 而拔濟之。時諸大臣共詣王所。悉舉其手高
399b11║ 聲唱言。大王當知。如太子意。毀壞王法禍及
399b12║ 萬人。若王愛念不責治者。王之寶祚亦不久
399b13║ 立。王聞此言赫然大怒。令誅太子及諸罪人。
399b14║ 王后聞之。愁憂號哭。毀形降服。與千采女馳
399b15║ 詣王所。舉身投地頂禮王足。俱作是言。唯願
399b16║ 大王。赦太子命。王即迴顧。語太子言。莫救罪
399b17║ 人。若救罪人必當殺汝。爾時太子。為欲專
399b18║ 求一切智故。為欲利益諸眾生故。為以大悲
399b19║ 普救攝故。其心堅固。無有退怯。復白王言。願
399b20║ 恕彼罪身當受戮。王言隨意。爾時王后白言。
399b21║ 大王。願聽太子。半月行施。恣意修福。然後治
399b22║ 罪。王即聽許。時都城北有一大園名曰日光。
399b23║ 是昔施場。太子往彼。設大施會。飲食衣服。華
399b24║ 鬘[2]瓔珞。塗香末香。幢幡寶蓋。諸莊嚴具。隨
399b25║ 有所求靡不周給。經半月已。於最後日。國王
399b26║ 大臣。長者居士。城邑人民。

简体字

我当云何令彼解脱？应舍身命而拔济之！’

“时，诸大臣共诣王所，悉举其手高声唱言：‘大王当知，如太子意，毁坏王法，祸及万人。若王爱念不责治者，王之宝祚亦不久立。’王闻此言，赫然大怒，令诛太子及诸罪人。

“王后闻之，愁忧号哭，毁形降服，与千采女驰诣王所，举身投地顶礼王足，俱作是言：‘唯愿大王，赦太子命！’王即回顾，语太子言：‘莫救罪人；若救罪人，必当杀汝！’尔时，太子为欲专求一切智故，为欲利益诸众生故，为以大悲普救摄故，其心坚固无有退怯，复白王言：‘愿恕彼罪，身当受戮！’王言：‘随意！’尔时，王后白言：‘大王，愿听太子，半月行施，恣意修福，然后治罪。’王即听许。

“时，都城北有一大园，名曰日光，是昔施场。太子往彼，设大施会；饮食、衣服、华鬘、璎珞、涂香、末香、幢幡、宝盖，诸庄严具，随有所求，靡不周给。经半月已，于最后日，国王、大臣、长者、居士、城邑人民

> How else then might I liberate them all? Therefore I should relinquish my body and life in order to rescue them.

All of those great officials then went to see the king where, raising their arms and shouting, they exclaimed:

> The great king must realize that, if we were we to act in accordance with the prince's intentions, this would violate the royal laws and bring disaster to a myriad other people. If, due to thoughts of affection, the king failed to enforce punishments, then even the king's own jeweled throne would not last long.

When the king heard these statements, he flew into a great fiery rage and ordered the execution of both the prince and all the criminals. When the Queen heard this, beset with sorrow and distress, she wailed and wept, made her appearance plain, donned her mourning clothes, and then went together with her thousand female attendants, hurrying to see the king. They then cast their bodies to the ground, bowing down in reverence at the feet of the king, and, speaking in unison, said, "Please, Great King, spare the prince's life."

The king then turned his gaze and said to the prince, "You must not attempt to rescue criminals. If you rescue these criminals, I will definitely have you executed."

Then, because the prince was single-mindedly intent on the quest for all-knowledge, because he wished to benefit all beings, and because he wished to use the great compassion to rescue them all, his resolve hardened and he refused to be intimidated. Thus, he then replied to the king by saying, "Please pardon those criminals and let me be executed in their place."

To this, the king replied, "However you wish."

The Queen then addressed him, saying, "Please permit the prince to carry out acts of giving for a half a month in order to freely cultivate merit and only then be punished for his crime." The king then permitted this.

North of that capital city, there was an immense park called "Sunlight" that, in the past, had served as an open area for charitable giving. The prince went there and established a great giving assembly in which he gave away food, drink, clothing, flower garlands, necklaces, perfumes, powdered incense, banners, pennants, jeweled canopies, and all kinds of adornments, ensuring that whatever was sought was provided to everyone.

After a half month had passed, on the very last day, the king, the great officials, the elders, the merchants, the citizens of that city,

正體字

及諸外道。悉來集
399b27║ 會。時法輪音虛空燈王如來。知諸眾生調伏
399b28║ 時至。與大眾俱。天王圍遶。龍王供養。夜叉王
399b29║ 守護。乾闥婆王讚歎。阿脩羅王曲躬頂禮。迦
399c01║ 樓羅王以清淨心散諸寶華。緊那羅王歡喜
399c02║ 勸請。摩睺羅伽王一心瞻仰。來入彼會。爾
399c03║ 時太子及諸大眾。遙見佛來。端嚴殊特諸根
399c04║ 寂定。如調順象。心無垢濁。如清淨池。現大神
399c05║ 通。示大自在。顯大威德。種種相好。莊嚴其
399c06║ 身。放大光明。普照世界。一切毛孔出香焰雲。
399c07║ [*]震動十方無量佛剎。隨所至處。普雨一切
399c08║ 諸莊嚴具。以佛威儀。以佛功德。眾生見者。心
399c09║ 淨歡喜煩惱[3]銷滅。爾時太子及諸大眾。五
399c10║ 體投地頂禮其足。安施床座。合掌白言。善來
399c11║ 世尊。善來善逝。唯願哀愍。攝受於我。處于此
399c12║ 座。以佛神力。淨居諸天。即變此座。為香摩尼
399c13║ 蓮華之座。佛坐其上。諸菩薩眾。亦皆就座。周
399c14║ 匝圍遶。時彼會中。一切眾生。因見如來。苦滅
399c15║ 障除。堪受聖法。

简体字

及诸外道，悉来集会。

“时，法轮音虚空灯王如来，知诸众生调伏时至，与大众俱，天王围绕，龙王供养，夜叉王守护，乾闼婆王赞叹，阿修罗王曲躬顶礼，迦楼罗王以清净心散诸宝华，紧那罗王欢喜劝请，摩睺罗伽王一心瞻仰，来入彼会。

“尔时，太子及诸大众，遥见佛来，端严殊特，诸根寂定如调顺象，心无垢浊如清净池，现大神通，示大自在，显大威德，种种相好庄严其身，放大光明普照世界，一切毛孔出香焰云，震动十方无量佛刹，随所至处普雨一切诸庄严具；以佛威仪，以佛功德，众生见者，心净欢喜，烦恼消灭。

“尔时，太子及诸大众五体投地，顶礼其足，安施床座，合掌白言：‘善来世尊！善来善逝！唯愿哀愍，摄受于我，处于此座！’以佛神力，净居诸天即变此座为香摩尼莲华之座。佛坐其上，诸菩萨众亦皆就座周匝围绕。时，彼会中一切众生，因见如来，苦灭障除，堪受圣法。

and all those who pursued the various heterodox paths all came and assembled together there.

At this time, King Illumining Space with the Voice of the Dharma Wheel Tathāgata knew that the time had arrived for the many beings to be trained. He was then accompanied with an immense congregation, surrounded by deva kings, dragon kings who were making offerings, *yakṣa* kings who were serving as protectors, *gandharva* kings who were singing praises, *asura* kings who were stooping down and bowing to him in reverence, *garuḍa* kings who, with pure minds, were scattering all kinds of jeweled flowers, *kiṃnara* kings who were joyfully requesting teachings, and *mahoraga* kings who were single-mindedly gazing up at him in reverence—these all came and entered that assembly.

The prince and that entire great assembly then saw the Buddha coming from afar, extraordinarily fine in his appearance, all of his faculties in quiescent absorption, like a well-disciplined elephant, his mind entirely free of defiling turbidities, like a pristinely clear pond, displaying great spiritual superknowledges, revealing his great powers of transformation, showing his immense awesome virtue, his body adorned with the many different major marks and secondary signs, emanating a great radiance everywhere illuminating the world, all of his pores sending forth fragrant clouds of flaming radiance, shaking and moving the countless *kṣetras* of the ten directions, and everywhere causing a rain of all kinds of adornments wherever he went. Due to the Buddha's awesome deportment and due to the meritorious qualities of the Buddha, whenever any of those beings there looked at him, their minds were purified, they were filled with joyous delight, and their afflictions were melted away.

The prince and everyone in that great assembly then bowed down in full reverential prostration at his feet. They arranged a seat for him, pressed their palms together, and addressed him, saying, "Welcome, O Bhagavat! Welcome, O Well Gone One! Please, out of pity for us, accept us in your presence and sit here on this seat."

Then, with the aid of the Buddha's spiritual powers, the devas of the Pure Abode Heavens immediately transformed this seat into a fragrant *maṇi* jewel lotus flower throne. The Buddha sat down on it and the congregation of bodhisattvas also sat down, sitting all around him. Then, because they had seen the Tathāgata, all the beings in that assembly had their sufferings extinguished and their obstacles removed so that they were then able to receive the Dharma of the *āryas*.

正體字

爾時如來。知其可化。以圓滿
399c16‖ 音。說修多羅。名普照因輪。令諸眾生。隨類各
399c17‖ 解。時彼會中。有八十那由他眾生。遠塵離垢。
399c18‖ 得[4]法眼淨。無量那由他眾生。得無學地。十
399c19‖ 千眾生。住大乘道。入普賢行。成滿大願。當爾
399c20‖ 之時。十方各百佛刹微塵數眾生。於大乘中。
399c21‖ 心得調伏。無量世界一切眾生。免離惡趣生
399c22‖ 於天上。善伏太子。即於此時。得菩薩教化眾
399c23‖ 生令生善根解脫門。善男子。爾時太子。豈異
399c24‖ 人乎。我身是也。我因往昔起大悲心。捨身
399c25‖ 命財。救苦眾生。開門大施。供養於佛。得此解
399c26‖ 脫。佛子當知。我於爾時。但為利益一切眾
399c27‖ 生。不著三界。不求果報。不貪名稱。不欲自讚
399c28‖ 輕毀於他。於諸境界。無所貪染。無所怖畏。但
399c29‖ 莊嚴大乘出要之道。常樂觀察一切智門。修
400a01‖ 行苦行。得此解脫。佛子。於汝意云何。彼時五
400a02‖ 百大臣。欲害我者。豈異人乎。今提婆達多等
400a03‖ 五百徒黨是也。是諸人等。蒙佛教化。皆當得
400a04‖ 阿耨多羅三藐三菩提。於未來世。過須彌山
400a05‖ 微塵數劫。

简体字

“尔时，如来知其可化，以圆满音，说修多罗，名普照因轮，令诸众生随类各解。时，彼会中有八十那由他众生，远尘离垢，得净法眼；无量那由他众生，得无学地；十千众生，住大乘道，入普贤行，成满大愿。当尔之时，十方各百佛刹微尘数众生，于大乘中，心得调伏；无量世界一切众生，免离恶趣，生于天上。善伏太子即于此时，得菩萨教化众生令生善根解脱门。

“善男子，尔时太子岂异人乎？我身是也。我因往昔起大悲心，舍身命财救苦众生，开门大施供养于佛，得此解脱。佛子当知，我于尔时，但为利益一切众生，不著三界，不求果报，不贪名称，不欲自赞轻毁于他，于诸境界无所贪染、无所怖畏，但庄严大乘出要之道，常乐观察一切智门，修行苦行，得此解脱。

“佛子，于汝意云何？彼时五百大臣，欲害我者，岂异人乎？今提婆达多等五百徒党是也。是诸人等，蒙佛教化，皆当得阿耨多罗三藐三菩提，于未来世，过须弥山微尘数劫，

Then the Tathāgata, knowing that they could now receive instruction, with his perfectly full voice, taught a sutra known as the Universal Illumination of the Maṇḍala of Causality, while enabling all the beings there to understand it in accordance with their individual capacities. There were at that time eighty nayutas of beings in that assembly who became far removed from the dust and defilement of the world and acquired the purified Dharma eye. There were countless nayutas of beings there who reached the ground beyond training and there were ten thousand beings there who came to abide in the path of the Great Vehicle, entered the practices of Samantabhadra, and accomplished the fulfillment of great vows.

At that very time, in each of the ten directions, there were beings as numerous as the atoms in a hundred buddha *kṣetras* whose minds submitted to training in the Great Vehicle. All the beings in countless worlds avoided rebirth in the wretched destinies and took rebirth in the heavens.

At this time, the Prince, Fine Conqueror, immediately acquired the liberation gateway known as "teaching beings to produce roots of goodness."

Son of Good Family, as for he who was the prince at that time, who else might it have been? It was none other than myself. It was due to my past development of the mind of great compassion, my relinquishing of my body, life, and wealth, my rescuing of beings afflicted by sufferings, my opening up of the gates of great giving, and my making offerings to buddhas that I then acquired this liberation.

Son of the Buddha, one should realize that, at that time, I acted solely to benefit all beings and not out of any attachment to the three realms of existence, not out of any wish for karmic rewards, not out of any desire for fame, and not out of any wish to praise myself and disparage others. I had no desire for any realms of the senses and I was entirely fearless. It was only because I wished to adorn the Great Vehicle's path to emancipation, because I always delighted in contemplating the gateways leading to all-knowledge, and because I cultivated austerities that I acquired this liberation.

Son of the Buddha, what do you think? As for those five hundred great officials who wished to harm me at that time, who else might they have been? They were none other than the five hundred followers of the man we now know as Devadatta. All of these men then received the Buddha's instruction and became bound in the future to attain *anuttara-samyak-saṃbodhi*. In a future age, beyond a number of kalpas as numerous as Mount Sumeru's atoms, there

正體字

爾時有劫。名善光。世界名寶光。於
400a06 中成佛。其五百佛次第興世。最初如來名曰
400a07 大悲。第二名饒益世間。第三名大悲師子。第
400a08 四名救護眾生。乃至最後名曰醫王。雖彼諸
400a09 佛大悲平等。然其國土。種族父母。受生誕生。
400a10 出家學道。往詣道場。轉正法輪。說修多羅。語
400a11 言音聲。光明眾會。壽命法住。及其名號。各各
400a12 差別。佛子。彼諸罪人。我所救者。即拘留孫等
400a13 賢劫千佛。及百萬阿僧祇諸大菩薩。於無量
400a14 精進力名稱功德慧如來所。發阿耨多羅三
400a15 藐三菩提心。今於十方國土。行菩薩道。修習
400a16 增長。此[1]菩薩。教化眾生。令生善根解脫者
400a17 是。時勝光王。今薩遮尼乾子大論師是。時
400a18 王宮人及諸眷屬。即彼尼乾六萬弟子。與師
400a19 俱來。建大論幢。共佛論議。悉降伏之。授阿耨
400a20 多羅三藐三菩提記者是。此諸人等。皆當作
400a21 佛。國土莊嚴。劫數名號。各各有異。佛子。我
400a22 於爾時。救罪人已。父母聽我。捨離國土。妻子
400a23 財寶。於法輪音虛空燈王佛所。出家學道。五
400a24 百歲中。淨修梵行。即得成就百萬陀羅尼。百
400a25 萬神通。

简体字

尔时有劫，名善光，世界名宝光，于中成佛。其五百佛次第兴世，最初如来，名曰大悲；第二，名饶益世间；第三，名大悲师子；第四，名救护众生；乃至最后，名曰医王。虽彼诸佛大悲平等，然其国土、种族、父母、受生、诞生、出家、学道、往诣道场、转正法轮、说修多罗、语言、音声、光明、众会、寿命、法住及其名号，各各差别。

“佛子，彼诸罪人，我所救者，即拘留孙等贤劫千佛，及百万阿僧祇诸大菩萨——于无量精进力名称功德慧如来所，发阿耨多罗三藐三菩提心，今于十方国土，行菩萨道，修习增长此菩提，教化众生，令生善根解脱者是。时胜光王，今萨遮尼乾子大论师是。时王宫人及诸眷属，即彼尼乾六万弟子，与师俱来，建大论幢，共佛论议，悉降伏之，授阿耨多罗三藐三菩提记者是。此诸人等，皆当作佛，国土庄严、劫数、名号，各各有异。

“佛子，我于尔时救罪人已，父母听我舍离国土、妻子、财宝，于法轮音虚空灯王佛所出家学道。五百岁中，净修梵行，即得成就百万陀罗尼、百万神通、

will be a kalpa known as Fine Radiance and a world known as Jewel Radiance in which they will attain buddhahood. Those five hundred buddhas will appear in the world sequentially. The first among them will be a tathāgata known as Great Compassion. The second of them will be named Liberally Benefiting the World. The third of them will be known as Lion of Great Compassion. The fourth will be named Rescuer of Beings. And so it shall continue in this way up to the very last of them who shall be named Medicine King.

Although all of those buddhas will be the same as regards their possession of the great compassion, each of them will possess individual differences as regards their land, their clan, their parents, their coming forth to take birth, their leaving behind the home life and training in the path, their going forth to the site of enlightenment, their turning of the wheel of right Dharma, their teaching of the sutras, their languages, their voice, their radiance, their congregations, their life spans, their Dharma's period of remaining in the world, and their names.

Son of the Buddha, all those criminals I saved at that time are now none other than Krakucchanda, the rest of the thousand buddhas of this Worthy Kalpa, and the hundred myriads of asaṃkheyas of great bodhisattvas. They made the resolve to attain *anuttara-samyak-saṃbodhi* under the *tathāgata* known as Merit and Wisdom Famed for the Power of Measureless Vigor. They are now practicing the bodhisattva path throughout the lands of the ten directions while growing in their cultivation of this bodhisattva's liberation known as "teaching beings to produce roots of goodness."

That king then known as "Supreme Radiance" is the Satyaka-nirgranthī-putra of our present era. Those abiding in that king's palace and those serving as members of his retinue are none other than those sixty thousand present Nirgrantha disciples who come together with their teacher to erect the banner of a great doctrine, engaged in doctrinal debate with the Buddha, and were then utterly vanquished by him even as he bestowed predictions on all these people foretelling their future realization of *anuttara-samyak-saṃbodhi,* their future buddhahood, and their separate lands, adornments, intervening kalpas, and names, each of which differ.

Son of the Buddha, after I rescued those criminals, my parents permitted me to leave behind my country, wife, children, and wealth to leave the home life and train in the path with King Illumining Space with the Voice of the Dharma Wheel Buddha. Then, for five hundred years, I cultivated the pure *brahmacarya,* whereupon I then perfected a million *dhāraṇīs,* a million spiritual superknowledges,

正體字

百萬法藏。[2]百萬求一切智勇猛精
400a26‖ 進。淨治百萬堪忍門。增長百萬思惟心。成就
400a27‖ 百萬菩薩力。入百萬菩薩智門。得百萬般若
400a28‖ 波羅蜜門。見十方百萬諸佛。生百萬菩薩大
400a29‖ 願。念念中十方各照百萬佛刹。念念中憶念
400b01‖ 十方世界前後際劫百萬諸佛。念念中知十方
400b02‖ 世界百萬諸佛變化海。念念中見十方百萬
400b03‖ 世界所有眾生種種諸趣。隨業所受。生時死
400b04‖ 時。善趣惡趣。好色惡色。其諸眾生。種種心
400b05‖ 行。種種欲樂。種種根性。種種業習。種種成
400b06‖ 就。皆悉明了。佛子。我於爾時。命終之後。還
400b07‖ 復於彼王家受生。作轉輪王。彼法輪音虛空
400b08‖ 燈王如來滅後。次即於此。值法空王如來。承
400b09‖ 事供養。次為帝釋。即此道場值天王藏如來。
400b10‖ 親近供養。次為夜摩天王。即於此世界值大
400b11‖ 地威力山如來。親近供養。次為兜率天王。即
400b12‖ 於此世界值法輪光音聲王如來。親近供養。
400b13‖ 次為化樂天王。即於此世界值虛空智王如
400b14‖ 來。親近供養。

简体字

百万法藏、百万求一切智勇猛精进，净治百万堪忍门，增长百万思惟心，成就百万菩萨力，入百万菩萨智门，得百万般若波罗蜜门，见十方百万诸佛，生百万菩萨大愿；念念中，十方各照百万佛刹；念念中，忆念十方世界前后际劫百万诸佛；念念中，知十方世界百万诸佛变化海；念念中，见十方百万世界所有众生种种诸趣，随业所受生时、死时、善趣、恶趣、好色、恶色，其诸众生种种心行、种种欲乐、种种根性、种种业习、种种成就，皆悉明了。

“佛子，我于尔时命终之后，还复于彼王家受生，作转轮王，彼法轮音虚空灯王如来灭后，次即于此值法空王如来，承事供养；次为帝释，即此道场值天王藏如来，亲近供养；次为夜摩天王，即于此世界值大地威力山如来，亲近供养；次为兜率天王，即于此世界值法轮光音声王如来，亲近供养；次为化乐天王，即于此世界值虚空智王如来，亲近供养；

a million treasuries of Dharma, and a million forms of courageous vigor in seeking all-knowledge. I also purified a million gateways of patience, developed a million varieties of contemplative thoughts, perfected a million bodhisattva powers, entered a million gateways to bodhisattva wisdom, acquired a million gateways into the *prajñāpāramitā,* saw a million buddhas of the ten directions, and made a million great bodhisattva vows.

In each successive mind-moment and in each of the ten directions, I illuminated a million buddha *kṣetras.* In each successive mind-moment, I brought to mind a million past and future buddhas throughout the worlds of the ten directions. In each successive mind-moment, I came to know throughout the worlds of the ten directions the ocean of transformations of a million buddhas.

And in each successive mind-moment, I saw all the beings in their many different rebirth destinies in a million worlds throughout the ten directions, seeing what they undergo in accordance with their karma when they are born and when they die, seeing whether they are reborn in the good rebirth destinies or in the wretched rebirth destinies, and seeing whether they take on fine physical forms or inferior physical forms. I also saw with regard to all those beings their various kinds of mental actions, their various inclinations, the various natures of their faculties, their various kinds of habitual karmic propensities, and their various kinds of successes, all of which I completely understood.

Son of the Buddha, at that time, after my life came to an end, I returned yet again to take birth in the family of that king where I became a wheel-turning king. After that King Illumining Space with the Voice of the Dharma Wheel Tathāgata had passed into nirvāṇa, I next met in this place Dharma Emptiness King Tathāgata to whom I rendered service and presented offerings.

Next, I became an Indra and then met at this very site of enlightenment Heavenly King Treasury Tathāgata to whom I drew near and presented offerings.

Next, I became a Yāma Heaven king and then met in this world Great Earth's Mountain of Awesome Power Tathāgata to whom I drew near and presented offerings.

Next, I became a Tuṣita Heaven king and then met in this world King Voice of the Light of the Dharma Wheel Tathāgata to whom I drew near and presented offerings.

Next, I became a Nirmāṇarati Heaven king and then met in this world Empty Space Wisdom King Tathāgata to whom I drew near and presented offerings.

正體字

次為他化自在天王。即於此
400b15‖ 世界值無能壞幢如來。親近供養。次為阿脩
400b16‖ 羅王。即於此世界值一切法雷音王如來。親
400b17‖ 近供養。次為梵王。即於此世界值普現化演
400b18‖ 法音如來。親近供養。佛子。此寶光世界善光
400b19‖ 劫中。有一萬佛。出興于世。我皆親近承事
400b20‖ 供養。次復有劫名曰日光。有六十億佛。出
400b21‖ 興於世。最初如來名妙相山。我時為王名曰
400b22‖ 大慧。於彼佛所承事供養。次有佛出名圓滿
400b23‖ 肩。我為居士。親近供養。次有佛出名離垢童
400b24‖ 子。我為大臣。親近供養。次有佛出名勇猛持。
400b25‖ 我為阿脩羅王。親近供養。次有佛出名須彌
400b26‖ 相。我為樹神。親近供養。次有佛出。名離垢
400b27‖ 臂。我為商主。親近供養。次有佛出名師子遊
400b28‖ 步。我為城神。親近供養。次有佛出名為寶髻。
400b29‖ 我為毘沙門天王。親近供養。次有佛出名最
400c01‖ 上法稱。我為乾闥婆王。親近供養。次有佛
400c02‖ 出名光明冠。我為鳩槃[3]荼王。親近供養。於
400c03‖ 彼劫中。如是次第。有六十億如來。出興於世。
400c04‖ 我常於此。受種種身。一一佛所。親近供養。教
400c05‖ 化成就無量眾生。

简体字

次为他化自在天王，即于此世界值无能坏幢如来，亲近供养；次为阿修罗王，即于此世界值一切法雷音王如来，亲近供养；次为梵王，即于此世界值普现化演法音如来，亲近供养。

“佛子，此宝光世界善光劫中，有一万佛出兴于世，我皆亲近承事供养。次复有劫，名曰日光，有六十亿佛出兴于世，最初如来，名妙相山，我时为王，名曰大慧，于彼佛所承事供养；次有佛出，名圆满肩，我为居士，亲近供养；次有佛出，名离垢童子，我为大臣，亲近供养；次有佛出，名勇猛持，我为阿修罗王，亲近供养；次有佛出，名须弥相，我为树神，亲近供养；次有佛出，名离垢臂，我为商主，亲近供养；次有佛出，名师子游步，我为城神，亲近供养；次有佛出，名为宝髻，我为毗沙门天王，亲近供养；次有佛出，名最上法称，我为乾闼婆王，亲近供养；次有佛出，名光明冠，我为鸠槃荼王，亲近供养。

“于彼劫中，如是次第有六十亿如来出兴于世。我常于此受种种身，一一佛所亲近供养，教化成就无量众生；

Next, I became a Paranirmita Vaśavartin Heaven king and then met in this world Invincible Banner Tathāgata to whom I drew near and presented offerings.

Next, I became an *asura* king and then met in this world All Dharmas' Thunder King Tathāgata to whom I drew near and presented offerings.

Next, I became a Brahma Heaven king and then met in this world Universally Appearing Transformations Proclaiming Dharma's Sounds Tathāgata to whom I drew near and presented offerings.

Son of the Buddha, in this Jewel Radiance World, during the Fine Radiance Kalpa, there were a myriad buddhas who appeared in the world, to all of whom I drew near and presented offerings.

There was next another kalpa that was named Sunlight in which sixty *koṭīs* of buddhas arose in the world. The very first *tathāgata* was named Mountain of Marvelous Marks. I was then a king named Great Wisdom who served and made offerings to that buddha.

Next there appeared a buddha named Perfect Shoulders. I was then a layman who drew near and made offerings to him.

Next there appeared a buddha named Pure Youth. I was then a great official who drew near and made offerings to him.

Next there appeared a buddha named Courageous Upholder. I was then an *asura* king who drew near and made offerings to him.

Next there appeared a buddha named Sumeru of the Marks. I was then a tree spirit who drew near and made offerings to him.

Next there appeared a buddha named Stainless Arms. I was then a caravan leader who drew near and made offerings to him.

Next there appeared a buddha named Lion's Stride. I was then a city spirit who drew near and made offerings to him.

Next there appeared a buddha named Jeweled Topknot. I was then a Vaiśravaṇa deva king who drew near and made offerings to him.

Next there appeared a buddha named Supreme Dharma Renown. I was then a *gandharva* king who drew near and made offerings to him.

Next there appeared a buddha named Radiant Crown. I was then a *kumbhāṇḍa* king who drew near and made offerings to him.

Throughout the course of that kalpa, sixty koṭīs of tathāgatas sequentially arose in the world. During this time, I always took on many different kinds of bodies here and then drew near and made offerings to every one of those buddhas as I also taught and ripened countless beings.

正體字

於一一佛所。得種種三昧
400c06║ 門。種種陀羅尼門。[4]種種神通門。種種辯才
400c07║ 門。種種一切智門。種種法明門。種種智慧門。
400c08║ 照種種十方海。入種種佛剎海。見種種諸佛
400c09║ 海。清淨成就增長廣大。如於此劫中親近供
400c10║ 養。爾所諸佛。於一切處一切世界海微塵數
400c11║ 劫。所有諸佛出興于世。親近供養。聽聞說法。
400c12║ 信受護持。亦復如是。如是一切諸如來所。皆
400c13║ 悉修習此解脫門。復得無量解脫方便。爾時
400c14║ 救護一切眾生主夜神。欲重宣此解脫義。即
400c15║ 為善財。而說頌言
400c16║ 汝以歡喜信樂心　問此難思解脫法
400c17║ 我承如來護念力　為汝宣說應聽受
400c18║ 過去無邊廣大劫　過於剎海微塵數
400c19║ 時有世界名寶光　其中有劫號善光
400c20║ 於此善光大劫中　一萬如來出興世
400c21║ 我皆親近而供養　從其修學此解脫
400c22║ 時有王都名喜嚴　縱廣寬平極殊麗
400c23║ 雜業眾生所居住　或心清淨或作惡
400c24║ 爾時有王名勝光　恒以正法御群生
400c25║ 其王太子名善伏　形體端正備眾相

简体字

于一一佛所，得种种三昧门、种种陀罗尼门、种种神通门、种种辩才门、种种一切智门、种种法明门、种种智慧门，照种种十方海，入种种佛刹海，见种种诸佛海，清净成就，增长广大。如于此劫中亲近供养尔所诸佛，于一切处、一切世界海微尘数劫，所有诸佛出兴于世，亲近供养，听闻说法，信受护持，亦复如是。如是，一切诸如来所，皆悉修习此解脱门，复得无量解脱方便。”

尔时，救护一切众生主夜神，欲重宣此解脱义，即为善财而说颂言：

“汝以欢喜信乐心，问此难思解脱法；
我承如来护念力，为汝宣说应听受。
过去无边广大劫，过于刹海微尘数，
时有世界名宝光，其中有劫号善光。
于此善光大劫中，一万如来出兴世，
我皆亲近而供养，从其修学此解脱。
时有王都名喜严，纵广宽平极殊丽，
杂业众生所居住，或心清净或作恶。
尔时有王名胜光，恒以正法御群生；
其王太子名善伏，形体端正备众相。

Under each of those buddhas, I acquired many different samādhi gateways, many different *dhāraṇī* gateways, many different gateways of the spiritual superknowledges, many different gateways of eloquence, many different gateways leading to all-knowledge, many different gateways to understanding Dharma, and many different gateways to wisdom as I illuminated many different oceans of the ten directions, entered many different oceans of buddha *kṣetras*, and saw many different oceans of buddhas. [All of these gateways that I acquired], I purified, perfected, developed, and enlarged.

Just as in these kalpas I drew near to and made offerings to so very many buddhas as these, so too, in all places, for kalpas as numerous as the atoms in all the oceans of worlds, whenever those buddhas arose in the world, I also drew near and made offerings to them, listened to them teach the Dharma, accepted those teachings with faith, and guarded and preserved them. In this way, under all tathāgatas, in every case, I cultivated this liberation gateway and also acquired countless additional means of liberation.

At that time, wishing to once again proclaim the meaning of this liberation, Sarvajagadrakṣāpraṇidhānavīryaprabhā Night Spirit then spoke these verses for Sudhana:

With a mind of joyous delight and faithful aspiration,
you have asked about this inconceivable liberation.
Aided by the power of the Tathāgata's protective mindfulness,
I shall expound on this for you. You should listen and receive it.

In the past, beyond a boundless number of vast kalpas
exceeding in number the atoms in an ocean of worlds,
there was a world named Jewel Radiance
in which there was a kalpa named Fine Radiance.

In this great kalpa known as Fine Radiance,
there were a myriad *tathāgatas* who arose in the world.
I drew near and made offerings to each one of them
and acquired from them the cultivation and training in this liberation.

There was then a royal capital known as Jewel Adornment that,
broad and flat in length and breadth, was especially beautiful,
and that was occupied by beings who engaged in mixed karma,
some with pure minds, and some committing evil deeds.

At that time, there was a king named Light of Victory
who constantly relied on right Dharma to rule the many beings.
The king's son, the prince, who was named Fine Conqueror
had a handsome body with many of the auspicious physical marks.

正體字

400c26 | 時有無量諸罪人　繫身牢獄當受戮
400c27 | 太子見已生悲愍　上啟於王請寬宥
400c28 | 爾時諸臣共白王　今此太子危王國
400c29 | 如是罪人應受戮　如何悉救令除免
401a01 | 時勝光王語太子　汝救彼罪自當受
401a02 | 太子哀念情轉深　誓救眾生無退怯
401a03 | 時王夫人采女等　俱來王所白王言
401a04 | 願放太子半月中　布施眾生作功德
401a05 | 時王聞已即聽許　設大施會濟貧乏
401a06 | 一切眾生靡不臻　隨有所求咸給與
401a07 | 如是半月日云滿　太子就戮時將至
401a08 | 大眾百千萬億人　同時瞻仰俱號泣
401a09 | 彼佛知眾根將熟　而來此會化群生
401a10 | 顯現神變大莊嚴　靡不親近而恭敬
401a11 | 佛以一音方便說　法燈普照修多羅
401a12 | 無量眾生意柔軟　悉蒙與授菩提記
401a13 | 善伏太子生歡喜　發興無上正覺心
401a14 | 誓願承事於如來　普為眾生作依處
401a15 | 便即出家依佛住　修行一切種智道
401a16 | 爾時便得此解脫　大悲廣濟諸群生

简体字

时有无量诸罪人，系身牢狱当受戮；
太子见已生悲愍，上启于王请宽宥。
尔时诸臣共白王：今此太子危王国，
如是罪人应受戮，如何悉救令除免？
时胜光王语太子：汝救彼罪自当受！
太子哀念情转深，誓救众生无退怯。
时王夫人采女等，俱来王所白王言：
愿放太子半月中，布施众生作功德。
时王闻已即听许，设大施会济贫乏，
一切众生靡不臻，随有所求咸给与。
如是半月日云满，太子就戮时将至，
大众百千万亿人，同时瞻仰俱号泣。
彼佛知众根将熟，而来此会化群生，
显现神变大庄严，靡不亲近而恭敬。
佛以一音方便说，法灯普照修多罗，
无量众生意柔软，悉蒙与授菩提记。
善伏太子生欢喜，发兴无上正觉心，
誓愿承事于如来，普为众生作依处。
便即出家依佛住，修行一切种智道，
尔时便得此解脱，大悲广济诸群生。

At that time, there were countless criminals
who were tied up in prison and bound to be executed.
When the prince saw them, he was so filled with compassionate pity
that he petitioned the king, requesting that they be pardoned.

All the officials then together addressed the king,
claiming, "This prince is now endangering the king's country.
Criminals such as these deserve to be put to death.
How can one propose rescuing them all, allowing them to go free?"

Then the king, Supreme Radiance, told the prince,
"If you rescue those criminals, you yourself must undergo their fate."
The prince's deeply felt mindful concern became even deeper yet,
so that, refusing to be intimidated, he vowed to rescue those beings.

Then the king's wife and her female attendants
all went to the king and addressed him, saying,
"Please allow the prince for half a month
to give gifts to beings to create karmic merit."

When the king heard this, he immediately assented.
Thus a great giving assembly was set up to rescue the poor.
Of all those types of beings, there were none who did not gather there.
Whatever any of them sought, it was all provided to them.

And so it went for a half month till the days were declared complete
and the time of the prince's execution was about to arrive.
That great assembly of a hundred thousand myriads of *koṭīs* of people
all together gazed up, all of them wailing and weeping.

That Buddha knew that those beings' faculties were about to ripen
and then came to this assembly to instruct the many beings there.
As he displayed magnificently adorned spiritual transformations,
no one there failed to draw near and revere him.

The Buddha then used a single voice to teach with expedient means
the Dharma Lamp's Universal Illumination Sutra.
Countless beings then attained mental pliancy
and all of them received the predictions of bodhi that he bestowed.

That prince, Fine Conqueror, was filled with joyous delight
and made the resolve to attain the unsurpassed awakening.
He then vowed to serve the Tathāgata
and to everywhere become a refuge for beings.

He then left the home life and dwelt in reliance on the Buddha
as he cultivated the path to the knowledge of all modes.
At that time, he then acquired this liberation
and his great compassion extensively rescued many beings.

正體字

401a17 [1] 於中止住經劫海　諦觀諸法真實性
401a18 常於苦海救眾生　如是修習菩提道
401a19 劫中所有諸佛現　悉皆承事無有餘
401a20 咸以清淨信解心　聽聞持護所說法
401a21 次於佛剎微塵數　無量無邊諸劫海
401a22 所有諸佛現世間　一一供養皆如是
401a23 我念往昔為太子　見諸眾生在牢獄
401a24 誓願捨身而救護　因其證此解脫門
401a25 經於佛剎微塵數　廣大劫海常修習
401a26 念念[2]令其得增長　復獲無邊巧方便
401a27 彼中所有諸如來　我悉得見蒙開悟
401a28 令我增明此解脫　及以種種方便力
401a29 我於無量千億劫　學此難思解脫門
401b01 諸佛法海無有邊　我悉一時能普飲
401b02 十方所有一切剎　其身普入無所礙
401b03 三世種種國土名　念念了知皆悉盡
401b04 三世所有諸佛海　一一明見盡無餘
401b05 亦能示現其身相　普詣於彼如來所
401b06 又於十方一切剎　一切諸佛導師前
401b07 普雨一切莊嚴雲　供養一切無上覺

简体字

于中止住经劫海，谛观诸法真实性，
常于苦海救众生，如是修习菩提道。
劫中所有诸佛现，悉皆承事无有余，
咸以清净信解心，听闻持护所说法。
次于佛刹微尘数，无量无边诸劫海，
所有诸佛现世间，一一供养皆如是。
我念往昔为太子，见诸众生在牢狱，
誓愿舍身而救护，因其证此解脱门。
经于佛刹微尘数，广大劫海常修习，
念念令其得增长，复获无边巧方便。
彼中所有诸如来，我悉得见蒙开悟，
令我增明此解脱，及以种种方便力。
我于无量千亿劫，学此难思解脱门；
诸佛法海无有边，我悉一时能普饮。
十方所有一切刹，其身普入无所碍；
三世种种国土名，念念了知皆悉尽。
三世所有诸佛海，一一明见尽无余；
亦能示现其身相，普诣于彼如来所。
又于十方一切刹，一切诸佛导师前，
普雨一切庄严云，供养一切无上觉。

He dwelt there throughout an ocean of kalpas
in which he closely contemplated the true nature of all dharmas.
He always rescued beings from the ocean of suffering,
cultivating in this manner the path to bodhi.

As during those kalpas all those buddhas appeared,
he served them all without exception.
Under all of them, with a mind of pure resolute faith,
he listened to, retained, and guarded the Dharma they proclaimed.

Thereafter, in an ocean of measurelessly and boundlessly many kalpas
as numerous as the atoms in a buddha *kṣetra,*
whenever all of those buddhas appeared in the world,
he made offerings to each of them in the very same way.

I recall that time long ago when, as that prince,
I saw all those beings confined in prison
and vowed to sacrifice my life to rescue them.
It was because of this that I realized this gateway to liberation.

Then, throughout a vast ocean of kalpas
as numerous as the atoms in a buddha *kṣetra,* I always cultivated it
and, in every mind-moment, caused it to grow
as I also acquired boundlessly many skillful expedients.

Of all those *tathāgatas* throughout that time,
I was able to see and experience awakening under all of them.
They enabled me to grow in my understanding of this liberation
and also acquire the power of many different skillful means.

For countless thousands of *koṭīs* of kalpas,
I trained in this inconceivable gateway of liberation
so that then, all at once, I was able to completely imbibe
the boundless ocean of the Dharma of all buddhas.

My bodies everywhere unimpededly entered
all the *kṣetras* throughout the ten directions.
In each successive mind-moment, I completely knew
the names of all the many different lands of the three periods of time.

Within the ocean of all buddhas of the three periods of time,
I clearly saw every one of them without exception
and also became able to manifest my body's appearance
everywhere to pay respects to all those *tathāgatas.*

Further, in the *kṣetras* throughout the ten directions,
in the direct presence of all the buddhas, those guiding teachers,
I everywhere spread clouds raining down all kinds of adornments
as offerings to all those of unsurpassed awakening.

正體字

401b08 ‖ 又以無邊大問海　啟請一切諸世尊
401b09 ‖ 彼佛所雨妙法雲　皆悉受持無忘失
401b10 ‖ 又於十方無量刹　一切如來眾會前
401b11 ‖ 坐於眾妙莊嚴座　示現種種神通力
401b12 ‖ 又於十方無量刹　示現種種諸神變
401b13 ‖ 一身示現無量身　無量身中現一身
401b14 ‖ 又於一一毛孔中　悉放無數大光明
401b15 ‖ 各以種種巧方便　除滅眾生煩惱火
401b16 ‖ 又於一一毛孔中　出現無量化身雲
401b17 ‖ 充滿十方諸世界　普雨法雨濟群品
401b18 ‖ 十方一切諸佛子　入此難思解脫門
401b19 ‖ 悉盡未來無量劫　安住修行菩薩行
401b20 ‖ 隨其心樂為說法　令彼皆除邪見網
401b21 ‖ 示以天道及二乘　乃至如來一切智
401b22 ‖ 一切眾生受生處　示現無邊種種身
401b23 ‖ 悉同其類現眾像　普應其心而說法
401b24 ‖ 若有得此解脫門　則住無邊功德海
401b25 ‖ 譬如刹海微塵數　不可思議無有量
401b26 ‖ 善男子。我唯知此教化眾生令生善根解脫
401b27 ‖ 門。如諸菩薩摩訶薩。超諸世間。現諸趣身。

简体字

又以无边大问海，启请一切诸世尊；
彼佛所雨妙法云，皆悉受持无忘失。
又于十方无量刹，一切如来众会前，
坐于众妙庄严座，示现种种神通力。
又于十方无量刹，示现种种诸神变，
一身示现无量身，无量身中现一身。
又于一一毛孔中，悉放无数大光明，
各以种种巧方便，除灭众生烦恼火。
又于一一毛孔中，出现无量化身云，
充满十方诸世界，普雨法雨济群品。
十方一切诸佛子，入此难思解脱门，
悉尽未来无量劫，安住修行菩萨行。
随其心乐为说法，令彼皆除邪见网，
示以天道及二乘，乃至如来一切智。
一切众生受生处，示现无边种种身，
悉同其类现众像，普应其心而说法。
若有得此解脱门，则住无边功德海，
譬如刹海微尘数，不可思议无有量。

“善男子，我唯知此教化众生令生善根解脱门。如诸菩萨摩诃萨，超诸世间，现诸趣身，

Moreover, with an ocean of boundlessly many questions,
I posed requests for teaching to all those *bhagavats*.
Of those clouds of sublime Dharma rained down by those buddhas,
I fully absorbed and retained them all, never forgetting any.

Furthermore, in the countless *kṣetras* throughout the ten directions,
in the front of all those *tathāgatas'* congregations,
I sat on seats with many marvelous adornments
and manifested many different powers of spiritual superknowledges.

Furthermore, in the countless *kṣetras* throughout the ten directions,
I manifested many different kinds of spiritual transformations
in which, with but one body, I manifested countless bodies
and, in countless bodies, I manifested but one body.

Moreover, from every pore,
I emanated innumerable brilliant rays of light,
each of which used many different clever expedients
to extinguish the fires of beings' afflictions.

Furthermore, from every pore,
I manifested countless clouds of transformation bodies
that filled all the worlds throughout the ten directions
and everywhere rained the Dharma rain, rescuing the many beings.

All sons of the Buddha throughout the ten directions
enter this inconceivable liberation gateway
in which they all exhaust all the countless kalpas of the future
securely established in the cultivation of the bodhisattva practices.

Thus, adapting to others' mental inclinations, they teach the Dharma
to enable them all to rid themselves of the net of wrong views
and show them the path to the heavens as well as to the two vehicles,
and so forth on up to the all-knowledge of the Tathāgata.

In all the places in which all beings are reborn,
they manifest boundlessly many different bodies,
all of which present many appearances that match their types,
and everywhere adapt to their minds as they teach them the Dharma.

If there is anyone who acquires this liberation gateway,
they abide in an ocean of boundlessly many meritorious qualities
that, like the number of atoms in an ocean of *kṣetras*,
is inconceivably and measurelessly vast.

Son of Good Family, I know only this "teaching beings to produce roots of goodness" liberation gateway. As for the bodhisattva-mahāsattvas:

Who have transcended the world;
Who manifest bodies in all the rebirth destinies;

正體字

不
401b28‖ 住攀緣。無有障礙。了達一切諸法自性。善能
401b29‖ 觀察一切諸法。得無我智。證無我法。教化調
401c01‖ 伏一切眾生。恒無休息。心常安住無二法門。
401c02‖ 普入一切諸言辭海。我今云何能知能說彼
401c03‖ 功德海。彼勇猛智。彼心行處。彼三昧境。彼解
401c04‖ 脫力。善男子。此閻浮提。有一園林名嵐毘尼。
401c05‖ 彼園有神名妙德圓滿。汝詣彼問。菩薩云何
401c06‖ 修菩薩行。生如來家。為世光明。盡未來劫。而
401c07‖ 無厭倦。時善財童子。頂禮其足。遶無量匝。合
401c08‖ 掌瞻仰。辭退而去
401c12‖ [4]大方廣佛華嚴經卷[5]第七十四
401c15‖ [9]入法界品第三十九之十五
401c16‖ 爾時善財童子。於大願精進力救護一切眾
401c17‖ 生夜神所。得菩薩解脫已。憶念修習。了達增
401c18‖ 長。漸次遊行。至嵐毘尼林。周遍尋覓彼妙德
401c19‖ 神。見在一切寶樹莊嚴樓閣中。坐寶蓮華師
401c20‖ 子之座。二十億那由他諸天。恭敬圍遶。為說
401c21‖ 菩薩受生海經。令其皆得生如來家。增長菩
401c22‖ 薩大功德海。善財見已。頂禮其足。

简体字

不住攀缘，无有障碍，了达一切诸法自性，善能观察一切诸法，得无我智，证无我法，教化调伏一切众生恒无休息，心常安住无二法门，普入一切诸言辞海；我今云何能知能说彼功德海、彼勇猛智、彼心行处、彼三昧境、彼解脱力？

“善男子，此阎浮提，有一园林，名岚毗尼；彼园有神，名妙德圆满。汝诣彼问：菩萨云何修菩萨行、生如来家、为世光明，尽未来劫而无厌倦？”

时，善财童子顶礼其足，绕无量匝，合掌瞻仰，辞退而去。

大方广佛华严经卷第七十四

入法界品第三十九之十五

尔时，善财童子于大愿精进力救护一切众生夜神所，得菩萨解脱已，忆念修习，了达增长。

渐次游行，至岚毗尼林，周遍寻觅彼妙德神，见在一切宝树庄严楼阁中，坐宝莲华师子之座，二十亿那由他诸天恭敬围绕，为说菩萨受生海经，令其皆得生如来家，增长菩萨大功德海。善财见已，顶礼其足，

Who do not abide in the manipulation of conditions;
Who are unimpeded in all that they do;
Who completely comprehend the nature of all dharmas;
Who are well able to contemplate all dharmas;
Who have acquired the wisdom of non-self;
Who have realized the dharma of non-self;
Who constantly teach and train all beings without resting;
Whose minds always securely dwell in the Dharma gateway of non-duality; and
Who everywhere enter the ocean of all verbal expressions—

How could I know of or be able to speak about their ocean of meritorious qualities, their courageous exercise of wisdom, the places where their minds are acting, the domain of their samādhis, or the powers of their liberations?

Son of Good Family, on this continent of Jambudvīpa, there is a garden and grove known as Lumbinī. In that garden, there is a spirit named Sutejomaṇḍalaratiśrī, or "Completely Perfected Marvelous Virtue." You should go there, pay your respects, and ask that spirit, "How should the bodhisattva tirelessly cultivate the bodhisattva practices, attain birth into the family of the Tathāgata, and become a shining light for the world to the very end of all future kalpas.

Sudhana the Youth then bowed down in reverence at her feet and circumambulated her countless times as, with palms together, he gazed up at her in admiration. He then respectfully withdrew and departed.

39 – Sutejomaṇḍalaratiśrī

At that time, after Sudhana the Youth had acquired that bodhisattva liberation from the Night Spirit, Sarvajagadrakṣāpraṇidhānavīry aprabhā, he bore it in mind, cultivated it, completely comprehended it, and developed it. He then gradually traveled on until he reached the grove at Lumbinī where he searched all around for that spirit known as Sutejomaṇḍalaratiśrī or "Marvelous Virtue" until he saw her in a tower beautified by trees adorned with all kinds of jewels. She was sitting on a jeweled lotus flower lion throne, respectfully surrounded by a following of twenty *koṭīs* of *nayutas* of devas for whom she was teaching a sutra known as The Bodhisattva's Ocean of Births with which she enabled them all to be reborn into the family of the Tathāgata and grow in the bodhisattva's ocean of great meritorious qualities. After he saw her there, Sudhana then went and bowed down in reverence at her feet, pressed his palms together as he stood

正體字

合掌前立。
401c23‖ 白言大聖。我已先發阿耨多羅三藐三菩提
401c24‖ 心。而未能知菩薩云何修菩薩行。生如來家
401c25‖ 為世大明。彼神答言。善男子。菩薩有十種
401c26‖ 受生藏。若菩薩。成就此法。則生如來家。念念
401c27‖ 增長菩薩善根。[10]不疲不懈不厭不退。無斷無
401c28‖ 失。離諸迷惑。不生怯劣惱悔之心。趣一切智。
401c29‖ 入法界門。發廣大心。增長諸度。成就諸佛無
402a01‖ 上菩提。捨世間趣。入如來地。獲勝神通。諸佛
402a02‖ 之法常現在前。順一切智真實義境。何等為
402a03‖ 十。一者願常供養一切諸佛受生藏。二者發
402a04‖ 菩提心受生藏。三者觀諸法門勤修行受生
402a05‖ 藏。四者以深淨心普照三世受生藏。五者平
402a06‖ 等光明受生藏。六者生如來家受生藏。七者
402a07‖ 佛力光明受生[1]藏。

简体字

合掌前立，白言：“大圣，我已先发阿耨多罗三藐三菩提心，而未能知菩萨云何修菩萨行、生如来家、为世大明？”

彼神答言：“善男子，菩萨有十种受生藏，若菩萨成就此法，则生如来家，念念增长菩萨善根，不疲不懈，不厌不退，无断无失，离诸迷惑，不生怯劣、恼悔之心，趣一切智，入法界门，发广大心，增长诸度，成就诸佛无上菩提，舍世间趣，入如来地，获胜神通，诸佛之法常现在前，顺一切智真实义境。

“何等为十？一者、愿常供养一切诸佛受生藏；二者、发菩提心受生藏；三者、观诸法门勤修行受生藏；四者、以深净心普照三世受生藏；五者、平等光明受生藏；六者、生如来家受生藏；七者、佛力光明受生藏；

before her, and addressed her, saying, "O Great Āryā, I am one who has already resolved to attain *anuttara-samyak-saṃbodhi*. Still, I do not yet understand how the bodhisattva is to cultivate the bodhisattva path, achieve rebirth in the family of the Tathāgata, and become a great shining light for the world."

That spirit then replied, saying:

Son of Good Family, the bodhisattva has ten kinds of rebirth treasuries. If the bodhisattva perfects these dharmas:

He will be reborn into the family of the Tathāgata;

In every mind-moment, he will increase the bodhisattva's roots of goodness;

He will not become tired, will not desist from his efforts, will not become weary, will not retreat, will not quit, and will not fail;

He will abandon all delusions;

He will not have thoughts that are timid, inferior, afflicted, or regretful;

He will progress toward all-knowledge;

He will enter the gates of the Dharma realm;

He will make the vast resolve;

He will grow in all the perfections;

He will succeed in reaching the unsurpassed bodhi of all buddhas;

He will abandon the worldly rebirth destinies;

He will enter the ground of the Tathāgata;

He will acquire the supreme spiritual superknowledges;

He will have the Dharma of all buddhas always manifest directly before him; and

He will accord with the realm of the true meaning of all-knowledge.

What then are those ten? They are as follows:

First, the rebirth treasury of vowing to always make offerings to all buddhas;

Second, the rebirth treasury of resolving to attain bodhi;

Third, the rebirth treasury of contemplating all Dharma gateways and diligently cultivating them;

Fourth, the rebirth treasury of everywhere illuminating all three periods of time with a purified earnest resolve;[1]

Fifth, the rebirth treasury of uniformly equal illumination;

Sixth, the rebirth treasury of being born into the family of the Tathāgata;

Seventh, the rebirth treasury of the light of the Buddha's powers;

正體字

八者觀普智門受生藏。九
402a08‖ 者普現莊嚴受生藏。十者入如來地受生藏。
402a09‖ 善男子。云何名願常供養一切佛受生藏。善
402a10‖ 男子。菩薩初發心時。作如是願。我當尊重恭
402a11‖ 敬供養一切諸佛。見佛無厭。於諸佛所。常生
402a12‖ 愛樂。常起深信修諸功德。恒無休息。[2]是為
402a13‖ 菩薩為一切智始集善根受生藏。云何名發菩
402a14‖ 提心受生藏。善男子。此菩薩。發阿耨多羅三
402a15‖ 藐三菩提心。所謂起大悲心。救護一切眾生
402a16‖ 故。起供養佛心。究竟承事故。起普求正法心。
402a17‖ 一切無[3]吝故。起廣大趣向心。求一切智故。
402a18‖ 起慈無量心。普攝眾生故。起不捨一切眾生
402a19‖ 心。被求一切智堅誓甲故。起無諂誑心。得
402a20‖ 如實智故。起如說行心。修菩薩道故。起不誑
402a21‖ 諸佛心。守護一切佛大誓願故。起一切智願
402a22‖ 心。盡未來化眾生不休息故。菩薩以如是等
402a23‖ 佛剎微塵數菩提心功德故。得生如來家。是
402a24‖ 為菩薩第二受生藏。

简体字

八者、观普智门受生藏；九者、普现庄严受生藏；十者、入如来地受生藏。

“善男子，云何名愿常供养一切佛受生藏？善男子，菩萨初发心时，作如是愿：‘我当尊重、恭敬、供养一切诸佛，见佛无厌，于诸佛所，常生爱乐，常起深信，修诸功德，恒无休息。’是为菩萨为一切智始集善根受生藏。

“云何名发菩提心受生藏？善男子，此菩萨发阿耨多罗三藐三菩提心。所谓：起大悲心，救护一切众生故；起供养佛心，究竟承事故；起普求正法心，一切无悋故；起广大趣向心，求一切智故；起慈无量心，普摄众生故；起不舍一切众生心，被求一切智坚誓甲故；起无谄诳心，得如实智故；起如说行心，修菩萨道故；起不诳诸佛心，守护一切佛大誓愿故；起一切智愿心，尽未来化众生不休息故。菩萨以如是等佛刹微尘数菩提心功德故，得生如来家。是为菩萨第二受生藏。

Eighth, the rebirth treasury of contemplating the gateways to universal knowledge;

Ninth, the rebirth treasury of everywhere manifesting adornments; and

Tenth, the rebirth treasury of entering the ground of the Tathāgata.

Son of Good Family, what is meant by "the rebirth treasury of vowing to always make offerings to all buddhas"? Son of Good Family, when the bodhisattva first makes the resolve, he makes this vow: "I shall honor, revere, and make offerings to all buddhas, shall be tireless in going to see all buddhas, shall always feel delight toward all buddhas, shall always produce deep faith in them, and shall constantly and incessantly cultivate the meritorious qualities." This is what is meant by the first rebirth treasury by which the bodhisattva accumulates roots of goodness for the sake of reaching all-knowledge.

What is meant by "the bodhisattva's rebirth treasury of resolving to attain bodhi"? Son of Good Family, this bodhisattva's resolve to attain *anuttara-samyak-saṃbodhi* entails the following:

He produces mind of great compassion in order to rescue all beings;

He resolves to make offerings to the buddhas in order to serve them in the ultimate way;

He resolves to everywhere seek right Dharma in order to remain free of miserliness in all things;

He resolves to make great progress in order to seek all-knowledge;

He produces the mind of immeasurable kindness in order to everywhere gather in beings;

He resolves to never forsake any beings in order to don the armor of solid vows to attain all-knowledge;

He resolves to be free of flattery and deviousness in order to acquire the wisdom that accords with reality;

He resolves to practice in accordance with his words in order to cultivate the bodhisattva path;

He resolves to never deceive the buddhas in order to preserve the great vow of all buddhas; and

He vows to attain all-knowledge in order to teach beings without ever resting to the very end of future time.

It is due to such meritorious qualities of the bodhi resolve that are as numerous as the atoms in a buddha *kṣetra* that he succeeds in being reborn into the family of the Tathāgata. This is what is meant by the second of the bodhisattva's rebirth treasuries.

正體字

云何名觀諸法門勤修
402a25 行受生藏。善男子。此菩薩摩訶薩。起觀一
402a26 切法門海心。起迴向一切智圓滿道心。起正
402a27 念無過失業心。起一切菩薩三昧海清淨心。
402a28 起修成一切菩薩功德心。起莊嚴一切菩薩
402a29 道心。起求一切智大精進行修諸功德如劫
402b01 火熾然無休息心。起修普賢行教化一切眾
402b02 生心。起善學一切威儀修菩薩功德捨離一
402b03 切所有住無所有真實心。是為菩薩第三受
402b04 生藏。云何名以深淨心普照三世受生藏。善
402b05 男子。此菩薩。具清淨增上心。得如來菩提光。
402b06 入菩薩方便海。其心堅固。猶若金剛背捨一
402b07 切諸有趣生。成就一切佛自在力。修殊勝行。
402b08 具菩薩根。其心明潔。願力不動。常為諸佛之
402b09 所護念。破壞一切諸障[4]礙山。普為眾生作所
402b10 依處。

简体字

“云何名观诸法门勤修行受生藏？善男子，此菩萨摩诃萨，起观一切法门海心，起回向一切智圆满道心，起正念无过失业心，起一切菩萨三昧海清净心，起修成一切菩萨功德心，起庄严一切菩萨道心，起求一切智大精进行、修诸功德如劫火炽然无休息心，起修普贤行教化一切众生心，起善学一切威仪、修菩萨功德、舍离一切所有、住无所有真实心。是为菩萨第三受生藏。

“云何名以深净心普照三世受生藏？善男子，此菩萨具清净增上心，得如来菩提光，入菩萨方便海，其心坚固犹若金刚，背舍一切诸有趣生，成就一切佛自在力，修殊胜行，具菩萨根，其心明洁，愿力不动，常为诸佛之所护念，破坏一切诸障碍山，普为众生作所依处。

What is meant by "the rebirth treasury of contemplating all Dharma gateways and diligently cultivating them"? Son of Good Family, as for this bodhisattva:

He resolves to contemplate the ocean of all gateways into the Dharma;

He resolves to dedicate himself to completely fulfilling all aspects of the path to all-knowledge;

He resolves to maintain right mindfulness in remaining free of any karmic transgressions;

He resolves to purify the ocean of all bodhisattvas' samādhis;

He resolves to cultivate and perfect all of the bodhisattva's meritorious qualities;

He resolves to adorn the path of all bodhisattvas;

He resolves that, as he pursues his quest to attain all-knowledge, he will be as unresting in his practice of great vigor in cultivating all the meritorious qualities as the blazing flames that rage on at the end of the kalpa;

He resolves to cultivate Samantabhadra's practices and teach all beings; and

He resolves to thoroughly train in all aspects of the awesome deportment, to cultivate the bodhisattva's meritorious qualities, to relinquish everything, and to abide in the reality of the nonexistence of anything at all.

This is what is meant by the third of the bodhisattva's rebirth treasuries.

What is meant by "the rebirth treasury of everywhere illuminating all three periods of time with a purified earnest resolve"? Son of Good Family, as for this bodhisattva:

He possesses an especially superior purified resolve with which he acquires the light of the Tathāgata's bodhi and enters the ocean of the bodhisattva's methods;

His resolve is as solid as vajra;

He has been liberated from rebirths in all the rebirth destinies throughout all realms of existence;

He perfects all buddhas' miraculous powers;

He cultivates the especially superior practices and is equipped with the faculties of the bodhisattva;

His mind is bright and pure;

His vow power is unshakable;

He is always afforded the protection of all buddhas;

He demolishes the mountain of all obstacles; and

He everywhere serves as a refuge for beings.

正體字

是為菩薩第四受生藏。[5]云何名平等光
402b11‖ 明受生藏。善男子。此菩薩。具足眾行。普化眾
402b12‖ 生。一切所有。悉皆能捨。住佛究竟淨戒境界。
402b13‖ 具足忍法。成就諸佛法忍光明。以大精進。趣
402b14‖ 一切智。到於彼岸。修習諸禪得普門定。淨
402b15‖ 智圓滿。以智慧日明照諸法。得無礙眼。見
402b16‖ 諸佛海。悟入一切真實法性。一切世間。見
402b17‖ 者歡喜。善能修習如實法門。是為菩薩第五
402b18‖ 受生藏。云何名生如來家受生藏。善男子。此
402b19‖ 菩薩。生如來家。隨諸佛住。成就一切甚深法
402b20‖ 門。具三世佛清淨大願。得一切佛同一善根。
402b21‖ 與諸如來。共一體性。具出世行白淨善法。安
402b22‖ 住廣大功德法門。入諸三昧。見佛神力。隨
402b23‖ 所應化。淨諸眾生。

简体字

是为菩萨第四受生藏。

“云何名平等光明受生藏？善男子，此菩萨具足众行，普化众生；一切所有，悉皆能舍；住佛究竟净戒境界；具足忍法，成就诸佛法忍光明；以大精进，趣一切智，到于彼岸；修习诸禅，得普门定；净智圆满，以智慧日，明照诸法；得无碍眼，见诸佛海，悟入一切真实法性；一切世间，见者欢喜，善能修习如实法门。是为菩萨第五受生藏。

“云何名生如来家受生藏？善男子，此菩萨生如来家，随诸佛住，成就一切甚深法门，具三世佛清净大愿，得一切佛同一善根，与诸如来共一体性，具出世行白净善法，安住广大功德法门；入诸三昧，见佛神力；随所应化，净诸众生；

This is what is meant by the fourth of the bodhisattva's rebirth treasuries.

What is meant by "the rebirth treasury of uniformly equal illumination"? Son of Good Family, as for this bodhisattva:

He is fully possessed of the many practices;

He everywhere teaches beings;

He is able to relinquish everything he possesses;

He abides in the realm of the Buddha's ultimately pure moral virtue;

He is fully possessed of the dharmas of patience and has acquired the light of all buddhas' dharmas' patience;

He uses great vigor in progressing toward all-knowledge and reaching the far shore;

He cultivates all the *dhyāna* concentrations and acquires the universal gateway meditative absorption;

He becomes perfectly complete in pure wisdom and brightly illuminates all dharmas with the sun of wisdom;

He acquires the unimpeded eye and sees the ocean of all buddhas;

He awakens to and enters the nature of all true dharmas;

He is one who everyone in the world delights in seeing; and

He is well able to cultivate the gateways that accord with genuine Dharma.

This is what is meant by the fifth of the bodhisattva's rebirth treasuries.

What is meant by "the rebirth treasury of being born into the family of the Tathāgata"? Son of Good Family, as for this bodhisattva:

He is born into the family of the Tathāgata and dwells together with the buddhas;

He perfects all the extremely profound Dharma gateways;

He accomplishes the pure and great vows of the buddhas of the three periods of time;

He acquires the same roots of goodness as all buddhas;

He shares the same essential nature as all *tathāgatas;*

He is equipped with the good and pure dharmas of the world-transcending practices;

He securely abides in the Dharma gateways to vast meritorious qualities;

He enters all the samādhis and witnesses the Buddha's spiritual powers;

He adapts to those amenable to teaching and thus purifies beings; and

正體字

如問而對。辯才無盡。是為
402b24‖ 菩薩第六受生藏。云何名佛力光明受生藏。
402b25‖ 善男子。此菩薩。深入佛力。遊諸佛刹。心無退
402b26‖ 轉。供養承事菩薩眾會。無有疲厭。了一切
402b27‖ 法皆如幻起。知諸世間如夢所見。一切色相
402b28‖ 猶如光影。神通所作皆如變化。一切受生悉
402b29‖ 皆如影。諸佛說法皆如谷響。開示法界咸令
402c01‖ 究竟。是為菩薩第七受生藏。云何名觀普智
402c02‖ 門受生藏。善男子。此菩薩。住童真位。觀一切
402c03‖ 智。一一智門。盡無量劫。開演一切菩薩所行。
402c04‖ 於諸菩薩甚深三昧。心得自在。念念生於十
402c05‖ 方世界諸如來所。於有差別境入無差別定。
402c06‖ 於無差別法現有差別智。於無量境知無境
402c07‖ 界。於少境界入無量境。

简体字

如问而对，辩才无尽。是为菩萨第六受生藏。

“云何名佛力光明受生藏？善男子，此菩萨深入佛力，游诸佛刹心无退转，供养承事菩萨众会无有疲厌，了一切法皆如幻起，知诸世间如梦所见，一切色相犹如光影，神通所作皆如变化，一切受生悉皆如影，诸佛说法皆如谷响，开示法界咸令究竟。是为菩萨第七受生藏。

“云何名观普智门受生藏？善男子，此菩萨住童真位，观一切智一一智门，尽无量劫开演一切菩萨所行，于诸菩萨甚深三昧心得自在，念念生于十方世界诸如来所，于有差别境入无差别定，于无差别法现有差别智，于无量境知无境界，于少境界入无量境，

He responds in a manner suited to the inquiry, doing so with inexhaustible eloquence.

This is what is meant by the sixth of the bodhisattva's rebirth treasuries.

What is meant by "the rebirth treasury of the light of the Buddha's powers"? Son of Good Family, as for this bodhisattva:

He deeply enters the powers of the buddha;

In traveling to all buddha *kṣetras*, his resolve is irreversible;

He is tireless in serving and making offerings to congregations of bodhisattvas;

He completely understands all dharmas as like magical conjurations;

He knows all worlds as like things seen in a dream;

He sees all forms and their signs as like reflections;

He sees everything created by the spiritual superknowledges as like magical transformations;

He sees all rebirths as like shadows;

He sees all buddhas' teachings on Dharma as like echoes resounding in a valley; and

He explains the Dharma realm so that everyone is able to achieve the ultimate.

This is what is meant by the seventh of the bodhisattva's rebirth treasuries.

What is meant by "the rebirth treasury of contemplating the gateways to universal knowledge"? Son of Good Family, as for this bodhisattva:

He dwells at the stage of the pure youth[2] in which he contemplates all-knowledge.

In relation to every one of the wisdom gateways, he exhausts countless kalpas expounding on all the bodhisattva practices;

His mind acquires sovereign mastery of all the bodhisattva's extremely profound samādhis;

In each successive mind-moment, he is born in the presence of all *tathāgatas* in the worlds of the ten directions;

He enters non-differentiating meditative absorptions on differentiated objective realms;

He manifests differentiating knowledge with regard to undifferentiated dharmas;

In measureless objective realms, he knows what is not an objective realm at all;

In but few objective realms, he penetrates measureless objective realms;

正體字

通達法性廣大無際。
402c08║ 知諸世間悉假施設。一切皆是識心所起。是
402c09║ 為菩薩第八受生藏。云何名普現莊嚴受生
402c10║ 藏。善男子。此菩薩。能種種莊嚴無量佛刹。普
402c11║ 能化現一切眾生。及諸佛身。得無所畏。演清
402c12║ 淨法。周流法界。無所障礙。隨其心樂普使知
402c13║ 見。示現種種成菩提行。令生無礙一切智道。
402c14║ 如是所作不失其時。而常在三昧毘盧遮那
402c15║ 智慧之藏。是為菩薩第九受生藏。云何名入
402c16║ 如來地受生藏。善男子。此菩薩。悉於三世
402c17║ 諸如來所。受灌頂法。普知一切境界次第。所
402c18║ 謂知一切眾生。前際後際沒生次第。一切菩
402c19║ 薩修行次第。一切眾生心念次第。三世如來
402c20║ 成佛次第。善巧方便說法次第。亦知一切初
402c21║ 中後際。所有諸劫。若成若壞。名號次第。

简体字

通达法性广大无际，知诸世间悉假施设，一切皆是识心所起。是为菩萨第八受生藏。

“云何名普现庄严受生藏？善男子，此菩萨能种种庄严无量佛刹，普能化现一切众生及诸佛身，得无所畏，演清净法，周流法界，无所障碍；随其心乐，普使知见，示现种种成菩提行，令生无碍一切智道；如是所作不失其时，而常在三昧毗卢遮那智慧之藏。是为菩萨第九受生藏。

“云何名入如来地受生藏？善男子，此菩萨悉于三世诸如来所受灌顶法，普知一切境界次第。所谓：知一切众生前际后际殁生次第、一切菩萨修行次第、一切众生心念次第、三世如来成佛次第、善巧方便说法次第，亦知一切初、中、后际所有诸劫若成若坏名号次第。

He gains a penetrating comprehension of the nature of dharmas as boundlessly vast; and

He realizes that all worlds are merely conventionally established and that they are all produced by the conscious mind.

This is what is meant by the eighth of the bodhisattva's rebirth treasuries.

What is meant by "the rebirth treasury of everywhere manifesting adornments"? Son of Good Family, as for this bodhisattva:

He is able to adorn countless buddha *kṣetras* with many different adornments;

He is everywhere able to transformationally manifest the bodies of all kinds of beings up to and including those of buddhas;

He has acquired fearlessness in expounding on pure Dharma;

He is unimpeded in circulating everywhere throughout the Dharma realm;

He adapts to the mental dispositions of others and thus everywhere enables them to acquire knowledge and vision;

He manifests the many different kinds of practices leading to the realization of bodhi;

He causes the arising of the unimpeded path to all-knowledge; and

In all endeavors such as these he never misses the right time and yet he always abides in samādhi with Vairocana's treasury of wisdom.

This is what is meant by the ninth of the bodhisattva's rebirth treasuries.

What is meant by "the rebirth treasury of entering the ground of the Tathāgata"? Son of Good Family, as for this bodhisattva:

He receives the dharma of the crown-anointing consecration in the presence of all *tathāgatas* of the three periods of time.

He knows the sequence in all realms, in particular:

He knows the sequences of all beings' past and future deaths and rebirths;

He knows the sequences in all bodhisattvas' cultivation;

He knows the sequences in all beings' thoughts;

He knows the sequences in the realization of buddhahood as it occurs with all *tathāgatas* of the three periods of time;

He knows the sequences in the use of skillful means when teaching the Dharma; and

He also knows the sequences in the past, present, and future of all kalpas, whether it be in their creation, their destruction, or their naming.

正體字

隨
402c22║ 諸眾生所應化度。為現成道功德莊嚴。神通
402c23║ 說法方便調伏。是為菩薩第十受生藏。佛子。
402c24║ 若菩薩摩訶薩。於此十法。修[6]習增長圓滿
402c25║ 成就。則能於一莊嚴中。現種種莊嚴。如是
402c26║ 莊嚴一切國土。開導示悟一切眾生。盡未來
402c27║ 劫無有休息。演說一切諸[7]佛法海。種種境
402c28║ 界。種種成熟。展轉傳來。無量諸法。現不思議
402c29║ 佛自在力。充滿一切虛空法界。於諸眾生心
403a01║ 行海中。而轉法輪。於一切世界。示現成佛。恒
403a02║ 無間斷。以不可說清淨言音。說一切法。住
403a03║ 無量處。通達無礙。以一切法莊嚴道場。隨
403a04║ 諸眾生欲解差別。而現成佛。開示無量。甚深
403a05║ 法藏。教化成就一切世間。爾時嵐毘尼林神。
403a06║ 欲重明其義。以佛神力。普觀十方。而說頌
403a07║ 言
403a08║ 最上離垢清淨心　見一切佛無厭足
403a09║ 願盡未來常供養　此明慧者受生藏

简体字

随诸众生所应化度，为现成道功德庄严，神通说法，方便调伏。是为菩萨第十受生藏。

“佛子，若菩萨摩诃萨，于此十法修习增长圆满成就，则能于一庄严中，现种种庄严；如是庄严一切国土，开导示悟一切众生，尽未来劫无有休息；演说一切诸佛法海种种境界、种种成熟，展转传来无量诸法；现不思议佛自在力，充满一切虚空法界；于诸众生心行海中而转法轮，于一切世界示现成佛，恒无间断；以不可说清净言音说一切法，住无量处通达无碍；以一切法庄严道场，随诸众生欲解差别而现成佛，开示无量甚深法藏，教化成就一切世间。”

尔时，岚毗尼林神，欲重明其义，以佛神力，普观十方而说颂言：

“最上离垢清净心，见一切佛无厌足，
愿尽未来常供养，此明慧者受生藏。

Adapting to what is appropriate for the beings who are amenable to teaching, he manifests for them the realization of enlightenment, the meritorious qualities, the adornments, the spiritual superknowledges, the proclamation of Dharma, the skillful means, and the training.

This is what is meant by the tenth of the bodhisattva's rebirth treasuries.

Son of the Buddha, if the bodhisattva-mahāsattva cultivates, develops, completely fulfills, and perfects these ten dharmas, then:

He becomes able to manifest the many different kinds of adornments even within one adornment, thereby adorning all lands;

He guides, instructs, and awakens all beings, continuing to do so without ever resting throughout all future kalpas;

He expounds on all buddhas' ocean of dharmas, on the many different kinds of objective realms, and on the many different factors involved in maturation, thereby passing on forward the countless dharmas;

In manifesting the Buddha's inconceivable miraculous powers, he fills the entire realm of empty space throughout the Dharma realm;

He turns the wheel of Dharma in [accordance with] the ocean of all beings' mental activities;

He constantly and uninterruptedly manifests the realization of buddhahood in all worlds;

Using an ineffable number of pure voices, he teaches all dharmas for those dwelling in countless places, doing so with unimpeded penetrating comprehension;

He adorns the site of enlightenment with all dharmas, adapts to the differences in all beings' aspirations and understandings, and manifests the realization of buddhahood;

He opens and reveals the treasury of the countless extremely profound dharmas; and

He teaches and promotes the development of all beings throughout the entire world.

At that time, wishing to restate and clarify these meanings, aided by the Buddha's spiritual powers, the spirit of the Lumbinī Grove regarded all the ten directions and then spoke these verses:

Those who possess the most supreme, immaculate, and pure mind,
who are insatiable in seeing all buddhas,
and who vow to always give them offerings throughout the future—
This is the rebirth treasury of those of such shining wisdom.

正體字

403a10 [1] 一切三世國土中　所有眾生及諸佛
403a11 悉願度脫恒瞻奉　此難思者受生藏
403a12 聞法無厭樂觀察　普於三世無所礙
403a13 身心清淨如虛空　此名稱者受生藏
403a14 其心恒住大悲海　堅如金剛及寶山
403a15 了達一切種智門　此最勝者受生藏
403a16 大慈普覆於一切　妙行常增諸度海
403a17 以法光明照群品　此雄猛者受生藏
403a18 了達法性心無礙　生於三世諸佛家
403a19 普入十方法界海　此明智者受生藏
403a20 法身清淨心無礙　普詣十方諸國土
403a21 一切佛力靡不成　此不思議受生藏
403a22 入深智慧已自在　於諸三昧亦究竟
403a23 觀一切智如實門　此真身者受生藏
403a24 淨治一切諸佛土　勤修普化眾生法
403a25 顯現如來自在力　此大名者受生藏
403a26 久已修行薩婆若　疾能趣入如來位
403a27 了知法界皆無礙　此諸佛子受生藏
403a28 善男子。菩薩具此十法。生如來家。為一切世
403a29 間清淨光明。善男子。我從無量劫來。得是自
403b01 在受生解脫門。

简体字

一切三世国土中，所有众生及诸佛，
悉愿度脱恒瞻奉，此难思者受生藏。
闻法无厌乐观察，普于三世无所碍，
身心清净如虚空，此名称者受生藏。
其心恒住大悲海，坚如金刚及宝山，
了达一切种智门，此最胜者受生藏。
大慈普覆于一切，妙行常增诸度海，
以法光明照群品，此雄猛者受生藏。
了达法性心无碍，生于三世诸佛家，
普入十方法界海，此明智者受生藏。
法身清净心无碍，普诣十方诸国土，
一切佛力靡不成，此不思议受生藏。
入深智慧已自在，于诸三昧亦究竟，
观一切智如实门，此真身者受生藏。
净治一切诸佛土，勤修普化众生法，
显现如来自在力，此大名者受生藏。
久已修行萨婆若，疾能趣入如来位，
了知法界皆无碍，此诸佛子受生藏。

“善男子，菩萨具此十法，生如来家，为一切世间清净光明。善男子，我从无量劫来，得是自在受生解脱门。”

All the beings on up to the buddhas themselves
in all lands throughout the three periods of time—
they vow to liberate or constantly look up to and serve them.
This is a rebirth treasury of those who are inconceivable.

Listening to Dharma insatiably, delighting in contemplations,
remaining unimpeded in this throughout the three periods of time
while both body and mind are as pure as empty space—
This is a rebirth treasury of those who are famed for this.

Their resolve constantly abides in the ocean of the great compassion,
and is as solid as vajra or a mountain of jewels.
They completely understand the gates to the knowledge of all modes.
This is a rebirth treasury of those who are most excellent.

Their great kindness extends to cover all beings,
their marvelous practices ever increase in the ocean of the perfections,
and they illuminate the many classes of beings with Dharma's light.
This is a rebirth treasury for those who are heroically brave.

Their minds are unimpeded in completely knowing dharmas' nature
and they gain birth into the family of all buddhas of the three times.
They everywhere enter the ten directions' ocean of the Dharma realm.
This is a rebirth treasury of those possessed of radiant wisdom.

The Dharma body is pure and their resolve is unimpeded
in everywhere going to pay respects in the lands of the ten directions.
Of all the Buddha's powers, there are none they do not perfect.
This is a rebirth treasury of those who are inconceivable.

They have achieved sovereign mastery in entering deep wisdom,
have already reached the ultimate in all the samādhis, and
contemplate the gateways to all-knowledge in accordance with reality.
This is a rebirth treasury of those possessed of the true body.

They engage in the purification of all buddha lands,
diligently cultivate the dharma of everywhere teaching all beings,
and reveal the Tathāgata's miraculous powers.
This is a rebirth treasury of those of great renown.

Having already long cultivated the path to all-knowledge,
they are able to swiftly progress toward the station of the Tathāgata,
and are unimpeded in completely knowing the entire Dharma realm.
This is a rebirth treasury of all sons of the Buddha.

Son of Good Family, the bodhisattva who possesses these ten dharmas is born into the family of the Tathāgatas and becomes a source of pure light for everyone in the world.

Son of Good Family, it has been countless kalpas since I acquired this liberation gateway of sovereign mastery in taking on births.

正體字

善財白言。聖者。此解脫門。境
403b02‖ 界云何。答言。善男子。我先發願。願一切菩薩
403b03‖ 示受生時。皆得親近。願入毘盧遮那如來無
403b04‖ 量受生海。以昔願力。生此世界閻浮提中嵐
403b05‖ 毘尼園。專念菩薩。何時下生。經於百年。世尊
403b06‖ 果從兜率陀天而來生此。時此林中。現十種
403b07‖ 相。何等為十。一者此園中地。忽自平坦。坑坎
403b08‖ 堆阜。悉皆不現。二者金剛為地。眾寶莊嚴。無
403b09‖ 有瓦礫。荊棘株杌。三者寶多羅樹。周匝行列。
403b10‖ 其根深植。至於水際。四者生眾香[2]芽。現眾
403b11‖ 香藏。寶香為樹。扶踈蔭映。其諸香氣。皆逾天
403b12‖ 香。五者諸妙華鬘。寶莊嚴具。行列分布。處處
403b13‖ 充滿。六者園中所有一切諸樹。皆自然開摩
403b14‖ 尼寶華。七者諸池沼中。皆自生華。從地[3]涌
403b15‖ 出。周布水上。八者時此林中。娑婆世界。欲色
403b16‖ 所住。天龍夜叉乾闥婆阿脩羅迦樓羅緊那
403b17‖ 羅摩睺羅伽一切諸王。莫不來集。合掌而住。
403b18‖ 九者此世界中。所有天女。乃至摩睺羅伽女。
403b19‖ 皆生歡喜。各各捧持諸供養具。向畢洛叉樹
403b20‖ 前。恭敬而立。

简体字

善财白言："圣者，此解脱门境界云何？"

答言："善男子，我先发愿：'愿一切菩萨示受生时皆得亲近；愿入毗卢遮那如来无量受生海。'以昔愿力，生此世界阎浮提中岚毗尼园，专念菩萨何时下生；经于百年，世尊果从兜率陀天而来生此。

"时，此林中现十种相。何等为十？一者、此园中地忽自平坦，坑坎、堆阜悉皆不现。二者、金刚为地，众宝庄严，无有瓦砾、荆棘、株杌。三者、宝多罗树周匝行列，其根深植至于水际。四者、生众香芽，现众香藏，宝香为树，扶疏荫映，其诸香气皆逾天香。五者、诸妙华鬘宝庄严具，行列分布，处处充满。六者、园中所有一切诸树，皆自然开摩尼宝华。七者、诸池沼中，皆自生华，从地涌出，周布水上。八者、时此林中，娑婆世界欲色所住天、龙、夜叉、乾闼婆、阿修罗、迦楼罗、紧那罗、摩睺罗伽，一切诸王，莫不来集，合掌而住。九者、此世界中所有天女，乃至摩睺罗伽女皆生欢喜，各各捧持诸供养具，向毕洛叉树前，恭敬而立。

Sudhana then addressed the spirit, saying, "O Āryā, what is the sphere of experience of this liberation like?"

The spirit replied, saying:

Son of Good Family, in the past I made a vow: "I vow that, whenever any bodhisattvas manifest as taking on birth, I will draw near to them." I also vowed to enter the ocean of Vairocana Tathāgata's countless births.

It was due to the power of that past vow that I was born in this world, in Jambudvīpa, in the park at Lumbinī where I single-mindedly thought about when the bodhisattva would descend to take birth here. Then, after a hundred years had passed, the Bhagavat descended from the Tuṣita Heaven to take birth here. When this occurred, ten kinds of signs appeared in this grove. What were those ten? They were as follows:

First, the land in this park suddenly became level so that pits and mounds no longer appeared there;

Second, the ground turned into vajra adorned with the many kinds of jewels. There were no longer any broken tiles, rubble, thorns, thickets, roots, or stumps;

Third, jeweled *tāla* trees arose in encircling rows, the roots of which penetrated deeply until they reached the water;

Fourth, the many kinds of fragrant incense sprouts grew forth, repositories of the many kinds of incense appeared. Jewels and incense formed those trees with their spreading branches, shade, and jewel radiance. The fragrance of all those types of incense was in every case superior to the incense in the heavens;

Fifth, many kinds of marvelous flower garlands and jewel adornments arranged in rows everywhere filled that place;

Sixth, all of the trees in those gardens spontaneously blossomed with *maṇi* jewel flowers;

Seventh, flowers spontaneously grew up from the soil in the bottoms of all the pools and ponds and twirled about as they floated on the surface of the waters;

Eighth, within this grove, of all of the kings of the desire and form realm beings throughout the Sahā World, including the devas, dragons, *yakṣas, gandharvas, asuras, garuḍas, kiṃnaras,* and *mahoragas,* there were none who did not come and assemble there where they stood with their palms pressed together;

Ninth, all the deva maidens in this world including even the *mahoraga* maidens were filled with joyous delight. Each of them held up offering gifts before that *plakṣa* fig tree as they reverently stood there; and

正體字

十者十方一切諸佛[4]臍中。皆
403b21‖ 放光明。名菩薩受生自在燈。普照此林。一一
403b22‖ 光中。悉現諸佛受生誕生。所有神變。及一
403b23‖ 切菩薩受生功德。又出諸佛種種言音。是為
403b24‖ 林中十種瑞相。此相現時。諸天王等。即知
403b25‖ 當有菩薩下生。我見此瑞。歡喜無量。善男子。
403b26‖ 摩耶夫人。出迦毘羅城。入此林時。復現十
403b27‖ 種光明瑞相。令諸眾生得法光明。[5]何等為
403b28‖ 十。所謂一切寶華藏光。寶香藏光。寶蓮華
403b29‖ 開演出真實妙音聲光。十方菩薩初發心光。
403c01‖ 一切菩薩得入諸地現神變光。一切菩薩修
403c02‖ 波羅蜜圓滿智光。一切菩薩大願智光。一切
403c03‖ 菩薩教化眾生方便智光。一切菩薩證於法
403c04‖ 界真實[6]智光。一切菩薩得佛自在受生出家
403c05‖ 成正覺光。此十光明。普照無量諸眾生心。善
403c06‖ 男子。摩耶夫人。於畢洛叉樹下坐時。

简体字

十者、十方一切诸佛脐中，皆放光明，名菩萨受生自在灯，普照此林；一一光中，悉现诸佛受生，诞生所有神变，及一切菩萨受生功德，又出诸佛种种言音。是为林中十种瑞相。此相现时，诸天王等即知当有菩萨下生；我见此瑞，欢喜无量。

“善男子，摩耶夫人出迦毗罗城，入此林时，复现十种光明瑞相，令诸众生得法光明。何等为十？所谓：一切宝华藏光、宝香藏光、宝莲华开演出真实妙音声光、十方菩萨初发心光、一切菩萨得入诸地现神变光、一切菩萨修波罗蜜圆满智光、一切菩萨大愿智光、一切菩萨教化众生方便智光、一切菩萨证于法界真实智光、一切菩萨得佛自在受生出家成正觉光。此十光明，普照无量诸众生心。

“善男子，摩耶夫人于毕洛叉树下坐时，

Tenth, from the navels of all buddhas of the ten directions, there emanated beams of light known as "the magical lamp illuminating the birth of the bodhisattva." They everywhere illuminated this entire grove. Within each of those beams of light there appeared images of all buddhas' taking birth, the spiritual transformations connected with their birth, and the meritorious qualities of all those bodhisattvas who had been born. They also emanated the sounds of the many different voices of all buddhas.

These were the ten kinds of auspicious signs that appeared then within this grove. When these signs appeared, all the deva kings and the others immediately realized that the bodhisattva was about to descend to take birth there. When I saw these auspicious portents, I was filled with measureless joyous delight.

Son of Good Family, when the Lady Māyā came from Kapilavastu and entered this grove, yet again, there appeared ten kinds of radiant auspicious signs that enabled those beings there to acquire the light of Dharma. What were those ten? Those signs that appeared then were as follows:

Light from all the treasuries of jeweled flower blossoms;

Light from the treasuries of precious incense;

Light from jeweled lotus flowers which opened and emanated the sounds of truly sublime voices;

Light emanating from the initial generation of resolve by the bodhisattvas of the ten directions;

Light emanating from all bodhisattvas' entering the grounds and manifesting spiritual transformations;

The perfectly full wisdom light emanating from all bodhisattvas' cultivation of the *pāramitās*;

The wisdom light emanating from all bodhisattvas' great vows;

The wisdom light emanating from all bodhisattvas' use of skillful means in teaching beings;

The wisdom light emanating from all bodhisattvas' realization of the reality of the Dharma realm; and

The light emanating from all bodhisattvas' attainment [of the knowledge] of the Buddha's miraculous displays of taking birth, leaving the home life, and realizing right enlightenment.

These ten kinds of light everywhere illuminated the minds of countless beings.

Son of Good Family, when the Lady Māyā sat beneath the *plakṣa* fig tree, there also appeared ten kinds of spiritual transformations

正體字

復現
403c07‖ 菩薩將欲誕生。十種神變。何等為十。善男子。
403c08‖ 菩薩將欲誕生之時。欲界諸天天子天女。及
403c09‖ 以色界一切諸天諸龍夜叉乾闥婆阿脩羅迦
403c10‖ 樓羅緊那羅摩睺羅伽并其眷屬。為供養故。
403c11‖ 悉皆雲集。摩耶夫人。威德殊勝。身諸毛孔。咸
403c12‖ 放光明。普照三千大千世界。無所障礙。一切
403c13‖ 光明悉皆不現。除滅一切眾生煩惱。及惡道
403c14‖ 苦。是為菩薩將欲誕生第一神變。又善男子。
403c15‖ 當爾之時。摩耶夫人。腹中悉現三千世界一
403c16‖ 切形像。其百億閻浮提內。各有都邑。各有
403c17‖ 園林。名號不同。皆有摩耶夫人。於中止住。天
403c18‖ 眾圍遶。悉為顯現菩薩將生不可思議神變
403c19‖ 之相。是為菩薩將欲誕生第二神變。又善男
403c20‖ 子。摩耶夫人一切毛孔。皆現如來往昔修行
403c21‖ 菩薩道時。恭敬供養一切諸佛。及聞諸佛說
403c22‖ 法音聲。譬如明鏡及以水中。能現虛空日月
403c23‖ 星宿。雲雷等像。摩耶夫人身諸毛孔。亦復
403c24‖ 如是。能現如來往昔因緣。是為菩薩將欲誕
403c25‖ 生第三神變。又善男子。摩耶夫人。身諸毛孔。
403c26‖ 一一皆現如來往修菩薩行時。所住世界。城
403c27‖ 邑聚落。

简体字

复现菩萨将欲诞生十种神变。何等为十？

"善男子，菩萨将欲诞生之时，欲界诸天天子、天女，及以色界一切诸天、诸龙、夜叉、乾闼婆、阿修罗、迦楼罗、紧那罗、摩睺罗伽并其眷属，为供养故，悉皆云集。摩耶夫人威德殊胜，身诸毛孔咸放光明，普照三千大千世界无所障碍，一切光明悉皆不现，除灭一切众生烦恼及恶道苦。是为菩萨将欲诞生第一神变。

"又，善男子，当尔之时，摩耶夫人腹中悉现三千世界一切形像，其百亿阎浮提内，各有都邑，各有园林，名号不同，皆有摩耶夫人于中止住、天众围绕，悉为显现菩萨将生不可思议神变之相。是为菩萨将欲诞生第二神变。

"又，善男子，摩耶夫人一切毛孔，皆现如来往昔修行菩萨道时，恭敬供养一切诸佛，及闻诸佛说法音声。譬如明镜及以水中，能现虚空日月、星宿、云雷等像；摩耶夫人身诸毛孔亦复如是，能现如来往昔因缘。是为菩萨将欲诞生第三神变。

"又，善男子，摩耶夫人身诸毛孔，一一皆现如来往修菩萨行时，所住世界，城邑聚落，

just before the bodhisattva was born. What were those ten? They were as follows:

Son of Good Family, when the Bodhisattva was about to take birth, all of the desire realm devas, devas' sons, and devas' daughters as well as all the form realm's devas, dragons, *yakṣas, gandharvas, asuras, garuḍas, kiṃnaras, mahoragas,* and their retinues assembled like clouds in order to present offerings. The Lady Māyā, extraordinarily excellent in her awesome virtue, emanated light from all the pores on her body which everywhere and unimpededly illuminated the worlds of the great trichiliocosm, caused all other forms of light there to no longer appear at all, and extinguished the afflictions of all beings as well as the sufferings in the wretched destinies. This is the first of the spiritual transformations that occurred when the Bodhisattva was about to be born.

Also, Son of Good Family, at that very time, within the belly of the Lady Māya, there appeared all of the images of the phenomena throughout the great trichiliocosm. Among them, in the hundred koṭīs of Jambudvīpa continents, there were in each case cities, each of which had parks and groves of different names, and all of which had the Lady Māya abiding within them, surrounded by a congregation of devas. In all of those scenes there appeared these signs of the inconceivable spiritual transformations occurring at the time when the Bodhisattva was about to take birth. This is the second of the spiritual transformations that occurred when the Bodhisattva was about to be born.

Also, Son of Good Family, within all of the Lady Māyā's pores were revealed the appearances of the Tathāgata's cultivation of the bodhisattva path throughout the distant past during which he respectfully made offerings to all buddhas and listened to the voices of all buddhas as they taught the Dharma. They appeared there in the same way as a brightly polished mirror or the surface of water is able to show the appearances of the sun, moon, stars, constellations, thunder clouds, and other such phenomena appearing up in the sky. So too it was with the pores of the Lady Māyā's body that were able to reveal the causes and conditions of the Tathāgata's distant past. This is the third of the spiritual transformations that occurred when the Bodhisattva was about to be born.

Also, Son of Good Family, in each of the Lady Māyā's pores there appeared scenes from the time in the distant past when the Tathāgata cultivated the bodhisattva practices, including the worlds in which he dwelt, their cities, villages, mountains,

正體字

山林河海。眾生劫數。值佛出世。入淨
403c28‖ 國土。隨所受生。壽命長短。依善知識。修行善
403c29‖ 法。於一切剎。在在生處。摩耶夫人。常為其
404a01‖ 母。如是一切。於毛孔中。靡不皆現。是為菩薩
404a02‖ 將欲誕生第四神變。又善男子。摩耶夫人一
404a03‖ 一毛孔。顯現如來往昔修行菩薩行時。隨所
404a04‖ 生處。色相形貌。衣服飲食。苦樂等事。一一
404a05‖ [1]普現。分明[2]辯了。是為菩薩將欲誕生第五
404a06‖ 神變。又善男子。摩耶夫人。身諸毛孔。一一皆
404a07‖ 現世尊往昔修施行時。捨所難捨。頭目耳鼻。
404a08‖ 脣舌牙齒。身體手足。血[3]肉筋骨。男女妻妾。
404a09‖ 城邑宮殿。衣服瓔珞。金銀寶貨。如是一切內
404a10‖ 外諸物。亦見受者形貌音聲。及其處所。是為
404a11‖ 菩薩將欲誕生第六神變。又善男子。摩耶夫
404a12‖ 人。入此園時。其林普現過去所有一切諸佛。
404a13‖ 入母胎時。國土園林。衣服華鬘。塗香末香。
404a14‖ 幡繒幢蓋。一切眾寶莊嚴之事。[4]妓樂歌詠。
404a15‖ 上妙音聲。令諸眾生普得見聞。是為菩薩將
404a16‖ 誕生時第七神變。

简体字

山林河海，众生劫数，值佛出世，入净国土，随所受生，寿命长短，依善知识修行善法，于一切刹在在生处，摩耶夫人常为其母；如是一切，于毛孔中靡不皆现。是为菩萨将欲诞生第四神变。

“又，善男子，摩耶夫人一一毛孔，显现如来往昔修行菩萨行时，随所生处，色相形貌，衣服饮食，苦乐等事，一一普现，分明辨了。是为菩萨将欲诞生第五神变。

“又，善男子，摩耶夫人身诸毛孔，一一皆现世尊往昔修施行时，舍所难舍——头目耳鼻，唇舌牙齿，身体手足，血肉筋骨，男女妻妾，城邑宫殿，衣服璎珞，金银宝货。——如是一切内外诸物，亦见受者形貌、音声及其处所。是为菩萨将欲诞生第六神变。

“又，善男子，摩耶夫人入此园时，其林普现过去所有一切诸佛入母胎时国土、园林、衣服、华鬘、涂香、末香、幡缯、幢盖——一切众宝庄严之事，妓乐歌咏上妙音声，令诸众生普得见闻。是为菩萨将诞生时第七神变。

forests, rivers, oceans, the numbers of beings and kalpas, his encounters with buddhas who appeared in the world, his entry into pure lands, the length of his lives whenever he was reborn, his reliance upon good spiritual guides, and his cultivation of the good dharmas. In all those *kṣetras,* wherever he was born, the Lady Māyā always served as his mother. Of all such circumstances as these, there were none that did not appear within her pores. This is the fourth of the spiritual transformations that occurred when the Bodhisattva was about to be born.

Also, Son of Good Family, within every one of the Lady Māyā's pores there appeared images from the time in the distant past when the Tathāgata cultivated the bodhisattva practices, including, wherever he was born, his physical characteristics and appearances, his clothes, his food and drink, his sufferings and pleasures, and other such phenomena. Every one of these matters was fully revealed there in ways that were distinctly and completely discernible.[3] This is the fifth of the spiritual transformations that occurred when the Bodhisattva was about to be born.

Also, Son of Good Family, within every one of the Lady Māyā's pores there appeared images from the time in the distant past when the Bhagavat cultivated the practice of giving by relinquishing what is difficult to relinquish, including when he gave up his head, eyes, ears, nose, lips, tongue, teeth, physical body, hands, feet, blood, flesh, sinews, and bones, including too when he gave up his sons and daughters, his wives and consorts, his cities and palaces, his robes and jewelry, his gold, silver and precious possessions, all such inward and outward things as these. One also saw there the appearances and voices of those who received these gifts as well as the places where they dwelt. This is the sixth of the spiritual transformations that occurred when the Bodhisattva was about to be born.

Also, Son of Good Family, when the Lady Māyā entered these gardens, its grove everywhere showed the events from the times in which all buddhas of the past descended into their mothers' wombs, including their lands, their gardens and groves, their clothing and flower garlands, their topically applied scents, powdered incense, pennants, streamers, banners, canopies, and all of their other adornments as well as their many different kinds of precious jewels and the exquisite sounds of their instrumental music, singing, and chanting, all of which manifested in ways that all the beings there could see and hear in their entirety. This is the seventh of the spiritual transformations that occurred when the Bodhisattva was about to be born.

正體字

又善男子。摩耶夫人。入
404a17║ 此園時。從其身出菩薩所住摩尼寶王宮殿
404a18║ 樓閣。超過一切天龍夜叉乾闥婆阿脩羅迦
404a19║ 樓羅緊那羅摩睺羅伽。及諸人王之所住者。
404a20║ 寶網覆上。妙香普熏。眾寶莊嚴。內外清淨。各
404a21║ 各差別。不相雜亂。周匝遍滿嵐毘尼園。是為
404a22║ 菩薩將誕生時第八神變。又善男子。摩耶夫
404a23║ 人。入此園時。從其身出十不可說百千億那
404a24║ 由他佛剎微塵數菩薩。其諸菩薩。身形容貌。
404a25║ 相好光明。進止威儀。神通眷[5]屬。皆與毘盧
404a26║ 遮那菩薩。等無有異。悉共同時。讚歎如來。是
404a27║ 為菩薩將誕生時第九神變。又善男子。摩耶
404a28║ 夫人。將欲誕生菩薩之時。忽於其前。從金
404a29║ 剛際。出大蓮華。名為一切寶莊嚴藏。金剛
404b01║ 為莖。眾寶為鬚。如意寶王以為其臺。有十佛
404b02║ 剎微塵數葉。一切皆以摩尼所成寶網寶蓋。
404b03║ 以覆其上。一切天王。所共執持。一切龍王降
404b04║ 注香雨。一切夜叉王恭敬圍遶。散諸天華。一
404b05║ 切乾闥婆王出微妙音。歌讚菩薩往[6]昔供養
404b06║ 諸佛功德。一切阿脩羅王捨憍慢心。稽首敬
404b07║ 禮。一切迦樓羅王垂寶繒幡。遍滿虛空。

简体字

“又，善男子，摩耶夫人入此园时，从其身出菩萨所住摩尼宝王宫殿、楼阁，超过一切天、龙、夜叉、乾闼婆、阿修罗、迦楼罗、紧那罗、摩睺罗伽及诸人王之所住者，宝网覆上，妙香普熏，众宝庄严，内外清净，各各差别，不相杂乱，周匝遍满岚毗尼园。是为菩萨将诞生时第八神变。

“又，善男子，摩耶夫人入此园时，从其身出十不可说百千亿那由他佛刹微尘数菩萨，其诸菩萨身形容貌、相好光明、进止威仪、神通眷属，皆与毗卢遮那菩萨等无有异，悉共同时赞叹如来。是为菩萨将诞生时第九神变。

“又，善男子，摩耶夫人将欲诞生菩萨之时，忽于其前，从金刚际出大莲华，名为一切宝庄严藏。金刚为茎，众宝为须，如意宝王以为其台，有十佛刹微尘数叶，一切皆以摩尼所成宝网、宝盖以覆其上。一切天王所共执持；一切龙王降注香雨；一切夜叉王恭敬围绕，散诸天华；一切乾闼婆王出微妙音，歌赞菩萨往昔供养诸佛功德；一切阿修罗王舍憍慢心，稽首敬礼；一切迦楼罗王垂宝缯幡，遍满虚空；

Also, Son of Good Family, when the Lady Māyā entered these gardens, there emerged from her body a palatial tower made of sovereign *maṇi* jewels in which the Bodhisattva resided. It surpassed those in which all the kings of the devas, dragons, *yakṣas, gandharvas, asuras, garuḍas, kiṃnaras, mahoragas,* and humans lived. Sheltered by a jeweled net canopy overhead, it was everywhere imbued with marvelous scents and was adorned with the many kinds of jewels. It was purified within and without, none of its various details were at all disordered, and it completely encompassed and filled all of the Lumbinī gardens. This is the eighth of the spiritual transformations that occurred when the Bodhisattva was about to be born.

Also, Son of Good Family, when the Lady Māyā entered these gardens, there emerged from her body bodhisattvas as numerous as the atoms in ten ineffable numbers of hundreds of thousands of *koṭīs* of *nayutas* of buddha *kṣetras*. Those bodhisattvas' bodies, appearances, major marks, secondary signs, radiance, deportment when moving or stopping, their spiritual superknowledges, and their retinues—these were all equivalent to and no different from those of Vairocana Bodhisattva. They all joined then in simultaneously proclaiming the praises of the Tathāgata. This is the ninth of the spiritual transformations that occurred when the Bodhisattva was about to be born.

Also, Son of Good Family, when the Lady Māyā was about to give birth to the Bodhisattva, an immense lotus flower from the vajra realm suddenly appeared directly before her. Known as Treasury of all Jewel Adornments, it had a stem made of vajra, stamens made of the many kinds of jewels, a seed pod made from sovereign wishing jewels, and petals as numerous as the atoms in ten buddha *kṣetras*.

It was entirely sheltered by an overhanging net of *maṇi* jewels and by a jeweled canopy.

It was jointly held up by all the heavenly kings.

All the dragon kings sent down a sprinkling rain of perfume.

All the *yakṣa* kings reverently circumambulated it, scattering down celestial flowers.

All the *gandharva* kings sang with sublime voices songs in praise of the Bodhisattva's merit from past offerings to all buddhas.

All the *asura* kings relinquished their arrogance and prostrated themselves in reverence.

All the *garuḍa* kings hung down jeweled streamers and banners that everywhere filled the sky.

正體字

一
404b08 ‖ 切緊那羅王歡喜瞻仰。歌詠讚歎菩薩功德。
404b09 ‖ 一切摩睺羅伽王皆生歡喜。歌詠讚歎。普雨
404b10 ‖ 一切寶莊嚴雲。是為菩薩將誕生時第十神
404b11 ‖ 變。善男子。嵐毘尼園。示現如是十種相已。然
404b12 ‖ 後菩薩。其身誕生。如虛空中現淨日輪。如高
404b13 ‖ 山頂出於慶雲。如密雲中而[7]耀電光。如夜
404b14 ‖ 闇中而然[8]大炬。爾時菩薩。從母脇生。身相
404b15 ‖ 光明。亦復如是。善男子。菩薩爾時。雖現初
404b16 ‖ 生。悉已了達一切諸法如夢如幻。如影如像。
404b17 ‖ 無來無去。不生不滅。善男子。當我見佛。於此
404b18 ‖ 四天下閻浮提內嵐毘尼園。示現初生種種
404b19 ‖ 神變時。亦見如來於三千大千世界百億四
404b20 ‖ 天下閻浮提內嵐毘尼園中。示現初生種種
404b21 ‖ 神變。[9]亦見三千大千世界一一塵中無量佛
404b22 ‖ 剎。亦見百佛世界。千佛世界。乃至十方一
404b23 ‖ 切世界。一一塵中。無量佛剎。如是一切諸佛
404b24 ‖ 剎中。皆有如來。示現受生種種神變。如是
404b25 ‖ 念念。常無間斷。時善財童子。白彼神言。大天
404b26 ‖ 得此解脫。其已久如。

简体字

`一切紧那罗王欢喜瞻仰，歌咏赞叹菩萨功德；一切摩睺罗伽王皆生欢喜，歌咏赞叹，普雨一切宝庄严云。是为菩萨将诞生时第十神变。

“善男子，岚毗尼园示现如是十种相已，然后菩萨其身诞生。如虚空中现净日轮，如高山顶出于庆云，如密云中而耀电光，如夜暗中而燃大炬；尔时，菩萨从母胁生，身相光明亦复如是。善男子，菩萨尔时，虽现初生，悉已了达一切诸法，如梦如幻，如影如像，无来无去，不生不灭。

“善男子，当我见佛于此四天下阎浮提内岚毗尼园示现初生种种神变时，亦见如来于三千大千世界百亿四天下阎浮提内岚毗尼园中示现初生种种神变；亦见三千大千世界一一尘中无量佛刹，亦见百佛世界、千佛世界乃至十方一切世界一一尘中无量佛刹，如是一切诸佛刹中，皆有如来示现受生种种神变。如是念念，常无间断。”

时，善财童子白彼神言：“大天得此解脱，其已久如？”

All the *kiṃnara* kings gazed up in joyful admiration, singing praises of the Bodhisattva's meritorious qualities.

All the *mahoraga* kings, filled with joyous delight, sang praises as they everywhere rained down clouds of adornments made of all varieties of jewels.

This is the tenth of the spiritual transformations that occurred when the Bodhisattva was about to be born.

Son of Good Family, after the manifestation in the Lumbinī Gardens of these ten kinds of signs, the Bodhisattva was born there. As if the brightly shining orb of the sun had appeared in the midst of the sky, as if the peak of a high mountain had emerged from behind the clouds, as if a dazzling flash of lightning appeared out of the midst of dense clouds, and as if a great torch appeared in the darkness of the night, just so were the manifestations of light that shone forth from the Bodhisattva's physical marks when he was born from his mother's side.

Son of Good Family, although the Bodhisattva appeared then to be newly born, he had already fully comprehended all dharmas as like a dream, like a magical conjuration, like reflections, like mere images, as neither coming nor going, and as neither produced nor destroyed.

Son of Good Family, when I saw all these many different spiritual transformations that occurred when the Buddha appeared as being newly born in the gardens at Lumbinī on the Jambudvīpa continent of this four-continent world, I also saw the many different spiritual transformations that occurred when the Tathāgata appeared as being newly born in the Lumbinī Gardens on the Jambudvīpa continents of a hundred *koṭīs* of four-continent worlds throughout the great trichiliocosm.

I also saw this in the countless buddha *kṣetras* in every atom throughout the great trichiliocosm and also saw this in the countless buddha *kṣetras* in each atom in a hundred buddha worlds, in a thousand buddha worlds, and so forth until we come to in all worlds throughout the ten directions. So it is that, in all those buddha *kṣetras,* there are *tathāgatas* who appear to be taking birth attended by many different spiritual transformations. This continues on in this way constantly and uninterruptedly in each successive mind-moment.

Sudhana the Youth then addressed the Spirit, asking, "O Great Goddess, how long has it been now since you acquired this liberation?"

正體字

答言。善男子。乃往古
404b27 世。過億佛刹微塵數劫。復過是數。時有世界
404b28 名為普寶。劫名悅樂。八十那由他佛。於中
404b29 出現。其第一佛。名自在功德幢。十號具足。彼
404c01 世界中。有四天下。名妙光莊嚴。其四天下閻
404c02 浮提中。有一王都。名須彌莊嚴幢。其中有王
404c03 名寶焰眼。其王夫人名曰喜光。善男子。如此
404c04 世界摩耶夫人。為毘盧遮那如來之母。彼世
404c05 界中喜光夫人。為初佛母。亦復如是。善男
404c06 子。其喜光夫人。將欲誕生菩薩之時。與二
404c07 十億那由他采女。詣金華園。園中有樓。名
404c08 妙寶峯。其邊有樹。名一切施。喜光夫人。攀彼
404c09 樹枝。而生菩薩。諸天王眾。各持香水。共以洗
404c10 沐。時有乳母。名為淨光。侍立其側。既洗沐
404c11 已。諸天王眾授與乳母。乳母敬受生大歡喜。
404c12 即得菩薩普眼三昧。得此三昧已。普見十方
404c13 無量諸佛。復得菩薩於一切處示現受生自
404c14 在解脫。如初受胎識。速疾無礙。得此解脫故。
404c15 見一切佛乘本願力。受生自在。亦復如是。善
404c16 男子。於汝意云何。彼乳母者。豈異人乎。我身
404c17 是也。我從是來。

简体字

答言："善男子，乃往古世，过亿佛刹微尘数劫，复过是数。时，有世界名为普宝，劫名悦乐，八十那由他佛于中出现；其第一佛，名自在功德幢，十号具足。彼世界中，有四天下，名妙光庄严；其四天下阎浮提中，有一王都，名须弥庄严幢；其中有王，名宝焰眼；其王夫人，名曰喜光。善男子，如此世界摩耶夫人，为毗卢遮那如来之母；彼世界中喜光夫人，为初佛母，亦复如是。

"善男子，其喜光夫人将欲诞生菩萨之时，与二十亿那由他采女诣金华园；园中有楼，名妙宝峰；其边有树，名一切施。喜光夫人攀彼树枝而生菩萨，诸天王众各持香水共以洗沐。时，有乳母名为净光，侍立其侧。既洗沐已，诸天王众授与乳母。乳母敬受，生大欢喜，即得菩萨普眼三昧；得此三昧已，普见十方无量诸佛，复得菩萨于一切处示现受生自在解脱。如初受胎识，速疾无碍；得此解脱故，见一切佛乘本愿力受生自在，亦复如是。善男子，于汝意云何？彼乳母者，岂异人乎？我身是也。我从是来，

The Spirit replied:

Son of Good Family, it was long ago in the ancient past, back beyond kalpas as numerous as the atoms in a *koṭī* of buddha *kṣetras* and then back again once more, before just as long as this, there was a world known as Ubiquitous Jewels in which, in a kalpa named Blissful Happiness, eighty *nayutas* of buddhas appeared.

Among those buddhas, the first was a buddha named Banner of Sovereign Qualities, one referred to by all ten titles of a buddha. In that world there was a four-continent array known as Adorned with Sublime Light. On the Jambudvīpa continent of that four-continent array, there was a royal capital city known as Banner of Sumeru's Adornments in which there was a king named Jewel Light Eyes. That king's wife was named Joyous Light.

Son of Good Family, just as the Lady Māyā served as the mother of Vairocana Tathāgata in this world, so too did Lady Joyous Light serve as the mother of the first of those buddhas. Son of Good Family, when Lady Joyous Light was about to give birth to the Bodhisattva, she went with twenty *koṭīs* of *nayutas* of female attendants to Golden Flower Gardens. Within those gardens there was a tower known as Marvelous Jeweled Spire, alongside which there was a tree known as Giving All. Lady Joyous Light then grasped a branch of that tree and gave birth to the Bodhisattva.

Then a congregation of heavenly kings each took up perfumed waters and together showered him. There was then a wet nurse known as Pure Light who stood at his side. When the shower had been performed, the congregation of heavenly kings passed him on to the wet nurse. The wet nurse respectfully received him and became filled with great joy, whereupon she immediately acquired "the bodhisattva's universal eye samādhi." Having acquired this samādhi, she everywhere saw the countless buddhas of the ten directions. She then also acquired the liberation known as "the bodhisattvas' sovereign manifestation of birth in all places." Just as when the consciousness of the embryo is first received into the womb, its arrival is swift and unimpeded, so too, because she acquired this liberation, in this same way, she could easily see all buddhas using the power of their original vows to freely take on births.

Son of Good Family, what do you think? As for that wet nurse, could it have been anyone else? It was none other than myself. From that time on forward, in every mind-moment, I have always seen the ocean of Vairocana Buddha's manifestations as the bodhisattva

正體字

念念常見毘盧遮那佛示現
404c18║ 菩薩受生海調伏眾生自在神力。如見毘盧
404c19║ 遮那佛。乘本願力。念念於此三千大千。乃至
404c20║ 十方。一切世界微塵之內。皆現菩薩受生神
404c21║ 變。見一切佛。悉亦如是。我皆恭敬承事供養。
404c22║ 聽所說法如說修行。時嵐毘尼林神。欲重宣
404c23║ 此解脫義。承佛神力。普觀十方而說頌言
404c24║ 佛子汝所問　諸佛甚深境
404c25║ 汝今應聽受　我說其因緣
404c26║ 過億剎塵劫　有劫名悅樂
404c27║ 八十那由他　如來出興世
404c28║ 最初如來號　自在功德幢
404c29║ 我在金華園　見彼初生日
405a01║ 我時為乳母　智慧極聰利
405a02║ 諸天授與我　菩薩金色身
405a03║ 我時疾捧持　諦觀不見頂
405a04║ 身相皆圓滿　一一無邊際
405a05║ 離垢清淨身　相好以莊嚴
405a06║ 譬如妙寶像　見已自欣慶
405a07║ 思惟彼功德　疾增眾福海
405a08║ 見此神通事　發大菩提心

简体字

念念常见毗卢遮那佛示现菩萨受生海调伏众生自在神力。如见毗卢遮那佛乘本愿力，念念于此三千大千，乃至十方一切世界微尘之内，皆现菩萨受生神变；见一切佛悉亦如是，我皆恭敬承事供养，听所说法，如说修行。”

时，岚毗尼林神，欲重宣此解脱义，承佛神力，普观十方而说颂言：

“佛子汝所问，诸佛甚深境；
汝今应听受，我说其因缘。
过亿刹尘劫，有劫名悦乐；
八十那由他，如来出兴世。
最初如来号，自在功德幢；
我在金华园，见彼初生日。
我时为乳母，智慧极聪利；
诸天授与我，菩萨金色身。
我时疾捧持，谛观不见顶，
身相皆圆满，一一无边际。
离垢清净身，相好以庄严，
譬如妙宝像，见已自欣庆。
思惟彼功德，疾增众福海；
见此神通事，发大菩提心。

taking on birth, thereby using his miraculous spiritual powers to train beings.

And just as I have witnessed Vairocana Buddha's spiritual transformations in which, using the power of his original vows, he in every mind-moment manifested the bodhisattva's taking on of births in the atoms of all worlds, so too have I witnessed all buddhas doing this in this very same way. In all those instances, I have reverently served them all, made offerings to them all, listened to the Dharma they all taught, and then practiced in accordance with their teachings.

Then, wishing to once again proclaim the meaning of this liberation, aided by the Buddha's powers, the spirit of the Lumbinī grove regarded all the ten directions and spoke these verses:

Son of the Buddha, as for what you have asked
about the extremely profound sphere of action of all buddhas,
you should now listen attentively
as I speak about those very causes and conditions.

Back beyond kalpas as numerous as the atoms in a *koṭī* of *kṣetras,*
there was a kalpa known as Blissful Happiness
in which eighty *nayutas*
of *tathāgatas* appeared in the world.

Of those *tathāgatas,* the very first was named
Banner of Sovereign Qualities.
In Golden Flower Gardens,
I saw him on that day when he took birth.

At that time, I was his wet nurse,
one who was possessed of especially acute wisdom.
Those devas then passed on to me
the Bodhisattva's gold-colored body.

I then quickly raised him up with both hands
and attentively regarded his summit [mark] that one cannot see.
His physical signs were perfectly complete
and each one of them was boundless.

His immaculate pure body,
adorned with the major marks and secondary signs,
resembled an image made of marvelous jewels.
Having seen him, I was filled with exultant joy.

On merely contemplating his meritorious qualities,
I swiftly established an ocean of manifold merit.
On seeing these supernatural phenomena,
I made the great resolve to attain bodhi.

正體字

405a09 [1] 專求佛功德　增廣諸大願
405a10 嚴淨一切剎　滅除三惡道
405a11 普於十方土　供養無數佛
405a12 修行本誓願　救脫眾生苦
405a13 我於彼佛所　聞法得解脫
405a14 億剎微塵數　無量劫修行
405a15 劫中所有佛　我悉曾供養
405a16 護持其正法　淨此解脫海
405a17 億剎微塵數　過去十力尊
405a18 盡持其法輪　增明此解脫
405a19 我於一念頃　見此剎塵中
405a20 一一有如來　所淨諸剎海
405a21 剎內悉有佛　園中示誕生
405a22 各現不思議　廣大神通力
405a23 或見不思議　億剎諸菩薩
405a24 住於天宮上　將證佛菩提
405a25 無量剎海中　諸佛現受生
405a26 說法眾圍遶　於此我皆見
405a27 一念見億剎　微塵數菩薩
405a28 出家趣道場　示現佛境界

简体字

专求佛功德，增广诸大愿，
严净一切刹，灭除三恶道。
普于十方土，供养无数佛，
修行本誓愿，救脱众生苦。
我于彼佛所，闻法得解脱，
亿刹微尘数，无量劫修行。
劫中所有佛，我昔曾供养，
护持其正法，净此解脱海。
亿刹微尘数，过去十力尊，
尽持其法轮，增明此解脱。
我于一念顷，见此刹尘中，
一一有如来，所净诸刹海。
刹内悉有佛，园中示诞生，
各现不思议，广大神通力。
或见不思议，亿刹诸菩萨，
住于天宫上，将证佛菩提。
无量刹海中，诸佛现受生，
说法众围绕，于此我皆见。
一念见亿刹，微尘数菩萨，
出家趣道场，示现佛境界。

I single-mindedly sought a buddha's meritorious qualities
and broadened all the great vows
to purify all the *kṣetras*
and do away with the three wretched destinies.

Everywhere throughout the lands of the ten directions,
I made offerings to countless buddhas,
cultivated my original vows,
and sought to liberate beings from their sufferings.

In the presence of that buddha,
I listened to the teaching of Dharma, acquired liberations,
and cultivated for countless kalpas
as numerous as the atoms in a *koṭī* of *kṣetras.*

I then made offerings to
all the buddhas who appeared in that kalpa,
guarded and preserved their legacy of right Dharma
and purified this ocean of liberations.

Past *bhagavats* possessed of the ten powers
as numerous as the atoms in a *koṭī* of *kṣetras*—
I preserved all their turnings of the Dharma wheel
and increased the brightness of this liberation.

In the instant of but a single mind-moment,
I see that, in the atoms of this *kṣetra,*
every one of them contains
an ocean of *kṣetras* purified by *tathāgatas.*

In all those *kṣetras,* there are buddhas
manifesting the taking on of birth in gardens.
Each manifests the inconceivable powers
of his vast spiritual superknowledges.

In some instances, I see all the bodhisattvas
in inconceivably many *koṭīs* of *kṣetras*
dwelling in their heavenly palaces
as they are about to realize the bodhi of the buddhas.

In oceans of countless *kṣetras,*
buddhas manifest the taking on of births,
then teach the Dharma surrounded by their congregations.
I have seen them all.

In but a single mind-moment, I see bodhisattvas
as numerous as the atoms in a *koṭī* of *kṣetras*
leave the home life and go to the site of enlightenment
where they manifest the realms of a buddha.

正體字

405a29‖ 我見剎塵內　無量佛成道
405b01‖ 各現諸方便　度脫苦眾生
405b02‖ 一一微塵中　諸佛轉法輪
405b03‖ 悉以無盡音　普雨甘露法
405b04‖ 億剎微塵數　一一剎塵內
405b05‖ 悉見於如來　示現般涅槃
405b06‖ 如是無量剎　如來示誕生
405b07‖ 而我悉分身　現前興供養
405b08‖ 不思議剎海　無量趣差別
405b09‖ 我悉現其前　雨於大法雨
405b10‖ 佛子我知此　難思解脫門
405b11‖ 無量億劫中　稱揚不可盡
405b12‖ 善男子。我唯知此菩薩於無量劫遍一切處
405b13‖ 示現受生自在解脫。如諸菩薩摩訶薩。能以
405b14‖ 一念為諸劫藏。觀一切法。以善方便而現受
405b15‖ 生。周遍供養一切諸佛。究竟通達一切佛法。
405b16‖ 於一切趣皆現受生。一切佛前坐蓮華座。知
405b17‖ 諸眾生應可度時。為現受生方便調伏。於一
405b18‖ 切剎現諸神變。猶如影像悉現其前。

简体字

我见刹尘内，无量佛成道，
各现诸方便，度脱苦众生。
一一微尘中，诸佛转法轮，
悉以无尽音，普雨甘露法。
亿刹微尘数，一一刹尘内，
悉见于如来，示现般涅槃。
如是无量刹，如来示诞生；
而我悉分身，现前兴供养。
不思议刹海，无量趣差别；
我悉现其前，雨于大法雨。
佛子我知此，难思解脱门，
无量亿劫中，称扬不可尽。

“善男子，我唯知此菩萨于无量劫遍一切处示现受生自在解脱。如诸菩萨摩诃萨，能以一念为诸劫藏，观一切法，以善方便而现受生；周遍供养一切诸佛，究竟通达一切佛法；于一切趣皆现受生，一切佛前坐莲华座；知诸众生应可度时，为现受生方便调伏；于一切刹现诸神变，犹如影像悉现其前。

I see within a *kṣetra*'s atoms
countless buddhas attaining enlightenment.
They each manifest all kinds of skillful means
to then liberate suffering beings.

Within every mote of dust,
buddhas turn the wheel of the Dharma.
In all of them they use endless voices
to everywhere rain the Dharma of the elixir of immortality.

In numbers equal to the atoms in a *koṭī* of *kṣetras,*
within the atoms of every *kṣetra,*
I see there all the *tathāgatas*
manifesting entry into *parinirvāṇa.*

In this way, in the countless *kṣetras,*
the *tathāgatas* manifest the taking on of births,
whereupon, for all of them, I issue division bodies
that appear before them, presenting offerings.

Throughout the oceans of inconceivably many *kṣetras,*
for the countless different beings in the rebirth destinies,
I appear directly before them all
and rain down the great Dharma's rain.

Son of the Buddha, I have come to know this
gateway of inconceivable liberation that,
if one praised it for countless *koṭīs* of kalpas,
even then, one could never finish doing so.

Son of the Buddha, I know only this liberation known as "the bodhisattvas' miraculous taking on births in all places for countless kalpas." As for the bodhisattva-mahāsattvas:

Who are able to turn one mind-moment into a treasury of kalpas in which they contemplate all dharmas;

Who use skillful means to appear to take on births;

Who go everywhere to make offerings to all buddhas;

Who have achieved the ultimate comprehension of the dharmas of all buddhas;

Who manifest the taking on of births in all the rebirth destinies;

Who sit before all buddhas on a lotus seat;

Who know when all beings can be liberated;

Who then manifest the taking on of births for them and use skillful means to train them;

Who manifest all kinds of spiritual transformations in all *kṣetras;* and

Who, like reflected images, manifest directly before all beings—

正體字

我當云
405b19 ‖ 何能知能說彼功德行。善男子。此迦毘羅城。
405b20 ‖ 有釋種女。名曰瞿波。汝詣彼問。菩薩云何於
405b21 ‖ 生死中。教化眾生。時善財童子。頂禮其足。遶
405b22 ‖ 無數匝。慇懃瞻仰。辭退而去
405c02 ‖ [3]大方廣佛華嚴經卷[4]第七十五
405c05 ‖ 入法界品第三十九之十六
405c06 ‖ 爾時善財童子。向迦毘羅城。思惟修習受生
405c07 ‖ 解脫。增長廣大。憶念不捨。漸次遊行。至菩薩
405c08 ‖ 集會普現法界光明講堂。其中有神。號無憂
405c09 ‖ 德。與一萬主宮殿神俱。來迎善財。作如是
405c10 ‖ 言。善來丈夫有大智慧。有大勇猛。能修菩薩
405c11 ‖ 不可思議自在解脫。心恒不捨廣大誓願。善
405c12 ‖ 能觀察諸法境界。安住法城。入於無量諸方
405c13 ‖ 便門。成就如來功德大海。得妙辯才。善調眾
405c14 ‖ 生。獲聖智身。恒順修行。知諸眾生心行差別。
405c15 ‖ 令其歡喜趣向佛道。我觀仁者修諸妙行。心
405c16 ‖ 無暫懈。威儀所行。悉皆清淨。汝當不久。得諸
405c17 ‖ 如來清淨莊嚴無上三業。以諸相好莊嚴其
405c18 ‖ 身。以十力智瑩飾其心。遊諸世間。我觀仁
405c19 ‖ 者勇猛精進而無有比。

简体字

我当云何能知能说彼功德行？

“善男子，此迦毗罗城，有释种女，名曰瞿波。汝诣彼问：菩萨云何于生死中教化众生？”

时，善财童子顶礼其足，绕无数匝，殷勤瞻仰，辞退而去。

大方广佛华严经卷第七十五

入法界品第三十九之十六

尔时，善财童子向迦毗罗城，思惟修习受生解脱，增长广大，忆念不舍。

渐次游行，至菩萨集会普现法界光明讲堂，其中有神，号无忧德，与一万主宫殿神俱，来迎善财，作如是言：“善来丈夫！有大智慧，有大勇猛，能修菩萨不可思议自在解脱，心恒不舍广大誓愿，善能观察诸法境界；安住法城，入于无量诸方便门，成就如来功德大海；得妙辩才，善调众生，获圣智身，恒顺修行，知诸众生心行差别，令其欢喜趣向佛道。

“我观仁者修诸妙行心无暂懈，威仪所行悉皆清净，汝当不久得诸如来清净庄严无上三业，以诸相好庄严其身，以十力智莹饰其心，游诸世间。我观仁者勇猛精进而无有比，

How could I know of or be able speak about their meritorious qualities and practices?

Son of Good Family, in this city of Kapilavastu, there is a maiden in the lineage of the Śākya clan known as Gopā. You should go there, pay your respects, and ask her, "How should the bodhisattva teach beings in *saṃsāra*?"

Sudhana the Youth then bowed down in reverence at her feet and circumambulated her countless times as he gazed up at her in attentive admiration. He then respectfully withdrew and departed.

40 – Gopā

At that time, Sudhana the Youth proceeded to the city of Kapilavastu as he contemplated and cultivated the "taking on births" liberation, expanding it, bearing it in mind, and never relinquishing it. He gradually traveled onward until he reached the congregation of bodhisattvas that had gathered at the lecture hall known as Universally Manifesting the Light of the Dharma Realm, in which there was a spirit named Sorrowless Virtue who, together with a myriad palace spirits there, came out to welcome Sudhana. She said:

It is good that you have come, Good Man, for you who are one possessed of great wisdom and immense courage. You have been able to cultivate the bodhisattva's inconceivable masterful liberations, doing so with a resolve that never relinquishes the vast vow. You are well able to contemplate the sphere of all dharmas, to dwell securely in the city of the Dharma, to enter the gateways of countless skillful means, to perfect the immense ocean of the Tathāgata's meritorious qualities, to acquire marvelous eloquence, to skillfully train beings, to acquire the wisdom body of the *āryas* and constantly accord with it in your cultivation, to know the differences in all beings' mental actions, and to enable them to happily progress along the path to buddhahood.

I have seen, Worthy One, that you cultivate the sublime practices with unremitting resolve and that the deportment you practice is entirely pure. Before long, you should be able to acquire the unexcelled purity and adornment of the three classes of actions of the *tathāgatas* by which all the major marks and secondary signs will adorn your body, the lustrous radiance of the wisdom of the ten powers will grace your mind, and you will travel to all worlds.

I have seen, Worthy One, that you are possessed of incomparable courage and vigor. You are bound before long to be able to everywhere see all buddhas of the three periods of time and listen to them

正體字

不久當得[8]普[9]見三
405c20 世一切諸佛。聽受其法。[10]不久當得一切菩薩
405c21 禪定解脫諸三昧樂。不久當入諸佛如來甚
405c22 深解脫。何以故。見善知識。親近供養。聽受其
405c23 教。憶念修行。不懈不退。無憂無悔。無有障
405c24 礙。魔及魔民。不能為難。不久當成無上果故。
405c25 善財童子言。聖者。如向所說。願我皆得。聖
405c26 者。我願一切眾生息諸熱惱。離諸惡業。生
405c27 諸安樂。修諸淨行。聖者。一切眾生起諸煩惱。
405c28 造諸惡業。墮諸惡趣。若身若心恒受楚毒。菩
405c29 薩見已心生憂惱。聖者。譬如有人唯有一子。
406a01 愛念情至。忽見被人割截[1]肢體。其心痛切不
406a02 能自安。菩薩摩訶薩。亦復如是。見諸眾生以
406a03 煩惱業。墮三惡趣受種種苦。心大憂惱。若見
406a04 眾生起身語意三種善業。生天人趣。受身心
406a05 樂。菩薩爾時。生大歡喜。[2]何以故。菩薩不自
406a06 為故求一切智。不貪生死諸欲快樂。不隨想
406a07 倒見倒心倒諸結隨眠愛見力轉。不起眾生
406a08 種種樂想。亦不味著諸禪定樂。

简体字

不久当得普见三世一切诸佛听受其法，不久当得一切菩萨禅定解脱诸三昧乐，不久当入诸佛如来甚深解脱。何以故？见善知识亲近供养，听受其教，忆念修行，不懈不退，无忧无悔，无有障碍，魔及魔民不能为难，不久当成无上果故。”

善财童子言：“圣者，如向所说，愿我皆得。圣者，我愿一切众生，息诸热恼，离诸恶业，生诸安乐，修诸净行。圣者，一切众生，起诸烦恼，造诸恶业，堕诸恶趣，若身若心恒受楚毒，菩萨见已心生忧恼。圣者，譬如有人，唯有一子，爱念情至，忽见被人割截肢体，其心痛切不能自安。菩萨摩诃萨亦复如是，见诸众生以烦恼业堕三恶趣受种种苦，心大忧恼。若见众生起身、语、意三种善业，生天人趣受身心乐，菩萨尔时生大欢喜。何以故？菩萨不自为故求一切智，不贪生死诸欲快乐，不随想倒、见倒、心倒、诸结、随眠、爱见力转，不起众生种种乐想，亦不味著诸禅定乐，

teaching the Dharma. You are bound before long to acquire the bliss of the samādhis of all bodhisattvas' *dhyāna* absorptions and liberations and you are bound before long to enter the extremely profound liberations of all buddhas, the *tathāgatas.*

And why is this so? You have seen the good spiritual guides, have drawn near to and made offerings to them, have listened to their teachings, have borne them in mind and cultivated them, and have not grown weary or retreated from your efforts. You are free of worry, free of regrets, and free of obstacles. Māra and his minions are unable to create difficulties for you, for you are bound before long to achieve the unsurpassed karmic fruition.

Sudhana the Youth then addressed her, saying:

O Āryā, may I be able to acquire all the qualities as you have just now described them. O Āryā, I hope that all beings may extinguish all their feverish afflictions, abandon all their evil karmic actions, develop all kinds of happiness, and cultivate all the pure practices.

O Āryā, all beings produce all kinds of afflictions, create all kinds of evil karmic deeds, and fall down into the wretched rebirth destinies in which, both physically and mentally, they are then subjected to constant excruciating cruelties. Once a bodhisattva has seen this, his mind becomes afflicted by sorrow.

O Āryā, suppose that there was a man who had but one son for whom his feelings of fond concern were extremely strong who then suddenly saw his son having his limbs sliced off by someone. The piercing pain he would feel would be unbearable. So too it is with the bodhisattva-mahāsattva. When he sees that, due to karmic actions rooted in the afflictions, beings fall into the three wretched destinies and undergo the many different kinds of sufferings, his mind is then afflicted by great sorrow. If he sees beings producing the three kinds of good physical, verbal, and mental karmic actions by which they are reborn in the rebirth destinies of devas and humans where they then enjoy both physical and mental bliss, the bodhisattva is filled with great happiness.

And why is this so? It is not for himself that the bodhisattva strives to attain all-knowledge, nor is it because he covets the various pleasures associated with desire in *saṃsāra.* Nor is it due to being swayed by the power of inverted conceptions, inverted views, inverted thoughts, the various fetters, latent afflictions, craving, or views. Nor is it due to producing beings' many different kinds of conceptions of what is pleasurable. Nor is it due to becoming attached to the delectability of the various *dhyāna* absorptions. Nor

正體字

非有障礙。疲
406a09║ 厭退轉住於生死。但見眾生。於諸有中。具
406a10║ 受無量種種諸苦。起大悲心。以大願力而普
406a11║ 攝取。悲願力故。修菩薩行。為斷一切眾生煩
406a12║ 惱。為求如來一切智智。為供養一切諸佛如
406a13║ 來。為嚴淨一切廣大國土。為淨治一切眾生
406a14║ 樂欲。及其所有身心諸行。於生死中無有疲
406a15║ 厭。聖者菩薩摩訶薩。於諸眾生為莊嚴。令
406a16║ 生人天富貴樂故。為父母。為其安立菩提心
406a17║ 故。為養育令其成就菩薩道故。為衛護。令其
406a18║ 遠離三惡道故。為[3]船師。令其得度生死海
406a19║ 故。為歸依。令捨諸魔煩惱怖故。為究竟。令其
406a20║ 永得清涼樂故。為津濟。令入一切諸佛海故。
406a21║ 為導師。令至一切法寶洲故。為妙華。開敷諸
406a22║ 佛功德心故。為嚴具。常放福德智慧光故。為
406a23║ 可樂。凡有所作悉端嚴故。為可尊。遠離一切
406a24║ 諸惡業故。

简体字

非有障碍、疲厌、退转住于生死。但见众生于诸有中，具受无量种种诸苦，起大悲心，以大愿力而普摄取。悲愿力故，修菩萨行，为断一切众生烦恼，为求如来一切智智，为供养一切诸佛如来，为严净一切广大国土，为净治一切众生乐欲及其所有身心诸行，于生死中无有疲厌。

“圣者，菩萨摩诃萨于诸众生，为庄严，令生人天富贵乐故；为父母，为其安立菩提心故；为养育，令其成就菩萨道故；为卫护，令其远离三恶道故；为船师，令其得度生死海故；为归依，令舍诸魔烦恼怖故；为究竟，令其永得清凉乐故；为津济，令入一切诸佛海故；为导师，令至一切法宝洲故；为妙华，开敷诸佛功德心故；为严具，常放福德智慧光故；为可乐，凡有所作悉端严故；为可尊，远离一切诸恶业故；

is it that he encounters obstacles and grows weary and so retreats from his quest and instead dwells in *saṃsāra.*

Rather it is because he sees beings in all the realms of existence undergoing in full measure the countless forms of sufferings that he then arouses the mind of great compassion and then, by the power of great vows, everywhere gathers them in.

It is because of the power of compassion and vows that he cultivates the bodhisattva practices. It is because he wishes to cut off all beings' afflictions, because he seeks to acquire the Tathāgata's wisdom of all-knowledge, because he wishes to make offerings to all buddhas, the *tathāgatas,* because he wishes to purify all the vast lands, and because he wishes to purify all beings' inclinations and all physical and mental actions that he never grows weary of remaining in *saṃsāra.*

O Āryā, as for these bodhisattva-mahāsattvas:

They serve as adornments for beings by enabling them to acquire the happiness associated with the wealth and nobility of humans and devas;

They serve as their parents by establishing them in the resolve to attain bodhi;

They serve them as nurturers by enabling them to perfect the bodhisattva path;

They serve them as protectors by enabling them to abandon the three wretched rebirth destinies;

They serve them as ship captains by enabling them to cross beyond the ocean of *saṃsāra;*

They serve them as refuges by enabling them to leave behind the afflictions and fear produced by the *māras;*

They serve them as sources of what is ultimate by enabling them to forever acquire the bliss of clarity and coolness;

They serve them as rescuing ferries by enabling them to set sail into the ocean of all buddhas;

They serve them as guiding teachers by enabling them to reach the isle of all Dharma jewels;

They serve them as marvelous flowers by causing their minds to blossom with the meritorious qualities of all buddhas;

They serve them as adornments by always emanating the light of merit and wisdom;

They serve as sources of delight by their majesty in all that they do;

They serve them as objects of veneration by renouncing all bad actions;

正體字

為普賢。具足一切端嚴身故。為大
406a25 明。常[4]放智慧淨光明故。為大雲。常雨一切
406a26 甘露法故。聖者。菩薩如是修諸行時。令一切
406a27 眾生。皆生愛樂具足法樂。爾時善財童子。將
406a28 [5]昇法堂。其無憂德及諸神眾。以出過諸天上
406a29 妙華鬘。塗香末香。及以種種寶莊嚴具。散善
406b01 財上。而說頌言
406b02 汝今出世間　為世大明燈
406b03 普為諸眾生　勤求無上覺
406b04 無量億千劫　難可得見汝
406b05 功德日今出　滅除諸世[6]闇
406b06 汝見諸眾生　顛倒惑所覆
406b07 而興大悲意　求證無師道
406b08 汝以清淨心　尋求佛菩提
406b09 承事善知識　不自惜身命
406b10 [7]　汝於諸世間　無依無所著
406b11 其心普無礙　清淨如虛空
406b12 汝修菩提行　功德悉圓滿
406b13 放大智慧光　普照一切世
406b14 汝不離世間　亦不著於世

简体字

为普贤，具足一切端严身故；为大明，常放智慧净光明故；为大云，常雨一切甘露法故。圣者，菩萨如是修诸行时，令一切众生皆生爱乐、具足法乐。”

尔时，善财童子将升法堂，其无忧德及诸神众，以出过诸天上妙华鬘、涂香、末香，及以种种宝庄严具，散善财上，而说颂言：

“汝今出世间，为世大明灯，
普为诸众生，勤求无上觉。
无量亿千劫，难可得见汝；
功德日今出，灭除诸世暗。
汝见诸众生，颠倒惑所覆，
而兴大悲意，求证无师道。
汝以清净心，寻求佛菩提，
承事善知识，不自惜身命。
汝于诸世间，无依无所著，
其心普无碍，清净如虚空。
汝修菩提行，功德悉圆满，
放大智慧光，普照一切世。
汝不离世间，亦不著于世，

They serve as those who are universally worthy by having bodies that are majestic in all respects;

They serve them as great lights by always emanating the pure light of wisdom; and

They serve them as great clouds by always raining down all the elixir-of-immortality dharmas.

O Āryā, when the bodhisattva cultivates all the practices in these ways, he causes all beings to feel fond delight and reach the complete fulfillment of Dharma bliss.

As Sudhana the Youth prepared to ascend to the Dharma hall, that Spirit, Sorrowless Virtue, and the rest of that congregation of spirits scattered over Sudhana marvelous flower garlands, perfumes, powdered incense, and many different jeweled adornments, all of which were superior to those found in the heavens. She then spoke these verses:

You have now come forth into the world
and serve the world as a great bright lamp
as, out of universal concern for all beings,
you diligently seek the unexcelled enlightenment.

In countless *koṭīs* of thousands of kalpas,
it would be difficult to ever be able to see you.
Your sun of meritorious qualities has now risen
and extinguishes the darkness of the entire world.

You see that all beings
are blanketed by inverted views and delusion
and so bring forth your greatly compassionate resolve
to seek to realize the teacherless path.

With pure intentions
you search out the bodhi of the Buddha
and serve the good spiritual guides,
not cherishing even your own body or life.

You are free of any dependence on or attachment to
anything that exists in the world
and your mind is everywhere unimpeded
and as pure as empty space.

In your cultivation of the practices leading to bodhi,
your meritorious qualities have all become perfectly full.
You emanate the light of great wisdom
that everywhere illuminates all worlds.

You refrain from abandoning the world,
but still are not attached to the world.

正體字

406b15 ‖ 行世無障礙 如風遊虛空
406b16 ‖ 譬如火災起 一切無能滅
406b17 ‖ 汝修菩提行 精進火亦然
406b18 ‖ 勇猛大精進 堅固不可動
406b19 ‖ 金剛慧師子 遊行無所畏
406b20 ‖ 一切法界中 所有諸剎海
406b21 ‖ 汝悉能往詣 親近善知識
406b22 ‖ 爾時無憂德神。說此頌已。為愛樂法故。隨逐
406b23 ‖ 善財。恒不捨離。爾時善財童子。入普現法界
406b24 ‖ 光明講堂。周遍推求彼釋氏女。見在堂內。坐
406b25 ‖ 寶蓮華師子之座。八萬四千采女所共圍遶。
406b26 ‖ 是諸采女。靡不皆從王種中生。悉於過去。修
406b27 ‖ 菩薩行同種善根。布施愛語普攝眾生。已能
406b28 ‖ 明見一切智境。已共修集佛菩提行。恒住正
406b29 ‖ 定。常遊大悲。普攝眾生猶如一子。慈心具
406c01 ‖ 足眷屬清淨。已於過去。成就菩薩不可思議
406c02 ‖ 善巧方便。皆於阿耨多羅三藐三菩提。得不
406c03 ‖ 退轉。

简体字

行世无障碍，如风游虚空。
譬如火灾起，一切无能灭；
汝修菩提行，精进火亦然。
勇猛大精进，坚固不可动，
金刚慧师子，游行无所畏。
一切法界中，所有诸刹海，
汝悉能往诣，亲近善知识。”

尔时，无忧德神说此颂已，为爱乐法故，随逐善财，恒不舍离。

尔时，善财童子入普现法界光明讲堂，周遍推求彼释氏女，见在堂内，坐宝莲华师子之座，八万四千采女所共围绕。是诸采女，靡不皆从王种中生，悉于过去修菩萨行同种善根，布施、爱语普摄众生；已能明见一切智境，已共修集佛菩提行；恒住正定，常游大悲，普摄众生犹如一子；慈心具足，眷属清净；已于过去成就菩萨不可思议善巧方便，皆于阿耨多罗三藐三菩提得不退转，

You are as unimpeded in traveling through the world
as the wind that roams through empty space.

Just as when the great conflagration arises,
there will be no one who is able to extinguish it,
so too, in your cultivation of the bodhisattva practices,
the fire of your vigor burns on in this very same way.

Courageous and possessed of great vigor
that is steadfast and unshakable,
you are a lion of vajra wisdom
who is fearless wherever he roams.

Throughout the entire Dharma realm,
in the oceans of all *kṣetras,*
you are able to go and pay your respects,
thus drawing near to the good spiritual guides.

Then, after speaking these verses, out of love for the Dharma, the spirit, Sorrowless Virtue, followed along after Sudhana, never leaving him.

Sudhana the Youth then entered that lecture hall known as Universally Manifesting the Light of the Dharma Realm, in which he searched everywhere for that maiden from the Śākya clan until he saw her in the hall, seated on a jeweled lotus lion throne, surrounded by eighty-four thousand female attendants.

As for all these female attendants:

There were none who had not been born into a royal lineage;

In the past, all of them had cultivated the bodhisattva practices and planted roots of goodness together;

They had everywhere attracted beings using giving and pleasing words;

They were already able to clearly perceive the realm of all-knowledge;

They had all already jointly cultivated and accumulated the practices leading to the bodhi of the Buddha;

They constantly dwelt in right meditative absorption;

They constantly roamed in the great compassion with which they everywhere gathered in beings as if they were their only sons;

They were fully possessed of the mind of kindness;

Their retinues were pure;

Throughout the past, they had already perfected the bodhisattva's inconceivable skillful means;

They had all achieved irreversibility in their progress toward *anuttara-samyak-saṃbodhi;*

正體字

具足菩薩諸波羅蜜。離諸取著。不樂
406c04 生死。[8]雖行諸有心常清淨。恒勤觀察一切智
406c05 道。離障蓋網。超諸著處。從於法身而示化形。
406c06 生普賢行。長菩薩力。智日慧燈悉已圓滿。爾
406c07 時善財童子。詣彼釋女瞿波之所。頂禮[9]其足
406c08 合掌而住。作如是言。聖者。我已[10]先發阿耨
406c09 多羅三藐三菩提心。而未知菩薩云何於生死
406c10 中。而不為生死過患所染。了法自性。而不住
406c11 聲聞辟支佛地。具足佛法。而修菩薩行。住菩
406c12 薩地。而入佛境界。[11]超過世間。而於世受生。
406c13 成就法身。而示現無邊種種色身。證無相法。
406c14 而為眾生示現諸相。知法無說。而廣為眾生
406c15 演說諸法。知眾生空。而恒不捨化眾生事。雖
406c16 知諸佛不生不滅。而勤供養。無有退轉。

简体字

具足菩萨诸波罗蜜；离诸取著，不乐生死；虽行诸有，心常清净，恒勤观察一切智道；离障盖网，超诸著处，从于法身而示化形；生普贤行，长菩萨力，智日慧灯悉已圆满。

尔时，善财童子诣彼释女瞿波之所，顶礼其足，合掌而住，作如是言："圣者，我已先发阿耨多罗三藐三菩提心，而未知菩萨云何于生死中，而不为生死过患所染？了法自性，而不住声闻、辟支佛地？具足佛法，而修菩萨行？住菩萨地，而入佛境界？超过世间，而于世受生？成就法身，而示现无边种种色身？证无相法，而为众生示现诸相？知法无说，而广为众生演说诸法？知众生空，而恒不舍化众生事？虽知诸佛不生不灭，而勤供养无有退转？

They had completely fulfilled all of the bodhisattva's *pāramitās;*
They had abandoned all attachments;
They did not delight in *saṃsāra;*
Although they traveled through all realms of existence, their minds were always pure;
They constantly and diligently contemplated the path to all-knowledge;
They had escaped the net of the obstacles and hindrances;
They had gone beyond all bases of attachment;
From within the Dharma body, they manifested transformations;
They had given birth to the practices of Samantabhadra;
They grew in the powers of the bodhisattva; and
Their lamps of wisdom were already fully bright with the sun of knowledge.

Sudhana the Youth then went to pay his respects to that Śākya maiden, Gopā, and bowed down in reverence at her feet. He then stood before her with palms pressed together and spoke thus:

O Āryā, I am one who has already resolved to attain *anuttara-samyak-saṃbodhi.* Still, I do not yet understand:

How can bodhisattvas remain in *saṃsāra* and yet avoid being defiled by the faults of *saṃsāra*?
How can they completely know the essential nature of dharmas and yet avoid dwelling on the grounds of the *śrāvaka* disciples or *pratyekabuddhas*?
How can they completely fulfill the dharmas of a buddha and yet still cultivate the bodhisattva practices?
How can they dwell on the bodhisattva grounds and yet still enter the realm of a buddha?
How can they transcend the world and yet still take on births in the world?
How can they perfect the Dharma body and yet still manifest countless different kinds of form bodies?
How can they realize the dharma of signlessness and yet manifest all kinds of signs for beings?
How can they realize the ineffability of the Dharma and yet still extensively expound on all dharmas for beings?
How can they realize the emptiness of beings and yet still never abandon the work of teaching beings?
How is it that, even though they realize all buddhas are neither produced nor destroyed, they can still diligently make offerings to them and never retreat from this practice?

正體字

雖
406c17‖ 知諸法無業無報。而修諸善行恒不止息。時
406c18‖ 瞿波女。告善財言。善哉善哉。善男子。汝今能
406c19‖ 問菩薩摩訶薩。如是行法。修習普賢諸行願
406c20‖ 者。能如是問。諦聽諦聽。善思念之。我當承佛
406c21‖ 神力。為汝宣說。善男子。若諸菩薩。成就十
406c22‖ 法。則能圓滿因陀羅網普智光明菩薩之行。
406c23‖ 何等為十。所謂依善知識故。得廣大勝解故。
406c24‖ 得清淨欲樂故。集一切福智故。於諸佛所聽
406c25‖ 聞法故。心恒不捨三世佛故。同於一切菩薩
406c26‖ 行故。一切如來所護念故。大悲妙願皆清淨
406c27‖ 故。能以智力普斷一切諸生死故。是為十。若
406c28‖ 諸菩薩。成就此法。則能圓滿因陀羅網普智
406c29‖ 光明菩薩之行。[12]佛子。若菩薩親近善知識。
407a01‖ 則能精進不退修習出生無盡佛法。佛子。菩
407a02‖ 薩以十種法。承事善知識。何等為十。所謂於
407a03‖ 自身命無所顧惜。於世樂具心不貪求。知一
407a04‖ 切法性皆平等。永不退捨一切智願。觀察一
407a05‖ 切法界實相。

简体字

虽知诸法无业无报，而修诸善行恒不止息？”

时，瞿波女告善财言：“善哉！善哉！善男子，汝今能问菩萨摩诃萨如是行法，修习普贤诸行愿者能如是问。谛听谛听！善思念之！我当承佛神力，为汝宣说。

“善男子，若诸菩萨成就十法，则能圆满因陀罗网普智光明菩萨之行。何等为十？所谓：依善知识故，得广大胜解故，得清净欲乐故，集一切福智故，于诸佛所听闻法故，心恒不舍三世佛故，同于一切菩萨行故，一切如来所护念故，大悲妙愿皆清净故，能以智力普断一切诸生死故。是为十。若诸菩萨成就此法，则能圆满因陀罗网普智光明菩萨之行。

“佛子，若菩萨亲近善知识，则能精进不退修习出生无尽佛法。佛子，菩萨以十种法，承事善知识。何等为十？所谓：于自身命无所顾惜，于世乐具心不贪求，知一切法性皆平等，永不退舍一切智愿，观察一切法界实相，

How is it that, even though they know dharmas are free of any karmic actions and free of any karmic retributions, they can still constantly and incessantly cultivate all good deeds?

The maiden, Gopā, then addressed Sudhana, saying:

It is good indeed, good indeed, Son of Good Family, that you are now able ask about bodhisattva-mahāsattvas' practices such as these. One who cultivates the practices and vows of Samantabhadra is able to pose questions such as these. Listen well, listen well, and then skillfully consider this as, aided by the Buddha's spiritual powers, I expound on these matters for you.

Son of Good Family, if bodhisattvas develop ten dharmas, then they can completely fulfill the bodhisattva practices of the light of universal knowledge of Indra's net. What are those ten? They are:

Reliance on good spiritual guides;
Attainment of vast resolute faith;
Attainment of pure aspirations;
Accumulation of all forms of merit and wisdom;
Listening to the Dharma from the buddhas;
Having a mind that never relinquishes its devotion to all buddhas of the three periods of time;
Following the same practices as all bodhisattvas;
Receiving the protection of all *tathāgatas;*
Purifying all of one's greatly compassionate and marvelous vows; and
Being able to use the power of wisdom to cut off all transmigration in *saṃsāra.*

These are the ten. If bodhisattvas perfect these dharmas, then they can completely fulfill the bodhisattva practices of the light of universal knowledge of Indra's net.

Son of the Buddha, if a bodhisattva draws near to the good spiritual guides, then he can vigorously and irreversibly cultivate and generate the endless dharmas of the Buddha.

Son of the Buddha, the bodhisattva uses ten kinds of dharmas in serving the good spiritual guides. What are those ten? They are as follows:

He is free of any cherishing concern for his own body or life;
His mind does not covet any of the means for attaining worldly pleasures;
He realizes the uniform equality of the nature of all dharmas;
He never retreats from his vow to attain all-knowledge;
He contemplates the true character of all dharma realms;

正體字

心恒捨離一切有海。知法如空
407a06 心無所依。成就一切菩薩大願。常能示現一
407a07 切刹海。淨修菩薩無礙智輪。佛子。應以此法。
407a08 承事一切諸善知識。無所違逆。爾時釋迦瞿
407a09 波女。欲重明此義。承佛神力。觀察十方。而說
407a10 頌言
407a11 菩薩為利諸群生　正念親承善知識
407a12 敬之如佛心無怠　此行於世帝網行
407a13 勝解廣大如虛空　一切三世悉入中
407a14 國土眾生佛皆爾　此是普智光明行
407a15 [1] 志樂如空無有際　永斷煩惱離諸垢
407a16 一切佛所修功德　此行於世身雲行
407a17 菩薩修習一切智　不可思議功德海
407a18 淨諸福德智慧身　此行於世不染行
407a19 一切諸佛如來所　聽受其法無厭足
407a20 能生實相智慧燈　此行於世普照行
407a21 十方諸佛無有量　一念一切悉能入
407a22 心恒不捨諸如來　此向菩提大願行
407a23 能入諸佛大眾會　一切菩薩三昧海
407a24 願海及以方便海　此行於世帝網行
407a25 一切諸佛所加持　盡未來際無邊劫

简体字

心恒舍离一切有海，知法如空心无所依，成就一切菩萨大愿，常能示现一切刹海，净修菩萨无碍智轮。佛子，应以此法承事一切诸善知识，无所违逆。”

尔时，释迦瞿波女，欲重明此义，承佛神力，观察十方，而说颂言：

“菩萨为利诸群生，正念亲承善知识，
敬之如佛心无怠，此行于世帝网行。
胜解广大如虚空，一切三世悉入中，
国土众生佛皆尔，此是普智光明行。
志乐如空无有际，永断烦恼离诸垢，
一切佛所修功德，此行于世身云行。
菩萨修习一切智，不可思议功德海，
净诸福德智慧身，此行于世不染行。
一切诸佛如来所，听受其法无厌足，
能生实相智慧灯，此行于世普照行。
十方诸佛无有量，一念一切悉能入，
心恒不舍诸如来，此向菩提大愿行。
能入诸佛大众会，一切菩萨三昧海，
愿海及以方便海，此行于世帝网行。
一切诸佛所加持，尽未来际无边劫，

His mind constantly abandons the ocean of all realms of existence;
He realizes dharmas are like space and thus his mind depends on nothing whatsoever;
He perfects all of the bodhisattva's great vows;
He is ever able to manifest throughout the ocean of all *kṣetras;* and
He purifies the bodhisattva's sphere of unimpeded wisdom.

Son of the Buddha, one should rely on these dharmas in serving all good spiritual guides without ever opposing them.

At that time, wishing to restate and clarify this meaning, aided by the Buddha's spiritual powers, the maiden, Gopā, regarded the ten directions and then spoke these verses:

To bestow benefit on the many kinds of beings, the bodhisattva uses
right mindfulness to draw near to and serve good spiritual guides,
revering them like buddhas, maintaining a mind free of indolence.
This practice in the world is the practice that is like Indra's net.

His resolute faith is as vast as empty space.
Everything in the three periods of time enters into it
along with all lands, beings, and buddhas, all in this same way.
This is the practice of he who shines the light of universal knowledge.

With aspirations as boundless as space itself,
one forever severs the afflictions, abandons all defilement,
and cultivates the meritorious qualities under all buddhas.
This is the practice of he who has a cloud of bodies in the world.

The bodhisattva cultivates all-knowledge
and an ocean of inconceivable meritorious qualities.
He purifies his bodies possessed of merit and wisdom.
This is the practice of he who is undefiled by the world.

In the presence of all buddhas, the *tathāgatas,*
he is insatiable in listening to their Dharma with which
he can create a lamp of wisdom [illumining dharmas'] true character.
This is the practice of he who everywhere illuminates the world.

Though the buddhas of the ten directions are countless,
in but one mind-moment, he can enter the presence of them all.
His mind never leaves any of the *tathāgatas.*
This is the practice of he who has the great vows that lead to bodhi.

He is able to enter the great congregations of all buddhas,
the ocean of all bodhisattvas' samādhis,
the ocean of vows, and also the ocean of skillful means.
This practice in the world is the practice that is like Indra's net.

Being aided and supported by all buddhas,
throughout boundlessly many kalpas to the end of future time,

正體字

407a26 處處修行普賢道　此是菩薩分身行
407a27 見諸眾生受大苦　起大慈悲現世間
407a28 演法光明除闇冥　此是菩薩智日行
407a29 見諸眾生在諸趣　為集無邊妙法輪
407b01 令其永斷生死流　此是修行普賢行
407b02 菩薩修行此方便　隨眾生心而現身
407b03 普於一切諸趣中　化度無量諸含識
407b04 以大慈悲方便力　普遍世間而現身
407b05 隨其解欲為說法　皆令趣向菩提道
407b06 時釋迦瞿波。說此頌已。告善財童子言。善男
407b07 子。我已成就觀察一切菩薩三昧海解脫門。
407b08 善財言。大聖。此解脫門境界云何。答言。善男
407b09 子。我入此解脫。知此娑婆世界佛剎微塵數
407b10 劫。所有眾生於諸趣中。死此生彼。作善作惡。
407b11 受諸果報。有求出離。不求出離。[2]正定邪定。
407b12 及以不定。有煩惱善根。無煩惱善根。具足善
407b13 根。不具足善根。不善根所攝善根。善根所攝
407b14 不善根。如是所集。善不善法。我皆知見。

简体字

处处修行普贤道，此是菩萨分身行。
见诸众生受大苦，起大慈悲现世间，
演法光明除暗冥，此是菩萨智日行。
见诸众生在诸趣，为集无边妙法轮，
令其永断生死流，此是修行普贤行。
菩萨修行此方便，随众生心而现身，
普于一切诸趣中，化度无量诸含识。
以大慈悲方便力，普遍世间而现身，
随其解欲为说法，皆令趣向菩提道。”

时，释迦瞿波说此颂已，告善财童子言：“善男子，我已成就观察一切菩萨三昧海解脱门。”

善财言：“大圣，此解脱门境界云何？”

答言：“善男子，我入此解脱，知此娑婆世界佛刹微尘数劫，所有众生于诸趣中，死此生彼，作善作恶，受诸果报，有求出离、不求出离，正定、邪定及以不定，有烦恼善根，无烦恼善根，具足善根，不具足善根，不善根所摄善根，善根所摄不善根；如是所集善、不善法，我皆知见。

in place after place, he cultivates the path of Samantabhadra.
This is the bodhisattva's division body practice.

He sees all beings undergoing great suffering,
arouses the great kindness and compassion, appears in the world,
spreads the light of the Dharma, and dispels their darkness.
This is the bodhisattva's wisdom sun practice.

He sees all beings abiding in all rebirth destinies and, for their sakes,
turns the wheel of the boundless sublime Dharma he has gathered,
thus enabling them to forever cut off the stream of *saṃsāra*.
This is the cultivation of the practices of Samantabhadra.

The bodhisattva cultivates these skillful means
by which, adapting to the minds of beings, he then manifests bodies
with which he teaches and liberates the countless sentient beings
everywhere throughout all the destinies of rebirth.

By the power of great kindness, compassion, and skillful means,
he manifests bodies everywhere throughout the world.
Then, adapting to their dispositions, he teaches the Dharma for them,
thereby enabling them all to progress along the path to bodhi.

Having spoken these verses, the Śākya maiden, Gopā, then told Sudhana the Youth: "Son of Good Family, I have already perfected the liberation gateway of 'contemplating the ocean of all bodhisattvas' samādhis.'"

Sudhana then asked: "O Great Āryā, what is the sphere of experience of this liberation gateway like?"

She replied:

Son of Good Family, having entered this liberation, I know with respect to this Sahā world, as it has occurred across the course of kalpas as numerous as the atoms in a buddha *kṣetra*, with regard to all beings in all rebirth destinies, their dying in this place and being reborn in that place, their good deeds and bad deeds, their undergoing of all kinds of karmic retributions, their seeking emancipation, their not seeking emancipation, their being fixed in what is right, fixed in what is wrong, or unfixed,[4] their possession of roots of goodness accompanied by the afflictions, their possession of roots of goodness unaccompanied by the afflictions, their completely developed roots of goodness, their incompletely developed roots of goodness, their roots of goodness gathered through roots of unwholesomeness, and their roots of unwholesomeness gathered through roots of goodness.[5] I know and see in their entirety all such good or bad dharmas that they have accumulated.

正體字

又彼
407b15‖ 劫中所有諸佛。名號次第。我悉了知。彼佛世
407b16‖ 尊。從初發心。及以方便。求一切智。出生一切
407b17‖ 諸大願海。供養諸佛。修菩薩行。成等正覺。轉
407b18‖ 妙法輪。現大神通。化度眾生。我悉了知。亦知
407b19‖ 彼佛眾會差別。其眾會中。有諸眾生依聲聞
407b20‖ 乘。而得出離。其聲聞眾。過去修習一切善根。
407b21‖ 及其所得種種智慧。我悉了知。有諸眾生依
407b22‖ 獨覺乘。而得出離。其諸獨覺。所有善根。所得
407b23‖ 菩提。寂滅解脫。神通變化。成熟眾生。入於涅
407b24‖ 槃。我悉了知。亦知彼佛諸菩薩眾。其諸菩薩。
407b25‖ 從初發心。修習善根。出生無量諸大願行。成
407b26‖ 就滿足諸波羅蜜種種莊嚴菩薩之道。以自
407b27‖ 在力。入菩薩地。住菩薩地。觀菩薩地。淨菩薩
407b28‖ 地。菩薩地相。菩薩地智。菩薩攝智。菩薩教化
407b29‖ 眾生智。菩薩建立智。菩薩廣大行境界菩薩
407c01‖ 神通行。菩薩三昧海。菩薩方便。菩薩於念念
407c02‖ 中所入三昧海。所得一切智光明。所獲一切
407c03‖ 智電光雲。

简体字

又彼劫中所有诸佛名号、次第，我悉了知。彼佛世尊从初发心，及以方便求一切智，出生一切诸大愿海，供养诸佛，修菩萨行，成等正觉，转妙法轮，现大神通，化度众生，我悉了知。亦知彼佛众会差别，其众会中有诸众生依声闻乘而得出离，其声闻众过去修习一切善根，及其所得种种智慧，我悉了知。有诸众生依独觉乘而得出离，其诸独觉所有善根、所得菩提、寂灭解脱、神通变化、成熟众生、入于涅槃，我悉了知。亦知彼佛诸菩萨众，其诸菩萨从初发心，修习善根，出生无量诸大愿行，成就满足诸波罗蜜种种庄严菩萨之道，以自在力，入菩萨地，住菩萨地，观菩萨地，净菩萨地，菩萨地相、菩萨地智、菩萨摄智、菩萨教化众生智、菩萨建立智、菩萨广大行境界、菩萨神通行、菩萨三昧海、菩萨方便，菩萨于念念中所入三昧海、所得一切智光明、所获一切智电光云、

Also, with regard to all the buddhas in all those kalpas, I know all their names and the sequence of their appearance and also know with respect to those buddhas, those *bhagavats*, from the time they first made the resolve, their use of skillful means in their quest to attain all-knowledge, their generation of an ocean of all the great vows, their offerings to all buddhas, their cultivation of the bodhisattva practices, their attainment of the universal and right enlightenment, their turning of the wheel of the sublime Dharma, their manifestation of the great spiritual superknowledges, and their teaching and liberation of beings. I know all these matters.

I also know the differences in the congregations of those buddhas. Thus I know that, within those congregations, there are beings who have gained emancipation by relying on the *śrāvaka*-disciple vehicle. I also know with respect to those *śrāvaka*-disciple congregations, their past cultivation of all kinds of roots of goodness as well as their acquisition of the many different kinds of wisdom. I know all these matters.

I know where there are beings who have achieved emancipation by relying on the *pratyekabuddha* vehicle and know with respect to those *pratyekabuddha* practitioners all the roots of goodness they have acquired, the bodhi they have acquired, their quiescent liberations, their spiritual superknowledges and transformations, their ripening of beings, and their entry into *nirvāṇa*. I know all these matters.

I also know with respect to the bodhisattva congregations of those buddhas when it was that they first made the resolve, their cultivation of roots of goodness, their generation of countless great vows and practices, their accomplishment and perfect fulfillment of all the *pāramitās*, their many different kinds of adornments of the bodhisattva path, their use of the power of sovereign mastery to enter the bodhisattva grounds, dwell on the bodhisattva grounds, contemplate the bodhisattva grounds, and purify the bodhisattva grounds, the characteristics of the bodhisattva grounds, the knowledge of the bodhisattva grounds, the bodhisattvas' knowledge in using the means of attraction, the bodhisattvas' knowledge in teaching beings, the bodhisattvas' knowledge in becoming established, the bodhisattvas' sphere of vast practice, the bodhisattvas' practice of the spiritual superknowledges, the bodhisattvas' ocean of samādhis, the bodhisattvas' skillful means, and, in every mind-moment, the ocean of samādhis the bodhisattvas enter, the light of all-knowledge they acquire, the lightning flashes and clouds of all-knowledge they acquire, the patience with respect to the true

正體字

所得實相忍。所通達一切智。所
407c04║ 住剎海。所入法海。所知眾生海。所住方便。所
407c05║ 發誓願。所現神通。我悉了知。善男子。此娑婆
407c06║ 世界盡未來際所有劫海。展轉不斷。我皆了
407c07║ 知。如知娑婆世界。亦知娑婆世界內微塵數
407c08║ 世界。亦知娑婆世界內一切世界。亦知娑婆
407c09║ 世界微塵內所有世界。亦知娑婆世界外十
407c10║ 方無間所住世界。亦知娑婆世界世界種所
407c11║ 攝世界。亦知毘盧遮那世尊此華藏世界海
407c12║ 中十方無量諸世界種所攝世界。所謂世界
407c13║ 廣博。世界安立。世界輪。世界場。世界差別。
407c14║ 世界轉。世界蓮華。世界須彌。世界名號。盡此
407c15║ 世界海。一切世界。由毘盧遮那世尊本願力
407c16║ 故。我悉能知。亦能憶念。亦念如來往昔所有
407c17║ 諸因緣海。所謂修集一切諸乘方便。無量劫
407c18║ 中住菩薩行。淨佛國土。教化眾生。承事諸佛。
407c19║ 造立住處。聽受說法。獲諸三昧。得諸自在。

简体字

所得实相忍、所通达一切智、所住刹海、所入法海、所知众生海、所住方便、所发誓愿、所现神通，我悉了知。

“善男子，此娑婆世界，尽未来际，所有劫海，展转不断，我皆了知。如知娑婆世界，亦知娑婆世界内微尘数世界，亦知娑婆世界内一切世界，亦知娑婆世界微尘内所有世界，亦知娑婆世界外十方无间所住世界，亦知娑婆世界世界种所摄世界，亦知毗卢遮那世尊此华藏世界海中十方无量诸世界种所摄世界，所谓：世界广博、世界安立、世界轮、世界场、世界差别、世界转、世界莲华、世界须弥、世界名号。尽此世界海一切世界，由毗卢遮那世尊本愿力故，我悉能知，亦能忆念。

“亦念如来往昔所有诸因缘海。所谓：修习一切诸乘方便，无量劫中，住菩萨行，净佛国土，教化众生，承事诸佛，造立住处，听受说法，获诸三昧，得诸自在；

character of dharmas they acquire, the all-knowledge they penetrate, the ocean of *kṣetras* in which they dwell, the Dharma ocean they enter, the ocean of beings they know, the skillful means in which they dwell, the vows they make, and the spiritual superknowledges they manifest. I know all these matters.

Son of Good Family, I completely know all these matters as they occur in this Sahā World throughout all the oceans of kalpas and as they ceaselessly continue to occur on to the very end of future time.

And just as I know these matters with respect to the Sahā World, so too do I know these matters with respect to worlds as numerous as the atoms in the Sahā World that are contained within it, so too do I know these matters with respect to all worlds within this Sahā World, so too do I know these matters with respect to all the worlds within the atoms of the Sahā World, so too do I know these matters with respect to the worlds throughout the ten directions beyond the Sahā World in which they continuously dwell, so too do I know these matters with respect to the worlds inside of the world systems that the Sahā World belongs to, and so too do I know these matters with respect to all the worlds subsumed within the countless world systems of the ten directions contained in Vairocana, the Bhagavat's, flower treasury ocean of worlds.

In particular, I know the relative vastness of those worlds, know those worlds' establishment, know those worlds' spheres, know those worlds' fields, know those worlds' differences, know those worlds' transformations, know those worlds' lotus flowers, know those worlds' Mount Sumerus, and know those worlds' names, knowing these matters with respect to all worlds in these oceans of worlds, all of this due to the power of the original vows of Vairocana, the Bhagavat. I am able to completely know all these matters and am also able to retain them in memory even as I also bear in mind the ocean of long past causes and conditions of the Tathāgata, in particular:

His cultivation and accumulation of the skillful means of all vehicles;
His dwelling in the bodhisattva practices for countless kalpas;
His purification of buddha lands;
His teaching of beings;
His serving of all buddhas;
His creation of dwelling places;
His listening to discourses on the Dharma;
His acquisition of the samādhis;
His acquisition of the sovereign masteries;

正體字

修
407c20║ 檀波羅蜜。入佛功德海。持戒苦行。具足諸忍。
407c21║ 勇猛精進。成就諸禪。圓滿淨慧。於一切處。示
407c22║ 現受生。普賢行願悉皆清淨。普入諸剎。普
407c23║ 淨佛土。普入一切如來智海。普攝一切諸佛
407c24║ 菩提。得於如來大智光明。證於諸佛一切智
407c25║ 性。成等正覺。轉妙法輪。及其所有道場眾會。
407c26║ 其眾會中一切眾生。往世已來。所種善根。從
407c27║ 初發心。成熟眾生。修行方便。念念增長。獲諸
407c28║ 三昧神通解脫。如是一切。我悉了知。何以故。
407c29║ 我此解脫。能知一切眾生心行。一切眾生修
408a01║ 行善根。一切眾生雜染清淨。一切眾生種種
408a02║ 差別。一切聲聞諸三昧門。一切緣覺寂靜三
408a03║ 昧神通解脫。一切菩薩一切如來解脫光明。皆
408a04║ 了知故。爾時善財童子。白瞿波言。聖者。得
408a05║ 此解脫。其已久如。答言。善男子。我於往世過
408a06║ 佛剎微塵數劫。有劫名勝行。世界名無畏。彼
408a07║ 世界中。有四天下。名為安隱。其四天下閻
408a08║ 浮提中。有一王城名高勝樹。於八十王城中
408a09║ 最為上首。

简体字

修檀波罗蜜入佛功德海，持戒苦行，具足诸忍，勇猛精进，成就诸禅，圆满净慧；于一切处示现受生，普贤行愿悉皆清净，普入诸刹，普净佛土，普入一切如来智海，普摄一切诸佛菩提，得于如来大智光明，证于诸佛一切智性，成等正觉，转妙法轮；及其所有道场众会，其众会中一切众生，往世已来所种善根，从初发心，成熟众生，修行方便，念念增长，获诸三昧神通解脱。如是一切，我悉了知。何以故？我此解脱，能知一切众生心行、一切众生修行善根、一切众生杂染清净、一切众生种种差别、一切声闻诸三昧门、一切缘觉寂静三昧神通解脱、一切菩萨一切如来解脱光明，皆了知故。”

尔时，善财童子白瞿波言：“圣者得此解脱，其已久如？”

答言：“善男子，我于往世，过佛刹微尘数劫，有劫名胜行，世界名无畏。彼世界中，有四天下，名为安隐。其四天下阎浮提中，有一王城，名高胜树，于八十王城中最为上首。

His cultivation of *dāna pāramitā;*
His entry into the buddhas' ocean of meritorious qualities;
His observance of moral precepts and practice of austerities;
His complete fulfillment of all types of patience;
His courageous vigor;
His perfection of the *dhyānas;*
His complete fulfillment and purification of wisdom;
His manifesting the taking on of births in all places;
His purification of all the practices and vows of Samantabhadra;
His everywhere entering all *kṣetras;*
His everywhere purifying buddha lands;
His everywhere entering the ocean of all *tathāgatas'* wisdom;
His comprehensive realization of all buddhas' bodhi;
His acquisition of the Tathāgata's light of great wisdom;
His realization of the all-knowledge of all buddhas;[6]
His realization of the universal and right enlightenment; and
His turning of the wheel of the sublime Dharma.

Also, as regards all the beings[7] in all his congregations from the distant past on forward to the present, [I recall] all their planting of roots of goodness as well as, from the time they made their initial resolve, their ripening of beings, their cultivation of skillful means, their continual growth in every mind-moment, and their acquisition of the samādhis, spiritual superknowledges, and liberations.

I know all these matters. And why is this so? It is because I have acquired this liberation that I am able to know all beings' mental actions, all beings' cultivation of roots of goodness, all beings' mixture of defilement and purity, all beings' many kinds of differences, all *śrāvaka* disciples' samādhi gateways, all *pratyekabuddhas'* quiescent samādhis, spiritual superknowledges, and liberations, and the light of liberation of all bodhisattvas and all *tathāgatas.* I know all these matters.

Sudhana the Youth then addressed Gopā, saying, "O Āryā, how long has it been now since that time when you acquired this liberation?"

She replied:

Son of Good Family, in the distance past, back beyond a number of kalpas as numerous as the atoms in a buddha *kṣetra,* there was a kalpa named Supreme Conduct and a world named Fearless. Within that world, there was a set of four continents known as Security. Among those four continents, on the continent of Jambudvīpa, there was a royal city known as Towering Tree. Of all the eighty royal cities, this one was foremost.

正體字

彼時有王名曰財主。其王具有六
408a10║ 萬采女五百大臣五百王子。其諸王子。皆悉
408a11║ 勇健。能伏怨敵。其王太子名威德主。端正
408a12║ 殊特。人所樂見。足下平滿。輪相備具。足趺隆
408a13║ 起。手足指間皆有網縵。足跟齊正。手足柔
408a14║ 軟。伊尼耶鹿王腨。七處圓滿[1]陰藏隱密。其
408a15║ 身上分如師子王。兩肩平滿。雙臂傭長。身相
408a16║ 端直。頸文三道。頰如師子。[2]具四十齒。悉皆
408a17║ 齊密。四牙鮮白。其舌長廣。出梵音聲。眼目紺
408a18║ 青。睫如牛王。眉間毫相。頂上肉髻。皮膚細
408a19║ 軟。如真金色。身毛上靡。髮帝青色。其身洪
408a20║ 滿。如尼拘陀樹。爾時太子受父王教。與十千
408a21║ 采女。詣香[3]芽園。遊觀戲樂。太子是時。乘妙
408a22║ 寶車。其車具有種種嚴飾。置大摩尼師子之
408a23║ 座。而坐其上。

简体字

彼时，有王名曰财主，其王具有六万采女、五百大臣、五百王子；其诸王子皆悉勇健，能伏怨敌。其王太子，名威德主，端正殊特，人所乐见，足下平满，轮相备具，足趺隆起，手足指间皆有网缦，足跟齐正，手足柔软，伊尼耶鹿王腨，七处圆满，阴藏隐密，其身上分如师子王，两肩平满，双臂[月+庸]长，身相端直，颈文三道，颊如师子，具四十齿悉皆齐密，四牙鲜白，其舌长广出梵音声，眼目绀青，睫如牛王，眉间毫相，顶上肉髻，皮肤细软如真金色，身毛上靡，发帝青色，其身洪满如尼拘陀树。

"尔时，太子受父王教，与十千采女诣香牙园游观戏乐。太子是时，乘妙宝车，其车具有种种严饰，置大摩尼师子之座而坐其上；

There was a king at that time called Lord of Wealth. That king had sixty thousand female attendants, five hundred great officials, and five hundred sons who were princes. All of those princes were brave and strong and well able to defeat any adversaries. Among them, the Crown Prince was named Lord of Awesome Virtue. Being extraordinarily handsome, he was one who people delighted in seeing. In particular:

The soles of his feet were flat and complete with the wheel emblem;
His feet had prominent arches;
His fingers and toes had proximate webs between them;
His heels were even and straight;
His hands and feet were soft;
His legs resembled those of the *aiṇeya* antelope royal stag;
His body was full in the seven places;
He possessed the well-retracted male organ;
The upper part of his body resembled that of the lion king;
His two shoulders were evenly shaped and full;
His two arms were long;
His body was upright and straight;
His neck had the three creases;
His jaw resembled that of the lion;
He had forty teeth all of which were evenly spaced and close-set;
He had the four front teeth that were pure white;
His tongue was long and broad;
He spoke with the pure and resounding voice;
His eyes were indigo;
He had eyelashes like the king of bulls;
He had the mark of the mid-brow hair tuft;
The top of his head had the fleshy *uṣṇīṣa* prominence;
His skin was fine, soft, and the color of real gold;
His bodily hair grew in an upward direction;
His hair was the color of sapphires; and
His body was large and full like the trunk of the *nyagrodha* tree.

The Crown Prince who was then in training under the tutelage of his father, the king, went out with ten thousand female attendants to the Garden of Fragrant Buds to wander about, see the sights, and enjoy themselves. The prince then ascended into his wonderfully jeweled carriage. His carriage was replete with all the many different kinds of adornments and was fitted with a lion seat where he sat that was decorated with immense *maṇi* jewels. Five hundred female

正體字

五百采女。各執寶繩牽馭而行。
408a24‖ 進止有度。不遲不速。百千萬人持諸寶蓋。百
408a25‖ 千萬人持諸寶幢。百千萬人持諸寶幡。百千
408a26‖ 萬人作諸[4]妓樂。百千萬人燒諸名香。百千
408a27‖ 萬人散諸妙華。前後圍遶。而為翊從。道路
408a28‖ 平正。無有高下。眾寶雜華散布其上。寶樹行
408a29‖ 列。寶網彌覆。種種樓閣延袤其間。其樓閣
408b01‖ 中。或有積聚種種珍寶。或有陳列諸莊嚴具。
408b02‖ 或有供設種種飲食。或有懸布種種衣服。或
408b03‖ 有備擬諸資生物。或復安置端正女人。及以
408b04‖ 無量僮僕侍從。隨有所須悉皆施與。時有[5]母
408b05‖ 人名為善現。將一童女名具足妙德。顏容端
408b06‖ 正。色相嚴潔。洪纖得所。修短合度。目髮紺
408b07‖ 青。聲如梵音。善達工巧。精通辯論。恭勤匪
408b08‖ 懈。慈愍不害。具足慚愧。柔和質直。離癡寡
408b09‖ 欲。無諸諂誑。乘妙寶車。[6]采女圍遶。及與其
408b10‖ 母從王城出。先太子行。見其太子言[7]辭諷
408b11‖ 詠。心生愛染而白母言。我心願得敬事此人。
408b12‖ 若不遂情當自殞滅。母告女言。

简体字

五百采女各执宝绳牵驭而行，进止有度，不迟不速；百千万人持诸宝盖，百千万人持诸宝幢，百千万人持诸宝幡，百千万人作诸妓乐，百千万人烧诸名香，百千万人散诸妙华，前后围绕而为翊从。道路平正，无有高下，众宝杂华散布其上；宝树行列，宝网弥覆，种种楼阁延袤其间。其楼阁中，或有积聚种种珍宝，或有陈列诸庄严具，或有供设种种饮食，或有悬布种种衣服，或有备拟诸资生物，或复安置端正女人，及以无量僮仆侍从；随有所须，悉皆施与。

“时，有母人名为善现，将一童女名具足妙德，颜容端正，色相严洁，洪纤得所，修短合度，目发绀青，声如梵音，善达工巧，精通辩论，恭勤匪懈，慈愍不害，具足惭愧，柔和质直，离痴寡欲，无诸谄诳，乘妙宝车，采女围绕，及与其母从王城出，先太子行。见其太子言辞讽咏，心生爱染，而白母言：‘我心愿得敬事此人，若不遂情，当自殒灭。’母告女言：

attendants each grasped its jeweled ropes and pulled it along at a measured pace, neither slow nor fast.

There were a hundred thousand myriads of people who held up jeweled parasols, a hundred thousand myriads of people who held jeweled banners, a hundred thousand myriads of people who held up jeweled pennants, a hundred thousand myriads of people who played all kinds of music, a hundred thousand myriads of people who burned all kinds of prized incenses, and a hundred thousand myriads of people who, scattering all kinds of marvelous flower blossoms, surrounded them all and served as a retinue of assistants.

The road was level and free of any high or low places. The many kinds of jewels and various kinds of flowers were scattered over it. Rows of jeweled trees were covered with nets made of jewels. Many different kinds of towers stood between them.

Some of those towers contained heaps of the many kinds of precious jewels, some contained arrays of various adornments, some had set out gifts of many different kinds of food and drink, some contained abundantly prepared provisions of many different kinds, and some contained beautiful women or countless servants and attendants. In this manner, whatever one might need was provided.

At that time, there was a mother named Most Beautiful who brought along with her a young daughter named Replete in Marvelous Virtue whose countenance was beautiful, whose form and features were immaculate, whose fullness and slenderness were perfectly arranged, whose height was fitting, whose eyes and hair were indigo, whose voice was like that of Brahmā, who was skilled in the arts, who was proficient in discussing the treatises, who was respectful, diligent, and conscientious, who was kind, sympathetic, and devoted to non-harming, who was fully endowed with a sense of shame and dread of blame, who was gentle, congenial, and straightforward in character, who abandoned whatever was foolish, who had but few desires, and who never engaged in flattery or deception.

Riding in a marvelously jeweled carriage attended by female attendants and accompanied by her mother, she rode out of that royal city just ahead of the prince. On seeing the prince and hearing the intonation of his speech, she fell in love with him and then told her mother, "I only hope that I will be able to respectfully serve this man. If I am unable to follow through on these sentiments, I am bound to kill myself."

Her mother then told her:

正體字

莫生此念。何
408b13║ 以故。此甚難得。此人具足輪王諸相。後當嗣
408b14║ 位作轉輪王。有寶女出。騰空自在。我等卑
408b15║ 賤非其匹偶。此處難得勿生是念。彼香[*]芽園
408b16║ 側。有一道場。名法雲光明。時有如來。名勝
408b17║ 日身。十號具足。於中出現已經七日。時彼
408b18║ 童女。暫時假寐。夢見[8]其佛。從夢覺已。空中
408b19║ 有天。而告之言。勝日身如來。於法雲光明道
408b20║ 場。成等正覺。已經七日。諸菩薩眾。前後圍
408b21║ 遶。天龍夜叉乾闥婆阿脩羅迦樓羅緊那羅
408b22║ 摩睺羅伽。梵天乃至。色究竟天。諸地神風神。
408b23║ 火神水神。河神海神。山神樹神。園神藥神。主
408b24║ 城神等。為見佛故。皆來集會。時妙德童女。夢
408b25║ 覩如來故。聞佛功德故。其心安隱。無有怖畏。
408b26║ 於太子前。而說頌言
408b27║ 我身最端正　名聞遍十方
408b28║ 智慧無等倫　善達諸工巧
408b29║ 無量百千眾　見我皆貪染
408c01║ 我心不於彼　而生少愛欲
408c02║ 無瞋亦無恨　無嫌亦無喜
408c03║ 但發廣大心　利益諸眾生

简体字

‘莫生此念。何以故？此甚难得。此人具足轮王诸相，后当嗣位作转轮王，有宝女出，腾空自在。我等卑贱，非其匹偶。此处难得，勿生是念。’

“彼香牙园侧，有一道场，名法云光明。时，有如来名胜日身，十号具足，于中出现已经七日。时，彼童女暂时假寐，梦见其佛；从梦觉已，空中有天而告之言：‘胜日身如来，于法云光明道场成等正觉已经七日，诸菩萨众前后围绕。天、龙、夜叉、乾闼婆、阿修罗、迦楼罗、紧那罗、摩睺罗伽、梵天乃至色究竟天，诸地神、风神、火神、水神、河神、海神、山神、树神、园神、药神、主城神等，为见佛故，皆来集会。’

“时，妙德童女梦睹如来故，闻佛功德故，其心安隐，无有怖畏，于太子前而说颂言：

“‘我身最端正，名闻遍十方，
智慧无等伦，善达诸工巧。
无量百千众，见我皆贪染；
我心不于彼，而生少爱欲。
无瞋亦无恨，无嫌亦无喜，
但发广大心，利益诸众生。

> Do not think in this way. Why? This would be impossible to accomplish. This man has all the marks of a wheel-turning king. Later on, he is bound to assume the throne and be crowned as the wheel-turning king at which time his precious female consort will come forth, soar into the air, freely doing as she pleases.
>
> Those of humble station such as ourselves could never be betrothed to someone like him. This would be impossible. You must not think in this way.

Off to the side of that Garden of Fragrant Buds, there was a site of enlightenment known as Dharma Cloud Radiance. At that very time, there was a *tathāgata* known as Supreme Solar Body, complete with all ten of a buddha's titles, who had appeared there seven days earlier.

At that time, that young maiden had drifted off to sleep for a brief nap in which she saw that buddha in a dream. On awakening from that dream, a goddess appeared in the sky and told her:

> Seven days ago, Supreme Solar Body Tathāgata attained the universal and right enlightenment at the Dharma Cloud Radiance site of enlightenment where he is now surrounded by a congregation of bodhisattvas. Dragons, *yakṣas, gandharvas, asuras, garuḍas, kiṃnaras, mahoragas,* Brahma Heaven kings, and the other devas on up to the Akaniṣṭha Heaven devas, earth spirits, wind spirits, fire spirits, water spirits, river spirits, ocean spirits, mountain spirits, tree spirits, garden spirits, herb spirits, city spirits, and others have all assembled there to see the Buddha.

Then, because she had seen the Tathāgata in this dream and because she had heard of the meritorious qualities of the Buddha, the mind of that maiden, Marvelous Virtue, became peaceful and fearless, whereupon, standing directly before the prince, she spoke these verses:

This body of mine is most beautiful,
renowned throughout the ten directions.
In wisdom I have no peer
and I thoroughly comprehend all skills and arts.

Countless hundreds of thousands of men,
on seeing me, are all filled with thoughts of lust.
My own mind, however, does not see in them
any basis for the least bit of desire.

Free of anger, free of hatred,
free of either disdain or delight,
I only bring forth the vast resolve
to serve the benefit of all beings.

正體字

408c04 我今見太子　具諸功德相
408c05 其心大欣慶　諸根咸悅樂
408c06 色如光明寶　髮美而右旋
408c07 額廣眉纖曲　我心願事汝
408c08 我觀太子身　譬[9]若真金像
408c09 亦如大寶山　相好有光明
408c10 目廣紺青色　月面師子頰
408c11 喜顏美妙音　願垂哀納我
408c12 舌相廣長妙　猶如赤銅色
408c13 梵音緊那聲　聞者皆歡喜
408c14 口方不褰縮　齒白悉齊密
408c15 發言現笑時　見者心歡喜
408c16 離垢清淨身　具相三十二
408c17 必當於此界　而作轉輪位
408c18 爾時太子。告彼女言。汝是誰女。為誰守護。若
408c19 先屬人。我則不應起愛染心。爾時太子。以頌
408c20 問言
408c21 汝身極清淨　功德相具足
408c22 我今問於汝　汝於誰所住
408c23 誰為汝父母　汝今繫屬誰
408c24 若已屬於人　彼人攝受汝

简体字

我今见太子，具诸功德相，
其心大欣庆，诸根咸悦乐。
色如光明宝，发美而右旋，
额广眉纤曲，我心愿事汝。
我观太子身，譬若真金像，
亦如大宝山，相好有光明。
目广绀青色，月面师子颊，
喜颜美妙音，愿垂哀纳我！
舌相广长妙，犹如赤铜色；
梵音紧那声，闻者皆欢喜。
口方不褰缩，齿白悉齐密，
发言现笑时，见者心欢喜。
离垢清净身，具相三十二，
必当于此界，而作转轮位。’

“尔时，太子告彼女言：‘汝是谁女？为谁守护？若先属人，我则不应起爱染心。’

“尔时，太子以颂问言：

“‘汝身极清净，功德相具足；
我今问于汝，汝于谁所住？
谁为汝父母？汝今系属谁？
若已属于人，彼人摄受汝。

Now, as I see you, Prince,
replete with the marks of the meritorious qualities,
my mind feels such great joyous elation
and all my faculties are suffused with blissful delight.

With a physical form like a radiant jewel,
with hair that is so beautiful in its rightward spirals,
and the broad forehead with brows long and curved,
you are the one my mind wishes to serve.

As I look upon the prince's body,
it appears like an icon made of real gold,
and like an immense mountain of jewels
with its marks and signs all shining with light.

With your indigo-colored wide eyes,
with your face like the moon and jaws like a lion,
your delightful countenance, and your exquisite voice—
Please have compassion for me and accept me as your own.

With your sign of the tongue that is broad, long, and wondrous
which in its color resembles red copper,
your voice of Brahmā with its *kiṃnara*-like sound
fills all who hear you with joyous delight.

With your mouth framed by lips that are neither slack nor pursed,
and your teeth that are white, even, and close-set,
when you speak or reveal a smile,
those who see you are moved to joyous delight.

Your immaculately pure body
is replete in all thirty-two marks.
You are certainly bound to serve in this realm
as he who assumes the throne of the wheel-turning king.

The prince then spoke to that maiden, saying, "Whose daughter are you? Under whose protection are you held? If you are already in the retinue of someone else, then it would not be fitting for me to indulge thoughts of desire for you." The prince then asked her in verse:

Your body is extremely lovely
and replete with the signs of meritorious qualities.
I am now moved to ask you:
With whom do you reside?

Who are your father and mother?
To whose retinue are you now bound?
If you already belong to someone else,
that man will select you as his own.

正體字

408c25 汝不盜他物　汝不有害心
408c26 汝不作邪婬　汝依何語住
408c27 不說他人惡　不壞他所親
408c28 不侵他境界　不於他恚怒
408c29 不生邪險見　不作相違業
409a01 不以諂曲力　方便誑世間
409a02 尊重父母不　敬善知識不
409a03 見諸貧窮人　能生攝心不
409a04 若有善知識　[1]誨示於汝法
409a05 能生堅固心　究竟尊重不
409a06 愛樂於佛不　了知菩薩不
409a07 眾僧功德海　汝能恭敬不
409a08 汝能知法不　能淨眾生不
409a09 為住於法中　為住於非法
409a10 見諸孤獨者　能起慈心不
409a11 見惡道眾生　能生大悲不
409a12 見他得榮樂　能生歡喜不
409a13 他來逼迫汝　汝無瞋惱不
409a14 汝發菩提意　開悟眾生不
409a15 無邊劫修行　[無能>能無]疲倦不

简体字

汝不盗他物，汝不有害心，
汝不作邪淫，汝依何语住？
不说他人恶，不坏他所亲，
不侵他境界，不于他恚怒。
不生邪险见，不作相违业，
不以谄曲力，方便诳世间。
尊重父母不？敬善知识不？
见诸贫穷人，能生摄心不？
若有善知识，诲示于汝法，
能生坚固心，究竟尊重不？
爱乐于佛不？了知菩萨不？
众僧功德海，汝能恭敬不？
汝能知法不？能净众生不？
为住于法中，为住于非法？
见诸孤独者，能起慈心不？
见恶道众生，能生大悲不？
见他得荣乐，能生欢喜不？
他来逼迫汝，汝无瞋恼不？
汝发菩提意，开悟众生不？
无边劫修行，能无疲倦不？’

Are you one who does not steal others' possessions?
Are you one who has no harmful intentions?
Are you one who does not engage in sensual misconduct?
On what sort of speech do you rely?

Do you refrain from speaking of others' wrong deeds?
Do you refrain from disparaging others' friends?
Do you refrain from invading the domain of others?
Do you become enraged at others?

Do you refrain from adopting wrong or dangerous views?
Do you refrain from engaging in transgressive actions?
Do you refrain from using the power of flattery and deviousness?
Do you use false means to deceive the world?

Do you venerate your parents?
Do you revere your good spiritual guides?
On encountering those who are poor,
can you to be motivated to treat them hospitably?

If there are any good spiritual guides
who provide you with instruction in the Dharma,
are you able to maintain an enduring motivation
to forever treat them with reverence?

Are you fond of the buddhas?
Do you appreciate the bodhisattvas?
Are you able to extend reverential respect
to the Sangha community as an ocean of meritorious qualities?

Are you able to understand the Dharma?
Can you enable the purification of beings?
Are you one who dwells in the Dharma,
or one who dwells in what is not Dharma?

When you encounter orphans or the solitary,
are you able to arouse a mind of kindness for them?
On seeing beings in the wretched destinies,
can you feel great compassion for them?

When you see others who have gained glory and happiness,
are you able to respond with sympathetic joy?
If others come and subject you to coercive pressure,
do you remain entirely without anger or annoyance?

Have you resolved to attain bodhi
and to strive to awaken beings?
And, even when cultivating for boundlessly many kalpas,
are you able to remain free of weariness?

正體字

409a16 爾時女母。為其太子。而說頌言
409a17 太子汝應聽　我今說此女
409a18 初生及成長　一切諸因緣
409a19 太子始生日　即從蓮華生
409a20 其目淨[2]修廣　[3]肢節悉具足
409a21 我曾於春月　遊觀娑羅園
409a22 普見諸藥草　種種皆榮茂
409a23 奇樹發妙華　望之如[4]慶雲
409a24 好鳥相和鳴　林間共歡樂
409a25 同遊八百女　端正奪人心
409a26 被服皆嚴麗　歌詠悉殊美
409a27 彼園有浴池　名曰蓮華幢
409a28 我於池岸坐　采女眾圍遶
409a29 於彼蓮池內　忽生千葉華
409b01 寶葉瑠璃莖　閻浮金為臺
409b02 爾時夜分盡　日光初出現
409b03 其蓮正開剖　放大清淨光
409b04 其光極熾盛　譬如[5]日初出
409b05 普照閻浮提　眾歎未曾有
409b06 時見此玉女　從彼蓮華生

简体字

“尔时，女母为其太子而说颂言：
“‘太子汝应听，我今说此女，
初生及成长，一切诸因缘。
太子始生日，即从莲华生，
其目净修广，肢节悉具足。
我曾于春月，游观娑罗园，
普见诸药草，种种皆荣茂。
奇树发妙华，望之如庆云；
好鸟相和鸣，林间共欢乐。
同游八百女，端正夺人心，
被服皆严丽，歌咏悉殊美。
彼园有浴池，名曰莲华幢；
我于池岸坐，采女众围绕。
于彼莲池内，忽生千叶华，
宝叶琉璃茎，阎浮金为台。
尔时夜分尽，日光初出现，
其莲正开剖，放大清净光。
其光极炽盛，譬如日初出，
普照阎浮提，众叹未曾有。
时见此玉女，从彼莲华生，

The mother of the maiden then addressed the prince in verse, saying:

O Prince, you should listen
as I now speak about this daughter of mine
and relate all the causes and conditions
from when she was first born until she grew up.

O Prince, on the day she was first born,
she emerged from a lotus flower.
Her eyes were clear and wide
and her limbs were all perfectly formed.

It was in the months of spring
that I roamed to see the *sāla* tree gardens
and everywhere saw the herbs and greenery there
luxuriantly flourishing in all their variety.

Those extraordinary trees had put forth exquisite blossoms
on which I gazed as if they were auspicious clouds
in which lovely birds sang in harmony
as, within the forest, all was joined in joyous bliss.

I had roamed there with eight hundred maidens
so beautiful their appearance stole the attentions of men.
They were all dressed in magnificently beautiful robes
and sang and chanted in especially lovely ways.

In those gardens there was a bathing pond
known as "Lotus Flower Banner."
I sat there on the banks of that pond,
surrounded by my company of female attendants.

Then from within that lotus pond,
there suddenly arose a thousand-petalled flower
with jeweled petals, a stem of lapis lazuli,
and a seed pod of *jambūnada* gold.

Then, right as the night reached its end
and the light of the sun was first appearing,
that lotus was just then opening,
emanating a pure bright light.

That light blazed in its full radiance,
like the light of the sun when it first rises.
It everywhere illuminated the continent of Jambudvīpa
causing everyone to praise it as unprecedented.

It was then that I saw this jade girl
being born from within that lotus flower

正體字

409b07 | 其身甚清淨　[*]肢分皆圓滿
409b08 | 此是人間寶　從於淨業生
409b09 | 宿因無失壞　今受此果報
409b10 | 紺髮青蓮眼　梵聲金色光
409b11 | 華鬘眾寶髻　清淨無諸垢
409b12 | [*]肢節悉具足　其身無缺減
409b13 | 譬如真金像　安處寶華中
409b14 | 毛孔栴檀香　普熏於一切
409b15 | 口出青蓮香　常演梵音聲
409b16 | 此女所住處　常有天音樂
409b17 | 不應下劣人　而當如是偶
409b18 | 世間無有人　堪與此為夫
409b19 | 唯汝相嚴身　願垂見納受
409b20 | 非長亦非短　非麁亦非細
409b21 | 種種悉端嚴　願垂見納受
409b22 | 文字算數法　工巧諸技藝
409b23 | 一切皆通達　願垂見納受
409b24 | 善了諸兵法　巧斷眾諍訟
409b25 | 能調難可調　願垂見納受
409b26 | 其身甚清淨　見者無厭足

简体字

其身甚清净，肢分皆圆满。
此是人间宝，从于净业生，
宿因无失坏，今受此果报。
绀发青莲眼，梵声金色光，
华鬘众宝髻，清净无诸垢。
肢节悉具足，其身无缺减，
譬如真金像，安处宝华中。
毛孔栴檀香，普熏于一切；
口出青莲香，常演梵音声。
此女所住处，常有天音乐；
不应下劣人，而当如是偶。
世间无有人，堪与此为夫，
唯汝相严身，愿垂见纳受！
非长亦非短，非粗亦非细，
种种悉端严，愿垂见纳受！
文字算数法，工巧诸技艺，
一切皆通达，愿垂见纳受！
善了诸兵法，巧断众诤讼，
能调难可调，愿垂见纳受！
其身甚清净，见者无厌足，

with her body so very immaculate
and her limbs all so perfectly formed.

This is a jewel among all of humanity
who was born from her pure karmic deeds.
The causes from past lives never perish,
hence she now received this as their karmic fruition.

With indigo hair, eyes the color of the blue lotus,
a voice like Brahmā, emanating golden light,
graced with flower garlands and a jewel topknot,
she was one who is immaculately lovely.

Her limbs were all perfect
and her body was not deficient in any way.
She was like a gold statue
standing in a jewel flower.

Her pores emanate the fragrance of sandalwood incense
that everywhere spreads its scent to everything.
Her mouth exhales the fragrance of a blue lotus
and she always speaks with a pure voice.

Wherever this maiden dwells,
there is always heavenly music.
It is not fitting that any inferior man
should become the mate of someone like her.

Indeed, there is no man in the entire world
who would be capable as serving as her husband
except for you whose body is adorned with these signs.
Please deign to accept her as your own.

She is neither too tall nor too short
and neither too stout nor too slight.
She is exquisitely beautiful in every way.
Please deign to accept her as your own.

Both literature and mathematics
as well as the technical skills and arts—
She has a penetrating comprehension of them all.
Please deign to accept her as your own.

She completely understands the art of war,
is skilled in resolving the many kinds of disputes,
and can discipline those who are hard to discipline.
Please deign to accept her as your own.

Her body is of the most lovely sort.
Whoever sees her gazes at it insatiably.

正體字

409b27 | 功德自莊嚴　汝應垂納受
409b28 | 眾生所有患　善達彼緣起
409b29 | 應病而與藥　一切能消滅
409c01 | 閻浮語言法　差別無量種
409c02 | 乃至[6]妓樂音　靡不皆通達
409c03 | 婦人之所能　此女一切知
409c04 | 而無女人過　願垂速納受
409c05 | 不嫉亦不慳　無貪亦無恚
409c06 | 質直性柔軟　離諸麁獷惡
409c07 | 恭敬於尊者　奉事無違逆
409c08 | 樂修諸善行　此能隨順汝
409c09 | 若見於老病　貧窮在苦難
409c10 | 無救無所依　常生大慈愍
409c11 | 常觀第一義　不求自利樂
409c12 | 但願益眾生　以此莊嚴心
409c13 | 行住與坐臥　一切無放逸
409c14 | 言說及默然　見者咸欣樂
409c15 | 雖於一切處　皆無染著心
409c16 | 見有功德人　樂觀無厭足
409c17 | 尊重善知識　樂見離惡人

简体字

功德自庄严，汝应垂纳受！
众生所有患，善达彼缘起，
应病而与药，一切能消灭。
阎浮语言法，差别无量种，
乃至妓乐音，靡不皆通达。
妇人之所能，此女一切知，
而无女人过，愿垂速纳受！
不嫉亦不悭，无贪亦无恚，
质直性柔软，离诸粗犷恶。
恭敬于尊者，奉事无违逆，
乐修诸善行，此能随顺汝。
若见于老病，贫穷在苦难，
无救无所依，常生大慈愍。
常观第一义，不求自利乐，
但愿益众生，以此庄严心。
行住与坐卧，一切无放逸；
言说及默然，见者咸欣乐。
虽于一切处，皆无染著心；
见有功德人，乐观无厌足。
尊重善知识，乐见离恶人；

She is naturally adorned with meritorious qualities.
You should deign to accept her as your own.

She well comprehends the originating conditions
of all the illnesses with which beings are beset.
She gives whichever medicine is right for the sickness at hand
and thus she is thereby able to completely dispel them all.

The languages throughout Jambudvīpa
in all their countless different varieties
and all other such matters, including musical performance—
There are none she does not thoroughly know.

Whatever a wife must be able to do,
this maiden understands it all.
She has none of the faults to which women are prone.
Please deign to quickly accept her as your own.

She is neither jealous nor miserly
and is free of lust and anger.
She is one of straightforward character and gentle nature
who has abandoned the faults of coarseness and rudeness.

She will respect you, Honorable Sir,
for, in serving others, she is never contrary.
She delights in cultivating all good practices.
In these ways, she will be able to comply with your wishes.

Whenever she sees those who are aged or ill,
those who are poor or in suffering hardship,
those with no one to rescue them or who have no refuge,
she always manifests great kindness and sympathy.

She always contemplates the supreme meaning
and does not seek her own benefit or happiness.
She only wishes to benefit beings
and in these ways adorns her mind.

Whether walking, standing, sitting, or lying down,
in all such things she is never neglectful.
Whether she is speaking or remaining silent,
all who see her experience blissful delight.

Although she may find herself in all kinds of situations,
she never indulges thoughts of defiling attachment.
Whenever she sees a person of meritorious qualities,
She delights in contemplating them and, in this, never tires.

She venerates the good spiritual guides
and delights in seeing any person who has abandoned evil.

正體字

409c18 其心不躁動　先思後作業
409c19 福智所莊嚴　一切無怨恨
409c20 女人中最上　宜應事太子
409c21 爾時太子。入香[*]芽園已。告其妙德及善現
409c22 言。善女。我趣求阿耨多羅三藐三菩提。當於
409c23 盡未來際無量劫。集一切智助道之法。修無
409c24 邊菩薩行。淨一切波羅蜜。供養一切諸如來。
409c25 護持一切諸佛教。嚴淨一切佛國土。當令一
409c26 切如來種性不斷。[7]當隨一切眾生種性而普
409c27 成熟。當滅一切眾生生死苦置於究竟安樂
409c28 處。當淨治一切眾生智慧眼。當修習一切菩
409c29 薩所修行。當安住一切菩薩平等心。當成就一
410a01 切菩薩所行地。當令一切眾生普歡喜。當捨
410a02 一切物盡未來際行。檀波羅蜜。令一切眾生
410a03 普得滿足衣服飲食。妻妾男女。頭目手足。如
410a04 是一切內外所有。悉當捨施無所吝惜。當於
410a05 爾時。汝或於我而作障難。施財物時汝心吝
410a06 惜。施男女時汝心痛惱。割[1]肢體時汝心憂
410a07 悶。捨汝出家汝心悔恨。[2]爾時太子。即為妙
410a08 德。而說頌言

简体字

其心不躁动，先思后作业。
福智所庄严，一切无怨恨，
女人中最上，宜应事太子。’

“尔时，太子入香牙园已，告其妙德及善现言：‘善女，我趣求阿耨多罗三藐三菩提，当于尽未来际无量劫，集一切智助道之法，修无边菩萨行，净一切波罗蜜，供养一切诸如来，护持一切诸佛教，严净一切佛国土，当令一切如来种性不断，当随一切众生种性而普成熟，当灭一切众生生死苦置于究竟安乐处，当净治一切众生智慧眼，当修习一切菩萨所修行，当安住一切菩萨平等心，当成就一切菩萨所行地，当令一切众生普欢喜；当舍一切物，尽未来际行檀波罗蜜，令一切众生普得满足衣服饮食、妻妾男女、头目手足，如是一切内外所有，悉当舍施，无所吝惜。当于尔时，汝或于我而作障难：施财物时，汝心吝惜；施男女时，汝心痛恼；割肢体时，汝心忧闷；舍汝出家，汝心悔恨。’

“尔时，太子即为妙德而说颂言：

Her mind is invulnerable to agitation
and she first reflects on matters and only later acts.

She is one who is adorned with both merit and wisdom
and there is no one at all who dislikes her.
Of all women, she is the most superior.
It would only be fitting that she serve you, O Prince.

After he entered the Garden of Fragrant Buds, the prince told the maiden, Marvelous Virtue, and her mother, Most Beautiful:

Good Ladies, I am one who has set out on the quest to attain *anuttara-samyak-saṃbodhi* in which:

I must accumulate the provisions for the path to all-knowledge throughout the countless kalpas of the future while also cultivating the boundless bodhisattva practices, purifying all the *pāramitās,* making offerings to all *tathāgatas,* guarding and preserving the teachings of all buddhas, and purifying all buddha lands;

I must ensure that the lineage of all *tathāgatas* is never cut off;

I must adapt to the natures of all beings and ripen them all;

I must extinguish the suffering of all beings in *saṃsāra* and establish them in a state of ultimate bliss;

I must purify the wisdom eyes of all beings;

I must cultivate the practices cultivated by all bodhisattvas;

I must become established in all bodhisattvas' mind of equanimity;

I must perfect the grounds on which all bodhisattvas practice;

I must enable the happiness of all beings; and

I must relinquish everything throughout all future time by practicing *dāna* pāramitā, thereby enabling all beings to become completely satisfied. Whether it be clothing, food and drink, wives, consorts, sons, daughters, or my head, eyes, hands, and feet, all inward and outward possessions such as these—I must be unstinting in relinquishing them all.

At such times, you are bound to become an obstacle for me, for when I give valuables, you will cling to them out of miserliness, when I give away sons and daughters, you will be struck with painful afflictions, when I cut off my limbs, you will fall into sorrowful depression, and when I abandon you to leave the householder's life, you will feel regrets and resentment.

The prince then spoke these verses for the maiden, Marvelous Virtue:

正體字	410a09	哀愍眾生故	我發菩提心
	410a10	當於無量劫	習行一切智
	410a11	無量大劫中	淨修諸願海
	410a12	入地及治障	悉經無量劫
	410a13	三世諸佛所	學六波羅蜜
	410a14	具足方便行	成就菩提道
	410a15	十方垢穢刹	我當悉嚴淨
	410a16	一切惡道難	我當令永出
	410a17	我當以方便	廣度諸群生
	410a18	令滅愚癡暗	住於佛智道
	410a19	當供一切佛	當淨一切地
	410a20	起大慈悲心	悉捨內外物
	410a21	汝見來乞者	[3]或生慳吝心
	410a22	我心常樂施	汝勿違於我
	410a23	若見我施頭	慎勿生憂惱
	410a24	我今先語汝	令汝心堅固
	410a25	乃至截手足	汝勿嫌乞者
	410a26	汝今聞我語	應可諦思惟
	410a27	男女所愛物	一切我皆捨
	410a28	汝能順我心	我當成汝意

简体字

"'哀愍众生故，我发菩提心，
当于无量劫，习行一切智。
无量大劫中，净修诸愿海，
入地及治障，悉经无量劫。
三世诸佛所，学六波罗蜜，
具足方便行，成就菩提道。
十方垢秽刹，我当悉严净；
一切恶道难，我当令永出。
我当以方便，广度诸群生，
令灭愚痴暗，住于佛智道。
当供一切佛，当净一切地，
起大慈悲心，悉舍内外物。
汝见来乞者，或生悭吝心；
我心常乐施，汝勿违于我。
若见我施头，慎勿生忧恼；
我今先语汝，令汝心坚固。
乃至截手足，汝勿嫌乞者；
汝今闻我语，应可谛思惟。
男女所爱物，一切我皆舍；
汝能顺我心，我当成汝意。'

It is because of deep sympathy for beings
that I have made the resolve to attain bodhi
by which, for a period of countless kalpas,
I must carry out the practices leading to all-knowledge.

Throughout countless great kalpas,
I will purely cultivate the ocean of all vows,
enter the grounds, and purify the obstacles,
doing all of this for countless kalpas.

Under all buddhas of the three periods of time,
I must train in the six *pāramitās,*
completely fulfill the practice of skillful means,
and accomplish the path that leads to bodhi.

I must purify all the defiled *kṣetras*
throughout the ten directions
and I must enable everyone in the wretched destinies
and the difficulties[8] to forever escape from them.

Through the use of skillful means,
I must engage in the extensive liberation of all beings,
extinguishing the darkness of their delusions,
and establishing them in the path to the Buddha's wisdom.

I shall make offerings to all buddhas,
must purify all the grounds,
and, arousing the mind of great kindness and great compassion,
I must relinquish all inward and outward possessions.

On seeing that supplicants have come,
it might be that you would have miserly thoughts.
Since my mind will always delight in giving,
you must not oppose me in this.

If you see that I am about to give up my own head,
take care, for you must not become tormented by sorrow.
I am now telling you in advance
to enable you to fortify your mind.

If I even go so far as to cut off my hands and feet,
you must not resent the supplicant.
Now that you have heard my words on these matters,
it should be that you can now carefully ponder them.

Sons, daughters, and whatever one cherishes—
I will forsake them all.
If you are able to comply with my resolve,
then I shall indeed fulfill your wishes.

正體字

410a29 爾時童女。白太子言。敬奉來教。即說頌言
410b01 無量劫海中　地獄火焚身
410b02 若能眷納我　甘心受此苦
410b03 無量受生處　碎身如微塵
410b04 若能眷納我　甘心受此苦
410b05 無量劫頂戴　廣大金剛山
410b06 若能眷納我　甘心受此苦
410b07 無量生死海　以我身肉施
410b08 汝得法王處　願令我亦然
410b09 若能眷納我　與我為主者
410b10 生生行施處　願常以我施
410b11 為愍眾生苦　而發菩提心
410b12 既已攝眾生　亦當攝受我
410b13 我不求豪富　不貪五欲樂
410b14 但為共行法　願以仁為主
410b15 [4]　紺青[*]修廣眼　慈愍觀世間
410b16 不起染著心　必成菩薩道
410b17 太子所行處　地出眾寶華
410b18 必作轉輪王　願能眷納我
410b19 我曾夢見此　妙法菩提場

简体字

“尔时，童女白太子言：‘敬奉来教。’即说颂言：
“‘无量劫海中，地狱火焚身；
若能眷纳我，甘心受此苦。
无量受生处，碎身如微尘；
若能眷纳我，甘心受此苦。
无量劫顶戴，广大金刚山；
若能眷纳我，甘心受此苦。
无量生死海，以我身肉施；
汝得法王处，愿令我亦然！
若能眷纳我，与我为主者，
生生行施处，愿常以我施！
为愍众生苦，而发菩提心；
既已摄众生，亦当摄受我。
我不求豪富，不贪五欲乐，
但为共行法，愿以仁为主！
绀青修广眼，慈愍观世间，
不起染著心，必成菩萨道。
太子所行处，地出众宝华，
必作转轮王，愿能眷纳我！
我曾梦见此，妙法菩提场，

The maiden then said to the prince: "I shall respectfully uphold your instructions." She then spoke these verses:

Even if I had to endure the fires of the hells
burning up my body for an ocean of countless kalpas—
If then you could but select me as yours,
I would gladly undergo such suffering as this.

Even if, in countless stations of rebirth,
I had to have my body ground to dust—
If then you could but select me as yours,
I would gladly undergo such suffering as this.

Even if, for countless kalpas, I had to hold atop my head
the vast mountains of vajra—
If then you could but select me as yours,
I would gladly undergo such suffering as this.

Even if, throughout an ocean of births and deaths,
you were to give away my body—
If then you could reach the station of a Dharma king,
then I wish that you would allow me to be used in this way.

If you could but select me as yours
so that you will then serve as my husband,
then, in life after life, wherever you are practicing giving,
Please always use me thus as one of your gifts.

Since it is out of pity for the sufferings of beings,
that you have made the resolve to attain bodhi,
having already gathered in living beings,
then you should also gather me in as well.

I do not seek aristocratic status or wealth
nor do I covet the five types of sensual pleasure.
Rather, it is only to practice the Dharma together
that I wish to have you as my husband.

You with your wide indigo-colored eyes,
who look with kindly pity on the world,
and do not indulge any thoughts of attachment,
will surely succeed in the bodhisattva path.

O Prince, wherever you walk,
the earth sends up flowers made of the many jewels.
Surely you will become a wheel-turning king.
Please deign to select me as yours.

I had a dream in which I saw this:
The site of enlightenment to the wondrous Dharma

正體字

410b20║ 如來樹下坐　無量眾圍遶
410b21║ 我夢彼如來　身如真金山
410b22║ 以手摩我頂　寤已心歡喜
410b23║ 往昔眷屬天　名曰喜光明
410b24║ 彼天為我說　道場佛興世
410b25║ 我曾生是念　願見太子身
410b26║ 彼天報我言　汝今當得見
410b27║ 我昔所志願　於今悉成滿
410b28║ 唯願俱往詣　供養彼如來
410b29║ 爾時太子。聞勝日身如來名。生大歡喜。願見
410c01║ 彼佛。以五百摩尼寶。散其女上。冠以妙藏光
410c02║ 明寶[5]冠。被以火焰摩尼寶衣。其女爾時。心
410c03║ 不動搖。亦無喜相。但合掌恭敬。瞻仰太子。目
410c04║ 不暫捨。其母善現。於太子前。而說頌言
410c05║ 此女極端正　功德莊嚴身
410c06║ 昔願奉太子　今意已滿足
410c07║ 持戒有智慧　具足諸功德
410c08║ 普於一切世　最勝無倫匹
410c09║ 此女蓮華生　種姓無譏醜
410c10║ 太子同行業　遠離一切過

简体字

如来树下坐，无量众围绕。
我梦彼如来，身如真金山，
以手摩我顶，寤已心欢喜。
往昔眷属天，名曰喜光明；
彼天为我说，道场佛兴世。
我曾生是念：愿见太子身。
彼天报我言：汝今当得见。
我昔所志愿，于今悉成满；
唯愿俱往诣，供养彼如来！’

“尔时，太子闻胜日身如来名，生大欢喜，愿见彼佛，以五百摩尼宝散其女上，冠以妙藏光明宝冠，被以火焰摩尼宝衣。其女尔时，心不动摇，亦无喜相；但合掌恭敬，瞻仰太子，目不暂舍。

“其母善现，于太子前而说颂言：

“‘此女极端正，功德庄严身；
昔愿奉太子，今意已满足。
持戒有智慧，具足诸功德；
普于一切世，最胜无伦匹。
此女莲华生，种姓无讥丑，
太子同行业，远离一切过。

in which the Tathāgata sat beneath the tree,
surrounded by countless beings.

In my dream that Tathāgata
with a body like a mountain of real gold
stretched out his hand and rubbed the crown of my head.
When I awakened, my mind was filled with joyous delight.

Previously, there was a goddess in my retinue
by the name of Joyous Light.
That goddess told me that, at the site of enlightenment,
the Buddha had appeared in the world.

Earlier, I had this thought:
"May I be able to see the prince in person,"
whereupon that goddess responded to me, saying,
"You will now be able to see him."

What I had previously wished for
has now all been completely fulfilled.
I only hope we will go together to pay our respects
and then present offerings to that *tathāgata*.

Then, having heard the name of Solar Body Tathāgata, the prince became filled with joyous delight and wished to see that buddha. He then showered the maiden with five hundred *maṇi* jewels, crowned her with a crown of marvelous glowing gems, and dressed her in a robe of flaming-radiance *maṇi* jewels.

At that time, the maiden's mind remained unwavering, without showing any signs of joy. She merely pressed her palms together respectfully and gazed up in admiration at the prince, never letting her eyes leave him for even a moment. Standing before the prince, her mother, Most Beautiful, then spoke these verses:

This maiden is the most beautiful,
with a body adorned with meritorious qualities.
In the past, I wished to present her to the prince
and now my wish has already been fulfilled.

She observes the moral precepts, possesses wisdom,
is replete with all the meritorious qualities.
Everywhere, throughout all worlds,
she is supreme and without a peer.

This maiden was born from within a lotus flower,
from a lineage well beyond reproach.
She has the karma to join the prince in practice,
for she has distanced herself from every sort of fault.

正體字

410c11 此女身柔軟　猶如天繒纊
410c12 其手所觸摩　眾患悉除滅
410c13 毛孔出妙香　芬馨最無比
410c14 眾生若聞者　悉住於淨戒
410c15 [6] 身色如真金　端坐華臺上
410c16 眾生若見者　離害具慈心
410c17 言音極柔軟　聽之無不喜
410c18 眾生若得聞　悉離諸惡業
410c19 心淨無瑕垢　遠離諸諂曲
410c20 稱心而發言　聞者皆歡喜
410c21 調柔具慚愧　恭敬於尊宿
410c22 無貪亦無誑　憐愍諸眾生
410c23 此女心不恃　色相及眷屬
410c24 但以清淨心　恭敬一切佛
410c25 爾時太子。與妙德女及十千采女并其眷屬。
410c26 出香[*]芽園。詣法雲光明道場。至已下車。步
410c27 進詣如來所。見佛身相端嚴寂靜。諸根調順。
410c28 內外清淨。如大龍池。無諸垢濁。皆生淨信。踊
410c29 躍歡喜。頂禮佛足。遶無數匝。于時太子及
411a01 妙德女。

简体字

此女身柔软，犹如天缯纩；
其手所触摩，众患悉除灭。
毛孔出妙香，芬馨最无比；
众生若闻者，悉住于净戒。
身色如真金，端坐华台上；
众生若见者，离害具慈心。
言音极柔软，听之无不喜；
众生若得闻，悉离诸恶业。
心净无瑕垢，远离诸谄曲，
称心而发言，闻者皆欢喜。
调柔具惭愧，恭敬于尊宿，
无贪亦无诳，怜愍诸众生。
此女心不恃，色相及眷属；
但以清净心，恭敬一切佛。’

“尔时，太子与妙德女及十千采女并其眷属，出香牙园，诣法云光明道场。至已下车，步进诣如来所。见佛身相端严寂静，诸根调顺，内外清净，如大龙池无诸垢浊；皆生净信，踊跃欢喜，顶礼佛足，绕无数匝。于时，太子及妙德女，

The body of this maiden is just as supple
as silks that one encounters in the heavens.
Whoever her hands touch and then massage
will soon be rid of all their many ills.

Her pores all emanate a wondrous fragrance,
the bouquet of which is beyond compare.
Whichever beings happen to smell this scent
all stay within the pure moral precepts.

The color of her body is like that of real gold.
As she sits erect atop a lotus dais,
if there is any being who so much as sees her,
he abandons all harming and possesses the mind of kindness.

Her voice's sound is most especially soft.
Of all who hear it, none are not delighted.
If there are any beings who are able to hear it,
they will all leave behind all evil deeds.

Her intentions are pure and free of faults or defilements.
She shuns all kinds of flattery and deception.
The words she speaks all match what is in her mind
and those who hear her speaking are all pleased.

Restrained and pliant, she has a sense of shame and dread of blame
and reveres all those who are her venerable elders.
She is free of any covetousness or deception,
and feels sympathetic pity for all beings.

This maiden's mind will not rely
on her physical beauty or her retinue.
It is only with pure intentions
that she reveres all buddhas.

Then the prince, the maiden, her myriad female attendants, and his retinue all left the Garden of Fragrant Buds to pay respects at the Dharma Cloud Radiance site of enlightenment. After arriving there, they descended from their carriages and walked in to pay their respects to the Tathāgata.

There they saw the Buddha's body with its characteristic signs, sitting there erect, adorned, and still, with all of his faculties well restrained, pure within and without. In this, he was like an immense dragon pond entirely free of turbidity. Filled with pure faith and exultant joy, they all bowed down in reverence at the Buddha's feet and circumambulated him countless times.

Then the prince and the maiden, Marvelous Virtue, each took five hundred marvelous jeweled lotus flowers and scattered them

正體字

各持五百妙寶蓮華。供散彼佛。太子
411a02║ 為佛。造五百精舍。一一皆以香木所成。眾寶
411a03║ 莊嚴。五百摩尼以為間錯。時佛為說普眼燈
411a04║ 門修多羅。聞是經已。於一切法中得三昧海。
411a05║ [1]所謂得普照一切佛願海三昧。普照三世藏
411a06║ 三昧。現見一切佛道場三昧。普照一切眾生
411a07║ 三昧。普照一切世間智燈三昧。普照一切眾
411a08║ 生根智燈三昧。救護一切眾生光明雲三昧。
411a09║ 普照一切眾生大明燈三昧。演一切佛法輪
411a10║ 三昧。具足普賢清淨行三昧。時妙德女。得三
411a11║ 昧。名難勝海藏。於阿耨多羅三藐三菩提。永
411a12║ 不退轉。時彼太子。與妙德女并其眷屬。頂禮
411a13║ 佛足。遶無數匝。辭退還宮。詣父王所。拜跪畢
411a14║ 已。奉白王言。大王當知。勝日身如來出興於
411a15║ 世。於此國內法雲光明菩提場中。成等正覺。
411a16║ 于今[2]未久。爾時大王語太子言。是誰為汝說
411a17║ 如是事。天耶[3]人耶。太子白言。是此具足妙
411a18║ 德女說。

简体字

各持五百妙宝莲华供散彼佛。太子为佛造五百精舍，一一皆以香木所成，众宝庄严，五百摩尼以为间错。时，佛为说普眼灯门修多罗；闻是经已，于一切法中得三昧海，所谓：得普照一切佛愿海三昧、普照三世藏三昧、现见一切佛道场三昧、普照一切众生三昧、普照一切世间智灯三昧、普照一切众生根智灯三昧、救护一切众生光明云三昧、普照一切众生大明灯三昧、演一切佛法轮三昧、具足普贤清净行三昧。时，妙德女得三昧，名难胜海藏，于阿耨多罗三藐三菩提永不退转。

“时，彼太子与妙德女并其眷属，顶礼佛足，绕无数匝，辞退还宫；诣父王所，拜跪毕已，奉白王言：‘大王当知，胜日身如来出兴于世，于此国内法云光明菩提场中成等正觉，于今未久。’尔时，大王语太子言：‘是谁为汝说如是事？天耶？人耶？’太子白言：‘是此具足妙德女说。’

as offerings to the Buddha. The prince arranged to build five hundred monastic dwellings, each of which was to be constructed of fragrant wood adorned with various gems and inlaid with five hundred *maṇi* jewels.

Then the Buddha taught them a sutra known as The Gateway of the Lamp of the Universal Eye. After they heard this sutra, they acquired an ocean of samādhis on all dharmas. In particular:

The samādhi of the universal illumination of the ocean of vows of all buddhas;

The samādhi of the universal illumination of the treasuries of the three periods of time;

The samādhi of directly seeing all buddhas' sites of enlightenment;

The samādhi of the universal illumination of all beings;

The samādhi of the wisdom lamp universally illuminating all worlds;

The samādhi of the wisdom lamp universally illuminating the faculties of all beings;

The samādhi of the cloud of light that rescues all beings;

The samādhi of the lamp of great radiance that illuminates all beings;

The samādhi of the proclamation of the Dharma wheel of all buddhas; and

The samādhi of the complete fulfillment of Samantabhadra's pure practices.

The maiden, Marvelous Virtue, then acquired a samādhi known as "treasury of the ocean of invincibility" and became forever irreversible in progressing toward *anuttara-samyak-saṃbodhi.*

Then the prince, the maiden, Marvelous Virtue, and their retinues all bowed down in reverence at the Buddha's feet and circumambulated him countless times. They then respectfully took their leave and returned to the palace where they went to pay their respects to the king, the prince's father. After bowing and kneeling before him, they addressed the king, saying, "The Great King should be informed that Supreme Solar Body Tathāgata has appeared in this world and has quite recently achieved the universal and right enlightenment in this country's Dharma Cloud Radiance site of enlightenment.

The great king then asked the prince, "Who told you of this matter? Was it a deva or a person?"

The prince replied, "It is this very maiden, Replete in Marvelous Virtue, who informed me of this."

正體字

時王聞已。歡喜無量。譬如貧人得
411a19 大伏藏。作如是念。佛無上寶難可值遇。若得
411a20 見佛永斷一切惡道怖畏。佛如醫王能治一
411a21 切諸煩惱病。能救一切生死大苦。佛如導師。
411a22 能令眾生至於究竟安隱住處。作是念已。集
411a23 諸小王群臣眷屬及以剎利婆羅門等一切大
411a24 眾。便捨王位。[4]授與太子。灌頂訖已。與萬人
411a25 俱。往詣佛所。到已禮足。遶無數匝。并其眷
411a26 屬。悉皆退坐。爾時如來。觀察彼王及諸大眾。
411a27 白毫相中放大光明。名一切世間心燈。普照
411a28 十方無量世界。住於一切世主之前。示現如
411a29 來不可思議大神通力。普令一切應受化者。
411b01 心得清淨。爾時如來。以不[5]思議自在神力。
411b02 現身超出一切世間。以圓滿音。普為大眾。說
411b03 陀羅尼。名一切法義離闇燈。佛剎微塵數陀
411b04 羅尼。而為眷屬。彼王聞已。即時獲得大智光
411b05 明。其眾會中。有閻浮提微塵數菩薩。俱時
411b06 證得此陀羅尼。六十[6]萬那由他人。盡諸有
411b07 漏心得解脫。十千眾生遠塵離垢。得法眼淨。
411b08 無量眾生發菩提心。時佛又以不思議力。廣
411b09 現神變。

简体字

时，王闻已，欢喜无量，譬如贫人得大伏藏，作如是念：‘佛无上宝难可值遇，若得见佛，永断一切恶道怖畏。佛如医王，能治一切诸烦恼病，能救一切生死大苦；佛如导师，能令众生至于究竟安隐住处。’作是念已，集诸小王、群臣、眷属，及以刹利、婆罗门等一切大众，便舍王位，授与太子；灌顶讫已，与万人俱，往诣佛所；到已礼足，绕无数匝，并其眷属悉皆退坐。

“尔时，如来观察彼王及诸大众，白毫相中放大光明，名一切世间心灯，普照十方无量世界，住于一切世主之前，示现如来不可思议大神通力，普令一切应受化者心得清净。尔时，如来以不思议自在神力，现身超出一切世间，以圆满音普为大众说陀罗尼，名一切法义离暗灯，佛刹微尘数陀罗尼而为眷属。彼王闻已，即时获得大智光明；其众会中，有阎浮提微尘数菩萨，俱时证得此陀罗尼；六十万那由他人，尽诸有漏，心得解脱；十千众生，远尘离垢，得法眼净；无量众生，发菩提心。时，佛又以不思议力广现神变，

On hearing this, the king was filled with measureless joy, like a poor man who has acquired a great hidden treasure. He thought:

> The Buddha is the unexcelled jewel who is rarely ever met. If one is able to see the Buddha, then one forever severs all fear of falling into the wretched rebirth destinies. The Buddha is like a king of physicians who is able to cure all diseases of the afflictions. He is able to rescue one from all the immense sufferings of *saṃsāra*. The Buddha is like a master guide who can lead beings to the most ultimately peaceful and secure dwelling place.

Having had this thought, he then assembled all the lesser kings, the many officials, his retinue, and the *kṣatriyas*, brahmans, and others within his entire great assembly, whereupon he ceded his kingship and passed it on to the prince. After the crown-anointing consecration ceremony had concluded, he went together with a myriad others to pay his respects to the Buddha. Having arrived, he bowed down in reverence at the Buddha's feet and circumambulated him countless times. Then, together with his retinue, he sat off to one side.

Then the Tathāgata contemplated that king and his great assembly of followers, whereupon, from the white hair mark between his brows, he emanated an immense light known as "the mind lamp of all worlds" that everywhere illuminated the countless worlds of the ten directions. It remained before the rulers of all those worlds, displayed the Tathāgata's inconceivable power of the great spiritual superknowledges, and everywhere enabled all who were amenable to instruction to purify their minds.

The Tathāgata then used his inconceivable miraculous spiritual powers to manifest a body surpassing any others anywhere in the world and, with his perfectly full voice, for that immense congregation, he spoke a *dhāraṇī* known as "the darkness-transcending lamp of the meanings of all dharmas" that had a retinue of *dhāraṇīs* as numerous as the atoms in a buddha *kṣetra*.

Having heard this, the king immediately acquired the light of great wisdom. Of those in that congregation, there were bodhisattvas as numerous as the atoms in Jambudvīpa who all simultaneously gained the realization of this *dhāraṇī*. Sixty myriads of *nayutas* of people put an end to all the contaminants, whereupon their minds were liberated. A myriad beings attained the dust-free, stainless, purified Dharma eye and countless beings resolved to attain bodhi.

Then, with his inconceivable powers, the Buddha further extensively manifested spiritual transformations through which he

正體字

普於十方無量世界。演三乘法。化
411b10║ 度眾生。時彼父王作如是念。我若在家。不能
411b11║ 證得如是妙法。若於佛所。出家學道。即當
411b12║ 成就。作是念已。前白佛言。願得從佛出家修
411b13║ 學。佛言隨意。宜自知時。時財主王。與十千
411b14║ 人。皆於佛所同時出家。未久之間。悉得成
411b15║ 就一切法義離闇燈陀羅尼。亦得如上諸三
411b16║ 昧門。又得菩薩十神通門。又得菩薩無邊辯
411b17║ 才。又得菩薩無礙淨身。往詣十方諸如來所。
411b18║ 聽受其法。為大法師演說妙法。[7]復以神力
411b19║ 遍十方剎。隨眾生心而為現身。讚佛出現。說
411b20║ 佛本行。示佛本緣。稱揚如來自在神力。護持
411b21║ 於佛所說教法。爾時太子。於十五日。在正
411b22║ 殿上。采女圍遶。七寶自至。一者輪寶名無礙
411b23║ 行。二者象寶名金剛身。三者馬寶名迅疾風。
411b24║ 四者珠寶名日光藏。五者女寶名具妙德。六
411b25║ 藏臣寶名為大財。七主兵寶名離垢眼。七寶
411b26║ 具足為轉輪王。

简体字

普于十方无量世界演三乘法化度众生。

“时，彼父王作如是念：‘我若在家，不能证得如是妙法；若于佛所出家学道，即当成就。’作是念已，前白佛言：‘愿得从佛出家修学！’佛言：‘随意，宜自知时。’时，财主王与十千人，皆于佛所同时出家。未久之间，悉得成就一切法义离暗灯陀罗尼，亦得如上诸三昧门，又得菩萨十神通门，又得菩萨无边辩才，又得菩萨无碍净身，往诣十方诸如来所听受其法，为大法师演说妙法；复以神力遍十方刹，随众生心而为现身，赞佛出现，说佛本行，示佛本缘，称扬如来自在神力，护持于佛所说教法。

“尔时，太子于十五日在正殿上，采女围绕，七宝自至——一者、轮宝，名无碍行；二者、象宝，名金刚身；三者、马宝，名迅疾风；四者、珠宝，名日光藏；五者、女宝，名具妙德；六、藏臣宝，名为大财；七、主兵宝，名离垢眼。——七宝具足，为转轮王，

everywhere expounded the Dharma of the Three Vehicles throughout the countless worlds of the ten directions. At that time, the king reflected: "If I continue to be a householder, I will not be able to realize such a sublime Dharma as this. But if I leave behind the household life and train in the path under the Buddha, I should then succeed in this."

After he had this thought, he came before the Buddha and addressed him, saying, "Please allow me to leave the household life under the Buddha so that I may cultivate this training."

To this, the Buddha replied, "You may proceed according to your wishes when you know the time is right."

At that time, King Lord of Wealth and a myriad others all left the household life at the same time under the Buddha. Then, before long, they all perfected the *dhāraṇī*, "darkness-transcending lamp of the meaning of all dharmas," and also gained the samādhi gateways described above. They also acquired the bodhisattva's ten spiritual superknowledges, also acquired the bodhisattva's boundless eloquences, and also acquired the bodhisattva's unimpeded pure bodies with which they went to pay their respects to the *tathāgatas* of the ten directions, listened to their Dharma teachings, and became great masters of the Dharma who expounded on the sublime Dharma.

They also used the spiritual powers to go everywhere throughout the *kṣetras* of the ten directions where, adapting to beings' dispositions, they manifested bodies for their benefit, praised the Buddha's appearance in the world, spoke of the Buddha's practices in previous lifetimes, revealed the Buddha's causal circumstances in previous lifetimes, praised the Tathāgata's miraculous spiritual powers, and guarded and preserved the teaching dharmas taught by the Buddha.

Then, on the fifteenth day of the month, when the prince was in the main palace surrounded by his female attendants, his seven treasures spontaneously arrived:

First, the wheel treasure known as Unimpeded Travel;
Second, the elephant treasure known as Vajra Body;
Third, the horse treasure known as Swift Wind;
Fourth, the pearl treasure known as Sunlight Treasury;
Fifth, the female treasure known as Replete in Marvelous Virtue;
Sixth, the treasurer treasure known as Great Wealth; and
Seventh, the military treasure known as Stainless Eye.

Having thus become complete with the seven treasures, he became a wheel-turning king, one who ruled over the continent of

正體字

王閻浮提。正法治世。人民快
411b27 樂。王有千子端正勇健。能伏怨敵。其閻浮提
411b28 中。有八十王城。一一城中有五百僧坊。一一
411b29 僧坊立佛支提。皆悉高廣。以眾妙寶而為校
411c01 飾。一一王城。皆請如來。以不思議眾妙供具。
411c02 而為供養。佛[8]入城時。現大神力。令無量眾
411c03 生種諸善根。無量眾生心得清淨。見佛歡喜。
411c04 發菩提意。起大悲心。利益眾生。勤修佛法。入
411c05 真實義。住於法性。了法平等。獲三世智。等觀
411c06 三世。知一切佛出興次第。說種種法。攝取
411c07 眾生。發菩薩願。入菩薩道。知如來法。成就法
411c08 海。能普現身。遍一切剎。知眾生根及其性欲。
411c09 令其發起一切智願。佛子。於汝意云何。彼時
411c10 太子得輪王位。供養佛者。豈異人乎。今釋迦
411c11 牟尼佛是也。財主王者寶華佛是。其寶華佛。
411c12 現在東方過世界海微塵數佛剎。有世界海。
411c13 名現法界虛空影像雲。中有世界種。名普現
411c14 三世影摩尼王。彼世界種中。有世界名圓滿
411c15 光。中有道場名現一切世主身。

简体字

王阎浮提，正法治世，人民快乐。王有千子，端正勇健，能伏冤敌。其阎浮提中有八十王城，一一城中有五百僧坊，一一僧坊立佛支提，皆悉高广，以众妙宝而为校饰；一一王城皆请如来，以不思议众妙供具而为供养。佛入城时，现大神力，令无量众生种诸善根，无量众生心得清净，见佛欢喜，发菩提意，起大悲心，利益众生，勤修佛法，入真实义，住于法性，了法平等，获三世智，等观三世，知一切佛出兴次第，说种种法摄取众生，发菩萨愿，入菩萨道，知如来法，成就法海，能普现身遍一切刹，知众生根及其性欲，令其发起一切智愿。

“佛子，于汝意云何？彼时太子得轮王位供养佛者，岂异人乎？今释迦牟尼佛是也。财主王者，宝华佛是。其宝华佛，现在东方过世界海微尘数佛刹有世界海，名现法界虚空影像云，中有世界种，名普现三世影摩尼王，彼世界种中有世界，名圆满光，中有道场，名现一切世主身，

Jambudvīpa and governed the world with right Dharma so that the people enjoyed happiness.

That king had a thousand sons who were handsome, courageous, strong, and able to subdue any adversary. Within that continent of Jambudvīpa, there were eighty royal cities. Each of those cities had five hundred monastic residences. At each of those monastic residences, buddha *caityas* were erected, all of which were tall and wide and adorned with many kinds of marvelous jewels. Each of those royal cities invited the Tathāgata to come and made offerings to him of many different marvelous kinds of inconceivable offering gifts.

When the Buddha entered the city, he displayed great spiritual powers, enabling countless beings to plant roots of goodness and enabling countless beings to purify their minds. On seeing the Buddha, they were filled with joyous delight, resolved to attain bodhi, aroused the mind of the great compassion, promoted the benefit of beings, diligently cultivated the Buddha's Dharma, [and directed their minds] to penetrating the genuine meaning, to dwelling in the nature of dharmas, to completely understanding the uniform equality of dharmas, to acquiring the knowledge of the three periods of time and contemplating all three periods of time, to knowing the sequence of all buddhas' appearance in the world, to teaching the many different kinds of dharmas for gathering in beings, to making the bodhisattva vows, to entering the bodhisattva path, to knowing the Dharma of the Tathāgata, to perfecting an ocean of dharmas, to manifesting bodies everywhere in all *kṣetras*, to knowing beings' faculties and dispositions, and to enabling them to vow to attain all-knowledge.

Son of the Buddha, what do you think? As for the prince who then acquired the position of the wheel-turning king and made offerings to the Buddha, could it have been anyone else? It was none other than our present Śākyamuni Buddha.

As for King Lord of Wealth, that was the present Jewel Flower Buddha. Jewel Flower Buddha now dwells off in the east beyond a number of buddha *kṣetras* as numerous as the atoms in an ocean of worlds in a place where there is an ocean of worlds known as Cloud Displaying the Reflected Images of the Dharma Realm and Empty Space. In that ocean of worlds, there is a world system known as Sovereign Maṇi Jewel Everywhere Displaying Reflected Images of the Three Periods of Time. Within that world system, there is a world known as Perfectly Full Radiance in which there is a site of enlightenment known as Displaying Images of All World Leaders. It is in this place that Jewel Flower Tathāgata attained

正體字

寶華如來。於
411c16‖ 此成阿耨多羅三藐三菩提。不可說佛刹微
411c17‖ 塵數諸菩薩眾。前後圍遶。而為說法。寶華如
411c18‖ 來。往昔修行菩薩道時。淨此世界海。其世
411c19‖ 界海中去來今佛。出興世者。皆是寶華如來
411c20‖ 為菩薩時。教化令發阿耨多羅三藐三菩提
411c21‖ 心。彼時女母善現者。今我母善目是。其王眷
411c22‖ 屬。今如來所眾會是也。皆具修行普賢諸行。
411c23‖ 成滿大願。雖恒在此眾會道場。而能普現一
411c24‖ 切世間。住諸菩薩平等三昧。常得現見一切
411c25‖ 諸佛。一切如來。[9]以等虛空妙音聲雲。演正
411c26‖ 法輪。悉能聽受。於一切法悉得自在。名稱
411c27‖ 普聞諸佛國土。普詣一切道場之所。普現一
411c28‖ 切眾生之前。隨其所應。教化調伏。盡未來劫。
411c29‖ 修菩薩道。恒無間斷。成滿普賢廣大誓願。佛
412a01‖ 子。其妙德女。與威德主轉輪聖王。以四事供
412a02‖ 養勝日身如來者。我身是也。彼佛滅後。其世
412a03‖ 界中。六十億百千那由他佛。出興於世。我皆
412a04‖ 與王。承事供養。其第一佛名清淨身。次名一
412a05‖ 切智月光明身。[1]次名閻浮檀金光明王。次名
412a06‖ 諸相莊嚴身。次名妙月光。

简体字

宝华如来于此成阿耨多罗三藐三菩提，不可说佛刹微尘数诸菩萨众前后围绕而为说法。宝华如来往昔修行菩萨道时，净此世界海；其世界海中去、来、今佛出兴世者，皆是宝华如来为菩萨时教化令发阿耨多罗三藐三菩提心。彼时女母善现者，今我母善目是。其王眷属，今如来所众会是也，皆具修行普贤诸行成满大愿，虽恒在此众会道场而能普现一切世间，住诸菩萨平等三昧，常得现见一切诸佛，一切如来以等虚空妙音声云演正法轮悉能听受，于一切法悉得自在，名称普闻诸佛国土，普诣一切道场之所，普现一切众生之前，随其所应教化调伏，尽未来劫修菩萨道恒无间断，成满普贤广大誓愿。

“佛子，其妙德女与威德主转轮圣王以四事供养胜日身如来者，我身是也。彼佛灭后，其世界中，六十亿百千那由他佛出兴于世，我皆与王承事供养。其第一佛，名清净身；次名一切智月光明身；次名阎浮檀金光明王；次名诸相庄严身；次名妙月光；

anuttara-samyak-saṃbodhi. He is surrounded by a congregation of bodhisattvas as numerous as the atoms in an ineffable number of buddha *kṣetras* to whom he teaches the Dharma.

When in the distant past Jewel Flower Tathāgata was cultivating the bodhisattva path, he purified this ocean of worlds. All the past, future, and present era buddhas who appear in this ocean of worlds are those Jewel Flower Tathāgata taught and induced to resolve to attain *anuttara-samyak-saṃbodhi* during that time when he was a bodhisattva.

As for that maiden's mother, Most Beautiful, that is my present-life mother, Eyes of Goodness.

As for that king's retinue, they currently comprise the congregation of this present era's *tathāgata.* They have all completely cultivated the practices of Samantabhadra and have completely fulfilled great vows. Although they constantly reside in the congregation at this site of enlightenment, they are still able to appear everywhere in all worlds.

They dwell in the bodhisattva's samādhi of uniform equality in which they are always able to directly see all buddhas. As all *tathāgatas* expound on right Dharma and turn the Dharma wheel with clouds of sublime voices as vast as space, they are able to hear them all.

They have acquired sovereign mastery in all dharmas and their fame is heard everywhere throughout all buddha lands. They travel everywhere, paying their respects at all sites of enlightenment. They everywhere appear directly before all beings, adapt to what is fitting for them, and then teach and train them. Throughout all kalpas of the future, they constantly and uninterruptedly continue to cultivate the bodhisattva path and fulfill the great vows of Samantabhadra.

Son of the Buddha, as for the maiden, Marvelous Virtue, who, together with the wheel-turning king, Lord of Awesome Virtue, offered the four requisites to Supreme Solar Body Tathāgata, that was none other than myself. After that buddha entered *nirvāṇa,* sixty *koṭīs* of hundreds of thousands of *nayutas* of buddhas appeared in the world. Together with that king, I served and made offerings to them.

The first of those buddhas was named Pure Body.

The next was named All-Knowledge Moonlight Body.

The next was named King of the Radiance of Jambūnada Gold.

The next was named Body Adorned with All the Signs.

The next was named Marvelous Moonlight.

正體字

次名智觀幢。次名
412a07 大智光。次名金剛那羅延精進。次名智力無
412a08 能勝。次名普安詳智。次名離垢勝智雲。次名
412a09 師子智光明。次名光明髻。次名功德光明幢。
412a10 次名智日幢。次名寶蓮華開敷身。次名福德
412a11 嚴淨光。次名智焰雲。次名普照月。次名莊嚴
412a12 蓋妙音聲。次名師子勇猛智光明。次名法界
412a13 月。次名現虛空影像開悟眾生心。次名恒嗅
412a14 寂滅香。次名普震寂靜音。次名甘露山。次
412a15 名法海音。次名堅固網。次名佛影髻。次名
412a16 月光毫。次名辯才口。次名覺華智。次名寶焰
412a17 山。次名功德星。次名寶月幢。次名三昧身。次
412a18 名寶光王。次名普智行。次名焰海燈。次名離
412a19 垢法音王。次名無比德名稱幢。次名修臂。次
412a20 名本願清淨月。次名照義燈。次名深遠音。

简体字

次名智观幢；次名大智光；次名金刚那罗延精进；次名智力无能胜；次名普安详智；次名离垢胜智云；次名师子智光明；次名光明髻；次名功德光明幢；次名智日幢；次名宝莲华开敷身；次名福德严净光；次名智焰云；次名普照月；次名庄严盖妙音声；次名师子勇猛智光明；次名法界月；次名现虚空影像开悟众生心；次名恒嗅寂灭香；次名普震寂静音；次名甘露山；次名法海音；次名坚固网；次名佛影髻；次名月光毫；次名辩才口；次名觉华智；次名宝焰山；次名功德星；次名宝月幢；次名三昧身；次名宝光王；次名普智行；次名焰海灯；次名离垢法音王；次名无比德名称幢；次名修臂；次名本愿清净月；次名照义灯；次名深远音；

The next was named Banner of Wisdom Contemplation.
The next was named Light of Great Wisdom.
The next was named Vajra Nārāyaṇa Vigor.
The next was named Invincible Wisdom Power.
The next was named Universally Calm Wisdom.
The next was named Cloud of Stainless Supreme Wisdom.
The next was named Light of the Lion of Wisdom.
The next was named Radiant Topknot.
The next was named Banner of the Light of Meritorious Qualities.
The next was named Banner of the Sun of Wisdom.
The next was named Blooming Jeweled Lotus Body.
The next was named Light of Purified Merit.
The next was named Flaming Light of the Cloud of Wisdom.
The next was named Universally Shining Moon.
The next was named Adorned Canopy's Marvelous Voice.
The next was named Light of the Lion's Courageous Wisdom.
The next was named Dharma Realm Moon.
The next was named Manifesting Reflected Images in Space, Awakening Beings' Minds.
The next was named Constantly Sensing Nirvāṇa's Fragrance.
The next was named Quiescent Sound Shaking All Places.
The next was named Sweet-Dew Mountain.
The next was named Sound of the Dharma Ocean.
The next was named Durable Net.
The next was named Buddha Reflections Topknot.
The next was named Moonlight Hair-Tuft.
The next was named Eloquent Mouth.
The next was named Wisdom of the Flower of Enlightenment.
The next was named Mountain of Jewels' Flaming Radiance.
The next was named Star of Meritorious Qualities.
The next was named Jewel Moon Banner.
The next was named Samādhi Body.
The next was named Jewel Light King.
The next was named Universal Wisdom Practice.
The next was named Lamp of the Sea of Flaming Radiance.
The next was named King of the Sound of Stainless Dharma.
The next was named Banner of Peerless Virtue's Fame.
The next was named Long Arms.
The next was named Pure Moon of Original Vows.
The next was named Meaning-Illuminating Lamp.
The next was named Deep and Far-Reaching Sound.

正體字

次
412a21‖ 名毘盧遮那勝藏王。次名諸乘幢。次名法海
412a22‖ 妙蓮華。佛子。彼劫中。有如是等六十億百千
412a23‖ 那由他佛。出興于世。我皆親近。承事供養。其
412a24‖ 最後佛。名廣大解。於彼佛所。得淨智眼。爾時
412a25‖ 彼佛。入城教化。我為王妃。與王禮覲。以眾妙
412a26‖ 物而為供養。[2]於其佛所。聞說出生一切如來
412a27‖ 燈法門。即時獲得觀察一切菩薩三昧海境
412a28‖ 界解脫。佛子。我得此解脫已。與菩薩於佛
412a29‖ 剎微塵數劫。勤加修習。於佛剎微塵數劫中。
412b01‖ 承事供養無量諸佛。或於一劫。承事一佛。或
412b02‖ 二或三。或不可說。或值佛剎微塵數佛。悉皆
412b03‖ 親近承事供養。而未能知菩薩之身形量色
412b04‖ 貌。及其身業心行智慧三昧境界。佛子。若
412b05‖ 有眾生。得見菩薩修菩提行。若疑若信。菩薩
412b06‖ 皆以世出世間種種方便。而攝取之。以為眷
412b07‖ 屬。令於阿耨多羅三藐三菩提得不退[3]轉。佛
412b08‖ 子。我見彼佛。得此解脫已。與菩薩於百佛剎
412b09‖ 微塵數劫。而共修習。於其劫中。

简体字

次名毗卢遮那胜藏王；次名诸乘幢；次名法海妙莲华。佛子，彼劫中，有如是等六十亿百千那由他佛出兴于世，我皆亲近承事供养。

“其最后佛，名广大解，于彼佛所，得净智眼。尔时，彼佛入城教化。我为王妃，与王礼觐，以众妙物而为供养，于其佛所闻说出生一切如来灯法门，即时获得观察一切菩萨三昧海境界解脱。佛子，我得此解脱已，与菩萨于佛刹微尘数劫勤加修习，于佛刹微尘数劫中承事供养无量诸佛；或于一劫承事一佛，或二、或三、或不可说，或值佛刹微尘数佛，悉皆亲近承事供养，而未能知菩萨之身形量色貌及其身业、心行智慧、三昧境界。

“佛子，若有众生，得见菩萨修菩提行，若疑若信；菩萨皆以世、出世间种种方便而摄取之，以为眷属，令于阿耨多罗三藐三菩提得不退转。佛子，我见彼佛得此解脱已，与菩萨于百佛刹微尘数劫而共修习；于其劫中，

The next was named King of Vairocana's Supreme Treasury.
The next was named Banner of the Vehicles.
And the next was named Marvelous Lotus of the Dharma Ocean.

Son of the Buddha, throughout that kalpa, there were sixty *koṭīs* of hundreds of thousands of *nayutas* of buddhas such as these who appeared in the world. I drew near to all of them, served them, and made offerings to them. The very last of those buddhas was named "Vast Liberation." It was under that buddha that I purified the wisdom eye.

At that time when that buddha entered the city to give teachings, I was a consort of the king who had gone with the king to bow in reverence and pay respects to him. We made offerings to him of many marvelous things and, in the presence of that buddha, heard him teach a Dharma gateway called "the appearance of the lamp of all *tathāgatas*," whereupon I immediately acquired the liberation known as "sphere of the contemplation of the ocean of all bodhisattvas' samādhis."

Son of the Buddha, after I acquired this liberation, together with the bodhisattva, I diligently cultivated it for kalpas as numerous as the atoms in a buddha *kṣetra* during which I also served and made offerings to countless buddhas for kalpas as numerous as the atoms in a buddha *kṣetra*. In some instances I served one buddha in one kalpa, in some instances two buddhas, in some instances three buddhas, in some instances an ineffable number of buddhas, and in some instances I encountered buddhas as numerous as the atoms in a buddha *kṣetra*. I drew near to all of them, served them, and made offerings to them.

Even so, I was still unable to know the extent of the bodhisattva's body, his physical forms and appearances, his bodily deeds, his mental deeds, his wisdom, or the spheres of experience of his samādhis.

Son of the Buddha, if any being encounters the bodhisattva cultivating the bodhi practices, no matter whether he is someone who has doubts about him or someone who has faith in him, in all such cases, the bodhisattva uses many different kinds of mundane and world-transcending skillful means to draw him in so that he becomes one of his retinue who he enables to gain irreversibility in the path to *anuttara-samyak-saṃbodhi.*

Son of the Buddha, after I saw that buddha and acquired this liberation, together with the bodhisattva, I cultivated it for kalpas as numerous as the atoms in a hundred buddha *kṣetras*. Throughout those kalpas, I drew near to, served, and made offerings to all the

正體字

所有諸佛
412b10 出興于世。我皆親近承事供養。聽所說法讀
412b11 誦受持。於彼一切諸如來所。得此解脫種種
412b12 法門。知種種三世。入種種刹海。見種種成正
412b13 覺。入種種佛眾會。發菩薩種種大願。修菩薩
412b14 種種妙行。得菩薩種種解脫。然未能知菩薩
412b15 所得普賢解脫門。何以故。菩薩普賢解脫門。
412b16 如太虛空。如眾生名。如三世海。如十方海。如
412b17 法界海。無量無邊。佛子。菩薩普賢解脫門。與
412b18 如來境界等。佛子。我於佛刹微塵數劫。觀菩
412b19 薩身。無有厭足。如多欲人男女集會。遞相
412b20 愛染。起於無量妄想思覺。我亦如是觀菩薩
412b21 身一一毛孔。念念見無量無邊廣大世界。種
412b22 種安住。種種莊嚴。種種形狀。有種種山。種種
412b23 地。種種雲。種種名。種種佛興。種種道場。種
412b24 種眾會。演種種修多羅。說種種灌頂。種種
412b25 諸乘。種種方便。種種清淨。又於菩薩一一
412b26 毛孔。念念常見無邊佛海。坐種種道場。現
412b27 種種神變。轉種種法輪。說種種修多羅。恒不
412b28 斷絕。

简体字

所有诸佛出兴于世，我皆亲近承事供养，听所说法读诵受持。于彼一切诸如来所，得此解脱种种法门，知种种三世，入种种刹海，见种种成正觉，入种种佛众会，发菩萨种种大愿，修菩萨种种妙行，得菩萨种种解脱，然未能知菩萨所得普贤解脱门。何以故？菩萨普贤解脱门，如太虚空，如众生名，如三世海，如十方海，如法界海，无量无边。佛子，菩萨普贤解脱门，与如来境界等。

“佛子，我于佛刹微尘数劫，观菩萨身无有厌足。如多欲人男女集会，递相爱染，起于无量妄想思觉。我亦如是，观菩萨身一一毛孔，念念见无量无边广大世界种种安住、种种庄严、种种形状，有种种山、种种地、种种云、种种名、种种佛兴、种种道场、种种众会，演种种修多罗，说种种灌顶、种种诸乘、种种方便、种种清净。又于菩萨一一毛孔，念念常见无边佛海，坐种种道场，现种种神变，转种种法轮，说种种修多罗，恒不断绝。

buddhas who appeared in the world, listened to the Dharma they taught, studied it, recited it, absorbed it, and retained it.

Under all those *tathāgatas,* I acquired many different Dharma gateways to this liberation. I came to know the three periods of time in many different ways, entered oceans of many different *kṣetras,* witnessed many different realizations of right enlightenment, entered many different congregations of buddhas, made many different great bodhisattva vows, cultivated many different marvelous bodhisattva practices, and acquired many different bodhisattva liberations. Even so, I was still unable to know the liberation gateways of Samantabhadra that the bodhisattva had acquired.

And why was this so? In their measurelessness and boundlessness, the bodhisattva's liberation gateways of Samantabhadra are like empty space, like all beings' names, like the oceans of the three periods of time, like the ocean of the ten directions, and like the ocean of the Dharma realm. Son of the Buddha, the bodhisattva's liberation gateways of Samantabhadra are equal in scope to the realm of the Tathāgata.

Son of the Buddha, for kalpas as numerous as the atoms in a buddha *kṣetra,* I have insatiably contemplated the bodhisattva's body in much the same way as when men and women with much desire meet and feel passion for each other, they have countless kinds of discursive thinking and ideation.

In the same way, as I contemplate each of the pores of the bodhisattva's body, in every mind-moment I see measurelessly and boundlessly many vast worlds and the many different ways they are established, their many different adornments, their many different shapes and appearances, their many different mountains, their many different grounds, their many different clouds, their many different names, their many different ways in which buddhas appear, their many different sites of enlightenment, their many different congregations, their expounding of many different sutras, their teaching of many different crown-anointing consecrations, their many different vehicles to emancipation, their many different skillful means, and their many different kinds of purity.

Further, in every pore of the bodhisattva and in every mind-moment I always see the boundless ocean of buddhas sitting in many different sites of enlightenment, manifesting many different spiritual transformations while constantly and incessantly turning the Dharma wheel in many different ways as they teach many different kinds of sutras.

正體字

又於菩薩一一毛孔。見無邊眾生海。種
412b29║ 種住處。種種形貌。種種作業。種種諸根。又於
412c01║ 菩薩一一毛孔。見三世諸菩薩無邊行門。所
412c02║ 謂無邊廣大願。無邊差別地。無邊波羅蜜。無
412c03║ 邊往昔事。無邊大慈門。無邊大悲雲。無邊
412c04║ 大喜心。無邊攝取眾生方便。佛子。我於佛剎
412c05║ 微塵數劫。念念如是觀於菩薩一一毛孔。已
412c06║ 所至處而不重至。已所見處而不重見。求其
412c07║ 邊際竟不可得。乃至見彼悉達太子。住於宮
412c08║ 中。采女圍遶。我以解脫力。觀於菩薩一一毛
412c09║ 孔。悉見三世法界中事。佛子。我唯得此觀
412c10║ 察菩薩三昧海解脫。如諸菩薩摩訶薩。究竟
412c11║ 無量諸方便海。為一切眾生現隨類身。為一
412c12║ 切眾生說隨樂行。於一一毛孔現無邊色相
412c13║ 海。知諸法性無性為性。知眾生性同虛空相
412c14║ 無有分別。知佛神力同於如如。

简体字

又于菩萨一一毛孔，见无边众生海种种住处、种种形貌、种种作业、种种诸根。又于菩萨一一毛孔，见三世诸菩萨无边行门，所谓：无边广大愿、无边差别地、无边波罗蜜、无边往昔事、无边大慈门、无边大悲云、无边大喜心、无边摄取众生方便。

“佛子，我于佛刹微尘数劫，念念如是观于菩萨一一毛孔，已所至处而不重至，已所见处而不重见，求其边际竟不可得，乃至见彼悉达太子住于宫中、采女围绕。我以解脱力，观于菩萨一一毛孔，悉见三世法界中事。

“佛子，我唯得此观察菩萨三昧海解脱。如诸菩萨摩诃萨，究竟无量诸方便海，为一切众生现随类身，为一切众生说随乐行，于一一毛孔现无边色相海；知诸法性无性为性，知众生性同虚空相无有分别，知佛神力同于如如，

Further, in every pore of the bodhisattva, I see the boundless ocean of beings in their many different kinds of abodes, in their many different forms and appearances, engaging in their many different kinds of karmic actions, and possessed of their many different kinds of faculties.

Further, in every pore of the bodhisattva, I see the boundlessly many gateways of practice of all bodhisattvas of the three periods of time, namely their boundlessly many vast vows, their boundlessly many different grounds, their boundlessly many *pāramitās*, their boundlessly many endeavors in previous lives, their boundlessly many gateways of great kindness, their boundlessly many clouds of great compassion, their boundlessly many thoughts of great rejoicing, and their boundlessly many skillful means in drawing forth beings.

Son of the Buddha, for kalpas as numerous as the atoms in a buddha *kṣetra*, in every mind-moment, I have contemplated in this way every pore of the bodhisattva, never revisiting any place already visited and never seeing again any place already seen. I proceeded in this way as I sought to find their far boundaries, but I was finally never able to discover them, even when I reached the point where I eventually saw Prince Siddhārtha dwelling in his palace, surrounded by female attendants.

With the power of the liberations, I have contemplated every pore of the bodhisattva and have seen in them all phenomena throughout the three periods of time and throughout the Dharma realm.

Son of the Buddha, I have acquired only this liberation known as "[sphere of] the contemplation of the ocean of all bodhisattvas' samādhis". As for the bodhisattva-mahāsattvas:

Who have reached the ultimate point of the ocean of the measureless ocean of skillful means;

Who appear for all beings in bodies adapted to their particular types;

Who teach all beings practices that accord with their inclinations;

Who in every pore manifest an ocean of boundlessly many different forms and appearances;

Who know the nature of all dharmas as consisting of the absence of any inherent nature whatsoever;

Who are without discrimination due to knowing that the nature of beings is characterized by their identity to empty space;

Who know the spiritual powers of the Buddha as identical to the suchness of suchness;

正體字

遍一切處示
412c15‖ 現無邊解脫境界。於一念中。能自在入廣大
412c16‖ 法界。遊戲一切諸地法門。而我云何能知能
412c17‖ 說彼功德行。善男子。此世界中。有佛母摩耶。
412c18‖ 汝詣彼問。菩薩云何修菩薩行。於諸世間無
412c19‖ 所染著。供養諸佛恒無休息。作菩薩業永不
412c20‖ 退轉。離一切障礙。入菩薩解脫不由於他。住
412c21‖ 一切菩薩道。詣一切如來所。攝一切眾生界。
412c22‖ 盡未來劫。修菩薩行。發大乘願。增長一切眾
412c23‖ 生善根。常無休息。爾時釋迦瞿波女。欲重明
412c24‖ 此解脫義。承佛神力。即說頌言
412c25‖ 若有見菩薩　修行種種行
412c26‖ 起善不善心　菩薩皆攝取
412c27‖ 乃往久遠世　過百剎塵劫
412c28‖ 有劫名清淨　世界名光明

简体字

遍一切处示现无边解脱境界；于一念中，能自在入广大法界，游戏一切诸地法门。而我云何能知能说彼功德行？

“善男子，此世界中，有佛母摩耶。汝诣彼问：菩萨云何修菩萨行，于诸世间无所染著，供养诸佛恒无休息，作菩萨业永不退转，离一切障碍、入菩萨解脱不由于他，住一切菩萨道，诣一切如来所，摄一切众生界，尽未来劫修菩萨行、发大乘愿，增长一切众生善根常无休息？”

尔时，释迦瞿波女，欲重明此解脱义，承佛神力即说颂言：

“若有见菩萨，修行种种行，
起善不善心，菩萨皆摄取。
乃往久远世，过百刹尘劫，
有劫名清净，世界名光明。

Who pervade all places manifesting boundless spheres of liberation;

Who, in but a single mind-moment, are able to freely enter the vast Dharma realm; and

Who possess easeful mastery of the Dharma gateways of all the grounds—

How could I know of or be able to speak about their meritorious qualities and practices?

Son of the Buddha, in this very world there is the mother of the Buddha, the Lady Māyā. You should go to her, pay your respects, and ask her:

How bodhisattvas cultivate the bodhisattva practices;

How they do so in all worlds and yet remain free of defiling attachments;

How they constantly make offerings to all buddhas without resting;

How they remain forever irreversible in doing the bodhisattva's works;

How they leave behind all obstacles;

How they enter the bodhisattva liberations without depending on others;

How they remain on the path of all bodhisattvas;

How they pay their respects to all *tathāgatas;*

How they gather in beings from all realms;

How they cultivate the bodhisattva practices throughout all kalpas of the future;

How they make the vows of the Great Vehicle; and

How they never desist from promoting the growth of all beings' roots of goodness.

Then, wishing to once again clarify the meaning of this liberation, aided by the Buddha's spiritual powers, the Śākya maiden, Gopā, spoke these verses:

Wherever there are those who see the bodhisattva
as he cultivates his various practices,
whether they think good or ill of him,
the bodhisattva gathers in all of them.

It was long ago in a far-off time
back beyond kalpas as numerous as the atoms in a hundred *kṣetras*
that there was a kalpa known as Pure
in which there was a world known as Radiance.

正體字

412c29 此劫佛興世　六十千萬億
413a01 最後天人主　號曰法幢燈
413a02 彼佛涅槃後　有王名智山
413a03 統領閻浮提　一切無怨敵
413a04 王有五百子　端正能勇健
413a05 其身悉清淨　見者皆歡喜
413a06 彼王及王子　信心供養佛
413a07 護持其法藏　亦樂勤修法
413a08 太子名善光　離垢多方便
413a09 諸相皆圓滿　見者無厭足
413a10 五百億人俱　出家行學道
413a11 勇猛堅精進　護持其佛法
413a12 王都名智樹　千億城圍遶
413a13 有林名靜德　眾寶所莊嚴
413a14 善光住彼林　廣宣佛正法
413a15 辯才智慧力　令眾悉清淨
413a16 有時因乞食　入彼王都城
413a17 行止極安詳　正知心不亂
413a18 城中有居士　號曰善名稱
413a19 我時為彼女　名為淨日光

简体字

此劫佛兴世，六十千万亿；
最后天人主，号曰法幢灯。
彼佛涅槃后，有王名智山，
统领阎浮提，一切无冤敌。
王有五百子，端正能勇健，
其身悉清净，见者皆欢喜。
彼王及王子，信心供养佛，
护持其法藏，亦乐勤修法。
太子名善光，离垢多方便，
诸相皆圆满，见者无厌足。
五百亿人俱，出家行学道，
勇猛坚精进，护持其佛法。
王都名智树，千亿城围绕；
有林名静德，众宝所庄严。
善光住彼林，广宣佛正法，
辩才智慧力，令众悉清净。
有时因乞食，入彼王都城，
行止极安详，正知心不乱。
城中有居士，号曰善名称；
我时为彼女，名为净日光。

In this kalpa, the buddhas who entered the world
were sixty thousand myriads of *koṭīs* in number.
The last among those lords of devas and men
was one then known as Dharma Banner Lamp.

After that Buddha passed into *nirvāṇa,*
there was a king whose name was Wisdom Mountain
who governed over all of Jambudvīpa
so that nowhere were there any adversaries there.

That monarch had in all five hundred sons
who were handsome and able to be brave and strong,
with bodies that were so completely pure
that those who saw them were all filled with joy.

That king as well as all his princely sons,
with faithful minds made offerings to the Buddha,
then guarded and preserved his Dharma treasury
while also enjoying the earnest cultivation of Dharma.

The crown prince who was known as Light of Goodness,
was possessed of immaculate purity and many skillful means.
All his signs were perfectly complete
so that all who saw him gazed at him insatiably.

Together with five hundred *koṭīs* of other people,
he left the home life to train there in the path.
Then he marshaled courage and solid vigor
to guard and preserve the Dharma of that buddha.

The royal capital known as Wisdom Tree
was ringed then by a thousand *koṭīs* of cities.
It had a forest known as Quiescent Virtue
adorned with all the many kinds of jewels.

Light of Goodness dwelt within that forest,
extensively teaching the right Dharma of the Buddha,
using the power of eloquence and wisdom
to enable al the multitudes to attain purity.

Once, in order to go on the almsround,
he entered into that royal capital city.
His deportment in moving or stopping was most serene,
and he was rightly aware, with undistracted mind.

Within that city, there was then a layman
known then by the name of Well Renowned.
At that time, it was I who was his daughter
known then by the name of Pure Sunlight.

正體字

413a20 時我於城中　遇見善光明
413a21 諸相極端嚴　其心生染著
413a22 次乞至我門　我心增愛染
413a23 即解身[1]瓔珞　并珠置鉢中
413a24 雖以愛染心　供養彼佛子
413a25 二百五十劫　不墮三惡趣
413a26 或生天王家　或作人王女
413a27 恒見善光明　妙相莊嚴身
413a28 此後所經劫　二百有五十
413a29 生於善現家　名為具妙德
413b01 時我見太子　而生尊重心
413b02 願得備瞻侍　幸蒙哀納受
413b03 我時與太子　覲佛勝日身
413b04 恭敬供養畢　即發菩提意
413b05 [2]於彼一劫中　六十億如來
413b06 最後佛世尊　名為廣大解
413b07 於彼得淨眼　了知諸法相
413b08 普見受生處　永除顛倒心
413b09 我得觀菩薩　三昧境解脫
413b10 一念入十方　不思議刹海

简体字

时我于城中，遇见善光明，
诸相极端严，其心生染著。
次乞至我门，我心增爱染，
即解身璎珞，并珠置钵中。
虽以爱染心，供养彼佛子；
二百五十劫，不堕三恶趣。
或生天王家，或作人王女，
恒见善光明，妙相庄严身。
此后所经劫，二百有五十，
生于善现家，名为具妙德。
时我见太子，而生尊重心，
愿得备瞻侍，幸蒙哀纳受。
我时与太子，觐佛胜日身，
恭敬供养毕，即发菩提意。
于彼一劫中，六十亿如来，
最后佛世尊，名为广大解。
于彼得净眼，了知诸法相，
普见受生处，永除颠倒心。
我得观菩萨，三昧境解脱，
一念入十方，不思议刹海。

At that time when I was in that city,
when I encountered there this Light of Goodness
who with all his marks was most majestic,
there arose within my mind an affectionate attachment.

When on his alms round, he next arrived at my door,
the taint of desire increased within my mind.
Right then I removed the necklace from my body
and placed it together with pearls into his almsbowl.

Although it had been due to desirous thoughts
that I made that offering to that son of the Buddha,
then, for a full two hundred and fifty kalpas,
I did not fall down into the three wretched destinies.

I was sometimes born into the clan of a deva king
and sometimes became the daughter of a human king,
but I always saw the body of Light of Goodness
that was adorned with all its marvelous marks.

After this, the kalpas through which I passed
came in all to a total of two hundred and fifty.
Then I was born into the family of Most Beautiful
where then I was named Replete in Marvelous Qualities.

It was at that time that I saw that prince
and brought forth thoughts of veneration for him.
I vowed to be able to fully serve him in the future
and enjoy the good fortune of his choosing to take me in.

Then I went together with the prince
to pay our respects to that Buddha, Supreme Solar Body.
When we had paid reverence to him and finished making offerings,
I right then made the resolve to realize bodhi.

It was during that single kalpa that there came
sixty *koṭīs* of *tathāgatas* arising in the world.
The very last of those buddhas, those *bhagavats*,
was known by the name of Vast Liberation.

It was under him that I attained the purified eye,
fully understood the characteristics of dharmas,
everywhere saw the places in which rebirth took place,
and forever rid myself of thoughts arising from inverted views.

I succeeded then in contemplating the bodhisattvas,
their spheres of samādhi and their liberations,
and then, in but a single mind-moment, I entered the ocean
of the inconceivably many *kṣetras* of the ten directions.

正體字

413b11 我見諸世界　淨穢種種別
413b12 於淨不貪樂　於穢不憎惡
413b13 普見諸世界　如來坐道場
413b14 皆於一念中　悉放無量光
413b15 一念能普入　不可說眾會
413b16 亦知彼一切　所得三昧門
413b17 一念能悉知　彼諸廣大行
413b18 無量地方便　及以諸願海
413b19 我觀菩薩身　無邊劫修行
413b20 一一毛孔量　求之不可得
413b21 一一毛孔剎　無數不可說
413b22 地水火風輪　靡不在其中
413b23 種種諸建立　種種諸形狀
413b24 種種體名號　無邊種莊嚴
413b25 我見諸剎海　不可說世界
413b26 及見其中佛　說法化眾生
413b27 不了菩薩身　及彼身諸業
413b28 亦不知心智　諸劫所行道
413b29 爾時善財童子。頂禮其足。遶無數匝。辭退而
413c01 去

简体字

我见诸世界，净秽种种别，
于净不贪乐，于秽不憎恶。
普见诸世界，如来坐道场，
皆于一念中，悉放无量光。
一念能普入，不可说众会；
亦知彼一切，所得三昧门。
一念能悉知，彼诸广大行，
无量地方便，及以诸愿海。
我观菩萨身，无边劫修行，
一一毛孔量，求之不可得。
一一毛孔刹，无数不可说，
地水火风轮，靡不在其中。
种种诸建立，种种诸形状，
种种体名号，无边种庄严。
我见诸刹海，不可说世界；
及见其中佛，说法化众生。
不了菩萨身，及彼身诸业；
亦不知心智，诸劫所行道。”

尔时，善财童子顶礼其足，绕无数匝，辞退而去。

It was then that I saw all the worlds,
both pure and defiled, with many different distinctions.
For those that are pure I did not have any attraction,
and for those that are defiled, I did not have any loathing.

Everywhere I saw within all worlds
the *tathāgatas* sitting at their sites of enlightenment,
all of whom, in but a single mind-moment,
then emanated measureless displays of light.

In a single mind-moment, I could everywhere enter
an ineffable number of their congregations
while also coming to know with regard to them all,
the samādhi gateways that each of them had gained.

In a single mind-moment, I was able to know
all the vast practices that those there had pursued,
the countless skillful means used on their grounds,
and also the ocean of all the vows they had made.

I contemplated the bodhisattva's body
and the practices he cultivated for boundless kalpas,
but, as for the measure of what was in every pore,
seeking to assess it, one could never know it all.

The *kṣetras* there in each and every pore
were so numberless as to be ineffably many.
Of the spheres of earth, of water, fire, and wind,
there were none of them not present there within them.

They had many different bases for their foundations,
many different kinds of shapes and appearances,
many different substances and names,
and boundlessly many varieties of adornments.

I saw within all the oceans of *kṣetras*
the ineffable number of worlds that they contained
and also saw the buddhas there within them
as they taught the Dharma there to teach those beings.

I never fully fathomed the bodhisattva's body
or all the deeds that his body carries out.
I also never understood the wisdom of his mind
or all the paths he has traveled in all those kalpas.

Sudhana the Youth then bowed down in reverence at her feet and circumambulated her countless times. He then respectfully withdrew and departed.

正體字

413c05‖ [3]大方廣佛華嚴經卷[4]第七十六
413c08‖ [8]入法界品第三十九之十七
413c09‖ 爾時善財童子。一心欲詣摩耶夫人所。即時
413c10‖ 獲得觀佛境界智。作如是念。是善知識。遠離
413c11‖ 世間。住無所住。超過六處。離一切著。知無礙
413c12‖ 道。具淨法身。以如幻業而現化身。以如幻智
413c13‖ 而觀世間。以如幻願而持佛身。隨意生身。無
413c14‖ 生滅身。無來去身。非虛實身。不變壞身。[9]無
413c15‖ 起盡身。所有諸相皆一相身。離二邊身。無依
413c16‖ 處身。無窮盡身。離諸分別如影現身。知如夢
413c17‖ 身。了如像身。如淨日身。普於十方而化現身。
413c18‖ 住於三世無變異身。非身心身。猶如虛空所
413c19‖ 行無礙。超諸世眼。唯是普賢淨目所見。如是
413c20‖ 之人。我今云何而得親近承事供養。與其同
413c21‖ 住。觀其狀貌。聽其音聲。思其語言。受其教
413c22‖ 誨。

简体字

大方广佛华严经卷第七十六

入法界品第三十九之十七

尔时，善财童子一心欲诣摩耶夫人所，即时获得观佛境界智，作如是念："是善知识，远离世间，住无所住，超过六处，离一切著，知无碍道，具净法身，以如幻业而现化身，以如幻智而观世间，以如幻愿而持佛身、随意生身、无生灭身、无来去身、非虚实身、不变坏身、无起尽身、所有诸相皆一相身、离二边身、无依处身、无穷尽身、离诸分别如影现身、知如梦身、了如像身、如净日身、普于十方而化现身、住于三世无变异身、非身心身，犹如虚空，所行无碍，超诸世眼，唯是普贤净目所见。如是之人，我今云何而得亲近承事供养、与其同住、观其状貌、听其音声、思其语言、受其教诲？"

41 – Māyā

At that time, as Sudhana the Youth formed a single-minded wish to go and pay his respects to the Lady Māyā, he immediately acquired the knowledge that enabled him to contemplate the sphere of a buddha. He then thought in this way:

> These good spiritual guides have become detached from the world and dwell without having anywhere they dwell. They have transcended the six sense faculties, have abandoned all attachments, know the unimpeded path, and possess the pure Dharma body. With their illusion-like actions, they manifest transformation bodies, with their illusion-like knowledge, they contemplate the world, and with their illusion-like vows, they sustain the bodies of a buddha. They have:
>
> Bodies that are created at will by the mind;
> Bodies that are neither produced nor destroyed;
> Bodies that have no coming or going;
> Bodies that are neither unreal nor real;
> Bodies that do not deteriorate;
> Bodies that have neither any arising nor any cessation;
> Bodies whose signs are all included in one sign;
> Bodies that transcend duality;
> Bodies that have no place on which they rely;
> Bodies that are endless;
> Bodies that transcend all discriminations and appear as mere reflections;
> Bodies that are known like dreams;
> Bodies that are perceived like images [in a mirror];
> Bodies that are like the clearly shining sun;
> Bodies that are transformationally created throughout the ten directions;
> Bodies that remain unchanging throughout the three periods of time; and
> Bodies that are neither physical nor mental.
>
> These [good spiritual guides] are as unimpeded in their movement as if they were traveling through empty space. They surpass the worldly eye's ability to see and are seen only by the purified eyes of Samantabhadra. How could I draw near to people such as these, serve them, make offerings to them, dwell together with them, contemplate their appearance, listen to their voice, reflect on their words, and receive their instructions?

正體字

作是念已。有主城神。名曰寶眼。眷屬圍
413c23‖ 遶。於虛空中。而現其身。種種妙物以為嚴飾。
413c24‖ 手持無量眾色寶華。以散善財。作如是言。善
413c25‖ 男子。應守護心城。謂不貪一切生死境界。應
413c26‖ 莊嚴心城。謂專意趣求如來十力。[10]應淨治心
413c27‖ 城。謂畢究斷除慳嫉諂誑。應清涼心城。謂
413c28‖ 思惟一切諸法實性。應增長心城。謂成[11]辦一
413c29‖ 切助道之法。應嚴飾心城。謂造立諸禪解脫
414a01‖ 宮殿。應照[1]耀心城。謂普入一切諸佛道場聽
414a02‖ 受般若波羅蜜[2]法。應增益心城。謂普攝一切
414a03‖ 佛方便道。應堅固心城。謂恒勤修習普賢行
414a04‖ 願。應防護心城。謂常專禦扞惡友魔軍。應廓
414a05‖ 徹心城。謂開引一切佛智光明。應善補心城。
414a06‖ 謂聽受一切佛所說法。應扶助心城。謂深信
414a07‖ 一切佛功德海。應廣大心城。謂大慈普及一
414a08‖ 切世間。應善覆心城。謂集眾善法。以覆其
414a09‖ 上應寬廣心城。謂大悲哀愍一切眾生。應開
414a10‖ 心城門。謂悉捨所有隨應給施。

简体字

作是念已，有主城神，名曰宝眼，眷属围绕，于虚空中而现其身，种种妙物以为严饰，手持无量众色宝华以散善财，作如是言："善男子，应守护心城，谓不贪一切生死境界；应庄严心城，谓专意趣求如来十力；应净治心城，谓毕究断除悭嫉谄诳；应清凉心城，谓思惟一切诸法实性；应增长心城，谓成办一切助道之法；应严饰心城，谓造立诸禅解脱宫殿；应照耀心城，谓普入一切诸佛道场听受般若波罗蜜法；应增益心城，谓普摄一切佛方便道；应坚固心城，谓恒勤修习普贤行愿；应防护心城，谓常专御捍恶友、魔军；应廓彻心城，谓开引一切佛智光明；应善补心城，谓听受一切佛所说法；应扶助心城，谓深信一切佛功德海；应广大心城，谓大慈普及一切世间；应善覆心城，谓集众善法以覆其上；应宽广心城，谓大悲哀愍一切众生；应开心城门，谓悉舍所有随应给施；

After he had this thought, a city spirit name Jewel Eye manifested her body in the sky, surrounded by her retinue and adorned with many different marvelous adornments. She held in her hands countless jewel flowers of various colors that she scattered over Sudhana. She then spoke to him, saying:

Son of Good Family:

You should guard the city of the mind by not craving any of *saṃsāra*'s spheres of sense experience;

You should adorn the city of the mind by focusing your resolve on the quest to attain the Tathāgata's ten powers;

You should purify the city of the mind by completely cutting off all miserliness, jealousy, flattery, and deviousness;

You should bring clarity and coolness to the city of the mind by meditative contemplation on the true nature of all dharmas;

You should grow the city of the mind by becoming completely accomplished in all the provisions for enlightenment;

You should beautify the city of the mind by creating palaces of the *dhyāna* concentrations and liberations;

You should illuminate the city of the mind by entering the congregations of all buddhas and listening to their teachings on the *prajñāpāramitā*;

You should augment the city of the mind by gathering together the requisites for all buddhas' path of skillful means;

You should fortify the city of the mind by constant and diligent cultivation of the conduct and vows of Samantabhadra;

You should defend the city of the mind by always focusing on resisting bad friends and the armies of Māra;

You should enlarge the city of the mind by opening it up and letting in the wisdom light of all buddhas;

You should thoroughly restore the city of the mind by listening to the Dharma taught by all buddhas;

You should support the city of the mind by deep faith in all buddhas' ocean of meritorious qualities;

You should expand the city of the mind by extending great kindness to the entire world;

You should skillfully shelter the city of the mind by accumulating the many kinds of good dharmas with which to cover it;

You should broaden the city of the mind by extending great compassion and deep sympathy to all beings;

You should open the gates of the city of the mind by relinquishing all your possessions and bestowing them on others in accordance with their needs;

正體字

應密護心城。
414a11‖ 謂防諸惡欲不令得入。應嚴肅心城。謂逐諸
414a12‖ 惡法不令其住。應決定心城。謂集一切智助
414a13‖ 道之法恒無退轉。應安立心城。謂正念三世
414a14‖ 一切如來所有境界。應瑩徹心城。謂明達一
414a15‖ 切佛正法輪修多羅中所有法門種種緣起。
414a16‖ 應部分心城。謂普曉示一切眾生皆令得見
414a17‖ 薩婆若道。應住持心城。謂發一切三世如來
414a18‖ 諸大願海。應富[3]實心城。謂集一切周遍法界
414a19‖ 大福德聚。應令心城明了。謂普知眾生根欲
414a20‖ 等法。應令心城自在。謂普攝一切十方法界。
414a21‖ 應令心城清淨。謂正念一切諸佛如來。應知
414a22‖ 心城自性。謂知一切法皆無有性。應知心城
414a23‖ 如幻。謂以一切智了諸法性。

简体字

应密护心城，谓防诸恶欲不令得入；应严肃心城，谓逐诸恶法不令其住；应决定心城，谓集一切智助道之法恒无退转；应安立心城，谓正念三世一切如来所有境界；应莹彻心城，谓明达一切佛正法轮修多罗中所有法门种种缘起；应部分心城，谓普晓示一切众生皆令得见萨婆若道；应住持心城，谓发一切三世如来诸大愿海；应富贵心城，谓集一切周遍法界大福德聚；应令心城明了，谓普知众生根欲等法；应令心城自在，谓普摄一切十方法界；应令心城清净，谓正念一切诸佛如来；应知心城自性，谓知一切法皆无有性；应知心城如幻，谓以一切智了诸法性。

You should tightly guard the city of the mind by warding off all unwholesome desires and never allowing them to enter;

You should impose strict discipline on the city of the mind by banishing all evil dharmas and never allowing them to remain within;

You should impose resolute decisiveness on the city of the mind by becoming forever irreversible in accumulating the provisions for the path to all-knowledge;

You should securely establish the city of the mind by abiding in right mindfulness of the domain of all *tathāgatas* of the three periods of time;

You should brighten and clarify the city of the mind by gaining a clear comprehension of the many different conditions for the arising of all the Dharma gateways contained in the sutras produced by all buddhas' turning of the wheel of right Dharma;

You should govern the city of the mind by everywhere instructing all beings, thereby enabling them to see the path to all-knowledge;

You should preserve the city of the mind by establishing the ocean of great vows of all *tathāgatas* of the three periods of time;

You should enrich the city of the mind by collecting an immense accumulation of merit that pervades the entire Dharma realm;

You should brighten the city of the mind by thoroughly knowing beings' faculties, dispositions, and other such dharmas;

You should achieve sovereign mastery over the city of the mind by gathering in everyone throughout the ten directions of the Dharma realm;

You should cleanse the city of the mind by right mindfulness of all buddhas, all *tathāgatas*;

You should know the essential nature of the city of the mind by realizing that all dharmas are devoid of any [inherently existent] nature; and

You should know the city of the mind to be like a magical conjuration by completely understanding the nature of all dharmas with all-knowledge.

Son of the Buddha, if the bodhisattva-mahāsattva can purify the city of the mind in these ways, then he will be able to accumulate all good dharmas. And how is this accomplished? This is accomplished by becoming entirely rid of all obstacles, namely obstacles to seeing the Buddha, obstacles to hearing the Dharma, obstacles to making offerings to the Tathāgata, obstacles to gathering in all beings, and obstacles to purifying buddha lands.

正體字

佛子。菩薩摩訶
414a24| 薩。若能如是淨修心城。則能積集一切善法。
414a25| 何以故。蠲除一切諸障難故。所謂見佛障。聞
414a26| 法障。供養如來障。攝諸眾生障。淨佛國土障。
414a27| 善男子。菩薩摩訶薩。以離如是諸障難故。若
414a28| 發希求善知識心。不用功力。則便得見。乃
414a29| 至究竟必當成佛。爾時有身眾神。名蓮華法
414b01| 德。及妙華光明無量諸神。前後圍遶。從道場
414b02| 出住虛空中。於善財前。以妙音聲。種種稱歎
414b03| 摩耶夫人。從其耳璫放無量色相光明網。普
414b04| 照無邊諸佛世界。令善財見十方國土一切
414b05| 諸佛。其光明網。右遶世間。經一匝已。然後還
414b06| 來。入善財頂。乃至遍入身諸毛孔。善財即得
414b07| 淨光明眼。永離一切愚癡闇故。得離翳眼。能
414b08| 了一切眾生性故。得離垢眼。能觀一切法性
414b09| 門故。[4]得淨慧眼。能觀一切佛國性故。得毘盧
414b10| 遮那眼。見佛法身故。得普光明眼。見佛平等
414b11| 不思議身故。得無礙光眼。觀察一切剎海成
414b12| 壞故。得普照眼。見十方佛起大方便轉正法
414b13| 輪故。得普境界眼。見無量佛以自在力調伏
414b14| 眾生故。得普見眼。覩一切剎諸佛出興故。時
414b15| 有守護菩薩法堂羅剎鬼王。名曰善眼。與其
414b16| 眷屬萬羅剎俱。於虛空中。以眾妙華。散善財
414b17| 上。作如是言。

简体字

“佛子，菩萨摩诃萨若能如是净修心城，则能积集一切善法。何以故？蠲除一切诸障难故，所谓：见佛障、闻法障、供养如来障、摄诸众生障、净佛国土障。善男子，菩萨摩诃萨以离如是诸障难故，若发希求善知识心，不用功力则便得见，乃至究竟必当成佛。”

尔时，有身众神，名莲华法德及妙华光明，无量诸神前后围绕，从道场出，住虚空中，于善财前，以妙音声，种种称叹摩耶夫人，从其耳珰放无量色相光明网，普照无边诸佛世界，令善财见十方国土一切诸佛。其光明网，右绕世间，经一匝已，然后还来，入善财顶，乃至遍入身诸毛孔。善财即得净光明眼，永离一切愚痴暗故；得离翳眼，能了一切众生性故；得离垢眼，能观一切法性门故；得净慧眼，能观一切佛国性故；得毗卢遮那眼，见佛法身故；得普光明眼，见佛平等不思议身故；得无碍光眼，观察一切刹海成坏故；得普照眼，见十方佛起大方便转正法轮故；得普境界眼，见无量佛以自在力调伏众生故；得普见眼，睹一切刹诸佛出兴故。

时，有守护菩萨法堂罗刹鬼王，名曰善眼，与其眷属万罗刹俱，于虚空中，以众妙华，散善财上，作如是言：

Son of Good Family, by abandoning all such obstacles as these, if the bodhisattva-mahāsattva wishes to find good spiritual guides, even without needing to exert any effort, he will be able to encounter them and then he will finally become definitely bound to attain buddhahood.

There was then a many-bodied spirit named "Lotus Dharma Virtue" who, surrounded by countless spirits emanating a marvelous floral radiance, came there from the site of enlightenment and dwelt in space directly before Sudhana. Then, with a sublime voice, she praised the Lady Māya in many different ways. From her earrings, she emanated a web of light rays of countless hues that everywhere illuminated boundlessly many buddha worlds and enabled Sudhana to see all buddhas in the lands of the ten directions. The web of light rays went around the world in a rightward direction and then, after having encircled it one time, it returned and entered the crown of Sudhana's head, proceeding then to enter all the pores of his body. Sudhana then acquired the following:

He acquired the eye of pure light with which he forever left behind all the darkness of delusion;

He acquired the eye that is free of all obscurations with which he was able to completely understand the nature of all beings;

He acquired the immaculately pure eye with which he contemplated the gateway to the nature of all dharmas;

He acquired the eye of pure wisdom with which he was able to contemplate the nature of all buddha lands;

He acquired the eye of Vairocana with which he saw the Dharma body of the buddha;

He acquired the eye of universal radiance with which he saw the uniformly identical and inconceivable body of the Buddha;[9]

He acquired the eye of unimpeded light with which he contemplated the creation and destruction of the ocean of all *kṣetras;*

He acquired the eye of universal illumination with which he saw the buddhas of the ten directions producing great skillful means to turn the wheel of right Dharma;

He acquired the eye of the universal realms with which he saw countless buddhas using their miraculous powers to train beings; and

He acquired the eye of universal vision with which he saw the arising of all buddhas in all *kṣetras.*

Then there was a king of the *rākṣasas* by the name of Good Eye, a guardian of the bodhisattvas' Dharma halls, who appeared there in space together with his retinue of a myriad *rākṣasas.* He scattered many marvelous flowers over Sudhana and then said:

正體字

善男子。菩薩。成就十法。則得
414b18‖ 親近諸善知識。何等為十。所謂其心清淨離
414b19‖ 諸諂誑。大悲平等普攝眾生。[5]知諸眾生無有
414b20‖ 真實趣一切智心不退轉。以信解力普入一
414b21‖ 切諸佛道場。得淨慧眼了諸法性。大慈平等
414b22‖ 普覆眾生。以智光明廓諸妄境。以甘露雨滌
414b23‖ 生死熱。以廣大眼徹鑒諸法。心常隨順諸善
414b24‖ 知識。是為十。復次佛子。菩薩。成就十種三
414b25‖ 昧門。則常現見諸善知識。何等為十。所謂法
414b26‖ 空清淨輪三昧。觀察十方海三昧。於一切境
414b27‖ 界不捨離不缺減三昧。普見一切佛出興三
414b28‖ 昧。集一切功德藏三昧。心恒不捨善知識三
414b29‖ 昧。常見一切善知識生諸佛功德三昧。常不
414c01‖ 離一切善知識三昧。常供養一切善知識三
414c02‖ 昧。常於一切善知識所無過失三昧。

简体字

“善男子，菩萨成就十法，则得亲近诸善知识。何等为十？所谓：其心清净离诸谄诳；大悲平等普摄众生，知诸众生无有真实；趣一切智，心不退转；以信解力普入一切诸佛道场；得净慧眼了诸法性；大慈平等普覆众生；以智光明廓诸妄境；以甘露雨涤生死热；以广大眼彻鉴诸法；心常随顺诸善知识。是为十。

“复次，佛子，菩萨成就十种三昧门，则常现见诸善知识。何等为十？所谓：法空清净轮三昧、观察十方海三昧、于一切境界不舍离不缺减三昧、普见一切佛出兴三昧、集一切功德藏三昧、心恒不舍善知识三昧、常见一切善知识生诸佛功德三昧、常不离一切善知识三昧、常供养一切善知识三昧、常于一切善知识所无过失三昧。

Son of Good Family, if a bodhisattva perfects ten dharmas, then he can draw near to good spiritual guides. What are these ten? They are as follows:

With a pure mind, he abandons all flattery and deception.

With great compassion, he equally gathers in all beings;

He knows that all beings are devoid of any true reality;

His resolve to progress toward all-knowledge is irreversible;

Through the power of resolute faith, he everywhere enters the sites of enlightenment of all buddhas;

He acquires the purified wisdom eye by which he completely understands the nature of all dharmas;

With great kindness, he equally shelters all beings;

With the light of wisdom, he clears away all false spheres of experience;

He uses the rain of the elixir of immortality to rinse away the feverish heat of *saṃsāra*; and

He uses the eye of vast vision to engage in a penetrating examination of all dharmas with a mind that always complies with the guidance of his good spiritual guides.

These are the ten. Further, Son of the Buddha, if the bodhisattva perfects ten kinds of samādhi gateways, then he is always able to directly see all good spiritual guides. What are those ten? They are as follows:

The samādhi of the Dharma sky's sphere of purity;

The samādhi in which one contemplates the ocean of the ten directions;

The samādhi in which one neither relinquishes nor insufficiently attends to the objective sphere;

The samādhi in which one everywhere sees all buddhas appearing in the world;

The samādhi in which one accumulates the treasury of all meritorious qualities;

The samādhi in which one's mind never abandons the good spiritual guides;

The samādhi in which one always sees all good spiritual guides and develops the meritorious qualities of all buddhas;

The samādhi in which one is never separated from all the good spiritual guides;

The samādhi in which one always makes offerings to all good spiritual guides; and

The samādhi in which one never transgresses against the good spiritual guides.

正體字

佛子。菩
414c03‖ 薩。成就此十三昧門。常得親近諸善知識。又
414c04‖ 得善知識轉一切佛法輪三昧。得此三昧已。
414c05‖ 悉知諸佛體性平等。處處值遇諸善知識。說
414c06‖ 是語時。善財童子。仰[6]視空中而答之言。善
414c07‖ 哉善哉。汝為哀愍攝受我故。方便教我。見
414c08‖ 善知識。願為我說。云何往詣善知識所。於
414c09‖ 何方處城邑聚落。求善知識。羅剎答言。善男
414c10‖ 子。汝應普禮十方求善知識。正念思惟一切
414c11‖ 境界。求善知識。勇猛自在遍遊十方。求善知
414c12‖ 識。觀身觀心如夢如影。求善知識。爾時善財。
414c13‖ 受行其教。即時覩見。大寶蓮華從地[7]涌出。
414c14‖ [8]金剛為莖。妙寶為藏。摩尼為葉。光明寶王
414c15‖ 以為其[9]臺。眾寶色香以為其鬚。無數寶網彌
414c16‖ 覆其上。於其臺上有一樓觀。名普[10]納十方法
414c17‖ 界藏。奇妙嚴飾。金剛為地。千柱行列。一切皆
414c18‖ 以摩尼寶成。閻浮檀金以為其壁。眾寶[11]瓔珞
414c19‖ 四面垂下。階陛欄楯。周匝莊嚴。其樓觀中。有
414c20‖ 如意寶蓮華之座。種種眾寶以為嚴飾。

简体字

佛子，菩萨成就此十三昧门，常得亲近诸善知识，又得善知识转一切佛法轮三昧；得此三昧已，悉知诸佛体性平等，处处值遇诸善知识。”

说是语时，善财童子仰视空中而答之言：“善哉！善哉！汝为哀愍摄受我故，方便教我见善知识。愿为我说：云何往诣善知识所？于何方处城邑聚落求善知识？”

罗刹答言：“善男子，汝应普礼十方，求善知识；正念思惟一切境界，求善知识；勇猛自在遍游十方，求善知识；观身观心如梦如影，求善知识。”

尔时，善财受行其教，即时睹见大宝莲华从地涌出，金刚为茎，妙宝为藏，摩尼为叶，光明宝王以为其台，众宝色香以为其须，无数宝网弥覆其上。于其台上，有一楼观，名普纳十方法界藏，奇妙严饰，金刚为地，千柱行列，一切皆以摩尼宝成，阎浮檀金以为其壁，众宝璎珞四面垂下，阶陛、栏楯周匝庄严。其楼观中，有如意宝莲华之座，种种众宝以为严饰，

Son of the Buddha, if the bodhisattva perfects these ten samādhi gateways, then he is always able to draw near to the good spiritual guides and is also able to acquire "the samādhi of the good spiritual guides' turning of the Dharma wheel of all buddhas." After he acquires this samādhi, he knows the uniform equality of the essential nature of all buddhas and then meets the good spiritual guides in place after place.

When he spoke these words, Sudhana the Youth looked up into the sky and replied to him, saying:

This is good indeed, good indeed, that, to take pity on me and assist me, you used skillful means to teach me how to see the good spiritual guides. Please teach me how to go and pay my respects to the good spiritual guides by showing me in which region, city, or village I may search for the good spiritual guides.

The *rākṣasa* then replied, saying:

Son of Good Family:

You should seek the good spiritual guides by paying reverence in all ten directions;

You should seek the good spiritual guides by reflecting with right mindfulness on all spheres of experience;

You should seek the good spiritual guides by courageously and freely roaming the ten directions; and

You should seek the good spiritual guides by contemplating the body and mind as like mere dreams and mere reflections.

Sudhana then accepted and began to carry out his instructions when, all of a sudden, he saw an immense jeweled lotus flower spring forth from the earth. It had a stem made of vajra, a pod made of marvelous jewels, petals made of *maṇi* jewels, a dais made of light-emanating sovereign jewels, and stamens made of incense the color of the many kinds of jewels. It was sheltered by countless jeweled nets suspended over it.

Atop the lotus dais, there was a viewing tower known as the Chamber Completely Containing the Ten Directions of the Dharma Realm. It was adorned in exotic and marvelous ways. Its grounds were made of vajra. It had a thousand pillars arranged in rows that were all made of *maṇi* jewels. Its walls were made of *jambūnada* gold. Strands of the many kinds of jewels hung down on all four sides and it was adorned with stairways and railings all around it.

Within that viewing tower was a lotus throne made of wish-fulfilling jewels that was adorned with the many different kinds of jewels.

正體字

妙寶
414c21‖ 欄楯。寶衣間列。寶帳寶網。以覆其上。眾寶
414c22‖ 繒幡。周匝垂下。微風徐動。光流響發。寶華幢
414c23‖ 中雨眾妙華。寶鈴鐸中出美音聲。寶戶牖間
414c24‖ 垂諸[*]瓔珞。摩尼身中流出香水。寶象口中出
414c25‖ 蓮華網。寶師子口吐妙香雲。梵形寶輪出隨
414c26‖ 樂音。金剛寶鈴出諸菩薩大願之音。寶月幢
414c27‖ 中出佛化形。淨藏寶王現三世佛受生次第。
414c28‖ 日藏摩尼放大光明遍照十方一切佛剎。摩
414c29‖ 尼寶王。放一切佛圓滿光明。毘盧遮那摩尼
415a01‖ 寶王。興供養雲供養一切諸佛如來。如意珠
415a02‖ 王。念念示現普賢神變充滿法界。須彌寶王。
415a03‖ 出天宮殿天諸采女。種種妙音。歌讚如來不
415a04‖ 可思議。微妙功德。爾時善財。見如是座。復有
415a05‖ 無量眾座圍遶。摩耶夫人。在彼座上於一切
415a06‖ 眾生前。現淨色身。所謂超三界色身已出一
415a07‖ 切諸有趣故。[1]隨心樂色。身於一切世間無所
415a08‖ 著故。普周遍色身等於一切眾生數故。無等
415a09‖ 比色身令一切眾生滅倒見故。

简体字

妙宝栏楯，宝衣间列，宝帐、宝网以覆其上，众宝缯幡周匝垂下，微风徐动，光流响发；宝华幢中雨众妙华，宝铃铎中出美音声，宝户牖间垂诸璎珞，摩尼身中流出香水，宝象口中出莲华网，宝师子口吐妙香云，梵形宝轮出随乐音，金刚宝铃出诸菩萨大愿之音，宝月幢中出佛化形，净藏宝王现三世佛受生次第，日藏摩尼放大光明遍照十方一切佛刹，摩尼宝王放一切佛圆满光明，毗卢遮那摩尼宝王兴供养云供养一切诸佛如来，如意珠王念念示现普贤神变充满法界，须弥宝王出天宫殿，天诸采女种种妙音歌赞如来不可思议微妙功德。

尔时，善财见如是座，复有无量众座围绕，摩耶夫人在彼座上，于一切众生前，现净色身。所谓：超三界色身，已出一切诸有趣故；随心乐色身，于一切世间无所著故；普周遍色身，等于一切众生数故；无等比色身，令一切众生灭倒见故；

It had railings made of marvelous gems along which hung jeweled robes. It was covered from above by jeweled banners and jeweled netting and was surrounded by hanging adornments of jeweled streamers and jeweled pennants.

As a soft breeze slowly wafted through, there came a flow of radiant light and the emanation of echoing sounds. A rain of many marvelous flowers descended from the jeweled floral banners and the jeweled chimes and bells rang with exquisitely lovely sounds.

There were gemstone necklace strands dangling from the jambs of the jeweled doors and windows. Perfume flowed from the body of *maṇi* jewels, nets of lotus flowers came forth from the mouths of jeweled elephants, clouds of marvelous incense streamed forth from the mouths of jeweled lions, a jeweled wheel like that owned by Brahmā created delightful sounds, bells adorned with vajra and jewels emanated the sounds of all bodhisattvas' great vows, jeweled moon banners issued buddhas' transformation bodies, sovereign treasury-of-purity jewels displayed the sequence of the births of all buddhas of the three periods of time, solar-core *maṇi* jewels emanated bright lights that everywhere illuminated all the *kṣetras* of the buddhas of the ten directions, sovereign *maṇi* jewels emanated light like the aura of all buddhas, sovereign *vairocana maṇi* jewels emanated clouds of offerings as gifts to all the buddhas, the *tathāgatas,* in every mind-moment, sovereign wish-fulfilling pearls displayed the spiritual transformations of Samantabhadra as they completely fill the Dharma realm, and a sovereign *sumeru* jewel streamed forth heavenly palaces as celestial maidens sang in many different marvelous voices their praises of the Tathāgata's inconceivable and sublime meritorious qualities.

When Sudhana saw this throne, he also saw an immeasurably large congregation seated all around it as the Lady Māyā sat on that throne, directly manifesting before all those beings pure form bodies of these sorts:

Form bodies that have transcended the three realms of existence, by having already escaped all rebirth destinies in the realms of existence;

Form bodies adapted to beings' mental dispositions, by having no attachment to anything in the world;

Form bodies that are pervasively present in all places, by existing in numbers equal to that of all beings;

Form bodies that are incomparable, by enabling all beings to extinguish their inverted views;

正體字

無量種色身隨
415a10‖ 眾生心種種現故。無邊相色身普現種種諸
415a11‖ 形相故。普對現色身以大自在而示現故。化
415a12‖ 一切色身隨其所應而現前故。恒示現色身
415a13‖ 盡眾生界而無盡故。無去色身於一切趣無
415a14‖ 所滅故。無來色身於諸世間無所出故。不生
415a15‖ 色身無生起故。不滅色身離語言故。非實色
415a16‖ 身得如實故。非虛色身隨世現故。無動色
415a17‖ 身生滅永離故。不壞色身法性不壞故。無相
415a18‖ 色身言語道斷故。一相色身無相為相故。如
415a19‖ 像色身隨心應現故。如幻色身幻智所生故。
415a20‖ 如焰色身但[2]想所持故。如影色身隨願現生
415a21‖ 故。如夢色[3]身隨心而現故。法界色身性淨
415a22‖ 如空故。

简体字

无量种色身，随众生心种种现故；无边相色身，普现种种诸形相故；普对现色身，以大自在而示现故；化一切色身，随其所应而现前故；恒示现色身，尽众生界而无尽故；无去色身，于一切趣无所灭故；无来色身，于诸世间无所出故；不生色身，无生起故；不灭色身，离语言故；非实色身，得如实故；非虚色身，随世现故；无动色身，生灭永离故；不坏色身，法性不坏故；无相色身，言语道断故；一相色身，无相为相故；如像色身，随心应现故；如幻色身，幻智所生故；如焰色身，但想所持故；如影色身，随愿现生故；如梦色身，随心而现故；法界色身，性净如空故；

Form bodies of countless types, because they manifest in many different ways adapted to the minds of beings;

Form bodies with boundlessly many different appearances, because they manifest with many different forms and features;

Form bodies that appear everywhere before beings, through manifesting great miraculous powers;

Form bodies that are transformationally produced for everyone, by appearing before beings in accordance with what is fitting for them;

Form bodies that are constantly manifested, by never ending even when the realms of beings come to an end;

Form bodies that never depart, by never disappearing from any of the rebirth destinies;

Form bodies that have no coming forth, because they have no going forth into the world;

Form bodies that are unborn, by having no arising at all;

Form bodies that are not destroyed, that are beyond the grasp of verbal descriptions;

Form bodies that are not real, for they have attained the reality of suchness;

Form bodies that are not false, because they appear in accordance with the circumstances in the world;

Form bodies that are unshakable, because they have transcended both arising and cessation;

Form bodies that are indestructible, because the nature of dharmas is indestructible;

Form bodies that are signless, for they have completely cut short the path of verbal description;

Form bodies that have but one characteristic sign, for their characteristic sign is signlessness;

Form bodies that resemble mere reflected images, because they are manifested in accordance with what is appropriate for beings' minds;

Form bodies that are like illusory conjurations, because they are produced by wisdom that knows all phenomena to be like illusory conjurations;

Form bodies that are like mirages, because they are sustained solely through perceptions;

Form bodies that are like reflections, because they are manifested in accordance with vows;

Form bodies that are like dreams, because they are manifested as adaptations to others' minds;

Form bodies that are like the Dharma realm, because their nature is as pure as empty space;

正體字

大悲色身常護眾生故。無礙色身念
415a23‖ 念周遍法界故。無邊色身普淨一切眾生故。
415a24‖ 無量色身超出一切語言故。無住色身願度
415a25‖ 一切世間故。無處色身恒化眾生不斷故。無
415a26‖ 生色身幻願所成故。無勝色身超諸世間故。
415a27‖ 如實色身定心所現故。不生色身隨眾生業
415a28‖ 而出現故。如意珠色身普滿一切眾生願故。
415a29‖ 無分別色身。但隨眾生分別起故。離分別色
415b01‖ 身一切眾生不能知故。無盡色身盡諸眾生
415b02‖ 生死際故。清淨色身同於如來無分別故。如
415b03‖ 是身者。非色所有。色相如影像故。非受。世間
415b04‖ 苦受究竟滅故。非想。但隨眾生想所現故。非
415b05‖ 行。依如幻業而成就故。離識。菩薩願智空無
415b06‖ 性故。

简体字

大悲色身，常护众生故；无碍色身，念念周遍法界故；无边色身，普净一切众生故；无量色身，超出一切语言故；无住色身，愿度一切世间故；无处色身，恒化众生不断故；无生色身，幻愿所成故；无胜色身，超诸世间故；如实色身，定心所现故；不生色身，随众生业而出现故；如意珠色身，普满一切众生愿故；无分别色身，但随众生分别起故；离分别色身，一切众生不能知故；无尽色身，尽诸众生生死际故；清净色身，同于如来无分别故。如是身者，非色，所有色相如影像故；非受，世间苦受究竟灭故；非想，但随众生想所现故；非行，依如幻业而成就故；离识，菩萨愿智空无性故，

Form bodies associated with the great compassion, because they always protect beings;

Form bodies that are unimpeded, because they are pervasively present in every mind-moment throughout the Dharma realm;

Form bodies that are boundless, because they everywhere purify all beings;

Form bodies that are measureless, for they go beyond all verbal descriptions;

Form bodies that have no place in which they abide, because of the vow to liberate everyone in the entire world;

Form bodies that have no location, because they are constantly teaching beings without any interruption;

Form bodies that have no birth, because they are mere illusory conjurations created by vows;

Form bodies that are unsurpassed, because they surpass everything in the world;

Form bodies that are a mere semblance of reality, because they are manifested by the mind of meditative absorption;

Form bodies that are not born, because they are manifested in accordance with the karmic actions of beings;

Form bodies that are like wish-fulfilling pearls, because they everywhere fulfill the aspirations of all beings;

Form bodies with no discriminations, because they only arise as adaptations to discriminations made by beings;

Form bodies that are beyond discriminations, because no being could ever know them;

Form bodies that are endless, because they have put an end to the bounds imposed by the birth and death of beings; and

Form bodies that are pure, because they are the same as the Tathāgata in their absence of discriminations.

Bodies such as these are not included among forms, for forms and their features are like mere reflected images.

They are not included among feelings, for they have accomplished the ultimate cessation of the world's painful feelings.

These are not included among perceptions, for they are only manifested as adaptations to beings' perceptions.

These are not included among karmic formative factors, for they are produced through actions that are like illusory conjurations.

And they have transcended consciousness, because they are products of the bodhisattva's vows and wisdom that are empty and devoid of any inherently existent nature, because they cut short all beings'

正體字

一切眾生語言斷故。已得成就寂滅身
415b07‖ 故。爾時善財童子。又見摩耶夫人。隨諸眾生
415b08‖ 心之所樂。現超過一切世間色身。所謂或現
415b09‖ 超過他化自在天女身。乃至超過四大天王
415b10‖ 天女身。或現超過龍女身。乃至超過人女身。
415b11‖ 現如是等無量色身。饒益眾生。集一切智助
415b12‖ 道之法。行於平等檀波羅蜜。大悲普覆一切
415b13‖ 世間。出生如來無量功德。[4]修習增長一切智
415b14‖ 心。觀察思惟諸法實性。獲深忍海。具眾定
415b15‖ 門。住於平等三昧境界。得如來定圓滿光明。
415b16‖ 銷竭眾生煩惱巨海。心常正定未嘗動亂。恒
415b17‖ 轉清淨不退法輪。善能了知一切佛法。恒以
415b18‖ 智慧觀法實相。見諸如來心無厭足。知三世
415b19‖ 佛出興次第。見佛三昧常現在前。了達如來
415b20‖ 出現於世。無量無數諸清淨道。行於諸佛虛
415b21‖ 空境界。

简体字

一切众生语言断故，已得成就寂灭身故。

尔时，善财童子又见摩耶夫人，随诸众生心之所乐，现超过一切世间色身。所谓：或现超过他化自在天女身乃至超过四大天王天女身，或现超过龙女身乃至超过人女身，现如是等无量色身，饶益众生。集一切智助道之法，行于平等檀波罗蜜，大悲普覆一切世间。出生如来无量功德，修习增长一切智心，观察思惟诸法实性；获深忍海，具众定门，住于平等三昧境界，得如来定圆满光明，销竭众生烦恼巨海；心常正定，未尝动乱，恒转清净不退法轮，善能了知一切佛法，恒以智慧观法实相；见诸如来心无厌足，知三世佛出兴次第，见佛三昧常现在前，了达如来出现于世无量无数诸清净道，行于诸佛虚空境界；

attempts to describe them, and because of having already acquired the body that has accomplished the realization of quiescence.

At this time, Sudhana the Youth also saw the Lady Māyā adapting to beings' inclinations by manifesting form bodies surpassing those of any form bodies in the world. For instance, in some cases, she manifested women's bodies surpassing those found in the Paranirmita Vaśavartin Heaven, and so forth until we come to her manifestation of women's bodies surpassing those found in the realms of the Four Great Heavenly Kings. In other cases, she manifested women's bodies surpassing those found in the dragon realms, and so forth until we come to her manifestation of women's bodies surpassing those found in the human realm. She manifested countless form bodies such as these with which:

She benefited beings;
She accumulated the provisions for the path to all-knowledge;
She practiced the impartial perfection of giving;[10]
She extended her great compassion to shelter everyone in the world;
She produced the countless meritorious qualities of the Tathāgata;
She cultivated and increased her resolve to attain all-knowledge;
She contemplated and reflected upon the true nature of dharmas;
She acquired a deep ocean of patience;
She perfected many gateways to meditative absorption;
She dwelt in the sphere of the samādhi of uniform equality;
She acquired the perfectly full radiance of the Tathāgata's meditative absorptions;
She dried up beings' immense ocean of afflictions;
She was constantly immersed in right meditative absorption in which she was never shaken or disturbed;
She constantly turned the irreversible wheel of the pure Dharma;
She was well able to completely understand all the dharmas of the Buddha;
She constantly contemplated with wisdom the true character of dharmas;
She was insatiable in her resolve to see all *tathāgatas;*
She knew the sequence of the arising of all buddhas of the three periods of time;
She experienced the seeing-all-buddhas samādhi always manifesting directly before her;
She fully comprehended the tathāgatas' appearance in the world and their measurelessly and numberlessly many paths of purity;
She traveled in the space-like realm of all buddhas;

正體字

普攝眾生各隨其心。教化成就。入
415b22‖ 佛無量清淨法身。成就大願。淨諸佛剎。究
415b23‖ 竟調伏一切眾生。心恒遍入諸佛境界。出生
415b24‖ 菩薩自在神力。已得法身清淨無染。而恒示
415b25‖ 現無量色身。摧一切魔力。成大善根力。出生
415b26‖ 正法力。具足諸佛力。得諸菩薩自在之力。速
415b27‖ 疾增長一切智力。得佛智光。普照一切。悉知
415b28‖ 無量眾生心海。根性欲解種種差別。其身普
415b29‖ 遍十方剎海。悉知諸剎成壞之相。以廣大眼
415c01‖ 見十方海。以周遍智知三世海。身普承事一
415c02‖ 切佛海。心恒納受一切法海。修習一切如來
415c03‖ 功德。出生一切菩薩智慧。常樂觀察一切菩
415c04‖ 薩。從初發心。乃至成就所行之道。常勤守
415c05‖ 護一切眾生。常樂稱揚諸佛功德。願為一切
415c06‖ 菩薩[5]之母。爾時善財童子。見摩耶夫人現
415c07‖ 如是等閻浮提微塵數諸方便門。既見是已。
415c08‖ 如摩耶夫人所現身數。善財亦現作爾許身。
415c09‖ 於一切處摩耶之前。恭敬禮拜。

简体字

普摄众生，各随其心，教化成就；入佛无量清净法身，成就大愿，净诸佛刹，究竟调伏一切众生，心恒遍入诸佛境界；出生菩萨自在神力，已得法身清净无染，而恒示现无量色身；摧一切魔力，成大善根力，出生正法力，具足诸佛力，得诸菩萨自在之力，速疾增长一切智力；得佛智光，普照一切，悉知无量众生心海，根、性、欲、解种种差别；其身普遍十方刹海，悉知诸刹成坏之相，以广大眼见十方海，以周遍智知三世海，身普承事一切佛海，心恒纳受一切法海；修习一切如来功德，出生一切菩萨智慧，常乐观察一切菩萨从初发心乃至成就所行之道，常勤守护一切众生，常乐称扬诸佛功德，愿为一切菩萨之母。

尔时，善财童子见摩耶夫人现如是等阎浮提微尘数诸方便门。既见是已，如摩耶夫人所现身数，善财亦现作尔许身，于一切处摩耶之前恭敬礼拜，

She everywhere gathered in beings by adapting to each of their minds as she taught and ripened them;
She entered the Buddha's measureless pure Dharma body, perfected great vows and purified buddha *kṣetras;*
She was ultimately able to train all beings;
Her mind constantly and pervasively penetrated the realm of all buddhas;
She manifested the bodhisattvas' miraculous spiritual powers;
She had already acquired the pure and undefiled Dharma body and yet she constantly manifested countless form bodies;
She demolished all the powers of Māra;
She perfected the power of great roots of goodness;
She manifested the power of right Dharma;
She completely fulfilled the powers of the buddhas;
She acquired the bodhisattvas' powers of sovereign mastery;
She swiftly grew in the powers of all-knowledge;
She acquired the Buddha's light of wisdom with which she everywhere illuminated all things; and
She completely knew the ocean of the minds of countless beings and the many differences in their faculties, dispositions, and convictions.

Her bodies were present everywhere throughout the oceans of the *kṣetras* of the ten directions. She completely knew the signs of the creation and destruction of all *kṣetras.* With the vast vision of her eyes, she could see the ocean of the ten directions. With her universally pervasive wisdom, she knew the ocean of the three periods of time. Her bodies everywhere served the ocean of all buddhas. Her mind constantly took in the ocean of all dharmas. She cultivated the meritorious qualities of all *tathāgatas,* aroused the wisdom of all bodhisattvas, and always delighted in contemplating all bodhisattvas from the time when they made their initial resolve all the way up to the time when they completed the path they had practiced. She always diligently protected all beings, always delighted in proclaiming the praises of all buddhas' meritorious qualities, and she vowed to serve as the mother of all bodhisattvas.

At that time, Sudhana the Youth saw the Lady Māyā manifesting gateways of skillful means such as these that were as numerous as the atoms in Jambudvīpa. Having seen this, Sudhana also manifested just so very many bodies as were manifested by the Lady Māyā and then bowed down in reverence before the Lady Māyā wherever she appeared. He then immediately acquired measurelessly and

正體字

即時證得無
415c10‖ 量無數諸三昧門。分別觀察。修行證入。從三
415c11‖ 昧起。右遶摩耶并其眷屬。合掌而立。白言大
415c12‖ 聖。文殊師利菩薩。教我發阿耨多羅三藐三
415c13‖ 菩提心。求善知識。親近供養。我於一一善
415c14‖ 知識所。皆往承事。無空過者。漸來至此。願為
415c15‖ 我說。菩薩云何學菩薩行。而得成就。答言。佛
415c16‖ 子。我已成就菩薩大願智幻解脫門。是故。常
415c17‖ 為諸菩薩母。佛子。如我於此閻浮提中迦毘
415c18‖ 羅城淨飯王家。右脇而生悉達太子。現不思
415c19‖ 議自在神變。如是乃至盡此世界海。所有一
415c20‖ 切毘盧遮那如來。皆入我身。示現誕生自在
415c21‖ 神變。又善男子。我於淨飯王宮。菩薩將欲
415c22‖ 下生之時。見菩薩身。一一毛孔咸放光明。名
415c23‖ 一切如來受生功德輪。[6]一一毛孔。皆現不
415c24‖ 可說不可說佛刹微塵數菩薩受生莊嚴。彼
415c25‖ 諸光明。皆悉普照一切世界。照世界已。來
415c26‖ 入我頂乃至一切諸毛孔中。又彼光中。普現
415c27‖ 一切菩薩名號。受生神變。宮殿眷屬。五欲
415c28‖ 自娛。又見出家。往詣道場。成等正覺。

简体字

即时证得无量无数诸三昧门，分别观察，修行证入。从三昧起，右绕摩耶并其眷属，合掌而立，白言："大圣，文殊师利菩萨教我发阿耨多罗三藐三菩提心，求善知识，亲近供养。我于一一善知识所，皆往承事，无空过者；渐来至此，愿为我说：菩萨云何学菩萨行而得成就？"

答言："佛子，我已成就菩萨大愿智幻解脱门，是故常为诸菩萨母。佛子，如我于此阎浮提中迦毗罗城净饭王家，右胁而生悉达太子，现不思议自在神变；如是，乃至尽此世界海，所有一切毗卢遮那如来，皆入我身，示现诞生自在神变。

"又，善男子，我于净饭王宫，菩萨将欲下生之时，见菩萨身一一毛孔咸放光明，名一切如来受生功德轮，一一毛孔皆现不可说不可说佛刹微尘数菩萨受生庄严。彼诸光明，皆悉普照一切世界；照世界已，来入我顶乃至一切诸毛孔中。又，彼光中普现一切菩萨名号、受生神变、宫殿眷属、五欲自娱；又见出家、往诣道场、成等正觉、

numberlessly many samādhi gateways, accomplished their contemplations, cultivated them, and realized entry into them.

He then arose from samādhi and, with his right side facing her, he circumambulated the Lady Māyā and her retinue. He then stood before her with his palms pressed together and addressed her, saying:

O Great Āryā, Mañjuśrī Bodhisattva instructed me in resolving to attain *anuttara-samyak-saṃbodhi,* in searching out the good spiritual guides, in drawing near to them, and in making offerings to them. I have visited and served every one of those good spiritual guides and have never done so in vain. In this way, I gradually arrived here. Please explain for me how the bodhisattva should train in the bodhisattva practices and thus achieve success in this.

She then replied to him, saying:

Son of the Buddha, I have already perfected the bodhisattva liberation known as "the illusion-like manifestation of the knowledge of great vows." It is because of this that I always serve as the mother of all bodhisattvas.

Son of the Buddha, just as I appeared here in Jambudvīpa in the family of King Śuddhodana of Kapilavastu where I gave birth to Prince Siddhārtha from my right side, thereby manifesting inconceivable magical spiritual transformations, so too, in this very same manner, throughout this ocean of worlds, all of the Vairocana Tathāgatas enter my body and then manifest their inconceivable miraculous spiritual transformation of appearing to take birth.

Further, Son of Good Family, when I was abiding in the palace of Śuddhodana and the Bodhisattva was about to descend to take birth, I saw the Bodhisattva's body emanating from every one of his pores a light known as "the sphere of qualities associated with the birth of all *tathāgatas,*" by which, in each of those pores, there appeared the adornments manifesting at the birth of bodhisattvas as numerous as the atoms in an ineffable-ineffable number of buddha *kṣetras.* All those rays of light everywhere illuminated all worlds and then came and entered the crown of my head and went to all the pores of my body.

Further, within that light, the names of those bodhisattvas were shown along with the spiritual transformations that occurred when they were born, their palaces, their retinues, and their enjoyment of the pleasures of the five senses. I also saw their leaving the home life, their going to the site of enlightenment, their realization of the universal and right enlightenment, their sitting on the lion seat

正體字

坐師子
415c29‖ 座。菩薩圍遶。諸王供養。為諸大眾。轉正法
416a01‖ 輪。又見如來往昔修行菩薩道時。於諸佛所。
416a02‖ 恭敬供養。發菩提心。淨佛國土。念念示現無
416a03‖ 量化身。充遍十方一切世界。乃至最後入般
416a04‖ 涅槃。如是等事靡不皆見。又善男子。彼妙光
416a05‖ 明入我身時。我身形量雖不逾本。然其實已
416a06‖ 超諸世間。所以者何。我身爾時。量同虛空。悉
416a07‖ 能容受十方菩薩受生莊嚴諸宮殿故。爾時
416a08‖ 菩薩。從兜率天。將降神時。有十佛剎微塵數
416a09‖ 諸菩薩。皆與菩薩。同願同行。同善根同莊嚴。
416a10‖ 同解脫同智慧。諸地諸力。法身色身。乃至
416a11‖ 普賢神通行願。悉皆同等。如是菩薩。前後
416a12‖ 圍遶。又有八萬諸龍王等。一切世主乘其宮
416a13‖ 殿。俱來供養。菩薩爾時。以神通力。與諸菩
416a14‖ 薩。普現一切兜率天宮。一一宮中。悉現十
416a15‖ 方一切世界。閻浮提內受生影像。方便教化
416a16‖ 無量眾生。令諸菩薩。離諸懈怠。無所執著。又
416a17‖ 以神力。放大光明。普照世間。[1]破諸黑闇。滅
416a18‖ 諸苦惱。令諸眾生。皆識宿世所有業行。永出
416a19‖ 惡道。

简体字

坐师子座、菩萨围绕、诸王供养、为诸大众转正法轮；又见如来往昔修行菩萨道时，于诸佛所恭敬供养，发菩提心，净佛国土，念念示现无量化身，充遍十方一切世界，乃至最后入般涅槃。如是等事，靡不皆见。

“又，善男子，彼妙光明入我身时，我身形量虽不逾本，然其实已超诸世间。所以者何？我身尔时量同虚空，悉能容受十方菩萨受生庄严诸宫殿故。尔时，菩萨从兜率天将降神时，有十佛刹微尘数诸菩萨，皆与菩萨同愿、同行、同善根、同庄严、同解脱、同智慧，诸地、诸力、法身、色身，乃至普贤神通行愿，悉皆同等，如是菩萨前后围绕；又有八万诸龙王等、一切世主，乘其宫殿，俱来供养。菩萨尔时，以神通力，与诸菩萨普现一切兜率天宫；一一宫中，悉现十方一切世界阎浮提内受生影像，方便教化无量众生，令诸菩萨离诸懈怠无所执著。又以神力，放大光明，普照世间，破诸黑暗，灭诸苦恼；令诸众生，皆识宿世所有业行，永出恶道。

surrounded by bodhisattvas, their receiving the offerings of all those kings, and their turning the wheel of right Dharma for all those immense congregations.

I also saw [within that light] the scenes from the distant past when the Tathāgata was cultivating the bodhisattva path, revering and making offerings to all buddhas, resolving to attain bodhi, purifying buddha lands, manifesting countless transformation bodies in every mind-moment, filling all worlds of the ten directions, and so forth on up to the very last when he entered *parinirvāṇa*. There were none of these matters that I did not see there.

Further, Son of Good Family, when that marvelous light entered my body, although my body did not grow beyond its original size, still, it was actually larger than the entire world. How could this be? This is because my body then became as large as empty space, for it was able to completely contain within it the palaces that adorned the birth of all bodhisattvas of the ten directions.

At that time, when the Bodhisattva was about to descend from the Tuṣita Heaven, he was accompanied by bodhisattvas as numerous as the atoms in ten buddha *kṣetras* who had the same vows as the Bodhisattva, the same practices, the same roots of goodness, the same adornments, the same liberations, the same wisdom, the same grounds, the same powers, the same Dharma body, the same form body, and so forth, including even the same spiritual superknowledges, practices, and vows of Samantabhadra. He was surrounded then by bodhisattvas such as these. There were also eighty thousand dragon kings and such as well as all the rulers of the worlds who, riding in their palaces, all simultaneously came along to make offerings to him.

At that time, through the power of his spiritual superknowledges, the Bodhisattva revealed himself and all those other bodhisattvas, each in their own Tuṣita Heaven palace. He also showed images of them all taking birth in the Jambudvīpa continents of all the worlds of the ten directions and also showed them all using skillful means to teach countless beings and encourage all bodhisattvas to abandon indolence and remain free of attachments to anything.

He also used his spiritual powers to emanate a bright light that everywhere illuminated the world, dispelled all darkness, extinguished all suffering and afflictions, and enabled all those beings to become conscious of all of their karmic actions in previous lives and then forever escape further existences in the wretched destinies of rebirth.

正體字

又為救護一切眾生。普現其前。作諸
416a20 神變。現如是等諸奇特事。與眷屬俱。來入我
416a21 身。彼諸菩薩。於我腹中。遊行自在。或以三千
416a22 大千世界。而為一步。或以不可說不可說佛
416a23 剎微塵數世界。而為一步。又念念中。十方
416a24 不可說不可說一切世界。諸如來所。菩薩眾
416a25 會。及四天王天。三十三天。乃至色界諸梵天
416a26 王。欲見菩薩處胎神變。恭敬供養。聽受正法。
416a27 皆入我身。雖我腹中。悉能容受如是眾會。而
416a28 身不廣大亦不迫窄。其諸菩薩。各見自處眾
416a29 會道場。清淨嚴飾。善男子。如此四天下閻
416b01 浮提中。菩薩受生我為其母。三千大千世界
416b02 百億四天下閻浮提中。悉亦如是。然我此身
416b03 本來無二。非一處住。非多處住。何以故。以修
416b04 菩薩大願智幻莊嚴解脫門故。善男子。如今
416b05 世尊我為其母。往昔所有無量諸佛悉亦如
416b06 是而為其母。善男子。我昔曾作蓮華池神。時
416b07 有菩薩。於蓮華藏。忽然化生。我即捧持。瞻侍
416b08 養育。一切世間。皆共號我。為菩薩母。又我昔
416b09 為菩提場神。時有菩薩。於我懷中。忽然化生。

简体字

又为救护一切众生，普现其前，作诸神变。现如是等诸奇特事，与眷属俱，来入我身。彼诸菩萨于我腹中，游行自在，或以三千大千世界而为一步，或以不可说不可说佛刹微尘数世界而为一步。又，念念中，十方不可说不可说一切世界诸如来所、菩萨众会，及四天王天、三十三天，乃至色界诸梵天王，欲见菩萨处胎神变，恭敬供养，听受正法，皆入我身。虽我腹中悉能容受如是众会，而身不广大亦不迫窄；其诸菩萨各见自处众会道场，清净严饰。

“善男子，如此四天下阎浮提中，菩萨受生，我为其母；三千大千世界百亿四天下阎浮提中，悉亦如是。然我此身本来无二，非一处住，非多处住。何以故？以修菩萨大愿智幻庄严解脱门故。善男子，如今世尊，我为其母；往昔所有无量诸佛，悉亦如是而为其母。

“善男子，我昔曾作莲华池神，时有菩萨于莲华藏忽然化生，我即捧持瞻侍养育，一切世间皆共号我为：菩萨母。又，我昔为菩提场神，时有菩萨于我怀中忽然化生，

Also, in order to rescue all beings, he everywhere appeared directly before them, performing feats of spiritual transformation. Then, having manifested extraordinary phenomena such as these, he came together with his retinue and entered my body. There all those bodhisattvas roamed about freely within my belly. Thus, in some cases, they traversed an entire great trichiliocosm in but a single footstep. In other cases, in but a single footstep, they traversed worlds as numerous as the atoms in an ineffable-ineffable number of buddha *kṣetras*.

Further, in each successive mind-moment, from the abodes of all buddhas in an ineffable-ineffable number of worlds throughout the ten directions, there came congregations of bodhisattvas together with devas from their Heavens of the Four Heavenly Kings, their Trāyastriṃśa Heavens, and so forth up to and including Brahma Heaven kings from their form realms. Wishing to witness the Bodhisattva's spiritual transformation of dwelling in the womb and wishing to pay reverence to him, make offerings to him, and listen to his teaching of right Dharma, they all entered my body.

Although I was able to contain congregations such as these in my belly, my body still did not expand nor did any crowding occur. All those bodhisattvas saw themselves abiding there in the midst of that purified and beautifully adorned congregation.

Son of Good Family, just as I served as the mother of the Bodhisattva as he took birth here in this Jambudvīpa continent within this fourfold array of continents, so too did this also occur in this very same way in all the Jambudvīpa continents in the hundred *koṭīs* of fourfold continent arrays throughout the worlds of this great trichiliocosm. Even so, from the very beginning on up to the present, this body of mine has always been non-dual, abiding neither in one place nor in many places.

How could this be so? This is due to my cultivation of the bodhisattva liberation gateway [known as] "the illusion-like manifestation of the knowledge of great vows."

Son of Good Family, just as I have served as the mother of this present *bhagavat*, so too have I also served as the mother of all the countless buddhas from the distant past on forward to the present.

Son of Good Family, in the past, when I was a lotus pool spirit, a bodhisattva was suddenly spontaneously born from a lotus flower's seed pod. I then held him up high, respectfully served him, and raised him. As a result, wherever I went in the world, everyone referred to me as "the bodhisattva's mother."

Again, in the past, when I was a *bodhimaṇḍa* spirit, there was a bodhisattva who was suddenly spontaneously born into my lap.

正體字

416b10‖ 世亦號我。為菩薩母。善男子。有無量最後
416b11‖ 身菩薩。於此世界種種方便示現受生。我皆
416b12‖ 為母。善男子。如此世界賢劫之中。過去世
416b13‖ 時。拘留孫佛。拘那含牟尼佛。迦葉佛。及今世
416b14‖ 尊釋迦牟尼佛。現受生時。我為其母。未來
416b15‖ 世中彌勒菩薩。從兜率天將降神時。放大光
416b16‖ 明。普照法界。示現一切諸菩薩眾。受生神變。
416b17‖ 乃於人間。生大族家。調伏眾生。我於彼時
416b18‖ 亦為其母。如是次第。有師子佛。[2]法幢佛。善
416b19‖ 眼佛。淨華佛。華德佛。提舍佛。弗沙佛。善意
416b20‖ 佛。金剛佛。離垢佛。月光佛。持炬佛。名稱佛。
416b21‖ 金剛楯佛。清淨義佛。紺身佛。到彼岸佛。寶焰
416b22‖ 山佛。持[3]炬佛。蓮華德佛。名稱佛。無量功德
416b23‖ 佛。最勝燈佛。莊嚴身佛。善威儀佛。慈德佛。
416b24‖ 無住佛。大威光佛。無邊音佛。勝怨敵佛。離疑
416b25‖ 惑佛。清淨佛。大光佛。淨心佛。雲德佛。莊嚴
416b26‖ 頂髻佛。樹王佛。寶璫佛。海慧佛。妙寶佛。華
416b27‖ 冠佛。滿願佛。大自在佛。妙德王佛。最尊勝
416b28‖ 佛。栴檀雲佛。紺眼佛。勝慧佛。觀察慧佛。熾
416b29‖ 盛王佛。堅固慧佛。自在名佛。師子王佛。自在
416c01‖ 佛。

简体字

世亦号我为：菩萨母。善男子，有无量最后身菩萨，于此世界种种方便示现受生，我皆为母。

“善男子，如此世界贤劫之中，过去世时，拘留孙佛、拘那含牟尼佛、迦葉佛及今世尊释迦牟尼佛现受生时，我为其母。未来世中，弥勒菩萨从兜率天将降神时，放大光明普照法界，示现一切诸菩萨众受生神变，乃于人间生大族家，调伏众生；我于彼时，亦为其母。如是次第，有师子佛、法幢佛、善眼佛、净华佛、华德佛、提舍佛、弗沙佛、善意佛、金刚佛、离垢佛、月光佛、持炬佛、名称佛、金刚楯佛、清净义佛、绀身佛、到彼岸佛、宝焰山佛、持明佛、莲华德佛、名称佛、无量功德佛、最胜灯佛、庄严身佛、善威仪佛、慈德佛、无住佛、大威光佛、无边音佛、胜冤敌佛、离疑惑佛、清净佛、大光佛、净心佛、云德佛、庄严顶髻佛、树王佛、宝珰佛、海慧佛、妙宝佛、华冠佛、满愿佛、大自在佛、妙德王佛、最尊胜佛、栴檀云佛、绀眼佛、胜慧佛、观察慧佛、炽盛王佛、坚固慧佛、自在名佛、师子王佛、自在佛、

Then, too, those in the world referred to me as "the bodhisattva's mother."

Son of Good Family, there are countless bodhisattvas who, coming into their very last physical body, use many different skillful means to manifest the appearance of taking birth into this world. I serve as the mother of them all.

Son of Good Family, for example, in this world, in the Bhadra Kalpa, I have served as the mother for Krakucchanda Buddha, Kanakamuni Buddha, Kāśyapa Buddha, and the present *bhagavat*, Śākyamuni Buddha, when they manifested the taking on of birth here. So too, in the future age, when Maitreya Bodhisattva descends from the Tuṣita Heaven, emanates a bright light everywhere illuminating the Dharma realm, manifests for all bodhisattva congregations the feat of spiritual transformation by which he takes birth, and then is born into a great clan in the human realm to take up the training of beings—then too, I shall be the one who serves as his mother.

In this way, in the order of their appearance, there will be:[11]

Lion Buddha, Dharma Banner Buddha, Eye of Goodness Buddha, Pure Blossom Buddha, Floral Virtue Buddha, Tiṣya Buddha, Puṣya Buddha, Fine Mind Buddha, Vajra Buddha, and Immaculate Buddha.

Moonlight Buddha, Torchbearer Buddha, Praised Name Buddha, Vajra Railing Buddha, Pure Meaning Buddha, Purple Body Buddha, Perfection Buddha, Mountain of Flaming Jewel Radiance Buddha, Firebrand Bearer Buddha,[12] and Lotus Virtue Buddha.

Renowned Name Buddha,[13] Measureless Qualities Buddha, Supreme Lamp Buddha, Adorned Body Buddha, Fine Comportment Buddha, Kindly Virtue Buddha, Nonabiding Buddha, Great Awesome Radiance Buddha, Boundless Voice Buddha, and Adversary Conqueror Buddha.

Delusion Transcendence Buddha, Pure Buddha, Great Light Buddha, Pure Mind Buddha, Cloud of Virtue Buddha, Adorned Topknot Buddha, Tree King Buddha, Jewel Earring Buddha, Oceanic Wisdom Buddha, and Marvelous Jewel Buddha.

Flower Crown Buddha, Fulfilled Vows Buddha, Great Sovereign Mastery Buddha, King of Marvelous Virtues Buddha, Most Honored Victor Buddha, Sandalwood Cloud Buddha, Blue Eyes Buddha, Supreme Wisdom Buddha, Contemplating Wisdom Buddha, and Blazing Flame King Buddha.

Solid Wisdom Buddha, Sovereign Mastery Fame Buddha, Lion King Buddha, Sovereign Mastery Buddha, Supreme Summit

正體字

最勝頂佛。金剛智山佛。妙德藏佛。寶網嚴
416c02‖ 身佛。善慧佛。自在天佛。大天王佛。無依德
416c03‖ 佛。善施佛。焰慧佛。水天佛。得上味佛。出生
416c04‖ 無上功德佛。仙人侍衛佛。隨世語言佛。功德
416c05‖ 自在幢佛。光幢佛。觀身佛。妙身佛。香焰佛。
416c06‖ 金剛寶嚴佛。喜眼佛。離欲佛。高大身佛。財天
416c07‖ 佛。無上天佛。順寂滅佛。智覺佛。滅貪佛。大
416c08‖ 焰王佛。寂諸有佛。毘舍佉天佛。金剛山佛。智
416c09‖ 焰德佛。安隱佛。師子出現佛。圓滿清淨佛。清
416c10‖ 淨賢佛。第一義佛。百光明佛。最增上佛。深自
416c11‖ 在佛。大地王佛。莊嚴王佛。解脫佛。妙音佛。
416c12‖ 殊勝佛。自在佛。無上醫王佛。功德月佛。無礙
416c13‖ 光佛。功德聚佛。月現佛。日天佛。出諸有佛。
416c14‖ 勇猛名稱佛。光明門佛。娑羅王佛。最勝佛。藥
416c15‖ 王佛。寶勝佛。金剛慧佛。無能勝佛。無能映蔽
416c16‖ 佛。眾會王佛。大名稱佛。敏持佛。無量光佛。
416c17‖ 大願光佛。法自在不虛佛。不退地佛。淨天佛。
416c18‖ 善天佛。堅固苦行佛。一切善友佛。解脫音佛。
416c19‖ 遊戲王佛。滅邪曲佛。[4]薝蔔淨光佛。

简体字

最胜顶佛、金刚智山佛、妙德藏佛、宝网严身佛、善慧佛、自在天佛、大天王佛、无依德佛、善施佛、焰慧佛、水天佛、得上味佛、出生无上功德佛、仙人侍卫佛、随世语言佛、功德自在幢佛、光幢佛、观身佛、妙身佛、香焰佛、金刚宝严佛、喜眼佛、离欲佛、高大身佛、财天佛、无上天佛、顺寂灭佛、智觉佛、灭贪佛、大焰王佛、寂诸有佛、毗舍佉天佛、金刚山佛、智焰德佛、安隐佛、师子出现佛、圆满清净佛、清净贤佛、第一义佛、百光明佛、最增上佛、深自在佛、大地王佛、庄严王佛、解脱佛、妙音佛、殊胜佛、自在佛、无上医王佛、功德月佛、无碍光佛、功德聚佛、月现佛、日天佛、出诸有佛、勇猛名称佛、光明门佛、娑罗王佛、最胜佛、药王佛、宝胜佛、金刚慧佛、无能胜佛、无能映蔽佛、众会王佛、大名称佛、敏持佛、无量光佛、大愿光佛、法自在不虚佛、不退地佛、净天佛、善天佛、坚固苦行佛、一切善友佛、解脱音佛、游戏王佛、灭邪曲佛、瞻卜净光佛、

Buddha, Mountain of Vajra Wisdom Buddha, Treasury of Marvelous Qualities Buddha, Body Adorned with a Net of Jewels Buddha, Fine Wisdom Buddha, and Sovereign Mastery Heaven Buddha.

Great Celestial Monarch Buddha, Independent Virtue Buddha, Fine Giving Buddha, Flaming Wisdom Buddha, Water Heaven Buddha, Supreme Flavor Buddha, Generating Unsurpassed Qualities Buddha, Served by Rishis Buddha, Adapting to Worldly Discourse Buddha, and Banner of Sovereign Mastery of the Qualities Buddha.

Radiant Banner Buddha, Body Contemplation Buddha, Marvelous Body Buddha, Fragrant Flaming Light Buddha, Vajra Jewel Adornment Buddha, Joyous Eyes Buddha, Desire Transcendence Buddha, Lofty and Immense Body Buddha, Heaven of Wealth Buddha, and Unexcelled Heaven Buddha.

Accordance with Quiescence Buddha, Wise Awakening Buddha, Desire Extinguishing Buddha, Great Flaming Radiance King Buddha, Stilling All Existences Buddha, Viśākha Heaven Buddha, Vajra Mountain Buddha, Wisdom's Flaming Virtue Buddha, Peaceful Security Buddha, and Lion Manifestation Buddha.

Perfectly Full Purity Buddha, Pure Worthy Buddha, Ultimate Meaning Buddha, Hundred-Fold Radiance Buddha, Most Dominant Buddha, Profound Sovereign Mastery Buddha, Great Earth King Buddha, Adorned King Buddha, Liberation Buddha, and Marvelous Voice Buddha.

Especially Supreme Buddha, Sovereign Mastery Buddha, Unsurpassable Physician King Buddha, Qualities Moon Buddha, Unimpeded Light Buddha, Accumulated Qualities Buddha, Lunar Appearance Buddha, Solar Heaven Buddha, Transcending All Existences Buddha, and Renowned Bravery Buddha.

Radiant Gateway Buddha, Śālendra King Buddha, Utter Supremacy Buddha, Medicine King Buddha, Bejeweled Supremacy Buddha, Vajra Wisdom Buddha, Invincible Buddha, Outshone by None Buddha, Congregation King Buddha, and Immensely Well Known Buddha.

Swift Retention Buddha, Measureless Radiance Buddha, Great Vows Radiance Buddha, Non-False Dharma Freedom Buddha, Irreversible Ground Buddha, Pure Heaven Buddha, Goodness Heaven Buddha, Solid Austerities Buddha, Fine Friend of All Buddha, and Voice of Liberation Buddha.

Joyful Wanderer King Buddha, Extinguisher of the False and Devious Buddha, Campaka's Pure Radiance Buddha, Embodying

正體字

具眾德
416c20‖ 佛。最勝月佛。執明炬佛。殊妙身佛。不可說
416c21‖ 佛。最清淨佛。友安眾生佛。無量光佛。無畏音
416c22‖ 佛。水天德佛。不動慧光佛。華勝佛。月焰佛。
416c23‖ 不退慧佛。離愛佛。無著慧佛。集功德蘊佛。滅
416c24‖ 惡趣佛。普散華佛。師子吼佛。第一義佛。無礙
416c25‖ 見佛。破他軍佛。不著相佛。離分別海佛。端嚴
416c26‖ 海佛。須彌山佛。無著智佛。無邊座佛。清淨住
416c27‖ 佛。隨師行佛。最上施佛。常月佛。饒益王佛。
416c28‖ 不動聚佛。普攝受佛。饒益慧佛。持壽佛。無滅
416c29‖ 佛。具足名稱佛。大威力佛。種種色相佛。無相
417a01‖ 慧佛。不動天佛。妙德難思佛。滿月佛。解脫月
417a02‖ 佛。無上王佛。希有身佛。梵供養佛。不瞬佛。
417a03‖ 順先古佛。最上業佛。順法智佛。無勝天佛。不
417a04‖ 思議功德光佛。隨法行佛。無量賢佛。普隨
417a05‖ 順自在佛。最尊天佛。如是乃至樓至如來。在
417a06‖ 賢劫中。於此三千大千世界。[1]當成佛者。悉
417a07‖ 為其母。如於此三千大千世界。如是於此世
417a08‖ 界海十方無量諸世界一切劫中。諸有修行
417a09‖ 普賢行願。為化一切諸眾生者。我自見身悉
417a10‖ 為其母。爾時善財童子。白摩耶夫人言。大聖。
417a11‖ 得此解脫。經今幾時。

简体字

具众德佛、最胜月佛、执明炬佛、殊妙身佛、不可说佛、最清净佛、友安众生佛、无量光佛、无畏音佛、水天德佛、不动慧光佛、华胜佛、月焰佛、不退慧佛、离爱佛、无著慧佛、集功德蕴佛、灭恶趣佛、普散华佛、师子吼佛、第一义佛、无碍见佛、破他军佛、不著相佛、离分别海佛、端严海佛、须弥山佛、无著智佛、无边座佛、清净住佛、随师行佛、最上施佛、常月佛、饶益王佛、不动聚佛、普摄受佛、饶益慧佛、持寿佛、无灭佛、具足名称佛、大威力佛、种种色相佛、无相慧佛、不动天佛、妙德难思佛、满月佛、解脱月佛、无上王佛、希有身佛、梵供养佛、不瞬佛、顺先古佛、最上业佛、顺法智佛、无胜天佛、不思议功德光佛、随法行佛、无量贤佛、普随顺自在佛、最尊天佛，如是乃至楼至如来，在贤劫中，于此三千大千世界，当成佛者，悉为其母。如于此三千大千世界，如是于此世界海十方无量诸世界一切劫中，诸有修行普贤行愿，为化一切诸众生者，我自见身悉为其母。”

尔时，善财童子白摩耶夫人言：“大圣得此解脱，经今几时？”

the Many Qualities Buddha, Utterly Supreme Moon Buddha, Bearer of the Radiant Torch Buddha, Especially Marvelous Bodhi Buddha, Ineffable Buddha, Utter Purity Buddha, and Friend and Pacifier of Beings Buddha.

Measureless Radiance Buddha, Fearless Voice Buddha, Water Heaven Virtue Buddha, Unshakable Wisdom Light Buddha, Floral Victor Buddha, Lunar Radiance Buddha, Irreversible Wisdom Buddha, Affection Transcending Buddha, Unattached Wisdom Buddha, and Aggregation of Collected Qualities Buddha.

Extinguisher of Wretched Destinies Buddha, Everywhere Scattering Flowers Buddha, Lion's Roar Buddha, Supreme Meaning Buddha, Unimpeded Vision Buddha, Destroyer of Others' Armies Buddha, Detached From Signs Buddha, Transcending the Ocean of Discriminations Buddha, Majestic Ocean Buddha, and Sumeru Mountain Buddha.

Unattached Wisdom Buddha, Boundless Throne Buddha, Pure Dwelling Buddha, Follower of the Master's Practice Buddha, Supreme Giving Buddha, Constant Moon Buddha, Beneficence King Buddha, Unshakable Aggregates Buddha, Universal Attraction Buddha, and Beneficent Wisdom Buddha.

Life-Sustaining Buddha, Non-Cessation Buddha, Replete in Renown Buddha, Immense Awesome Power Buddha, Various Forms and Features Buddha, Signless Wisdom Buddha, Unshakable Heaven Buddha, Marvelous and Inconceivable Virtue Buddha, Full Moon Buddha, and Liberation Moon Buddha.

Insuperable King Buddha, Rare Body Buddha, Pure Offerings Buddha, Unblinking Buddha, Following the Ancients Buddha, Supreme Works Buddha, Dharma-Compliant Wisdom Buddha, Invincible Deva Buddha, Light of Inconceivable Qualities Buddha, and Dharma-Compliant Practice Buddha.

Measureless Worthiness Buddha, Everywhere According with Sovereign Mastery Buddha, Most Venerable Deva Buddha, and all the others such as these up to and including Rucika Tathāgata.

For all of these who will become buddhas in this trichiliocosm during this Bhadra Kalpa, I will serve as the mother of them all. And just as this is so in this great trichiliocosm, so too, in this very same way, throughout this ocean of worlds, in all the countless worlds of the ten directions, and throughout all kalpas, wherever there are those who have cultivated the conduct and vows of Samantabhadra in order to teach all beings, I will manifest my body to serve as the mother of them all.

Sudhana the Youth then addressed the Lady Māyā, saying, "O Great Āryā, how much time has now passed since you first acquired this liberation?"

正體字

答言。善男子。乃往古
417a12‖ 世。過不可思議。非最後身菩薩。神通道眼
417a13‖ 所知劫數。爾時有劫名淨光。世界名須彌德。
417a14‖ 雖有諸山五趣雜居。然其國土眾寶所成。清
417a15‖ 淨莊嚴無諸穢惡。有千億四天下。有一四天
417a16‖ 下。名師子幢。於中有八十億王城。有一王城。
417a17‖ 名自在幢。有轉輪王。名大威德。彼王城北。有
417a18‖ 一道場。名滿月光明。其道場神。名曰慈德。時
417a19‖ 有菩薩。名離垢幢。坐於道場。將成正覺。有一
417a20‖ 惡魔。名金色光。與其眷屬無量眾俱。至菩
417a21‖ 薩所。彼大威德轉輪聖王。已得菩薩神通自
417a22‖ 在。化作[2]兵眾。其數倍多。圍遶道場。諸魔惶
417a23‖ 怖。悉自奔散。故彼菩薩。得成阿耨多羅三藐
417a24‖ 三菩提。時道場神。見是事已。歡喜無量。便於
417a25‖ 彼王而生子想。頂禮佛足。作是願言。此轉輪
417a26‖ 王。在在生處乃至成佛。願我常得與其為母。
417a27‖ 作是願已。於此道場。復曾供養十那由他佛。
417a28‖ 善男子。於汝意云何。彼道場神。豈異人乎。我
417a29‖ 身是也。轉輪王者。今世尊毘盧遮那是。我從
417b01‖ 於彼發願已來。

简体字

答言："善男子，乃往古世，过不可思议非最后身菩萨神通道眼所知劫数，尔时有劫名净光，世界名须弥德，虽有诸山五趣杂居，然其国土众宝所成，清净庄严无诸秽恶。有千亿四天下，有一四天下，名师子幢，于中有八十亿王城。有一王城，名自在幢；有转轮王，名大威德。彼王城北，有一道场，名满月光明；其道场神，名曰慈德。时，有菩萨，名离垢幢，坐于道场，将成正觉。有一恶魔，名金色光，与其眷属无量众俱，至菩萨所。彼大威德转轮圣王已得菩萨神通自在，化作兵众，其数倍多，围绕道场；诸魔惶怖，悉自奔散；故彼菩萨得成阿耨多罗三藐三菩提。时，道场神见是事已，欢喜无量，便于彼王而生子想，顶礼佛足，作是愿言：'此转轮王，在在生处，乃至成佛，愿我常得与其为母。'作是愿已，于此道场，复曾供养十那由他佛。

"善男子，于汝意云何？彼道场神岂异人乎？我身是也。转轮王者，今世尊毗卢遮那是。我从于彼发愿已来，

She then replied, saying:

Son of Good Family, it has been since a time in the ancient past so long ago that the number of kalpas that have gone by exceeds the range of vision[14] of the spiritual superknowledges of a bodhisattva in his very last incarnation prior to buddhahood.

At that time, there was a kalpa known as Pure Light and a world named Sumeru Qualities. Although that land had mountains and the mixed presence of those in the five rebirth destinies, it was still composed of many kinds of jewels, was pure in its adornments, and was entirely free of any filthy or loathsome aspects.

Within it there were a thousand *koṭīs* of four-continent arrays among which there was one four-continent array named Lion Banner in which there were eighty *koṭīs* of royal capital cities. Among them was one royal city named Banner of Sovereign Mastery in which there was a wheel-turning king named Immense Awesome Virtue. To the north of that royal city there was a site of enlightenment known as Full Moon Light in which there was a *bodhimaṇḍa* spirit named Kindly Virtue.

At that time, in that site of enlightenment, there sat a bodhisattva by the name of Banner of Immaculate Purity who was just then on the verge of realizing right enlightenment. There was then an evil *māra* known as Golden Light who, accompanied by a measurelessly large horde of followers, began to approach the bodhisattva.

Because the wheel-turning sage king, Immense Awesome Virtue, had already acquired sovereign mastery in the bodhisattva's spiritual superknowledges, he used his spiritual powers to conjure an army twice the size [of the *māras'* hordes] with which he surrounded the site of enlightenment. Those *māras* were then so seized with terror that they all ran off and scattered of their own accord. As a consequence, that bodhisattva was then able to attain *anuttara-samyak-saṃbodhi.*

When that *bodhimaṇḍa* spirit witnessed this event, her joyous delight was measureless and she then thought of that king as if he were her own son. Bowing down in reverence at the feet of the Buddha, she made this vow: "May I always be able to be the mother of this wheel-turning king wherever he is reborn up until he finally becomes a buddha." After she made this vow, she made offerings to ten *nayutas* of buddhas at this site of enlightenment.

Son of Good Family, what do you think? Could that *bodhimaṇḍa* spirit have been anyone else? It was indeed myself. As for that wheel-turning king, he was none other than our present era's *bhagavat,* Vairocana Buddha. From the time when I made that vow up

正體字

此佛世尊。於十方剎一切諸
417b02║ 趣。處處受生。種諸善根。修菩薩行。教化成就
417b03║ 一切眾生。乃至示現住最後身。念念普於一
417b04║ 切世界。示現菩薩受生神變。常為我子我常
417b05║ 為母。善男子。過去現在十方世界無量諸佛。
417b06║ 將成佛時。皆於[3]齎中。放大光明。來照我身
417b07║ 及我所住宮殿屋宅。彼最後生。我悉為母。善
417b08║ 男子。[4]我唯知此菩薩大願智幻解脫門。如諸
417b09║ 菩薩摩訶薩。具大悲藏。教化眾生常無厭足。
417b10║ 以自在力。一一毛孔。示現無量諸佛神變。我
417b11║ 今云何能知能說彼功德行。善男子。於此世
417b12║ 界三十三天。有王名正念。其王有女。名天
417b13║ 主光。汝詣彼問。菩薩云何學菩薩行。修菩
417b14║ 薩道。時善財童子。敬受其教。頭面作禮。遶無
417b15║ 數匝。戀慕瞻仰。却行而退
417b16║ 遂往天宮。見彼天女。禮足圍遶。合掌前住。白
417b17║ 言。

简体字

此佛世尊，于十方刹一切诸趣，处处受生，种诸善根，修菩萨行，教化成就一切众生，乃至示现住最后身，念念普于一切世界，示现菩萨受生神变，常为我子，我常为母。善男子，过去、现在十方世界无量诸佛将成佛时，皆于脐中放大光明，来照我身及我所住宫殿屋宅；彼最后生，我悉为母。

“善男子，我唯知此菩萨大愿智幻解脱门。如诸菩萨摩诃萨，具大悲藏，教化众生常无厌足，以自在力，一一毛孔示现无量诸佛神变；我今云何能知能说彼功德行？

“善男子，于此世界三十三天，有王名正念，其王有女名天主光。汝诣彼问：菩萨云何学菩萨行、修菩萨道？”

时，善财童子敬受其教，头面作礼，绕无数匝，恋慕瞻仰，却行而退。

遂往天宫，见彼天女，礼足围绕，合掌前住，白言：

until the present, he has always been my son and I have always been his mother. This has been so whenever this buddha, this *bhagavat,* has taken birth in all the rebirth destinies throughout the *kṣetras* of the ten directions as he planted all kinds of roots of goodness, as he cultivated the bodhisattva practices, and as he taught all beings and brought them to maturity. It has continued even up to when, as he manifested coming to dwell in his very last body, in each successive mind-moment, he manifested everywhere and in all worlds the spiritual transformations that occur when the Bodhisattva takes on birth. During all this time, he has always been my son and I have always been his mother.

Son of Good Family, whenever the countless past and present buddhas throughout the worlds of the ten directions were about to become buddhas, they emanated a bright light from their navels that came and illuminated my body and the palaces or residences in which I dwelt. I then served as their mothers as they took on their very last birth.

Son of Good Family, I know only this bodhisattva liberation gateway of "the illusion-like manifestation of the knowledge of great vows." As for the bodhisattva-mahāsattvas who possess a treasury of great compassion, who are ever insatiable in teaching beings, and who, by their powers of sovereign mastery, manifest in every pore the measureless spiritual transformations of all buddhas, how could I know of or be able to speak about their meritorious qualities and practices?

Son of Good Family, in the Trāyastriṃśa Heaven of this world, there is a king known as Rightly Mindful. That king has a daughter named Surendrābhā, or "Celestial Lord's Light." You should go there, pay your respects, and ask her, "How should the bodhisattva train in the bodhisattva practices and how should he cultivate the bodhisattva path?"

Sudhana the Youth then respectfully accepted her instruction, bowed down in reverence at her feet, and circumambulated her countless times as he gazed up at her in fond admiration. He then respectfully withdrew and departed.

42 – Surendrābhā

[Sudhana] then went to that palace in the heavens where he saw that celestial maiden, bowed down in reverence at her feet, and circumambulated her. He then stood before her with his palms pressed together and addressed her, saying:

正體字

聖者。我已先發阿耨多羅三藐三菩提心。
417b18‖ 而未知菩薩云何學菩薩行。云何修菩薩道。
417b19‖ 我聞聖者。善能誘誨。願為我說。天女答言。
417b20‖ 善男子。我得菩薩解脫。名無礙念清淨莊嚴。
417b21‖ 善男子。我以此解脫力。憶念過去。有最勝劫。
417b22‖ 名青蓮華。我於彼劫中。供養恒河沙數諸佛
417b23‖ 如來。彼諸如來。從初出家。我皆瞻奉。守護供
417b24‖ 養。造僧伽藍。營[5]辨什物。又彼諸佛。從為菩
417b25‖ 薩住母胎時。誕生之時。行七步時。大師子
417b26‖ 吼時。住童子位在宮中時。向菩提樹成正覺
417b27‖ 時。轉正法輪現佛神變。教化調伏眾生之時。
417b28‖ 如是一切諸所作事。從初發心。乃至法盡。我
417b29‖ 皆明憶。無有遺餘。常現在前。念持不忘。又憶
417c01‖ 過去劫名善地。我於彼供養十恒河沙數諸
417c02‖ 佛如來。[6]又過去劫。名為妙德。我於彼供養
417c03‖ 一佛世界微塵數諸佛如來。又劫名無所得。
417c04‖ 我於彼供養八十四億百千那由他諸佛如
417c05‖ 來。又劫名善光。我於彼供養閻浮提微塵數
417c06‖ 諸佛如來。

简体字

“圣者，我已先发阿耨多罗三藐三菩提心，而未知菩萨云何学菩萨行？云何修菩萨道？我闻圣者善能诱诲，愿为我说！”

天女答言：“善男子，我得菩萨解脱，名无碍念清净庄严。善男子，我于此解脱力，忆念过去，有最胜劫，名青莲华。我于彼劫中，供养恒河沙数诸佛如来。彼诸如来，从初出家，我皆瞻奉，守护供养，造僧伽蓝，营办什物。又，彼诸佛从为菩萨住母胎时，诞生之时，行七步时，大师子吼时，住童子位在宫中时，向菩提树成正觉时，转正法轮现佛神变教化调伏众生之时；如是一切诸所作事，从初发心乃至法尽，我皆明忆，无有遗余，常现在前，念持不忘。又，忆过去劫，名善地，我于彼供养十恒河沙数诸佛如来；又，过去劫名为妙德，我于彼供养一佛世界微尘数诸佛如来；又，劫名无所得，我于彼供养八十四亿百千那由他诸佛如来；又，劫名善光，我于彼供养阎浮提微尘数诸佛如来；

O Āryā, I am one who has already resolved to attain *anuttara-samyak-saṃbodhi*. Still, I do not yet know how the bodhisattva should train in the bodhisattva practices or how he should cultivate the bodhisattva path. I have heard that the Āryā is well able to provide guidance and instructions in these matters. Please explain this for me.

The heavenly maiden replied, saying:

Son of Good Family, I have acquired a bodhisattva liberation known as "the purified adornment of unimpeded recollection." Son of Good Family, by the power of this liberation, I remember that in the past there was a kalpa known as Blue Lotus Flower. During that kalpa I made offerings to buddhas, *tathāgatas*, as numerous as the sands of the Ganges. Even from the time those *tathāgatas* first left the home life, I looked up to them with admiration, served them, protected them, made offerings to them, built monastic dwellings[15] for them, and saw to their being provided[16] with their various material needs.

Further, regarding all those buddhas, from the time when, as bodhisattvas, they dwelt in their mother's womb, took birth, walked seven steps, roared the great lion's roar, dwelt as a youth in the palace, went to the bodhi tree, attained the right enlightenment, turned the wheel of right Dharma, manifested a buddha's spiritual transformations, and taught and trained beings—all those deeds they did from the time they made their initial resolve until their Dharma legacy finally disappeared from the world—I remember it all clearly and without any exceptions as if it were all constantly manifesting directly before me. I recall it all and never forget it.

I also remember that, in the past, there was a kalpa named "Ground of Goodness" in which I made offerings to all of its buddhas, its *tathāgatas*, that were as numerous as the sands in ten Ganges Rivers.

There was also a kalpa in the past known as Marvelous Virtues in which I made offerings to buddhas, *tathāgatas*, as numerous as the atoms in one buddha world.

There was also a kalpa named Unattainable in which I made offerings to eighty-four *koṭīs* of hundreds of thousands of *nayutas* of buddhas, *tathāgatas*.

There was also a kalpa named Fine Radiance in which I made offerings to all the buddhas, *tathāgatas*, as numerous as the atoms in the continent of Jambudvīpa.

正體字

又劫名無量光。我於彼供養二十
417c07‖ 恒河沙數諸佛如來。又劫名最勝德。我於彼
417c08‖ 供養一恒河沙數諸佛如來。又劫名善悲。我
417c09‖ 於彼供養八十恒河沙數諸佛如來。又劫名
417c10‖ 勝遊。我於彼供養六十恒河沙數諸佛如來。
417c11‖ 又劫名妙月。我於彼供養七十恒河沙數諸
417c12‖ 佛如來。善男子。如是憶念恒河沙劫。我常
417c13‖ 不捨諸佛如來應正等覺。從彼一切諸如來
417c14‖ 所。聞此無礙念清淨莊嚴菩薩解脫。受持修
417c15‖ 行恒不忘失。[7]如是先劫所有如來。從初菩
417c16‖ 薩。乃至法盡。一切所作。我以淨嚴解脫之力。
417c17‖ 皆隨憶念。明了現前。持而順行曾無懈廢。善
417c18‖ 男子。我唯知此無礙念清淨解脫。如諸菩薩
417c19‖ 摩訶薩。出生死夜朗然明徹。永離癡冥未嘗
417c20‖ 惛寐。心無諸蓋身行輕安。於諸法性清淨覺
417c21‖ 了。成就十力。開悟群生。

简体字

又，劫名无量光，我于彼供养二十恒河沙数诸佛如来；又，劫名最胜德，我于彼供养一恒河沙数诸佛如来；又，劫名善悲，我于彼供养八十恒河沙数诸佛如来；又，劫名胜游，我于彼供养六十恒河沙数诸佛如来；又，劫名妙月，我于彼供养七十恒河沙数诸佛如来。

“善男子，如是忆念恒河沙劫，我常不舍诸佛如来、应、正等觉，从彼一切诸如来所，闻此无碍念清净庄严菩萨解脱，受持修行恒不忘失。如是，先劫所有如来，从初菩萨，乃至法尽，一切所作，我以净严解脱之力，皆随忆念，明了现前，持而顺行，曾无懈废。

“善男子，我唯知此无碍念清净解脱。如诸菩萨摩诃萨，出生死夜朗然明彻，永离痴冥未尝惛寐，心无诸盖、身行轻安，于诸法性清净觉了，成就十力开悟群生；

There was also a kalpa named Measureless Light in which I made offerings to all the buddhas, *tathāgatas,* as numerous as the sands in twenty Ganges Rivers.

There was also a kalpa named Supreme Virtues in which I made offerings to all the buddhas, *tathāgatas,* as numerous as the sands in one Ganges River.

There was also a kalpa named Fine Compassion in which I made offerings to all the buddhas, *tathāgatas,* as numerous as the sands in eighty Ganges Rivers.

There was also a kalpa named Victorious Roaming in which I made offerings to all the buddhas, *tathāgatas,* as numerous as the sands in sixty Ganges Rivers.

There was also a kalpa named Marvelous Moon in which I made offerings to all the buddhas, *tathāgatas,* as numerous as the sands in seventy Ganges Rivers.

Son of Good Family, in this same way I recall kalpas as numerous as the sands in the Ganges River during which I never left any of those buddhas, those *tathāgatas,* arhats, possessed of right and universal enlightenment. It was in the presence of all those *tathāgatas* that I heard this bodhisattva liberation known as "the purified adornment of unimpeded recollection," absorbed it, retained it, cultivated it, and never forgot it.

So it is that, with regard to everything done by all those *tathāgatas* from past kalpas, beginning with when they first became bodhisattvas and continuing on until the complete disappearance of their Dharma legacy—by the power of this "purified adornment" liberation, I remember it all with complete and directly present clarity, retain it all, and accord with it in practice that never diminishes.

Son of Good Family, I know only this liberation known as "the purified adornment of unimpeded recollection." As for the bodhisattva-mahāsattvas:

Who have emerged with brilliant and penetrating radiance from the nighttime of *saṃsāra;*

Who have forever abandoned the abysmal darkness of delusion and never fall into the slumber of confusion;

Whose minds are free of all the hindrances and whose physical actions are imbued with meditative tranquility;

Who have attained the purified awakening to the nature of all dharmas;

Who have developed the ten powers; and

Who awaken the many kinds of beings—

正體字

而我云何能知能
417c22‖ 說彼功德行。善男子。迦毘羅城。有童子師。名
417c23‖ 曰遍友。汝詣彼問。菩薩云何學菩薩行。修
417c24‖ 菩薩道。時善財童子。以聞法故。歡喜踊躍。不
417c25‖ 思議善根。自然增廣。頂禮其足。遶無數匝。辭
417c26‖ 退而去。從天宮下。漸向彼城。至遍友所。禮足
417c27‖ 圍遶。合掌恭敬。於一面立。白言。聖者。我已
417c28‖ 先發阿耨多羅三藐三菩提心。而未知菩薩
417c29‖ 云何學菩薩行。云何修菩薩道。我聞聖者。善
418a01‖ 能誘誨。願為我說。遍友答言。善男子。此有童
418a02‖ 子。名善知眾藝。學菩薩字智。汝可問之。當為
418a03‖ 汝說。爾時善財。即至其所。頭頂禮敬。於一面
418a04‖ 立。白言。聖者。我已先發阿耨多羅三藐三菩
418a05‖ 提心。而未知菩薩云何學菩薩行。云何修菩
418a06‖ 薩道。

简体字

而我云何能知能说彼功德行？

“善男子，迦毗罗城有童子师，名曰遍友。汝诣彼问：菩萨云何学菩萨行、修菩萨道？”

时，善财童子以闻法故，欢喜踊跃，不思议善根自然增广；顶礼其足，绕无数匝，辞退而去。

从天宫下，渐向彼城。至遍友所，礼足围绕，合掌恭敬，于一面立，白言：“圣者，我已先发阿耨多罗三藐三菩提心，而未知菩萨云何学菩萨行？云何修菩萨道？我闻圣者善能诱诲，愿为我说！”

遍友答言：“善男子，此有童子，名善知众艺，学菩萨字智。汝可问之，当为汝说。”

尔时，善财即至其所，头顶礼敬，于一面立，白言：“圣者，我已先发阿耨多罗三藐三菩提心，而未知菩萨云何学菩萨行？云何修菩萨道？

How could I know of or be able to speak about their meritorious qualities and practices?

Son of Good Family, in the city of Kapilavastu there is a teacher of youths known as Viśvāmitra, or "Universally Friendly." You should go there, pay your respects, and ask him, "How should the bodhisattva train in the bodhisattva practices and how should he cultivate the bodhisattva path?"

Then, due to having heard this Dharma, Sudhana the Youth was filled with joyous exultation and his inconceivable roots of goodness naturally became ever more vast. He then bowed down in reverence at the feet of Surendrābhā and circumambulated her countless times, whereupon he respectfully took his leave and departed.

43 – Viśvāmitra

[At that time, Sudhana] descended from that heavenly palace and gradually traveled toward that city. When he arrived in the presence of Viśvāmitra, or "Universally Friendly," he bowed down at his feet and circumambulated him. Then, standing off to one side with his palms pressed together in respect, he addressed him, saying:

O Ārya, I am one who has already resolved to attain *anuttara-samyak-saṃbodhi*. Even so, I do not yet know how the bodhisattva should train in the bodhisattva practices or how he should cultivate the bodhisattva path. I have heard that the Ārya is well able to offer guidance and instruction in these matters. Please explain this for me.

Viśvāmitra then replied to him, saying: "There is a youth here known as Śilpābhijña, or 'Skilled in the Knowledge of the Many Arts,' who has trained in the knowledge of the bodhisattva syllabary. You could inquire of him on these matters and he should be able explain them for you."

44 – Śilpābhijña

At that time, Sudhana straightaway went to Śilpābhijña and bowed down in reverence at his feet, whereupon he stood off to one side and addressed him, saying:

O Ārya, I am one who has already made the resolve to attain *anuttara-samyak-saṃbodhi*. Even so, I do not yet know how the bodhisattva should train in the bodhisattva practices or how he should cultivate the bodhisattva path. I have heard that the Ārya is well

正體字

我聞聖者。善能誘誨。願為我說。時彼童
418a07║ 子。告善財言。善男子。我得菩薩解脫。名善知
418a08║ 眾藝。我恒唱持此之字母。唱阿字時。入般若
418a09║ 波羅蜜門。名以菩薩威力入無差別境界。唱
418a10║ 多字時。入般若波羅蜜門。名無邊差別門。
418a11║ [1]唱波字時。入般若波羅蜜門。名普照法界。
418a12║ 唱者字時。入般若波羅蜜門。名普輪斷差別。
418a13║ 唱那字時。入般若波羅蜜門。名得無依無上。
418a14║ 唱邏字時。入般若波羅蜜門。名離依止無垢。
418a15║ 唱[2]柂([3]輕呼)字時。入般若波羅蜜門。名不退轉
418a16║ 方便。唱婆([4]蒲我[5]切)字時。入般若波羅蜜門。名
418a17║ 金剛場。唱荼([6]徒解[*]切)字時。入般若波羅蜜門。名
418a18║ 曰普輪。唱沙([7]史我[*]切)字時。入般若波羅蜜門。名
418a19║ 為海藏。唱縛([8]房可[*]切)字時。入般若波羅蜜門。名
418a20║ 普生安住。唱哆([9]都我[*]切)字時。入般若波羅蜜門。
418a21║ 名圓滿光。唱也([10]以可[*]切)字時。入般若波羅蜜門。
418a22║ 名差別積聚。唱瑟吒字時。入般若波羅蜜門。
418a23║ 名普光明息煩惱。

简体字

我闻圣者善能诱诲，愿为我说！”

时，彼童子告善财言：“善男子，我得菩萨解脱，名善知众艺。我恒唱持此之字母：唱阿字时，入般若波罗蜜门，名以菩萨威力入无差别境界；唱多字时，入般若波罗蜜门，名无边差别门；唱波字时，入般若波罗蜜门，名普照法界；唱者字时，入般若波罗蜜门，名普轮断差别；唱那字时，入般若波罗蜜门，名得无依无上；唱逻字时，入般若波罗蜜门，名离依止无垢；唱拖（轻呼）字时，入般若波罗蜜门，名不退转方便；唱婆（蒲我切）字时，入般若波罗蜜门，名金刚场；唱荼（徒解切）字时，入般若波罗蜜门，名曰普轮；唱沙（史我切）字时，入般若波罗蜜门，名为海藏；唱缚（房可切）字时，入般若波罗蜜门，名普生安住；唱哆（都我切）字时，入般若波罗蜜门，名圆满光；唱也（以可切）字时，入般若波罗蜜门，名差别积聚；唱瑟吒字时，入般若波罗蜜门，名普光明息烦恼；

able to provide guidance and instruction in these matters. Please explain this for me.

That youth then spoke to Sudhana, saying:

Son of Good Family, I have acquired a bodhisattva liberation known as "skillful knowledge of the many arts." I constantly chant and bear in mind its syllabary in this way:

When I chant the *"a"* syllable, I enter the gateway of the *prajñāpāramitā* known as "entering the sphere of non-differentiation through the awesome power of the bodhisattva."

When I chant the *"ra"* syllable, I enter the gateway of the *prajñāpāramitā* known as "the gateway of boundless differentiation."

When I chant the *"pa"* syllable, I enter the gateway of the *prajñāpāramitā* known as "universal illumination of the Dharma realm."

When I chant the *"ca"* syllable, I enter the gateway of the *prajñāpāramitā* known as "the universal wheel that cuts off differentiation."

When I chant the *"na"* syllable, I enter the gateway of the *prajñāpāramitā* known as "acquisition of independent unsurpassability."

When I chant the *"la"* syllable, I enter the gateway of the *prajñāpāramitā* known as "stainless abandonment of dependence."

When I chant the *"da"* syllable, I enter the gateway of the *prajñāpāramitā* known as "irreversible effort."

When I chant the *"ba"* syllable, I enter the gateway of the *prajñāpāramitā* known as "the vajra *maṇḍala*."

When I chant the *"ḍa"* syllable, I enter the gateway of the *prajñāpāramitā* known as "the universal wheel."

When I chant the *"ṣa"* syllable, I enter the gateway of the *prajñāpāramitā* known as "oceanic matrix."

When I chant the *"va"* syllable, I enter the gateway of the *prajñāpāramitā* known as "universally arising establishment."

When I chant the *"ta"* syllable, I enter the gateway of the *prajñāpāramitā* known as "*maṇḍala* of light."

When I chant the *"ya"* syllable, I enter the gateway of the *prajñāpāramitā* known as "mass of differentiations."

When I chant the *"ṣṭa"* syllable, I enter the gateway of the *prajñāpāramitā* known as "universal light that extinguishes afflictions."

正體字

唱迦字時。入般若波羅蜜
418a24‖ 門。名無差別雲。唱娑([11]蘇我[＊]切)字時。入般若波羅
418a25‖ 蜜門。名降[12]霔大雨。唱麼字時。入般若波羅
418a26‖ 蜜門。名大流湍激眾峯齊峙。唱伽([13]上聲輕呼)字時。
418a27‖ 入般若波羅蜜門。名普安立。唱他([14]他可[15]切)字時。
418a28‖ 入般若波羅蜜門。名真如平等藏。唱社字時。
418a29‖ 入般若波羅蜜門。名入世間海清淨。唱鎖字
418b01‖ 時。入般若波羅蜜門。名念一切佛莊嚴。唱柂
418b02‖ 字時。入般若波羅蜜門。名觀察[16]揀擇一切法
418b03‖ 聚。唱奢([17]尸苛[＊]切)字時。入般若波羅蜜門。名隨順
418b04‖ 一切佛教輪光明。唱佉字時。入般若波羅蜜
418b05‖ 門。名修因地智慧藏。唱叉(楚我[18]切)字時。入般若
418b06‖ 波羅蜜門。名息諸業海藏。唱娑(蘇紇[＊]切)多([19]上聲[20]呼)字
418b07‖ 時。入般若波羅蜜門。名蠲諸惑障開淨光明。
418b08‖ 唱壤字時。入般若波羅蜜門。名作世間智慧
418b09‖ 門。唱曷攞多([21]上聲)字時。入般若波羅蜜門。名
418b10‖ 生死境界智慧輪。唱婆(蒲餓[22]切)字時。入般若波
418b11‖ 羅蜜門。名一切智宮殿圓滿莊嚴。

简体字

唱迦字时，入般若波罗蜜门，名无差别云；唱娑（苏我切）字时，入般若波罗蜜门，名降霔大雨；唱么字时，入般若波罗蜜门，名大流湍激众峰齐峙；唱伽（上声轻呼）字时，入般若波罗蜜门，名普安立；唱他（他可切）字时，入般若波罗蜜门，名真如平等藏；唱社字时，入般若波罗蜜门，名入世间海清净；唱锁字时，入般若波罗蜜门，名念一切佛庄严；唱柂字时，入般若波罗蜜门，名观察简择一切法聚；唱奢（尸何切）字时，入般若波罗蜜门，名随顺一切佛教轮光明；唱佉字时，入般若波罗蜜门，名修因地智慧藏；唱叉（楚我切）字时，入般若波罗蜜门，名息诸业海藏；唱娑（苏纥切）多（上声呼）字时，入般若波罗蜜门，名蠲诸惑障开净光明；唱壤字时，入般若波罗蜜门，名作世间智慧门；唱曷攞多（上声呼）字时，入般若波罗蜜门，名生死境界智慧轮；唱婆（蒲饿切）字时，入般若波罗蜜门，名一切智宫殿圆满庄严；

When I chant the "*ka*" syllable, I enter the gateway of the *prajñāpāramitā* known as "cloud of non-differentiation."

When I chant the "*sa*" syllable, I enter the gateway of the *prajñāpāramitā* known as "the deluge of great rain."

When I chant the "*ma*" syllable, I enter the gateway of the *prajñāpāramitā* known as "vast torrential rapids and the uniformly even range of many mountain peaks."

When I chant the "*ga*" syllable, I enter the gateway of the *prajñāpāramitā* known as "universal establishment."

When I chant the "*tha*" syllable, I enter the gateway of the *prajñāpāramitā* known as "treasury of the uniform equality of true suchness."

When I chant the "*ja*" syllable, I enter the gateway of the *prajñāpāramitā* known as "entering the purity of the ocean of worldly existence."

When I chant the "*sva*" syllable, I enter the gateway of the *prajñāpāramitā* known as "adornment of the mindfulness of all buddhas."

When I chant the "*dha*" syllable, I enter the gateway of the *prajñāpāramitā* known as "examination and investigation of the aggregation of all dharmas."

When I chant the "*śa*" syllable, I enter the gateway of the *prajñāpāramitā* known as "the light of accordance with the wheel of all buddhas' teachings."

When I chant the "*kha*" syllable, I enter the gateway of the *prajñāpāramitā* known as "cultivation of the treasury of wisdom pertaining to the causal ground."

When I chant the "*kṣa*" syllable, I enter the gateway of the *prajñāpāramitā* known as "the treasury of extinguishing the ocean of karma."

When I chant the "*sta*" syllable, I enter the gateway of the *prajñāpāramitā* known as "purging affliction-based obstacles and opening the light of purity."

When I chant the "*ña*" syllable, I enter the gateway of the *prajñāpāramitā* known as "the gateway to wisdom regarding the creation of the world."

When I chant the "*tha*" syllable, I enter the gateway of the *prajñāpāramitā* known as "the sphere of wisdom regarding the realm of *saṃsāra*."

When I chant the "*bha*" syllable, I enter the gateway of the *prajñāpāramitā* known as "the perfectly full adornments of the palace of all-knowledge."

正體字

唱車(上聲[＊]呼)
418b12‖ 字時。入般若波羅蜜門。名修行方便藏各別
418b13‖ 圓滿。唱娑(蘇紇[＊]切)麼字時。入般若波羅蜜門。名
418b14‖ 隨十方現見諸佛。唱訶婆([23]二字皆上聲呼)字時。入般
418b15‖ 若[24]波羅蜜門。名觀察一切無緣眾生方便攝
418b16‖ 受令出生無礙力。唱縒(七可[＊]切)字時。入般若波
418b17‖ 羅蜜門。名修行趣入一切功德海。唱伽(上聲[＊]呼)字
418b18‖ 時。入般若波羅蜜門。名持一切法雲堅固海
418b19‖ 藏。唱吒字時。入般若波羅蜜門。名隨願普見
418b20‖ 十方諸佛。唱拏(嬭可[＊]切)字時。入般若波羅蜜門。
418b21‖ 名觀察字輪有無盡諸億字。唱娑(蘇紇[＊]切)頗字時。
418b22‖ 入般若波羅蜜門。名化眾生究竟處。唱娑(同前音)
418b23‖ 迦字時。入般若波羅蜜門。名廣大藏無礙辯
418b24‖ 光明輪遍照。唱也(夷[25]舸[＊]切)娑(蘇舸[＊]切)字時。入般若
418b25‖ 波羅蜜門。名宣說一切佛法境界。唱室者字
418b26‖ 時。入般若波羅蜜門。名於一切眾生界法雷
418b27‖ 遍吼。唱侘(恥加[＊]切)字時。入般若波羅蜜門。名以
418b28‖ 無我法開曉眾生。唱陀字時。入般若波羅蜜
418b29‖ 門。名一切法輪差別藏。

简体字

唱车（上声呼）字时，入般若波罗蜜门，名修行方便藏各别圆满；唱娑（苏纥切）么字时，入般若波罗蜜门，名随十方现见诸佛；唱诃婆（诃婆二字皆上声呼）字时，入般若波罗蜜门，名观察一切无缘众生方便摄受令出生无碍力；唱縒（七可切）字时，入般若波罗蜜门，名修行趣入一切功德海；唱伽（上声呼）字时，入般若波罗蜜门，名持一切法云坚固海藏；唱吒字时，入般若波罗蜜门，名随愿普见十方诸佛；唱拏（奶可切）字时，入般若波罗蜜门，名观察字轮有无尽诸亿字；唱娑（苏纥切）颇字时，入般若波罗蜜门，名化众生究竟处；唱娑（同前音）迦字时，入般若波罗蜜门，名广大藏无碍辩光明轮遍照；唱也（夷舸切）娑（苏舸切）字时，入般若波罗蜜门，名宣说一切佛法境界；唱室者字时，入般若波罗蜜门，名于一切众生界法雷遍吼；唱侘（耻加切）字时，入般若波罗蜜门，名以无我法开晓众生；唱陀字时，入般若波罗蜜门，名一切法轮差别藏。

When I chant the "*cha*" syllable, I enter the gateway of the *prajñāpāramitā* known as "cultivation of the treasury of effort through which each one is differently fulfilled."

When I chant the "*sma*" syllable, I enter the gateway of the *prajñāpāramitā* known as "the direct seeing of all buddhas throughout the ten directions."

When I chant the "*hva*" syllable, I enter the gateway of the *prajñāpāramitā* known as "contemplating all incapable beings and using skillful means to gather them in and enable them to develop unimpeded power."

When I chant the "*tsa*" syllable, I enter the gateway of the *prajñāpāramitā* known as "cultivating and entering the ocean of all qualities."

When I chant the "*gha*" syllable, I enter the gateway of the *prajñāpāramitā* known as "the solid oceanic treasury supporting the cloud of all dharmas."

When I chant the "*ṭha*" syllable, I enter the gateway of the *prajñāpāramitā* known as "everywhere seeing the buddhas of the ten directions by according with one's vows."

When I chant the "*ṇa*" syllable, I enter the gateway of the *prajñāpāramitā* known as "contemplating the syllabary wheel's possession of an inexhaustible number of *koṭīs* of syllables."

When I chant the "*pha*" syllable, I enter the gateway of the *prajñāpāramitā* known as "the ultimate station for the ripening of beings."

When I chant the "*ska*" syllable, I enter the gateway of the *prajñāpāramitā* known as "the universally pervasive illumination of the sphere of light emanating from a vast treasury of unimpeded eloquence."

When I chant the "*ysa*" syllable, I enter the gateway of the *prajñāpāramitā* known as "the domain of the proclamation of all the dharmas of a buddha."

When I chant the "*śca*" syllable, I enter the gateway of the *prajñāpāramitā* known as "the universally pervasive roar of the thunder of the Dharma throughout all realms of beings."

When I chant the "*ṭa*" syllable, I enter the gateway of the *prajñāpāramitā* known as "instructing and awakening beings with the dharma of non-self."

And when I chant the "*ḍha*" syllable, I enter the gateway of the *prajñāpāramitā* known as "the treasury of distinctions arising from all turnings of the Dharma wheel."

正體字

善男子。我唱如是
418c01 字母時。此四十二般若波羅蜜門為首。入無
418c02 量無數般若波羅蜜門。善男子。我唯知此[26]善
418c03 知眾藝菩薩解脫。如諸菩薩摩訶薩。能於一
418c04 切世出世間善巧之法。以智通達。到於彼岸。
418c05 殊方異藝。咸綜無遺。文字算數。蘊其深解。醫
418c06 方呪術。善療眾病。有諸眾生。鬼魅所持。怨憎
418c07 呪詛。惡星變怪。死屍奔逐。癲癇羸瘦。種種諸
418c08 疾。咸能救之。使得痊愈。又善別知金玉珠貝。
418c09 珊瑚瑠璃。摩尼硨磲。雞薩羅等。一切寶藏
418c10 出生之處。品類不同。價直多少。村營鄉邑。大
418c11 小都城。宮殿苑園。巖泉藪澤。凡是一切人
418c12 眾所居。菩薩咸能隨方攝護。又善觀察天文
418c13 地理。人相吉凶。鳥獸音聲。雲霞氣候。年穀豐
418c14 儉。國土安危。如是世間。所有[27]技藝。莫不[28]該
418c15 練。盡其源本。

简体字

善男子，我唱如是字母时，此四十二般若波罗蜜门为首，入无量无数般若波罗蜜门。

“善男子，我唯知此善知众艺菩萨解脱。如诸菩萨摩诃萨，能于一切世、出世间善巧之法，以智通达到于彼岸；殊方异艺，咸综无遗；文字、算数，蕴其深解；医方、咒术，善疗众病；有诸众生，鬼魅所持，怨憎咒诅，恶星变怪，死尸奔逐，癫痫、羸瘦，种种诸疾，咸能救之，使得痊愈；又善别知金玉、珠贝、珊瑚、琉璃、摩尼、砗磲、鸡萨罗等一切宝藏，出生之处，品类不同，价值多少；村营乡邑、大小都城、宫殿苑园、岩泉薮泽，凡是一切人众所居，菩萨咸能随方摄护；又善观察天文地理、人相吉凶、鸟兽音声、云霞气候、年谷丰俭、国土安危，如是世间所有技艺，莫不该练，尽其源本；

Son of the Buddha, when I chant this syllabary, I then enter measurelessly and numberlessly many *prajñāpāramitā* gateways among which these forty-two *prajñāpāramitā* gateways are foremost.

Son of Good Family, I know only this bodhisattva liberation known as "skillful knowledge of the many arts." As for the bodhisattva-mahāsattvas:

Who use wisdom to achieve perfection in their penetrating comprehension of the dharmas of all mundane and world-transcending skills;

Who have comprehensively assembled all the extraordinary techniques and exotic arts without exception;

Who have assembled a profound understanding of literary and mathematical subjects;

Who use medical prescriptions and mantric techniques to skillfully treat the many kinds of disorders so that, wherever there are beings who are possessed by ghosts and goblins, who are under the influence of vengeful magical spells, who have undergone strange transformations due to the influence of evil stars, who are chased after by running corpses, who are afflicted by epileptic convulsions and wasting disorders, or who are afflicted by the many other different kinds of sicknesses, they are able to save them all and bring about a cure;

Who are also skilled in distinguishing and knowing with respect to gold, jade, pearls, cowries, coral, lapis lazuli, *maṇi* jewels, *musāragalva*, *keśara*, and all other kinds of contents of jewel treasuries the places from which they came, their different categories, and their particular valuations;

Who as bodhisattvas are also able, no matter what the location, to bring under their protection the inhabitants of hamlets, encampments, villages, towns, large and small cities, palaces, parks and gardens, caves, springs, jungles, marshes, and whatever other kinds of places in which communities of people reside;

Who are also skilled in the contemplative analysis and interpretation of matters pertaining to astronomy and geography, auspicious or inauspicious physiognomy, bird calls, animal cries, the arrangements of the clouds, the weather, the prospect of any year's crops to be either abundant or deficient, the safety or danger of a country, and other such worldly skills and arts of which there are none in which they have not acquired such comprehensive expertise that it exhaustively fathoms the very origins of such knowledge;

正體字

又能分別出世之法。正名[29]辨
418c16‖ 義。觀察體相。隨順修行。智入其中。無疑無
418c17‖ 礙。無愚暗。無頑鈍。無憂惱。無沈沒。無不現
418c18‖ 證。而我云何能知能說彼功德行。善男子。此
418c19‖ 摩竭提國有一聚落。彼中有城。名婆咀那。有
418c20‖ 優婆夷號曰賢勝。汝詣彼問。菩薩云何學菩
418c21‖ 薩行。修菩薩道。時善財童子。頭面敬禮知藝
418c22‖ 之足。遶無數匝。戀仰辭去
418c23‖ 向聚落城。至賢勝所。禮足圍遶。合掌恭敬。於
418c24‖ 一面立。白言。聖者。我已先發阿耨多羅三藐
418c25‖ 三菩提心。而未知菩薩云何學菩薩行。云何
418c26‖ 修菩薩道。我聞聖者。善能誘誨。願為我說。賢
418c27‖ 勝答言。善男子。我得菩薩解脫。名無依處道
418c28‖ 場。既自開解。復為人說。又得無盡三昧。非彼
418c29‖ 三昧法。有盡無盡。

简体字

又能分别出世之法，正名辩义，观察体相，随顺修行，智入其中，无疑、无碍、无愚暗、无顽钝、无忧恼、无沉没、无不现证。而我云何能知能说彼功德行？

“善男子，此摩竭提国，有一聚落，彼中有城，名婆咀那；有优婆夷，号曰贤胜。汝诣彼问：菩萨云何学菩萨行、修菩萨道？”

时，善财童子头面敬礼知艺之足，绕无数匝，恋仰辞去。

向聚落城，至贤胜所，礼足围绕，合掌恭敬，于一面立，白言：“圣者，我已先发阿耨多罗三藐三菩提心，而未知菩萨云何学菩萨行？云何修菩萨道？我闻圣者善能诱诲，愿为我说！”

贤胜答言：“善男子，我得菩萨解脱，名无依处道场；既自开解，复为人说。又得无尽三昧，非彼三昧法有尽、无尽，

Who are also well able to distinguish world-transcending dharmas and rightly determine their designation, distinguish their meanings, analytically contemplate and deduce their essential substance and signs, and comply with them in their cultivation; and

Whose knowledge so well penetrates these matters that it is free of doubt, unimpeded, free of the darkness of delusion, free of any sort of mental dullness, free of worry and distress, unsubmerged, and free of any failure to achieve directly present realization—

How could I know of or be able to speak about their meritorious qualities and practices?

Son of Good Family, in this state of Magadha there is a district in which there is a city named Vartanaka where an *upāsikā* named Bhadrottamā or "Supreme Among Worthies" dwells. You should go there, pay your respects, and ask her, "How should the bodhisattva train in the bodhisattva practices and how should he cultivate the bodhisattva path?"

Sudhana the Youth then bowed down in reverence at the feet of Śilpābhijña and circumambulated him countless times as he gazed up at him in fond admiration. He then respectfully withdrew and departed.

45 – Bhadrottamā

[At that time, Sudhana] proceeded toward the city in that district and went to the abode of Bhadrottamā or "Supreme Among Worthies," where he bowed down in reverence at her feet and circumambulated her. He then stood off to one side with his palms pressed together respectfully and addressed her, saying:

O Āryā, I am one who has already resolved to attain *anuttara-samyak-saṃbodhi*. Still, I do not yet understand how the bodhisattva should train in the bodhisattva practices or how he should cultivate the bodhisattva path. I have heard that the Āryā is well able to provide guidance and instruction in these matters. Please explain this for me.

Bhadrottamā replied to him, saying:

Son of Good Family, I have acquired a bodhisattva liberation known as "the *maṇḍala* of independence." Having understood it myself, I then teach it for others. I have also acquired an inexhaustible samādhi. It is not the case that the dharmas of that samādhi are either exhaustible or inexhaustible. [Rather]:

正體字

以能出生一切智性眼無
419a01 盡故。又能出生一切智性耳無盡故。又能出
419a02 生一切智性鼻無盡故。又能出生一切智性
419a03 舌無盡故。又能出生一切智性身無盡故。又
419a04 能出生一切智性意無盡故。又能出生一切
419a05 智性功德波濤無盡故。又能出生一切智性
419a06 智慧光明無盡故。又能出生一切智性速疾
419a07 神通無盡故。善男子。我唯知此無依處道場
419a08 解脫。如諸菩薩摩訶薩。一切無著功德行。而
419a09 我云何盡能知說。善男子。南方有城。名為
419a10 [1]沃田。彼有長者。名堅固解脫。汝可往問。菩
419a11 薩云何學菩薩行。修菩薩道。爾時善財。禮賢
419a12 勝足。遶無數匝。戀慕瞻仰。辭退南行
419a13 到於彼城。詣長者所。禮足圍遶。合掌恭敬。於
419a14 一面立。白言。聖者。我已先發阿耨多羅三藐
419a15 三菩提心。而未知菩薩云何學菩薩行。

简体字

以能出生一切智性眼无尽故，又能出生一切智性耳无尽故，又能出生一切智性鼻无尽故，又能出生一切智性舌无尽故，又能出生一切智性身无尽故，又能出生一切智性意无尽故，又能出生一切智性功德波涛无尽故，又能出生一切智性智慧光明无尽故，又能出生一切智性速疾神通无尽故。

“善男子，我唯知此无依处道场解脱。如诸菩萨摩诃萨一切无著功德行，而我云何尽能知说？

“善男子，南方有城，名为沃田；彼有长者，名坚固解脱。汝可往问：菩萨云何学菩萨行、修菩萨道？”

尔时，善财礼贤胜足，绕无数匝，恋慕瞻仰，辞退南行。

到于彼城，诣长者所，礼足围绕，合掌恭敬，于一面立，白言：“圣者，我已先发阿耨多罗三藐三菩提心，而未知菩萨云何学菩萨行？

It is because it is able to produce the eye of all-knowledge, which is inexhaustible;

It is because it is also able to produce the ear of all-knowledge, which is inexhaustible;

It is because it is also able to produce the nose of all-knowledge, which is inexhaustible;

It is because it is also able to produce the tongue of all-knowledge, which is inexhaustible;

It is because it is also able to produce the body of all-knowledge, which is inexhaustible;

It is because it is also able to produce the mind of all-knowledge, which is inexhaustible;

It is because it is also able to produce the waves of meritorious qualities of all-knowledge, which are inexhaustible;

It is because it is also able to produce the light of wisdom of all-knowledge, which is inexhaustible; and

It is because it is also able to produce the swiftly executed spiritual superknowledges of all-knowledge, which are inexhaustible.

Son of Good Family, I know only this "*maṇḍala* of independence" liberation. As for the meritorious practices of the bodhisattva-mahāsattvas who are free of attachment in all things, how could I be completely able to know of or speak about them?

Son of Good Family, off to the south, there is a city known as Bharukaccha in which there is an elder known as Muktisāra,[17] or "Solid Liberation." You could go to see him and ask him, "How should the bodhisattva train in the bodhisattva practices and how should he cultivate the bodhisattva path?"

Sudhana then bowed down in reverence at the feet of Bhadrottamā and circumambulated her countless times as he gazed up at her in fond admiration. He then respectfully withdrew and traveled south.

46 – Muktisāra

[At that time, when Sudhana] reached that city, he went to pay his respects at the abode of that elder where he bowed down in reverence at his feet and circumambulated him. He then stood off to one side with his palms pressed together respectfully and addressed him, saying:

O Ārya, I am one who has already resolved to attain *anuttara-samyak-saṃbodhi*. Still, I do not yet know how the bodhisattva should train in the bodhisattva practices or how he should cultivate

正體字

云何
419a16‖ 修菩薩道。我聞聖者。善能誘誨。願為我說。長
419a17‖ 者答言。善男子。我得菩薩解脫。名無著念
419a18‖ 清淨莊嚴。我自得是解脫已來。於十方佛所。
419a19‖ 勤求正法。無有休息。善男子。[2]我唯知此無
419a20‖ 著念淨莊嚴解脫。如諸菩薩摩訶薩。獲無所
419a21‖ 畏大師子吼安住廣大福智之聚。而我云何
419a22‖ 能知能說彼功德行。善男子。即此城中。有一
419a23‖ 長者。名為妙月。其長者宅。常有光明。汝詣彼
419a24‖ 問。菩薩云何學菩薩行。修菩薩道。時善財
419a25‖ 童子。禮堅固足。遶無數匝。辭退而行
419a26‖ 向妙月所。禮足圍遶。合掌恭敬。於一面立。白
419a27‖ 言。聖者。我已先發阿耨多羅三藐三菩提心。
419a28‖ 而未知菩薩云何學菩薩行。云何修菩薩道。
419a29‖ 我聞聖者。善能誘誨。願為我說。妙月答言。善
419b01‖ 男子。我得菩薩解脫。名淨智光明。[3]善男子。
419b02‖ 我唯知此智光解脫。如諸菩薩摩訶薩。證得
419b03‖ 無量解脫法門。而我云何能知能說彼功德
419b04‖ 行。

简体字

云何修菩萨道？我闻圣者善能诱诲，愿为我说！”

长者答言：“善男子，我得菩萨解脱，名无著念清净庄严。我自得是解脱已来，于十方佛所勤求正法无有休息。

“善男子，我唯知此无著念净庄严解脱。如诸菩萨摩诃萨，获无所畏大师子吼，安住广大福智之聚；而我云何能知能说彼功德行？

“善男子，即此城中，有一长者，名为妙月；其长者宅，常有光明。汝诣彼问：菩萨云何学菩萨行、修菩萨道？”

时，善财童子礼坚固足，绕无数匝，辞退而行。

向妙月所，礼足围绕，合掌恭敬，于一面立，白言：“圣者，我已先发阿耨多罗三藐三菩提心，而未知菩萨云何学菩萨行？云何修菩萨道？我闻圣者善能诱诲，愿为我说！”

妙月答言：“善男子，我得菩萨解脱，名净智光明。

“善男子，我唯知此智光解脱。如诸菩萨摩诃萨证得无量解脱法门，而我云何能知能说彼功德行？

the bodhisattva path. I have heard that the Ārya is well able to offer guidance and instruction in these matters. Please explain this for me.

The Elder replied to him, saying:

I have acquired a bodhisattva liberation known as "the pure adornment of unattached mindfulness." From the time I acquired this liberation on up to the present, I have incessantly and diligently sought right Dharma under the buddhas of the ten directions.

Son of Good Family, I know only this liberation, "the pure adornment of unattached mindfulness." As for the bodhisattva-mahāsattvas who have acquired the fearless lion's roar and have become established in the accumulations of vast merit and wisdom, how could I know of or be able to speak about their meritorious qualities and practices?

Son of Good Family, within this very city, there is an elder named Sucandra, or "Marvelous Moon." That elder's house always emanates light. You should go there, pay your respects, and ask him, "How should the bodhisattva train in the bodhisattva practices and how should he cultivate the bodhisattva path?"

Sudhana the Youth then bowed down in reverence at the feet of Muktisāra, circumambulated him countless times, and respectfully withdrew.

47 – Sucandra

[At that time, Sudhana] went to the abode of Sucandra where he bowed down in reverence at his feet and circumambulated him. Then, standing off to one side with his palms pressed together respectfully, he addressed him, saying:

O Ārya, I am one who has already resolved to attain *anuttara-samyak-saṃbodhi*. Even so, I still do not yet know how the bodhisattva should train in the bodhisattva practices or how he should cultivate the bodhisattva path. I have heard that the Ārya is well able to provide guidance and instruction in these matters. Please explain this for me.

Sucandra then replied to him, saying:

Son of Good Family, I have acquired a bodhisattva liberation known as "the light of pure wisdom." Son of Good Family, I know only this light of pure wisdom liberation. As for the bodhisattva-mahāsattvas who have realized and acquired countless Dharma gateways to liberation, how could I know of or be able to speak about their meritorious qualities and practices?

正體字

善男子。於此南方。有城名出生。彼有長
419b05‖ 者。名無勝軍。汝詣彼問。菩薩云何學菩薩行。
419b06‖ 修菩薩道。是時善財禮妙月足。遶無數匝。戀
419b07‖ 仰辭去
419b08‖ 漸向彼城。至長者所。禮足圍遶。合掌恭敬。於
419b09‖ 一面立。白言。聖者。我已先發阿耨多羅三藐
419b10‖ 三菩提心。而未知菩薩云何學菩薩行。云何
419b11‖ 修菩薩道。我聞聖者。善能誘誨。願為我說。長
419b12‖ 者答言。善男子。我得菩薩解脫。名無盡相。
419b13‖ [4]我以證此菩薩解脫。見無量佛得無盡藏。善
419b14‖ 男子。我唯知此無盡相解脫。如諸菩薩摩訶
419b15‖ 薩。得無限智無礙辯才。而我云何能知能說
419b16‖ 彼功德行。善男子。於此城南。有一聚落。名
419b17‖ 之為法。彼聚落中。有婆羅門。名最寂靜。汝詣
419b18‖ 彼問。菩薩云何學菩薩行。修菩薩道。時善
419b19‖ 財童子。禮無勝軍足。遶無數匝。戀仰辭去

简体字

“善男子，于此南方，有城名出生；彼有长者，名无胜军。汝诣彼问：菩萨云何学菩萨行、修菩萨道？”

是时，善财礼妙月足，绕无数匝，恋仰辞去。

渐向彼城，至长者所，礼足围绕，合掌恭敬，于一面立，白言：“圣者，我已先发阿耨多罗三藐三菩提心，而未知菩萨云何学菩萨行？云何修菩萨道？我闻圣者善能诱诲，愿为我说！”

长者答言：“善男子，我得菩萨解脱，名无尽相。我以证此菩萨解脱，见无量佛，得无尽藏。

“善男子，我唯知此无尽相解脱。如诸菩萨摩诃萨得无限智无碍辩才，而我云何能知能说彼功德行？

“善男子，于此城南，有一聚落，名之为：法；彼聚落中，有婆罗门，名最寂静。汝诣彼问：菩萨云何学菩萨行、修菩萨道？”

时，善财童子礼无胜军足，绕无数匝，恋仰辞去。

Son of Good Family, south of here there is a city known as Roruk, or "Generation," in which there is an elder known as Ajitasena or "Invincible Army." You should go there, pay your respects, and ask him, "How should the bodhisattva train in the bodhisattva practices and how should he cultivate the bodhisattva path?"

Sudhana bowed down in reverence at the feet of Sucandra and circumambulated him countless times as he gazed up at him in fond admiration. He then took his leave and departed.

48 – Ajitasena

[At that time, Sudhana] gradually traveled toward that city. When he arrived at the abode of that elder he bowed down in reverence at his feet and circumambulated him. Then, standing off to one side with his palms pressed together respectfully, he addressed him, saying:

O Ārya, I am one who has already resolved to attain *anuttara-samyak-saṃbodhi.* Even so, I still do not yet know how the bodhisattva should train in the bodhisattva practices or how he should cultivate the bodhisattva path. I have heard that the Ārya is well able to provide guidance and instruction in these matters. Please explain this for me.

The Elder then replied to him, saying:

Son of Good Family, I have acquired a bodhisattva liberation known as "inexhaustible appearance." It is due to realizing this bodhisattva liberation that I see countless buddhas and acquire their inexhaustible treasuries.

Son of Good Family, I know only this "inexhaustible appearance" liberation. As for the bodhisattva-mahāsattvas who have acquired such unlimited wisdom and unimpeded eloquence, how could I know of or be able to speak about their meritorious qualities and practices?

Son of Good Family, south of this city there is a village known as "Dharma" in which there is a brahman known as Śivarāgra or "Supreme Quiescence." You should go there, pay your respects, and ask him, "How should the bodhisattva train in the bodhisattva practices and how should he cultivate the bodhisattva path?"

Sudhana the Youth then bowed down in reverence at the feet of Ajitasena and circumambulated him countless times as he gazed up at him in fond admiration. He then took his leave and departed.

正體字

419b20‖ 漸次南行。詣彼聚落。見最寂靜。禮足圍遶。合
419b21‖ 掌恭敬。於一面立。白言。聖者。我已先發阿耨
419b22‖ 多羅三藐三菩提心。而未知菩薩云何學菩
419b23‖ 薩行。云何修菩薩道。我聞聖者。善能誘誨。願
419b24‖ 為我說。婆羅門答言。善男子。我得菩薩解脫。
419b25‖ 名誠願語。過去現在。未來菩薩。以是語故。乃
419b26‖ 至於阿耨多羅三藐三菩提。無有退轉。[5]無已
419b27‖ 退。無現退。無當退。善男子。我以住於誠願語
419b28‖ 故。隨意所作。莫不成滿。善男子。我唯知此誠
419b29‖ 語解脫。如諸菩薩摩訶薩。與誠願語。行止
419c01‖ 無違。言必以誠。未曾虛妄。無量功德。因之出
419c02‖ 生。而我云何。能知能說。善男子。於此南方。
419c03‖ 有城名妙意華門。彼有童子。名曰德生。復有
419c04‖ 童女。名為有德。汝詣彼問。菩薩云何。學菩薩
419c05‖ 行。修菩薩道。時善財童子。於法尊重。禮婆羅
419c06‖ 門足。遶無數匝。戀仰而去

简体字

渐次南行，诣彼聚落，见最寂静，礼足围绕，合掌恭敬，于一面立，白言：“圣者，我已先发阿耨多罗三藐三菩提心，而未知菩萨云何学菩萨行？云何修菩萨道？我闻圣者善能诱诲，愿为我说！”

婆罗门答言：“善男子，我得菩萨解脱，名诚愿语；过去、现在、未来菩萨，以是语故，乃至于阿耨多罗三藐三菩提，无有退转，无已退、无现退、无当退。

“善男子，我以住于诚愿语故，随意所作，莫不成满。善男子，我唯知此诚语解脱。如诸菩萨摩诃萨，与诚愿语，行止无违，言必以诚，未曾虚妄，无量功德因之出生；而我云何能知能说？

“善男子，于此南方，有城名妙意华门；彼有童子，名曰德生；复有童女，名为有德。汝诣彼问：菩萨云何学菩萨行、修菩萨道？”

时，善财童子于法尊重，礼婆罗门足，绕无数匝，恋仰而去。

49 – Śivarāgra

[At that time, Sudhana] gradually traveled toward the south and went to that village where he saw Śivarāgra, bowed down in reverence at his feet, and circumambulated him. Then, standing off to one side with his palms pressed together respectfully, he addressed him, saying:

O Ārya, I am one who has already resolved to attain *anuttara-samyak-saṃbodhi*. Even so, I still do not yet understand how the bodhisattva should train in the bodhisattva practices or how he should cultivate the bodhisattva path. I have heard that the Ārya is well able to provide guidance and instruction in these matters. Please explain this for me.

The Brahman then replied, saying:

Son of Good Family, I have acquired a bodhisattva liberation known as "speech arising from the vow to be truthful." It is due to speech such as this that the bodhisattvas of the past, future, and present have achieved everything up to the irreversibility in progressing toward *anuttara-samyak-saṃbodhi* by which they have never retreated in the past, do not retreat in the present, and will not retreat in the future. Son of Good Family, it is due to abiding in truthful aspirations and speech that, whatever I decide to do, there is nothing in which I am not completely successful.

Son of Good Family, I know only this "speech arising from the vow to be truthful" liberation. As for the bodhisattva-mahāsattvas who in whatever they do never contradict the vow to be truthful in speech, whose speech is definitely truthful and never false, and who produce measureless merit because of this, how could I know of or be able to speak about them?

Son of Good Family, south of here there is a city known as Sumanāmukha or "Gateway to the Flower of the Sublime Mind" in which there is a youth known as Śrīsaṃbhava or "Born of Virtue." There is also a maiden there known as Śrīmati or "Possessed of Virtue." You should go there, pay your respects to them, and ask them, "How should the bodhisattva train in the bodhisattva practices and how should he cultivate the bodhisattva path?"

Then, out of veneration for the Dharma, Sudhana the Youth bowed down in reverence at the feet of that brahman, circumambulated him countless times as he gazed up at him in fond admiration, and then departed.

正體字

419c10‖ [7]大方廣佛華嚴經卷[8]第七十七
419c13‖ [12]入法界品第三十九之十八
419c14‖ 爾時善財童子。漸次南行。至妙意華門城。見
419c15‖ 德生童子有德童女。頂禮其足。右遶畢已。於
419c16‖ 前合掌。而作是言。聖者。我已先發阿耨多羅
419c17‖ 三藐三菩提心。而未知菩薩云何學菩薩行。
419c18‖ 云何修菩薩道。唯願慈哀。為我宣說。時童子
419c19‖ 童女。告善財言。善男子。我等證得菩薩解脫。
419c20‖ 名為幻住。得此解脫故。見一切世界皆幻住。
419c21‖ 因緣所生故。一切眾生皆幻住。業煩惱所起
419c22‖ 故。[13]一切世間皆幻住。無明有愛等展轉緣生
419c23‖ 故。一切法皆幻住。我見等種種幻緣所生故。
419c24‖ 一切三世皆幻住。我見等顛倒智所生故。一
419c25‖ 切眾生生滅生老[14]病死憂悲苦惱皆幻住。虛
419c26‖ 妄分別所生故。一切國土皆幻住。想倒心倒
419c27‖ 見倒無明所現故。

简体字

大方广佛华严经卷第七十七

入法界品第三十九之十八

尔时，善财童子渐次南行，至妙意华门城，见德生童子、有德童女，顶礼其足，右绕毕已，于前合掌而作是言：“圣者，我已先发阿耨多罗三藐三菩提心，而未知菩萨云何学菩萨行？云何修菩萨道？唯愿慈哀，为我宣说！”

时，童子、童女告善财言：“善男子，我等证得菩萨解脱，名为幻住。得此解脱故，见一切世界皆幻住，因缘所生故；一切众生皆幻住，业烦恼所起故；一切世间皆幻住，无明、有、爱等展转缘生故；一切法皆幻住，我见等种种幻缘所生故；一切三世皆幻住，我见等颠倒智所生故；一切众生生灭、生老病死、忧悲苦恼皆幻住，虚妄分别所生故；一切国土皆幻住，想倒、心倒、见倒无明所现故；

50 – Śrīsambhava and Śrīmati

At that time, Sudhana the Youth gradually traveled southward to the city of Sumanāmukha, or "Gateway to the Flower of the Sublime Mind," where he saw the youth known as Śrīsaṃbhava or "Born of Virtue" and the maiden known as Śrīmati or "Possessed of Virtue." After bowing down in reverence at their feet and circumambulating them in a rightward direction, he stood before them with palms pressed together and said:

> O Āryas, I am one who has already resolved to attain *anuttara-samyak-saṃbodhi*. Even so, I still do not yet understand how the bodhisattva should train in the bodhisattva practices or how he should cultivate the bodhisattva path. Please explain these matters for me.

The youth and the maiden then replied to Sudhana, saying:

> Son of Good Family, we have realized a bodhisattva liberation known as "illusory existence." Due to having acquired this liberation:
>
> We see all worlds as having a merely illusory existence because they are produced by causes and conditions;
>
> We see all beings as having a merely illusory existence because they are produced by karmic actions and afflictions;
>
> We see everything in the world as having a merely illusory existence because they are all produced from the progressively occurring process of conditioned origination involving [the conditions of] ignorance, becoming, craving, and so forth;
>
> We see all dharmas as having a merely illusory existence because they are the product of the view imputing the existence of a self and many other kinds of illusory conditions;
>
> We see all three periods of time[18] as having a merely illusory existence because they are the product of the view imputing the existence of a self and other such cognitions arising from inverted views;
>
> We see as having a merely illusory existence all beings' arising and cessation, their birth, aging, sickness, and death, and their sorrow, lamentation, pain, and affliction because they are all the product of false discriminations;
>
> We see all lands as having a merely illusory existence because they are manifested due to inverted perceptions, inverted thoughts, inverted views, and ignorance;

正體字

一切聲聞辟支佛皆幻住。
419c28‖ 智斷分別所成故。一切菩薩皆幻住。能自調
419c29‖ 伏教化眾生諸行願法之所成故。一切菩薩
420a01‖ 眾會變化調伏諸所施為皆幻住。願智幻所
420a02‖ 成故。善男子。幻境自性不可思議。善男子。我
420a03‖ 等二人。但能知此幻住解脫。如諸菩薩摩訶
420a04‖ 薩。善入無邊諸事幻網。彼功德行。我等云何
420a05‖ 能知能說。時童子童女。說自解脫已。以不
420a06‖ 思議諸善根力。令善財身柔軟光澤。而告之
420a07‖ 言。善男子。於此南方。有國名海岸。有園名大
420a08‖ 莊嚴。其中有一廣大樓閣。名毘盧遮那莊嚴
420a09‖ 藏。從菩薩善根果報生。從菩薩念力願力自
420a10‖ 在力神通力生。從菩薩善巧方便生。從菩薩
420a11‖ 福德智慧生。善男子。住不思議解脫菩薩。以
420a12‖ 大悲心。為諸眾生。現如是境界。集如是莊嚴。
420a13‖ 彌勒菩薩摩訶薩。安處其中。為欲攝受本所
420a14‖ 生處父母眷屬及諸人民。令成熟故。[1]又欲令
420a15‖ 彼同受生同修行眾生。於大乘中。得堅固故。

简体字

一切声闻、辟支佛皆幻住，智断分别所成故；一切菩萨皆幻住，能自调伏教化众生诸行愿法之所成故；一切菩萨众会、变化、调伏、诸所施为皆幻住，愿智幻所成故。善男子，幻境自性不可思议。

“善男子，我等二人但能知此幻住解脱。如诸菩萨摩诃萨善入无边诸事幻网，彼功德行，我等云何能知能说？”

时，童子、童女说自解脱已，以不思议诸善根力，令善财身柔软光泽，而告之言：“善男子，于此南方，有国名海岸，有园名大庄严，其中有一广大楼阁，名毗卢遮那庄严藏，从菩萨善根果报生，从菩萨念力、愿力、自在力、神通力生，从菩萨善巧方便生，从菩萨福德智慧生。

“善男子，住不思议解脱菩萨，以大悲心，为诸众生，现如是境界，集如是庄严。弥勒菩萨摩诃萨安处其中，为欲摄受本所生处父母、眷属及诸人民，令成熟故；又欲令彼同受生、同修行众生，于大乘中得坚固故；

We see all *śrāvaka* disciples and *pratyekabuddhas* as having a merely illusory existence because they are created by the severance of discriminations by cognition;

We see all bodhisattvas as having a merely illusory existence because they are created by the conduct and vows with which they train themselves and teach beings; and

We see all the transformations, training, and other endeavors carried out by all those congregations of bodhisattvas as having a merely illusory existence because they are all brought to fulfillment through their vows and wisdom which themselves are like mere conjured illusions.

Son of Good Family, the essential nature of these illusory spheres of experience is inconceivable. Son of Good Family, the two of us are only able to know this "illusory existence" liberation. As for the bodhisattva-mahāsattvas who skillfully enter into the boundless web of all phenomena's illusory existence, how could we know of or be able to speak about their meritorious qualities and practices?

Having described their liberations, the youth and the maiden then used the power of their inconceivable roots of goodness to cause Sudhana's body to become suffused with pliancy and glow with radiance, whereupon they spoke to him, saying:

Son of Good Family, south of here there is a country known as Samudrakaccho or "Ocean Shores" in which there is a park known as "Great Adornment" where there is a vast tower known as "the Chamber of Vairocana's Adornments" that has been produced from the karmic fruition of the bodhisattva's roots of goodness, that has been produced from the bodhisattva's power of mindfulness, power of vows, powers of sovereign mastery, and powers of the spiritual superknowledges, that has been produced from the bodhisattva's skillful means, and that has been produced from the bodhisattva's merit and wisdom.

Son of Good Family, it is inhabited by a bodhisattva who abides in inconceivable liberations and relies upon the mind of great compassion to manifest for beings such spheres of objective experience in which adornments such as these are brought together. It is Maitreya Bodhisattva-mahāsattva who dwells within it, doing so:

Because he wished to gather in and ripen his parents, retinue, and the peoples of those lands where he had previously been born;

Also because he wished to enable the solid establishment in the Great Vehicle of those beings with whom he has previously been born together and together with whom he has previously cultivated;

正體字

420a16‖ 又欲令彼一切眾生。隨住地隨善根皆成就
420a17‖ 故。又欲為汝顯示菩薩解脫門故。顯示菩薩
420a18‖ 遍一切處受生自在故。顯示菩薩以種種身
420a19‖ 普現一切眾生之前常教化故。顯示菩薩以
420a20‖ 大悲力普攝一切世間資財。而不厭故。顯示
420a21‖ 菩薩具修諸行。知一切行。離諸相故。顯示菩
420a22‖ 薩處處受生。了一切生皆無相故。汝詣彼問。
420a23‖ 菩薩云何行菩薩行。云何修菩薩道。云何學
420a24‖ 菩薩戒。云何淨菩薩心。云何發菩薩願。云
420a25‖ 何集菩薩助道具。云何入菩薩所住地。云何
420a26‖ 滿菩薩波羅蜜。云何獲菩薩無生忍。云何具
420a27‖ 菩薩功德法。云何事菩薩善知識。何以故。善
420a28‖ 男子。彼菩薩摩訶薩。通達一切菩薩行。了
420a29‖ 知一切眾生心。常現其前。教化調伏。彼菩薩。
420b01‖ 已滿一切波羅蜜。

简体字

又欲令彼一切众生，随住地、随善根皆成就故；又欲为汝显示菩萨解脱门故，显示菩萨遍一切处受生自在故，显示菩萨以种种身普现一切众生之前常教化故，显示菩萨以大悲力普摄一切世间资财而不厌故，显示菩萨具修诸行知一切行离诸相故，显示菩萨处处受生了一切生皆无相故。汝诣彼问：菩萨云何行菩萨行？云何修菩萨道？云何学菩萨戒？云何净菩萨心？云何发菩萨愿？云何集菩萨助道具？云何入菩萨所住地？云何满菩萨波罗蜜？云何获菩萨无生忍？云何具菩萨功德法？云何事菩萨善知识？

“何以故？善男子，彼菩萨摩诃萨通达一切菩萨行，了知一切众生心，常现其前教化调伏。彼菩萨已满一切波罗蜜，

Also because he wished to enable all beings to succeed in accordance with the grounds on which they dwelt and in accordance with the roots of goodness they possess; and also because he wished:

To reveal for you the liberation gateways of the bodhisattva;

To reveal for you the bodhisattva's sovereign mastery in being born everywhere;

To reveal for you the bodhisattva's use of many different kinds of bodies to appear everywhere before all beings and always teach them;

To reveal for you the bodhisattva's use of the power of great compassion to tirelessly accumulate all forms of wealth in the world [to benevolently give it to beings];[19]

To reveal for you the bodhisattva's complete cultivation of all practices, knowledge of all practices, and transcendence of all signs; and

To reveal for you the bodhisattva's taking on of births everywhere, completely understanding that all births are signless.

You should go there, pay your respects, and ask him with regard to the bodhisattva:

How he should practice the bodhisattva practices;

How he should cultivate the bodhisattva path;

How he should train in the bodhisattva precepts;

How he should purify the bodhisattva's resolve;

How he should make the bodhisattva vows;

How he should accumulate the bodhisattva's provisions for the path;

How he should enter the grounds on which the bodhisattva dwells;

How he should fulfill the bodhisattva's *pāramitās;*

How he should acquire the bodhisattva's unproduced-dharmas patience;

How he should perfect the dharmas of the bodhisattva's meritorious qualities; and

How he should serve the bodhisattva's good spiritual guides.

And why should you do this? Son of Good Family, that bodhisattva-mahāsattva has a penetrating comprehension of all the bodhisattva practices, completely knows the minds of all beings, and always appears before them to teach and train them. That bodhisattva has already fulfilled all the *pāramitās,* has already dwelt on all

正體字

已住一切菩薩地。[2]已證一
420b02‖ 切菩薩忍。已入一切菩薩位。已蒙授與具足
420b03‖ 記。已遊一切菩薩境。已得一切佛神力。已
420b04‖ 蒙一切如來以一切智。甘露法水。而灌其頂。
420b05‖ 善男子。彼善知識。能潤澤汝諸善根。能增
420b06‖ 長汝菩提心。能堅汝志。能益汝善。能長汝菩
420b07‖ 薩根。能示汝無礙法。能令汝入普賢地。能
420b08‖ 為汝說菩薩願。能為汝說普賢行。能為汝說
420b09‖ 一切菩薩行願所成功德。[3]善男子。汝不應修
420b10‖ 一善。照一法。行一行。發一願。得一記。住一
420b11‖ 忍。生究竟想。不應以限量心。行於六度。住於
420b12‖ 十地。淨佛國土。事善知識。何以故。善男子。
420b13‖ 菩薩摩訶薩。應種無量諸善根。應集無量菩
420b14‖ 提具。應修無量菩提因。應學無量巧迴向。應
420b15‖ 化無量眾生界。應知無量眾生心。應知無量
420b16‖ 眾生根。應識無量眾生解。應觀無量眾生行。
420b17‖ 應調伏無量眾生。應斷無量煩惱。應淨無量
420b18‖ 業習。應滅無量邪見。應除無量雜染心。

简体字

已住一切菩萨地，已证一切菩萨忍，已入一切菩萨位，已蒙授与具足记，已游一切菩萨境，已得一切佛神力，已蒙一切如来以一切智甘露法水而灌其顶。善男子，彼善知识能润泽汝诸善根，能增长汝菩提心，能坚汝志，能益汝善，能长汝菩萨根，能示汝无碍法，能令汝入普贤地，能为汝说菩萨愿，能为汝说普贤行，能为汝说一切菩萨行愿所成功德。

“善男子，汝不应修一善、照一法、行一行、发一愿、得一记、住一忍，生究竟想；不应以限量心，行于六度，住于十地，净佛国土，事善知识。何以故？善男子，菩萨摩诃萨应种无量诸善根，应集无量菩提具，应修无量菩提因，应学无量巧回向，应化无量众生界，应知无量众生心，应知无量众生根，应识无量众生解，应观无量众生行，应调伏无量众生，应断无量烦恼，应净无量业习，应灭无量邪见，应除无量杂染心，

the bodhisattva grounds, has already realized all the bodhisattva patiences, has already entered the stations of all bodhisattvas, has already received the complete prediction, has already roamed in all the bodhisattva realms, has already acquired the spiritual powers of all buddhas, and has already received all *tathāgatas'* crown-anointing consecration with the Dharma's elixir of immortality of the omniscient ones.

Son of Good Family, that good spiritual guide:

Is able to moisten all your roots of goodness;

Is able to produce growth in your resolve to attain bodhi;

Is able to strengthen your determination;

Is able to increase your goodness;

Is able to produce growth in your bodhisattva faculties;

Is able to show you the unimpeded Dharma;

Is able to cause you to enter the grounds of Samantabhadra;

Is able to explain the bodhisattva vows for you;

Is able to explain the practices of Samantabhadra for you; and

Is able to explain the meritorious qualities developed by the conduct and vows of all bodhisattvas.

Son of Good Family, you should not cultivate only one type of goodness, illuminate only one dharma, practice only one practice, make only one vow, receive only one prediction, and dwell in only one type of patience and think you have achieved the ultimate. You should not rely on a limited resolve to practice the six perfections, dwell on the ten grounds, purify the buddha lands and serve one's good spiritual guides.

Why? Son of Good Family, the bodhisattva-mahāsattva:

Should plant countless roots of goodness;

Should accumulate countless provisions for the path to bodhi;

Should cultivate countless causes for the realization of bodhi;

Should train in countless skillful dedications of merit;

Should teach countless realms of beings;

Should know the minds of countless beings;

Should know the faculties of countless beings;

Should recognize the understandings of countless beings;

Should contemplate the practices of countless beings;

Should train countless beings;

Should sever countless afflictions;

Should purify countless habitual karmic propensities;

Should extinguish countless wrong views;

Should rid himself of countless defiled states of mind;

正體字

應
420b19║ 發無量清淨心。應拔無量苦毒箭。應涸無量
420b20║ 愛欲海。應破無量無明暗。應摧無量我慢山。
420b21║ 應斷無量生死縛。應度無量諸有流。應竭無
420b22║ 量受生海。應令無量眾生出五欲淤泥。應使
420b23║ 無量眾生。離三界牢獄。應置無量眾生於聖
420b24║ 道中。[4]應[5]消滅無量貪欲行。應淨治無量瞋
420b25║ 恚行。應摧破無量愚癡行。應超無量魔網。應
420b26║ 離無量魔業。應淨治菩薩無量欲樂。應增長
420b27║ 菩薩無量方便。應出生菩薩無量增上根。應
420b28║ 明潔菩薩無量決定解。應趣入菩薩無量平
420b29║ 等。應清淨菩薩無量功德。應修治菩薩無量
420c01║ 諸行。應示現菩薩無量隨順世間行。應生無
420c02║ 量淨信力。應住無量精進力。應淨無量正念
420c03║ 力。應滿無量三昧力。應起無量淨慧力。應
420c04║ 堅無量勝解力。應集無量福德力。應長無量
420c05║ 智慧力。應發起無量菩薩力。應圓滿無量如
420c06║ 來力。應分別無量法門。應了知無量法門。應
420c07║ 清淨無量法門。

简体字

应发无量清净心，应拔无量苦毒箭，应涸无量爱欲海，应破无量无明暗，应摧无量我慢山，应断无量生死缚，应度无量诸有流，应竭无量受生海，应令无量众生出五欲淤泥，应使无量众生离三界牢狱，应置无量众生于圣道中，应消灭无量贪欲行，应净治无量瞋恚行，应摧破无量愚痴行，应超无量魔网，应离无量魔业，应净治菩萨无量欲乐，应增长菩萨无量方便，应出生菩萨无量增上根，应明洁菩萨无量决定解，应趣入菩萨无量平等，应清净菩萨无量功德，应修治菩萨无量诸行，应示现菩萨无量随顺世间行，应生无量净信力，应住无量精进力，应净无量正念力，应满无量三昧力，应起无量净慧力，应坚无量胜解力，应集无量福德力，应长无量智慧力，应发起无量菩萨力，应圆满无量如来力，应分别无量法门，应了知无量法门，应清净无量法门，

Should produce countless types of pure states of mind;
Should remove countless arrows of intense suffering;
Should dry up the measurelessly vast ocean of craving;
Should dispel the measureless darkness of ignorance;
Should demolish the measureless mountain of arrogance;
Should sever the countless bonds of *saṃsāra;*
Should cross beyond the measureless flood of the realms of existence;
Should dry up the measureless ocean of rebirths;
Should enable countless beings to escape the mud of the five types of desires;
Should enable countless beings to escape the prison of the three realms of existence;
Should establish countless beings on the path of the *āryas;*
Should eliminate countless actions influenced by the desires;
Should purify the countless actions influenced by hatred;
Should demolish the countless actions influenced by delusion;
Should step over the countless net-traps set by Māra;
Should abandon the countless works of the *māras;*
Should purify the bodhisattva's countless aspirations;
Should increase the countless bodhisattva skillful means;
Should produce the bodhisattva's countless superior faculties;
Should purify the bodhisattva's countless resolute convictions;
Should enter the bodhisattva's countless acts of impartiality;
Should purify the bodhisattva's countless meritorious qualities;
Should cultivate and refine the bodhisattva's countless practices;
Should manifest the bodhisattva's countless actions in adapting to those in the world;
Should develop the power of measureless pure faith;
Should dwell in the power of measureless vigor;
Should purify the power of measureless right mindfulness;
Should fulfill the power of measureless samādhi;
Should bring forth the power of measureless pure wisdom;
Should strengthen the power of measureless resolute faith;[20]
Should accumulate the power of measureless merit;
Should produce growth in the power of measureless wisdom;
Should manifest the measureless powers of the bodhisattva;
Should completely fulfill the measureless powers of the Tathāgata;
Should distinguish the countless gateways to the Dharma;
Should completely know the countless gateways to the Dharma;
Should purify the countless gateways to the Dharma;

正體字

應生無量法光明。應作無
420c08‖ 量法照耀。應照無量品類根。應知無量煩惱
420c09‖ 病。應集無量妙法藥。應療無量眾生疾。應
420c10‖ 嚴[6]辨無量甘露供。應往詣無量佛國土。應
420c11‖ 供養無量諸如來。應入無量菩薩會。應受無
420c12‖ 量諸佛教。應忍無量眾生罪。應滅無量惡道
420c13‖ 難。應令無量眾生生善道。應以四攝攝無量
420c14‖ 眾生。應修無量總持門。應生無量大願門。應
420c15‖ 修無量大慈大願力。應勤求無量法常無休
420c16‖ 息。應起無量思惟力。應起無量神通事。應
420c17‖ 淨無量智光明。應往無量眾生趣。應受無量
420c18‖ 諸有生。應現無量差別身。應知無量言辭法。
420c19‖ 應入無量差別心。應知菩薩大境界。應住菩
420c20‖ 薩大宮殿。應觀菩薩甚深妙法。應知菩薩難
420c21‖ 知境界。

简体字

应生无量法光明，应作无量法照耀，应照无量品类根，应知无量烦恼病，应集无量妙法药，应疗无量众生疾，应严办无量甘露供，应往诣无量佛国土，应供养无量诸如来，应入无量菩萨会，应受无量诸佛教，应忍无量众生罪，应灭无量恶道难，应令无量众生生善道，应以四摄摄无量众生，应修无量总持门，应生无量大愿门，应修无量大慈、大愿力，应勤求无量法常无休息，应起无量思惟力，应起无量神通事，应净无量智光明，应往无量众生趣，应受无量诸有生，应现无量差别身，应知无量言辞法，应入无量差别心，应知菩萨大境界，应住菩萨大宫殿，应观菩萨甚深妙法，应知菩萨难知境界，

Should manifest the measureless light of the Dharma;
Should create measureless bright illumination of the Dharma;
Should illuminate the faculties of countless types of beings;
Should know the countless disorders created by the afflictions;
Should accumulate countless medicines of the sublime Dharma;
Should treat the disorders of the countless beings;
Should make countless majestic offerings of the elixir of immortality;[21]
Should go and pay his respects in the lands of countless buddhas;
Should make offerings to countless *tathāgatas*;
Should enter countless bodhisattva congregations;
Should receive the teachings of countless buddhas;
Should maintain patience with the karmic transgressions of countless beings;
Should extinguish the measureless [suffering of] the wretched destinies and the difficulties;[22]
Should enable countless beings to be born in the good rebirth destinies;
Should use the four means of attraction to attract countless beings;
Should cultivate the countless complete-retention *dhāraṇī* gateways;
Should initiate the practice of countless gateways of the great vows;
Should cultivate the power of measureless great kindness and great vows;
Should be diligent and never rest in seeking to acquire countless dharmas;
Should bring forth the power of measureless meditative reflections;
Should undertake countless endeavors using the spiritual superknowledges;
Should purify the light of measureless wisdom;
Should go forth into the rebirth destinies of countless beings;
Should take on births in the countless stations of existence;
Should manifest countless different kinds of bodies;
Should know the countless dharmas of verbal expression;[23]
Should penetrate the countless different mind states [of beings];
Should know the bodhisattva's great spheres of action;[24]
Should dwell in the great palace of the bodhisattvas;
Should contemplate the bodhisattva's extremely profound and marvelous dharmas;
Should know the bodhisattva's recondite spheres of cognition;[25]

正體字

應行菩薩難行諸行。應具菩薩尊重
420c22║ 威德。應踐菩薩難入正位。應知菩薩種種諸
420c23║ 行。應現菩薩普遍神力。應受菩薩平等法雲。
420c24║ 應廣菩薩無邊行網。應滿菩薩無邊諸度。應
420c25║ 受菩薩無量記[7]別。應入菩薩無量忍門。應
420c26║ 治菩薩無量諸地。應淨菩薩無量法門。應同
420c27║ 諸菩薩安住無邊劫。供養無量佛。嚴淨不可
420c28║ 說佛國土。出生不可說菩薩願。善男子。舉
420c29║ 要言之。應普修一切菩薩行。應普化一切眾
421a01║ 生界。應普入一切劫。應普生一切處。應普
421a02║ 知一切世。應普行一切法。應普淨一切剎。應
421a03║ 普滿一切願。應普供一切佛。應普同一切菩
421a04║ 薩願。應普事一切善知識。善男子。汝求善知
421a05║ 識。不應疲倦。見善知識。勿生厭足。請問善知
421a06║ 識。勿憚勞苦。

简体字

应行菩萨难行诸行，应具菩萨尊重威德，应践菩萨难入正位，应知菩萨种种诸行，应现菩萨普遍神力，应受菩萨平等法云，应广菩萨无边行网，应满菩萨无边诸度，应受菩萨无量记莂，应入菩萨无量忍门，应治菩萨无量诸地，应净菩萨无量法门，应同诸菩萨，安住无边劫，供养无量佛，严净不可说佛国土，出生不可说菩萨愿。善男子，举要言之，应普修一切菩萨行，应普化一切众生界，应普入一切劫，应普生一切处，应普知一切世，应普行一切法，应普净一切刹，应普满一切愿，应普供一切佛，应普同一切菩萨愿，应普事一切善知识。

“善男子，汝求善知识，不应疲倦；见善知识，勿生厌足；请问善知识，勿惮劳苦；

Should enact the bodhisattva's difficult-to-implement practices;
Should possess the bodhisattva's venerable awesome virtue;
Should ascend to the bodhisattva's difficult-to-enter right and definite position;[26]
Should know the bodhisattva's many different kinds of practices;
Should manifest the bodhisattva's universally pervasive spiritual powers;
Should receive the bodhisattva's cloud of impartial Dharma;
Should broaden the bodhisattva's boundless web of practices;
Should fulfill the practice of the bodhisattva's boundless perfections;
Should receive the bodhisattva's countless predictions;
Should enter the gateways of the bodhisattva's measureless patience;
Should refine [his practice of] the bodhisattva's countless grounds;
Should purify the bodhisattva's countless gateways into the Dharma; and
Should dwell together with bodhisattvas for boundless kalpas, make offerings to countless buddhas, purify an ineffable number of buddha lands, and produce an ineffable number of bodhisattva vows.

Son of Good Family, to speak of what is most essential here:
He should everywhere cultivate all the bodhisattva practices;
He should everywhere teach all realms of beings;
He should everywhere enter all kalpas;
He should everywhere take birth in all places;
He should everywhere know all worlds;
He should everywhere practice all dharmas;
He should everywhere purify all *kṣetras;*
He should everywhere fulfill all vows;
He should everywhere make offerings to all buddhas;
He should everywhere make the same vows as all bodhisattvas; and
He should everywhere serve all good spiritual guides.

Son of Good Family:
You should not become weary in searching for good spiritual guides;
You must not become complacent in going to see good spiritual guides;
You must not fear the wearisome suffering of [traveling to] question good spiritual guides;

正體字

親近善知識。勿懷退轉。供養善
421a07‖ 知識。不應休息。受善知識教不應倒錯。學
421a08‖ 善知識行不應疑惑。聞善知識演說出離門
421a09‖ 不應猶豫。見善知識隨[1]順煩惱行勿生嫌怪。
421a10‖ 於善知識所生深信尊敬心不應變改。何以
421a11‖ 故。善男子。菩薩因善知識。聽聞一切菩薩諸
421a12‖ 行。成就一切菩薩功德。出生一切菩薩大願。
421a13‖ 引發一切菩薩善根。積集一切菩薩助道。開
421a14‖ 發一切菩薩法光明。顯示一切菩薩出離門。
421a15‖ 修學一切菩薩清淨戒。安住一切菩薩功德
421a16‖ 法。清淨一切菩薩廣大志。增長一切菩薩堅
421a17‖ 固心。具足一切菩薩陀羅尼辯才門。得一切
421a18‖ 菩薩清淨藏。生一切菩薩定光明。得一切菩
421a19‖ 薩殊勝願。與一切菩薩同一願。聞一切菩薩
421a20‖ 殊勝法。得一切菩薩祕密處。至一切菩薩法
421a21‖ 寶洲。增一切菩薩善根[2]芽。長一切菩薩智
421a22‖ 慧身。護一切菩薩深[3]密藏。持一切菩薩福
421a23‖ 德聚。

简体字

亲近善知识，勿怀退转；供养善知识，不应休息；受善知识教，不应倒错；学善知识行，不应疑惑；闻善知识演说出离门，不应犹豫；见善知识随烦恼行，勿生嫌怪；于善知识所生深信尊敬心，不应变改。何以故？善男子，菩萨因善知识，听闻一切菩萨诸行，成就一切菩萨功德，出生一切菩萨大愿，引发一切菩萨善根，积集一切菩萨助道，开发一切菩萨法光明，显示一切菩萨出离门，修学一切菩萨清净戒，安住一切菩萨功德法，清净一切菩萨广大志，增长一切菩萨坚固心，具足一切菩萨陀罗尼辩才门，得一切菩萨清净藏，生一切菩萨定光明，得一切菩萨殊胜愿，与一切菩萨同一愿，闻一切菩萨殊胜法，得一切菩萨秘密处，至一切菩萨法宝洲，增一切菩萨善根芽，长一切菩萨智慧身，护一切菩萨深密藏，持一切菩萨福德聚，

You must not think of retreating from your attempts to draw near to good spiritual guides;
You should never desist from making offerings to good spiritual guides;
You should never err in how you receive teachings from good spiritual guides;
You should not cherish doubts regarding your training in the practices of the good spiritual guides;
You should not become hesitant in listening to the good spiritual guides' teachings on the gateways to emancipation;
You must not disapprove of or criticize the good spiritual guides if you see them according with afflicted behavior; and
You should never waver in your profound faith, veneration, and reverence for good spiritual guides.

Why? Son of Good Family, it is because of the good spiritual guides that the bodhisattva:

Hears of the practices of all bodhisattvas;
Perfects the meritorious qualities of all bodhisattvas;
Makes the vows of all bodhisattvas;
Instigates the [growth of] all bodhisattvas' roots of goodness;
Accumulates all bodhisattvas' provisions for the path;
Initiates the light of all bodhisattvas' dharmas;
Reveals all bodhisattvas' gateways of emancipation;
Cultivates and trains in the precepts of all bodhisattvas;
Becomes established in the dharmas of all bodhisattvas' meritorious qualities;
Purifies all bodhisattvas' vast resolve;
Increases all bodhisattvas' strength of resolve;
Completely fulfills all bodhisattvas' *dhāraṇī* and eloquence gateways;
Acquires all bodhisattvas' treasury of purity;
Produces all bodhisattvas' light of meditative absorptions;
Acquires all bodhisattvas' especially excellent vows;
Shares the same single vow with all bodhisattvas;
Listens to all bodhisattvas' especially excellent Dharma;
Attains all bodhisattvas' esoteric stations [of the path];
Reaches all bodhisattvas' isle of Dharma jewels;
Increases the sprouts of all bodhisattvas' roots of goodness;
Produces growth in all bodhisattvas' wisdom body;
Guards all bodhisattvas' treasuries of the deeply esoteric;
Retains all bodhisattvas' accumulation of merit;

正體字

淨一切菩薩受生道。受一切菩薩正法
421a24‖ 雲。入一切菩薩大願路。趣一切如來菩提果。
421a25‖ 攝取一切菩薩妙行。開示一切菩薩功德。往
421a26‖ 一切方聽受妙法。讚一切菩薩廣大威德。生
421a27‖ 一切菩薩大慈悲力。攝一切菩薩勝自在力。
421a28‖ 生一切菩薩菩提分。作一切菩薩利益事。善
421a29‖ 男子。菩薩由善知識任持不墮惡趣。由善知
421b01‖ 識攝受不退大乘。由善知識護念不毀犯菩
421b02‖ 薩戒。由善知識守護不隨逐惡知識。由善知
421b03‖ 識養育不缺減菩薩法。由善知識攝取超越
421b04‖ 凡夫地。由善知識教誨超越二乘地。由善知
421b05‖ 識示導得出離世間。[4]由善知識長養能不染
421b06‖ 世法。由承事善知識修一切菩薩行。由供養
421b07‖ 善知識具一切助[5]道法。由親近善知識不為
421b08‖ 業惑之所摧伏。由恃怙善知識勢力堅固不
421b09‖ 怖諸魔。

简体字

净一切菩萨受生道，受一切菩萨正法云，入一切菩萨大愿路，趣一切如来菩提果，摄取一切菩萨妙行，开示一切菩萨功德，往一切方听受妙法，赞一切菩萨广大威德，生一切菩萨大慈悲力，摄一切菩萨胜自在力，生一切菩萨菩提分，作一切菩萨利益事。

"善男子，菩萨由善知识任持，不堕恶趣；由善知识摄受，不退大乘；由善知识护念，不毁犯菩萨戒；由善知识守护，不随逐恶知识；由善知识养育，不缺减菩萨法；由善知识摄取，超越凡夫地；由善知识教诲，超越二乘地；由善知识示导，得出离世间；由善知识长养，能不染世法；由承事善知识，修一切菩萨行；由供养善知识，具一切助道法；由亲近善知识，不为业惑之所摧伏；由恃怙善知识，势力坚固，不怖诸魔；

Purifies all bodhisattvas' path of rebirth;
Receives all bodhisattvas' cloud of right Dharma;
Enters all bodhisattvas' road of the great vows;
Progresses toward the fruit of bodhi of all *tathāgatas;*
Gathers together the marvelous practices of all bodhisattvas;
Reveals all bodhisattvas' meritorious qualities;
Travels everywhere to listen to the sublime Dharma;
Praises all bodhisattvas' vast awesome virtue;
Produces all bodhisattvas' power of great kindness and compassion;
Gathers all bodhisattvas' supreme powers of sovereign mastery;
Develops all bodhisattvas' enlightenment factors; and
Engages in all bodhisattvas' beneficial endeavors.

Son of Good Family, as for the bodhisattvas:

It is due to being supported by the good spiritual guides that they do not fall into the wretched destinies;
It is due to being taken in by the good spiritual guides that they do not retreat from the Great Vehicle;
It is due to being borne in the protective mindfulness of the good spiritual guides that they do not transgress against the bodhisattva precepts;
It is due to being guarded by the good spiritual guides that they do not follow bad spiritual guides;
It is due to being nurtured by the good spiritual guides that they do not become deficient in the bodhisattva dharmas;
It is due to being gathered in by the good spiritual guides that they step beyond the grounds of the common person;
It is due to the good spiritual guides' teachings that they step beyond the grounds of the two vehicles;
It is due to the good spiritual guides' instructive guidance that they succeed in escaping from the world;
It is due to being raised up by the good spiritual guides that they are able to remain undefiled by worldly dharmas;
It is due to serving the good spiritual guides that they cultivate all the bodhisattva practices;
It is due to making offerings to the good spiritual guides that they become equipped with all the aids to realization of the path;
It is due to drawing near to the good spiritual guides that they are not vanquished by their karma and afflictions;
It is due to relying on the good spiritual guides' powers that their strength is steadfast and they do not fear the *māras;* and

正體字

由依止善知識增長一切菩提分法。
421b10‖ 何以故。善男子。善知識者。能淨諸障。能滅
421b11‖ 諸罪。能除諸難。能止諸惡。能破無明長夜
421b12‖ 黑暗。能壞諸見堅固牢獄。能出生死城。能
421b13‖ 捨世俗家。能截諸魔網。能拔眾苦箭。能離無
421b14‖ 智險難處。能出邪見大曠野。能度諸有流。能
421b15‖ 離諸邪道。能示菩提路。能教菩薩法。能令安
421b16‖ 住菩薩行。能令趣向一切智。能淨智慧眼。能
421b17‖ 長菩提心。能生大悲。能演妙行。能說波羅蜜。
421b18‖ 能擯惡知識。能令住諸地。能令獲諸忍。能
421b19‖ 令修習一切善根。[6]能令成[7]辦一切道具。能
421b20‖ 施與一切大功德。

简体字

由依止善知识，增长一切菩提分法。何以故？善男子，善知识者，能净诸障，能灭诸罪，能除诸难，能止诸恶，能破无明长夜黑暗，能坏诸见坚固牢狱，能出生死城，能舍世俗家，能截诸魔网，能拔众苦箭，能离无智险难处，能出邪见大旷野，能度诸有流，能离诸邪道，能示菩提路，能教菩萨法，能令安住菩萨行，能令趣向一切智，能净智慧眼，能长菩提心，能生大悲，能演妙行，能说波罗蜜，能摈恶知识，能令住诸地，能令获诸忍，能令修习一切善根，能令成办一切道具，能施与一切大功德，

It is due to depending on the good spiritual guides that they bring about the growth of all the enlightenment factors.

And why is this so? Son of Good Family, as for the good spiritual guides:

They enable one to purify all obstacles;
They enable one to extinguish all karmic offenses;
They enable one to do away with the difficulties;
They enable one to stop all evil;
They enable one to dispel the darkness of the long night of ignorance;
They enable one to destroy the solidly fortified prison of the various views;
They enable one to escape from the city of *saṃsāra;*
They enable one to abandon the house of worldly existence;
They enable one to rend the net of Māra;
They enable one to remove the arrows of the many kinds of suffering;
They enable one to leave behind circumstances made dangerous and difficult by ignorance;
They enable one to escape from the vast wilderness of wrong views;
They enable one to cross over the river of the stations of existence;
They enable one to abandon all wrong paths;
They are able to reveal the road to the realization of bodhi;
They are able to teach the bodhisattva dharmas;
They are able to induce one to become established in the bodhisattva practices;
They are able to induce one to progress toward the realization of all-knowledge;
They enable the purification of one's wisdom eye;
They are able to increase one's resolve to attain bodhi;
They are able to promote the birth of the great compassion;
They are able to expound on the sublime practices;
They are able to teach the *pāramitās;*
They enable one to cast aside bad teachers;
They are able to cause one to dwell on the grounds;
They are able to cause one to acquire the patiences;
They are able to cause one to cultivate all roots of goodness;
They are able to cause one to successfully acquire all the provisions for the path;
They are able to bestow all the great meritorious qualities;

正體字

能令到一切種智位。能令
421b21‖ 歡喜集功德。能令踊躍修諸行。能令趣入甚
421b22‖ 深義。能令開示出離門。能令杜絕諸惡道。能
421b23‖ 令以法光照[8]耀。能令以法雨潤澤。能令[9]消
421b24‖ 滅一切惑。能令捨離一切見。能令增長一切
421b25‖ 佛智慧。能令安住一切佛法門。善男子。善
421b26‖ 知識者如慈母。出生佛種故。如慈父。廣大
421b27‖ 利益故。如乳母。守護不令作惡故。如教師。
421b28‖ 示其菩薩所學故。如善導。能示波羅蜜道故。
421b29‖ [10]如良醫。能治煩惱諸病故。如雪山。增長一
421c01‖ 切智藥故。如勇將。殄除一切怖[11]畏故。如濟
421c02‖ 客。令出生死暴流故。如船師。令到智慧寶
421c03‖ 洲故。善男子。常當如是正念思惟諸善知識。
421c04‖ [12]復次善男子。汝承事一切善知識。

简体字

能令到一切种智位，能令欢喜集功德，能令踊跃修诸行，能令趣入甚深义，能令开示出离门，能令杜绝诸恶道，能令以法光照耀，能令以法雨润泽，能令消灭一切惑，能令舍离一切见，能令增长一切佛智慧，能令安住一切佛法门。

“善男子，善知识者，如慈母，出生佛种故；如慈父，广大利益故；如乳母，守护不令作恶故；如教师，示其菩萨所学故；如善导，能示波罗蜜道故；如良医，能治烦恼诸病故；如雪山，增长一切智药故；如勇将，殄除一切怖畏故；如济客，令出生死暴流故；如船师，令到智慧宝洲故。善男子，常当如是正念思惟诸善知识。

“复次，善男子，汝承事一切善知识，

They are able to cause one to reach the station of the knowledge of all modes;

They are able to cause one to delight in the accumulation of meritorious qualities;

They are able to cause one to rejoice in cultivating all the practices;

They are able to cause one to penetrate the extremely profound meaning;

They are able to cause one to open the gates to emancipation;

They are able to cause one to block access to the wretched destinies;

They are able to cause one to use the light of Dharma for illumination;

They are able to cause one to rely on the rain of Dharma for moisture;

They are able to cause one to extinguish all afflictions;

They are able to cause one to relinquish all wrong views;

They are able to cause one to grow in the wisdom of all buddhas; and

They are able to cause one to become established in the dharmas of a buddha.

Son of Good Family, again, as for the good spiritual guides:

They are like a kindly mother, for they give birth to the lineage of the Buddha;

They are like a kindly father, for they bestow vast benefit;

They are like a foster mother, for they protect one and do not allow one to do what is evil;

They are like a teacher, for they provide instruction in the bodhisattva training;

They are like a good guide, for they are able to reveal the path of the *pāramitās*;

They are like a fine physician, for they are able to cure all the diseases caused by the afflictions;

They are like the Himalaya Mountains, for they are able to bring about the growth of the medicinal herbs of all-knowledge;

They are like a courageous general, for they vanquish all perils;

They are like a ferryman, for they enable one to escape the raging flood waters of *saṃsāra*; and

They are like a ship captain, for they enable one to reach the isle of the jewels of wisdom.

Son of Good Family, one should always reflect with right mindfulness on all good spiritual guides. Furthermore, Son of Good Family, in supporting and serving all good spiritual guides:

正體字

應發如
421c05‖ 大地心。荷負重任。無疲倦故。應發如金剛心。
421c06‖ 志願堅固不可壞故。應發如鐵圍山心。一切
421c07‖ 諸苦無能動故。應發如給侍心。所有教令。皆
421c08‖ 隨順故。應發如弟子心。所有訓誨。無違逆故。
421c09‖ 應發如僮僕心。不厭一切諸作務故。應發如
421c10‖ 養母心。受諸勤苦不告勞故。應發如傭作心。
421c11‖ 隨所受教無違逆故。應發如除糞人心。離憍
421c12‖ 慢故。應發如已熟稼心。能低下故。應發如
421c13‖ 良馬心。離惡性故。應發如大車心。能運重故。
421c14‖ 應發如調順象心。恒伏從故。應發如須彌山
421c15‖ 心。不傾動故。應發如良犬心。不害主故。應發
421c16‖ 如旃荼羅心。離憍慢故。應發如犗牛心。無威
421c17‖ 怒故。應發如舟船心。往來不倦故。應發如
421c18‖ 橋梁心。濟渡忘疲故。應發如孝子心。承順
421c19‖ 顏色故。應發如王子心。遵行教命故。

简体字

应发如大地心，荷负重任无疲倦故；应发如金刚心，志愿坚固不可坏故；应发如铁围山心，一切诸苦无能动故；应发如给侍心，所有教令皆随顺故；应发如弟子心，所有训诲无违逆故；应发如僮仆心，不厌一切诸作务故；应发如养母心，受诸勤苦不告劳故；应发如佣作心，随所受教无违逆故；应发如除粪人心，离憍慢故；应发如已熟稼心，能低下故；应发如良马心，离恶性故；应发如大车心，能运重故；应发如调顺象心，恒伏从故；应发如须弥山心，不倾动故；应发如良犬心，不害主故；应发如旃荼罗心，离憍慢故；应发如犗牛心，无威怒故；应发如舟船心，往来不倦故；应发如桥梁心，济渡忘疲故；应发如孝子心，承顺颜色故；应发如王子心，遵行教命故。

You should manifest a mind like the great earth with which you remain tireless even in bearing a heavy responsibility;
You should manifest a mind like vajra with which your determination is indestructibly solid;
You should manifest a mind like the Iron Ring Mountains with which no suffering can cause you to waver in the least;
You should manifest a mind like that of an attendant with which you remain compliant in response to all orders;
You should manifest a mind like that of a disciple with which you never oppose any instruction;
You should manifest a mind like that of a servant with which you do not disdain any of the responsibilities you discharge;
You should manifest a mind like that of a nursemaid with which you take on all kinds of difficult work yet never complain;
You should manifest a mind like that of a wage laborer with which, no matter what instructions you receive, you never oppose them;
You should manifest a mind like that of one who disposes of excrement with which you abandon all arrogance;
You should manifest a mind like the seed head of already ripened grain with which you are well able to bend down low;
You should manifest a mind like that of a fine horse with which you abandon any ill-natured tendencies;
You should manifest a mind like an immense vehicle with which you are able to carry a heavy load;
You should manifest a mind like a well-trained elephant with which you are constantly compliant;
You should manifest a mind like Mount Sumeru with which you do not quaver in the least;
You should manifest a mind like a good dog with which you do not injure your master;
You should manifest a mind like that of an untouchable with which you abandon arrogance and pride;
You should manifest a mind like a gelded bull with which you are free of anger;
You should manifest a mind like a ship with which, in all your goings and comings, you never grow weary;
You should manifest a mind like a bridge with which, in taking others across, you forget your own weariness;
You should manifest a mind like that of a filial son with which you serve with an agreeably compliant demeanor; and
You should manifest a mind like that of a prince with which you respectfully carry out all decrees.

正體字

復次
421c20 善男子。汝應於自身生病苦想。於善知識生
421c21 醫王想。於所說法生良藥想。於所修行生除
421c22 病想。又應於自身生遠行想。於善知識生導
421c23 師想。於所說法生正道想。於所修行生遠達
421c24 想。又應於自身生求度想。於善知識生船師
421c25 想。於所說法生舟[13]檝想。於所修行生到岸
421c26 想。又應於自身生苗稼想。於善知識生龍王
421c27 想。於所說法生時雨想。於所修行生成熟想。
421c28 又應於自[14]身生貧窮想。於善知識生毘沙門
421c29 王想。於所說法生財寶想。於所修行生富饒
422a01 想。[1]又應於自身生弟子想。於善知識生良工
422a02 想。於所說法生技藝想。於所修行生了知想。
422a03 又應於自身生恐怖想。於善知識生勇健想。
422a04 於所說法生器仗想。於所修行生破怨想。又
422a05 應於自身生商人想。於善知識生導師想。於
422a06 所說法生珍寶想。於所修行生捃拾想。又應
422a07 於自身生兒子想。於善知識生父母想。

简体字

“复次，善男子，汝应于自身生病苦想，于善知识生医王想，于所说法生良药想，于所修行生除病想；又应于自身生远行想，于善知识生导师想，于所说法生正道想，于所修行生远达想；又应于自身生求度想，于善知识生船师想，于所说法生舟楫想，于所修行生到岸想；又应于自身生苗稼想，于善知识生龙王想，于所说法生时雨想，于所修行生成熟想；又应于自身生贫穷想，于善知识生毗沙门王想，于所说法生财宝想，于所修行生富饶想；又应于自身生弟子想，于善知识生良工想，于所说法生技艺想，于所修行生了知想；又应于自身生恐怖想，于善知识生勇健想，于所说法生器仗想，于所修行生破冤想；又应于自身生商人想，于善知识生导师想，于所说法生珍宝想，于所修行生捃拾想；又应于自身生儿子想，于善知识生父母想，

Furthermore, Son of Good Family:

You should think of yourself as afflicted by a disease, should think of the good spiritual guide as the king of physicians, should think of the Dharma that he teaches as fine medicine, and should think of the practice you cultivate as getting rid of your disease;

You should also think of yourself as one who is traveling far, should think of the good spiritual guide as a guide, should think of the Dharma that he teaches as the right path, and should think of the practice you cultivate as what will lead to your distant destination;

You should also think of yourself as one who is being rescued and ferried across, should think of the good spiritual guide as a ship captain, should think of the Dharma that he teaches as a ship, and should think of the practice you cultivate as the means of reaching the far shore;

You should also think of yourself as like a grain seedling, should think of the good spiritual guide as like the dragon king, should think of the Dharma that he teaches as the seasonal rains, and should think of the practice you cultivate as what causes the seedling's maturation;

You should also think of yourself as one who is poverty stricken, should think of the good spiritual guide as King Vaiśravaṇa, should think of the Dharma that he teaches as wealth and jewels, and should think of the practice you cultivate as bestowing abundant wealth;

You should also think of yourself as an apprentice, should think of the good spiritual guide as the fine artisan, should think of the Dharma that he teaches as the artisan's techniques, and should think of the practice you cultivate as the complete knowledge of those matters;

You should also think of yourself as involved in a frightful situation, should think of the good spiritual guide as a heroically brave stalwart, should think of the Dharma that he teaches as weapons, and should think of the practice you cultivate as what will defeat the enemy;

You should also think of yourself as a merchant, should think of the good spiritual guide as an expedition guide, should think of the Dharma that he teaches as precious jewels, and should think of the practice you cultivate as the means for gathering them;

You should also think of yourself as a young boy, should think of the good spiritual guide as your parent, should think of the

正體字

於所
422a08‖ 說法生家業想。於所修行生紹繼想。[2]又應
422a09‖ 於自身生王子想。於善知識生大臣想。於所
422a10‖ 說法生王教想。於所修行生冠王冠想。服王
422a11‖ 服想。繫王繒想。坐王殿想。善男子。汝應發如
422a12‖ 是心作如是意近善知識。何以故。以如是心
422a13‖ 近善知識。令其志願永得清淨。復次善男子。
422a14‖ 善知識者長諸善根。譬如雪山長諸藥草。善
422a15‖ 知識者是佛法器。譬如大海吞納眾流。善
422a16‖ 知識者是功德處。譬如大海出生眾寶。善知
422a17‖ 識者淨菩提心。譬如猛火能[3]鍊真金。善知
422a18‖ 識者出過世法。如須彌山出於大海。善知識
422a19‖ 者不染世法。譬如蓮華不著於水。善知識者
422a20‖ 不受諸惡。譬如大海不宿死屍。善知識者增
422a21‖ 長白法。譬如白月光色圓滿。善知識者照明
422a22‖ 法界。譬如盛日照四天下。

简体字

于所说法生家业想，于所修行生绍继想；又应于自身生王子想，于善知识生大臣想，于所说法生王教想，于所修行生冠王冠想、服王服想、系王缯想、坐王殿想。

“善男子，汝应发如是心，作如是意近善知识。何以故？以如是心近善知识，令其志愿永得清净。

“复次，善男子，善知识者长诸善根，譬如雪山长诸药草；善知识者是佛法器，譬如大海吞纳众流；善知识者是功德处，譬如大海出生众宝；善知识者净菩提心，譬如猛火能炼真金；善知识者出过世法，如须弥山出于大海；善知识者不染世法，譬如莲华不著于水；善知识者不受诸恶，譬如大海不宿死尸；善知识者增长白法，譬如白月光色圆满；善知识者照明法界，譬如盛日照四天下；

Dharma that he teaches as the family livelihood, and should think of the practice you cultivate as the means by which you inherit it and carry it forward; and

You should also think of yourself as a crown prince, should think of the good spiritual guide as a great official, should think of the Dharma that he teaches as the king's teachings, and should think of the practice you cultivate as enabling you to be crowned with the king's crown, to don the king's robes, to tie on the king's headband, and to take the throne in the king's palace.

Son of Good Family, in drawing near to the good spiritual guides, you should have these kinds of thoughts and should form these kinds of intentions. And why? Due to having thoughts such as these, in drawing near to the good spiritual guides, one's resolve is caused to be forever pure.

Furthermore, Son of Good Family:

Those who follow good spiritual guides produce growth in their roots of goodness just as the Himalaya Mountains produce growth in the various types of medicinal herbs;

Those who follow good spiritual guides become vessels who contain the Dharma of the Buddha just as the great ocean is a vessel that swallows up the many rivers;

Those who follow good spiritual guides become a place for the production of meritorious qualities just as the great ocean is a place that produces the many kinds of jewels.

Those who follow good spiritual guides are able to purify the resolve to attain bodhi just as a fierce fire is able to refine real gold.

Those who follow good spiritual guides rise above worldly dharmas just as Mount Sumeru rises above the great ocean.

Those who follow good spiritual guides are not defiled by worldly dharmas just as the lotus flower is no longer even touched by the water.

Those who follow good spiritual guides do not take in any sort of evil just as the great ocean does not abide the presence of a corpse.

Those who follow good spiritual guides bring about the growth of pure dharmas just as the full moon shines with perfectly full radiance.

Those who follow good spiritual guides brightly illuminate the Dharma realm just as the brightly shining sun illuminates all four continents; and

正體字

善知識者長菩薩
422a23‖ 身。譬如父母養育兒子。善男子。以要言之。菩
422a24‖ 薩摩訶薩。若能隨順善知識教。得十不可說
422a25‖ 百千億那由他功德。淨十不可說百千億那
422a26‖ 由他深心。長十不可說百千億那由他菩薩
422a27‖ 根。淨十不可說百千億那由他菩薩力。斷十
422a28‖ 不可說百千億阿僧祇障。超十不可說百千
422a29‖ 億阿僧祇魔境。入十不可說百千億阿僧祇
422b01‖ 法門。滿十不可說百千億阿僧祇助道。修十
422b02‖ 不可說百千億阿僧祇妙行。發十不可說百
422b03‖ 千億阿僧祇大願。[4]善男子。我復略說一切
422b04‖ 菩薩行。一切菩薩波羅蜜。一切菩薩地。一
422b05‖ 切菩薩忍。一切菩薩總持門。一切菩薩三昧
422b06‖ 門。一切菩薩神通智。一切菩薩迴向。一切
422b07‖ 菩薩願。一切菩薩成就佛法。皆由善知識力。
422b08‖ 以善知識而為根本。依善知識生。依善知識
422b09‖ 出。依善知識長。依善知識住。善知識為因緣。
422b10‖ 善知識能發起。時善財童子。聞善知識如是
422b11‖ 功德。

简体字

善知识者长菩萨身，譬如父母养育儿子。

“善男子，以要言之，菩萨摩诃萨若能随顺善知识教，得十不可说百千亿那由他功德，净十不可说百千亿那由他深心，长十不可说百千亿那由他菩萨根，净十不可说百千亿那由他菩萨力，断十不可说百千亿阿僧祇障，超十不可说百千亿阿僧祇魔境，入十不可说百千亿阿僧祇法门，满十不可说百千亿阿僧祇助道，修十不可说百千亿阿僧祇妙行，发十不可说百千亿阿僧祇大愿。

“善男子，我复略说一切菩萨行、一切菩萨波罗蜜、一切菩萨地、一切菩萨忍、一切菩萨总持门、一切菩萨三昧门、一切菩萨神通智、一切菩萨回向、一切菩萨愿。一切菩萨成就佛法，皆由善知识力，以善知识而为根本，依善知识生，依善知识出，依善知识长，依善知识住，善知识为因缘，善知识能发起。”

时，善财童子闻善知识如是功德，

Those who follow good spiritual guides bring about the growth of their bodhisattva body just as parents raise up their sons.

Son of Good Family, to speak of what is most essential here, if the bodhisattva-mahāsattva is able to comply with the good spiritual guides' teachings:

He acquires ten ineffable numbers of hundreds of thousands of *koṭīs* of *nayutas* of meritorious qualities;

He purifies ten ineffable numbers of hundreds of thousands of *koṭīs* of *nayutas* of earnest intentions;

He causes the growth of ten ineffable numbers of hundreds of thousands of *koṭīs* of *nayutas* of bodhisattva faculties;

He purifies ten ineffable numbers of hundreds of thousands of *koṭīs* of *nayutas* of bodhisattva powers;

He cuts off ten ineffable numbers of hundreds of thousands of *koṭīs* of *nayutas* of obstacles;

He steps beyond ten ineffable numbers of hundreds of thousands of *koṭīs* of *nayutas* of realms of the *māras;*

He enters ten ineffable numbers of hundreds of thousands of *koṭīs* of *nayutas* of Dharma gateways;

He fulfills ten ineffable numbers of hundreds of thousands of *koṭīs* of *nayutas* of provisions for the path;

He cultivates ten ineffable numbers of hundreds of thousands of *koṭīs* of *nayutas* of marvelous practices; and

He makes ten ineffable numbers of hundreds of thousands of *koṭīs* of *nayutas* of great vows.

Son of Good Family, I shall summarize this again: As for all bodhisattva practices, all bodhisattva *pāramitās,* all bodhisattva grounds, all bodhisattva patiences, all bodhisattva complete-retention *dhāraṇī* gateways, all bodhisattva samādhi gateways, all bodhisattva spiritual superknowledges and wisdom, all bodhisattva dedications, all bodhisattva vows, and all bodhisattva accomplishment of buddha dharmas, they all arise from the powers of the good spiritual guides, take the good spiritual guides as their very origin, are produced in reliance on the good spiritual guides, come forth in reliance on the good spiritual guides, grow in reliance on the good spiritual guides, and abide in reliance on the good spiritual guides. The good spiritual guides are both their cause and their condition, and the good spiritual guides are those who have the capacity to enable them to arise.

Then, having heard of such qualities possessed by the good spiritual guides, having heard that they are able to open and reveal the

正體字

能開示無量菩薩妙行。能成就無量廣
422b12‖ 大佛法。踊躍歡喜。頂禮德生及有德足。遶無
422b13‖ 量匝。慇懃瞻仰。辭退而去
422b14‖ 爾時善財童子。[5]善知識教。潤澤其心。正念
422b15‖ 思惟諸菩薩行。向海岸國。自憶往世不修禮
422b16‖ 敬。即時發意勤力而行。復憶往世身心不淨。
422b17‖ 即時發意專自治潔。復憶往世作諸惡業。即
422b18‖ 時發意專自防斷。[6]復憶往世起諸妄想。即
422b19‖ 時發意恒正思惟。復憶往世所修諸行但為
422b20‖ 自身。即時發意令心廣大普及含識。復憶往
422b21‖ 世追求欲境常自損耗無有滋味。即時發意
422b22‖ 修行佛法長養諸根以自安隱。復憶往世起
422b23‖ 邪思念顛倒相應。即時發意生正見心起菩
422b24‖ 薩願。復憶往世日夜劬勞作諸惡事。即時發
422b25‖ 意起大精進成就佛法。

简体字

能开示无量菩萨妙行，能成就无量广大佛法，踊跃欢喜，顶礼德生及有德足，绕无量匝，殷勤瞻仰，辞退而去。

尔时，善财童子闻善知识教，润泽其心，正念思惟诸菩萨行，向海岸国。自忆往世不修礼敬，即时发意勤力而行；复忆往世身心不净，即时发意专自治洁；复忆往世作诸恶业，即时发意专自防断；复忆往世起诸妄想，即时发意恒正思惟；复忆往世所修诸行但为自身，即时发意令心广大普及含识；复忆往世追求欲境常自损耗无有滋味，即时发意修行佛法长养诸根以自安隐；复忆往世起邪思念颠倒相应，即时发意生正见心起菩萨愿；复忆往世日夜劬劳作诸恶事，即时发意起大精进成就佛法；

countless marvelous bodhisattva practices, and having heard that they are able to bring about the successful development of the countless vast dharmas of a buddha, Sudhana the Youth was filled with joyous exultation and happiness. He then bowed down in reverence at the feet of Śrīsaṃbhava and Śrīmati and circumambulated them countless times as he gazed up at them in attentive admiration. He then respectfully withdrew and departed.

51 – Maitreya

At that time, with his mind moistened by the teachings about the good spiritual guides, Sudhana the Youth reflected with right mindfulness on the bodhisattva practices as he traveled on toward the country of Samudrakaccho or "Ocean Shores." In doing so:

He recalled how in previous lives he failed to cultivate reverential respect, whereupon he immediately resolved to practice it with diligent effort;

He also recalled how in previous lives he had not been pure in body and mind, whereupon he immediately resolved to focus on purifying himself;

He also recalled how in previous lives he had committed all kinds of bad actions, whereupon he immediately resolved to focus on guarding against and cutting off such behavior;

He also recalled how in previous lives he had given rise to all kinds of wrong thinking,[27] whereupon he immediately resolved to constantly engage in right reflection;

He also recalled how in previous lives he had cultivated practices solely for his own benefit, whereupon he immediately resolved to expand the scope of his intentions to include all beings;

He also recalled how in previous lives he had chased after desirable sense objects which were always self-destructive and flavorless, whereupon he immediately resolved to cultivate the Dharma of the Buddha, nourish the growth of all his faculties, and thereby produce personal peace and security;

He also recalled how in previous lives he had indulged in erroneous thought reflective of the inverted views, whereupon he immediately resolved to generate thoughts aligned with right views while also making the bodhisattva vows;

He also recalled how in previous lives, day and night, he had labored strenuously in doing all kinds of evil deeds, whereupon he immediately resolved to arouse great vigor in becoming accomplished in the dharmas of a buddha; and

正體字

復憶往世受五趣生
422b26‖ 於自他身皆無利益。即時發意願以其身饒
422b27‖ 益眾生成就佛法承事一切諸善知識。如是
422b28‖ 思惟生大歡喜。復觀此身。是生老病死眾苦
422b29‖ 之宅。願盡未來劫。修菩薩道。教化眾生。見諸
422c01‖ 如來成就佛法。遊行一切佛剎。承事一切法
422c02‖ 師。住持一切佛教。尋求一切法侶。見一切
422c03‖ 善知識。集一切諸佛法。與一切菩薩願智身。
422c04‖ 而作因緣。作是念時。長不思議無量善根。
422c05‖ [7]即於一切菩薩。深信尊重。生希有想。生大
422c06‖ 師想。諸根清淨善法增益。起一切菩薩恭敬
422c07‖ 供養。作一切菩薩曲躬合掌。生一切菩薩普
422c08‖ 見世間眼。起一切菩薩普念眾生想。現一切
422c09‖ 菩薩無量願化身。出一切菩薩清淨讚說音。
422c10‖ 想見過現一切諸佛及諸菩薩。於一切處。示
422c11‖ 現成道。神通變化。乃至無有一毛端處而
422c12‖ 不周遍。

简体字

复忆往世受五趣生于自他身皆无利益，即时发意愿以其身饶益众生成就佛法承事一切诸善知识。如是思惟，生大欢喜。复观此身是生、老、病、死众苦之宅，愿尽未来劫，修菩萨道教化众生，见诸如来成就佛法，游行一切佛刹，承事一切法师，住持一切佛教，寻求一切法侣，见一切善知识，集一切诸佛法，与一切菩萨愿智身而作因缘。

作是念时，长不思议无量善根，即于一切菩萨深信尊重，生希有想，生大师想；诸根清净，善法增益，起一切菩萨恭敬供养，作一切菩萨曲躬合掌，生一切菩萨普见世间眼，起一切菩萨普念众生想，现一切菩萨无量愿化身，出一切菩萨清净赞说音；想见过、现一切诸佛及诸菩萨，于一切处示现成道神通变化，乃至无有一毛端处而不周遍；

He also recalled how in previous lives he had taken on births in the five rebirth destinies that brought no benefit to either himself or others, whereupon he immediately vowed to devote himself to benefiting beings, to becoming accomplished in the dharmas of a buddha, and to serving all good spiritual guides.

Having reflected in this manner, he was filled with great happiness. He then also contemplated this body as being the house of the manifold sufferings of birth, aging, sickness, death and then vowed that, throughout all future kalpas:

He would cultivate the bodhisattva path;

He would teach beings;

He would see all *tathāgatas;*

He would become accomplished in the dharmas of a buddha;

He would travel to all buddha *kṣetras;*

He would serve all teachers of the Dharma;

He would preserve the teachings of all buddhas;

He would search for all his companions in the Dharma;

He would see all good spiritual guides;

He would accumulate the dharmas of all buddhas; and

He would create causes and conditions with all bodhisattvas' vow bodies and wisdom bodies.

Even as he was having these thoughts, he was growing inconceivable and measureless roots of goodness. He then felt deep faith in and veneration for all bodhisattvas, thinking of them as only rarely encountered and thinking of them as great teachers. His faculties all became purified and his good dharmas increased. Then:

He brought forth all bodhisattvas' reverence and offerings;

He adopted all bodhisattvas' bowing posture with palms pressed together;

He developed all bodhisattvas' eye that sees everything in the world;

He produced all bodhisattvas' thought devoted to mindful concern for all beings;

He manifested all bodhisattvas' countless vow-generated transformation bodies;

He produced all bodhisattvas' pure voice of praise;

He visualized and saw with regard to all buddhas and bodhisattvas of the past and present their everywhere manifesting the realization of enlightenment, their spiritual transformations produced with the spiritual superknowledges, and so forth, even seeing that there was not one place the size of the tip of a hair that they did not completely pervade;

正體字

又得清淨智光明眼。見一切菩薩所
422c13 行境界。其心普入十方剎網。其願普遍虛空
422c14 法界。三世平等無有休息。如是一切皆以信
422c15 受善知識教之所致耳。善財童子。以如是尊
422c16 重。如是供養。如是稱讚。如是觀察。如是願
422c17 力。如是想念。如是無量智慧境界。於毘盧
422c18 遮那莊嚴藏大樓閣前。五體投地。暫時斂念。
422c19 思惟觀察。以深信解。大願力故。入遍一切
422c20 處智慧身平等門。普現其身。在於一切如來
422c21 前。一切菩薩前。一切善知識前。一切如來
422c22 塔廟前。一切如來形像前。一切諸佛諸菩薩
422c23 住處前。一切法寶前。一切聲聞辟支佛及其
422c24 塔廟前。一切聖眾福田前。一切父母尊者前。
422c25 一切十方眾生前。皆如上說。尊重禮讚。盡未
422c26 來際無有休息。等虛空無邊量故。等法界無
422c27 障礙故。[8]等實際遍一切故。等如來無分別
422c28 故。猶如影。隨智現故。猶如夢。從思起故。

简体字

又得清净智光明眼，见一切菩萨所行境界；其心普入十方刹网，其愿普遍虚空法界，三世平等，无有休息。如是一切，皆以信受善知识教之所致耳。

善财童子以如是尊重、如是供养、如是称赞、如是观察、如是愿力、如是想念、如是无量智慧境界，于毗卢遮那庄严藏大楼阁前，五体投地，暂时敛念，思惟观察。以深信解、大愿力故，入遍一切处智慧身平等门，普现其身在于一切如来前、一切菩萨前、一切善知识前、一切如来塔庙前、一切如来形像前、一切诸佛诸菩萨住处前、一切法宝前、一切声闻辟支佛及其塔庙前、一切圣众福田前、一切父母尊者前、一切十方众生前，皆如上说，尊重礼赞，尽未来际无有休息。等虚空，无边量故；等法界，无障碍故；等实际，遍一切故；等如来，无分别故。犹如影，随智现故；犹如梦，从思起故；

He also acquired the eye of the pure light of wisdom with which he saw all the realms in which all bodhisattvas act;

His mind everywhere entered the net of the *kṣetras* of the ten directions; and

His vows extended everywhere throughout the realm of empty space and the Dharma realm, doing so equally and incessantly throughout all three periods of time.

All of this was brought about through his faithful acceptance of the teachings bestowed by the good spiritual guides.

It was with just such veneration as this, just such offerings as these, just such praises as these, just such contemplations as these, just such vow power as this, just such visualizing thought as this, and just such measureless realms of wisdom as these that, in front of the Chamber of Vairocana's Adornments, Sudhana the Youth bowed down in full reverential prostration, briefly gathered his thoughts, and used a contemplative reflection by which, through deep resolute faith and the power of great vows, he entered the wisdom body's uniformly equal gateway to pervasive presence in all places and everywhere manifested his body:

Directly before all *tathāgatas;*

Directly before all bodhisattvas;

Directly before all good spiritual guides;

Directly before the stupas of all *tathāgatas;*

Directly before the images of all *tathāgatas;*

Directly before the abodes of all buddhas and bodhisattvas;

Directly before all Dharma jewels;

Directly before all *śrāvaka* disciples and *pratyekabuddhas* and their stupas;

Directly before the fields of merit in the congregations of all *āryas;*

Directly before all parents and venerable persons; and

Directly before all beings of the ten directions.

So it was that he incessantly venerated, revered, and praised all those aforementioned beings until the very end of the future, doing so:

The same as empty space, due to being boundless;

The same as the Dharma realm, due to being unimpeded;

The same as the apex of reality, due to pervading everything;

The same as the Tathāgata, due to having no discriminations;

The same as a reflection, due to manifesting in accordance with wisdom;

The same as a dream, due to arising from thought;

正體字

猶
422c29‖ 如像。示一切故。猶如響。緣所發故。無有生。
423a01‖ 遞興謝故。無有性。隨緣轉故。又決定知一切
423a02‖ 諸報皆從業起。一切諸果皆從因起。一切諸
423a03‖ 業皆從習起。一切佛興皆從信起。一切化現
423a04‖ 諸供養事。皆悉從於決定解起。一切化佛從
423a05‖ 敬心起。一切佛法從善根起。一切化身從方
423a06‖ 便起。一切佛事從大願起。一切菩薩所修諸
423a07‖ 行。從迴向起。一切法界廣大莊嚴。從一切智
423a08‖ 境界而起。離於斷見知迴向故。離於常見知
423a09‖ 無生故。離無因見知正因故。離顛倒見知如
423a10‖ 實理故。離自在見知不由他故。離自他見知
423a11‖ 從緣起故。離邊執見知法界無邊故。離往來
423a12‖ 見知如影像故。離有無見知不生滅故。

简体字

犹如像，示一切故；犹如响，缘所发故；无有生，递兴谢故；无有性，随缘转故。

又决定知一切诸报皆从业起，一切诸果皆从因起，一切诸业皆从习起，一切佛兴皆从信起，一切化现诸供养事皆悉从于决定解起，一切化佛从敬心起，一切佛法从善根起，一切化身从方便起，一切佛事从大愿起，一切菩萨所修诸行从回向起，一切法界广大庄严从一切智境界而起。离于断见，知回向故；离于常见，知无生故；离无因见，知正因故；离颠倒见，知如实理故；离自在见，知不由他故；离自他见，知从缘起故；离边执见，知法界无边故；离往来见，知如影像故；离有无见，知不生灭故；

The same as an image, due to showing everything;
The same as an echo, due to being produced by conditions;
Being unproduced, due to alternating waxing and waning; and
Having no [inherent] nature, due to changing in accordance with conditions.

He also then decisively understood:

How all karmic retributions arise from actions;
How all effects arise from causes;
How all karmic actions arise from habitual karmic propensities;
How all buddhas' appearances in the world all arise from faith;
How all transformationally produced offerings arise from resolute understanding;
How all emanation buddhas arise from the reverential mind;
How all dharmas of the buddhas arise from roots of goodness;
How all emanation bodies arise from skillful means;
How all works of buddhas arise from great vows;
How all the practices cultivated by all bodhisattvas arise from dedications of merit;
How all the vast adornments of the Dharma realm arise from the sphere of all-knowledge;
How abandonment of the annihilationist view occurs due to knowing the nature of how ripening [of karma] occurs;[28]
How abandonment of the eternalist view occurs due to knowing non-production;
How abandonment of the view denying causality occurs due to knowing right causality;
How abandonment of inverted views occurs due to knowing principles in accordance with reality;
How abandonment of the view seizing on Maheśvara [as a creator god] occurs due to knowing [that one's circumstances] are not determined by others;[29]
How abandonment of the view that seizes on the inherent existence of self and others occurs due to knowing that they arise due to conditions;
How abandonment of views seizing on bounds occurs due to knowing that the Dharma realm is boundless;
How abandonment of the view that seizes on the existence of going and coming occurs due to knowing they are like reflected images;
How abandonment of the view that seizes on entities' existence or nonexistence occurs due to knowing they are neither produced nor destroyed;

正體字

離一
423a13║ 切法見知空無生故。知不自在故。知願力出
423a14║ 生故。離一切相見入無相際故。知一切法如
423a15║ 種生[1]芽故。如印生文故。[2]知質如像故。知聲
423a16║ 如響故。知境如夢故。知業如幻故。了世心現
423a17║ 故。了果因起故。了報業集故。了知一切諸
423a18║ 功德法。皆從菩薩善巧方便所流出故。善財
423a19║ 童子。入如是智。端心潔念。於樓觀前。舉體
423a20║ 投地。慇懃頂禮。不思議善根。流注身心。清涼
423a21║ 悅[3]澤。從地而起。一心瞻仰。目不暫捨。合掌
423a22║ 圍遶。經無量匝。作是念言。此大樓閣。是解空
423a23║ 無相無願者之所住處。是於一切法無分別
423a24║ 者之所住處。是了法界無差別者之所住處。
423a25║ [4]是知一切眾生不可得者之所住處。

简体字

离一切法见，知空无生故，知不自在故，知愿力出生故；离一切相，见入无相际故。知一切法如种生芽故，如印生文故。知质如像故，知声如响故，知境如梦故，知业如幻故。了世心现故，了果因起故，了报业集故，了知一切诸功德法皆从菩萨善巧方便所流出故。

善财童子入如是智，端心洁念；于楼观前，举体投地，殷勤顶礼；不思议善根流注身心，清凉悦泽。从地而起，一心瞻仰，目不暂舍，合掌围绕，经无量匝，作是念言："此大楼阁，是解空、无相、无愿者之所住处；是于一切法无分别者之所住处；是了法界无差别者之所住处；是知一切众生不可得者之所住处；

How abandonment of the view that seizes on the existence of all dharmas occurs due to knowing they are empty and are unproduced, due to knowing they do not possess any inherent existence, and due to knowing they arise due to the power of vows; and

How abandonment of the view that seizes on the existence of signs occurs:

Through entering the apex of signlessness;

Through knowing all dharmas are like sprouts grown from seeds;

Through knowing they are like words produced by a seal stamp;

Through knowing that their appearance of substantiality is like a mere image;

Through knowing sounds are like mere echoes;

Through knowing that objective states are like mere dreams;

Through knowing karmic actions are like mere conjured illusions;

Through completely understanding that signs manifest due to mundane thought;

Through completely understanding that effects arise from their causes;

Through completely understanding that karmic consequences arise from the accumulation of karmic actions; and

Through completely understanding that all dharmas associated with all meritorious qualities all flow forth from the bodhisattva's skillfully invoked expedient means.

Having entered right thought and pure mindfulness due to entering knowledge such as this, Sudhana the Youth completely prostrated his body there on the ground before that tower. As he earnestly bowed down in reverence there, inconceivable roots of goodness flowed into his body and mind, whereupon he felt refreshed and full of delight. He then rose from the ground and single-mindedly gazed up in admiration, his eyes not straying for even a moment as, with palms pressed together, he circumambulated it countless times, reflecting thus:

This immense tower:

Is the abode of those who understand emptiness, signlessness, and wishlessness;

Is the abode of those who are free of discriminations regarding any dharma;

Is the abode of those who completely understand that the Dharma realm is devoid of distinctions;

Is the abode of those who understand that no beings can be found at all;

正體字

是知一
423a26 切法無生者之所住處。是不著一切世間者
423a27 之所住處。是不著一切窟宅者之所住處。是
423a28 不樂一切聚落者之所住處。是不依一切境
423a29 界者之所住處。是離一切想者之所住處。是
423b01 知一切法無自性者之所住處。是斷一切分
423b02 別業者之所住處。是離一切想心意識者之
423b03 所住處。是不入不出一切道者之所住處。是
423b04 入一切甚深般若波羅蜜者之所住處。是能
423b05 以方便住普門法界者之所住處。是息滅一
423b06 切煩惱火者之所住處。是以增上慧除斷一
423b07 切見愛慢者之所住處。是出生一切諸禪解
423b08 脫三昧通明而遊戲者之所住處。是觀察一
423b09 切菩薩三昧境界者之所住處。是安住一切
423b10 如來所者之所住處。是以一劫入一切劫。以
423b11 一切劫入一劫。而不壞其相者之所住處。是
423b12 以一剎入一切剎。以一切剎入一剎。而不壞
423b13 其相者之所住處。是以一法入一切法。以一
423b14 切法入一法。而不壞其相者之所住處。

简体字

是知一切法无生者之所住处；是不著一切世间者之所住处；是不著一切窟宅者之所住处；是不乐一切聚落者之所住处；是不依一切境界者之所住处；是离一切想者之所住处；是知一切法无自性者之所住处；是断一切分别业者之所住处；是离一切想心、意、识者之所住处；是不入不出一切道者之所住处；是入一切甚深般若波罗蜜者之所住处；是能以方便住普门法界者之所住处；是息灭一切烦恼火者之所住处；是以增上慧除断一切见、爱、慢者之所住处；是出生一切诸禅解脱三昧通明而游戏者之所住处；是观察一切菩萨三昧境界者之所住处；是安住一切如来所者之所住处；是以一劫入一切劫，以一切劫入一劫，而不坏其相者之所住处；是以一刹入一切刹，以一切刹入一刹，而不坏其相者之所住处；是以一法入一切法，以一切法入一法，而不坏其相者之所住处；

Is the abode of those who understand that all dharmas are characterized by non-arising;

Is the abode of those who are not attached to anything in the world;

Is the abode of those who are not attached to any home;

Is the abode of those who do not delight in any village;

Is the abode of those who do not rely on any of the sense objects;

Is the abode of those who have transcended all perceptions;

Is the abode of those who realize all dharmas are devoid of any inherently existent nature;

Is the abode of those who have cut off all actions based on discriminations;

Is the abode of those who have transcended all conceptual thought and [discriminations] of the intellectual mind consciousness;[30]

Is the abode of those who neither enter into nor leave any of the paths;

Is the abode of those who have entered all [gateways into] the extremely profound *prajñāpāramitā;*

Is the abode of those who are able to use skillful means to abide in the Dharma realm of the universal gateway;

Is the abode of those who have extinguished the fire of all the afflictions;

Is the abode of those who have used especially excellent wisdom to cut off all views, cravings, and conceit;

Is the abode of those who have developed all the *dhyānas,* liberations, samādhis, superknowledges, and clear knowledges and thus exercise easeful mastery of them;

Is the abode of those who contemplate the sphere of action of all bodhisattvas' samādhis;[31]

Is the abode of those who securely abide wherever all *tathāgatas* reside;

Is the abode of those who subsume any single kalpa within all kalpas and subsume all kalpas within any single kalpa and accomplish this without interfering with any of their characteristic features;

Is the abode of those who subsume any single *kṣetra* within all *kṣetras* and subsume all *kṣetras* within any single *kṣetra* and accomplish this without interfering with any of their characteristic features;

Is the abode of those who subsume any single dharma within all dharmas and subsume all dharmas within any single dharma and accomplish this without interfering with any of their characteristic features;

正體字

是以
423b15‖ 一眾生入一切眾生。以一切眾生入一眾生。
423b16‖ 而不壞其相者之所住處。是以一佛入一切
423b17‖ 佛。以一切佛入一佛。而不壞其相者之所住
423b18‖ 處。是於一念中而知一切三世者之所住處。
423b19‖ 是於一念中往詣一切國土者之所住處。是
423b20‖ 於一切眾生前悉現其身者之所住處。是心
423b21‖ 常利益一切世間者之所住處。是能遍至一
423b22‖ 切處者之所住處。是雖已出一切世間。為化
423b23‖ 眾生故而恒於中現身者之所住處。是不著
423b24‖ 一切剎為供養諸佛故而遊一切剎者之所住
423b25‖ 處。是不動本處能普詣一切佛剎而莊嚴者
423b26‖ 之所住處。是親近一切佛而不起佛想者之
423b27‖ 所住處。是依止一切善知識而不起善知識
423b28‖ 想者之所住處。是住一切魔宮而不耽著欲
423b29‖ 境界者之所住處。是永離一切心想者之所
423c01‖ 住處。是雖於一切眾生中而現其身。然於自
423c02‖ 他不生二想者之所住處。是能普入一切世
423c03‖ 界。而於法界無差別想者之所住處。

简体字

是以一众生入一切众生，以一切众生入一众生，而不坏其相者之所住处；是以一佛入一切佛，以一切佛入一佛，而不坏其相者之所住处；是于一念中而知一切三世者之所住处；是于一念中往诣一切国土者之所住处；是于一切众生前悉现其身者之所住处；是心常利益一切世间者之所住处；是能遍至一切处者之所住处；是虽已出一切世间，为化众生故而恒于中现身者之所住处；是不著一切刹，为供养诸佛故而游一切刹者之所住处；是不动本处，能普诣一切佛刹而庄严者之所住处；是亲近一切佛而不起佛想者之所住处；是依止一切善知识而不起善知识想者之所住处；是住一切魔宫而不耽著欲境界者之所住处；是永离一切心想者之所住处；是虽于一切众生中而现其身，然于自他不生二想者之所住处；是能普入一切世界而于法界无差别想者之所住处；

Is the abode of those who subsume any single being within all beings and subsume all beings within any single being and accomplish this without interfering with any of their characteristic features;

Is the abode of those who subsume any single buddha within all buddhas and subsume all buddhas within any single buddha and accomplish this without interfering with any of their characteristic features;

Is the abode of those who, in but a single mind-moment, know all three periods of time;

Is the abode of those who, in but a single mind-moment, travel to all lands to pay their respects;

Is the abode of those who manifest their bodies directly before all beings;

Is the abode of those whose minds always benefit everyone in the entire world;

Is the abode of those who are able to go forth everywhere to all places;

Is the abode of those who, even though they have already transcended everything in the entire world, still constantly manifest bodies within it in order to teach beings;

Is the abode of those who are not attached to any *kṣetra* and yet travel to all *kṣetras* to make offerings to all buddhas;

Is the abode of those who, even without ever moving from their original place, are able to travel everywhere to all buddha *kṣetras* to pay their respects and adorn them;

Is the abode of those who draw near to all buddhas and yet never even give rise to a thought [attached to] the idea of a buddha;[32]

Is the abode of those who rely upon all good spiritual guides and yet never even give rise to the idea of [the existence of] a good spiritual guide;

Is the abode of those who, even if they dwelt in the palace of Māra, would still never indulge in the objects of sensual desire;

Is the abode of those who have forever abandoned all conceptual thought;

Is the abode of those who, even though they manifest their bodies among all beings, still never raise any dualistic thought conceiving of "self" or "other";

Is the abode of those who are able to everywhere enter all worlds and yet still have no thoughts conceiving of any differences in the Dharma realm;

正體字

是願住
423c04‖ 未來一切劫。而於諸劫無長短想者之所住
423c05‖ 處。是不離一毛端處而普現身一切世界者
423c06‖ 之所住處。是能演說難遭遇法者之所住處。
423c07‖ 是能住難知法甚深法無二法無相法無對治
423c08‖ 法無所得法無戲論法者之所住處。是住大
423c09‖ 慈大悲者之所住處。是已度一切二乘智。已
423c10‖ 超一切魔境界。已於世法無所染。已到菩薩
423c11‖ 所到岸。已住如來所住處者之所住處。是雖
423c12‖ 離一切諸相而亦不入聲聞正位。雖了一切
423c13‖ 法無生而亦不住無生法性者之所住處。是
423c14‖ 雖觀不淨而不證離貪法亦不與貪欲俱。雖
423c15‖ 修於慈而不證離瞋法亦不與瞋垢俱。雖觀
423c16‖ 緣起而不證離癡法亦不與癡惑俱者之所住
423c17‖ 處。是雖住四禪而不隨禪生。雖行四無量。為
423c18‖ 化眾生故而不生色界。

简体字

是愿住未来一切劫而于诸劫无长短想者之所住处；是不离一毛端处而普现身一切世界者之所住处；是能演说难遭遇法者之所住处；是能住难知法、甚深法、无二法、无相法、无对治法、无所得法、无戏论法者之所住处；是住大慈大悲者之所住处；是已度一切二乘智、已超一切魔境界、已于世法无所染、已到菩萨所到岸、已住如来所住处者之所住处；是虽离一切诸相而亦不入声闻正位，虽了一切法无生而亦不住无生法性者之所住处；是虽观不净而不证离贪法亦不与贪欲俱，虽修于慈而不证离瞋法亦不与瞋垢俱，虽观缘起而不证离痴法亦不与痴惑俱者之所住处；是虽住四禅而不随禅生，虽行四无量为化众生故而不生色界，

Is the abode of those who vow to abide throughout all kalpas of the future and yet do not conceive of any kalpas as either long or short;

Is the abode of those who, even without ever leaving a place the size of the tip of a hair, still manifest their bodies everywhere in all worlds;

Is the abode of those who are able to expound even on rarely encountered dharmas;

Is the abode of those who are able to abide in recondite dharmas, extremely profound dharmas, non-dual dharmas, signless dharmas, non-counteractive dharmas, dharmas that cannot be found anywhere at all, and dharmas that are free of all conceptual proliferation;

Is the abode of those who abide in the great kindness and the great compassion;

Is the abode of those who have already gone beyond all wisdom of the two vehicles, who have already stepped beyond all realms of Māra, who are already beyond defilement by worldly dharmas, who have already reached the far shore of perfection reached by bodhisattvas, and who already abide in the station where the Tathāgata abides; and

Is the abode of those who, although they have transcended all signs, still refrain from entering the right and fixed position of *śrāvaka* disciples and, although they have completely realized all dharmas' non-arising, still do not abide in the unproduced nature of dharmas.

It is the abode of:

Those who, although they contemplate unloveliness, do not realize the dharma of dispassion, yet still do not coexist with desire;

Those who, although they cultivate kindness, do not realize the dharma of non-hatred, yet still do not coexist with the defilement of hatred; and

Those who, although they contemplate conditioned arising, do not realize the dharma of non-delusion, yet still do not coexist with delusion.

It is the abode of:

Those who, although they abide in the four *dhyānas*, still do not take rebirth in accordance with the *dhyānas*;

Those who, although they practice the four immeasurable minds for the purpose of teaching beings, still do not take rebirth in the form realm; and

正體字

雖修四無色定以大
423c19‖ 悲故而不住無色界者之所住處。是雖勤修
423c20‖ 止觀為化眾生故而不證[5]明脫。雖行於捨而
423c21‖ 不捨化眾生事者之所住處。是雖觀於空而
423c22‖ 不起空見。雖行無相而常化著相眾生。雖行
423c23‖ 無願而不捨菩提行願者之所住處。是雖於
423c24‖ 一切業煩惱中而得自在。為化眾生故而現
423c25‖ 隨順諸業煩惱。雖無生死為化眾生故示受
423c26‖ 生死雖已離一切趣為化眾生故示入諸趣者
423c27‖ 之所住處。是雖行於慈而於諸眾生無所愛
423c28‖ 戀。雖行於悲而於諸眾生無所取著。雖行
423c29‖ 於喜而觀苦眾生心常哀愍。雖行於捨而不
424a01‖ 廢捨利益他事者之所住處。

简体字

虽修四无色定以大悲故而不住无色界者之所住处；是虽勤修止观为化众生故而不证明脱，虽行于舍而不舍化众生事者之所住处；是虽观于空而不起空见，虽行无相而常化著相众生，虽行无愿而不舍菩提行愿者之所住处；是虽于一切业烦恼中而得自在为化众生故而现随顺诸业烦恼，虽无生死为化众生故示受生死，虽已离一切趣为化众生故示入诸趣者之所住处；是虽行于慈而于诸众生无所爱恋，虽行于悲而于诸众生无所取著，虽行于喜而观苦众生心常哀愍，虽行于舍而不废舍利益他事者之所住处；

Those who, even though they cultivate the four formless concentrations, still, due to the great compassion, do not abide in the formless realm.

It is the abode of:

Those who, although they diligently cultivate calming and contemplative insight, in order to continue teaching beings, they still refrain from realizing clear knowledge and liberation, and

Those who, although they practice equanimity, still never relinquish their works in the service of teaching beings.

It is the abode of:

Those who, although they contemplate emptiness of inherent existence, still do not generate an emptiness-centered view;

Those who, although they practice signlessness, still always teach beings who are attached to signs; and

Those who, although they practice wishlessness, still never abandon the vow to pursue the practices leading to bodhi.

It is the abode of:

Those who, although they have achieved sovereign mastery over all karma and afflictions, in order to teach beings, still manifest the appearance of following karma and afflictions;

Those who, although they have become free of births and deaths, in order to teach beings, still manifest the appearance of being subject to birth and death; and

Those who, although they have already transcended all the rebirth destinies, in order to teach beings, still manifest the appearance of entering into the rebirth destinies.

It is the abode of:

Those who, although they practice kindness, still have no loving affection for any being;

Those who, although they practice compassion, still have no attachment to any being;

Those who, although they practice sympathetic joy, still contemplate suffering beings with a mind that always feels deep pity for them; and

Those who, although they practice equanimity, still never neglect endeavors that benefit others.

And it is the abode of:

正體字

是雖行九次第
424a02 定而不厭離欲界受生。雖知一切法無生無
424a03 滅而不於實際作證。雖入三解脫門而不取
424a04 聲聞解脫。雖觀四聖諦而不住小乘聖果。雖
424a05 觀甚深緣起而不住究竟寂滅。雖修八聖道
424a06 而不求永出世間。雖超凡夫地而不墮聲聞
424a07 辟支佛地。雖觀五取蘊而不永滅諸蘊。雖超
424a08 出四魔而不分別諸魔。雖不著六處而不永
424a09 滅六處。雖安住真如而不墮實際。雖說一切
424a10 乘而不捨大乘。此大樓閣是住如是等一切
424a11 諸功德者之所住處。爾時善財童子。而說頌
424a12 言
424a13 此是大悲清淨智　利益世間慈氏尊
424a14 灌頂地中佛長子　入如來境之住處
424a15 一切名聞諸佛子　已入大乘解脫門

简体字

是虽行九次第定而不厌离欲界受生，虽知一切法无生无灭而不于实际作证，虽入三解脱门而不取声闻解脱，虽观四圣谛而不住小乘圣果，虽观甚深缘起而不住究竟寂灭，虽修八圣道而不求永出世间，虽超凡夫地而不堕声闻、辟支佛地，虽观五取蕴而不永灭诸蕴，虽超出四魔而不分别诸魔，虽不著六处而不永灭六处，虽安住真如而不堕实际，虽说一切乘而不舍大乘。此大楼阁，是住如是等一切诸功德者之所住处。”

尔时，善财童子而说颂言：

“此是大悲清净智，利益世间慈氏尊，
灌顶地中佛长子，入如来境之住处。
一切名闻诸佛子，已入大乘解脱门，

Those who, although they practice the nine sequential meditative absorptions,[33] still do not renounce taking birth in the desire realm;

Those who, although they have realized that all dharmas are neither produced nor destroyed, still refrain from realizing the apex of reality;

Those who, although they enter the three gates to liberation, still refrain from opting for the *śrāvaka* disciple's liberation;

Those who, although they contemplate the four truths of the *ārya,* still refrain from abiding in the Small Vehicle's fruits of the *ārya;*

Those who, although they contemplate the extremely profound doctrine of conditioned arising, still refrain from abiding in final quiescent cessation;

Those who, although they cultivate the eightfold path of the *ārya,* still do not seek to escape from the world forever;

Those who, although they have stepped beyond the grounds of the common person, still refrain from falling down to the grounds of the *śrāvaka* disciples and *pratyekabuddhas;*

Those who, although they contemplate the five appropriated aggregates, they still refrain from forever extinguishing the aggregates;

Those who, although they have gone beyond the four types of *māras,* still do not make discriminations among the types of *māras;*[34]

Those who, although they do not become attached to the six sense bases, still do not forever extinguish the six sense bases;

Those who, although they securely abide in true suchness, still do not fall into [final realization of] the apex of reality; and

Those who, although they teach all the vehicles, still never abandon the Great Vehicle.

This immense tower is the abode of those who abide in all such meritorious qualities as these.

Sudhana the Youth then spoke these verses:

This is the abode of the one of great compassion and pure wisdom
who benefits those in the world, the Venerable Maitreya,
the Buddha's senior son on the crown-anointing consecration ground
who is on the verge of entering the realm of the Tathāgatas.

All of those renowned sons of the Buddha
who have already entered the Great Vehicle's gates of liberation

正體字

424a16 遊行法界心無著　此無等者之住處
424a17 施戒忍進禪智慧　方便願力及神通
424a18 如是大乘諸度法　悉具足者之住處
424a19 [1] 智慧廣大如虛空　普知三世一切法
424a20 無礙無依無所取　了諸有者之住處
424a21 善能解了一切法　無性無生無所依
424a22 如鳥飛空得自在　此大智者之住處
424a23 了知三毒真實性　分別因緣虛妄起
424a24 亦不厭彼而求出　此寂靜人之住處
424a25 三解脫門八聖道　諸蘊處界及緣起
424a26 悉能觀察不趣寂　此善巧人之住處
424a27 十方國土及眾生　以無礙智咸觀察
424a28 了性皆空不分別　此寂滅人之住處
424a29 普行法界悉無礙　而求行性不可得
424b01 如風行空無所行　此無依者之住處
424b02 普見惡道群生類　受諸楚毒無所歸
424b03 放大慈光悉除滅　此哀愍者之住處
424b04 見諸眾生失正道　譬如生盲踐畏途
424b05 引其令入解脫城　此大導師之住處
424b06 見諸眾生入魔網　生老病死常逼迫

简体字

游行法界心无著，此无等者之住处。
施戒忍进禅智慧，方便愿力及神通，
如是大乘诸度法，悉具足者之住处。
智慧广大如虚空，普知三世一切法，
无碍无依无所取，了诸有者之住处。
善能解了一切法，无性无生无所依，
如鸟飞空得自在，此大智者之住处。
了知三毒真实性，分别因缘虚妄起，
亦不厌彼而求出，此寂静人之住处。
三解脱门八圣道，诸蕴处界及缘起，
悉能观察不趣寂，此善巧人之住处。
十方国土及众生，以无碍智咸观察，
了性皆空不分别，此寂灭人之住处。
普行法界悉无碍，而求行性不可得，
如风行空无所行，此无依者之住处。
普见恶道群生类，受诸楚毒无所归，
放大慈光悉除灭，此哀愍者之住处。
见诸众生失正道，譬如生盲践畏途，
引其令入解脱城，此大导师之住处。
见诸众生入魔网，生老病死常逼迫，

and roam throughout the Dharma realm with unattached minds—
This is the abode of these peerless ones.

Giving, moral virtue, patience, vigor, *dhyāna*, and wisdom as well as
skillful means, vows, the powers, and the spiritual superknowledges,
all such dharmas associated with the Great Vehicle's perfections—
This is the abode of those who have completely fulfilled them all.

Those whose wisdom is as vast as empty space,
who know all dharmas of the three periods of time,
and who are unimpeded, non-dependent, and cling to nothing—
This is the abode of those who fully know all the stations of existence.

Those who completely understand all dharmas as without a nature
and as unproduced—those who, depending on nothing, are like birds
flying across the sky in their attainment of the sovereign masteries—
This is the abode of those who possess such great wisdom as this.

Those who fully know the true nature of the three poisons,
those who distinguish arising based on causes and conditions as false,
and those who do not, due to weariness of them, then seek to escape—
This is the abode of the quiescent ones such as these.

The three gates to liberation, the eightfold path of the *ārya*,
the aggregates, sense bases, sense realms, and conditioned arising—
They can contemplate them all, yet do not proceed into quiescence.
This is the abode of those who are skilled in expedient means.

With unimpeded wisdom, they contemplate
all the lands of the ten directions as well as all their beings.
Knowing the nature of them all as empty, they do not discriminate.
This is the abode of those who have become quiescent.

They are unimpeded in traveling all throughout the Dharma realm,
yet, in seeking such actions' inherent nature, it cannot be found.
Like the wind moving through space, there are no actions that they do.
This is the abode of those who have nothing they depend on.

When they everywhere see the many beings in the wretched destinies
enduring all kinds of intense cruelties from which there is no refuge,
they emanate the light of great kindness to extinguish them all.
This is the abode of those who possess such deep sympathy.

When they see beings who have lost the right road,
as if they were people born blind traveling on a fearsome path,
they lead them along and enable them to enter the city of liberation.
This is the abode of the great Master Guides.

When they see beings entering the net of Māra
who are then driven along by birth, aging, sickness, and death,

正體字

424b07 | 令其解脫得慰安　此勇健人之住處
424b08 | 見諸眾生嬰惑病　而興廣大悲愍心
424b09 | 以智慧藥悉除滅　此大醫王之住處
424b10 | 見諸群生沒有海　沈淪憂迫受眾苦
424b11 | 悉以法船而救之　此善度者之住處
424b12 | 見諸眾生在惑海　能發菩提妙寶心
424b13 | 悉入其中而濟拔　此善漁[2]人之住處
424b14 | 恒以大願慈悲眼　普觀一切諸眾生
424b15 | 從諸有海而拔出　此金翅王之住處
424b16 | 譬如日月在虛空　一切世間靡不燭
424b17 | 智慧光明亦如是　此照世者之住處
424b18 | 菩薩為化一眾生　普盡未來無量劫
424b19 | 如為一人一切爾　此救世者之住處
424b20 | 於一國土化眾生　盡未來劫無休息
424b21 | 一一國土咸如是　此堅固意之住處
424b22 | 十方諸佛所說法　一座普受咸令盡
424b23 | 盡未來劫恒悉然　此智海人之住處
424b24 | 遍遊一切世界海　普入一切道場海
424b25 | 供養一切如來海　此修行者之住處
424b26 | [3]　修行一切妙行海　發起無邊大願海

简体字

令其解脱得慰安，此勇健人之住处。
见诸众生婴惑病，而兴广大悲愍心，
以智慧药悉除灭，此大医王之住处。
见诸群生没有海，沉沦忧迫受众苦，
悉以法船而救之，此善度者之住处。
见诸众生在惑海，能发菩提妙宝心，
悉入其中而济拔，此善渔人之住处。
恒以大愿慈悲眼，普观一切诸众生，
从诸有海而拔出，此金翅王之住处。
譬如日月在虚空，一切世间靡不烛，
智慧光明亦如是，此照世者之住处。
菩萨为化一众生，普尽未来无量劫，
如为一人一切尔，此救世者之住处。
于一国土化众生，尽未来劫无休息，
一一国土咸如是，此坚固意之住处。
十方诸佛所说法，一座普受咸令尽，
尽未来劫恒悉然，此智海人之住处。
遍游一切世界海，普入一切道场海，
供养一切如来海，此修行者之住处。
修行一切妙行海，发起无边大愿海，

they help them to escape and gain comfort and security.
This is the abode of those who are courageous and strong.

When they see beings beset by the sickness of the afflictions,
they arouse the mind of vast compassion and pity
and use the medicine of wisdom to completely cure them.
This is the abode of the great king of physicians.

When they see the many beings submerged in the ocean of existences,
sunken therein, driven by sorrows, and enduring the many sufferings,
they use the ship of the Dharma to rescue them all.
This is the abode of those who are skilled in ferrying others across.

Seeing all beings abiding in the ocean of afflictions,
they are able to make the wondrously precious resolve to attain bodhi
with which they enter into it and rescue them all.
This is the dwelling place of those who are skilled as fishers of men.

They always use great vows and the eyes of kindness and compassion
to everywhere contemplate all beings
and pull them out of the ocean of existences.
This is the abode of the kings of the golden-winged *garuḍas*.

Just as the sun and the moon that hover in the sky
have nothing in the world on which they do not shine,
so too it is with the light of their wisdom.
This is the abode of those who illuminate the world.

In order to teach but a single being, all bodhisattvas
will remain for all the countless kalpas of the future,
and as they do so for but one person, so too will they do so for all.
This is the abode of those who would rescue the entire world.

Just as, in but a single land, they teach the beings there,
and incessantly continue this throughout all future kalpas,
so too, in each and every land, they do so in this way.
This is the abode of those possessed of just such solid resolve.

All the Dharma taught by all buddhas throughout the ten directions—
They take in every part of it in but a single sitting
and constantly continue to do so throughout all future kalpas.
This is the abode of those who possess an ocean of wisdom.

They roam everywhere throughout the oceans of all worlds,
everywhere enter the ocean of all assemblies,
and then make offerings to the ocean of all *tathāgatas*.
This is the abode of those pursuing such cultivation.

They cultivate an ocean of all the marvelous practices,
make a boundless ocean of great vows,

正體字

424b27 | 如是經於眾劫海　此功德者之住處
424b28 | 一毛端處無量剎　佛眾生劫不可說
424b29 | 如是明見靡不周　此無礙眼之住處
424c01 | 一念普攝無邊劫　國土諸佛及眾生
424c02 | 智慧無礙悉正知　此具德人之住處
424c03 | 十方國土碎為塵　一切大海以毛滴
424c04 | 菩薩發願數如是　此無礙者之住處
424c05 | [4] 成就總持三昧門　大願諸禪及解脫
424c06 | 一一皆住無邊劫　此真佛子之住處
424c07 | 無量無邊諸佛子　種種說法度眾生
424c08 | 亦說世間眾技術　此修行者之住處
424c09 | 成就神通方便智　修行如幻妙法門
424c10 | 十方五趣悉現生　此無礙者之住處
424c11 | 菩薩始從初發心　具足修行一切行
424c12 | 化身無量遍法界　此神力者之住處
424c13 | 一念成就菩提道　普作無邊智慧業
424c14 | 世情思慮悉發狂　此難量者之住處
424c15 | 成就神通無障礙　遊行法界靡不周
424c16 | 其心未嘗有所得　此淨慧者之住處
424c17 | 菩薩修行無礙慧　入諸國土無所著

简体字

如是经于众劫海，此功德者之住处。
一毛端处无量刹，佛众生劫不可说，
如是明见靡不周，此无碍眼之住处。
一念普摄无边劫，国土诸佛及众生，
智慧无碍悉正知，此具德人之住处。
十方国土碎为尘，一切大海以毛滴，
菩萨发愿数如是，此无碍者之住处。
成就总持三昧门，大愿诸禅及解脱，
一一皆住无边劫，此真佛子之住处。
无量无边诸佛子，种种说法度众生，
亦说世间众技术，此修行者之住处。
成就神通方便智，修行如幻妙法门，
十方五趣悉现生，此无碍者之住处。
菩萨始从初发心，具足修行一切行，
化身无量遍法界，此神力者之住处。
一念成就菩提道，普作无边智慧业，
世情思虑悉发狂，此难量者之住处。
成就神通无障碍，游行法界靡不周，
其心未尝有所得，此净慧者之住处。
菩萨修行无碍慧，入诸国土无所著，

and do so throughout an ocean of many kalpas.
This is the abode of those who possess the meritorious qualities.

On the tip of but a single hair, there are countless *kṣetras*
in which there are ineffably many buddhas, beings, and kalpas.
They clearly see things such as these, having none not completely so.
This is the abode of those who have the unimpeded eye.

Within but a single mind-moment, they subsume
all the boundlessly many kalpas, lands, buddhas, and living beings
that, with unimpeded wisdom, they completely and rightly know.
This is the abode of those who have perfected the qualities.

If the lands of the ten directions were all ground to atoms
and all the great oceans were ladled out drop-by-drop with a hair,
the vows the bodhisattvas have made are of just such a number.
This is the abode of those whose actions are so unimpeded.

Of all the complete-retention *dhāraṇīs,* samādhi gateways,
great vows, *dhyānas,* and liberations they have perfected,
they dwell in each of them for boundless kalpas.
This is the abode of those who are the true sons of the Buddha.

These measurelessly and boundlessly many sons of the Buddha
have in many different ways taught the Dharma, liberated beings,
and presented teachings on the many kinds of worldly skills and arts.
This is the abode of those whose cultivation is of this sort.

Adept in the spiritual superknowledges, skillful means, and wisdom,
they cultivate the marvelous Dharma gate of the illusory nature of all
and manifest births in all five destinies throughout the ten directions.
This is the abode of those who are unimpeded in these things.

From when these bodhisattvas first made their resolve,
they have completely fulfilled the cultivation of all the practices
and have emanated countless bodies throughout the Dharma realm.
This is the abode of those possessed of such spiritual powers.

In but a single mind-moment, they have realized enlightenment[35]
and everywhere performed works of boundless wisdom that, whoever
pondered them with only worldly sentiment would all be driven mad.
This is the abode of those who are so very difficult to assess as this.

Having perfected the unimpeded spiritual superknowledges,
they roam the Dharma realm and have no place they do not pervade,
yet their minds have never found anything that is apprehensible.
This is the abode of those possessed of such pure wisdom.

These bodhisattvas cultivate unimpeded wisdom,
enter all lands without having anything to which they are attached,

正體字

424c18║ 以無二智普照明　此無我者之住處
424c19║ 了知諸法無依止　本性寂滅同虛空
424c20║ 常行如是境界中　此離垢人之住處
424c21║ 普見群生受諸苦　發大仁慈智慧心
424c22║ 願常利益諸世間　此悲愍者之住處
424c23║ 佛子住於此　普現眾生前
424c24║ 猶如日月輪　遍除生死暗
424c25║ 佛子住於此　普順眾生心
424c26║ 變現無量身　充滿十方剎
424c27║ 佛子住於此　遍遊諸世界
424c28║ 一切如來所　無量無數劫
424c29║ 佛子住於此　思量諸佛法
425a01║ 無量無數劫　其心無厭倦
425a02║ [1] 佛子住於此　念念入三昧
425a03║ 一一三昧門　闡明諸佛境
425a04║ 佛子住於此　悉知一切剎
425a05║ 無量無數劫　眾生佛名號
425a06║ 佛子住於此　一念攝諸劫
425a07║ 但隨眾生心　而無分別想
425a08║ 佛子住於此　修習諸三昧

简体字

以无二智普照明，此无我者之住处。
了知诸法无依止，本性寂灭同虚空，
常行如是境界中，此离垢人之住处。
普见群生受诸苦，发大仁慈智慧心，
愿常利益诸世间，此悲愍者之住处。
佛子住于此，普现众生前，
犹如日月轮，遍除生死暗。
佛子住于此，普顺众生心，
变现无量身，充满十方刹。
佛子住于此，遍游诸世界，
一切如来所，无量无数劫。
佛子住于此，思量诸佛法，
无量无数劫，其心无厌倦。
佛子住于此，念念入三昧，
一一三昧门，阐明诸佛境。
佛子住于此，悉知一切刹，
无量无数劫，众生佛名号。
佛子住于此，一念摄诸劫，
但随众生心，而无分别想。
佛子住于此，修习诸三昧，

and use non-dual wisdom to shine their illumination everywhere.
This is the abode of those who are free of the idea of a self.

They completely know all dharmas are devoid of any basis
and that their fundamental nature is quiescence, just like space.
They always course in spheres of cognition such as these.
This is the abode of those who have abandoned the defilements.

Everywhere seeing the many beings undergoing all kinds of suffering,
they arouse the mind of great humane kindness and wisdom
and vow to always benefit everyone in the world.
This is the abode of those possessed of compassionate pity.

The sons of the Buddha who abide herein
everywhere appear before all beings.
Like the orbs of the sun and moon
they everywhere dispel the darkness of *saṃsāra*.

The sons of the Buddha who abide herein
everywhere adapt to the minds of beings
and transformationally manifest countless bodies
that completely fill the *kṣetras* of the ten directions.

The sons of the Buddha who abide herein
travel everywhere to all worlds,
going to the abodes of all *tathāgatas*
for measurelessly and numberlessly many kalpas.

The sons of the Buddha who abide herein
contemplate the Dharma of all buddhas,
doing so for measurelessly and numberlessly many kalpas
in which their minds never grow weary.

The sons of the Buddha who abide herein,
in every mind-moment enter samādhis
in which each of these samādhi gateways
clearly reveals the realms of all buddhas.

The sons of the Buddha who abide herein
all know all of the *kṣetras,*
their measurelessly and numberlessly many kalpas,
their beings, and the names of their buddhas.

The sons of the Buddha who abide herein
subsume all kalpas within but a single mind-moment.
They merely accord with the minds of beings
while remaining free of any discriminating thought.

The sons of the Buddha who abide herein
cultivate all the samādhis.

正體字

425a09 ║ 一一心念中　了知三世法
425a10 ║ 佛子住於此　結[2]跏身不動
425a11 ║ 普現一切剎　一切諸趣中
425a12 ║ 佛子住於此　飲諸佛法海
425a13 ║ 深入智慧海　具足功德海
425a14 ║ 佛子住於此　悉知諸剎數
425a15 ║ 世數眾生數　佛名數亦然
425a16 ║ 佛子住於此　一念悉能了
425a17 ║ 一切三世中　國土之成壞
425a18 ║ [3] 佛子住於此　普知佛行願
425a19 ║ 菩薩所修行　眾生根性欲
425a20 ║ 佛子住於此　見一微塵中
425a21 ║ 無量剎道場　眾生及諸劫
425a22 ║ 如一微塵內　一切塵亦然
425a23 ║ 種種咸具足　處處皆無礙
425a24 ║ 佛子住於此　普觀一切法
425a25 ║ 眾生剎及世　無起無所有
425a26 ║ 觀察眾生等　法等如來等
425a27 ║ 剎等諸願等　三世悉平等
425a28 ║ 佛子住於此　教化諸群生

简体字

一一心念中，了知三世法。
佛子住于此，结跏身不动，
普现一切刹，一切诸趣中。
佛子住于此，饮诸佛法海，
深入智慧海，具足功德海。
佛子住于此，悉知诸刹数，
世数众生数，佛名数亦然。
佛子住于此，一念悉能了，
一切三世中，国土之成坏。
佛子住于此，普知佛行愿，
菩萨所修行，众生根性欲。
佛子住于此，见一微尘中，
无量刹道场，众生及诸劫。
如一微尘内，一切尘亦然，
种种咸具足，处处皆无碍。
佛子住于此，普观一切法，
众生刹及世，无起无所有。
观察众生等，法等如来等，
刹等诸愿等，三世悉平等。
佛子住于此，教化诸群生，

In each and every mind-moment,
they know the dharmas of the three periods of time.

The sons of the Buddha who abide herein
sit in the lotus posture, their bodies unmoving,
even as they appear in all *kṣetras*
and in all the rebirth destinies.

The sons of the Buddha who abide herein
drink in the ocean of all buddhas' Dharma,
deeply enter the ocean of wisdom,
and perfect the ocean of meritorious qualities.

The sons of the Buddha who abide herein
know the number of all the *kṣetras*
and know the number of worlds, the number of beings,
and the number of buddha names in just the same way.

The sons of the Buddha who abide herein
are able to completely know in a single mind-moment
the creation and destruction of all lands
throughout all three periods of time.

The sons of the Buddha who abide herein
know the conduct and vows of all buddhas,
the practices cultivated by the bodhisattvas,
and the faculties and desires of beings.

The sons of the Buddha who abide herein
see in but a single atom
countless *kṣetras,* congregations,
living beings, and kalpas.

Just as this is so within but a single atom,
so too is this so in all atoms
in which everything is fully present in all its variations,
and all places are present there with no mutual interference.

The sons of the Buddha who abide herein
everywhere contemplate all dharmas,
beings, *kṣetras,* and periods of time
as having no arising and as having no inherent existence.

They contemplate the equality of beings,
the equality of dharmas, the equality of *tathāgatas,*
the equality of *kṣetras,* the equality of vows,
and the equality of all three periods of time.

The sons of the Buddha who abide herein
teach all the many kinds of beings,

正體字

425a29 供養諸如來　思惟諸法性
425b01 無量千萬劫　所修願智行
425b02 廣大不可量　稱揚莫能盡
425b03 彼諸大勇猛　所行無障礙
425b04 安住於此中　我合掌敬禮
425b05 諸佛之長子　聖德慈氏尊
425b06 我今恭敬禮　願垂顧念我
425b07 爾時善財童子。以如是等一切菩薩無量稱
425b08 揚讚歎法。而讚毘盧遮那莊嚴藏大樓閣中
425b09 諸菩薩已。曲躬合掌恭敬頂禮。一心願見彌
425b10 勒菩薩親近供養。乃見彌勒菩薩摩訶薩。從
425b11 別處來。無量天龍夜叉乾闥婆阿脩羅迦樓
425b12 羅緊那羅摩睺羅伽王。釋梵護世。及本生
425b13 處。無量眷屬。婆羅門眾。及餘無數。百千眾
425b14 生。前後圍遶。而共來向莊嚴藏大樓觀所。善
425b15 財見已。歡喜踊躍。五體投地。時彌勒菩薩。觀
425b16 察善財。指示大眾。歎其功德。而說頌曰
425b17 汝等觀善財　智慧心清淨
425b18 為求菩提行　而來至我所
425b19 善來圓滿慈　善來清淨悲
425b20 善來寂滅眼　修行無懈倦

简体字

供养诸如来，思惟诸法性。
无量千万劫，所修愿智行，
广大不可量，称扬莫能尽。
彼诸大勇猛，所行无障碍，
安住于此中，我合掌敬礼。
诸佛之长子，圣德慈氏尊；
我今恭敬礼，愿垂顾念我！”

尔时，善财童子以如是等一切菩萨无量称扬赞叹法，而赞毗卢遮那庄严藏大楼阁中诸菩萨已，曲躬合掌，恭敬顶礼，一心愿见弥勒菩萨亲近供养；乃见弥勒菩萨摩诃萨从别处来，无量天、龙、夜叉、乾闼婆、阿修罗、迦楼罗、紧那罗、摩睺罗伽王，释、梵、护世，及本生处无量眷属、婆罗门众，及余无数百千众生，前后围绕而共来向庄严藏大楼观所。善财见已，欢喜踊跃，五体投地。

时，弥勒菩萨观察善财，指示大众，叹其功德，而说颂曰：

“汝等观善财，智慧心清净，
为求菩提行，而来至我所。
善来圆满慈，善来清净悲，
善来寂灭眼，修行无懈倦。

make offerings to all *tathāgatas,*
and meditate on the nature of all dharmas.

The vows, wisdom, and practices they have cultivated
for countless thousands of myriads of kalpas
are so vast as to be immeasurable
and are such that no one could ever finish praising them.

I press my palms together in respect and bow down in reverence
to all those greatly courageous ones who,
with their unimpeded spheres of action,
dwell here in this place.

I now bow down in reverence
to this eldest son of the buddhas
so possessed of the *āryas'* qualities, the Venerable Maitreya.
May he extend his kindly concern to me.

Then, having used countless bodhisattva praises such as these to praise the bodhisattvas dwelling in that immense tower, the Chamber of Vairocana's Adornments, Sudhana the Youth bent forward humbly with his palms pressed together in respect and bowed down in reverence, single-mindedly praying to be able to see Maitreya Bodhisattva, draw near to him, and make offerings to him. He then saw Maitreya Bodhisattva-mahāsattva arriving from some other place surrounded by a measureless retinue of countless kings of the devas, dragons, *yakṣas, gandharvas, asuras, garuḍas, kiṃnaras,* and *mahoragas,* as well as by Śakra, Brahmā, the World-Protecting Deva Kings, a measureless retinue from the land of his birth, congregations of brahmans, and countless other hundreds of thousands of beings, all of whom came together with him to that immense Chamber of Adornments tower.

When Sudhana saw this, he was overcome with joyous exultation and bowed down in a complete reverential prostration, whereupon Maitreya Bodhisattva looked at Sudhana, pointed him out to that huge congregation, praised his meritorious qualities, and then spoke these verses:

You should all regard this Sudhana
whose aspiration for wisdom is pure.
It is to seek the bodhi practices
that he comes here into my presence.

Welcome, O you of completely full kindness.
Welcome, O you of pure compassion.
Welcome, O you whose gaze is quiescent.
May you be free of weariness in your cultivation.

正體字

425b21	善來清淨意	善來廣大心
425b22	善來不退根	修行無懈倦
425b23	善來不動行	常求善知識
425b24	了達一切法	調伏諸群生
425b25	善來行妙道	善來住功德
425b26	善來趣佛果	未曾有疲倦
425b27	[4] 善來德為體	善來法所滋
425b28	善來無邊行	世間難可見
425b29	善來離迷惑	世法不能染
425c01	利衰毀譽等	一切無分別
425c02	善來施安樂	調柔堪受化
425c03	諂誑瞋慢心	一切悉除滅
425c04	善來真佛子	普詣於十方
425c05	增長諸功德	調柔無懈惓
425c06	善來三世智	遍知一切法
425c07	普生功德藏	修行不疲厭
425c08	文殊德雲等	一切諸佛子
425c09	令汝至我所	示汝無礙處
425c10	具修菩薩行	普攝諸群生
425c11	如是廣大人	今來至我所

简体字

善来清净意，善来广大心，
善来不退根，修行无懈倦。
善来不动行，常求善知识，
了达一切法，调伏诸群生。
善来行妙道，善来住功德，
善来趣佛果，未曾有疲倦。
善来德为体，善来法所滋，
善来无边行，世间难可见。
善来离迷惑，世法不能染，
利衰毁誉等，一切无分别。
善来施安乐，调柔堪受化；
谄诳瞋慢心，一切悉除灭。
善来真佛子，普诣于十方，
增长诸功德，调柔无懈倦。
善来三世智，遍知一切法，
普生功德藏，修行不疲厌。
文殊德云等，一切诸佛子，
令汝至我所，示汝无碍处。
具修菩萨行，普摄诸群生；
如是广大人，今来至我所。

Welcome, O you of pure aspiration.
Welcome, O you who are possessed of vast mind.
Welcome, O you of irreversible faculties.
May you be free of weariness in your cultivation.

Welcome, O you of unshakable practice,
you who always search for good spiritual guides,
you who completely understand all dharmas,
you who are devoted to training the many kinds of beings.

Welcome, O you who practice the marvelous path.
Welcome, O you who dwell in the meritorious qualities.
Welcome, O you who progress toward the fruit of buddhahood
and have never succumbed to weariness.

Welcome, O you for whom the qualities are your very essence.
Welcome, O you who take the Dharma as your source of sustenance.
Welcome, O you of the boundless practices.
You are one who is only rarely encountered in the world.

Welcome, O you who have abandoned delusion,
whom worldly dharmas are unable to sully,
and who, in issues of gain, loss, disrepute, fame, and such,[36]
make no discriminations at all.

Welcome, O you who are a bestower of happiness,
who are pliant and capable of accepting teaching,
and who have completely rid yourself of all thoughts
of flattery, deception, anger, and pride.

Welcome, O you who are a true son of the Buddha
who travels to pay respects in all the ten directions,
increasing the growth of your meritorious qualities
while remaining pliant and free of indolence and weariness.

Welcome, O you who possess the knowledge of the three times,
who everywhere know all dharmas,
who give birth to a treasury of all meritorious qualities,
and whose cultivation never succumbs to weariness.

Mañjuśrī, Meghaśrī, and the rest,
all those sons of the Buddha,
sent you here to my abode,
so that I can show you the realm of the unimpeded.

You have completely cultivated the bodhisattva practices
and have everywhere gathered in the many beings.
A person of such vast qualities as this
has now arrived here at my abode.

正體字

425c12 為求諸如來　清淨之境界
425c13 問諸廣大願　而來至我所
425c14 去來現在佛　所成諸行業
425c15 汝欲皆修學　而來至我所
425c16 汝於善知識　欲求微妙法
425c17 欲受菩薩行　而來至我所
425c18 汝念善知識　諸佛所稱歎
425c19 令汝成菩提　而來至我所
425c20 汝念善知識　生我如父母
425c21 養我如乳母　增我菩提分
425c22 如醫療眾疾　如天灑甘露
425c23 如日示正道　如月轉淨輪
425c24 如山不動搖　如海無增減
425c25 如船師濟渡　而來至我所
425c26 [5]　汝觀善知識　猶如大猛將
425c27 亦如大商主　又如大導師
425c28 能建正法幢　能示佛功德
425c29 能滅諸惡道　能開善趣門
426a01 能顯諸佛身　能守諸佛藏
426a02 能持諸佛法　是故願瞻奉

简体字

为求诸如来，清净之境界，
问诸广大愿，而来至我所。
去来现在佛，所成诸行业，
汝欲皆修学，而来至我所。
汝于善知识，欲求微妙法，
欲受菩萨行，而来至我所。
汝念善知识，诸佛所称叹，
令汝成菩提，而来至我所。
汝念善知识，生我如父母，
养我如乳母，增我菩提分，
如医疗众疾，如天洒甘露，
如日示正道，如月转净轮，
如山不动摇，如海无增减，
如船师济渡，而来至我所。
汝观善知识，犹如大猛将，
亦如大商主，又如大导师，
能建正法幢，能示佛功德，
能灭诸恶道，能开善趣门，
能显诸佛身，能守诸佛藏，
能持诸佛法，是故愿瞻奉。

It was in order to seek out
the pure realms of all *tathāgatas*
that he has inquired about all the vast vows
and thus has come here to my abode.

It was due to your aspiration to cultivate the training
in all the practices and works accomplished
by the buddhas of the past, future, and present
that you have come here to my abode.

It was because you wished to seek the sublime Dharma
and wished to receive the bodhisattva practices
from the good spiritual guides
that you have come here to my abode.

It was because you recalled that the good spiritual guides
are those who are praised by all buddhas
and are the cause for your attainment of bodhi
that you have come here to my abode.

It was because you recalled, "The good spiritual guides
give birth to me like my own parents,
raise me like nursemaids,
enable the growth of my limbs of bodhi,

cure my many disorders like physicians,
shower me with the elixir of immortality like devas,
show me the right road like the sun,
are like the purifying orb of the moon,

are like the mountains that are unshakable,
are like the ocean that never increases or decreases,
and are like the ship captain who rescues me and takes me across."
Hence you have come here to my abode.

You look upon the good spiritual guides
as like great valiant generals,
as like great leaders of merchants,
as like great caravan guides,

as able to erect the banner of right Dharma,
as able to show the buddhas' meritorious qualities,
as able to destroy all the wretched rebirth destinies,
as able to open the gates to the good rebirth destinies,

as able to reveal the bodies of all buddhas
as able to guard the treasury of all buddhas,
and as able to preserve the Dharma of all buddhas.
Therefore you wish to look up to and serve them.

正體字

426a03 | 欲滿清淨智　欲具端正身
426a04 | 欲生尊貴家　而來至我所
426a05 | 汝等觀此人　親近善知識
426a06 | 隨其所修學　一切應順行
426a07 | 以昔福因緣　文殊令發心
426a08 | 隨順無違逆　修行不懈倦
426a09 | 父母與親屬　宮殿及財產
426a10 | 一切皆捨離　謙下求知識
426a11 | 淨治如是意　永離世間身
426a12 | 當生佛國土　受諸勝果報
426a13 | 善財見眾生　生老病死苦
426a14 | 為發大悲意　勤修無上道
426a15 | 善財見眾生　五趣常流轉
426a16 | 為求金剛智　破彼諸苦輪
426a17 | 善財見眾生　心田甚荒穢
426a18 | 為除三毒刺　專求利智犁
426a19 | 眾生處癡暗　盲冥失正道
426a20 | 善財為導師　示其安隱處
426a21 | 忍鎧解脫乘　智慧為利劍
426a22 | 能於三有內　破諸煩惱賊

简体字

欲满清净智，欲具端正身，
欲生尊贵家，而来至我所。
汝等观此人，亲近善知识，
随其所修学，一切应顺行。
以昔福因缘，文殊令发心，
随顺无违逆，修行不懈倦。
父母与亲属，宫殿及财产，
一切皆舍离，谦下求知识。
净治如是意，永离世间身，
当生佛国土，受诸胜果报。
善财见众生，生老病死苦，
为发大悲意，勤修无上道。
善财见众生，五趣常流转，
为求金刚智，破彼诸苦轮。
善财见众生，心田甚荒秽，
为除三毒刺，专求利智犁。
众生处痴暗，盲冥失正道；
善财为导师，示其安隐处。
忍铠解脱乘，智慧为利剑，
能于三有内，破诸烦恼贼。

It is because you wish to reach fulfillment in pure wisdom,
because you wish to be fully endowed with the fine body,
and because you wish to be born into the venerable and noble clan
that you have come here to my abode.

You should all look at this person
who has drawn near to the good spiritual guides
and followed what they have cultivated and trained in.
You should accord in practice with all that he has done.

Due to the causes and conditions of past merit,
Mañjuśrī enabled him to make the resolve,
accord with [the teachings], never oppose them,
and cultivate them without becoming lax or weary.

His father, his mother, and his relatives
as well as his palace and his wealth—
He relinquished all of this
to humbly seek the good spiritual guides.

He has purified resolve such as this,
has forever renounced the mundane body,
and will be born in a buddha land
where he will enjoy the supreme karmic rewards.

Sudhana saw the sufferings of beings
undergoing birth, aging, sickness, and death, and
for their sakes, made the greatly compassionate resolve
to diligently cultivate the unexcelled path.

Sudhana saw beings forever flowing on
and turning about in the five destinies of rebirth,
and sought for their sakes to acquire the vajra wisdom
that breaks the cycle of all their sufferings.

Sudhana saw that beings' fields of the mind
are as if deserted and overgrown with weeds,
and single-mindedly sought the plow of sharp wisdom,
to rid them of the thorns of the three poisons.

Beings abide in the darkness of delusion where,
blinded by benightedness, they have lost the right path.
Sudhana will serve them as a guide
who shows them the peaceful and secure place.

Taking patience as his armor, the liberations as his vehicle,
and wisdom as his sharp sword,
he will be able to destroy the brigands of the afflictions
throughout the three realms of existence.

正體字

426a23 [1] 善財法船師　普濟諸含識
426a24 令過爾焰海　疾至淨寶洲
426a25 善財正覺日　智光大願輪
426a26 周行法界空　普照群迷宅
426a27 善財正覺月　白法悉圓滿
426a28 慈定清涼光　等照眾生心
426a29 [2] 善財勝智海　依於直心住
426b01 菩提行漸深　出生眾法寶
426b02 善財大心龍　[3]昇於法界空
426b03 興雲霔甘澤　生成一切果
426b04 [4] 善財然法燈　信炷慈悲油
426b05 念器功德光　滅除三毒暗
426b06 覺心迦羅邏　悲胞慈為肉
426b07 菩提分[5]肢節　長於如來藏
426b08 增長福德藏　清淨智慧藏
426b09 開顯方便藏　出生大願藏
426b10 如是大莊嚴　救護諸群生
426b11 一切天人中　難聞難可見
426b12 如是智慧樹　根深不可動
426b13 眾行漸增長　普蔭諸群生

简体字

善财法船师，普济诸含识，
令过尔焰海，疾至净宝洲。
善财正觉日，智光大愿轮，
周行法界空，普照群迷宅。
善财正觉月，白法悉圆满，
慈定清凉光，等照众生心。
善财胜智海，依于直心住，
菩提行渐深，出生众法宝。
善财大心龙，升于法界空，
兴云霔甘泽，生成一切果。
善财燃法灯，信炷慈悲油，
念器功德光，灭除三毒暗。
觉心迦罗逻，悲胞慈为肉，
菩提分肢节，长于如来藏。
增长福德藏，清净智慧藏，
开显方便藏，出生大愿藏。
如是大庄严，救护诸群生；
一切天人中，难闻难可见。
如是智慧树，根深不可动，
众行渐增长，普荫诸群生。

Sudhana will become the captain of the ship of Dharma
that everywhere rescues all sentient beings
and enables them to cross the ocean of what should be known[37]
so that they swiftly reach the isle of the jewels of purity.

Sudhana will be a sun of right enlightenment
whose light of wisdom and shining orb of great vows
will travel throughout the sky of the Dharma realm,
everywhere illuminating the abodes of confused beings.

Sudhana will be a moon of right enlightenment
whose white dharmas of purity will become completely full.
The clear and cool light of his kindness and meditative absorptions
will equally illuminate the minds of beings.

Sudhana will become an ocean of supreme knowledge
abiding in reliance on his resolute intentions
and his ever-deepening bodhi practices
which shall then produce the many jewels of the Dharma.

Sudhana, the dragon of the great resolve,
is rising up into the sky of the Dharma realm where
he will spread the clouds and pour down the sweet rains
that will bring forth and ripen all the fruits [of the path].

Sudhana will light the lamp of the Dharma
with its wick of faith, its oil of kindness and compassion,
its font of mindfulness, and its light of meritorious qualities
that entirely extinguishes the darkness of the three poisons.

His bodhi resolve is the *kalala* embryo.
Compassion is the womb, kindness is the flesh,
and the limbs of enlightenment form the extremities
as it grows in the womb of the Tathāgata.

He will increase his treasury of merit,
purify his treasury of wisdom,
reveal a treasury of skillful means,
and produce a treasury of great vows.

With such great adornments as these
he will rescue the many beings
and will become one who, among all devas and men,
is only rarely ever heard of or encountered.

Such a tree of wisdom as this
is one whose roots go deep and that is unshakable.
His many practices will gradually grow
until he everywhere provides shade for all beings.

正體字	426b14 欲生一切德　欲問一切法 426b15 欲斷一切疑　專求善知識 426b16 欲破諸惑魔　欲除諸見垢 426b17 欲解眾生縛　專求善知識 426b18 當滅諸惡道　當示人天路 426b19 令修功德行　疾入涅槃城 426b20 當度諸見難　當截諸見網 426b21 當枯愛欲水　當示三有道 426b22 當為世依怙　當作世光明 426b23 當成三界師　示其解脫處 426b24 亦當令世間　普離諸想著 426b25 普覺煩惱睡　普出愛欲泥 426b26 當了種種法　當淨種種剎 426b27 一切咸究竟　其心大歡喜 426b28 汝行極調柔　汝心甚清淨 426b29 所欲修功德　一切當圓滿 426c01 不久見諸佛　了達一切法 426c02 嚴淨眾剎海　成就大菩提 426c03 當滿諸行海　當知諸法海 426c04 當度眾生海　如是修諸行
简体字	欲生一切德，欲问一切法， 欲断一切疑，专求善知识。 欲破诸惑魔，欲除诸见垢， 欲解众生缚，专求善知识。 当灭诸恶道，当示人天路， 令修功德行，疾入涅槃城。 当度诸见难，当截诸见网， 当枯爱欲水，当示三有道。 当为世依怙，当作世光明， 当成三界师，示其解脱处。 亦当令世间，普离诸想著， 普觉烦恼睡，普出爱欲泥。 当了种种法，当净种种刹； 一切咸究竟，其心大欢喜。 汝行极调柔，汝心甚清净， 所欲修功德，一切当圆满。 不久见诸佛，了达一切法， 严净众刹海，成就大菩提。 当满诸行海，当知诸法海， 当度众生海，如是修诸行。

Wishing to develop all the virtues,
wishing to inquire about all dharmas,
and wishing to sever all doubts,
he is devoted to the search for good spiritual guides.

Wishing to destroy all the *māras* of the afflictions,
wishing to do away with the defilement of the various views,
and wishing to liberate beings from their bonds,
he is devoted to searching for good spiritual guides.

He will destroy all the wretched rebirth destinies,
will reveal the road to rebirth among humans and devas, and
will enable cultivation of practices that produce meritorious qualities
and lead to swift entry into the city of nirvāṇa.

He will liberate others from the difficulties produced by views,
will cut through the net of views,
will dry up the waters of craving,
and will reveal the paths out of the three realms of existence.

He will become a refuge for the world,
will become a light for the world,
will become a teacher of those in the three realms,
and will show them the way to liberation from them.

He will also enable those in the world
to abandon their attachments to perceptions,
to awaken from their slumber among the afflictions,
and to escape from the mud of sensual desires.

He will completely understand the many different dharmas,
will purify the many kinds of *kṣetras*,
and will lead everyone to the ultimate destination,
thereby filling their minds with great joyous delight.

Your practice has become so extremely pliant
and your mind has become so very purified
that, whichever meritorious qualities you wish to cultivate,
they will all reach perfect fulfillment.

Before long, you will see all buddhas,
will completely comprehend all dharmas,
will purify the ocean of the many *kṣetras*,
and will completely realize the great bodhi.

Cultivating all the practices in this way,
you will fulfill the ocean of all practices,
will know the ocean of all dharmas,
and will liberate an ocean of beings.

正體字

426c05 | 當到功德岸　當生諸善品
426c06 | 當與佛子等　如是心決定
426c07 | 當斷一切惑　當淨一切業
426c08 | 當伏一切魔　滿足如是願
426c09 | 當生妙智道　當開正法道
426c10 | 不久當捨離　惑業諸苦道
426c11 | [6] 一切眾生輪　沈迷諸有輪
426c12 | 汝當轉法輪　令其斷苦輪
426c13 | 汝當持佛種　汝當淨法種
426c14 | 汝[能>當]集僧種　三世悉周遍
426c15 | 當斷眾愛網　當裂眾見網
426c16 | 當救眾苦網　當成此願網
426c17 | 當度眾生界　當淨國土界
426c18 | 當集智慧界　當成此心界
426c19 | 當令眾生喜　當令菩薩喜
426c20 | 當令諸佛喜　當成此歡喜
426c21 | 當見一切趣　當見一切剎
426c22 | 當見一切法　當成此佛見
426c23 | 當放破暗光　當放息熱光
426c24 | 當放滅惡光　滌除三有苦

简体字

当到功德岸，当生诸善品，
当与佛子等，如是心决定。
当断一切惑，当净一切业，
当伏一切魔，满足如是愿。
当生妙智道，当开正法道，
不久当舍离，惑业诸苦道。
一切众生轮，沉迷诸有轮；
汝当转法轮，令其断苦轮。
汝当持佛种，汝当净法种，
汝当集僧种，三世悉周遍。
当断众爱网，当裂众见网，
当救众苦网，当成此愿网。
当度众生界，当净国土界，
当集智慧界，当成此心界。
当令众生喜，当令菩萨喜，
当令诸佛喜，当成此欢喜。
当见一切趣，当见一切刹，
当见一切法，当成此佛见。
当放破暗光，当放息热光，
当放灭恶光，涤除三有苦。

Having achieved such decisive resolve as this,
you will reach the far shore of meritorious qualities,
will develop all the varieties of goodness,
and will become the equal of the sons of the Buddha.

You will cut off all the afflictions,
will purify all karma,
and will subdue all the *māras,*
thus completely fulfilling vows such as these.

You will produce the path of marvelous wisdom,
will open the path of right Dharma,
and before long will relinquish
the path of afflictions, karma, and suffering.[38]

The sphere of all beings is sunken and confused
in the wheel of all the realms of existence.
You will turn the wheel of Dharma
and enable them to cut off the cycle of suffering.

You will preserve the lineage of the Buddha,
you will purify the lineage of the Dharma,
and you will gather the lineage of the Sangha
and see that they pervade all three periods of time.

You will cut away the net of the many cravings,
will rend the net of the many views,
will rescue beings from the net of their many sufferings,
and will successfully fulfill this net of vows.

You will liberate the realms of beings,
will purify the realms of lands,
will accumulate the realms of wisdom,
and will succeed in the realm of your resolute intentions.

You will arouse joy in beings,
will arouse joy among the bodhisattvas,
and will arouse joy in the buddhas.
You will produce joyous delight such as this.

You will see all the rebirth destinies,
will see all the *kṣetras,*
will see all dharmas,
and will acquire the vision of this buddha.

You will emanate the light that dispels darkness,
will emanate the light that extinguishes heat,
will emanate the light that extinguishes evil
and will rinse away the sufferings of the three realms of existence.

正體字

426c25 當開天趣門　當開佛道門
426c26 當示解脫門　普使眾生入
426c27 [7] 當示於正道　當絕於邪道
426c28 如是勤修行　成就菩提道
426c29 當修功德海　當度三有海
427a01 普使群生海　出於眾苦海
427a02 當於眾生海　消竭煩惱海
427a03 令修諸行海　疾入大智海
427a04 汝當增智海　汝當修行海
427a05 諸佛大願海　汝當咸滿足
427a06 [1] 汝當入剎海　汝當觀眾海
427a07 汝當以智力　普飲諸法海
427a08 當覲諸佛雲　當起供養雲
427a09 當聽妙法雲　當興此願雲
427a10 普遊三有室　普壞眾惑室
427a11 普入如來室　當行如是道
427a12 普入三昧門　普遊解脫門
427a13 普住神通門　周行於法界
427a14 普現眾生前　普對諸佛前
427a15 譬如日月光　當成如是力

简体字

当开天趣门，当开佛道门，
当示解脱门，普使众生入。
当示于正道，当绝于邪道；
如是勤修行，成就菩提道。
当修功德海，当度三有海；
普使群生海，出于众苦海。
当于众生海，消竭烦恼海，
令修诸行海，疾入大智海。
汝当增智海，汝当修行海；
诸佛大愿海，汝当咸满足。
汝当入刹海，汝当观众海；
汝当以智力，普饮诸法海。
当觐诸佛云，当起供养云，
当听妙法云，当兴此愿云。
普游三有室，普坏众惑室，
普入如来室，当行如是道。
普入三昧门，普游解脱门，
普住神通门，周行于法界。
普现众生前，普对诸佛前，
譬如日月光，当成如是力。

You will open the gates to the celestial rebirth destinies,
will open the gates to the path to buddhahood,
will reveal the gates to liberation,
and will cause all beings to enter them.

You will show them the right path
and will cut off access to the wrong paths.
Diligently cultivating in this way,
you will succeed in completing the path to bodhi.

You will cultivate the ocean of meritorious qualities,
will liberate those in the ocean of the three realms of existence,
and will everywhere enable the ocean of all beings
to escape from the ocean of the many kinds of sufferings.

In the ocean of beings,
you will dry up the ocean of afflictions
and will enable them to cultivate the ocean of practices
and swiftly enter the ocean of great wisdom.

You will increase the ocean of wisdom,
you will cultivate the ocean of practices,
and you will completely fulfill
the ocean of all buddhas' great vows.

You will enter the ocean of *kṣetras,*
you will contemplate the ocean of congregations,
and you will use the power of wisdom
to drink the entire ocean of all dharmas.

You will seek audiences with the cloud of all buddhas,
will raise up clouds of offerings to them,
will listen to their clouds of sublime Dharma,
and will make a cloud of vows such as these.

Roaming everywhere in the house of the three realms of existence,
everywhere demolishing the house of the many afflictions,
and everywhere entering the house of the Tathāgatas—
You will practice a path such as this.

You will everywhere enter the gateways of samādhi,
will everywhere roam in the gates of liberation,
will everywhere abide in the gates of the spiritual superknowledges,
and will travel everywhere throughout the Dharma realm.

You will everywhere appear before beings
and will everywhere appear before all buddhas
like the light of the sun and the moon.
You will develop powers such as these.

正體字

427a16 | [2] 所行無動亂　所行無染著
427a17 | 如鳥行虛空　當成此妙用
427a18 | 譬如因陀網　剎網如是住
427a19 | 汝當悉往詣　如風無所礙
427a20 | 汝當入法界　遍往[3]諸世界
427a21 | 普見三世佛　心生大歡喜
427a22 | 汝於諸法門　已得及當得
427a23 | 應生大喜躍　無貪亦無厭
427a24 | 汝是功德器　能隨諸佛教
427a25 | 能修菩薩行　得見此奇特
427a26 | 如是諸佛子　億劫難可遇
427a27 | 況見其功德　所修諸妙道
427a28 | 汝生於人中　大獲諸善利
427a29 | 得見文殊等　無量諸功德
427b01 | 已離諸惡道　已出諸難處
427b02 | 已超眾苦患　善哉勿懈怠
427b03 | 已離凡夫地　已住菩薩地
427b04 | 當滿智慧地　速入如來地
427b05 | 菩薩行如海　佛智同虛空
427b06 | 汝願亦復然　應生大欣慶

简体字

所行无动乱，所行无染著，
如鸟行虚空，当成此妙用。
譬如因陀网，刹网如是住；
汝当悉往诣，如风无所碍。
汝当入法界，遍往诸世界，
普见三世佛，心生大欢喜。
汝于诸法门，已得及当得，
应生大喜跃，无贪亦无厌。
汝是功德器，能随诸佛教，
能修菩萨行，得见此奇特。
如是诸佛子，亿劫难可遇；
况见其功德，所修诸妙道！
汝生于人中，大获诸善利，
得见文殊等，无量诸功德。
已离诸恶道，已出诸难处，
已超众苦患，善哉勿懈怠。
已离凡夫地，已住菩萨地，
当满智慧地，速入如来地。
菩萨行如海，佛智同虚空，
汝愿亦复然，应生大欣庆。

In all that you practice, you will remain unwavering and undistracted,
and in all that you practice, you will be as free of defiling attachments
as a bird as it flies across the sky.
You will develop marvelous functions such as these.

Just as is so within the net of Indra,
so too will you dwell in the network of *kṣetras*.
You will go forth to visit them all,
being as unimpeded in your travels as the wind.

You will enter the Dharma realm
and go everywhere throughout all worlds,
everywhere seeing the buddhas of the three periods of time,
doing so with a mind filled with great joy.

With regard to all the Dharma gateways
you have already acquired or shall acquire in the future,
you should bring forth great exultant joyfulness,
while staying free of either covetousness or weariness.

You are a vessel filled with meritorious qualities
who is able to follow the teachings of all buddhas
and is able to cultivate the bodhisattva practices.
Hence you see these extraordinary phenomena.

Sons of the Buddha such as these
would be rarely met even in a *koṭī* of kalpas.
How much rarer it is to see their meritorious qualities
and the marvelous paths that they cultivate.

You have been born within the human realm
where you have reaped a vast harvest of excellent benefits.
You have succeeded in seeing Mañjuśrī and the others
as well as their countless meritorious qualities.

You have already escaped the wretched rebirth destinies,
have already escaped the places beset by the difficulties,[39]
and have already gone beyond the many sufferings and troubles.
This is so very good indeed! You must not indulge any indolence.

You have already left the grounds of the common person,
and have already come to dwell on the bodhisattva grounds.
You will fulfill the practice of the wisdom grounds
and soon enter the ground of the Tathāgata.

The bodhisattva practices are like an ocean,
the buddhas' wisdom is like empty space,
and so too are your vows.
You should rejoice greatly in this.

正體字

427b07║ 諸根不懈倦　志願恒決定
427b08║ 親近善知識　不久悉成滿
427b09║ [4] 菩薩種種行　皆為調眾生
427b10║ 普行諸法門　慎勿生疑惑
427b11║ 汝具難思福　及以真實信
427b12║ 是故於今日　得見諸佛子
427b13║ 汝見諸佛子　悉獲廣大利
427b14║ 一一諸大願　一切咸信受
427b15║ 汝於三有中　能修菩薩行
427b16║ 是故諸佛子　示汝解脫門
427b17║ 非是法器人　與佛子同住
427b18║ 設經無量劫　莫知其境界
427b19║ 汝見諸菩薩　得聞如是法
427b20║ 世間甚難有　應生大喜慶
427b21║ 諸佛護念汝　菩薩攝受汝
427b22║ 能順其教行　善哉住壽命
427b23║ 已生菩薩家　已具菩薩德
427b24║ 已長如來種　當[*]昇灌頂位
427b25║ 不久汝當得　與諸佛子等
427b26║ 見苦惱眾生　悉置安隱處

简体字

诸根不懈倦，志愿恒决定，
亲近善知识，不久悉成满。
菩萨种种行，皆为调众生，
普行诸法门，慎勿生疑惑。
汝具难思福，及以真实信；
是故于今日，得见诸佛子。
汝见诸佛子，悉获广大利，
一一诸大愿，一切咸信受。
汝于三有中，能修菩萨行；
是故诸佛子，示汝解脱门。
非是法器人，与佛子同住，
设经无量劫，莫知其境界。
汝见诸菩萨，得闻如是法，
世间甚难有，应生大喜庆。
诸佛护念汝，菩萨摄受汝，
能顺其教行，善哉住寿命。
已生菩萨家，已具菩萨德，
已长如来种，当升灌顶位。
不久汝当得，与诸佛子等，
见苦恼众生，悉置安隐处。

Your faculties are such that you do not grow lax or weary
and your resolve is always decisive.
Draw near to the good spiritual guides
and before long you will achieve complete success.

The bodhisattvas' many different practices
are all done for the sake of training beings.
Completely practice all the Dharma gateways
and take care not to doubt them.

You possess an inconceivable stock of merit
as well as genuine faith.
It is due to this that now, today,
you have been able to see these sons of the Buddha.

You have seen all these sons of the Buddha
and have acquired vast benefit from all of them.
Each and every one of their great vows
are such that you accept them with faith.

You are one who is able to cultivate the bodhisattva practices
throughout the three realms of existence.
Therefore those sons of the Buddha
revealed to you their gateways to liberation.

Though those who are not vessels of the Dharma
might dwell together with the sons of the Buddha,
even if they did so for countless kalpas,
none of them could ever know their spheres of experience.

You have seen the bodhisattvas
and have been able to hear dharmas such as these
that are found in the world only extremely rarely.
In this, you should greatly rejoice.

All buddhas are protectively mindful of you,
and the bodhisattvas gather you in and accept you.
You are one who is able to practice in accord with their teachings.
This is good indeed! May you live a long life.

You have already been born into the family of the bodhisattvas,
have already acquired the virtues of the bodhisattvas,
and you have already grown in the lineage of the Tathāgata,
and are bound to ascend to the crown-anointing consecration stage.

Before long, you are bound to succeed
in becoming the same as the other sons of the Buddha.
Whenever you see beings afflicted by sufferings,
you shall establish them all in a peaceful and secure place.

正體字

427b27 如下如是種　必獲如是果
427b28 我今慶慰汝　汝應大欣悅
427b29 無量諸菩薩　無量劫行道
427c01 未能成此行　今汝皆獲得
427c02 [5] 信樂堅進力　善財成此行
427c03 若有敬慕心　亦當如是學
427c04 一切功德行　皆從願欲生
427c05 善財已了知　常樂勤修習
427c06 如龍布密雲　必當霔大雨
427c07 菩薩起願智　決定修諸行
427c08 [6] 若有善知識　示汝普賢行
427c09 汝當好承事　慎勿生疑惑
427c10 汝於無量劫　為欲妄捨身
427c11 今為求菩提　此捨方為善
427c12 汝於無量劫　具受生死苦
427c13 不曾事諸佛　未聞如是行
427c14 汝今得人身　值佛善知識
427c15 聽受菩提行　云何不歡喜
427c16 雖遇佛興世　亦值善知識
427c17 其心不清淨　不聞如是法

简体字

如下如是种，必获如是果，
我今庆慰汝，汝应大欣悦。
无量诸菩萨，无量劫行道，
未能成此行，今汝皆获得。
信乐坚进力，善财成此行；
若有敬慕心，亦当如是学。
一切功德行，皆从愿欲生；
善财已了知，常乐勤修习。
如龙布密云，必当霔大雨；
菩萨起愿智，决定修诸行。
若有善知识，示汝普贤行；
汝当好承事，慎勿生疑惑。
汝于无量劫，为欲妄舍身；
今为求菩提，此舍方为善。
汝于无量劫，具受生死苦，
不曾事诸佛，未闻如是行。
汝今得人身，值佛善知识，
听受菩提行，云何不欢喜！
虽遇佛兴世，亦值善知识；
其心不清净，不闻如是法。

It is just as when one plants a seed of this particular sort,
one is then certain to harvest a fruit of this very same sort.
I now congratulate you and offer you my comforting assurance.
You should therefore feel greatly joyous happiness.

Countless bodhisattvas
have practiced the path for countless kalpas
and yet have still been unable to develop these practices,
all of which you have now already acquired.

Through the power of faith-filled aspiration and solid vigor,
Sudhana has succeeded in these practices.
Whoever feels respect and admiration for this
should also pursue training such as this.

All the meritorious qualities and practices
arise from vows and aspirations.
Sudhana has already completely understood this.
Hence he always aspires to diligently cultivate them.

Just as when the dragons spread forth dense clouds,
it is then certain that a great rain will pour down,
so too, when the bodhisattva brings forth vows and wisdom,
he will definitely pursue the cultivation of the practices.

If there are any good spiritual guides
who show you the practices of Samantabhadra,
You should serve them well
and take care not to doubt them.

For countless kalpas, because of sensual desires,
you have relinquished bodies in vain.
Now, if you were to do so for the sake of the quest for bodhi,
this relinquishing would then be good.

Throughout countless past kalpas,
you have fully endured the sufferings of births and deaths
without ever having served the buddhas
and without ever even hearing of practices such as these.

Now that you have acquired this human body,
have met the Buddha and the good spiritual guides,
and have heard the practices leading to bodhi,
how could you not be filled with joyous delight?

Even if one met a buddha appearing in the world
and also met good spiritual guides,
still, if one's mind was impure,
one would not get to hear dharmas such as these.

正體字

427c18 [7] 若於善知識　信樂心尊重
427c19 離疑不疲厭　乃聞如是法
427c20 若有聞此法　而興誓願心
427c21 當知如是人　已獲廣大利
427c22 如是心清淨　常得近諸佛
427c23 亦近諸菩薩　決定成菩提
427c24 [8] 若入此法門　則具諸功德
427c25 永離眾惡趣　不受一切苦
427c26 不久捨此身　往生佛國土
427c27 常見十方佛　及以諸菩薩
427c28 往因今淨解　及事善友力
427c29 增長諸功德　如水生蓮華
428a01 樂事善知識　勤供一切佛
428a02 專心聽聞法　常行勿懈倦
428a03 汝是真法器　當具一切法
428a04 當修一切道　當滿一切願
428a05 汝以信解心　而來禮敬我
428a06 不久當普入　一切諸佛會
428a07 善哉真佛子　恭敬一切佛
428a08 不久具諸行　到佛功德岸

简体字

若于善知识，信乐心尊重，
离疑不疲厌，乃闻如是法。
若有闻此法，而兴誓愿心；
当知如是人，已获广大利。
如是心清净，常得近诸佛，
亦近诸菩萨，决定成菩提。
若入此法门，则具诸功德，
永离众恶趣，不受一切苦。
不久舍此身，往生佛国土，
常见十方佛，及以诸菩萨。
往因今净解，及事善友力，
增长诸功德，如水生莲华。
乐事善知识，勤供一切佛，
专心听闻法，常行勿懈倦。
汝是真法器，当具一切法，
当修一切道，当满一切愿。
汝以信解心，而来礼敬我，
不久当普入，一切诸佛会。
善哉真佛子，恭敬一切佛，
不久具诸行，到佛功德岸。

If, toward the good spiritual guide,
one were to produce faith, aspiration, resolve, and reverence
while abandoning doubts and remaining free of weariness,
only then one might be able to hear Dharma such as this.

If there is anyone who hears this Dharma
and then produces a mind of resolute vows,
one should realize that a person such as this
has already reaped vast benefit.

If one's resolve is purified in this way,
he will always be able to draw near to the buddhas,
will also draw near to the bodhisattvas,
and will definitely succeed in realizing bodhi.

If one enters this gateway of the Dharma,
then he will acquire all the meritorious qualities,
will forever leave behind the many wretched destinies,
and will no longer undergo any of those sufferings.

Before long, you will relinquish this body
and go forth to rebirth in a buddha land
where you will always see the buddhas of the ten directions
as well as all the bodhisattvas.

Due to past causes by which your resolve is now purified
and also due to the power of having served the good spiritual guides,
you grow in all the meritorious qualities
just as a lotus flower grows forth from its waters.

Delight in serving the good spiritual guides,
be diligent in making offerings to all buddhas,
single-mindedly listen to the Dharma,
always practice, and never let yourself grow lax or weary.

You have become a true vessel of the Dharma.
You will become completely possessed of all dharmas,
will cultivate all the paths,
and will fulfill all the vows.

It is with a mind of resolute faith
that you have come here to pay your respects to me.
Before long, you will everywhere enter
the congregations of all buddhas.

It is good indeed, you true son of the Buddha.
You who revere all the buddhas
are bound before long to fully possess all the practices
and achieve perfection in the Buddha's meritorious qualities.

正體字

428a09‖ 　汝當往大智　　文殊師利所
428a10‖ 　彼當令汝得　　普賢深妙行
428a11‖ 爾時彌勒菩薩摩訶薩。在眾會前。稱讚善財
428a12‖ 大功德藏。善財聞已歡喜踊躍。身毛皆豎悲
428a13‖ 泣哽噎。起立合掌恭敬瞻仰。遶無量匝。以文
428a14‖ 殊師利心念力故。眾華瓔珞種種妙寶。不覺
428a15‖ 忽然自盈其手。善財歡喜。即以奉散彌勒菩
428a16‖ 薩摩訶薩上。時彌勒菩[1]薩。摩善財頂。為說
428a17‖ 頌言
428a18‖ 　善哉善哉真佛子　　普策諸根無懈倦
428a19‖ 　不久當具諸功德　　猶如文殊及與我
428a20‖ 時善財童子。以頌答曰
428a21‖ 　我念善知識　　億劫難值遇
428a22‖ 　今得咸親近　　而來詣尊所
428a23‖ 　我以文殊故　　見諸難見者
428a24‖ 　彼大功德尊　　願速還瞻覲
428b02‖ [3]大方廣佛華嚴經卷[4]第七十八
428b05‖ 　　[8]入法[9]界品第三十九之十九
428b06‖ 爾時善財童子。合掌恭敬。重白彌勒菩薩摩
428b07‖ 訶薩言。大聖。我已先發阿耨多羅三藐三菩
428b08‖ 提心。而我未知菩薩云何學菩薩行。云何修
428b09‖ 菩薩道。大聖。一切如來授尊者記。一生當得
428b10‖ 阿耨多羅三藐三菩提。

简体字

　　汝当往大智，文殊师利所；
　　彼当令汝得，普贤深妙行。”

　　尔时，弥勒菩萨摩诃萨在众会前，称赞善财大功德藏。善财闻已，欢喜踊跃，身毛皆竖，悲泣哽噎；起立合掌，恭敬瞻仰，绕无量匝。以文殊师利心念力故，众华、璎珞、种种妙宝不觉忽然自盈其手；善财欢喜，即以奉散弥勒菩萨摩诃萨上。

　　时，弥勒菩萨摩善财顶，为说颂言：

“善哉善哉真佛子，普策诸根无懈倦，
　不久当具诸功德，犹如文殊及与我。”

　　时，善财童子以颂答曰：

“我念善知识，亿劫难值遇；
　今得咸亲近，而来诣尊所。
　我以文殊故，见诸难见者；
　彼大功德尊，愿速还瞻觐。”

大方广佛华严经卷第七十八

入法界品第三十九之十九

　　尔时，善财童子合掌恭敬，重白弥勒菩萨摩诃萨言：“大圣，我已先发阿耨多罗三藐三菩提心，而我未知菩萨云何学菩萨行？云何修菩萨道？

　　“大圣，一切如来授尊者记，一生当得阿耨多罗三藐三菩提；

You should go forth to the abode
of the greatly wise Mañjuśrī.
He will enable you to acquire
the profound and sublime practices of Samantabhadra.

Then, having heard Maitreya Bodhisattva-mahāsattva in front of that congregation praising Sudhana's immense treasury of meritorious qualities, Sudhana felt joyous exultation and the hairs of his body all stood on end. Weeping and choked up, he then stood up with his palms pressed together respectfully, and gazed up in admiration at Maitreya Bodhisattva as he circumambulated him countless times.

Then, through the mental powers of Mañjuśrī and without Sudhana even being aware of it, many kinds of flowers, necklaces, and various marvelous jewels suddenly and spontaneously filled his hands. Overjoyed, Sudhana straightaway lifted them up as offerings and showered them over Maitreya Bodhisattva-mahāsattva, whereupon Maitreya Bodhisattva-mahāsattva rubbed the crown of Sudhana's head and spoke this verse:

It is so good indeed, so very good indeed, you true son of the Buddha.
You goaded all your faculties and stayed free of laxness or weariness.
Before long you will acquire all the meritorious qualities
by which you will become like Mañjuśrī and myself.

Sudhana the Youth then replied with these verses:

I am mindful that the good spiritual guides
are only rarely met even in a *koṭī* of kalpas.
Now, I have succeeded in drawing near to them all
and have come here to pay my respects to the Venerable One.

It is because of Mañjuśrī that I have seen
all of these who are so rarely seen.
May I swiftly return to gaze up at and have audiences with
that venerable one of such great meritorious qualities.

Sudhana the Youth then pressed his palms together respectfully and again addressed Maitreya Bodhisattva-mahāsattva, saying:

O Great Ārya. I am one who has already resolved to attain *anuttara-samyak-saṃbodhi*. Still, I do not yet know how the bodhisattva should train in the bodhisattva practices or how he should cultivate the bodhisattva path.

O Great Ārya, all *tathāgatas* have bestowed the prediction on the Venerable One, verifying that, in but one lifetime, he shall attain *anuttara-samyak-saṃbodhi*.

正體字

若一生當得無上菩
428b11‖ 提。則已超越一切菩薩所住處。則已出過一
428b12‖ 切菩薩離生位。則已圓滿一切波羅蜜。則已
428b13‖ 深入一切諸忍門。則已具足一切菩薩地。[10]則
428b14‖ 已遊戲一切解脫門。則已成就一切三昧法。
428b15‖ 則已通達一切菩薩行。則已證得一切陀羅
428b16‖ 尼辯才。則已於一切菩薩自在中而得自在
428b17‖ 則已積集一切菩薩助道法。則已遊戲智慧
428b18‖ 方便。則已出生大神通智。則已成就一切學
428b19‖ 處。則已圓滿一切妙行。則已滿足一切大願。
428b20‖ 則已領受一切佛所記。則已了知一切諸乘
428b21‖ 門。則已堪受一切如來所護念。則已能攝一
428b22‖ 切佛菩提。則已能持一切佛法藏。則已能持
428b23‖ 一切諸佛菩薩祕密藏。則已能於一切菩薩
428b24‖ 眾中為上首。則已能為破煩惱魔軍大勇將。
428b25‖ 則已能作出生死曠野大導師。則已能作治
428b26‖ 諸惑重病大醫王。

简体字

若一生当得无上菩提，则已超越一切菩萨所住处，则已出过一切菩萨离生位，则已圆满一切波罗蜜，则已深入一切诸忍门，则已具足一切菩萨地，则已游戏一切解脱门，则已成就一切三昧法，则已通达一切菩萨行，则已证得一切陀罗尼辩才，则已于一切菩萨自在中而得自在，则已积集一切菩萨助道法，则已游戏智慧方便，则已出生大神通智，则已成就一切学处，则已圆满一切妙行，则已满足一切大愿，则已领受一切佛所记，则已了知一切诸乘门，则已堪受一切如来所护念，则已能摄一切佛菩提，则已能持一切佛法藏，则已能持一切诸佛菩萨秘密藏，则已能于一切菩萨众中为上首，则已能为破烦恼魔军大勇将，则已能作出生死旷野大导师，则已能作治诸惑重病大医王，

If, in but one lifetime, one is bound to attain the unexcelled bodhi, then:

He has already stepped beyond the stations in which all bodhisattvas abide;

He has already gone beyond all bodhisattvas' station of emancipation from births;[40]

He has already completely fulfilled all the *pāramitās;*

He has already deeply entered all the gateways of patience;

He has already completed all the bodhisattva grounds;

He has achieved easeful mastery of all of the gates to liberation;

He has already accomplished all the samādhi dharmas;

He has already gained a penetrating comprehension of all bodhisattva practices;

He has already realized all the *dhāraṇīs* and types of eloquence;

He has already attained mastery of all the bodhisattvas' sovereign masteries;

He has already accumulated all of the bodhisattvas' provisions for the path to enlightenment;

He has already attained easeful mastery of wisdom and skillful means;

He has already developed all of the spiritual superknowledges and knowledges;

He has already perfected all the stations of training;

He has already perfectly fulfilled all the marvelous practices;

He has already completely fulfilled all the great vows;

He has already received the predictions from all buddhas;

He has already completely known the gateways to all the vehicles;

He is already able to receive the protective mindfulness of all *tathāgatas;*

He is already able to embrace the bodhi of all buddhas;

He is already able to preserve the Dharma treasury of all buddhas;

He is already able to preserve the treasury of esoteric teachings of all buddhas and bodhisattvas;

He is already able to serve as the supreme leader in all bodhisattva congregations;

He is already able to serve as a great and brave general who demolishes the armies of the affliction *māras;*

He is already able to serve as a great guide across the wilderness of *saṃsāra;*

He is already able to serve as a great physician king who cures all the serious illnesses rooted in the afflictions;

正體字

[11]則已能於一切眾生中為
428b27 最勝。則已能於一切世主中得自在。則已能
428b28 於一切聖人中最第一。則已能於一切聲聞
428b29 獨覺中最增上。則已能於生死海中為船師。
428c01 則已能布調伏一切眾生網。則已能觀一切
428c02 眾生根。則已能攝一切眾生界。則已能守
428c03 護一切菩薩眾。則已能談議一切菩薩事。則
428c04 已能[12]往詣一切如來所。則已能住止一切如
428c05 來會。則已能現身一切眾生前。則已能於
428c06 一切世法無所染。則已能超越一切魔境界。
428c07 則已能安住一切佛境界。則已能到一切菩
428c08 薩無礙境。則已能精勤供養一切佛。則已與
428c09 一切諸佛法同體性。已繫妙法繒。已受佛灌
428c10 頂。已住一切智。已能普生一切佛法。已能
428c11 速踐一切智位。大聖。菩薩云何學菩薩行。云
428c12 何修菩薩道。隨所修學。疾得具足一切佛法。
428c13 悉能度脫所念眾生。

简体字

则已能于一切众生中为最胜，则已能于一切世主中得自在，则已能于一切圣人中最第一，则已能于一切声闻、独觉中最增上，则已能于生死海中为船师，则已能布调伏一切众生网，则已能观一切众生根，则已能摄一切众生界，则已能守护一切菩萨众，则已能谈议一切菩萨事，则已能往诣一切如来所，则已能住止一切如来会，则已能现身一切众生前，则已能于一切世法无所染，则已能超越一切魔境界，则已能安住一切佛境界，则已能到一切菩萨无碍境，则已能精勤供养一切佛，则已与一切诸佛法同体性，已系妙法缯，已受佛灌顶，已住一切智，已能普生一切佛法，已能速践一切智位。

“大圣，菩萨云何学菩萨行？云何修菩萨道？随所修学，疾得具足一切佛法，悉能度脱所念众生，

He is already able to be supreme among all beings;
He is already able to prevail with sovereign mastery over all the rulers of the world;
He is already able to be foremost among all persons who are *āryas;*
He is already able to be most supreme among all the *śrāvaka* disciples and *pratyekabuddhas;*
He is already able to serve as a ship captain on the ocean of *saṃsāra;*
He is already able to cast the net that draws all beings into the training;
He is already able to contemplate and assess the faculties of all beings;
He is already able to gather in all realms of beings;
He is already able to guard all bodhisattva congregations;
He is already able to discuss all the works of bodhisattvas;
He is already able to travel and pay his respects to all *tathāgatas;*
He is already able to dwell within the congregations of all *tathāgatas;*
He is already able to manifest bodies that appear directly before all beings;
He is already able to remain undefiled by any of the worldly dharmas;
He is already able to go beyond the realms of all the *māras;*
He is already able to abide securely in the realms of all buddhas;
He is already able to reach the unimpeded realms of all bodhisattvas;
He is already able to diligently make offerings to all buddhas;
He has already become of the same essential nature as the Dharma of all buddhas;
He has already tied on the silken headband of the sublime Dharma;
He has already received the Buddha's crown-anointing consecration;
He has already come to abide in all-knowledge;
He is already able to everywhere manifest all the dharmas of a buddha; and
He is already able to swiftly ascend to the station of all-knowledge.

O Great Ārya, this being so, how should the bodhisattva train in the bodhisattva practices and how should he cultivate the bodhisattva path so that, as a consequence of his cultivation and training:

He will swiftly succeed in becoming fully equipped with all the dharmas of a buddha;
He will be able to liberate all beings he brings to mind;

正體字

普能成滿所發大願。普
428c14‖ 能究竟所起諸行。普能安慰一切天人。不負
428c15‖ 自身。不斷三寶。不虛一切佛菩薩種。能持
428c16‖ 一切諸佛法眼。如是等事願皆為說
428c17‖ 爾時。彌勒菩薩摩訶薩。觀察一切道場眾會。
428c18‖ 指示善財而作是言。諸仁者。汝等見此長者
428c19‖ 子今於我所問菩薩行諸功德不。諸仁者。此
428c20‖ 長者子勇猛精進志願無雜。深心堅固恒不
428c21‖ 退轉。具勝希望。如救頭然。無有厭足。樂善
428c22‖ 知識親近供養。處處尋求承事請法。諸仁者。
428c23‖ 此長者子。曩於福城受文殊教。展轉南行求
428c24‖ 善知識。經由一百一十善知識已。然後而來
428c25‖ 至於我所。未曾暫起一念疲懈。諸仁者。此
428c26‖ 長者子。甚為難有。趣向大乘。乘於大慧。發大
428c27‖ 勇猛。擐大悲甲。以大慈心救護眾生。起大
428c28‖ 精進波羅蜜行。

简体字

普能成满所发大愿，普能究竟所起诸行，普能安慰一切天人，不负自身，不断三宝，不虚一切佛菩萨种，能持一切诸佛法眼。如是等事，愿皆为说！”

尔时，弥勒菩萨摩诃萨观察一切道场众会，指示善财而作是言：“诸仁者，汝等见此长者子，今于我所问菩萨行诸功德不？诸仁者，此长者子，勇猛精进，志乐无杂，深心坚固，恒不退转；具胜希望，如救头燃，无有厌足；乐善知识，亲近供养，处处寻求，承事请法。诸仁者，此长者子，曩于福城受文殊教，展转南行求善知识，经由一百一十善知识已，然后而来至于我所，未曾暂起一念疲懈。

“诸仁者，此长者子甚为难有，趣向大乘，乘于大慧，发大勇猛，擐大悲甲，以大慈心救护众生，起大精进波罗蜜行，

He will be able to fulfill all the great vows he has made;
He will be able to finish all the practices he has started;
He will be able to everywhere comfort all devas and humans;
He will not fail his own responsibility to himself;
He will not cut off the lineage of the Three Jewels;
He will ensure that the lineage of all buddhas and bodhisattvas does not become vacant; and
He will be able to preserve the Dharma eye of all buddhas?

Please explain all such matters for me.

Maitreya Bodhisattva-mahāsattva then surveyed the entire congregation, pointed to Sudhana, and said:

Worthy Ones, do you see this son of an elder who now asks me about the meritorious qualities of the bodhisattva's practice?

Worthy Ones, as for this son of an elder:

He is heroically vigorous;
He is free of mixed motivations;
His deep resolve is solid;
He is forever irreversible;
He possesses supreme aspirations;
He [practices with such urgency that] he is like someone hastening to extinguish a fire in his own hair;
He is insatiable in this;
He delights in good spiritual guides;
He draws near to them and makes offerings; and
He searches for them everywhere, seeks to serve them, and requests Dharma teachings from them.

Worthy Ones, as for this son of an elder, he previously received teachings from Mañjuśrī in Dhanyākara or "Merit City" and then gradually traveled south in search of good spiritual guides. After having met with a hundred and ten good spiritual guides, he came to me. During all that time, he never had a single thought of weariness in his efforts.

Worthy Ones, this son of an elder is one who is extremely rare, for:

He has set out in the Great Vehicle;
He has ascended to its great wisdom;
He brings forth great courage;
He dons the armor of great compassion;
He uses the mind of great kindness to rescue beings;
He arouses great vigor in the practice of the *pāramitās*;

正體字

作大商主護諸眾生。為大法
428c29‖ 船度諸有海。住於大道。集大法寶。修諸廣
429a01‖ 大助道之法。如是之人。難可得聞。難可得見。
429a02‖ 難得親近同居共行。何以故。此長者子。發心
429a03‖ 救護一切眾生。令一切眾生解脫諸苦。超諸
429a04‖ 惡趣。離諸險難。破無明闇。出生死野。息諸趣
429a05‖ 輪。度魔境界。不著世法。出欲淤泥。斷貪鞅解
429a06‖ 見縛。壞想宅絕迷道。摧慢幢拔惑箭。撤睡
429a07‖ 蓋裂愛網。滅無明度有流。離諂幻淨心垢。斷
429a08‖ 癡惑出生死。諸仁者。此長者子。為被四流
429a09‖ 漂泊者造大法船。為被見泥沒溺者立大法
429a10‖ 橋。為被癡暗昏迷者然大智燈。

简体字

作大商主护诸众生，为大法船度诸有海，住于大道，集大法宝，修诸广大助道之法；如是之人，难可得闻，难可得见，难得亲近、同居、共行。何以故？此长者子发心救护一切众生，令一切众生，解脱诸苦，超诸恶趣，离诸险难，破无明暗，出生死野，息诸趣轮，度魔境界，不著世法，出欲淤泥，断贪鞅，解见缚，坏想宅，绝迷道，摧慢幢，拔惑箭，撤睡盖，裂爱网，灭无明，度有流，离谄幻，净心垢，断痴惑，出生死。

“诸仁者，此长者子，为被四流漂汩者，造大法船；为被见泥没溺者，立大法桥；为被痴暗昏迷者，燃大智灯；

He serves as a great leader of merchants who guards all beings;
He serves as a great Dharma ship that takes others across the ocean of all stations of existence;
He abides in the great path;
He gathers the jewels of the great Dharma; and
He cultivates the vast provisions for the path.

A person such as this would only rarely be heard about and would only rarely be seen. It be even more difficult to ever draw near to such a person, abide together with him, or join with him in carrying out the practices. And why is this so?

This son of an elder has resolved to rescue all beings and enable all beings:

To gain liberation from sufferings;
To step beyond the wretched destinies;
To abandon the dangers and the difficulties;
To dispel the darkness of ignorance;
To escape from the wilderness of *saṃsāra;*
To halt the wheel of the rebirth destinies;
To cross beyond the realms of Māra;
To cease their attachment to worldly dharmas;
To escape from the mud of sensual desires;
To cut off the halter of desire and untie the bonds of the various views;
To demolish the house of conceptual thought and cut off the path of confusion;
To knock down the banner of arrogance and extricate the arrows of delusion;
To remove the hindrance of drowsiness and rend the net of cravings;
To extinguish ignorance and cross beyond the river of existence;
To abandon flattery and deception and cleanse the mind of defilements; and
To cut off delusions and escape from *saṃsāra.*

Worthy Ones, as for this son of an elder:

For those adrift in the currents of four floods, he builds a great Dharma ship;
For those drowning in the mire of views, he erects a great Dharma bridge;
For those immersed in the confusion of delusion's darkness, he lights the lamp of great wisdom;

正體字

為行生死曠
429a11‖ 野者開示聖道。[1]為嬰煩惱重病者調和法藥。
429a12‖ 為遭生老死苦者飲以甘露令其安隱。為入
429a13‖ 貪恚癡火者沃以定水使得清涼。多憂惱者
429a14‖ 慰[2]諭使安。繫有獄者曉誨令出。入見網者開
429a15‖ 以智劍。住界城者示諸脫門。在險難者導安
429a16‖ 隱處。懼結賊者與無畏法。墮惡趣者授慈悲
429a17‖ 手。拘害蘊者示涅槃城。界蛇所纏解以聖道。
429a18‖ 著於六處空聚落者以智慧光引之令出。住
429a19‖ 邪濟者令入正濟。近惡友者示其善友。樂凡
429a20‖ 法者誨以聖法。著生死者令其趣入一切智
429a21‖ 城。諸仁者。此長者子。恒以此行。救護眾生。
429a22‖ 發菩提心未嘗休息。

简体字

为行生死旷野者，开示圣道；为婴烦恼重病者，调和法药；为遭生、老、死苦者，饮以甘露，令其安隐；为入贪、恚、痴火者，沃以定水，使得清凉；多忧恼者，慰喻使安；系有狱者，晓诲令出；入见网者，开以智剑；住界城者，示诸脱门；在险难者，导安隐处；惧结贼者，与无畏法；堕恶趣者，授慈悲手；拘害蕴者，示涅槃城；界蛇所缠，解以圣道；著于六处空聚落者，以智慧光引之令出；住邪济者，令入正济；近恶友者，示其善友；乐凡法者，诲以圣法；著生死者，令其趣入一切智城。

“诸仁者，此长者子，恒以此行救护众生，发菩提心未尝休息，

For those traveling through the wilderness of *saṃsāra,* he shows them the path of the *āryas;*

For those who have contracted the grave illnesses caused by the afflictions, he compounds Dharma medicines;

For those who have met with the sufferings of birth, aging, and death, he comforts them with the elixir of immortality;

For those who have entered into the fires of greed, hatred, and delusion, he gives them clarity and coolness by drenching them with the waters of meditative absorption;

For those who are beset by an abundance of sorrow and dejection, he comforts and encourages them so that they find peace;

For those who are confined in the prison of the realms of existence, he explains to them how to escape;

For those who have entered the net of views, he cuts it open with the sword of wisdom;

For those who dwell in the city of the realms of existence, he shows them the gates of liberation;

For those in danger and difficulty, he leads them to a place of peace and security;

For those terrorized by the thieves of the fetters, he provides them with the means to attain fearlessness;

For those who have fallen into the wretched rebirth destinies, he aids them with the hands of kindness and compassion;

For those caught in and injured by the aggregates, he shows them the city of nirvāṇa;

For those who are caught in the coils of the serpents of the sense realms, he frees them with the path of the *āryas;*

For those attached to the empty village of the six sense bases, he leads them out with the light of wisdom, thereby enabling their escape;

For those trying to ford [the river] in the wrong place, he assists to ford it at the right place;

For those who have drawn near to bad spiritual friends, he shows good spiritual friends;

For those who delight in mundane dharmas, he teaches them the dharmas of the *āryas;* and

For those who have become attached to *saṃsāra,* he enables their entry into the city of all-knowledge.

Worthy Ones, as for this son of an elder:

He constantly uses these practices to rescue beings;

He never rests in manifesting the resolve to attain bodhi;

正體字

求大乘道曾無懈倦。飲
429a23‖ 諸法水不生厭足。[3]恒勤積集助道之行。常
429a24‖ 樂清淨一切法門。修菩薩行不捨精進。成滿
429a25‖ 諸願善行方便。見善知識情無厭足。事善知
429a26‖ 識身不疲懈。聞善知識所有教誨。常樂順行
429a27‖ 未曾違逆。諸仁者。若有眾生。能發阿耨多
429a28‖ 羅三藐三菩提心。是為希有。若發心已。又
429a29‖ 能如是。精進方便。集諸佛法。倍為希有。[4]又
429b01‖ 能如是求菩薩道。又能如是淨菩薩行。又能
429b02‖ 如是事善知識。又能如是如救頭然。又能如
429b03‖ 是順知識教。又能如是堅固修行。又能如是
429b04‖ 集菩提分。又能如是不求一切名聞利養。又
429b05‖ 能如是不捨菩薩純一之心。又能如是不樂
429b06‖ 家宅。不著欲樂。不戀父母親戚知識。但樂
429b07‖ 追求菩薩伴侶。

简体字

求大乘道曾无懈倦，饮诸法水不生厌足，恒勤积集助道之行，常乐清净一切法门，修菩萨行不舍精进，成满诸愿善行方便，见善知识情无厌足，事善知识身不疲懈，闻善知识所有教诲常乐顺行未曾违逆。

“诸仁者，若有众生能发阿耨多罗三藐三菩提心，是为希有；若发心已，又能如是精进方便集诸佛法，倍为希有；又能如是求菩萨道，又能如是净菩萨行，又能如是事善知识，又能如是如救头燃，又能如是顺知识教，又能如是坚固修行，又能如是集菩提分，又能如是不求一切名闻利养，又能如是不舍菩萨纯一之心，又能如是不乐家宅、不著欲乐、不恋父母亲戚知识，但乐追求菩萨伴侣，

He never indulges any indolence or weariness in his pursuit of the path of the Great Vehicle;
He is insatiable in drinking the waters of the Dharma;
He constantly and diligently accumulates practices that are provisions for the path to enlightenment;
He always delights in purifying all Dharma gateways;
He never relinquishes his vigor in cultivating the bodhisattva practices;
He fulfills his vows and skillfully practices expedient means;
He is insatiable in his eagerness to see the good spiritual guides;
He is never weary or lax in serving the good spiritual guides; and
He listens to all the teachings of the good spiritual guides, always delights in complying with them, and never opposes them.

Worthy Ones, it would be rare enough to meet any being who is able to resolve to attain *anuttara-samyak-saṃbodhi*. But it is doubly rare to meet anyone who has made this resolve who is then also able to be as vigorous as this in his efforts to accumulate all the dharmas of a buddha. Furthermore:

If he were then also able in this same way to seek the bodhisattva path—
If he were then also able in this same way to purify the bodhisattva practices—
If he were then also able in this same way to serve good spiritual guides—
If he were then also able in this same way to act with the urgency of someone hastening to extinguish a fire in his own hair—
If he were then also able in this same way to comply with the good spiritual guides' teachings—
If he were then also able in this same way to persist with solid cultivation—
If he were then also able in this same way to accumulate the limbs of bodhi—
If he were then also able in this same way to never seek fame or offerings—
If he were then also able in this same way to never forsake the bodhisattva's purely singular resolve—
If he were then also able in this same way to never delight in house and home, to never become attached to desires, to never be fondly attached to parents, relatives, and friends, and to only delight in seeking bodhisattva companions—

正體字

又能如是不顧身命。唯願勤
429b08║ 修一切智道。應知展轉倍更難得。諸仁者。餘
429b09║ 諸菩薩。經於無量百千萬億那由他劫。乃能
429b10║ 滿足菩薩願行。乃能親近諸佛菩提。此長者
429b11║ 子。於一生內。則能淨佛刹。則能化眾生。則能
429b12║ 以智慧深入法界。則能成就諸波羅蜜。則能
429b13║ 增廣一切諸行。則能圓滿一切大願。則能超
429b14║ 出一切魔業。則能承事一切善友。則能清淨
429b15║ 諸菩薩道。則能具足普賢諸行。爾時彌勒菩
429b16║ 薩摩訶薩。如是稱歎善財童子種種功德。令
429b17║ 無量百千眾生。發菩提心已。告善財言。善
429b18║ 哉善哉。善男子。汝為饒益一切世間。汝為
429b19║ 救護一切眾生。汝為勤求一切佛法故。發阿
429b20║ 耨多羅三藐三菩提心。善男子。汝獲善利。汝
429b21║ 善得人身。汝善住壽命。汝善值如來出現。汝
429b22║ 善見文殊師利大善知識。

简体字

又能如是不顾身命，唯愿勤修一切智道，应知展转倍更难得。

“诸仁者，余诸菩萨经于无量百千万亿那由他劫，乃能满足菩萨愿行，乃能亲近诸佛菩提；此长者子，于一生内，则能净佛刹，则能化众生，则能以智慧深入法界，则能成就诸波罗蜜，则能增广一切诸行，则能圆满一切大愿，则能超出一切魔业，则能承事一切善友，则能清净诸菩萨道，则能具足普贤诸行。”

尔时，弥勒菩萨摩诃萨如是称叹善财童子种种功德，令无量百千众生发菩提心已，告善财言：“善哉！善哉！善男子，汝为饶益一切世间，汝为救护一切众生，汝为勤求一切佛法故，发阿耨多罗三藐三菩提心。

“善男子，汝获善利，汝善得人身，汝善住寿命，汝善值如来出现，汝善见文殊师利大善知识。

And if he were then also able in this same way to never cherish his own body and life and only wish to diligently cultivate the path to all-knowledge—

Were this to be the case, then one should realize that, in each successive instance, this person would thereby become doubly rare to ever encounter.

Worthy Ones, in the case of all the other bodhisattvas, they must pass through countless hundreds of thousands of myriads of *koṭīs* of *nayutas* of kalpas and only then can they fulfill the bodhisattva's vows and practices. Only then can they draw near to the bodhi of all buddhas.

However, in the case of this son of an elder, it has been in the course of but one lifetime that:

He has become able to purify buddha *kṣetras;*
He has become able to teach beings;
He has become able to deeply enter the Dharma realm with wisdom;
He has become able to perfect all the *pāramitās;*
He has become able to expand all the practices;
He has become able to fulfill all the great vows;
He has become able to step beyond all of Māra's works;
He has become able to serve all good spiritual guides;
He has become able to purify the path of all bodhisattvas; and
He has become able to fulfill the practices of Samantabhadra.

Then, after Maitreya Bodhisattva-mahāsattva had praised in this way the many different meritorious qualities of Sudhana the Youth, thereby causing countless hundreds of thousands of beings to resolve to attain bodhi, he spoke to Sudhana, saying:

It is good indeed, good indeed, Son of Good Family, that, for the sake of benefiting everyone in the world, for the sake of rescuing all beings, and for the sake of diligently seeking all the dharmas of a buddha, you have resolved to attain *anuttara-samyak-saṃbodhi.*

Son of Good Family:

You have reaped an excellent benefit;
You have done well in attaining the human body;
You have done well in abiding in this life;
You have done well in encountering the Tathāgata's appearance in the world;
You have done well in encountering Mañjuśrī, the great good spiritual guide;

正體字

[5]汝身是善器。為諸
429b23‖ 善根之所潤澤。汝為白法之所資持。所有解
429b24‖ 欲。悉已清淨。已為諸佛共所護念。已為善
429b25‖ 友共所攝受。何以故。善男子。菩提心者猶如
429b26‖ 種子。能生一切諸佛法故。菩提心者猶如良
429b27‖ 田。能長眾生白淨法故。菩提心者猶如大地。
429b28‖ 能持一切諸世間故。菩提心者猶如淨水。能
429b29‖ 洗一切煩惱垢故。菩提心者猶如大風。普於
429c01‖ 世間無所礙故。菩提心者猶如盛火。能燒一
429c02‖ 切諸見薪故。[6]菩提心者猶如淨日。普照一
429c03‖ 切諸世間故。菩提心者猶如盛月。諸白淨法
429c04‖ 悉圓滿故。菩提心者猶如明燈。能放種種法
429c05‖ 光明故。菩提心者猶如淨目。普見一切安危
429c06‖ 處故。菩提心者猶如大道。普令得入大智城
429c07‖ 故。菩提心者猶如正濟。令其得離諸邪法故。
429c08‖ 菩提心者猶如大車。普能運載諸菩薩故。菩
429c09‖ 提心者猶如門戶。開示一切菩薩行故。菩提
429c10‖ 心者猶如宮殿。安住修習三昧法故。菩提心
429c11‖ 者猶如園苑。於中遊戲受法樂故。

简体字

汝身是善器，为诸善根之所润泽。汝为白法之所资持，所有解欲悉已清净，已为诸佛共所护念，已为善友共所摄受。何以故？

“善男子，菩提心者，犹如种子，能生一切诸佛法故；菩提心者，犹如良田，能长众生白净法故；菩提心者，犹如大地，能持一切诸世间故；菩提心者，犹如净水，能洗一切烦恼垢故；菩提心者，犹如大风，普于世间无所碍故；菩提心者，犹如盛火，能烧一切诸见薪故；菩提心者，犹如净日，普照一切诸世间故；菩提心者，犹如盛月，诸白净法悉圆满故；菩提心者，犹如明灯，能放种种法光明故；菩提心者，犹如净目，普见一切安危处故；菩提心者，犹如大道，普令得入大智城故；菩提心者，犹如正济，令其得离诸邪法故；菩提心者，犹如大车，普能运载诸菩萨故；菩提心者，犹如门户，开示一切菩萨行故；菩提心者，犹如宫殿，安住修习三昧法故；菩提心者，犹如园苑，于中游戏受法乐故；

Your person has become a vessel of goodness sustained by roots of goodness;

You have been sustained and supported by the pure dharmas;

All your resolute intentions have become purified;

You have already become one whom all buddhas hold in their protective mindfulness; and

You are one who has already been gathered in and accepted by the good spiritual guides.

And why is this so? Son of Good Family:

The bodhi resolve is like a seed, for it is able to produce all the dharmas of a buddha;

The bodhi resolve is like a fine field, for it is able to grow beings' pure dharmas;

The bodhi resolve is like the great earth, for it is able to support everyone in the world;

The bodhi resolve is like pure water, for it is able to rinse away all the filth of the afflictions;

The bodhi resolve is like the great wind, for it is unimpeded everywhere in the world;

The bodhi resolve is like a raging fire, for it is able to burn up all the deadwood of views;

The bodhi resolve is like the clearly shining sun, for it everywhere illuminates the entire world;

The bodhi resolve is like the full moon, for it is perfectly full in the white dharmas of purity;

The bodhi resolve is like a brightly shining lamp, for it is able to emanate many different kinds of Dharma light;

The bodhi resolve is like the clearly seeing eye, for it everywhere perceives all the safe and hazardous places;

The bodhi resolve is like the great road, for it enables everyone to enter the city of great wisdom;

The bodhi resolve is like the right fording place, for it enables one to leave behind all wrong dharmas;

The bodhi resolve is like a great vehicle, for it is able to transport all bodhisattvas;

The bodhi resolve is like a door, for it opens and shows all the bodhisattva practices;

The bodhi resolve is like a palace, for, within it, one abides securely in the cultivation of the dharmas of samādhi;

The bodhi resolve is like a park, for one sports about in it, enjoying the bliss of the Dharma;

正體字

菩提心者
429c12 猶如舍宅。安隱一切諸眾生故。菩提心者則
429c13 為所歸。利益一切諸世間故。菩提心者則為
429c14 所依。諸菩薩行所依處故。菩提心者猶如慈
429c15 父。訓導一切諸菩薩故。菩提心者猶如慈母。
429c16 生長一切諸菩薩故。菩提心者猶如乳母。養
429c17 育一切諸菩薩故。[7]菩提心者猶如善友。成益
429c18 一切諸菩薩故。菩提心者猶如君主。勝出一
429c19 切二乘人故。菩提心者猶如帝王。一切願中
429c20 得自在故。菩提心者猶如大海。一切功德悉
429c21 入中故。菩提心者如須彌山。於諸眾生心平
429c22 等故。菩提心者如鐵圍山。攝持一切諸世間
429c23 故。菩提心者猶如雪山。長養一切智慧藥故。
429c24 [8]菩提心者猶如香山。出生一切功德香故。菩
429c25 提心者猶如虛空。諸妙功德廣無邊故。菩提
429c26 心者猶如蓮華。不染一切世間法故。菩提心
429c27 者如調慧象。其心善順不獷[9]戾故。菩提心者
429c28 如良善馬。遠離一切諸惡性故。菩提心者如
429c29 調御師。守護大乘一切法故。菩提心者猶如
430a01 良藥。能治一切煩惱病故。菩提心者猶如坑
430a02 穽。陷沒一切諸惡法故。

简体字

菩提心者，犹如舍宅，安隐一切诸众生故；菩提心者，则为所归，利益一切诸世间故；菩提心者，则为所依，诸菩萨行所依处故；菩提心者，犹如慈父，训导一切诸菩萨故；菩提心者，犹如慈母，生长一切诸菩萨故；菩提心者，犹如乳母，养育一切诸菩萨故；菩提心者，犹如善友，成益一切诸菩萨故；菩提心者，犹如君主，胜出一切二乘人故；菩提心者，犹如帝王，一切愿中得自在故；菩提心者，犹如大海，一切功德悉入中故；菩提心者，如须弥山，于诸众生心平等故；菩提心者，如铁围山，摄持一切诸世间故；菩提心者，犹如雪山，长养一切智慧药故；菩提心者，犹如香山，出生一切功德香故；菩提心者，犹如虚空，诸妙功德广无边故；菩提心者，犹如莲华，不染一切世间法故；菩提心者，如调慧象，其心善顺不犷戾故；菩提心者，如良善马，远离一切诸恶性故；菩提心者，如调御师，守护大乘一切法故；菩提心者，犹如良药，能治一切烦恼病故；菩提心者，犹如坑阱，陷没一切诸恶法故；

The bodhi resolve is like a house, for it provides peace and security for all beings;

The bodhi resolve is a place of refuge, for it benefits the entire world;

The bodhi resolve is a place of support, for it is the place upon which all bodhisattva practices depend;

The bodhi resolve is like a kindly father, for it trains and guides all bodhisattvas;

The bodhi resolve is like a kindly mother, for it gives birth to and raises all bodhisattvas;

The bodhi resolve is like a nursemaid, for it raises all bodhisattvas;

The bodhi resolve is like a good friend, for it brings success and benefit to all bodhisattvas;

The bodhi resolve is like a monarch, for it reigns supreme over all adherents of the two vehicles;

The bodhi resolve is like an imperial monarch, for it has gained sovereignty over all other vows;

The bodhi resolve is like the great ocean, for all the meritorious qualities flow into it;

The bodhi resolve is like Mount Sumeru, for it looks on all beings with equal regard;

The bodhi resolve is like the Iron Ring mountains, for it embraces the entire world;

The bodhi resolve is like the Himalaya Mountains, for it grows all the medicinal herbs of wisdom;

The bodhi resolve is like the Mount Gandhamādana, the mountain that produces fine fragrances, for it produces the fragrance of all the meritorious qualities;

The bodhi resolve is like empty space, for its marvelous qualities are boundlessly vast;

The bodhi resolve is like a lotus flower, for it is unsullied by any of the worldly dharmas;

The bodhi resolve is like the well-trained and intelligent elephant, for its mind is good and compliant, not fierce and unmanageable;

The bodhi resolve is like an especially fine horse, for it has abandoned all of its ill-tempered tendencies;

The bodhi resolve is like a charioteer, for it preserves and protects all the dharmas of the Great Vehicle;

The bodhi resolve is like especially fine medicine, for it is able to cure all the illnesses caused by the afflictions;

The bodhi resolve is like a pit trap, for all evil dharmas fall into it and disappear;

正體字

菩提心者猶如金剛。
430a03‖ 悉能穿徹一切法故。[1]菩提心者猶如香篋。能
430a04‖ 貯一切功德香故。菩提心者猶如妙華。一切
430a05‖ 世間所樂見故。菩提心者如白栴檀。除眾欲
430a06‖ 熱使清涼故。菩提心者如黑沈香。能熏法界
430a07‖ 悉周遍故。菩提心者如善見藥王。能破一切
430a08‖ 煩惱病故。菩提心者如毘笈摩藥。能拔一切
430a09‖ 諸惑箭故。菩提心者猶如帝釋。一切主中最
430a10‖ 為尊故。菩提心者如毘沙門。能斷一切貧窮
430a11‖ 苦故。菩提心者如功德天。一切功德所莊嚴
430a12‖ 故。菩提心者如莊嚴具。莊嚴一切諸菩薩故。
430a13‖ 菩提心者如劫燒火。能燒一切諸有為故。菩
430a14‖ 提心者如無生根藥。長養一切諸佛法故。菩
430a15‖ 提心者猶如龍珠。能消一切煩惱毒故。菩提
430a16‖ 心者如水清珠。能清一切煩惱濁故。菩提心
430a17‖ 者如如意珠。周給一切諸貧乏故。菩提心者
430a18‖ 如功德瓶。滿足一切眾生心故。菩提心者如
430a19‖ 如意樹。能雨一切莊嚴具故。菩提心者如鵝
430a20‖ 羽衣。不受一切生死垢故。菩提心者如白[疊*毛]
430a21‖ 線。從本已來性清淨故。菩提心者如快利犁。
430a22‖ 能治一切眾生田故。

简体字

菩提心者，犹如金刚，悉能穿彻一切法故；菩提心者，犹如香箧，能贮一切功德香故；菩提心者，犹如妙华，一切世间所乐见故；菩提心者，如白栴檀，除众欲热使清凉故；菩提心者，如黑沉香，能熏法界悉周遍故；菩提心者，如善见药王，能破一切烦恼病故；菩提心者，如毗笈摩药，能拔一切诸惑箭故；菩提心者，犹如帝释，一切主中最为尊故；菩提心者，如毗沙门，能断一切贫穷苦故；菩提心者，如功德天，一切功德所庄严故；菩提心者，如庄严具，庄严一切诸菩萨故；菩提心者，如劫烧火，能烧一切诸有为故；菩提心者，如无生根药，长养一切诸佛法故；菩提心者，犹如龙珠，能消一切烦恼毒故；菩提心者，如水清珠，能清一切烦恼浊故；菩提心者，如如意珠，周给一切诸贫乏故；菩提心者，如功德瓶，满足一切众生心故；菩提心者，如如意树，能雨一切庄严具故；菩提心者，如鹅羽衣，不受一切生死垢故；菩提心者，如白毡线，从本已来性清净故；菩提心者，如快利犁，能治一切众生田故；

The bodhi resolve is like vajra, for it is able to penetrate all dharmas;

The bodhi resolve is like an incense chest, for it stores the incense of the meritorious qualities;

The bodhi resolve is like a marvelous flower, for it is what the whole world loves to see;

The bodhi resolve is like white sandalwood, for it rids one of the fever of the many desires and enables one to experience clarity and coolness;

The bodhi resolve is like black *agaru* incense, for its fragrance is able to permeate the entire Dharma realm;

The bodhi resolve is like the king of medicines known as "lovely," for it is able to cure all the diseases caused by the afflictions;

The bodhi resolve is like the medicine known as *vigama* or "separation," for it is able to pull out all the arrows of the afflictions;

The bodhi resolve is like Indra, for it is the most revered of all rulers;

The bodhi resolve is like Vaiśravaṇa, for it is able to put an end to all the sufferings of poverty;

The bodhi resolve is like the goddess Śri or "the Goddess of Good Qualities," for it is adorned with all the meritorious qualities;

The bodhi resolve is like an adornment, for it adorns all bodhisattvas;

The bodhi resolve is like the kalpa-ending conflagration, for it is able to burn up all conditioned things;[41]

The bodhi resolve is like an herbal medicine that treats stunted roots, for it nourishes the growth of all dharmas of the Buddha;

The bodhi resolve is like the dragon's pearl, for it is able to eliminate the poison of all the afflictions;

The bodhi resolve is like the water-clarifying jewel, for it is able to clear away all the turbidity caused by the afflictions;

The bodhi resolve is like a wish-fulfilling jewel, for it everywhere provides for everyone who is poverty-stricken;

The bodhi resolve is like the vase of good fortune, for it fulfills the aspirations of all beings;

The bodhi resolve is like the wish-fulfilling tree, for it is able to rain down all kinds of adornments;

The bodhi resolve is like a goose-feather robe, for it remains unsullied by any of the defilements of *saṃsāra*;

The bodhi resolve is like white cotton thread, for it has always been pure by its very nature;

The bodhi resolve is like a sharp plow, for it is able to cultivate the field of all beings;

正體字

菩提心者如那羅延。能
430a23‖ 摧一切我見敵故。菩提心者猶如快箭。能破
430a24‖ 一切諸苦的故。[2]菩提心者猶如利矛。能穿
430a25‖ 一切煩惱甲故。菩提心者猶如堅甲。能護一
430a26‖ 切如理心故。菩提心者猶如利刀。能斬一切
430a27‖ 煩惱首故。菩提心者猶如利劍。能斷一切憍
430a28‖ 慢鎧故。菩提心者如勇將幢。能伏一切諸魔
430a29‖ 軍故。菩提心者猶如利鋸。能截一切無明樹
430b01‖ 故。菩提心者猶如利斧。能伐一切諸苦樹故。
430b02‖ 菩提心者猶如兵仗。能防一切諸苦難故。菩
430b03‖ 提心者猶如善手。防護一切諸度身故。菩提
430b04‖ 心者猶如好足。安立一切諸功德故。菩提心
430b05‖ 者猶如眼藥。滅除一切無明翳故。菩提心者
430b06‖ 猶如鉗鑷。能拔一切身見刺故。菩提心者猶
430b07‖ 如臥具。息除生死諸勞苦故。菩提心者如善
430b08‖ 知識。能解一切生死縛故。菩提心者如好珍
430b09‖ 財。能除一切貧窮事故。菩提心者如大導師。
430b10‖ 善知菩薩出要道故。菩提心者猶如伏藏。出
430b11‖ 功德財無匱乏故。菩提心者猶如涌泉。生智
430b12‖ 慧水無窮盡故。菩提心者猶如明鏡。普現一
430b13‖ 切法門像故。

简体字

菩提心者，如那罗延，能摧一切我见敌故；菩提心者，犹如快箭，能破一切诸苦的故；菩提心者，犹如利矛，能穿一切烦恼甲故；菩提心者，犹如坚甲，能护一切如理心故；菩提心者，犹如利刀，能斩一切烦恼首故；菩提心者，犹如利剑，能断一切憍慢铠故；菩提心者，如勇将幢，能伏一切诸魔军故；菩提心者，犹如利锯，能截一切无明树故；菩提心者，犹如利斧，能伐一切诸苦树故；菩提心者，犹如兵仗，能防一切诸苦难故；菩提心者，犹如善手，防护一切诸度身故；菩提心者，犹如好足，安立一切诸功德故；菩提心者，犹如眼药，灭除一切无明翳故；菩提心者，犹如钳镊，能拔一切身见刺故；菩提心者，犹如卧具，息除生死诸劳苦故；菩提心者，如善知识，能解一切生死缚故；菩提心者，如好珍财，能除一切贫穷事故；菩提心者，如大导师，善知菩萨出要道故；菩提心者，犹如伏藏，出功德财无匮乏故；菩提心者，犹如涌泉，生智慧水无穷尽故；菩提心者，犹如明镜，普现一切法门像故；

The bodhi resolve is like a *nārāyaṇa* warrior, for it is able to vanquish the enemy, all views of an [inherently existent] self;

The bodhi resolve is like the swift arrow, for it destroys its target, namely all sufferings;

The bodhi resolve is like a sharp spear, for it is able to pierce the armor of all afflictions;

The bodhi resolve is like solid armor, for it is able to protect all principled thought;

The bodhi resolve is like a sharp saber, for it is able to decapitate all afflictions;

The bodhi resolve is like sharp sword, for it is able to slice away the armor of arrogance;

The bodhi resolve is like the banner of a valiant general, for it is able to subdue all the armies of Māra;

The bodhi resolve is like a sharp saw, for it is able to cut down all the trees of ignorance;

The bodhi resolve is like a sharp axe, for it is able to fell all the trees of suffering;

The bodhi resolve is like a soldier's cudgel, for it is able to defend against all sufferings and difficulties;

The bodhi resolve is like good hands, for it is able to protect the body of the *pāramitās;*

The bodhi resolve is like fine feet, for it stabilizes all the meritorious qualities;

The bodhi resolve is like eye medicine, for it does away with all the cataracts of ignorance;

The bodhi resolve is like tweezers, for it is able to pull out the thorns of all kinds of personality view;

The bodhi resolve is like bedding, for it rids one of the suffering of the wearisomeness of *saṃsāra;*

The bodhi resolve is like the good spiritual guide, for it is able to free one from all the bonds of *saṃsāra;*

The bodhi resolve is like the wealth of fine jewels, for it is able to rid one of all poverty;

The bodhi resolve is like a great guide, for it thoroughly knows the bodhisattva's path to emancipation;

The bodhi resolve is like a hidden treasure trove, for it produces the endless wealth of meritorious qualities;

The bodhi resolve is like a gushing spring, for it produces endless waters of wisdom;

The bodhi resolve is like a brightly polished mirror, for it is able to show the appearance of all the Dharma gateways;

正體字

菩提心者猶如蓮華。不染一切
430b14‖ 諸罪垢故。[3]菩提心者猶如大河。流引一切
430b15‖ 度攝法故。菩提心者如大龍王。能雨一切妙
430b16‖ 法雨故。菩提心者猶如命根。[4]任持菩薩大
430b17‖ 悲身故。菩提心者猶如甘露。能令安住不死
430b18‖ 界故。菩提心者猶如大網。普攝一切諸眾生
430b19‖ 故。菩提心者猶如羂索。攝取一切所應化故。
430b20‖ 菩提心者猶如鉤餌。出有淵中所居者故。菩
430b21‖ 提心者如阿伽陀藥。能令無[5]病永安隱故。菩
430b22‖ 提心者如除毒藥。悉能[6]消歇貪愛毒故。菩
430b23‖ 提心者如善持呪。能除一切顛倒毒故。菩提
430b24‖ 心者猶如疾風。能卷一切諸障霧故。菩提心
430b25‖ 者如大寶洲。出生一切覺分寶故。菩提心者
430b26‖ 如好種性。出生一切白淨法故。菩提心者猶
430b27‖ 如住宅。諸功德法所依處故。菩提心者猶如
430b28‖ 市肆。菩薩商人貿易處故。[7]菩提心者如鍊
430b29‖ 金藥。能治一切煩惱垢故。菩提心者猶如好
430c01‖ 蜜。圓滿一切功德味故。菩提心者猶如正道。
430c02‖ 令諸菩薩入智城故。菩提心者猶如好器。能
430c03‖ 持一切白淨法故。

简体字

菩提心者，犹如莲华，不染一切诸罪垢故；菩提心者，犹如大河，流引一切度摄法故；菩提心者，如大龙王，能雨一切妙法雨故；菩提心者，犹如命根，任持菩萨大悲身故；菩提心者，犹如甘露，能令安住不死界故；菩提心者，犹如大网，普摄一切诸众生故；菩提心者，犹如罥索，摄取一切所应化故；菩提心者，犹如钩饵，出有渊中所居者故；菩提心者，如阿伽陀药，能令无病永安隐故；菩提心者，如除毒药，悉能消歇贪爱毒故；菩提心者，如善持咒，能除一切颠倒毒故；菩提心者，犹如疾风，能卷一切诸障雾故；菩提心者，如大宝洲，出生一切觉分宝故；菩提心者，如好种性，出生一切白净法故；菩提心者，犹如住宅，诸功德法所依处故；菩提心者，犹如市肆，菩萨商人贸易处故；菩提心者，如炼金药，能治一切烦恼垢故；菩提心者，犹如好蜜，圆满一切功德味故；菩提心者，犹如正道，令诸菩萨入智城故；菩提心者，犹如好器，能持一切白净法故；

The bodhi resolve is like a lotus flower, for it remains undefiled by the filth of all the karmic offenses;

The bodhi resolve is like a great river, for it draws in the streams of the *pāramitās* and the means of attraction;

The bodhi resolve is like a great dragon king, for it is able to shower down the rain of all the sublime dharmas;

The bodhi resolve is like the life faculty itself, for it sustains the body of the bodhisattva's great compassion;

The bodhi resolve is like the elixir of immortality, for it is able to establish one in the realm of the deathless;

The bodhi resolve is like an immense net, for it is able to everywhere gather in all beings;

The bodhi resolve is like a great lasso, for it is everywhere able to pull in all those who should be taught;

The bodhi resolve is like a baited hook, for it is able to pull out those abiding in the deep pool of the realms of existence;

The bodhi resolve is like the *agada* or "disease-free" medicine, for it is able to cause one to become free of illness and become forever safe and secure;

The bodhi resolve is like a poison-extracting medicine, for it is able to eliminate the poison of sensual lust;

The bodhi resolve is like skillfully used mantra, for it is able to rid one of the poisons of all inverted views;

The bodhi resolve is like a swift wind, for it is able to roll back the fog of all the obstacles;

The bodhi resolve is like a great isle of jewels, for it is able to produce all the jewels of the enlightenment factors;

The bodhi resolve is like a good lineage, for it produces all the white dharmas of purity;

The bodhi resolve is like a home, for it is the abode of all meritorious qualities;

The bodhi resolve is like a marketplace, for it is the place where the bodhisattva trader plies his trade;

The bodhi resolve is like the gold-refining elixir, for it is able to refine away all the dross of the afflictions;

The bodhi resolve is like fine honey, for it is perfectly full in all the flavors of the meritorious qualities;

The bodhi resolve is like the right road, for it enables the bodhisattvas to enter the city of wisdom;

The bodhi resolve is like a fine vessel, for it is able to hold all the white dharmas of purity;

正體字

菩提心者猶如時雨。能滅
430c04 一切煩惱塵故。菩提心者則為住處。一切菩
430c05 薩所住處故。菩提心者則為壽行。不取聲聞
430c06 解脫果故。菩提心者如淨瑠璃。自性明潔無
430c07 諸垢故。菩提心者如帝青寶。出過世間二乘
430c08 智故。菩提心者如更漏鼓。覺諸眾生煩惱睡
430c09 故。菩提心者如清淨水。性本澄潔無垢濁故。
430c10 菩提心者如閻浮金。映奪一切有為善故。菩
430c11 提心者如大山王。超出一切諸世間故。菩提
430c12 心者則為所歸。不拒一切諸來者故。菩提心
430c13 者則為義利。能除一切衰惱事故。菩提心者
430c14 則為妙寶。能令一切心歡喜故。菩提心者如
430c15 大施會。充滿一切眾生心故。菩提心者則為
430c16 尊勝。諸眾生心無與等故。菩提心者猶如伏
430c17 藏。能攝一切諸佛法故。菩提心者如因陀羅
430c18 網。能伏煩惱阿脩羅故。菩提心者如婆樓那
430c19 風。能動一切所應化故。菩提心者如因陀羅
430c20 火。能燒一切諸惑習故。菩提心者如佛支提。
430c21 一切世間應供養故。善男子。菩提心者。成
430c22 就如是無量功德。舉要言之。

简体字

菩提心者，犹如时雨，能灭一切烦恼尘故；菩提心者，则为住处，一切菩萨所住处故；菩提心者，则为寿行，不取声闻解脱果故；菩提心者，如净琉璃，自性明洁无诸垢故；菩提心者，如帝青宝，出过世间二乘智故；菩提心者，如更漏鼓，觉诸众生烦恼睡故；菩提心者，如清净水，性本澄洁无垢浊故；菩提心者，如阎浮金，映夺一切有为善故；菩提心者，如大山王，超出一切诸世间故；菩提心者，则为所归，不拒一切诸来者故；菩提心者，则为义利，能除一切衰恼事故；菩提心者，则为妙宝，能令一切心欢喜故；菩提心者，如大施会，充满一切众生心故；菩提心者，则为尊胜，诸众生心无与等故；菩提心者，犹如伏藏，能摄一切诸佛法故；菩提心者，如因陀罗网，能伏烦恼阿修罗故；菩提心者，如婆楼那风，能动一切所应化故；菩提心者，如因陀罗火，能烧一切诸惑习故；菩提心者，如佛支提，一切世间应供养故。

“善男子，菩提心者，成就如是无量功德；举要言之，

The bodhi resolve is like the timely rain, for it is able to settle all the dust of the afflictions;

The bodhi resolve is like a dwelling place, for it is the dwelling place of all bodhisattvas;

The bodhi resolve is like a magnet finding no attraction to the fruits of a *śrāvaka* disciple's liberations;

The bodhi resolve is like pure *vaiḍūrya,* for its essential nature is radiant purity free of all defilements;

The bodhi resolve is like a sapphire, for it surpasses the wisdom of worldlings and adherents of the two vehicles;

The bodhi resolve is like the drum that sounds the hours of the night watch, for it awakens beings from the slumber of the afflictions;

The bodhi resolve is like pure water, for its nature is fundamentally clear, pristinely pure, and free of the turbidity of the defilements;

The bodhi resolve is like *jambūnada* gold, for its brilliant light outshines that of every kind of conditioned goodness;

The bodhi resolve is like the great king of mountains, for it rises above everything in the entire world;

The bodhi resolve is a refuge, for it does not reject anyone who comes to it;

The bodhi resolve is meaningful and beneficial, for it is able to do away with all circumstances involving misfortune and anguish;

The bodhi resolve is like a marvelous jewel, for it is able to produce joy in the minds of everyone;

The bodhi resolve is like a great meeting for the bestowing of gifts, for it satisfies the minds of all beings;

The bodhi resolve is venerable and supreme, for no other thought of any being could even compare to it;

The bodhi resolve is like a treasure trove, for it is able to contain all the dharmas of all buddhas;

The bodhi resolve is like Indra's net, for it is able to subdue the *asuras* of the afflictions;

The bodhi resolve is like the wind of Varuṇa, for it is able to move everyone one should teach;

The bodhi resolve is like the fire of Indra, for it is able to burn up all affliction-based habitual karmic propensities; and

The bodhi resolve is like a *caitya* memorializing a buddha, for it is worthy of offerings from everyone in the world.

Son of Good Family, the bodhi resolve perfects all meritorious qualities such as these. To speak of what is most essential, one should

正體字

應知悉與一切
430c23║ 佛法諸功德等。何以故。因菩提心。出生一
430c24║ 切諸菩薩行。三世如來。從菩提心而出生故。
430c25║ 是故善男子。若有發阿耨多羅三藐三菩提
430c26║ 心者。則已出生無量功德。普能攝取一切智
430c27║ 道。善男子。譬如有人得無畏藥離五恐怖。何
430c28║ 等為五。所謂火不能燒。毒不能中。刀不能傷。
430c29║ 水不能漂。煙不能熏。菩薩摩訶薩亦復如是。
431a01║ 得一切智菩提心藥。貪火不燒。瞋毒不中。惑
431a02║ 刀不傷。有流不漂。諸覺觀煙不能熏害。善男
431a03║ 子。譬如有人得解脫藥終無橫難。菩薩摩訶
431a04║ 薩亦復如是。得菩提心解脫智藥。永離一切
431a05║ 生死橫難。善男子。譬如有人。持摩訶應伽藥。
431a06║ 毒蛇聞氣即皆遠去。菩薩摩訶薩亦復如是。
431a07║ 持菩提心大應伽藥。一切煩惱諸惡毒蛇。聞
431a08║ 其氣者悉皆散滅。[1]善男子。譬如有人。持無
431a09║ 勝藥。一切怨敵無能勝者。菩薩摩訶薩亦復
431a10║ 如是。持菩提心無能勝藥。悉能降伏一切魔
431a11║ 軍。善男子。譬如有人。持毘笈摩藥。能令毒箭
431a12║ 自然墮落。菩薩摩訶薩亦復如是。持菩提心
431a13║ 毘笈摩藥。

简体字

应知悉与一切佛法诸功德等。何以故？因菩提心出生一切诸菩萨行，三世如来从菩提心而出生故。是故，善男子，若有发阿耨多罗三藐三菩提心者，则已出生无量功德，普能摄取一切智道。

“善男子，譬如有人，得无畏药，离五恐怖。何等为五？所谓：火不能烧，毒不能中，刀不能伤，水不能漂，烟不能熏。菩萨摩诃萨亦复如是，得一切智菩提心药，贪火不烧，瞋毒不中，惑刀不伤，有流不漂，诸觉观烟不能熏害。

“善男子，譬如有人，得解脱药，终无横难。菩萨摩诃萨亦复如是，得菩提心解脱智药，永离一切生死横难。

“善男子，譬如有人，持摩诃应伽药，毒蛇闻气，即皆远去。菩萨摩诃萨亦复如是，持菩提心大应伽药，一切烦恼诸恶毒蛇，闻其气者，悉皆散灭。

“善男子，譬如有人，持无胜药，一切冤敌无能胜者。菩萨摩诃萨亦复如是，持菩提心无能胜药，悉能降伏一切魔军。

“善男子，譬如有人，持毗笈摩药，能令毒箭自然堕落。菩萨摩诃萨亦复如是，持菩提心毗笈摩药，

realize that it is equal in its meritorious qualities to those of all other dharmas of all buddhas.

How could this be so? This is because the bodhi resolve produces all the bodhisattva practices and all *tathāgatas* of the three periods of time are produced by the bodhi resolve.

Therefore, Son of Good Family, if there are any beings who have resolved to attain *anuttara-samyak-saṃbodhi,* they have already produced countless meritorious qualities and they are all able to take up the path leading to all-knowledge.

Son of Good Family, they are like the person who has acquired the medicine that bestows fearlessness with which he abandons five kinds of fear. What are those five? They are: fire is unable to burn him; poison is unable to enter him; knives are unable to injure him; water is unable to drown him; and smoke is unable to harm him.

So too it is with the bodhisattva-mahāsattva, for, once he has acquired the medicine of the bodhi resolve to attain all-knowledge, the fire of greed is unable to burn him, the poison of hatred is unable to enter him, the blade of delusion is unable to injure him, the flood of existence is unable to sweep him away in its currents, and the smoke of ideation and discursive thought is unable to injure him with its fumes.

Son of Good Family, it is as if there were someone who had acquired the "liberation" elixir with which he would be forever free of disasters. So too it is with the bodhisattva-mahāsattva, for, having acquired the bodhi resolve's elixir of liberating wisdom, he becomes forever free of all the disasters of *saṃsāra.*

Son of Good Family, it is as if there were someone who possessed the *maghī* elixir that causes any poisonous snakes smelling its fragrance to immediately go away. So too it is with the bodhisattva-mahāsattva, for, possessing the *maghī* elixir of the bodhi resolve, all the poisonous snakes of the afflictions smell its fragrance and then scatter and disappear.

Son of Good Family, it is as if there were someone who possessed an invincibility medicine that ensured no adversary could defeat him. So too it is with the bodhisattva-mahāsattva, for he possesses the invincibility elixir of the bodhi resolve with which he is able to vanquish all the armies of Māra.

Son of Good Family, it is as if there were someone who possessed the *vigama* or "separation" medicine with which he was able to cause even poisoned arrows to naturally drop away from his body. So too it is with the bodhisattva-mahāsattva, for he possesses the *vigama* or "separation" medicine of the bodhi resolve with which he causes

正體字

令貪恚癡諸邪見箭。自然墮落。善
431a14║ 男子。譬如有人。持善見藥。能除一切所有
431a15║ 諸病。菩薩摩訶薩亦復如是。持菩提心善見
431a16║ 藥王。悉除一切諸煩惱病。善男子。如有藥
431a17║ 樹名珊陀那。有取其皮以塗瘡者。瘡即除愈。
431a18║ 然其樹皮。隨取隨生終不可盡。菩薩摩訶薩。
431a19║ 從菩提心。生一切智樹。亦復如是。若有得見
431a20║ 而生信者。煩惱業瘡悉得消滅。一切智樹初
431a21║ 無所損。善男子。如有藥樹名無生根。以其力
431a22║ 故。增長一切閻浮提樹。菩薩摩訶薩菩提心
431a23║ 樹。亦復如是。以其力故。增長一切學與無學。
431a24║ 及諸菩薩所有善法。[2]善男子。譬如有藥名阿
431a25║ 藍婆。若用塗身。身之與心咸有堪能。菩薩
431a26║ 摩訶薩。得菩提心阿藍婆藥。亦復如是。令
431a27║ 其身心增長善法。善男子。譬如有人得念力
431a28║ 藥。凡所聞事憶持不忘。菩薩摩訶薩。得菩提
431a29║ 心念力妙藥。悉能聞持一切佛法。皆無忘失。
431b01║ 善男子。譬如有藥名大蓮華。其有服者住壽
431b02║ 一劫。菩薩摩訶薩。服菩提心大蓮華藥。亦復
431b03║ 如是。於無數劫壽命自在。善男子。譬如有人
431b04║ 執翳形藥。人與非人悉不能見。

简体字

令贪、恚、痴、诸邪见箭自然堕落。

“善男子，譬如有人，持善见药，能除一切所有诸病。菩萨摩诃萨亦复如是，持菩提心善见药王，悉除一切诸烦恼病。

“善男子，如有药树，名珊陀那，有取其皮以涂疮者，疮即除愈；然其树皮，随取随生，终不可尽。菩萨摩诃萨从菩提心生一切智树亦复如是，若有得见而生信者，烦恼业疮悉得消灭，一切智树初无所损。

“善男子，如有药树，名无生根，以其力故，增长一切阎浮提树。菩萨摩诃萨菩提心树亦复如是，以其力故，增长一切学与无学及诸菩萨所有善法。

“善男子，譬如有药，名阿蓝婆，若用涂身，身之与心咸有堪能。菩萨摩诃萨得菩提心阿蓝婆药亦复如是，令其身心增长善法。

“善男子，譬如有人，得念力药，凡所闻事忆持不忘。菩萨摩诃萨得菩提心念力妙药，悉能闻持一切佛法皆无忘失。

“善男子，譬如有药，名大莲华，其有服者住寿一劫。菩萨摩诃萨服菩提心大莲华药亦复如是，于无数劫，寿命自在。

“善男子，譬如有人，执翳形药，人与非人悉不能见。

the arrows of greed, anger, delusion, and wrong views to naturally drop away from him.

Son of Good Family, it is as if there were someone who possessed the *sudarśana* or "beautiful" medicine that is able to rid one of all diseases. So too it is with the bodhisattva-mahāsattva, for he possesses the king of "beautiful" medicines, the bodhi resolve, with which he rids himself of all the diseases of the afflictions.

Son of Good Family, it is as if there were a medicine tree known as *saṃtāna* or "continuous regeneration" that, if one applied its bark to wounds, they immediately healed and the bark grew back endlessly as soon as it was stripped from the tree. So too it is with the bodhisattva-mahāsattva, for the tree of all-knowledge growing from his bodhi resolve is such that, if anyone but sees it and has faith, the wounds of his affliction-based karma all disappear without that tree of all-knowledge being diminished by this.

Son of Good Family, it is as if there were a medicine tree known as "promoter of root growth"[42] by the power of which the growth of all trees on the continent of Jambudvīpa was enhanced. So too it is with the bodhisattva-mahāsattva's tree of the bodhi resolve, for, due to its power, growth is increased in all the good dharmas of all *śrāvaka* disciples in training and beyond training and of all bodhisattvas.

Son of Good Family, it is as if there were a medicine known as *ratilambha* or "attainment of pleasure" which, when smeared on the body, caused the body and mind to acquire enhanced capabilities. So too it is with the bodhisattva-mahāsattva who has acquired the *ratilambha* medicine of the bodhi resolve that enables his body and mind to acquire more good dharmas.

Son of Good Family, it is as if there were someone who possessed a memory-power medicine with which he remembered all he ever heard and then never forgot it. So too it is with the bodhisattva-mahāsattva, for he has acquired the wondrous memory-power medicine of the bodhi resolve with which he is able to hear and retain all dharmas of the Buddha without ever forgetting them.

Son of Good Family, it is as if there were a medicine named "great lotus," that, if one ingested it, one would live for an entire kalpa. So too it is with the bodhisattva-mahāsattva, for, having ingested the great lotus medicine of the bodhi resolve, he lives for countless kalpas with sovereign mastery over his life span.

Son of Good Family, it is as if there were someone who possessed an invisibility-invoking medicine with which no human or nonhuman could see him. So too it is with the bodhisattva-mahāsattva,

正體字

菩薩摩訶薩。
431b05| 執菩提心翳形妙藥。一切諸魔不能得見。[3]善
431b06| 男子。如海有珠名普集眾寶。此珠若在。假
431b07| 使劫火焚燒世間。能令此海減於一滴。無有
431b08| 是處。菩薩摩訶薩菩提心珠。亦復如是。住
431b09| 於菩薩大願海中。若常憶持不令退失。能壞
431b10| 菩薩一善根者。終無是處。若退其心。一切善
431b11| 法即皆散滅。善男子。如有摩尼名大光明。有
431b12| 以此珠瓔珞身者。映蔽一切寶莊嚴具。所有
431b13| 光明悉皆不現。菩薩摩訶薩菩提心寶。亦復
431b14| 如是。[4]瓔珞其身。映蔽一切二乘心寶。諸莊
431b15| 嚴具悉無光[5]彩。善男子。如水清珠能清濁
431b16| 水。菩薩摩訶薩菩提心珠。亦復如是。能清一
431b17| 切煩惱垢濁。善男子。譬如有人得住水寶。繫
431b18| 其身上入大海中不為水害。菩薩摩訶薩亦
431b19| 復如是。得菩提心住水妙寶。入於一切生死
431b20| 海中。終不沈沒。善男子。譬如有人得龍寶珠
431b21| 持入龍宮。一切龍蛇不能為害。菩薩摩訶薩
431b22| 亦復如是。得菩提心大龍寶珠。入欲界中。煩
431b23| 惱龍蛇不能為害。[6]善男子。譬如帝釋著摩尼
431b24| 冠。映蔽一切諸餘天眾。菩薩摩訶薩亦復如
431b25| 是。

简体字

菩萨摩诃萨执菩提心翳形妙药，一切诸魔不能得见。

“善男子，如海有珠，名普集众宝，此珠若在，假使劫火焚烧世间，能令此海减于一滴，无有是处。菩萨摩诃萨菩提心珠亦复如是，住于菩萨大愿海中，若常忆持不令退失，能坏菩萨一善根者，终无是处；若退其心，一切善法即皆散灭。

“善男子，如有摩尼，名大光明，有以此珠璎珞身者，映蔽一切宝庄严具，所有光明悉皆不现。菩萨摩诃萨菩提心宝亦复如是，璎珞其身，映蔽一切二乘心宝，诸庄严具悉无光彩。

“善男子，如水清珠，能清浊水。菩萨摩诃萨菩提心珠亦复如是，能清一切烦恼垢浊。

“善男子，譬如有人，得住水宝，系其身上，入大海中，不为水害。菩萨摩诃萨亦复如是，得菩提心住水妙宝，入于一切生死海中，终不沉没。

“善男子，譬如有人，得龙宝珠，持入龙宫，一切龙蛇不能为害。菩萨摩诃萨亦复如是，得菩提心大龙宝珠，入欲界中，烦恼龙蛇不能为害。

“善男子，譬如帝释，著摩尼冠，映蔽一切诸余天众。菩萨摩诃萨亦复如是，

for he possesses the wondrous invisibility-invoking medicine of the bodhi resolve with which none of the *māras* are able to even see him.

Son of Good Family, it is as if there were a jewel in the ocean which was known as "collector of the many kinds of jewels" and, so long as this jewel remained there, even if the kalpa-ending conflagration burned up the entire world, it would be impossible for this ocean to be diminished by even a single drop. So too it is with the bodhisattva-mahāsattva's jewel of the bodhi resolve that abides in the ocean of the bodhisattva's great vows. So long as he constantly bears it in mind and does not retreat from it, it is impossible that anything could damage even one of the bodhisattva's roots of goodness. However, if he were he to retreat from his resolve, all of his good dharmas would immediately scatter and disappear.

Son of Good Family, it is as if there were a *maṇi* jewel named "great radiance" that, if one wore it in a necklace on his body, it would so outshine all the other jewel adornments that their radiance would no longer be apparent at all. So too it is with the bodhisattva-mahāsattva's jewel of the bodhi resolve, for, when he adorns his person with a strand that includes it, it so outshines the mind jewels of the two vehicles that all those other adornments lose all their splendor.

Son of Good Family, it is as if there were a water-clarifying jewel which was able to clear waters of all their turbidity. So too it is with the bodhisattva-mahāsattva's jewel of the bodhi resolve, for it is able to clear away all the turbidity of the afflictions' defilements.

Son of Good Family, it is as if there were someone who acquired a "water-dwelling jewel" which was such that, if he tied it to his body, he could enter the great ocean without being harmed by its waters. So too it is with the bodhisattva-mahāsattva, for, having acquired the "water-dwelling jewel" of the bodhi resolve, he enters the ocean of *saṃsāra* and yet never sinks and drowns in it.

Son of Good Family, it is as if there were someone who had obtained the dragon's precious pearl and thus, by carrying it with him, he could enter the dragon palace and remain unharmed by any of those dragons or serpents. So too it is with the bodhisattva-mahāsattva who, having acquired the great dragon's precious pearl of the bodhi resolve, enters the desire realm and yet cannot be harmed by the dragons or serpents of the afflictions.

Son of Good Family, just as when Indra dons his *maṇi* jewel crown, his radiance outshines that of everyone else in the communities of devas, so too it is with the bodhisattva-mahāsattva, for,

正體字

著菩提心大願寶冠。超過一切三界眾生。
431b26 | 善男子。譬如有人得如意珠。除滅一切貧窮
431b27 | 之苦。菩薩摩訶薩亦復如是。得菩提心如意
431b28 | 寶珠。遠離一切邪命怖畏。善男子。譬如有
431b29 | 人得日精珠。持向日光而生於火。菩薩摩訶
431c01 | 薩亦復如是。得菩提心智日寶珠。持向智光
431c02 | 而生智火。善男子。譬如有人得月精珠。持向
431c03 | 月光而生於水。菩薩摩訶薩亦復如是。得菩
431c04 | 提心月精寶珠。持此心珠。鑒迴向光。而生一
431c05 | 切善根願水。[7]善男子。譬如龍王首戴如意摩
431c06 | 尼寶冠。遠離一切怨敵怖畏。菩薩摩訶薩亦
431c07 | 復如是。著菩提心大悲寶冠。遠離一切惡道
431c08 | 諸難。善男子。如有寶珠名一切世間莊嚴藏。
431c09 | 若有得者。令其所欲悉得充滿。而此寶珠無
431c10 | 所損減。菩提心寶亦復如是。若有得者。令
431c11 | 其所願悉得滿足。而菩提心無有損減。善男
431c12 | 子。如轉輪王有摩尼寶。置於宮中。放大光
431c13 | 明破一切暗。菩薩摩訶薩亦復如是。以菩提
431c14 | 心大摩尼寶。住於欲界。放大智光。悉破諸
431c15 | 趣無明黑暗。善男子。譬如帝青大摩尼寶。若
431c16 | 有為此光明所觸即同其色。菩薩摩訶薩菩
431c17 | 提心寶。亦復如是。

简体字

著菩提心大愿宝冠，超过一切三界众生。

“善男子，譬如有人，得如意珠，除灭一切贫穷之苦。菩萨摩诃萨亦复如是，得菩提心如意宝珠，远离一切邪命怖畏。

“善男子，譬如有人，得日精珠，持向日光而生于火。菩萨摩诃萨亦复如是，得菩提心智日宝珠，持向智光而生智火。

“善男子，譬如有人，得月精珠，持向月光而生于水。菩萨摩诃萨亦复如是，得菩提心月精宝珠，持此心珠，鉴回向光，而生一切善根愿水。

“善男子，譬如龙王，首戴如意摩尼宝冠，远离一切怨敌怖畏。菩萨摩诃萨亦复如是，著菩提心大悲宝冠，远离一切恶道诸难。

“善男子，如有宝珠，名一切世间庄严藏，若有得者，令其所欲悉得充满，而此宝珠无所损减。菩提心宝亦复如是，若有得者，令其所愿悉得满足，而菩提心无有损减。

“善男子，如转轮王，有摩尼宝，置于宫中，放大光明，破一切暗。菩萨摩诃萨亦复如是，以菩提心大摩尼宝，住于欲界，放大智光，悉破诸趣无明黑暗。

“善男子，譬如帝青大摩尼宝，若有为此光明所触，即同其色。菩萨摩诃萨菩提心宝亦复如是，

having donned the bodhi resolve's jeweled crown of great vows, he surpasses all beings in the three realms.

Son of Good Family, it is as if there were someone who had acquired a wish-fulfilling jewel with which he could do away with all the sufferings of poverty. So too it is with the bodhisattva-mahāsattva, for, having acquired the precious wish-fulfilling jewel of the bodhi resolve, he leaves behind any fear of entering into any wrong livelihoods.

Son of Good Family, it is as if there were someone who had acquired a solar-essence jewel which he could hold up toward the sunlight and thereby emanate fire. So too it is with the bodhisattva-mahāsattva, for, having acquired the bodhi resolve's precious jewel of the sun of wisdom, when he holds it up toward the light of wisdom, he emanates the fire of wisdom.

Son of Good Family, it is as if there were someone who had acquired a lunar-essence jewel that he could hold up toward the moonlight and thereby produce water. So too it is with the bodhisattva-mahāsattva, for, having acquired the bodhi resolve's precious lunar-essence jewel, when he holds up this mind jewel so that it reflects the light of the dedication of merit, he thereby produces the waters of all roots of goodness and vows.

Son of Good Family, just as when the dragon king places his wish-fulfilling *maṇi* jewel crown on his head, he leaves behind all fears of any adversaries, so too it is with the bodhisattva-mahāsattva, for, when he dons the bodhi resolve's jeweled crown of the great compassion, he leaves behind all the wretched destinies and the difficulties.

Son of Good Family, it is as if there were a precious jewel known as "treasury of the entire world's adornments" that, if one obtained it, it could cause all one's wishes to be fulfilled without this jewel being diminished in any way. So too it is with the jewel of the bodhi resolve, for, if one but acquires it, it causes all one's wishes to be fulfilled without the bodhi resolve being diminished in any way.

Son of Good Family, just as the wheel-turning king has a *maṇi* jewel placed within his palace that emanates a bright light that dispels all darkness, so too it is with the bodhisattva-mahāsattva who dwells in the desire realm with the great *maṇi* jewel of the bodhi resolve that emanates the light of great wisdom which dispels the darkness of ignorance in all the rebirth destinies.

Son of Good Family, just as whoever is touched by the light of a sapphire takes on its same color, so too it is with the bodhisattva's jewel of the bodhi resolve, for, when he contemplates dharmas and

正體字

觀察諸法迴向善根。靡不
431c18| 即同菩提心色。善男子。如瑠璃寶於百千歲。
431c19| 處不淨中。不為臭穢之所染著。性本淨故。菩
431c20| 薩摩訶薩菩提心寶。亦復如是。於百千劫住
431c21| 欲界中。不為欲界過患所染。猶如法界性清
431c22| 淨故。[8]善男子。譬如有寶名淨光明。悉能映
431c23| 蔽一切寶色。菩薩摩訶薩菩提心寶。亦復如
431c24| 是。悉能映蔽一切凡夫二乘功德。善男子。譬
431c25| 如有寶名為火焰。悉能除滅一切暗冥。菩薩
431c26| 摩訶薩菩提心寶。亦復如是。能滅一切無知
431c27| 暗冥。善男子。譬如海中有無價寶。商人[9]採
431c28| 得[10]船載入城。諸餘摩尼百千萬種。光色價
431c29| 直無與等者。菩提心寶亦復如是。住於生死
432a01| 大海之中。菩薩摩訶薩。乘大願船。深心相續。
432a02| 載之來入解脫城中。二乘功德無能及者。善
432a03| 男子。如有寶珠名自在王。處閻浮洲。去日
432a04| 月輪四萬由旬。日月宮中所有莊嚴。其珠影
432a05| 現悉皆具足。菩薩摩訶薩發菩提心淨功德
432a06| 寶。亦復如是。住生死中照法界空。佛智日
432a07| 月。一切功德悉於中現。[1]善男子。如有寶珠
432a08| 名自在王。日月光明所照之處。一切財寶衣
432a09| 服等物。所有價直悉不能及。

简体字

观察诸法回向善根，靡不即同菩提心色。

“善男子，如琉璃宝，于百千岁处不净中，不为臭秽之所染著，性本净故。菩萨摩诃萨菩提心宝亦复如是，于百千劫住欲界中，不为欲界过患所染，犹如法界性清净故。

“善男子，譬如有宝，名净光明，悉能映蔽一切宝色。菩萨摩诃萨菩提心宝亦复如是，悉能映蔽一切凡夫二乘功德。

“善男子，譬如有宝，名为火焰，悉能除灭一切暗冥。菩萨摩诃萨菩提心宝亦复如是，能灭一切无知暗冥。

“善男子，譬如海中有无价宝，商人采得，船载入城；诸余摩尼百千万种，光色、价值无与等者。菩提心宝亦复如是，住于生死大海之中，菩萨摩诃萨乘大愿船，深心相续，载之来入解脱城中，二乘功德无能及者。

“善男子，如有宝珠，名自在王，处阎浮洲，去日月轮四万由旬，日月宫中所有庄严，其珠影现悉皆具足。菩萨摩诃萨发菩提心净功德宝亦复如是，住生死中，照法界空，佛智日月一切功德悉于中现。

“善男子，如有宝珠，名自在王，日月光明所照之处，一切财宝、衣服等物，所有价值悉不能及。

dedicates his roots of goodness, none of them are not then colored by his bodhi resolve.

Son of Good Family, just as, because it is pure by nature, a *vaiḍūrya* gem can be placed in the midst of impurities for a hundred thousand years without being sullied by any sort of foul-smelling filth, so too it is with the bodhisattva-mahāsattva's jewel of the bodhi resolve. Because it is by nature as pure as the Dharma realm, it can dwell in the desire realm for a hundred thousand kalpas without being sullied by any of the faults or calamities of the desire realm.

Son of Good Family, just as there is a jewel known as "pure light" that is able to outshine the colors of all other jewels, so too it is with the bodhisattva-mahāsattva's jewel of the bodhi resolve that is able to outshine the meritorious qualities of all common people and practitioners of the two vehicles.

Son of Good Family, just as there is a jewel known as "flaming radiance" that is able to dispel all darkness, so too it is with the bodhisattva-mahāsattva's jewel of the bodhi resolve that is able to dispel all the darkness of ignorance.

Son of Good Family, suppose a merchant were to find a priceless jewel in the ocean, place it in his ship, and bring it into the city where its luster and value could not be matched by any of the other hundreds of thousands of myriads of *maṇi* jewels. So too it is with the jewel of the bodhi resolve that dwells in the midst of the great ocean of *saṃsāra*. The bodhisattva-mahāsattva boards the ship of great vows in which he continues with deep resolve to transport it into the city of liberation where, among all the meritorious qualities of the adherents of the two vehicles, there are none that can even compare to it.

Son of Good Family, just as the precious jewel known as "sovereign king" that is located in Jambudvīpa, a distance of forty thousand *yojanas* away from the orbs of the sun and moon, is still able to completely display the images of all the adornments in the solar and lunar palaces, so too it is with the jewel of the bodhi resolve's pure meritorious qualities that is produced by the bodhisattva-mahāsattva. Even as it resides within *saṃsāra*, it still illuminates the sky of the Dharma realm and reflects within itself all the meritorious qualities of the sun and moon of the Buddha's wisdom.

Son of Good Family, just as there is a precious jewel known as "sovereign king," the value of which could not even be approached by all the wealth, jewels, robes, and other precious things contained in the entire area illuminated by the light of the sun and moon, so too it is with the "sovereign king" jewel of the bodhi resolve

正體字

菩薩摩訶薩發
432a10 菩提心自在王寶。亦復如是。一切智光所照
432a11 之處。三世所有天人二乘。漏無漏善一切功
432a12 德。皆不能及。善男子。海中有寶名曰海藏。
432a13 普現海中諸莊嚴事。菩薩摩訶薩菩提心寶。
432a14 亦復如是。普能顯現一切智海諸莊嚴事。[2]善
432a15 男子。譬如天上閻浮檀金。唯除心王大摩尼
432a16 寶。餘無及者。菩薩摩訶薩發菩提心閻浮檀
432a17 金。亦復如是。除一切智心王大寶。餘無及
432a18 者。善男子。譬如有人善調龍法。於諸龍中而
432a19 得自在。菩薩摩訶薩亦復如是。得菩提心善
432a20 調龍法。於諸一切煩惱龍中。而得自在。善
432a21 男子。譬如勇士被執鎧仗。一切怨敵無能[3]降
432a22 伏。菩薩摩訶薩亦復如是。被執菩提大心鎧
432a23 [4]仗。一切業惑諸惡怨敵。無能屈伏。善男子。
432a24 譬如天上黑栴檀香。若燒一銖。其香普熏小
432a25 千世界。三千世界滿中珍寶。所有價直皆不
432a26 能及。菩薩摩訶薩菩提心香。亦復如是。一
432a27 念功德普熏法界。聲聞緣覺一切功德。皆所
432a28 不及。[5]善男子。如白栴檀若以塗身。悉能除
432a29 滅一切熱惱。令其身心普得清涼。菩薩摩訶
432b01 薩菩提心香。亦復如是。

简体字

菩萨摩诃萨发菩提心自在王宝亦复如是，一切智光所照之处，三世所有天人、二乘漏无漏善一切功德皆不能及。

“善男子，海中有宝，名曰海藏，普现海中诸庄严事。菩萨摩诃萨菩提心宝亦复如是，普能显现一切智海诸庄严事。

“善男子，譬如天上阎浮檀金，唯除心王大摩尼宝，余无及者。菩萨摩诃萨发菩提心阎浮檀金亦复如是，除一切智心王大宝，余无及者。

“善男子，譬如有人，善调龙法，于诸龙中而得自在。菩萨摩诃萨亦复如是，得菩提心善调龙法，于诸一切烦恼龙中而得自在。

“善男子，譬如勇士，被执铠仗，一切冤敌无能降伏。菩萨摩诃萨亦复如是，被执菩提大心铠仗，一切业惑诸恶冤敌无能屈伏。

“善男子，譬如天上黑栴檀香，若烧一铢，其香普熏小千世界，三千世界满中珍宝所有价值皆不能及。菩萨摩诃萨菩提心香亦复如是，一念功德普熏法界，声闻、缘觉一切功德皆所不及。

“善男子，如白栴檀，若以涂身，悉能除灭一切热恼，令其身心普得清凉；菩萨摩诃萨菩提心香亦复如是，

produced by the bodhisattva-mahāsattva the value of which cannot even be approached by the value of all the meritorious qualities of all the contaminated or uncontaminated goodness of all devas, humans, and two vehicles practitioners of the three periods of time in the entire area illuminated by the light of all-knowledge.

Son of Good Family, just as there is a jewel in the ocean known as "ocean treasury" that reveals all the items of adornment in the ocean, so too it is with the bodhisattva-mahāsattva's jewel of the bodhi resolve that everywhere reveals all the items of adornment in the ocean of all-knowledge.

Son of Good Family, just as the *jambūnada* gold in the heavens is unapproachable in its qualities by any other precious thing aside from the great mind-king *maṇi* jewel, so too it is with the *jambūnada* gold of the bodhisattva-mahāsattva's arousal of the bodhi resolve that is unapproachable in its qualities by any other precious thing aside from the great mind king jewel of all-knowledge itself.

Son of Good Family, it is as if there were a person who had become skilled in the methods of subduing dragons and thus was able to exercise mastery over the dragons. So too it is with the bodhisattva-mahāsattva, for, having acquired the bodhi resolve's skill in subduing dragons, he is able to exercise mastery over the dragons of all the afflictions.

Son of Good Family, just as a valiant soldier who had donned his armor and taken up arms might be unconquerable by any enemy, so too it is with the bodhisattva-mahāsattva who, having donned the armor and taken up the arms of the great bodhi resolve, then becomes unconquerable by any of the evil adversaries of karma and the afflictions.

Son of Good Family, just as a mere *karṣa*-weight of black sandalwood incense from the heavens can everywhere permeate a minor chiliocosm with its fragrance and just as its value cannot be matched even by a trichiliocosm full of precious jewels, so too it is with the incense of the bodhisattva-mahāsattva's bodhi resolve, for one mind-moment of its meritorious qualities everywhere permeates the Dharma realm and cannot be even approached by all the meritorious qualities of the *śrāvaka* disciples and *pratyekabuddhas.*

Son of Good Family, just as when one smears white sandalwood on one's body, it is able to rid one of all fevers and cause one's body and mind to become completely clear and cool, so too it is with the incense of the bodhisattva-mahāsattva's bodhi resolve, for it is able to rid one of all the fevers of false discriminations, greed, anger,

正體字

能除一切虛妄分別
432b02║ 貪恚癡等諸惑熱惱。令其具足智慧清涼。善
432b03║ 男子。如須彌山。若有近者即同其色。菩薩
432b04║ 摩訶薩菩提心山。亦復如是。若有近者。悉
432b05║ 得同其一切智色。善男子。譬如波利質多羅
432b06║ 樹。其皮香氣。閻浮提中。若婆師迦。若[6]薝蔔
432b07║ 迦。若蘇摩那。如是等華所有香氣皆不能及。
432b08║ 菩薩摩訶薩菩提心樹。亦復如是。所發大願
432b09║ 功德之香。一切二乘無漏戒定。智慧解脫。解
432b10║ 脫知見諸功德香悉不能及。[7]善男子。譬如波
432b11║ 利質多羅樹。雖未開華。應知即是無量諸華
432b12║ 出生之處。菩薩摩訶薩菩提心樹。亦復如是。
432b13║ 雖未開發一切智華。應知即是無數天人眾
432b14║ 菩提華所生之處。善男子。譬如波利質多羅
432b15║ 華。一日熏衣。[*]薝蔔迦華。婆利師華。蘇摩那
432b16║ 華。雖千歲熏亦不能及。菩薩摩訶薩菩提心
432b17║ 華。亦復如是。一生所熏諸功德香。普徹十
432b18║ 方一切佛所。一切二乘無漏功德。百千劫熏
432b19║ 所不能及。善男子。如海島中生椰子樹。根
432b20║ 莖枝葉及以華果。一切眾生。恒取受用無時
432b21║ 暫歇。

简体字

能除一切虚妄、分别、贪、恚、痴等诸惑热恼，令其具足智慧清凉。

“善男子，如须弥山，若有近者，即同其色。菩萨摩诃萨菩提心山亦复如是，若有近者，悉得同其一切智色。

“善男子，譬如波利质多罗树，其皮香气，阎浮提中若婆师迦、瞻卜迦，若苏摩那，如是等华所有香气皆不能及。菩萨摩诃萨菩提心树亦复如是，所发大愿功德之香，一切二乘无漏戒定、智慧解脱、解脱知见诸功德香悉不能及。

“善男子，譬如波利质多罗树，虽未开华，应知即是无量诸华出生之处。菩萨摩诃萨菩提心树亦复如是，虽未开发一切智华，应知即是无数天人众菩提华所生之处。

“善男子，譬如波利质多罗华，一日熏衣，瞻卜迦华、婆利师华、苏摩那华虽千岁熏亦不能及。菩萨摩诃萨菩提心华亦复如是，一生所熏诸功德香，普彻十方一切佛所，一切二乘无漏功德百千劫熏所不能及。

“善男子，如海岛中生椰子树，根、茎、枝、叶及以华果，一切众生恒取受用无时暂歇。菩萨摩诃萨菩提心树亦复如是，始从发起悲愿之心，乃至成佛，正法住世，常时利益一切世间无有间歇。

delusion, and the other afflictions while it also causes one to become completely imbued with the clarity and coolness of wisdom.

Son of Good Family, just as when someone draws near to Mount Sumeru, he becomes of the same color as the mountain, so too it is with the bodhisattva-mahāsattva's mountain of the bodhi resolve, for whoever draws near to it takes on its same hue of all-knowledge.

Son of Good Family, just as the fragrance of the *pārijātaka* tree's bark cannot be even approached by the fragrance of *vārṣikā* blossoms, *campaka* blossoms, *kusuma* blossoms, or any other such blossom on the continent of Jambudvīpa, so too it is with the bodhisattva-mahāsattva's tree of the bodhi resolve, for the fragrance of the meritorious qualities of the great vows he has made cannot even be approached by the fragrance of all the meritorious qualities of all two vehicles practitioners' uncontaminated moral virtue, meditative absorptions, wisdom, liberations, and knowledge and vision of liberation.

Son of Good Family, just as, even when it has not yet blossomed, one should still realize that the *pārijātaka* tree is the birthplace of countless blossoms, so too it is with the bodhisattva-mahāsattva's tree of the bodhi resolve, for, even when it has not yet opened its blossom of all-knowledge, one should still realize that it is the birthplace of countless blossoms of bodhi among devas and humans.

Son of Good Family, just as the fragrance of a robe exposed for but one day to the fragrance of the *pārijātaka* tree cannot be even approached by that of one exposed for even a thousand years to the fragrance of *campaka* blossoms, *vārṣikā* blossoms, or *kusuma* blossoms, so too it is with the blossom of the bodhisattva-mahāsattva's bodhi resolve, for the fragrance imparted by but one lifetime of exposure to the fragrance of its meritorious qualities everywhere penetrates the presence of all buddhas of the ten directions and it cannot be even approached by a hundred thousand kalpas of exposure to the fragrance of all the uncontaminated meritorious qualities of all two vehicles practitioners.

Son of Good Family, just as the roots, trunk, branches, leaves, blossoms, and fruit of an ocean island's coconut trees are constantly used by all the beings who take them and ceaselessly put them to their uses, so too it is with the bodhisattva-mahāsattva's tree of the bodhi resolve, for, from that very time when he first produces the resolve of his compassionate vow up until the time when he attains buddhahood and his right Dharma continues to abide in the world, during that entire time, it constantly and ceaselessly benefits the entire world.

正體字

菩薩摩訶薩菩提心樹。亦復如是。始
432b22 從發起悲願之心。乃至成佛。正法住世。常時
432b23 利益一切世間。無有間歇。[8]善男子。如有藥
432b24 汁名訶宅迦。人或得之。以其一兩變千兩銅。
432b25 悉成真金。非千兩銅能變此藥。菩薩摩訶薩
432b26 亦復如是。以菩提心迴向智藥。普變一切業
432b27 惑等法。悉使成於一切智相非業惑等。能變
432b28 其心。善男子。譬如小火隨所焚燒其焰轉熾。
432b29 菩薩摩訶薩菩提心火。亦復如是。隨所攀緣
432c01 智焰增長。善男子。譬如一燈然百千燈。其本
432c02 一燈無減無盡。菩薩摩訶薩菩提心燈。亦復
432c03 如是。普然三世諸佛智燈。而其心燈無減無
432c04 盡。善男子。譬如一燈入於闇室。百千年闇
432c05 悉能破盡。菩薩摩訶薩菩提心燈。亦復如是。
432c06 入於眾生心室之內。百千萬億不可說劫。諸
432c07 業煩惱種種闇障。悉能除盡。[9]善男子。譬如
432c08 燈炷隨其大小而發光明。若益膏油明終不
432c09 絕。菩薩摩訶薩菩提心燈。亦復如是。大願
432c10 為炷。光照法界。益大悲油。教化眾生。莊嚴國
432c11 土。施作佛事無有休息。善男子。譬如他化
432c12 自在天王冠閻浮檀真金天冠。欲界天子。諸
432c13 莊嚴具皆不能及。菩薩摩訶薩亦復如是。冠
432c14 菩提心大願天冠。一切凡夫二乘功德。皆不
432c15 能及。

简体字

“善男子，如有药汁，名诃宅迦，人或得之，以其一两变千两铜，悉成真金，非千两铜能变此药。菩萨摩诃萨亦复如是，以菩提心回向智药，普变一切业惑等法，悉使成于一切智相，非业惑等能变其心。

“善男子，譬如小火，随所焚烧，其焰转炽。菩萨摩诃萨菩提心火亦复如是，随所攀缘，智焰增长。

“善男子，譬如一灯，燃百千灯，其本一灯无减无尽。菩萨摩诃萨菩提心灯亦复如是，普燃三世诸佛智灯，而其心灯无减无尽。

“善男子，譬如一灯，入于暗室，百千年暗悉能破尽。菩萨摩诃萨菩提心灯亦复如是，入于众生心室之内，百千万亿不可说劫诸业烦恼、种种暗障悉能除尽。

“善男子，譬如灯炷，随其大小而发光明；若益膏油，明终不绝。菩萨摩诃萨菩提心灯亦复如是，大愿为炷，光照法界；益大悲油，教化众生，庄严国土，施作佛事，无有休息。

“善男子，譬如他化自在天王，冠阎浮檀真金天冠，欲界天子诸庄严具皆不能及。菩萨摩诃萨亦复如是，冠菩提心大愿天冠，一切凡夫、二乘功德皆不能及。

Son of Good Family, just as there is an herbal potion known as *hāṭaka* which, if one acquires it, he can use one ounce of it to transform a thousand ounces of copper into real gold without those thousand ounces of copper altering that potion, so too it is with the bodhisattva-mahāsattva who can use the wisdom potion of his bodhi resolve's dedications of merit to everywhere transform all karma, afflictions, and other such dharmas so that they all take on the character of all-knowledge without the karma, afflictions, and such being able to alter his resolve.

Son of Good Family, just as a small fire's flames will grow ever brighter in accordance with whatever it is burning, so too it is with the fire of a bodhisattva-mahāsattva's bodhi resolve, for it is in accordance with whatever it takes up that the flames of his wisdom will increase.

Son of Good Family, just as one lamp may light a hundred thousand lamps without that original single lamp being diminished or used up by them, so too it is with the bodhisattva-mahāsattva's lamp of the bodhi resolve, for it could everywhere light the wisdom lamps of all buddhas of the three periods of time even as the lamp of his resolve would still not be diminished or used up by them.

Son of Good Family, just as when one lamp is brought into a dark room, it is able to completely dispel the darkness of a hundred thousand years, so too it is with the lamp of the bodhisattva-mahāsattva's bodhi resolve, for when it enters the room of a being's mind, it is able to completely dispel all the different kinds of darkness-generated obstacles produced by the karma and afflictions of a hundred thousand myriads of *koṭīs* of ineffable numbers of kalpas.

Son of Good Family, just as it is in accordance with the relative size of a lamp's wick that it emanates its radiance and then endlessly burns brightly so long as more fuel continues to be added to it, so too it is with the lamp of the bodhisattva-mahāsattva's bodhi resolve in which his great vows form its wick and its light illuminates the Dharma realm so long as he adds the oil of the great compassion by which he can teach beings, adorn lands, and do the buddha's works without ever resting.

Son of Good Family, just as, when the king of the Paranirmita Vaśavartin Heaven dons his celestial crown of *jambūnada* gold, none of the adornments of the devas' sons of the desire-realm heavens are able to even approach it, so too it is with the bodhisattva-mahāsattva, for, when he dons the celestial crown of his bodhi resolve and great vows, none of the meritorious qualities of any of common people or two vehicles practitioners are able to even approach it.

正體字

善男子。如師子王哮吼之時。師子兒聞
432c16║ 皆增勇健。餘獸聞之即皆竄伏。佛師子王菩
432c17║ 提心吼。應知亦爾。諸菩薩聞增長功德。有
432c18║ 所得者聞皆退散。[10]善男子。譬如有人以師
432c19║ 子筋。而為樂絃。其音既奏餘絃悉絕。菩薩摩
432c20║ 訶薩亦復如是。以如來師子波羅蜜身菩提
432c21║ 心筋。為法樂絃。其音既奏。一切五欲及以二
432c22║ 乘諸功德絃。悉皆斷滅。善男子。譬如有人
432c23║ 以牛羊等種種諸乳。假使積集盈於大海。以
432c24║ 師子乳一滴投中。悉令變壞直過無礙。菩薩
432c25║ 摩訶薩亦復如是。以如來師子菩提心乳。著
432c26║ 無量劫業煩惱乳大海之中。悉令壞滅直過
432c27║ 無礙。終不住於二乘解脫。善男子。譬如迦
432c28║ 陵頻伽鳥。在卵[穀-禾+卵]中有大勢力。一切諸鳥所
432c29║ 不能及。菩薩摩訶薩亦復如是。於生死[穀-禾+卵]。發
433a01║ 菩提心所有大悲功德勢力。聲聞緣覺無能
433a02║ 及者。善男子。如金翅鳥王子初始生時。目則
433a03║ 明利飛則勁捷。一切諸鳥。雖久成長無能及
433a04║ 者。菩薩摩訶薩亦復如是。發菩提心為佛王
433a05║ 子。智慧清淨。大悲勇猛。

简体字

"善男子，如师子王哮吼之时，师子儿闻皆增勇健，余兽闻之即皆窜伏。佛师子王菩提心吼应知亦尔，诸菩萨闻增长功德，有所得者闻皆退散。

"善男子，譬如有人，以师子筋而为乐弦；其音既奏，余弦悉绝。菩萨摩诃萨亦复如是，以如来师子波罗蜜身菩提心筋为法乐弦；其音既奏，一切五欲及以二乘诸功德弦悉皆断灭。

"善男子，譬如有人，以牛羊等种种诸乳，假使积集盈于大海，以师子乳一滴投中，悉令变坏，直过无碍。菩萨摩诃萨亦复如是，以如来师子菩提心乳，著无量劫业烦恼乳大海之中，悉令坏灭，直过无碍，终不住于二乘解脱。

"善男子，譬如迦陵频伽鸟，在卵[穀-禾+卵]中有大势力，一切诸鸟所不能及。菩萨摩诃萨亦复如是，于生死[穀-禾+卵]发菩提心，所有大悲功德势力，声闻、缘觉无能及者。

"善男子，如金翅鸟王子，初始生时，目则明利，飞则劲捷，一切诸鸟虽久成长无能及者。菩萨摩诃萨亦复如是，发菩提心，为佛王子，智慧清净，大悲勇猛，

Son of Good Family, just as, when the lion king roars, the courage of all the lion cubs grows stronger, whereas, when other animals hear it, they flee and hide, one should realize that so too it is when the Buddha, the king of lions, roars his roar of the bodhi resolve, for, on hearing this, the bodhisattvas' meritorious qualities grow stronger, whereas, when all those who impute the actual existence of anything at all hear this, they all retreat and scatter.

Son of Good Family, just as there are those who use lion sinews to string their musical instruments because their music would cause any other kinds of strings to snap, so too it is with the bodhisattva-mahāsattvas, for they use the sinews of the bodhi resolve from the body of the Tathāgata's *pāramitā* lion as the strings for playing the music of the Dharma because the playing of that music would break the strings made from the meritorious qualities of those devoted to the five desires or to the practices of the two vehicles.

Son of Good Family, suppose there was someone who collected the milk of cows, sheep, and various other animals in such a great quantity that it exceeded the volume of the great ocean and then added to it but one drop of lion's milk which then caused it all to be destroyed and disappear so that there would then no longer be any obstacle to his passing directly beyond it. So too it is with the bodhisattva-mahāsattva, for he adds the lion's milk of the Tathāgata's bodhi resolve to the ocean of countless kalpas of his karma and afflictions and thereby causes it all to be completely destroyed so that he can then pass directly beyond it without encountering any obstacles and without ever abiding in the liberations of the two vehicles.

Son of Good Family, just as the *kalaviṅka* bird, even when still in its shell, is already possessed of immense power unmatched by that of any other bird, so too it is with the bodhisattva-mahāsattva, for, even while still within the eggshell of *saṃsāra*, he brings forth all of the power of the meritorious qualities of the bodhi resolve's great compassion, power that the *śrāvaka* disciples and *pratyekabuddhas* are unable to match.

Son of Good Family, just as when the sons of the king of the golden-winged *garuḍa* birds are first born, their vision is so clear and sharp and their flight is so powerful and swift that none of the other birds, even when already long since grown, can rival them in this, so too it is with the bodhisattva-mahāsattva, for, once he has aroused the bodhi resolve and become a son of the buddha king, his wisdom, purity, great compassion, and heroic bravery cannot be rivaled by the long-cultivated practice of the path of any of the two

正體字

一切二乘。雖百千
433a06‖ 劫。久修道行所不能及。[1]善男子。如有壯夫
433a07‖ 手執利矛刺堅密甲。直過無礙。菩薩摩訶薩
433a08‖ 亦復如是。執菩提心銛利快矛。刺諸邪見隨
433a09‖ 眠密甲。悉能穿徹無有障礙。善男子。譬如
433a10‖ 摩訶那伽大力勇士。若奮威怒。於其額上必
433a11‖ 生瘡疱。瘡若未合。閻浮提中一切人民。無能
433a12‖ 制伏。菩薩摩訶薩亦復如是。若起大悲。必定
433a13‖ 發於菩提之心。心未捨來。一切世間魔及魔
433a14‖ 民不能為害。善男子。譬如射師有諸弟子。雖
433a15‖ 未慣習其師[2]技藝。然其智慧方便善巧。餘
433a16‖ 一切人所不能及。菩薩摩訶薩初始發心。亦
433a17‖ 復如是。雖未慣習一切智行。然其所有願智
433a18‖ 解欲。一切世間凡夫二乘。悉不能及。善男
433a19‖ 子。如人學射先安其足後習其法。菩薩摩訶
433a20‖ 薩亦復如是。欲學如來一切智道。先當安住
433a21‖ 菩提之心。然後修行一切佛法。善男子。譬如
433a22‖ 幻師將作幻事。先當起意憶持幻法。然後所
433a23‖ 作悉得成就。菩薩摩訶薩亦復如是。將起一
433a24‖ 切諸佛菩薩神通幻事。先當起意發菩提心。
433a25‖ 然後一切悉得成就。

简体字

一切二乘虽百千劫久修道行所不能及。

“善男子，如有壮夫，手执利矛，刺坚密甲，直过无碍。菩萨摩诃萨亦复如是，执菩提心铦利快矛，刺诸邪见随眠密甲，悉能穿彻无有障碍。

“善男子，譬如摩诃那伽大力勇士，若奋威怒，于其额上必生疮疱；疮若未合，阎浮提中一切人民无能制伏。菩萨摩诃萨亦复如是，若起大悲，必定发于菩提之心；心未舍来，一切世间魔及魔民不能为害。

“善男子，譬如射师有诸弟子，虽未惯习其师技艺，然其智慧、方便、善巧，余一切人所不能及。菩萨摩诃萨初始发心亦复如是，虽未惯习一切智行，然其所有愿、智、解、欲，一切世间凡夫、二乘悉不能及。

“善男子，如人学射，先安其足，后习其法。菩萨摩诃萨亦复如是，欲学如来一切智道，先当安住菩提之心，然后修行一切佛法。

“善男子，譬如幻师，将作幻事，先当起意忆持幻法，然后所作悉得成就。菩萨摩诃萨亦复如是，将起一切诸佛菩萨神通幻事，先当起意发菩提心，然后一切悉得成就。

vehicles practitioners who have been practicing even for a hundred thousand kalpas.

Son of Good Family, just as a strong man holding a sharp spear could pierce through even tight-fitting body armor without any obstacle to its penetration, so too it is with the bodhisattva-mahāsattva, for, when he grasps the sharp spear of the bodhi resolve and stabs the tight-fitting armor of wrong views and latent tendencies, it penetrates straight through all of them without any obstacle to its penetration.

Son of Good Family, just as an immensely powerful and brave *mahānāga* elephant [in *musth*] who has become worked up and filled with awesome fury will certainly also develop *musth*-related sores on his temples and, so long as those sores have not healed, he will be uncontrollable by anyone in Jambudvīpa, so too it is with the bodhisattva-mahāsattva, for once he has produced the great compassion, he will certainly generate the bodhi resolve and, so long as he does not relinquish that resolve, no Māra or follower of Māra could ever harm him.

Son of Good Family, just as, although the disciples of a master archer are not yet fully proficient in their master's expertise even as their own knowledge, technique, and skill still cannot be rivaled by anyone else, so too it is with the bodhisattva-mahāsattva who has produced his initial resolve, for, even though he is not yet fully proficient in the practices leading to all-knowledge, all his vows, knowledge, and resolute zeal still cannot be rivaled by any of the world's common people or any of the practitioners of the two vehicles.

Son of Good Family, just as one who trains in archery first adopts a stable stance and only then practices its techniques, so too it is with the bodhisattva-mahāsattva, for, once he aspires to train in the Tathāgata's path to all-knowledge, he must first become securely established in the bodhi resolve and only afterward cultivate all the dharmas of a buddha.

Son of Good Family, just as when a master conjurer is preparing to produce his conjurations, he must first generate the will that sustains those conjured phenomena after which all that he does is successful, so too it is with the bodhisattva-mahāsattva, for when he is about to carry out the works of conjuration produced by the spiritual superknowledges of all buddhas and bodhisattvas, he must first generate the will with which he makes the bodhi resolve after which all that he does becomes successful.

正體字

善男子。譬如幻術無色
433a26| 現色。菩薩摩訶薩菩提心相。亦復如是。雖
433a27| 無有色不可覩見。然能普於十方法界。示現
433a28| 種種功德莊嚴。善男子。譬如猫狸纔見於鼠。
433a29| 鼠即入穴不敢復出。菩薩摩訶薩發菩提心。
433b01| 亦復如是。暫以慧眼觀諸惑業。皆即竄匿不
433b02| 復出生。善男子。譬如有人著閻浮金莊嚴之
433b03| 具。映蔽一切皆如聚墨。菩薩摩訶薩亦復如
433b04| 是。著菩提心莊嚴之具。映蔽一切凡夫二乘
433b05| 功德莊嚴。悉無光色。[3]善男子。如好[4]磁石少
433b06| 分之力。即能吸壞諸鐵鉤鎖。菩薩摩訶薩發
433b07| 菩提心。亦復如是。若起一念。悉能壞滅一
433b08| 切見欲無明鉤鎖。善男子。如有[*]磁石。鐵若
433b09| 見之。即皆散去無留住者。菩薩摩訶薩發菩
433b10| 提心。亦復如是。諸業煩惱二乘解脫。若暫
433b11| 見之即皆散滅。亦無住者。善男子。譬如有
433b12| 人善入大海。一切水族無能為害。假使入於
433b13| 摩竭魚口。亦不為彼之所吞噬。菩薩摩訶薩
433b14| 亦復如是。發菩提心入生死海。諸業煩惱不
433b15| 能為害。假使入於聲聞緣覺實際法中。亦不
433b16| 為其之所留難。善男子。譬如有人飲甘露漿。
433b17| 一切諸物不能為害。菩薩摩訶薩亦復如是。
433b18| 飲菩提心甘露法漿。

简体字

“善男子，譬如幻术，无色现色。菩萨摩诃萨菩提心相亦复如是，虽无有色，不可睹见，然能普于十方法界示现种种功德庄严。

“善男子，譬如猫狸，才见于鼠，鼠即入穴不敢复出。菩萨摩诃萨发菩提心亦复如是，暂以慧眼观诸惑业，皆即窜匿不复出生。

“善男子，譬如有人，著阎浮金庄严之具，映蔽一切皆如聚墨。菩萨摩诃萨亦复如是，著菩提心庄严之具，映蔽一切凡夫二乘功德庄严悉无光色。

“善男子，如好磁石，少分之力，即能吸坏诸铁钩锁。菩萨摩诃萨发菩提心亦复如是，若起一念，悉能坏灭一切见欲无明钩锁。

“善男子，如有磁石，铁若见之，即皆散去，无留住者。菩萨摩诃萨发菩提心亦复如是，诸业烦恼、二乘解脱，若暂见之，即皆散灭，亦无住者。

“善男子，譬如有人，善入大海，一切水族无能为害；假使入于摩竭鱼口，亦不为彼之所吞噬。菩萨摩诃萨亦复如是，发菩提心入生死海，诸业烦恼不能为害；假使入于声闻、缘觉实际法中，亦不为其之所留难。

“善男子，譬如有人，饮甘露浆，一切诸物不能为害。菩萨摩诃萨亦复如是，饮菩提心甘露法浆，

Son of Good Family, just as, by the techniques of conjuration, one manifests forms where there are no forms, so too it is with the appearance of the bodhisattva-mahāsattva's bodhi resolve, for, although it has no form and cannot be seen, it is still able to manifest throughout the ten directions of the Dharma realm the many different kinds of adornments with his meritorious qualities.

Son of Good Family, just as when a wildcat sees a rat, the rat immediately enters its burrow and dares not emerge again, so too it is with the bodhisattva-mahāsattva's arousing of the bodhi resolve, for even when he only momentarily directs the attention of his wisdom eye to contemplating any affliction-generated karma, it all immediately goes into hiding and does not emerge again.

Son of Good Family, just as, when someone dons an adornment made of *jambūnada* gold, its radiance outshines all others so completely that it is as if they were but lumps of ink, so too it is with the bodhisattva-mahāsattva, for, when he dons the adornment of the bodhi resolve, its radiance so outshines all adornments with meritorious qualities of all common persons and practitioners of the two vehicles that they seem as if they had no radiance at all.

Son of Good Family, just as but a small amount of the power of a strong magnet can break an iron chain, so too it is with the bodhisattva-mahāsattva's arousal of the bodhi resolve, for, if he produces it for but a single mind-moment, it can completely destroy the chain of all views, desires, and ignorance.

Son of Good Family, just as if one has a magnet, when [polarized] iron is exposed to it, it all scatters so that none remains, so too it is with the bodhisattva-mahāsattva's arousal of the bodhi resolve, for whenever any karma, afflictions, or liberations of practitioners of the two vehicles are exposed to it, they all disperse and no longer remain.

Son of Good Family, just as someone who is skilled in going out into the great ocean cannot be harmed by any of the creatures of the ocean and can even enter the mouth of the *makara* monster without being eaten by it, so it is with the bodhisattva-mahāsattva, for, having made the bodhi resolve and entered the ocean of *saṃsāra,* none of the karmic actions or afflictions are able to harm him and, even if he enters into the apex of reality dharmas of *śrāvaka* disciples or *pratyekabuddhas,* he still cannot be detained or troubled by them.

Son of Good Family, just as someone who drinks the elixir of immortality becomes invulnerable to harm by any creature, so too it is with the bodhisattva-mahāsattva, for, when he drinks the Dharma nectar of the bodhi resolve's elixir of immortality, because

正體字

不墮聲聞辟支佛地。以
433b19 | 具廣大悲願力故。善男子。譬如有人得安繕
433b20 | 那藥以塗其目。雖行人間人所不見。菩薩摩
433b21 | 訶薩亦復如是。得菩提心安繕那藥。能以方
433b22 | 便入魔境界。一切眾魔所不能見。善男子。譬
433b23 | 如有人依附於王。不畏餘人。菩薩摩訶薩亦
433b24 | 復如是。依菩提心大勢力王。不畏障蓋惡道
433b25 | 之難。善男子。譬如有人住於水中。不畏火
433b26 | 焚。菩薩摩訶薩亦復如是。住菩提心善根水
433b27 | 中。不畏二乘解脫智火。善男子。譬如有人
433b28 | 依倚猛將。即不怖畏一切怨敵。菩薩摩訶薩
433b29 | 亦復如是。依菩提心勇猛大將。不畏一切惡
433c01 | 行怨敵。善男子。如釋天王執金剛杵。摧伏一
433c02 | 切阿脩羅眾。菩薩摩訶薩亦復如是。持菩提
433c03 | 心金剛之杵。摧伏一切諸魔外道。[5]善男子。譬
433c04 | 如有人服延齡藥。長得充健不老不瘦。菩薩
433c05 | 摩訶薩亦復如是。服菩提心延齡之藥。於無
433c06 | 數劫修菩薩行。心無疲厭亦無染著。善男子。
433c07 | 譬如有人調和藥汁。必當先取好清淨水。菩
433c08 | 薩摩訶薩亦復如是。欲修菩薩一切行願。先
433c09 | 當發起菩提之心。善男子。如人護身先護命
433c10 | 根。菩薩摩訶薩亦復如是。護持佛法亦當先
433c11 | 護菩提之心。

简体字

不堕声闻、辟支佛地，以具广大悲愿力故。

“善男子，譬如有人，得安缮那药以涂其目，虽行人间，人所不见。菩萨摩诃萨亦复如是，得菩提心安缮那药，能以方便入魔境界，一切众魔所不能见。

“善男子，譬如有人，依附于王，不畏余人。菩萨摩诃萨亦复如是，依菩提心大势力王，不畏障、盖、恶道之难。

“善男子，譬如有人，住于水中，不畏火焚。菩萨摩诃萨亦复如是，住菩提心善根水中，不畏二乘解脱智火。

“善男子，譬如有人，依倚猛将，即不怖畏一切冤敌。菩萨摩诃萨亦复如是，依菩提心勇猛大将，不畏一切恶行冤敌。

“善男子，如释天王，执金刚杵，摧伏一切阿修罗众。菩萨摩诃萨亦复如是，持菩提心金刚之杵，摧伏一切诸魔外道。

“善男子，譬如有人，服延龄药，长得充健，不老不瘦。菩萨摩诃萨亦复如是，服菩提心延龄之药，于无数劫修菩萨行，心无疲厌亦无染著。

“善男子，譬如有人，调和药汁，必当先取好清净水。菩萨摩诃萨亦复如是，欲修菩萨一切行愿，先当发起菩提之心。

“善男子，如人护身，先护命根。菩萨摩诃萨亦复如是，护持佛法，亦当先护菩提之心。

he possesses the power of vast compassion and vows, he then never falls down onto the grounds of *śrāvaka* disciples or *pratyekabuddhas.*

Son of Good Family, just as when someone who acquires *añjana* medicine applies it to his eyes, although he travels among people, he remains invisible to them, so too it is with the bodhisattva-mahāsattva, for when he acquires the *añjana* medicine[43] of the bodhi resolve, he can use skillful means to enter the realms of the *māras* and he will remain invisible to the many kinds of *māras.*

Son of Good Family, just as someone who relies upon the support of a king has no fear of any other person, so too it is with the bodhisattva-mahāsattva, for he relies on the immensely powerful king of the bodhi resolve and thus does not fear the difficulties posed by the obstacles, hindrances, or wretched destinies.

Son of Good Family, just as someone who lives in the water has no fear of being burned by fire, so too it is with the bodhisattva-mahāsattva, for, because he abides in the waters of the roots of goodness arising from the bodhi resolve, he has no fear of the fire of the two vehicles' knowledge of liberation.

Son of Good Family, just as when someone relies on a brave general, he does not fear any adversary, so too it is with the bodhisattva-mahāsattva, for, relying on the courageous and great general of the bodhi resolve, he does not fear any of the adversaries of the evil actions.

Son of Good Family, just as when the heavenly king, Śakra, takes up his vajra pestle, he vanquishes all the *asura* hordes, so too it is with the bodhisattva-mahāsattva, for, when he takes up the vajra pestle of the bodhi resolve, he vanquishes all *māras* and followers of non-Buddhist paths.

Son of Good Family, just as when someone ingests an elixir of long life, he long enjoys robust health and neither ages nor wastes away, so too it is with the bodhisattva-mahāsattva, for, when he ingests the bodhi resolve's elixir of long life, he cultivates the bodhisattva practices for countless kalpas during which his mind never grows weary and he remains free of defiling attachments.

Son of Good Family, just as when someone blends an herbal elixir, he must first get good pure water, so too it is with the bodhisattva-mahāsattva, for when he cultivates all the bodhisattva's practices and vows, he must first make the bodhi resolve.

Son of Good Family, just as when someone protects his body, he first sees to the protection of his life faculty, so too it is with the bodhisattva-mahāsattva, for, even as he guards and preserves the Buddha's Dharma, he also first guards his bodhi resolve.

正體字

善男子。譬如有人命根若斷。不
433c12 ‖ 能利益父母宗親。菩薩摩訶薩亦復如是。捨
433c13 ‖ 菩提心。不能利益一切眾生。不能成就諸佛
433c14 ‖ 功德。善男子。譬如大海無能壞者。菩提心
433c15 ‖ 海亦復如是。諸業煩惱二乘之心。所不能壞。
433c16 ‖ [6]善男子。譬如日光。星宿光明不能映蔽。菩
433c17 ‖ 提心日亦復如是。一切二乘無漏智光。所不
433c18 ‖ 能蔽。善男子。如王子初生即為大臣之所尊
433c19 ‖ 重。以種性自在故。菩薩摩訶薩亦復如是。於
433c20 ‖ 佛法中。發菩提心。即為耆宿久修梵行。聲聞
433c21 ‖ 緣覺所共尊重。以大悲自在故。善男子。譬
433c22 ‖ 如王子年雖幼稚。一切大臣皆悉敬禮。菩薩
433c23 ‖ 摩訶薩亦復如是。雖初發心修菩薩行。二乘
433c24 ‖ 耆舊皆應敬禮。善男子。譬如王子雖於一切
433c25 ‖ 臣佐之中未得自在。已具王相。不與一切諸
433c26 ‖ 臣佐等。以生處尊勝故。菩薩摩訶薩亦復如
433c27 ‖ 是。雖於一切業煩惱中未得自在。然已具足
433c28 ‖ 菩提之相。不與一切二乘齊等。以種性第一
433c29 ‖ 故。善男子。譬如清淨摩尼妙寶。眼有翳故
434a01 ‖ 見為不淨。菩薩摩訶薩菩提心寶。亦復如是。
434a02 ‖ 無智不信謂為不淨。

简体字

“善男子，譬如有人，命根若断，不能利益父母、宗亲。菩萨摩诃萨亦复如是，舍菩提心，不能利益一切众生，不能成就诸佛功德。

“善男子，譬如大海，无能坏者。菩提心海亦复如是，诸业烦恼、二乘之心所不能坏。

“善男子，譬如日光，星宿光明不能映蔽。菩提心日亦复如是，一切二乘无漏智光所不能蔽。

“善男子，如王子初生，即为大臣之所尊重，以种性自在故。菩萨摩诃萨亦复如是，于佛法中发菩提心，即为耆宿久修梵行声闻、缘觉所共尊重，以大悲自在故。

“善男子，譬如王子，年虽幼稚，一切大臣皆悉敬礼。菩萨摩诃萨亦复如是，虽初发心修菩萨行，二乘耆旧皆应敬礼。

“善男子，譬如王子，虽于一切臣佐之中未得自在，已具王相，不与一切诸臣佐等，以生处尊胜故。菩萨摩诃萨亦复如是，虽于一切业烦恼中未得自在，然已具足菩提之相，不与一切二乘齐等，以种性第一故。

“善男子，譬如清净摩尼妙宝，眼有翳故见为不净。菩萨摩诃萨菩提心宝亦复如是，无智不信谓为不净。

Son of Good Family, just as when someone's life faculty has been severed, he is unable to benefit his parents or clan relatives, so too it is with the bodhisattva-mahāsattva, for, if he were to abandon his bodhi resolve, he would be unable to benefit all beings and he would be unable to perfect the meritorious qualities of a buddha.

Son of Good Family, just as the great ocean cannot be ruined by anyone, so too it is with the ocean of the bodhi resolve, for it cannot be ruined by karma, the afflictions, or the resolve of practitioners of the two vehicles.

Son of Good Family, just as the light of the sun can never be outshone by the light of the stars and constellations, so too it is with the sun of the bodhi resolve, for it can never be outshone by the light of the uncontaminated wisdom of any of the practitioners of the two vehicles.

Son of Good Family, just as when the son of the king is first born, due to the sovereignty of his clan lineage, he is immediately accorded the reverential esteem of the great officials, so too it is with the bodhisattva-mahāsattva, for, when he arouses the bodhi resolve for the dharma of buddhahood, because of the sovereignty of the great compassion, he is immediately revered and esteemed by those who have long cultivated *brahmacarya,* namely the *śrāvaka* disciples and the *pratyekabuddhas.*

Son of Good Family, just as, even though the son of the king may still be young, he is nonetheless revered by all the great officials, so too it is with the bodhisattva-mahāsattva, for, although he has only just produced his initial resolve to cultivate the bodhisattva practices, all the senior practitioners of the two vehicles should still revere him.

Son of Good Family, even though the son of the king has not yet acquired sovereign authority over all the officials and other retainers, because he possesses the mark of royalty and because his birth station is revered as supreme, he is unequaled by any of those officials or other retainers. So too it is with the bodhisattva-mahāsattva, for, even though he has not yet acquired sovereign mastery over all karmic actions and afflictions, because he already possesses the mark of bodhi and because his clan lineage is foremost, he is unequaled by any of the practitioners of the two vehicles.

Son of Good Family, just as a pure and marvelous *maṇi* jewel might nonetheless be perceived as having impurities by someone whose eyes were afflicted with cataracts, so too it is with the bodhisattva-mahāsattva's jewel of the bodhi resolve, for those without wisdom who have no faith might still regard it as impure.

正體字

善男子。譬如有藥為呪
434a03‖ 所持。若有眾生見聞同住。一切諸病皆得消
434a04‖ 滅。菩薩摩訶薩菩提心藥。亦復如是。一切
434a05‖ 善根。智慧方便。菩薩願智。共所攝持。若有眾
434a06‖ 生。見聞同住憶念之者。諸煩惱病悉得除滅。
434a07‖ 善男子。譬如有人常持甘露。其身畢竟不變
434a08‖ 不壞。菩薩摩訶薩亦復如是。若常憶持菩提
434a09‖ 心露。令願智身畢竟不壞。善男子。如機關
434a10‖ 木人若無有楔。身即離散不能運動。菩薩摩
434a11‖ 訶薩亦復如是。無菩提心行即分散。不能成
434a12‖ 就一切佛法。善男子。如轉輪王有沈香寶。名
434a13‖ 曰象藏。若燒此香。王四種兵悉騰虛空。菩薩
434a14‖ 摩訶薩菩提心香。亦復如是。若發此意。即
434a15‖ 令菩薩一切善根。永出三界行如來智無為
434a16‖ 空中。[1]善男子。譬如金剛唯從金剛處及金處
434a17‖ 生。非餘寶處生。菩薩摩訶薩菩提心金剛。亦
434a18‖ 復如是。唯從大悲救護眾生金剛處。一切智
434a19‖ 智殊勝境界金處而生。非餘眾生善根處生。
434a20‖ 善男子。譬如有樹名曰無根。不從根生。而
434a21‖ 枝葉華果悉皆繁茂。菩薩摩訶薩菩提心樹。
434a22‖ 亦復如是無根可得。

简体字

“善男子，譬如有药，为咒所持，若有众生见、闻、同住，一切诸病皆得消灭。菩萨摩诃萨菩提心药亦复如是，一切善根、智慧、方便、菩萨愿智共所摄持，若有众生见、闻、同住、忆念之者，诸烦恼病悉得除灭。

“善男子，譬如有人，常持甘露，其身毕竟不变不坏。菩萨摩诃萨亦复如是，若常忆持菩提心甘露，令愿智身毕竟不坏。

“善男子，如机关木人，若无有楔，身即离散，不能运动。菩萨摩诃萨亦复如是，无菩提心，行即分散，不能成就一切佛法。

“善男子，如转轮王，有沉香宝，名曰象藏；若烧此香，王四种兵悉腾虚空。菩萨摩诃萨菩提心香亦复如是，若发此意，即令菩萨一切善根永出三界，行如来智无为空中。

“善男子，譬如金刚，唯从金刚处及金处生，非余宝处生。菩萨摩诃萨菩提心金刚亦复如是，唯从大悲救护众生金刚处、一切智智殊胜境界金处而生，非余众生善根处生。

“善男子，譬如有树，名曰无根，不从根生，而枝、叶、华、果悉皆繁茂。菩萨摩诃萨菩提心树亦复如是，无根可得，

Son of Good Family, just when any being sees, hears of, or lives with a particular medicine that is sustained by a mantra, his illnesses are all done away with, so too it is with the bodhisattva-mahāsattva's medicine of the bodhi resolve that is jointly sustained by all his roots of goodness, wisdom, skillful means, bodhisattva vows, and knowledge in such a way that, if any being but sees him, hears his voice, remains together with him, or bears him in mind, then all of his diseases arising from the afflictions will all be done away with.

Son of Good Family, just as someone who is always in possession of the elixir of immortality is one whose body never changes or deteriorates, so too it is with the bodhisattva-mahāsattva, for, so long as he always bears in mind the elixir of the bodhi resolve, this will prevent his body of vows and wisdom from ever deteriorating.

Son of Good Family, just as the body of a wooden marionette, if deprived of its peg joints, would immediately scatter into pieces and become incapable of performing its movements, so too it is with the bodhisattva-mahāsattva, for, in the absence of his bodhi resolve, his practice would break apart and he would not be able to successfully develop any of the dharmas of a buddha.

Son of Good Family, just as a wheel-turning king possesses an *agaru* incense treasure known as "elephant treasury" that, when he lights this incense, it enables his fourfold army to soar up into the sky, so too it is with the bodhisattva-mahāsattva's incense of the bodhi resolve, for, when he makes this resolve, this immediately enables all the bodhisattva's roots of goodness to forever soar beyond the three realms of existence and travel through the unconditioned sky of the Tathāgata's wisdom.

Son of Good Family, just as vajra comes forth only from the places where vajra is found or where gold is found and not from any other place, so too it is with the vajra of the bodhisattva-mahāsattva's bodhi resolve, for it comes forth only from the place where one finds the vajra of the great compassion that rescues beings or from the place where one finds the gold of the especially excellent realm of the knowledge of omniscience and, as such, it does not come forth from the roots of goodness of any other being.

Son of Good Family, just as there is a tree known as "rootless" that does not grow from roots even as all of its branches, leaves, flowers, and fruit still flourish luxuriantly, so too it is with the tree of the bodhisattva-mahāsattva's bodhi resolve that has no roots that can be found even as it is able to generate the growth of the branches, leaves, flowers, and fruit of the knowledge of omniscience,

正體字

而能長養一切智智神
434a23 | 通大願。枝葉華果。扶疎蔭映。普覆世間。[2]善
434a24 | 男子。譬如金剛。非劣惡器及以破器所能容
434a25 | 持。唯除全具上妙之器。菩提心金剛亦復如
434a26 | 是。非下劣眾生慳嫉破戒。懈怠妄念無智器
434a27 | 中所能容持。亦非退失殊勝志願散亂惡覺
434a28 | 眾生器中所能容持。唯除菩薩深心寶器。善
434a29 | 男子。譬如金剛能穿眾寶。菩提心金剛亦復
434b01 | 如是。悉能穿徹一切法寶。善男子。譬如金
434b02 | 剛能壞眾山。菩提心金剛亦復如是。悉能摧
434b03 | 壞諸邪見山。善男子。譬如金剛雖破不全。一
434b04 | 切眾寶猶不能及。菩提心金剛亦復如是。雖
434b05 | 復志劣少有虧損。猶勝一切二乘功德。善男
434b06 | 子。譬如金剛雖有損缺。猶能除滅一切貧窮。
434b07 | 菩提心金剛亦復如是。雖有損缺不進諸行。
434b08 | 猶能捨離一切生死。[3]善男子。如[4]小金剛悉
434b09 | 能破壞一切諸物。菩提心金剛亦復如是。入
434b10 | 少境界即破一切無知諸惑。善男子。譬如金
434b11 | 剛非凡人所得。菩提心金剛亦復如是。非劣
434b12 | 意眾生之所能得。善男子。譬如金剛不識寶
434b13 | 人。不知其能

简体字

而能长养一切智智神通大愿；枝、叶、华、果，扶疏荫映，普覆世间。

"善男子，譬如金刚，非劣恶器及以破器所能容持，唯除全具上妙之器。菩提心金刚亦复如是，非下劣众生悭、嫉、破戒、懈怠、妄念、无智器中所能容持，亦非退失殊胜志愿、散乱、恶觉众生器中所能容持，唯除菩萨深心宝器。

"善男子，譬如金刚，能穿众宝。菩提心金刚亦复如是，悉能穿彻一切法宝。

"善男子，譬如金刚，能坏众山。菩提心金刚亦复如是，悉能摧坏诸邪见山。

"善男子，譬如金刚，虽破不全，一切众宝犹不能及。菩提心金刚亦复如是，虽复志劣，少有亏损，犹胜一切二乘功德。

"善男子，譬如金刚，虽有损缺，犹能除灭一切贫穷。菩提心金刚亦复如是，虽有损缺，不进诸行，犹能舍离一切生死。

"善男子，如少金刚，悉能破坏一切诸物。菩提心金刚亦复如是，入少境界，即破一切无知诸惑。

"善男子，譬如金刚，非凡人所得。菩提心金刚亦复如是，非劣意众生之所能得。

"善男子，譬如金刚，不识宝人不知其能、

the spiritual superknowledges, and the great vows that all together spread their shade and radiance in such a way that they everywhere provide shelter for the entire world.

Son of Good Family, just as vajra is something that cannot be contained in an inferior vessel, a broken vessel, or any other kind of vessel other than a perfectly intact and supremely marvelous vessel, so too it is with the vajra of the bodhi resolve, for it is not something that can be contained in the vessel of any inferior being, or in the vessel of any being who is miserly, envious, a breaker of precepts, indolent, wrong thinking, or ignorant. Nor can it be contained in the vessel of any being who has retreated from the especially excellent vows, who is scattered and confused, who courses in evil ideation, or who is anyone other than the precious vessel of a bodhisattva with deep resolve.

Son of Good Family, just as vajra is able to bore through the many different kinds of jewels, so too it is with the vajra of the bodhi resolve, for it is able to penetrate through all the jewels of the Dharma.

Son of Good Family, just as vajra is even able to shatter the many mountains, so too it is with the vajra of the bodhi resolve, for it is able to completely demolish the mountain of all wrong views.

Son of Good Family, just as vajra cannot be rivaled by any of the other kinds of jewels even when it has been broken and is no longer whole, so too it is with the vajra of the bodhi resolve, for, although that resolve may have become weakened or somewhat diminished, it is still superior to all the meritorious qualities of the practitioners of the two vehicles.

Son of Good Family, just as vajra, even when it has become damaged, is still able to do away with poverty, so too it is with the vajra of the bodhi resolve, for, even though it may have become damaged to the point that one is not progressing in the practices, it is still able to lead to abandoning all involvement in *saṃsāra*.

Son of Good Family, just as even a small vajra is still able to break all other things, so too it is with the vajra of the bodhi resolve, for whenever it enters any inferior mind state, it immediately crushes all of its ignorance-generated delusions.

Son of Good Family, just as vajra is not something acquired by common persons, so too it is with the vajra of the bodhi resolve, for it is not something that beings with inferior aspirations are able to acquire.

Son of Good Family, just as one who does not know jewels will be unable to understand the capabilities of vajra or be able to take

正體字

不得。其用。菩提心金剛亦復如
434b14 是。不知法人。不了其能不得其用。[5]善男子。
434b15 譬如金剛無能銷滅。菩提心金剛亦復如是。
434b16 一切諸法無能銷滅。善男子。如金剛杵。諸
434b17 大力人皆不能持。唯除有大那羅延力。菩提
434b18 之心亦復如是。一切二乘皆不能持。唯除菩
434b19 薩廣大因緣堅固善力。善男子。譬如金剛一
434b20 切諸物無能壞者。而能普壞一切諸物。然其
434b21 體性無所損減。菩提之心亦復如是。普於三
434b22 世無數劫中。教化眾生。修行苦行。聲聞緣
434b23 覺所不能者。咸能作之。然其畢竟。無有疲厭
434b24 亦無損壞。善男子。譬如金剛餘不能持。唯金
434b25 剛地之所能持。菩提之心亦復如是。聲聞緣
434b26 覺皆不能持。唯除趣向薩婆若者。善男子。如
434b27 金剛器無有瑕缺用盛於水。永不滲漏而入
434b28 於地。菩提心金剛器亦復如是。盛善根水。永
434b29 不滲漏。令入諸趣。善男子。如金剛際能持
434c01 大地不令墜沒。菩提之心亦復如是。能持菩
434c02 薩一切行願。不令墜沒入於三界。善男子。譬
434c03 如金剛久處水中不爛不濕。菩提之心亦復
434c04 如是。於一切劫處在生死業惑水中。無壞無
434c05 變。

简体字

不得其用。菩提心金刚亦复如是，不知法人不了其能、不得其用。

“善男子，譬如金刚，无能销灭。菩提心金刚亦复如是，一切诸法无能销灭。

“善男子，如金刚杵，诸大力人皆不能持，唯除有大那罗延力。菩提之心亦复如是，一切二乘皆不能持，唯除菩萨广大因缘坚固善力。

“善男子，譬如金刚，一切诸物无能坏者，而能普坏一切诸物，然其体性无所损减。菩提之心亦复如是，普于三世无数劫中，教化众生，修行苦行，声闻、缘觉所不能者咸能作之，然其毕竟无有疲厌亦无损坏。

“善男子，譬如金刚，余不能持，唯金刚地之所能持。菩提之心亦复如是，声闻、缘觉皆不能持，唯除趣向萨婆若者。

“善男子，如金刚器，无有瑕缺用盛于水，永不渗漏而入于地。菩提心金刚器亦复如是，盛善根水，永不渗漏，令入诸趣。

“善男子，如金刚际，能持大地，不令坠没。菩提之心亦复如是，能持菩萨一切行愿，不令坠没入于三界。

“善男子，譬如金刚，久处水中，不烂不湿。菩提之心亦复如是，于一切劫处，在生死业惑水中，无坏无变。

advantage of its uses, so too it is with the vajra of the bodhi resolve, for, one who does not know the Dharma will not understand its capabilities or be able to take advantage of its uses.

Son of Good Family, just as vajra cannot be melted away by anything at all, so too it is with the vajra of the bodhi resolve, for there is no dharma that is able to melt it away.

Son of Good Family, just as a vajra pestle cannot be wielded even by any strong men except for those who possess the powers of a great *nārāyaṇa* stalwart, so too it is with the bodhi resolve, for it cannot be taken up by anyone at all, including even the practitioners of the two vehicles, except for those who possess the power of the bodhisattvas' vast causes and conditions and steadfast goodness.

Son of Good Family, just as vajra cannot be destroyed by anything else and yet it can destroy anything else without its essential nature being diminished at all, so too it is with the bodhi resolve, for, everywhere throughout the three periods of time and across the course of countless kalpas, it persists in teaching beings and cultivating the austerities to an extent that cannot be matched by *śrāvaka* disciples or *pratyekabuddhas,* as it continues on with all such practices without ever growing weary and without their ever being diminished.

Son of Good Family, just as vajra cannot be held by anything aside from ground that is itself made of vajra, so too it is with the bodhi resolve, for it cannot be held by *śrāvaka* disciples or *pratyekabuddhas,* but rather only by those who are progressing toward the realization of omniscience.

Son of Good Family, just as a vessel made of vajra which is free of defects that is being used to hold water will never leak and allow that water to run off onto the ground, so too it is with the vajra vessel of the bodhi resolve, for once it has been filled with the waters of roots of goodness, they will never leak out and be allowed to enter the destinies of rebirth.

Son of Good Family, just as the vajra stratum is able to support the entire great earth and prevent it from collapsing, so too it is with the bodhi resolve, for it is able to support all the bodhisattva's practices and vows and thus prevent them from collapsing into the three realms of existence.

Son of Good Family, just as vajra can remain in the water for a long time and yet never decay or become soaked through with moisture, so too it is with the bodhi resolve, for it can reside even for the duration of all kalpas within the waters of *saṃsāra*'s karma and afflictions and yet still remain undamaged and unchanged by them.

正體字

[6]善男子。譬如金剛一切諸火不能燒然不
434c06 能令熱。菩提之心亦復如是。一切生死諸煩
434c07 惱火。不能燒然不能令熱。善男子。譬如三千
434c08 世界之中金剛座上能持諸佛。坐於道場。降
434c09 伏諸魔。成等正覺。非是餘座之所能持。菩提
434c10 心座亦復如是。能持菩薩一切願行諸波羅
434c11 蜜。諸忍諸地。迴向受記。修[7]集菩提助道之
434c12 法。供養諸佛。聞法受行。一切餘心所不能持。
434c13 善男子。菩提心者。成就如是無量無邊乃至
434c14 不可說不可說殊勝功德。若有眾生發阿耨
434c15 多羅三藐三菩提心。則獲如是勝功德法。是
434c16 故善男子。汝獲善利。汝發阿耨多羅三藐三
434c17 菩提心。求菩薩行。已得如是大功德故。善男
434c18 子。如汝所問。菩薩云何學菩薩行。修菩薩道。
434c19 善男子。汝可入此毘盧遮那莊嚴藏大樓閣
434c20 中。周遍觀察。則能了知學菩薩行。學已成就
434c21 無量功德
434c25 [9]大方廣佛華嚴經卷[10]第七十九
434c28 [14]入法界品第三十九之二十
434c29 爾時善財童子。恭敬右遶彌勒菩薩摩訶薩
435a01 已。而白之言。唯願大聖。開樓閣門令我得入。
435a02 時彌勒菩薩。前詣樓閣。彈指出聲。其門即開。
435a03 命善財入。善財心喜。入已還閉。見其樓閣。廣
435a04 博無量。同於虛空。

简体字

“善男子，譬如金刚，一切诸火不能烧燃、不能令热。菩提之心亦复如是，一切生死诸烦恼火不能烧燃、不能令热。

“善男子，譬如三千世界之中金刚座上，能持诸佛坐于道场、降伏诸魔、成等正觉，非是余座之所能持。菩提心座亦复如是，能持菩萨一切愿行、诸波罗蜜、诸忍、诸地、回向、受记、修习菩提助道之法、供养诸佛、闻法受行，一切余心所不能持。

“善男子，菩提心者，成就如是无量无边乃至不可说不可说殊胜功德。若有众生发阿耨多罗三藐三菩提心，则获如是胜功德法。是故，善男子，汝获善利！汝发阿耨多罗三藐三菩提心，求菩萨行，已得如是大功德故。

“善男子，如汝所问：菩萨云何学菩萨行、修菩萨道？善男子，汝可入此毗卢遮那庄严藏大楼阁中周遍观察，则能了知学菩萨行，学已成就无量功德。”

大方广佛华严经卷第七十九

入法界品第三十九之二十

尔时，善财童子恭敬右绕弥勒菩萨摩诃萨已，而白之言：“唯愿大圣开楼阁门，令我得入！”

时，弥勒菩萨前诣楼阁，弹指出声，其门即开，命善财入。善财心喜，入已还闭。

见其楼阁广博无量同于虚空，

Son of Good Family, just as vajra cannot be burned up or even made to become hot by any fire, so too it is with the bodhi resolve, for it cannot be burned up and cannot even be made to become hot by any of *saṃsāra*'s fires of the afflictions.

Son of Good Family, just as, within the worlds of the trichiliocosm, it is the vajra throne that is able to support all buddhas as they sit at the site of enlightenment, vanquish the *māras*, and attain the universal and right enlightenment, supporting what no other throne can support, so too it is with the throne of the bodhi resolve, for it is able to support all the bodhisattva's vows, practices, *pāramitās*, patiences, grounds, dedications, received predictions, cultivation of the provisions for the path, offerings to buddhas, listening to teachings on Dharma, absorbing them, practicing them, and all other things such as these that no other type of resolve is able to support.

Son of Good Family, the bodhi resolve enables the development of a measureless number, a boundless number, and so forth until we come to an ineffable-ineffable number of especially excellent meritorious qualities such as these. If any being arouses the resolve to attain *anuttara-samyak-saṃbodhi,* then he will acquire dharmas possessed of such supreme meritorious qualities as these.

Therefore, Son of Good Family, you have acquired such a fine benefit yourself and, having already resolved to attain *anuttara-samyak-saṃbodhi* and having sought the bodhisattva practices, you have also already acquired such great meritorious qualities as these.

Son of Good Family, as for your question about how a bodhisattva should train in the bodhisattva practices and how he should cultivate the bodhisattva path, Son of Good Family, you may now enter into this tower of the Chamber of Vairocana's Adornments and look all around in it. If you do so, you will then be able to completely understand how to train in the bodhisattva practices and how one who has trained in them perfects countless meritorious qualities.

Then, having finished respectfully circumambulating Maitreya Bodhisattva-mahāsattva with his right side facing him, Sudhana the Youth addressed him, saying, "I wish only that the Great Ārya would please open the tower door and allow me to enter."

Thereupon, Maitreya Bodhisattva approached the front of the tower and snapped his fingers, making a sound. The door immediately opened and he told Sudhana to enter. Sudhana was overjoyed.

After he entered, the door closed again and he saw that the interior of the palace was as measurelessly vast as empty space. [He saw that]

正體字

阿僧祇寶以為其地。阿僧
435a05 祇宮殿。阿僧祇門[1]闥。阿僧祇窓牖。阿僧祇
435a06 階陛。阿僧祇欄楯。阿僧祇道路。皆七寶成。阿
435a07 僧祇幡。阿僧祇幢。阿僧祇蓋。周迴間列。阿僧
435a08 祇眾寶[2]瓔珞。阿僧祇真珠[*]瓔珞。阿僧祇赤
435a09 真珠[*]瓔珞。阿僧祇師子珠瓔珞。處處垂下。
435a10 阿僧祇半月。阿僧祇繒帶。阿僧祇寶網以為
435a11 嚴飾。阿僧祇寶鐸風動成音。散阿僧祇天諸
435a12 雜華。懸阿僧祇天寶鬘帶。嚴阿僧祇眾寶香
435a13 [3]爐。雨阿僧祇細末金屑。懸阿僧祇寶鏡。然
435a14 阿僧祇寶燈。布阿僧祇寶衣。列阿僧祇寶帳。
435a15 設阿僧祇寶坐。阿僧祇寶繒以敷座上。阿僧
435a16 祇閻浮檀金童女像。阿僧祇雜寶諸形像。阿
435a17 僧祇妙寶菩薩像。處處充遍。阿僧祇眾鳥出
435a18 和雅音。阿僧祇寶優鉢羅華。阿僧祇寶波頭
435a19 摩華。阿僧祇寶拘物頭華。阿僧祇寶芬陀利
435a20 華。以為莊嚴。阿僧祇寶樹次第行列。阿僧
435a21 祇摩尼寶放大光明。如是等無量阿僧祇諸
435a22 莊嚴具。以為莊嚴。[4]又見其中。有無量百千
435a23 諸妙樓閣。一一嚴飾悉如上說。廣博嚴麗。皆
435a24 同虛空。不相障礙亦無雜亂。善財童子。於
435a25 一處中見一切處。一切諸處悉如是見。爾時
435a26 善財童子。見毘盧遮那莊嚴藏樓閣如是種
435a27 種不可思議自在境界。生大歡喜。踊躍無量。
435a28 身心柔軟。離一切想。除一切障。

简体字

阿僧祇宝以为其地；阿僧祇宫殿、阿僧祇门闼、阿僧祇窗牖、阿僧祇阶陛、阿僧祇栏楯、阿僧祇道路，皆七宝成；阿僧祇幡、阿僧祇幢、阿僧祇盖，周回间列；阿僧祇众宝璎珞、阿僧祇真珠璎珞、阿僧祇赤真珠璎珞、阿僧祇师子珠璎珞，处处垂下；阿僧祇半月、阿僧祇缯带、阿僧祇宝网，以为严饰；阿僧祇宝铎风动成音，散阿僧祇天诸杂华，悬阿僧祇天宝鬘带，严阿僧祇众宝香炉，雨阿僧祇细末金屑，悬阿僧祇宝镜，燃阿僧祇宝灯，布阿僧祇宝衣，列阿僧祇宝帐，设阿僧祇宝坐，阿僧祇宝缯以敷座上；阿僧祇阎浮檀金童女像、阿僧祇杂宝诸形像、阿僧祇妙宝菩萨像，处处充遍；阿僧祇众鸟出和雅音；阿僧祇宝优钵罗华、阿僧祇宝波头摩华、阿僧祇宝拘物头华、阿僧祇宝芬陀利华，以为庄严；阿僧祇宝树次第行列，阿僧祇摩尼宝放大光明。如是等无量阿僧祇诸庄严具，以为庄严。又见其中，有无量百千诸妙楼阁，一一严饰悉如上说；广博严丽皆同虚空，不相障碍亦无杂乱。善财童子于一处中见一切处，一切诸处悉如是见。

尔时，善财童子见毗卢遮那庄严藏楼阁如是种种不可思议自在境界，生大欢喜，踊跃无量，身心柔软，离一切想，除一切障，

there were *asaṃkhyeyas* of jewels that formed its grounds and there were *asaṃkhyeyas* of palaces, *asaṃkhyeyas* of gateways, *asaṃkhyeyas* of windows, *asaṃkhyeyas* of stairways, *asaṃkhyeyas* of railings, *asaṃkhyeyas* of paths made of the seven precious things, *asaṃkhyeyas* of pennants, *asaṃkhyeyas* of banners, *asaṃkhyeyas* of canopies in encircling arrays, *asaṃkhyeyas* of necklaces strung with the many kinds of jewels, *asaṃkhyeyas* of necklaces made from real pearls, *asaṃkhyeyas* of necklaces made from red-colored real pearls, *asaṃkhyeyas* of lion-pearl necklaces that hung down in place after place, *asaṃkhyeyas* of half-moons, *asaṃkhyeyas* of silken sashes, *asaṃkhyeyas* of jeweled nets serving as adornments, *asaṃkhyeyas* of jeweled bells that sounded in response to breezes, scatterings of *asaṃkhyeyas* of the various celestial flower blossoms, hangings of *asaṃkhyeyas* of celestial jewel-adorned garland sashes, adornments of *asaṃkhyeyas* of many-jeweled censors, rains of *asaṃkhyeyas* of finely-ground gold-dust, hangings of *asaṃkhyeyas* of jeweled mirrors, *asaṃkhyeyas* of burning jeweled lamps, drapes of *asaṃkhyeyas* of jeweled robes, arrays of *asaṃkhyeyas* of jeweled banners, arrangements of *asaṃkhyeyas* of jeweled seats, *asaṃkhyeyas* of jeweled silken cloth cushioning the thrones, *asaṃkhyeyas* of *jambūnada* gold figurines of young maidens, *asaṃkhyeyas* of all kinds of other figurines adorned with various jewels, rows of *asaṃkhyeyas* of bodhisattva images adorned with marvelous jewels that everywhere filled place after place, *asaṃkhyeyas* of many kinds of birds singing harmonious sounds, *asaṃkhyeyas* of jeweled *utpala* blossoms, *asaṃkhyeyas* of jeweled *padma* blossoms, *asaṃkhyeyas* of *kumuda* blossoms, *asaṃkhyeyas* of *puṇḍarīka* blossoms serving as adornments, *asaṃkhyeyas* of jeweled trees arranged in orderly rows, and *asaṃkhyeyas* of *maṇi* jewels emanating bright light. There were countless *asaṃkhyeyas* of adornments such as these that beautified the place.

He also saw within it countless hundreds of thousands of marvelous towers, each of which was adorned as just described. The adorned beauty of them all was as vast as space, yet they somehow did not interfere with each other. Sudhana saw all places in one place and saw all places in just this same way.

At that time when Sudhana saw in this Tower of the Treasury of Vairocana's Adornments all different kinds of inconceivable miraculous scenes such as these, he was filled with joyous delight and measureless exultation. As his body and mind became pliant, he abandoned all thought, became free of all obstacles, destroyed all

正體字

滅一切惑。所
435a29‖ 見不忘。所聞能憶。所思不亂。入於無礙解
435b01‖ 脫之門。普運其心。普見一切。普申敬禮。纔始
435b02‖ 稽首。以彌勒菩薩威神之力。自見其身。遍
435b03‖ 在一切諸樓閣中。具見種種不可思議自在
435b04‖ 境界。所謂或見彌勒菩薩。初發無上菩提心
435b05‖ 時。如是名字。如是種族。如是善友之所開悟。
435b06‖ [5]令其種植如是善根。住如是壽。在如是劫。
435b07‖ 值如是佛。處於如是莊嚴剎土。修如是行。發
435b08‖ 如是願。彼諸如來如是眾會。如是壽命。經爾
435b09‖ 許時。親近供養。悉皆明見。或見彌勒最初
435b10‖ 證得慈心三昧。從是已來。號為慈氏。或見彌
435b11‖ 勒修諸妙行。成滿一切諸波羅蜜。或見得忍。
435b12‖ 或見住地。或見成就清淨國土。或見護持如
435b13‖ 來正教。為大法師。得無生忍。某時某處。某如
435b14‖ 來所。受於無上菩提之記。或見彌勒為轉輪
435b15‖ 王勸[6]諸眾生。住十善道。[7]或為護世饒益眾
435b16‖ 生。或為釋天呵責五欲。或為焰摩天王讚不
435b17‖ 放逸。

简体字

灭一切惑，所见不忘，所闻能忆，所思不乱，入于无碍解脱之门。普运其心，普见一切，普申敬礼，才始稽首，以弥勒菩萨威神之力，自见其身遍在一切诸楼阁中，具见种种不可思议自在境界。

所谓：或见弥勒菩萨初发无上菩提心时如是名字、如是种族，如是善友之所开悟，令其种植如是善根、住如是寿、在如是劫、值如是佛、处于如是庄严刹土、修如是行、发如是愿；彼诸如来如是众会、如是寿命，经尔许时亲近供养。——悉皆明见。

或见弥勒最初证得慈心三昧，从是已来，号为慈氏；或见弥勒修诸妙行，成满一切诸波罗蜜；或见得忍，或见住地，或见成就清净国土，或见护持如来正教，为大法师，得无生忍，某时、某处、某如来所受于无上菩提之记。

或见弥勒为转轮王，劝诸众生住十善道；或为护世，饶益众生；或为释天，呵责五欲；或为焰摩天王，赞不放逸；

delusions, never forget anything he saw, remembered all that he heard, was never disordered in thought, entered into the gateways of unimpeded liberation, transported his mind to all places, and everywhere saw all things, whereupon he bowed down, directing his reverence everywhere.

Just as he lowered his head to the ground, due to Maitreya Bodhisattva's awesome spiritual powers, he saw his own body everywhere in all those towers and saw in their entirety all those different kinds of inconceivable miraculous scenes. In particular:

In one of those scenes, he saw Maitreya Bodhisattva when he first resolved to attain the unexcelled bodhi and saw too that he had this particular name, that he came from this particular clan, that he was awakened by this particular good spiritual guide who caused him to plant these particular roots of goodness, that he remained for the duration of this particular life span, that, in this particular kalpa, he met this particular buddha, that he dwelt in this particular adorned *kṣetra,* that he cultivated these particular practices, that he made these particular vows, that in the congregations of these particular *tathāgatas,* he had these particular life spans and passed through this particular length of time during which he drew near to and made offerings to them. In all these cases, he clearly saw all these matters.

In another of those scenes, he saw Maitreya at that very time when he first attained the samādhi of kindness after which he was always known as Maitreya, or "the Kindly One."

In another, he saw Maitreya cultivating the marvelous practices by which he fulfilled the *pāramitās.*

In another, he saw him acquiring the various types of patience.

In another, he saw him dwelling on the grounds.

In yet another scene, he saw him creating a pure land.

In yet another, he saw him guarding and preserving the Tathāgata's right teachings, serving as a great master of the Dharma, realizing the unproduced-dharmas patience, and, at this particular time, in this particular place, and in the congregation of this particular *tathāgata,* he saw him receiving the prediction that he would attain the unexcelled enlightenment.

In another, he saw Maitreya serving as a wheel-turning king encouraging beings to abide in the ten paths of good karmic action.

In another, he saw him as a world-protector benefiting beings.

In another, he saw him serving as Indra inveighing against pursuit of the five types of sensual pleasures.

In yet another scene, he saw him as a Yama Heaven deva king praising the avoidance of neglectfulness.

正體字

或為兜率天王稱歎一生菩薩功德。或
435b18‖ 為化樂天王。為諸天眾。現諸菩薩。變化莊嚴。
435b19‖ 或為他化自在天王。為諸天眾演說一切諸
435b20‖ 佛之法。或作魔王說一切法皆悉無常。或為
435b21‖ 梵王說諸禪定無量喜樂。或為[8]阿脩羅王入
435b22‖ 大智海。了法如幻。為其眾會常演說法。斷除
435b23‖ 一切憍慢醉傲。或復見其處閻羅界放大光
435b24‖ 明救地獄苦。或見在於餓鬼之處。施諸飲食
435b25‖ 濟彼飢渴。或見在於畜生之道。種種方便調
435b26‖ 伏眾生。或復見為護世天王眾會說法。或復
435b27‖ 見為忉利天王眾會說法。[9]或復見為焰摩天
435b28‖ 王眾會說法。或復見為兜率天王眾會說法。
435b29‖ 或復見為化樂天王眾會說法。或復見為他
435c01‖ 化自在天王眾會說法。或復見為大梵王眾
435c02‖ 會說法。或復見為龍王眾會說法。或復見為
435c03‖ 夜叉羅剎王眾會說法。

简体字

或为兜率天王，称叹一生菩萨功德；或为化乐天王，为诸天众现诸菩萨变化庄严；或为他化自在天王，为诸天众演说一切诸佛之法；或作魔王，说一切法皆悉无常；或为梵王，说诸禅定无量喜乐；或为阿修罗王，入大智海，了法如幻，为其众会常演说法，断除一切憍慢醉傲。

或复见其处阎罗界，放大光明，救地狱苦；或见在于饿鬼之处，施诸饮食，济彼饥渴；或见在于畜生之道，种种方便，调伏众生。

或复见为护世天王众会说法，或复见为忉利天王众会说法，或复见为焰摩天王众会说法，或复见为兜率天王众会说法，或复见为化乐天王众会说法，或复见为他化自在天王众会说法，或复见为大梵王众会说法，或复见为龙王众会说法，或复见为夜叉、罗刹王众会说法，

In yet another, he saw him as a Tuṣita Heaven king praising the qualities of the bodhisattva on the verge of his last incarnation.

In another, he saw him as a Sunirmita Heaven king manifesting for the celestial congregation the bodhisattva's supernatural emanation of adornments.

In another, he saw him as a Paranirmita Vaśavartin Heaven king expounding the Dharma of all buddhas to the celestial congregation.

In another, he saw him serving as a king of the *māras* teaching the complete impermanence of all dharmas.

In yet another scene, he saw him serving as a Brahma Heaven king teaching about the measureless joy and bliss of the *dhyāna* absorptions.

In yet another, he saw him serving as an *asura* king entering the ocean of great wisdom, comprehending dharmas as like mere illusions, forever expounding the Dharma for his congregation as he instructed them in the severance of arrogance and intoxication with self-pride.

In another, he saw him in Yama's realm, emanating an immense radiance that rescued beings from the sufferings of the hells.

In another, he saw him in the realm of the hungry ghosts, providing them with drink and food, thus rescuing them from their hunger and thirst.

In another, he saw him in the realm of the animals, using various skillful means to train those beings.

In yet another scene, he saw him teaching the Dharma for the congregation of a king of the World-Protecting devas.

In yet another, he saw him teaching the Dharma for the congregation of the king of the Trāyastriṃśa Heaven.

In another, he saw him teaching the Dharma for the congregation of the king of the Yama Heaven.

In another, he saw him teaching the Dharma for the congregation of the king of the Tuṣita Heaven.

In another, he saw him teaching the Dharma for the congregation of the king of the Nirmāṇarati Heaven.

In yet another scene, he saw him teaching the Dharma for the congregation of the king of the Paranirmita Vaśavartin Heaven.

In yet another, he saw him teaching the Dharma for the congregation of the king of the Great Brahma Heaven.

In another, he saw him teaching the Dharma for the congregation of a king of the dragons.

In another, he saw him teaching the Dharma for the congregations of the kings of the *yakṣas* and *rākṣasas*.

正體字

或復見為乾闥婆緊
435c04‖ 那羅王眾會說法。或復見為阿脩羅陀那婆
435c05‖ 王眾會說法。或復見為迦樓羅摩睺羅伽王
435c06‖ 眾會說法。或復見為其餘一切人非人等眾
435c07‖ 會說法。或復見為聲聞眾會說法。或復見為
435c08‖ 緣覺眾會說法。或復見為初發心乃至一生
435c09‖ 所繫已灌頂者諸菩薩眾。而演說法。[10]或見讚
435c10‖ 說初地乃至十地所有功德。或見讚說滿足
435c11‖ 一切諸波羅蜜。或見讚說入諸忍門。或見讚
435c12‖ 說諸大三昧門。或見讚說甚深解脫門。或見
435c13‖ 讚說諸禪三昧神通境界。或見讚說諸菩薩
435c14‖ 行。或見讚說諸大誓願。或見與諸同行菩薩。
435c15‖ 讚說世間資生工巧種種方便利眾生事。或
435c16‖ 見與諸一生菩薩。讚說一切佛灌頂門。或見
435c17‖ 彌勒於百千年。經行讀誦書寫經卷。勤求觀
435c18‖ 察為眾說法。[11]或入諸禪四無量心。

简体字

或复见为乾闼婆、紧那罗王众会说法，或复见为阿修罗、陀那婆王众会说法，或复见为迦楼罗、摩睺罗伽王众会说法，或复见为其余一切人非人等众会说法，或复见为声闻众会说法，或复见为缘觉众会说法，或复见为初发心乃至一生所系已灌顶者诸菩萨众而演说法。

或见赞说初地乃至十地所有功德，或见赞说满足一切诸波罗蜜，或见赞说入诸忍门，或见赞说诸大三昧门，或见赞说甚深解脱门，或见赞说诸禅三昧神通境界，或见赞说诸菩萨行，或见赞说诸大誓愿，或见与诸同行菩萨赞说世间资生工巧种种方便利众生事，或见与诸一生菩萨赞说一切佛灌顶门。

或见弥勒于百千年，经行、读诵、书写经卷，勤求观察，为众说法，或入诸禅四无量心，

In another, he saw him teaching the Dharma for the congregations of the kings of the *gandharvas* and *kiṃnaras*.

In yet another scene, he saw him teaching the Dharma for the congregations of the kings of the *asuras* and *dānavats*.[44]

In yet another, he saw him teaching the Dharma for the congregations of the kings of the *garuḍas* and *mahoragas*.

In another, he saw him teaching the Dharma for the congregations of other kinds of human and non-human beings.

In another, he saw him teaching the Dharma for congregations of *śrāvaka* disciples.

In another, he saw him teaching the Dharma for congregations of *pratyekabuddhas*.

In yet another scene, he saw him teaching the Dharma for congregations of bodhisattvas ranging from those who have just made their initial resolve all the way up to those who, having already received the crown-anointing consecration, have but one remaining incarnation prior to buddhahood.

In yet another, he saw him praising the meritorious qualities of bodhisattvas from the first ground to the tenth ground.

In another, he saw him praising the complete fulfillment of all the *pāramitās*.

In another, he saw him praising entry into the gateways of the various types of patience.

In another, he saw him praising the gateways leading into all the great samādhis.

In yet another scene, he saw him praising the gateway of the extremely profound liberations.

In yet another, he saw him praising the spheres of experience of all the *dhyāna* samādhis and spiritual superknowledges.

In another, he saw him praising all the bodhisattva practices.

In another, he saw him praising all the great vows.

In another, he saw him together with bodhisattvas pursuing the same practices, praising all life-supporting skills and the various methods for benefiting beings.

In yet another scene, he saw him together with bodhisattvas having but one incarnation prior to buddhahood, praising the crown-anointing gateway of all buddhas.

In yet another, he saw Maitreya across the course of a hundred thousand years engaged in the practices of meditative walking, studying, reciting, writing out sutra scrolls, diligently pursuing meditative contemplations, and teaching the Dharma for congregations.

In another, he saw him entering the *dhyāna* absorptions and the four measureless minds.

正體字

或入遍處
435c19‖ 及諸解脫。或入三昧以方便力現諸神變。或
435c20‖ 見諸菩薩入變化三昧。各於其身一一毛孔。
435c21‖ 出於一切變化身雲。或見出天眾身雲。或見
435c22‖ 出龍眾身雲。或見出夜叉乾闥婆緊那羅阿
435c23‖ 脩羅迦樓羅摩睺羅伽。釋梵護世轉輪聖王
435c24‖ 小王王子大臣官屬長者居士身雲。或見出
435c25‖ 聲聞緣覺及諸菩薩如來身雲。或見出一切
435c26‖ 眾生身雲。或見出妙音讚諸菩薩種種法門。
435c27‖ [12]所謂讚說菩提心功德門。讚說檀波羅蜜乃
435c28‖ 至智波羅蜜功德門。讚說諸攝諸禪。諸無量
435c29‖ 心。及諸三昧。三摩鉢底。諸通諸明。總持辯
436a01‖ 才。諸諦諸智。止觀解脫。諸緣諸依。諸說法
436a02‖ 門。讚說念處正勤。神足根力。七菩提分。八聖
436a03‖ 道分。諸聲聞乘。諸獨覺乘。諸菩薩乘。諸地諸
436a04‖ 忍。諸行諸願。如是等一切諸功德門。

简体字

或入遍处及诸解脱，或入三昧以方便力现诸神变。

或见诸菩萨入变化三昧，各于其身一一毛孔，出于一切变化身云；或见出天众身云，或见出龙众身云，或见出夜叉、乾闼婆、紧那罗、阿修罗、迦楼罗、摩睺罗伽、释、梵、护世、转轮圣王、小王、王子、大臣、官属、长者、居士身云，或见出声闻、缘觉及诸菩萨、如来身云，或见出一切众生身云。

或见出妙音，赞诸菩萨种种法门。所谓：赞说菩提心功德门；赞说檀波罗蜜乃至智波罗蜜功德门；赞说诸摄、诸禅、诸无量心，及诸三昧、三摩钵底、诸通、诸明、总持、辩才、诸谛、诸智、止观、解脱、诸缘、诸依、诸说法门；赞说念、处、正勤、神足、根、力、七菩提分、八圣道分、诸声闻乘、诸独觉乘、诸菩萨乘、诸地、诸忍、诸行、诸愿，如是等一切诸功德门。

In another, he saw him entering the universal bases meditations[45] and the liberations.

In another, he saw him entering samādhis and using the power of skillful means to manifest all kinds of spiritual transformations.

In other scenes, he saw all the bodhisattvas entering the transformational samādhis in which each of them emanated from every one of their pores clouds of all kinds of transformation bodies.

In some instances, he saw them emanating clouds of deva body congregations.

In other instances, he saw them emanating clouds of dragon body congregations.

In yet other instances, he saw them emanating clouds of the bodies of *yakṣas, gandharvas, kiṃnaras, asuras, garuḍas, mahoragas,* Indras, Brahma Heaven kings, world-protectors, wheel-turning sage kings, lesser kings, princes, great officials, subordinate officials, elders, and householders.

In other instances, he saw them emanating clouds of bodies of *śrāvaka* disciples, *pratyekabuddhas,* bodhisattvas, and *tathāgatas.*

In other instances, he saw them emanating clouds of the bodies of all kinds of beings.

In yet other scenes, he saw him emanating marvelous voices praising the many different Dharma gateways of the bodhisattvas, in particular:

He praised the gateways to the meritorious qualities of the bodhi resolve;

He praised the gateways to the meritorious qualities of *dāna pāramitā* and the others up to and including the *pāramitā* of knowledge;

He praised the gateways [to the meritorious qualities] of the means of attraction, the *dhyāna* absorptions, the measureless minds, the samādhis, the *samāpattis,* the superknowledges, the clear knowledges, the complete-retention *dhāraṇīs,* the types of eloquence, the truths, the types of knowledge, calming-and-contemplation, the liberations, conditioned origination, the reliances, and teaching Dharma; and

He praised the gateways to the meritorious qualities of the stations of mindfulness, the right efforts, the foundations of psychic power, the roots, the powers, the seven enlightenment factors, the eightfold path of the *āryas,* the *śrāvaka*-disciple vehicle, the *pratyekabuddha* vehicle, the bodhisattva vehicle, the grounds, the various types of patience, the practices, the vows, and all other such gateways to the meritorious qualities as these.

正體字

或復於
436a05‖ 中。見諸如來大眾圍遶。亦見其佛生處種姓
436a06‖ 身形壽命。剎劫名號。說法利益。教住久近。乃
436a07‖ 至所有道場眾會。種種不同。悉皆明見。又
436a08‖ 復於彼莊嚴藏內諸樓閣中。見一樓閣高廣
436a09‖ 嚴飾最上無比。於中悉見三千世界百億四
436a10‖ 天下百億兜率陀天。一一皆有彌勒菩薩。降
436a11‖ 神誕生。釋梵天王。捧持頂戴。遊行七步。觀察
436a12‖ 十方。大師子吼。現為童子。居處宮殿。遊戲園
436a13‖ 苑。為一切智。出家苦行。示受乳糜。往詣道
436a14‖ 場。降伏諸魔。成等正覺。觀菩提樹。梵王勸
436a15‖ 請。轉正法輪。[1]昇天宮殿。而演說法。劫數壽
436a16‖ 量。眾會莊嚴。所淨國土。[2]所修行願。教化成
436a17‖ 熟眾生方便。分布舍利。住持教法。皆悉不同
436a18‖ 爾時善財。自見其身。在彼一切諸如來所。亦
436a19‖ 見於彼一切眾會一切佛事。憶持不忘。通達
436a20‖ 無礙。

简体字

或复于中，见诸如来，大众围绕；亦见其佛生处、种姓、身形、寿命、刹劫、名号、说法利益、教住久近，乃至所有道场众会种种不同，悉皆明见。

又复于彼庄严藏内诸楼阁中，见一楼阁，高广严饰，最上无比；于中悉见三千世界百亿四天下、百亿兜率陀天，一一皆有弥勒菩萨降神诞生、释梵天王捧持顶戴、游行七步、观察十方、大师子吼、现为童子、居处宫殿、游戏园苑、为一切智出家苦行、示受乳糜、往诣道场、降伏诸魔、成等正觉、观菩提树、梵王劝请转正法轮、升天宫殿而演说法、劫数寿量、众会庄严、所净国土、所修行愿、教化成熟众生方便、分布舍利、住持教法，皆悉不同。

尔时，善财自见其身，在彼一切诸如来所；亦见于彼一切众会、一切佛事，忆持不忘，通达无碍。

In yet another scene, he saw *tathāgatas* surrounded by immense congregations and also saw those buddhas' birthplaces, clan origins, physical appearances, life spans, *kṣetras,* kalpas, buddha names, the benefits brought about by their proclamation of the Dharma, the duration, whether long or short, of their teachings, and so forth, including all of the many different kinds of differences in all their congregations.

He clearly saw all of these various phenomena.

In addition, within that Tower of the Treasury of Adornments, in the midst of all those towers within it, he saw one particular tower the height, breadth, and adornments of which were unsurpassed and peerless. Within it, he could see into the hundred *koṭīs* of Tuṣita Heavens of the trichiliocosm's hundred *koṭīs* of four-continent arrays.

Within every one of those Tuṣita Heavens, he saw Maitreya Bodhisattva descending to take birth where:

He was reverently raised above the heads of the deva kings, Indra and Brahmā;

He walked seven steps, surveyed the ten directions, and roared the lion's roar;

He manifested life as a youth who dwelt in the palace and roamed about, sporting in its gardens;

For the sake of gaining all-knowledge, he left the householder's life and took up the practice of austerities;

He manifested the appearance of accepting the offering of milk-rice;

He then went forth to the site of enlightenment;

He vanquished the *māras* and realized right enlightenment;

He contemplated the bodhi tree;

The Brahma Heaven King entreated him to turn the wheel of right Dharma; and

He then ascended to the heavenly palaces where he then proceeded to expound on the Dharma.

In all these instances, there were differences in the number of kalpas, life spans, congregations, adornments, lands that were purified, practices and vows that were cultivated, the skillful means used in teaching and ripening beings, the distribution of *śarīra* relics, and the duration of their teachings.

At that time, Sudhana saw his own body in the presence of all those *tathāgatas* as he also saw all the buddha works occurring in all those congregations, all of which he bore in mind, never forgot, and fathomed with unimpeded understanding. Moreover:

正體字

復聞一切諸樓閣內。寶網鈴鐸及諸樂
436a21‖ 器。皆悉演暢不可思議微妙法音。說種種法。
436a22‖ [3]所謂或說菩薩發菩提心。或說修行波羅蜜
436a23‖ 行。或說諸願。或說諸地。或說恭敬供養如來。
436a24‖ 或說莊嚴諸佛國土。或說諸佛說法差別。如
436a25‖ 上所說一切佛法。悉聞其音敷暢辯了。又聞
436a26‖ 某處。有某菩薩。聞某法門。某善知識之所
436a27‖ 勸導發菩提心。於某劫某剎。某如來所。某
436a28‖ 大眾中。聞於某佛如是功德。發如是心。起
436a29‖ 如是願。種於如是廣大善根。經若干劫。修
436b01‖ 菩薩行。於爾許時。當成正覺。如是名號。如是
436b02‖ 壽量。如是國土。具足莊嚴。滿如是願。化如是
436b03‖ 眾。如是聲聞菩薩眾會。般涅槃後。正法住
436b04‖ 世。經爾許劫。利益如是無量眾生。或聞某處。
436b05‖ 有某菩薩。布施持戒。忍辱精進。禪定智慧。修
436b06‖ 習如是諸波羅蜜。或聞某處。有某菩薩。為求
436b07‖ 法故。棄捨王位及諸珍寶。妻子眷屬手足頭
436b08‖ 目。一切身分皆無所吝。或聞某處。有某菩
436b09‖ 薩。守護如來所說正法。

简体字

复闻一切诸楼阁内，宝网铃铎及诸乐器，皆悉演畅不可思议微妙法音，说种种法。所谓：或说菩萨发菩提心，或说修行波罗蜜行，或说诸愿，或说诸地，或说恭敬供养如来，或说庄严诸佛国土，或说诸佛说法差别。如上所说一切佛法，悉闻其音，敷畅辩了。

又闻某处，有某菩萨，闻某法门，某善知识之所劝导发菩提心，于某劫、某刹、某如来所、某大众中，闻于某佛如是功德，发如是心，起如是愿，种于如是广大善根；经若干劫修菩萨行，于尔许时当成正觉，如是名号，如是寿量，如是国土，具足庄严，满如是愿，化如是众，如是声闻、菩萨众会；般涅槃后，正法住世，经尔许劫，利益如是无量众生。

或闻某处，有某菩萨，布施、持戒、忍辱、精进、禅定、智慧，修习如是诸波罗蜜。或闻某处有某菩萨，为求法故，弃舍王位及诸珍宝、妻子、眷属、手、足、头、目，一切身分皆无所吝。或闻某处，有某菩萨，守护如来所说正法，

He also heard within all of those towers the ringing of the bells and chimes on their jeweled nets as well as the music resonating from their musical instruments, all of which everywhere proclaimed the sounds of the inconceivable and sublime Dharma and the many different teachings on Dharma. In particular, some spoke of the bodhisattva's making the resolve to attain bodhi, some spoke of the cultivation of the *pāramitās,* some spoke of the vows, some spoke of the grounds, some spoke of revering and making offerings to the *tathāgatas,* some spoke of the adornment of all buddha lands, and some spoke of the differences in the Dharma discourses of the various buddhas. In all such instances, he heard all those voices as they spread the sounds of their eloquent proclamations regarding all of the above-mentioned buddha dharmas.

He also heard voices proclaiming that, in a particular place, there was a particular bodhisattva who, having heard a particular Dharma gateway, was encouraged and guided by a particular good spiritual guide to resolve to attain bodhi, this in a particular kalpa, in a particular *kṣetra,* under a particular *tathāgata,* in the midst of a particular great congregation where he heard of the meritorious qualities of a particular buddha, aroused just such a resolve, made just such particular vows, planted just such vast roots of goodness, passed through just so very many kalpas during which he cultivated the bodhisattva practices and became bound to achieve right enlightenment at just such a particular time in which he was then known by this particular name, remained for the duration of this particular life span, completely adorned these particular lands, fulfilled these particular vows, taught these particular congregations, was attended upon by these particular assemblies of *śrāvaka* disciples and bodhisattvas, and, after his *parinirvāṇa,* his right Dharma remained in the world for this particular number of kalpas during which it benefited such a countless number of beings.

In other instances, he heard voices proclaiming that, in a particular place, there is a particular bodhisattva who engages in the practices of giving, moral virtue, patience, vigor, *dhyāna* meditation, and wisdom, cultivating *pāramitās* such as these.

In other instances, he heard voices proclaiming that, in a particular place, there is a particular bodhisattva who, in order to seek the Dharma, abandoned the royal throne, his precious jewels, his wife, his children, and his retinue, and was unstinting in his willingness to give up even his hands, feet, head, eyes, or other parts of his body.

In other instances, he heard voices proclaiming that, in a particular place, there is a particular bodhisattva who preserves and protects the right Dharma proclaimed by the Tathāgata and serves as

正體字

為大法師。廣行法
436b10║ 施。建法幢。吹法[4]螺。擊法鼓。雨法雨。造佛塔
436b11║ 廟。作佛形像。施諸眾生一切樂具。[5]或聞某
436b12║ 處。有某如來。於某劫中。成等正覺。如是國
436b13║ 土。如是眾會。如是壽命。說如是法。滿如是
436b14║ 願。教化如是無量眾生。善財童子。聞如是等
436b15║ 不可思議微妙法音。身心歡喜。柔軟悅[6]澤。
436b16║ 即得無量諸總持門。諸辯才門。諸禪諸忍。諸
436b17║ 願諸度。諸通諸明。及諸解脫。諸三昧門。又見
436b18║ 一切諸寶鏡中種種形像。所謂或見諸佛眾
436b19║ 會道場。或見菩薩眾會道場。或見聲聞眾會
436b20║ 道場。或見緣覺眾會道場。或見淨世界。或
436b21║ 見不淨世界。或見淨不淨世界。或見不淨淨
436b22║ 世界。或見有佛世界。或見無佛世界。或見
436b23║ 小世界。或見中世界。或見大世界。或見因
436b24║ 陀羅網世界。或見覆世界。或見仰世界。或見
436b25║ 平坦世界。或見地獄畜生餓鬼所住世界。或
436b26║ 見天人充滿世界。

简体字

为大法师，广行法施，建法幢，吹法蠡，击法鼓，雨法雨，造佛塔庙，作佛形像，施诸众生一切乐具。或闻某处，有某如来，于某劫中，成等正觉，如是国土，如是众会，如是寿命，说如是法，满如是愿，教化如是无量众生。

善财童子闻如是等不可思议微妙法音，身心欢喜，柔软悦怿，即得无量诸总持门、诸辩才门、诸禅、诸忍、诸愿、诸度、诸通、诸明，及诸解脱、诸三昧门。

又见一切诸宝镜中种种形像。所谓：或见诸佛众会道场，或见菩萨众会道场，或见声闻众会道场，或见缘觉众会道场，或见净世界，或见不净世界，或见净不净世界，或见不净净世界，或见有佛世界，或见无佛世界，或见小世界，或见中世界，或见大世界，或见因陀罗网世界，或见覆世界，或见仰世界，或见平坦世界，或见地狱、畜生、饿鬼所住世界，或见天人充满世界。

great master of the Dharma who extensively practices the giving of Dharma, erects the Dharma banner, blows the Dharma conch, beats the Dharma drum, rains down the Dharma rain, builds the Buddha's stupas and temples, creates images of the Buddha, and gives beings everything that makes them happy.

In other instances, he heard voices proclaiming that, in a particular place, there is a particular *tathāgata* who, during a particular kalpa, attained the universal and right enlightenment in this particular land where he was attended upon by this particular congregation and remained for this particular span of life, taught these particular dharmas, fulfilled these particular vows, and taught such a measureless number of beings.

Having heard the sound of inconceivable sublime dharmas such as these, Sudhana the Youth felt joyous delight in body and mind and was suffused with feelings of pliancy and contentment, whereupon he immediately acquired countless complete-retention *dhāraṇī* gateways, eloquence gateways, *dhyāna* absorptions, the various types of patience, vows, perfections, superknowledges, and clear cognitions as well as all kinds of liberations and samādhi gateways.

Further, he saw within all of those jeweled mirrors many different kinds of images, for example:

In some, he saw the congregations of buddhas;
In others, he saw the congregations of bodhisattvas;
In yet others, he saw the congregations of *śrāvaka* disciples;
In still others, he saw the congregations of *pratyekabuddhas*;
In some, he saw pure worlds;
In others, he saw impure worlds;
In yet others, he saw impure worlds with some pure aspects;
In still others, he saw pure worlds with some impure aspects;
In some, he saw worlds with buddhas;
In others, he saw worlds with no buddhas;
In yet others, he saw small worlds;
In still others, he saw intermediate-sized worlds;
In some, he saw immense worlds;
In others, he saw worlds with Indra's nets;
In yet others, he saw inverted worlds;
In still others, he saw upward-facing worlds;
In some, he saw level worlds;
In others, he saw worlds inhabited by hell-dwellers, animals, and hungry ghosts; and
In yet others, he saw worlds full of devas and humans.

正體字

於如是等諸世界中。見有
436b27 無數大菩薩眾。或行或坐。作諸事業。或起大
436b28 悲憐愍眾生。或造諸論利益世間。或受或持。
436b29 或書或誦。或問或答。三時懺悔。迴向發願。又
436c01 見一切諸寶柱中。放摩尼王大光明網。或青
436c02 或黃。或赤或白。或[7]玻瓈色。或水精色。或帝
436c03 青色。或虹霓色。或閻浮檀金色。或作一切
436c04 諸光明色。又見彼閻浮檀金童女。及眾寶像。
436c05 或以其手而執華雲。或執衣雲。或執幢幡。或
436c06 執鬘蓋。或持種種塗香末香。或持上妙摩尼
436c07 寶網。或垂金鎖。或[8]挂[9]瓔珞。或舉其臂捧莊
436c08 嚴具。或低其首垂摩尼冠。曲躬瞻仰目不暫
436c09 捨。又見彼真珠瓔珞。常出香水。具八功德。
436c10 瑠璃瓔珞百千光明。同時照[10]耀。幢幡網蓋如
436c11 是等物。一切皆以眾寶莊嚴。又復見彼優鉢
436c12 羅華。波頭摩華。拘物頭華。芬陀利華。各各生
436c13 於無量諸華。或大一手。或長一肘。或復縱
436c14 廣猶如車輪。一一華中。皆悉示現種種色像。
436c15 以為嚴飾。所謂男色像女色像。

简体字

于如是等诸世界中，见有无数大菩萨众，或行或坐作诸事业，或起大悲怜愍众生，或造诸论利益世间，或受或持，或书或诵，或问或答，三时忏悔，回向发愿。

又见一切诸宝柱中，放摩尼王大光明网，或青、或黄、或赤、或白、或玻璃色、或水精色、或帝青色、或虹霓色、或阎浮檀金色，或作一切诸光明色。

又见彼阎浮檀金童女及众宝像，或以其手而执华云，或执衣云，或执幢幡，或执鬘盖，或持种种涂香、末香，或持上妙摩尼宝网，或垂金锁，或挂璎珞，或举其臂捧庄严具，或低其首垂摩尼冠，曲躬瞻仰，目不暂舍。

又见彼真珠璎珞，常出香水，具八功德；琉璃、璎珞，百千光明，同时照耀；幢、幡、网、盖，如是等物，一切皆以众宝庄严。

又复见彼优钵罗华、波头摩华、拘物头华、芬陀利华，各各生于无量诸华，或大一手，或长一肘，或复纵广犹如车轮，一一华中皆悉示现种种色像以为严饰。所谓：男色像、女色像、

In worlds such as these, he saw that there were countless congregations of great bodhisattvas, some walking along and some sitting still as they engaged in various works in which some were arousing great compassion and sympathy for beings, others were composing treatises benefiting the world, yet others were receiving particular teachings, others were seeing to their preservation, others were writing them out, others were reciting them, others were asking about them, others were answering their questions, and yet others were engaged in repentances in all three periods of the day, in dedicating merit, and in making vows.

He also saw in all those jeweled pillars the emanation of a net of bright light issuing from the sovereign *maṇi* jewels, lights that shone forth as blue, or yellow, or red, or white, or as the color of crystal, as the color of water-essence crystal, as the color of sapphires, as the colors of the rainbow, as the color of *jambūnada* gold, or as all the colors of all these lights.

He also saw those figurines of maidens made of *jambūnada* gold together with images made of the many kinds of jewels. Some held flower clouds in their hands, others held robe clouds, others held banners and pennants, others held garlands and canopies, others held various kinds of perfumes and powdered incenses, others held supremely marvelous *maṇi* jewel nets, others held dangling chains made of gold, others held dangling strands of pearls, and still others raised their arms to offer up adornments or lowered their heads and let their *maṇi*-jewel crowns hang down, or, with their bodies humbly bent low, they gazed up in admiration, never letting their gaze look away for even a moment.

He also saw those necklaces of real pearls constantly emanating perfume possessed of eight qualities, saw crystal necklaces emanating a hundred thousand rays of light, all of them simultaneously shining with dazzling illumination, and saw banners, pennants, nets, canopies, and other such objects, all of which were adorned with many kinds of jewels.

He also saw those *udumbara* blossoms, *padma* flowers, *kusuma* flowers, and *puṇḍarīka* flowers, all of which in turn produced countless other flowers, some of which were the diameter of one's hand, some of which were a cubit in diameter, and some of which were as wide as a carriage wheel. Each one of those flowers displayed the images of many different types of forms which appeared there as adornments. For example, there were images of men, images of women, images

正體字

童男色像。童
436c16 | 女色像。釋梵護世。天龍夜叉。乾闥婆阿脩
436c17 | 羅。迦樓羅緊那羅。摩睺羅伽。聲聞緣覺。及諸
436c18 | 菩薩。如是一切眾生色像。皆悉合掌曲躬禮
436c19 | 敬。亦見如來結[11]跏趺坐。三十二相莊嚴其
436c20 | 身。又復見彼淨瑠璃地一一步間。現不思議
436c21 | 種種色像。所謂世界色像。菩薩色像。如來色
436c22 | 像。及諸樓閣莊嚴色像。又於寶樹枝葉華果。
436c23 | 一一事中。悉見種種半身色像。所謂佛半身
436c24 | 色像。菩薩半身色像。天龍夜叉。乃至護世。轉
436c25 | 輪聖王。小王王子。大臣官長。及以四眾半身
436c26 | 色像。其諸色像。或執華鬘。或執瓔珞。或持一
436c27 | 切諸莊嚴具。或有曲躬合掌禮敬。一心瞻仰
436c28 | 目不暫捨。或有讚歎。或入三昧。其身悉以相
436c29 | 好莊嚴。普放種種諸色光明。所謂金色光明。
437a01 | 銀色光明。珊瑚色光明。兜沙羅色光明。帝青
437a02 | 色光明。毘盧遮那寶色光明。一切眾寶色光
437a03 | 明。瞻波迦華色光明。又見諸樓閣半月像中。
437a04 | 出阿僧祇日月星宿種種光明。普照十方。又
437a05 | 見諸樓閣周迴四壁。一一步內。一切眾寶以
437a06 | 為莊嚴。一一寶中皆現彌勒曩劫修行。菩
437a07 | 薩道時。

简体字

童男色像、童女色像、释、梵、护世、天、龙、夜叉、乾闼婆、阿修罗、迦楼罗、紧那罗、摩睺罗伽、声闻、缘觉及诸菩萨。如是一切众生色像，皆悉合掌，曲躬礼敬。

亦见如来结跏趺坐，三十二相庄严其身。

又复见彼净琉璃地，一一步间，现不思议种种色像。所谓：世界色像、菩萨色像、如来色像及诸楼阁庄严色像。

又于宝树枝、叶、华、果一一事中，悉见种种半身色像。所谓：佛半身色像、菩萨半身色像，天、龙、夜叉，乃至护世、转轮圣王、小王、王子、大臣、官长，及以四众半身色像。其诸色像，或执华鬘，或执璎珞，或持一切诸庄严具；或有曲躬合掌礼敬，一心瞻仰，目不暂舍；或有赞叹，或入三昧。其身悉以相好庄严，普放种种诸色光明，所谓：金色光明、银色光明、珊瑚色光明、兜沙罗色光明、帝青色光明、毗卢遮那宝色光明、一切众宝色光明、瞻波迦华色光明。

又见诸楼阁半月像中，出阿僧祇日月星宿种种光明普照十方。

又见诸楼阁周回四壁，一一步内，一切众宝以为庄严。一一宝中，皆现弥勒曩劫修行菩萨道时，

of pure youths, images of pure maidens, images of Indra, Brahmā, world protectors, devas, dragons, *yakṣas, gandharvas, asuras, garuḍas, kiṃnaras, mahoragas, śrāvaka* disciples, *pratyekabuddhas,* and bodhisattvas, images of all kinds of beings such as these. Each of those images appeared with their palms pressed together and their bodies humbly bending forward in reverence.

He also saw *tathāgatas* sitting in the lotus posture, their bodies adorned with the thirty-two major marks.

He also saw that, with every step, the pure lapis lazuli grounds revealed many different kinds of inconceivable images: images of world systems, images of bodhisattvas, and images of *tathāgatas* as well as images of the various adornments of all those towers.

He also saw that in the branches, leaves, flowers, and fruit of those jeweled trees, in every one of those phenomena, there appeared busts of the many different kinds of images: images of busts of buddhas, images of busts of bodhisattvas, and images of busts of devas, dragons, *yakṣas,* and so forth, including busts of world protectors, wheel-turning sage kings, lesser kings, princes, great officials, ministers, and members of the fourfold community.

Some of them held flower garlands. Others held necklaces. Others held various adornments. Then again, there were those with their palms pressed together and their bodies humbly bending forward in reverence as they single-mindedly gazed up in admiration, never letting their gaze look away for even a moment. And yet others were offering up praises.

There were also others who were immersed in samādhi, their bodies fully adorned with the major marks and secondary signs as they everywhere emanated light rays of many different colors: gold-colored light rays, silver-colored light rays, coral-colored light rays, light rays the color of *tuṣāra* frost,[46] light rays the color of sapphires, light rays the color of *vairocana* jewels, light rays the color of many different jewels, and light rays the color of *campaka* flowers.

He also saw that the half-moon images on all the towers emanated *asaṃkhyeyas* of many different kinds of lights of the sun, the moon, and the constellations which everywhere illuminated the ten directions.

He also saw that, with each step all around all four walls of all those towers, there were adornments consisting of all the many different kinds of jewels. In each of those jewels were displayed scenes of Maitreya in previous kalpas when he was cultivating the bodhisattva path:

正體字

或施頭目。或施手足。脣舌牙齒。耳鼻
437a08║ 血肉。皮膚骨髓。乃至爪髮。如是一切悉皆
437a09║ 能捨。妻妾男女。城邑聚落。國土王位。隨其所
437a10║ 須盡皆施與。處牢獄者令得出離。被繫縛者
437a11║ 使其解脫。有疾病者為其救療。入邪徑者示
437a12║ 其正道。或為船師令度大海。或為馬王救[1]護
437a13║ 惡難。或為大仙善說諸論。或為輪王勸修十
437a14║ 善。或為醫王善療眾病。或孝順父母。或親
437a15║ 近善友。或作聲聞。或作緣覺。或作菩薩。或作
437a16║ 如來。教化調伏一切眾生。或為法師奉行佛
437a17║ 教。受持讀誦。如理思惟。立佛支提。作佛形
437a18║ 像。若自供養。若勸於他。塗香散華。恭敬禮
437a19║ 拜。如是等事相續不絕。或見坐於師子之座。
437a20║ 廣演說法。勸諸眾生。安住十善。一心歸向佛
437a21║ 法僧寶。受持五戒及八[2]齋戒。出家聽法。受
437a22║ 持讀誦。如理修行。乃至見於彌勒菩薩。百
437a23║ 千億那由他阿僧祇劫。修行諸度一切色像。

简体字

或施头目，或施手足、唇舌、牙齿、耳鼻、血肉、皮肤、骨髓乃至爪发，如是一切，悉皆能舍；妻妾、男女、城邑、聚落、国土、王位，随其所须，尽皆施与。处牢狱者，令得出离；被系缚者，使其解脱；有疾病者，为其救疗；入邪径者，示其正道。或为船师，令度大海；或为马王，救护恶难；或为大仙，善说诸论；或为轮王，劝修十善；或为医王，善疗众病；或孝顺父母，或亲近善友，或作声闻，或作缘觉，或作菩萨，或作如来，教化调伏一切众生；或为法师，奉行佛教，受持读诵，如理思惟，立佛支提，作佛形像，若自供养，若劝于他，涂香散华，恭敬礼拜。如是等事，相续不绝。或见坐于师子之座，广演说法，劝诸众生安住十善，一心归向佛、法、僧宝，受持五戒及八斋戒，出家听法，受持读诵，如理修行。

乃至见于弥勒菩萨，百千亿那由他阿僧祇劫，修行诸度一切色像；

In some, he was seen to give away his own head or eyes or to give away his own hands, feet, lips, tongue, teeth, ears, nose, blood, flesh, skin, bones, marrow, and so forth, including even his fingernails and hair, being able to relinquish all such things. His wives, consorts, sons, daughters, cities, towns, lands, and royal throne—whatever others needed, he gave it all.

[In yet others], he was seen to enable those dwelling in the hells to gain emancipation, to liberate those who were tied up in bondage, to cure those who were sick, or to show the path of right action to those who had entered the path of wrongdoing.

In still other cases, he was seen as a ship captain enabling beings to cross a great ocean.

In some, he was seen as a king of horses rescuing beings from terrible difficulties.

In others, he was seen as a great rishi skillfully explaining the treatises.

In yet others, he was seen as a wheel-turning king exhorting beings to cultivate the ten good karmic deeds.

In still others, he was seen as a physician king skilled in the treatment of many diseases.

In some, he was seen as practicing filial obedience to his parents.

In others, he was seen as drawing near to good spiritual guides.

In yet others, he was seen as a *śrāvaka* disciple, as a *pratyekabuddha,* or as a bodhisattva.

In others, he was seen as a *tathāgata* teaching and training all beings.

In yet others, he was seen as a master of the Dharma who was upholding the practice of the Buddha's teachings, absorbing and preserving them, studying them, reciting them, and contemplating them in accordance with principle while also establishing buddha *caityas* and making buddha images, making offerings himself or encouraging others to do so, presenting offerings of perfume incense, scattering flowers, and bowing down in reverence, continuously and incessantly doing deeds such as these.

In still others, he was seen sitting on the lion seat, extensively teaching the Dharma, exhorting beings to establish themselves in the ten good karmic deeds, to single-mindedly take the refuges in the jewels of the Buddha, the Dharma and the Sangha, to take and uphold the five precepts or the eight lay abstinence precepts,[47] to leave the home life, to listen to the Dharma, to accept and uphold it, to study and recite it, to cultivate the practices in accordance with their principles, and so forth, including seeing all kinds of images of Maitreya Bodhisattva's cultivation of all the perfections throughout hundreds of thousands of *koṭīs* of *nayutas* of *asaṃkhyeyas* of kalpas.

正體字

437a24 | 又見彌勒曾所承事諸善知識。悉以一切功
437a25 | 德莊嚴。亦見彌勒在彼一一善知識所。親近
437a26 | 供養受行其教。乃至住於灌頂之地。時諸知
437a27 | 識。告善財言。善來童子。汝觀此菩薩不思
437a28 | 議事。莫生疲厭
437a29 | 爾時善財童子。得不忘失憶念力故。得見十
437b01 | 方清淨眼故。得善觀察無礙智故。得諸菩薩
437b02 | 自在智故。得諸菩薩已。[3]入智地廣大解故。於
437b03 | 一切樓閣一一物中。悉見如是及餘無量不
437b04 | 可思議自在境界諸莊嚴事。譬如有人。於睡
437b05 | 夢中。見種種物。所謂城邑聚落。宮殿園苑。山
437b06 | 林河池。衣服飲食。乃至一切資生之具。[4]或
437b07 | 見自身父母兄弟。內外親屬。或見大海須彌
437b08 | 山王。乃至一切諸天宮殿。閻浮提等四天下
437b09 | 事。或見其身形量廣大百千由旬。房舍衣服
437b10 | 悉皆相稱。謂於晝日經無量時不眠不寢受
437b11 | 諸安樂。從睡覺已乃知是夢。而能明記所見
437b12 | 之事。善財童子亦復如是。以彌勒菩薩力所
437b13 | 持故。

简体字

又见弥勒曾所承事诸善知识，悉以一切功德庄严；亦见弥勒在彼一一善知识所，亲近供养，受行其教，乃至住于灌顶之地。

时，诸知识告善财言：“善来童子！汝观此菩萨不思议事，莫生疲厌。”

尔时，善财童子得不忘失忆念力故，得见十方清净眼故，得善观察无碍智故，得诸菩萨自在智故，得诸菩萨已入智地广大解故，于一切楼阁一一物中，悉见如是及余无量不可思议自在境界诸庄严事。

譬如有人，于睡梦中见种种物，所谓：城邑、聚落、宫殿、园苑、山林、河池、衣服、饮食乃至一切资生之具；或见自身父母兄弟、内外亲属；或见大海须弥山王，乃至一切诸天宫殿、阎浮提等四天下事；或见其身形量广大百千由旬，房舍、衣服悉皆相称，谓于昼日经无量时不眠不寝受诸安乐。从睡觉已，乃知是梦，而能明记所见之事。善财童子亦复如是，以弥勒菩萨力所持故，

He also saw in them Maitreya's previous serving of all his good spiritual guides, all of whom were adorned with all the meritorious qualities.

And he also saw in those images Maitreya in the presence of each of those good spiritual guides as he was drawing near to them, making offerings to them, taking on the practice of their teachings, and so forth until he eventually dwelt on the ground of the crown-anointing consecration.

Then those good spiritual guides spoke directly to Sudhana, saying, "Welcome youth. As you observe this bodhisattva's inconceivable deeds, you must not allow yourself to feel weary."

It was because he had acquired the power of memory by which he never forgot anything, because he had acquired the purified eye that observes the ten directions, because he had acquired the unimpeded wisdom of skill in insight, because he had acquired sovereign mastery over the wisdom possessed by bodhisattvas, and because he had acquired the vast understanding of bodhisattvas who had already entered the wisdom grounds that Sudhana the Youth was then able to see in every object in these towers all such phenomena as these as well as the adorned phenomena of countless other inconceivable and miraculous spheres of experience.

It was just as a man might see many different kinds of things in a dream, seeing cities, towns, villages, palaces, parks, gardens, mountains, forests, rivers, ponds, and provisions such as robes, food, drink, and such, while also perhaps seeing himself, his parents, his siblings, his close and distant relatives, also perhaps seeing the great ocean, Sumeru, king of mountains, and so forth, including even the celestial palaces and all the phenomena present throughout Jambudvīpa and the other continents in the four-continent array, also seeing perhaps his own body assuming such vast dimensions that it came to encompass an area a hundred thousand *yojanas* in breadth, even as what he was seeing still completely matched the circumstances in his own room and in the very robes he was then wearing, all of this leading him to think that, in but a day, he had passed through a measurelessly long time in which he was experiencing peace and happiness without ever sleeping or lying down. Then, having finally awakened from his sleep, he then and only then would know that it was a dream even though he was still able to clearly remember all the phenomena he had seen [in that dream].

So too it was as experienced then by Sudhana the Youth. It was because he was supported by Maitreya Bodhisattva's powers, because

正體字

知三界法皆如夢故。[5]滅諸眾生狹劣
437b14‖ 想故。得無障礙廣大解故。住諸菩薩勝境界
437b15‖ 故。入不思議方便智故。能見如是自在境界。
437b16‖ 譬如有人將欲命終。見隨其業。所受報相。行
437b17‖ 惡業[6]者。見於地獄畜生餓鬼。所有一切眾
437b18‖ 苦境界。或見獄卒手持兵仗。或瞋或罵。囚
437b19‖ 執將去。亦聞號叫悲歎之聲。或見灰河。或見
437b20‖ 鑊湯。或見刀山。或見劍樹。種種逼迫受諸
437b21‖ 苦惱。作善業者。即見一切諸天宮殿。無量
437b22‖ 天眾天諸采女。種種衣服。具足莊嚴。宮殿
437b23‖ 園林。盡皆妙好。身雖未死。而由業力見如是
437b24‖ 事。善財童子亦復如是。以菩薩業不思議力。
437b25‖ 得見一切莊嚴境界。譬如有人為鬼所持。見
437b26‖ 種種事。隨其所問。悉皆能答。善財童子亦復
437b27‖ 如是。菩薩智慧之所持故。見彼一切諸莊嚴
437b28‖ 事。若有問者。靡不能答。譬如有人為龍所
437b29‖ 持。自謂是龍。入於龍宮。

简体字

知三界法皆如梦故，灭诸众生狭劣想故，得无障碍广大解故，住诸菩萨胜境界故，入不思议方便智故，能见如是自在境界。

譬如有人，将欲命终，见随其业所受报相：行恶业者，见于地狱、畜生、饿鬼所有一切众苦境界，或见狱卒手持兵仗或瞋或骂囚执将去，亦闻号叫、悲叹之声，或见灰河，或见镬汤，或见刀山，或见剑树，种种逼迫，受诸苦恼；作善业者，即见一切诸天宫殿无量天众、天诸采女，种种衣服具足庄严，宫殿、园林尽皆妙好。身虽未死，而由业力见如是事。善财童子亦复如是，以菩萨业不思议力，得见一切庄严境界。

譬如有人，为鬼所持，见种种事，随其所问，悉皆能答。善财童子亦复如是，菩萨智慧之所持故，见彼一切诸庄严事，若有问者，靡不能答。

譬如有人，为龙所持，自谓是龙，入于龙宫，

he had come to realize that the dharmas of the three realms of existence were like a dream, because he had extinguished the narrow and inferior conceptual thought typical of beings, because he had acquired an unimpededly vast understanding, because he had come to abide in the superior sphere of experience of a bodhisattva, and also because he had penetrated the knowledge of inconceivable methods that he was thus able to see such miraculous spheres of experience.

This is just as when a man who is approaching the end of his life sees in accordance with his karmic deeds the signs of the retribution he is about to receive.

Thus those who have engaged in evil karmic deeds see all kinds of scenes of the many different types of suffering experienced in the hell realms, the animal realms, and the realms of the hungry ghosts, sometimes seeing the hell guardians wielding their weapons, sometimes seeing them being wrathful or cursing as they put them in restraints and drag them away after which they hear the sounds of howling screams and pitiful sighing moans, sometimes seeing the river of hot coals, sometimes seeing the boiling cauldrons, sometimes seeing the mountain of knives, and sometimes seeing the sword trees, seeing all of these things along with their many different types of torments and the agonizing sufferings they inflict.

Those who have engaged in good karmic deeds then see all the heavenly palaces, the measureless congregations of devas, all kinds of celestial female attendants, and the various types of robes, all beautifully adorned. They also see palaces, parks, and groves, all of which are marvelously fine.

Although their bodies have not yet died, they still see phenomena such as these due to the power of their karmic deeds. So too it was then with Sudhana, for it was due to the inconceivable power of the bodhisattva's karmic deeds that he was able to see all these beautifully adorned spheres of experience.

This was just as when someone is possessed by a ghost and then sees many different kinds of phenomena so that, no matter what they are asked, they can answer accordingly. So too it was with Sudhana the Youth, for, due to being supported by the wisdom of the bodhisattva, he saw all of those adorned phenomena and, if anyone were to question him, there would be no question he could not answer.

This was just as when someone possessed by a dragon then thinks of himself as being a dragon and then enters the dragon palace, and,

正體字

於少時間。自謂已經
437c01‖ 日月年載。善財童子亦復如是。以住菩薩智
437c02‖ 慧想故。彌勒菩薩所加持故。於少時間謂無
437c03‖ 量劫。譬如梵宮[7]名莊嚴藏。於中悉見三千
437c04‖ 世界一切諸物。不相雜亂。善財童子亦[8]復
437c05‖ 如是。於樓觀中。普見一切莊嚴境界。種種差
437c06‖ 別不相雜亂。譬如比丘入遍處定。若行若住
437c07‖ 若坐若臥。隨所入定境界現前。善財童子亦
437c08‖ 復如是。入於樓觀。一切境界悉皆明了。譬
437c09‖ 如有人。於虛空中。見乾闥婆城具足莊嚴。悉
437c10‖ 分別知無有障礙。譬如夜叉宮殿與人宮殿。
437c11‖ 同在一處而不相雜。各隨其業所見不同。譬
437c12‖ 如大海於中悉見三千世界一切色像。譬如
437c13‖ 幻師以幻力故。現諸幻事種種作業。善財童
437c14‖ 子亦復如是。以彌勒菩薩威神力故。及不思
437c15‖ 議幻智力故。能以幻智知諸法故。得諸菩薩
437c16‖ 自在力故。見樓閣中一切莊嚴。自在境界
437c17‖ 爾時彌勒菩薩摩訶薩。即攝神力。入樓閣中。
437c18‖ 彈指作聲。告善財言。

简体字

于少时间，自谓已经日月年载。善财童子亦复如是，以住菩萨智慧想故，弥勒菩萨所加持故，于少时间谓无量劫。

譬如梵宫，名庄严藏，于中悉见三千世界一切诸物不相杂乱。善财童子亦复如是，于楼观中，普见一切庄严境界种种差别不相杂乱。

譬如比丘，入遍处定，若行、若住、若坐、若卧，随所入定，境界现前。善财童子亦复如是，入于楼观，一切境界悉皆明了。

譬如有人，于虚空中见乾闼婆城具足庄严，悉分别知，无有障碍；譬如夜叉宫殿与人宫殿，同在一处而不相杂，各随其业，所见不同；譬如大海，于中悉见三千世界一切色像；譬如幻师，以幻力故，现诸幻事种种作业。善财童子亦复如是，以弥勒菩萨威神力故，及不思议幻智力故，能以幻智知诸法故，得诸菩萨自在力故，见楼阁中一切庄严自在境界。

尔时，弥勒菩萨摩诃萨即摄神力入楼阁中，弹指作声，告善财言：

in but a short period of time, feels as if he has already passed through many days, months, and years. So too it was with Sudhana the Youth. Because he dwelt in the wise thought of a bodhisattva and because he was supported by Maitreya Bodhisattva, in but a short period of time, he felt as if he had already passed through countless kalpas.

This was also just as when, in the Brahma Heaven palace known as "Chamber of Adornments," one sees all things throughout the trichiliocosm without them being mixed up or confused with each other. So too it was with Sudhana the Youth, for within that tower, he saw all of the adorned realms everywhere in all their variety, none of which became mixed up or confused with any others.

This was also just as when a bhikshu who has entered into meditative absorption on one of the universal bases meditation objects[48] finds that, whether he is walking, standing, sitting, or lying down, the object of the absorption he has entered manifests directly before him. So too it was with Sudhana the Youth, for, when he entered that tower, all those objective spheres appeared before him with complete clarity.

This was also just as when someone sees the cities of the *gandharvas* in the sky, complete in all their adornments, all of which he is able to discern without any interference.

This was also just as when the palaces of the *yakṣas* and the palaces of humans exist together in the same place and yet they do not become mixed up with each other and what each of them sees differs in accordance with their respective karma.

This was also just as when one sees reflected on the surface of the great ocean everything throughout the trichiliocosm. It was also just as when a master conjurer is able to use his powers of conjuration to manifest the appearances of all kinds of illusory scenes and many different actions occurring in each of them. So too it was with Sudhana the Youth, for he was able to see within that tower all those adornments and independently observable scenes due to the awesome spiritual power of Maitreya Bodhisattva, due to the power of the inconceivable wisdom that realizes the illusory nature of phenomena, due to the ability to use the wisdom that realizes the illusory nature of dharmas, and due to having acquired the miraculous transformational powers of all bodhisattvas.

Maitreya Bodhisattva-mahāsattva then withdrew those spiritual powers, entered the tower, made a sound by snapping his fingers, and then spoke to Sudhana, saying:

正體字

善男子起。法性如是。
437c19‖ [9]此是菩薩知諸法智因緣聚集所現之相。如
437c20‖ 是自性。如幻如夢。如影如像。悉不成就。爾時
437c21‖ 善財。聞彈指聲。從三昧起。彌勒告言。善男
437c22‖ 子。汝住菩薩不可思議自在解脫。受諸菩薩
437c23‖ 三昧喜樂。能見菩薩神力所持。助道所流。願
437c24‖ 智所現。種種上妙莊嚴宮殿。見菩薩行。聞菩
437c25‖ 薩法。知菩薩德。了如來願。善財白言。唯然
437c26‖ 聖者。是善知識。加被憶念威神之力。聖者。此
437c27‖ 解脫門。其名何等。彌勒告言。善男子。此解脫
437c28‖ 門。名入三世一切境界不忘念智莊嚴藏。[10]善
437c29‖ 男子。此解脫門中。有不可說不可說解脫門。
438a01‖ 一生菩薩之所能得。善財問言。此莊嚴事。何
438a02‖ 處去耶。彌勒答言。於來處去。曰從何處來。曰
438a03‖ 從菩薩智慧神力中來。依菩薩智慧神力而
438a04‖ 住。無有去處。亦無住處。非集非常。遠離一
438a05‖ 切。善男子。如龍王降雨。不從身出

简体字

"善男子起！法性如是！此是菩萨知诸法智，因缘聚集所现之相，如是自性，如幻、如梦、如影、如像，悉不成就。"尔时，善财闻弹指声，从三昧起。

弥勒告言："善男子，汝住菩萨不可思议自在解脱，受诸菩萨三昧喜乐，能见菩萨神力所持、助道所流、愿智所现种种上妙庄严宫殿；见菩萨行，闻菩萨法，知菩萨德，了如来愿。"

善财白言："唯然！圣者，是善知识加被忆念威神之力。圣者，此解脱门，其名何等？"

弥勒告言："善男子，此解脱门，名入三世一切境界不忘念智庄严藏。善男子，此解脱门中，有不可说不可说解脱门，一生菩萨之所能得。"

善财问言："此庄严事，何处去耶？"

弥勒答言："于来处去。"

曰："从何处来？"

曰："从菩萨智慧神力中来，依菩萨智慧神力而住，无有去处，亦无住处，非集非常，远离一切。善男子，如龙王降雨，不从身出，

> Son of Good Family, arise. The nature of the Dharma is just thus. These are appearances manifested by the accumulation of causes and conditions associated with the bodhisattva's wisdom that knows all dharmas. The intrinsic nature of such phenomena is like an illusion, like a dream, like a reflection, and like an image, for none of them are actually established at all.

On hearing the sound of the snapping fingers, Sudhana emerged from samādhi. Maitreya then spoke to him, saying:

> Son of Good Family, you have been abiding in the bodhisattva's inconceivable and miraculous liberation, have been enjoying the joy and bliss of the bodhisattvas' samādhis, and have been able to see the various supremely marvelous adorned palaces sustained by bodhisattvas' spiritual powers that flow forth from the provisions for the path and that are manifested due to vows and wisdom. Hence you are able to see the practices of the bodhisattvas, are able to hear the Dharma of the bodhisattvas, are able to know the virtues of the bodhisattvas, and are able to completely understand the vows of the Tathāgata.[49]

Sudhana then addressed him, saying, "O Ārya, so it is. This has occurred through the power of the good spiritual guides' assistance, mindful attentiveness, and spiritual powers. O Ārya, what is the name of this gateway of liberation?"

Maitreya replied, saying, "Son of Good Family, this gateway of liberation is known as 'the treasury of adornments associated with the unforgetting mindfulness that enters the knowledge of all objects in the three periods of time.' Son of Good Family, within this gateway of liberation there are an ineffable-ineffable number of liberation gateways that the bodhisattva at the stage of but one more incarnation before buddhahood is capable of acquiring."

Sudhana then asked: "Where did these adornments go?"

Maitreya replied, "They went to the place from which they came."

Sudhana then asked, "Where then did they come from?"

Maitreya replied:

> They came forth from the bodhisattvas' wisdom and spiritual powers and they are sustained by the bodhisattvas' wisdom and spiritual powers. They have no place they go and no place they dwell. They are neither accumulated nor permanent and they transcend everything.
>
> Son of Good Family, it is just as when a dragon king sends down the rain, it does not come from his body, does not come from his

正體字

不從心出。
438a06║ 無有積集。而非不見。但以龍王心念力故。霈
438a07║ 然洪霔。周遍天下。如是境界不可思議。善男
438a08║ 子。彼莊嚴事亦復如是。不住於內。亦不住
438a09║ 外。而非不見。但由菩薩威神之力。汝善根
438a10║ 力。見如是事。[1]善男子。譬如幻師作諸幻事。
438a11║ 無所從來無所至去。雖無來去。以幻力故分
438a12║ 明可見。彼莊嚴事亦復如是。無所從來亦無
438a13║ 所去。雖無來去。然以慣習不可思議幻智力
438a14║ 故。及由往昔大願力故。如是顯現。善財童
438a15║ 子言。大聖。從何處來。彌勒言。善男子。諸菩
438a16║ 薩。無來無去。如是而來。無行無住。如是而
438a17║ 來。無處無著。不沒不生。不住不遷。不動不
438a18║ 起。無戀無著。無業無報。無起無滅。不斷不
438a19║ 常。如是而來。善男子。菩薩。從大悲處來。為
438a20║ 欲調伏諸眾生故。從大慈處來。為欲救護諸
438a21║ 眾生故。從淨戒處來。隨其所樂而受生故。從
438a22║ 大願處來。往昔願力之所持故。

简体字

不从心出，无有积集，而非不见；但以龙王心念力故，霈然洪霔，周遍天下，如是境界不可思议。善男子，彼庄严事亦复如是，不住于内，亦不住外，而非不见；但由菩萨威神之力、汝善根力，见如是事。善男子，譬如幻师作诸幻事，无所从来，无所至去；虽无来去，以幻力故，分明可见。彼庄严事亦复如是，无所从来，亦无所去；虽无来去，然以惯习不可思议幻智力故，及由往昔大愿力故，如是显现。”

善财童子言：“大圣从何处来？”

弥勒言：“善男子，诸菩萨无来无去，如是而来；无行无住，如是而来；无处无著，不没不生，不住不迁，不动不起，无恋无著，无业无报，无起无灭，不断不常，如是而来。善男子，菩萨从大悲处来，为欲调伏诸众生故；从大慈处来，为欲救护诸众生故；从净戒处来，随其所乐而受生故；从大愿处来，往昔愿力之所持故；

mind, and there is no process of accumulation, and yet it is not that one did not see it. It is solely due to the dragon king's power of thought that it pours down its vast torrential rains everywhere across the entire continent. A sphere of experience such as this is inconceivable.

Son of Good Family, so too it is with these adornments, for they do not exist inwardly, do not exist outwardly, and yet it is not that one does not see them. It is solely due to the awesome spiritual power of the bodhisattva and the power of your roots of goodness that you see phenomena such as these.

Son of Good Family, it is just as when a master conjurer creates all kinds of illusory conjurations, they have no place from which they come and no place to which they go, and yet, even though they have no coming or going, due to the power of that conjuration, one is able to clearly see them. So too it is with those adornments. They have no place from which they come and no place to which they go, yet, although they have no coming or going, still, due to repeated practice of the inconceivable powers of the knowledge of the illusory and also due to the power of great vows made in the distant past, appearances such as these are manifested.

Sudhana the Youth then asked: "O Great Ārya, where have you come from?"

Maitreya replied:

Son of Good Family, bodhisattvas have no coming and no going. Just so do they come. They have no moving and no stopping. Just so do they come. And, without residing and without attachment, without passing away and without taking rebirth, without dwelling and without moving thither, without motion and without origination, without affection and without attachment, without karmic actions and without karmic retributions, without arising and without cessation, and without any termination and without any permanence—just so do they come.

Son of Good Family, as for the bodhisattvas:

They come forth from the place of great compassion because they wish to train all beings;

They come forth from the place of great kindness because they wish to rescue and protect all beings;

They come forth from the place of pure moral virtue in order to take on births in whatever circumstance they please;

They come forth from the place of great vows because they are sustained by the power of vows they made in the distant past;

正體字

從神通處來。
438a23‖ 於一切處隨樂現故。[2]從無動搖處來。恒不捨
438a24‖ 離一切佛故。從無取捨處來。不役身心使往
438a25‖ 來故。從智慧方便處來。隨順一切諸眾生故。
438a26‖ 從示現變化處來。猶如影像而化現故。然善
438a27‖ 男子。汝問於我從何處來者。善男子。我從
438a28‖ 生處摩羅提國。而來於此。善男子。彼有聚落
438a29‖ 名為房舍。有長者子名瞿波羅。為化其人令
438b01‖ 入佛法。而住於彼。又為生處。一切人民。隨所
438b02‖ 應化。而為說法。亦為父母及諸眷屬婆羅門
438b03‖ 等。演說大乘。令其趣入故。住於彼。而從彼
438b04‖ 來。善財童子言。聖者。何者是菩薩生處。答
438b05‖ 言。善男子。菩薩有十種生處。何者為十。善男
438b06‖ 子。菩提心。是菩薩生處。生菩薩家故。深心。
438b07‖ 是菩薩生處。生善知識家故。諸地。是菩薩
438b08‖ 生處。生波羅蜜家故。大願。是菩薩生處。生妙
438b09‖ 行家故。大悲。是菩薩生處。生四攝家故。如理
438b10‖ 觀察。是菩薩生處。生般若波羅[3]蜜家故。大
438b11‖ 乘。是菩薩生處。生方便善巧家故。

简体字

从神通处来，于一切处随乐现故；从无动摇处来，恒不舍离一切佛故；从无取舍处来，不役身心使往来故；从智慧方便处来，随顺一切诸众生故；从示现变化处来，犹如影像而化现故。

“然，善男子，汝问于我从何处来者。善男子，我从生处摩罗提国而来于此。善男子，彼有聚落，名为房舍；有长者子，名瞿波罗。为化其人，令入佛法，而住于彼；又为生处一切人民随所应化而为说法，亦为父母及诸眷属、婆罗门等演说大乘，令其趣入故住于彼。而从彼来。”

善财童子言：“圣者，何者是菩萨生处？”

答言：“善男子，菩萨有十种生处。何者为十？善男子，菩提心是菩萨生处，生菩萨家故；深心是菩萨生处，生善知识家故；诸地是菩萨生处，生波罗蜜家故；大愿是菩萨生处，生妙行家故；大悲是菩萨生处，生四摄家故；如理观察是菩萨生处，生般若波罗蜜家故；大乘是菩萨生处，生方便善巧家故；

They come forth from the place of the spiritual superknowledges in order to appear in any place they please;

They come forth from the place of unshakability because they never leave all buddhas;

They come forth from the place of neither grasping nor rejecting because they do not order the body and mind to come or go;

They come forth from the place of wisdom and skillful means in order to adapt to all beings; and

They come forth from the place of transformational manifestations because they produce transformational appearances that are like reflected images.

Now, Son of Good Family, as for your question about where I came from, Son of Good Family, I came here from my birthplace in the state of Mālada. Son of Good Family, there is a village there known as Kuṭi where there is a son of an elder named Gopālaka. It was in order to teach that man and enable him to enter the Buddha's Dharma that I dwelt there. It was also to teach Dharma for the sake of everyone in my birthplace who was amenable to teaching. It was also in order to expound on the Great Vehicle for my parents as well as my relatives, the brahmans, and others with the aim of enabling them to enter it. That was why I dwelt there and then came here from there.

Sudhana the Youth then asked, "What is the birthplace of the bodhisattva?"

Maitreya replied:

Son of Good Family, the bodhisattva has ten kinds of birthplaces. What are those ten? Son of Good Family, they are as follows:

The bodhi resolve is the bodhisattva's birthplace because it enables his birth into the clan of the bodhisattvas;

Deep resolve is the bodhisattva's birthplace because it enables his birth into the clan of the good spiritual guides;

The grounds are the bodhisattva's birthplace because they enable his birth into the house of the *pāramitās*;

The great vows are the bodhisattva's birthplace because they enable his birth into the house of the marvelous practices;

The great compassion is the bodhisattva's birthplace because it enables his birth into the house of the four means of attraction;

Meditative contemplation in accordance with principle is the bodhisattva's birthplace because it enables his birth into the house of the *prajñāpāramitā*;

The Great Vehicle is the bodhisattva's birthplace because it enables his birth into the house of skillful means;

正體字

教化眾
438b12║ 生。是菩薩生處。生佛家故。智慧方便。是菩薩
438b13║ 生處。生無生法忍家故。修行一切法。是菩
438b14║ 薩生處。生過現未來一切如來家故。善男子。
438b15║ 菩薩摩訶薩。以般若波羅[*]蜜為母。方便善
438b16║ 巧為父。檀波羅[*]蜜為乳母。尸波羅[*]蜜為養
438b17║ 母。忍波羅[*]蜜為莊嚴具。勤波羅[*]蜜為養育
438b18║ 者。禪波羅[*]蜜為[4]澣濯人。善知識為教授師。
438b19║ 一切菩提分為伴侶。一切善法為眷屬。一切
438b20║ 菩薩為兄弟。菩提心為家。如理修行為家法。
438b21║ 諸地為家處。諸忍為家族。大願為家教。滿
438b22║ 足諸行為順家法。勸發大乘為紹家業。法水
438b23║ 灌頂一生所繫菩薩為王太子。成就菩提為
438b24║ 能淨家族。善男子。菩薩如是超凡夫地。入
438b25║ 菩薩位。生如來家。住佛種性。能修諸行。

简体字

教化众生是菩萨生处，生佛家故；智慧方便是菩萨生处，生无生法忍家故；修行一切法是菩萨生处，生过、现、未来一切如来家故。

“善男子，菩萨摩诃萨，以般若波罗蜜为母，方便善巧为父，檀波罗蜜为乳母，尸波罗蜜为养母，忍波罗蜜为庄严具，勤波罗蜜为养育者，禅波罗蜜为浣濯人，善知识为教授师，一切菩提分为伴侣，一切善法为眷属，一切菩萨为兄弟，菩提心为家，如理修行为家法，诸地为家处，诸忍为家族，大愿为家教，满足诸行为顺家法，劝发大乘为绍家业，法水灌顶一生所系菩萨为王太子，成就菩提为能净家族。

“善男子，菩萨如是超凡夫地，入菩萨位，生如来家，住佛种性，能修诸行，

The teaching of beings is the bodhisattva's birthplace because it enables his birth into the clan of the Buddha;

Wisdom and skillful means are the bodhisattva's birthplace because they enable his birth into the house of the unproduced-dharmas patience; and

The cultivation of all dharmas is the bodhisattva's birthplace because it enables his birth into the clan of all *tathāgatas* of the past, present, and future.

Son of Good Family, as for the bodhisattva-mahāsattva:

He takes the *prajñāpāramitā* as his mother;

He takes skillful means as his father;

He takes the *pāramitā* of giving as his wet nurse;

He takes the *pāramitā* of moral virtue as his nursemaid;

He takes the *pāramitā* of patience as his adornment;

He takes the *pāramitā* of vigor as the one that raises him;

He takes the *pāramitā* of meditation as the person who bathes him;

He takes the good spiritual guide as his master teacher;

He takes all the enlightenment factors as his companions;

He takes all good dharmas as his retinue;

He takes all the bodhisattvas as his brothers;

He takes the bodhi resolve as his clan;

He takes cultivation in accordance with principle as the law governing his clan;

He takes the grounds as the dwelling place of his clan;

He takes the patiences as his relatives;

He takes the great vows as the clan's teachings;

He takes the complete fulfillment of all the practices as compliance with the law governing his clan;

He takes promotion of the Great Vehicle as the continuance of the clan's karmic works;

He takes as the royal prince the bodhisattva at the stage of the crown-anointing consecration who has but one remaining incarnation prior to buddhahood; and

He takes the complete realization of bodhi as what purifies the clan.

Son of Good Family, it is in these ways that the bodhisattva:

Transcends the grounds of the common person;

Enters the stations of the bodhisattvas;

Is born into the family of the Tathāgata;

Dwells in the Buddha's lineage;

Is able to cultivate the practices;

正體字

不斷
438b26‖ 三寶。善能守護菩薩種族。淨菩薩種。生處
438b27‖ 尊勝。無諸過惡。一切世間。天人魔梵。沙門婆
438b28‖ 羅門。恭敬讚歎。善男子。菩薩摩訶薩。生於如
438b29‖ 是尊勝家已。知一切法如影像故。[5]於諸世
438c01‖ 間無所惡賤。知一切法如變化故。於諸有趣
438c02‖ 無所染著。知一切法無有我故。教化眾生心
438c03‖ 無疲厭。以大慈悲為體性故。攝受眾生不覺
438c04‖ 勞苦。了達生死猶如夢故。經一切劫而無怖
438c05‖ 畏。了知諸蘊皆如幻故。示現受生而無[6]憂
438c06‖ 厭。知諸界處同法界故。於諸境界無所壞滅。
438c07‖ 知一切想如陽焰故。入於諸趣不生倒惑。達
438c08‖ 一切法皆如幻故。入魔境界不起染著。知法
438c09‖ 身故。一切煩惱不能欺誑。得自在故。於一
438c10‖ 切趣通達無礙。善男子。我身普生一切法界。
438c11‖ 等一切眾生差別色相。等一切眾生殊異言
438c12‖ 音。

简体字

不断三宝，善能守护菩萨种族，净菩萨种，生处尊胜，无诸过恶，一切世间天、人、魔、梵、沙门、婆罗门恭敬赞叹。

“善男子，菩萨摩诃萨生于如是尊胜家已，知一切法如影像故，于诸世间无所恶贱；知一切法如变化故，于诸有趣无所染著；知一切法无有我故，教化众生心无疲厌；以大慈悲为体性故，摄受众生不觉劳苦；了达生死犹如梦故，经一切劫而无怖畏；了知诸蕴皆如幻故，示现受生而无疲厌；知诸界、处同法界故，于诸境界无所坏灭；知一切想如阳焰故，入于诸趣不生倒惑；达一切法皆如幻故，入魔境界不起染著；知法身故，一切烦恼不能欺诳；得自在故，于一切趣通达无碍。

“善男子，我身普生一切法界，等一切众生差别色相，等一切众生殊异言音，

Refrains from cutting short the lineage of the Three Jewels;
Is well able to preserve and protect the clan of the bodhisattvas;
Purifies the bodhisattva lineage;
Is born into venerable and superior circumstances;
Remains free of transgressions; and
Is revered and praised by everyone in the world including the devas, humans, Māra, Brahmā, the *śramaṇas,* and the brahmans.

Son of Good Family, once the bodhisattva-mahāsattvas have been born into such a venerable and esteemed clan as this:

Because they know all dharmas are like reflected images, there is nothing in the world that they disdain as inferior;
Because they know all dharmas are like transformationally-created phenomena, they have no defiling attachment to any of the stations of existence;
Because they know all dharmas are free of any self, their minds do not grow weary of teaching beings;
Because they take the great kindness and compassion as their essential nature, they do not find gathering in beings to be toilsome;
Because they completely comprehend *saṃsāra* as like a dream, they have no fear of passing through all kalpas;
Because they completely understand that the aggregates are all like illusions, they manifest the appearance of taking on births and yet are free of any distress or disdain in doing so;
Because they realize that all the sense realms and sense bases are the same as the Dharma realm itself, they remain uninjured by the sense realms;
Because they realize all perceptions are like a mirage, when they enter the rebirth destinies, they do not generate any of the delusions characteristic of the inverted views;
Because they have a penetrating comprehension of all dharmas as like illusions, even when they enter spheres of experience influenced by the *māras,* they still do not generate any defiling attachments;
Because they know the Dharma body, they cannot be deceived by any of the afflictions; and
Because they have acquired sovereign mastery over them, they have an unimpeded comprehension of all the rebirth destinies.

Son of Good Family, my bodies are born everywhere throughout the entire Dharma realm:

With forms and appearances the same as those of all beings;
With different languages the same as those of all beings;

正體字

等一切眾生種種名號。等一切眾生所樂
438c13‖ 威儀隨順世間教化調伏。等一切清淨眾生
438c14‖ 示現受生。等一切凡夫眾生所作事業。等一
438c15‖ 切眾生想。等一切菩薩願。而現其身充滿法
438c16‖ 界。善男子。我為化度與我往昔同修諸行。今
438c17‖ 時退失菩提心者。亦為教化父母親屬。亦為
438c18‖ 教化諸婆羅門。令其離於種族憍慢。得生如
438c19‖ 來種性之中。而生於此閻浮提界摩羅提國
438c20‖ 拘吒聚落婆羅門家。善男子。我住於此大樓
438c21‖ 閣中。隨諸眾生心之所樂。種種方便。教化
438c22‖ 調伏。善男子。我為隨順眾生心故。我為成
438c23‖ 熟兜率天中同行天故。我為示現菩薩福智。
438c24‖ 變化莊嚴。超過一切諸欲界故。令其捨離
438c25‖ 諸欲樂故。令知有為皆無常故。令知諸天盛
438c26‖ 必衰故。[7]為欲示現將降生時大智法門。與
438c27‖ 一生菩薩共談論故。

简体字

等一切众生种种名号，等一切众生所乐威仪，随顺世间教化调伏；等一切清净众生示现受生，等一切凡夫众生所作事业，等一切众生想，等一切菩萨愿，而现其身充满法界。

“善男子，我为化度与我往昔同修诸行，今时退失菩提心者；亦为教化父母、亲属；亦为教化诸婆罗门，令其离于种族憍慢，得生如来种性之中。——而生于此阎浮提界、摩罗提国、拘吒聚落、婆罗门家。善男子，我住于此大楼阁中，随诸众生心之所乐，种种方便教化调伏。善男子，我为随顺众生心故，我为成熟兜率天中同行天故，我为示现菩萨福智变化庄严；超过一切诸欲界故，令其舍离诸欲乐故，令知有为皆无常故，令知诸天盛必衰故，为欲示现将降生时大智法门；与一生菩萨共谈论故，

With many different kinds of names the same as those of all beings;

With modes of comportment matching the dispositions of all beings and conforming to the ways of the world in order to teach and train them;

With the manifestation of taking birth matching that of all the pure beings there;

With endeavors and livelihoods the same as all common beings;

With ways of thinking that match those of all beings; and

With vows matching those of all bodhisattvas.

It is in these ways that these bodies have come to completely fill the Dharma realm.

Son of Good Family, it was in order to teach and liberate those with whom I have cultivated the practices in the distant past who have now retreated from their bodhi resolve, it was also in order to teach parents and relatives, and it was also in order to teach brahmans so as to enable them to abandon caste-based arrogance and acquire birth into the lineage of the Tathāgata—it was for all these reasons that I have been born in this realm of Jambudvīpa in the state of Mālada, in the village of Kuṭi, in the household of a brahman.

Son of Good Family, as I abide in this great tower, I adapt to the dispositions of beings and thus use all kinds of skillful means to teach and train them.

Son of Good Family:

I do this to adapt to the inclinations of beings;

I do this to ripen the devas in the Tuṣita Heaven who are engaged in the same practices;

I do this to manifest transformations and adornments of a bodhisattva's merit and wisdom that surpass those of all others in the desire realm;

This is also done to enable beings to abandon the delights of sensual desires;

This is also done to enable beings to realize that all conditioned existence is impermanent;

This is also done to enable beings to realize that all the flourishing abundance of the heavens is bound to perish;

This is also done at the time bodhisattvas are about to descend to take birth, wishing to manifest "the Dharma gateway of great knowledge" by joining in reciting it together with other bodhisattvas having but one more birth [before buddhahood];[50]

正體字

為欲攝化諸同行故。為
438c28 欲教化釋迦如來所遣來者。令如蓮華悉開
438c29 悟故。於此命終。生兜率天。善男子。我願滿
439a01 足。成一切智。得菩提時。汝及文殊。俱得見
439a02 我。善男子。汝當往詣文殊師利善知識所。而
439a03 問之言。菩薩云何學菩薩行。云何而入普賢
439a04 行門。[1]云何成就。云何廣大。云何隨順。云何
439a05 清淨。云何圓滿。善男子。彼當為汝分別演
439a06 說。何以故。文殊師利。所有大願。非餘無量百
439a07 千億那由他菩薩之所能有。善男子。文殊師
439a08 利童子。其行廣大。其願無邊。出生一切菩薩
439a09 功德。無有休息。善男子。文殊師利。常為無量
439a10 百千億那由他諸佛母。常為無量百千億那
439a11 由他菩薩師。教化成[2]熟一切眾生。名稱普
439a12 聞十方世界。常於一切諸佛眾中。為說法師。
439a13 一切如來之所讚歎。住甚深智。[3]能如實見
439a14 一切諸法。通達一切解脫境界。究竟普賢所
439a15 行諸行。善男子。文殊師利童子。是汝善知識。
439a16 令汝得生如來家。長養一切諸善根。發起一
439a17 切助道法。值遇真實善知識。令汝修一切功
439a18 德。入一切願網。住一切大願。為汝說一切菩
439a19 薩祕密法。現一切菩薩難思行。與汝往昔。同
439a20 生同行。

简体字

为欲摄化诸同行故，为欲教化释迦如来所遣来者令如莲华悉开悟故，于此命终，生兜率天。善男子，我愿满足，成一切智，得菩提时，汝及文殊俱得见我。

“善男子，汝当往诣文殊师利善知识所而问之言：‘菩萨云何学菩萨行？云何而入普贤行门？云何成就？云何广大？云何随顺？云何清净？云何圆满？’善男子，彼当为汝分别演说。何以故？文殊师利所有大愿，非余无量百千亿那由他菩萨之所能有。

“善男子，文殊师利童子，其行广大，其愿无边，出生一切菩萨功德无有休息。善男子，文殊师利常为无量百千亿那由他诸佛母，常为无量百千亿那由他菩萨师，教化成就一切众生，名称普闻十方世界；常于一切诸佛众中为说法师，一切如来之所赞叹；住甚深智，能如实见一切诸法，通达一切解脱境界，究竟普贤所行诸行。

“善男子，文殊师利童子是汝善知识，令汝得生如来家，长养一切诸善根，发起一切助道法，值遇真实善知识；令汝修一切功德，入一切愿网，住一切大愿；为汝说一切菩萨秘密法，现一切菩萨难思行；与汝往昔同生同行。

This is also done wishing to attract and teach those who are engaged in the same practices;

This is also done wishing to teach those who have been sent here by Śākyamuni, with the intention of enabling them to open and awaken like blooming lotuses and then take rebirth in the Tuṣita Heaven at the end of this life.

Son of Good Family, you and Mañjuśrī will both see me again when my vows have been fulfilled and I attain all-knowledge.

Son of Good Family, you should go and pay your respects to Mañjuśrī, the good spiritual guide, and ask him how the bodhisattva should train in the bodhisattva practices, how he should enter Samantabhadra's gateways of practice, how he should perfect them, how he should broaden them, how he should accord with them, how he should purify them, and how he should completely fulfill them.

Son of Good Family, he shall distinguish and explain these matters for you. Why? All of Mañjuśri's great vows are of a sort that none of the other countless hundreds of thousands of *koṭīs* of *nayutas* of bodhisattvas could possess.

Son of Good Family, the practices of Mañjuśrī the Youth are vast, his vows are boundless, and he incessantly produces the meritorious qualities of all bodhisattvas. Son of Good Family, Mañjuśrī has always served as the mother of countless hundreds of thousands of *koṭīs* of *nayutas* of buddhas and he has always served as the master teacher of countless hundreds of thousands of *koṭīs* of *nayutas* of bodhisattvas. He teaches and ripens all beings. His fame extends everywhere throughout the worlds of the ten directions.

He has always served as a Dharma teacher in the congregations of all buddhas and he is praised by all *tathāgatas*. He abides in extremely deep wisdom and he is able to perceive all dharmas in accordance with reality. He has a penetrating comprehension of all the realms of liberation and he has completed all of Samantabhadra's practices.

Son of Good Family, Mañjuśrī is your good spiritual guide. He enables your birth into the clan of the Tathāgata, your growth of all the roots of goodness, your production of all the provisions for the path to enlightenment, and your meeting with genuine good spiritual guides. He enables your cultivation of all the meritorious qualities, your entry into the network of all vows, and your abiding in all the great vows. He explains all the bodhisattva's esoteric dharmas for you, shows you the inconceivable practices of all bodhisattvas, and in the past has been born together with you in the same places where you have both undertaken the same practices.

正體字

是故。善男子。汝應往詣文殊之所莫
439a21‖ 生疲厭。文殊師利。當為汝說一切功德。何以
439a22‖ 故。汝先所見諸善知識。聞菩薩行。入解脫門。
439a23‖ 滿足大願。皆是文殊威神之力。文殊師利。於
439a24‖ 一切處。咸得究竟。時善財童子。頂禮其足。遶
439a25‖ 無量匝。慇懃瞻仰。辭退而去
439b02‖ [5]大方廣佛華嚴經卷第八十
439b05‖ [9]入法界品第三十九之二十一
439b06‖ 爾時善財童子。依彌勒菩薩摩訶薩教。漸次
439b07‖ 而行。經[10]由一百一十餘城已。到普門國[11]蘇
439b08‖ 摩那城。住其門所。思惟文殊師利。隨順觀察。
439b09‖ 周旋求覓。希欲奉覲。是時文殊師利。遙伸右
439b10‖ 手。過一百一十由旬。按善財頂。作如是言。善
439b11‖ 哉善哉。善男子。若離信根。心劣憂悔。功行不
439b12‖ 具。退失精勤。於一善根。心生住著。於少功
439b13‖ 德。便[12]以為足。不能善巧發起行願。不為善
439b14‖ 知識之所攝護。不為如來之所憶念。不能了
439b15‖ 知如是法性。如是理趣。如是法門。如是所行。
439b16‖ 如是境界。若周遍知。若種種知。若盡源底。若
439b17‖ 解了。若趣入。若解說。若分別。

简体字

“是故，善男子，汝应往诣文殊之所莫生疲厌，文殊师利当为汝说一切功德。何以故？汝先所见诸善知识闻菩萨行、入解脱门、满足大愿，皆是文殊威神之力，文殊师利于一切处咸得究竟。”

时，善财童子顶礼其足，绕无量匝，殷勤瞻仰，辞退而去。

大方广佛华严经卷第八十

入法界品第三十九之二十一

尔时，善财童子依弥勒菩萨摩诃萨教，渐次而行，经由一百一十余城已，到普门国苏摩那城，住其门所，思惟文殊师利，随顺观察，周旋求觅，希欲奉觐。

是时，文殊师利遥伸右手，过一百一十由旬，按善财顶，作如是言：“善哉！善哉！善男子，若离信根，心劣忧悔，功行不具，退失精勤，于一善根心生住著，于少功德便以为足，不能善巧发起行愿，不为善知识之所摄护，不为如来之所忆念，不能了知如是法性、如是理趣、如是法门、如是所行、如是境界；若周遍知、若种种知、若尽源底，若解了、若趣入、若解说、若分别、

Therefore, Son of Good Family, you should be tireless in going to see Mañjuśrī to pay your respects to him, for Mañjuśrī will explain all the meritorious qualities for you. Why? All those good spiritual guides you have previously seen, all the teachings on the bodhisattva practices you have heard, all the gateways of liberation you have entered, and all the great vows you have fulfilled have all been due to the awesome spiritual powers of Mañjuśrī. Mañjuśrī has reached the ultimate degree of achievement in all these things.

Sudhana the Youth then bowed down in reverence at the feet of Maitreya and circumambulated him countless times as he gazed up at him in attentive admiration. He then respectfully withdrew and departed.

52 – Mañjuśrī

At that time, Sudhana the Youth, relying on the instructions provided by Maitreya Bodhisattva-mahāsattva, gradually traveled on until, after he had passed through more than a hundred and ten other cities, he reached the city of Sumana in the country of Samantamukha[51] where he stayed at the city gates. Then, thinking of Mañjuśrī, he looked for him, searching everywhere, hoping to pay his respects and have an audience with him.

Then, from afar, Mañjuśrī stretched his right hand across a distance of one hundred and ten *yojanas*, rubbed the crown of Sudhana's head, and said:

This is good indeed, good indeed! Son of Good Family, those who have abandoned the faculty of faith, whose minds have become weak and beset by sorrow and remorse, whose efforts are incomplete, who have retreated from energetic diligence, whose minds are attached to but one root of goodness, who have become satisfied with only a few meritorious qualities, who are unable to skillfully take up the practices and vows, who have not been gathered in and protected by good spiritual guides, and who are not borne in mind by the Tathāgatas—they are unable to completely know the nature of dharmas such as this, a principle and purport such as this, a Dharma gateway such as this, a practice such as this, or a realm such as this.[52]

Whether it be a universal knowing of them, a multi-faceted knowing of them, a complete fathoming of their very source, a complete understanding of them, a progression into them, an explanatory discussion of them, an analysis of them, a realized knowing of

正體字

若證知。若獲
439b18‖ 得。皆悉不能。是時文殊師利。宣說此法。示教
439b19‖ 利喜。令善財童子。成就阿僧祇法門。具足
439b20‖ 無量大智光明。令得菩薩無邊際陀羅尼。無
439b21‖ 邊際願。無邊際三昧。無邊際神通。無邊際智。
439b22‖ 令入普賢行道場。及置善財自所住處。文殊
439b23‖ 師利。還攝不現。於是善財。思惟觀察。一心
439b24‖ 願見文殊師利。及見三千大千世界微塵數
439b25‖ 諸善知識。悉皆親近。恭敬承事。受行其教。無
439b26‖ 有違逆。[13]增長趣求一切智慧。廣大悲海。益
439b27‖ 大慈雲。普觀眾生。生大歡喜。安住菩薩寂
439b28‖ 靜法門。普緣一切廣大境界。學一切佛廣大
439b29‖ 功德。入一切佛決定知見。增一切智助道之
439c01‖ 法。善修一切菩薩深心。知三世佛出興次第。
439c02‖ 入一切法海。轉一切法輪。生一切世間。入
439c03‖ 於一切菩薩願海。住一切劫。修菩薩行。照
439c04‖ 明一切如來境界。長養一切菩薩諸根。獲一
439c05‖ 切智清淨光明。普照十方。除諸暗障。智周法
439c06‖ 界於一切佛剎。一切諸有。普現其身。靡不周
439c07‖ 遍。

简体字

若证知、若获得，皆悉不能。”

是时，文殊师利宣说此法，示教利喜，令善财童子成就阿僧祇法门，具足无量大智光明，令得菩萨无边际陀罗尼、无边际愿、无边际三昧、无边际神通、无边际智，令入普贤行道场，及置善财自所住处；文殊师利还摄不现。

于是，善财思惟观察，一心愿见文殊师利，及见三千大千世界微尘数诸善知识，悉皆亲近，恭敬承事，受行其教，无有违逆；增长趣求一切智慧，广大悲海，益大慈云，普观众生，生大欢喜，安住菩萨寂静法门；普缘一切广大境界，学一切佛广大功德，入一切佛决定知见，增一切智助道之法，善修一切菩萨深心，知三世佛出兴次第；入一切法海，转一切法轮，生一切世间，入于一切菩萨愿海，住一切劫修菩萨行，照明一切如来境界，长养一切菩萨诸根；获一切智清净光明，普照十方，除诸暗障，智周法界；于一切佛刹、一切诸有，普现其身，靡不周遍；

them, or an acquisition of them—they would be unable to accomplish any of these.

Mañjuśrī then expounded on these dharmas, explained them, and used them to benefit and gladden Sudhana. He enabled Sudhana the Youth to become accomplished in an *asaṃkhyeya* of Dharma gateways, enabled him to become endowed with the light of measureless great wisdom, and enabled him to acquire the bodhisattva's boundless *dhāraṇīs*, boundless vows, boundless samādhis, boundless spiritual superknowledges, and boundless knowledge. He enabled him to enter the *maṇḍala* of Samantabhadra's practices and also established Sudhana in the very place in which he himself dwells,[53] whereupon Mañjuśrī withdrew and disappeared.

53 – Samantabhadra

At that time, Sudhana thought about, looked around for, and single-mindedly yearned to see Mañjuśrī and all the good spiritual guides as numerous as the atoms in the world systems of a great trichiliocosm. He wished to draw near to them all, wished to revere and serve them all, and wished to adopt and practice their teachings without ever turning away from them.

He advanced in his quest for all-knowledge, expanded his ocean of great compassion, increased his clouds of great kindness, everywhere contemplated beings, became filled with immense joyous delight, became established in the bodhisattva's Dharma gateways of quiescence, everywhere engaged with all the vast realms, trained in all buddhas' vast meritorious qualities, and entered all buddhas' definite knowledge and vision.

He increased his development of provisions for the path to all-knowledge, skillfully cultivated all bodhisattvas' resolute intentions, came to know the sequence of arising of all buddhas of the three periods of time, entered the ocean of all dharmas, turned the wheel of all dharmas, took on births in all world systems, entered the ocean of vows of all bodhisattvas, dwelt in all kalpas, cultivated the bodhisattva practices, clearly illuminated all realms of the *tathāgatas*, and increased his growth in the faculties of all bodhisattvas.

He acquired the pure light of all-knowledge and everywhere illuminated the ten directions, ridding them of the obstacles of darkness. His wisdom pervaded the Dharma realm as he everywhere manifested his body in all buddha *kṣetras* and in all of realms of existence, having none in which he was not everywhere present. He

正體字

摧一切障。入無礙法。住於法界平等之地。
439c08║ 觀察普賢解脫境界。即聞普賢菩薩摩訶薩
439c09║ 名字行願。助道正道。諸地地。方便地。入地。
439c10║ 勝進地。住地。修習地。境界地。威力地。同住
439c11║ 渴仰。欲見普賢菩薩。即於此金剛藏菩提場。
439c12║ 毘盧遮那如來師子座前一切寶蓮華藏座
439c13║ 上。起等虛空界廣大心。捨一切剎離一切著
439c14║ 無礙心。普行一切無礙法無礙心。遍入一切
439c15║ 十方海無礙心。普入一切[14]智境界清淨心。觀
439c16║ 道場莊嚴明了心。入一切佛法海廣大心。化
439c17║ 一切眾生界周遍心。淨一切國土無量心。住
439c18║ 一切劫無盡心。趣如來十力究竟心。善財童
439c19║ 子。起如是心時。由自善根力。一切如來所
439c20║ 加被力。普賢菩薩同善根力[15]故。見十種瑞
439c21║ 相。何等為十。所謂見一切佛剎清淨。一切
439c22║ 如來成正等覺。見一切佛剎清淨。無諸[16]惡
439c23║ 道。見一切佛剎清淨。眾妙蓮華。以為嚴飾。

简体字

摧一切障，入无碍法，住于法界平等之地；观察普贤解脱境界，即闻普贤菩萨摩诃萨名字、行愿、助道、正道、诸地地、方便地、入地、胜进地、住地、修习地、境界地、威力地，同住渴仰。

欲见普贤菩萨，即于此金刚藏菩提场，毗卢遮那如来师子座前，一切宝莲华藏座上，起等虚空界广大心、舍一切刹离一切著无碍心、普行一切无碍法无碍心、遍入一切十方海无碍心、普入一切智境界清净心、观道场庄严明了心、入一切佛法海广大心、化一切众生界周遍心、净一切国土无量心、住一切劫无尽心、趣如来十力究竟心。

善财童子起如是心时，由自善根力、一切如来所加被力、普贤菩萨同善根力故，见十种瑞相。何等为十？所谓：见一切佛刹清净，一切如来成正等觉；见一切佛刹清净，无诸恶道；见一切佛刹清净，众妙莲华以为严饰；

demolished all obstacles, entered the unimpeded Dharma, and dwelt on the Dharma realm's ground of uniform equality.

He contemplated Samantabhadra's realm of liberation and then immediately heard the name of Samantabhadra Bodhisattva-mahāsattva, his practices and vows, his provisions for enlightenment, his right path, his grounds, his skillful means on the grounds, his entry into the grounds, his vigor on the grounds, his dwelling on the grounds, his cultivation of the grounds, his realms of experience on the grounds, his awesome power on the grounds, and his dwelling together with others on the grounds.

As he was eagerly yearning to see Samantabhadra Bodhisattva, he then immediately came to be sitting in this vajra treasury site of enlightenment on a lotus flower seat adorned with all kinds of jewels, directly in front of Vairocana Tathāgata's lion throne. He then produced these types of mind that were as vast as the realm of empty space:

The unimpeded mind that relinquishes all *kṣetras* and abandons all attachments;
The unimpeded mind that everywhere practices all unimpeded dharmas;
The unimpeded mind that everywhere pervades the entire ocean of the ten directions;
The pure mind that everywhere enters the realm of all-knowledge;
The completely understanding mind that contemplates the site of enlightenment's adornments;
The vast mind that enters the ocean of all dharmas of the buddhas;
The universally pervasive mind devoted to teaching all beings;
The measureless mind that purifies all lands;
The inexhaustible mind that abides throughout all kalpas; and
The ultimate mind that enters the Tathāgata's ten powers.

When Sudhana the Youth produced types of mind such as these, due to the power of his own roots of goodness, due to the power of all *tathāgatas'* assistance, and due to the power of roots of goodness equivalent to Samantabhadra's, he then witnessed ten kinds of auspicious signs. What are those ten? They are as follows:

He beheld the purity of all buddha *kṣetras* in which all *tathāgatas* attained the right and universal enlightenment;
He beheld the purity of all buddha *kṣetras* in which there are no wretched destinies;
He beheld the purity of all buddha *kṣetras* adorned by the many kinds of marvelous lotus flowers;

正體字

見
439c24 一切佛剎清淨。一切眾生。身心清淨。見一
439c25 切佛剎清淨。種種眾寶之所莊嚴。見一切佛
439c26 剎清淨。一切眾生諸相嚴身。見一切佛剎清
439c27 淨。諸莊嚴雲以覆其上。見一切佛剎清淨。一
439c28 切眾生互起慈心遞相利益不為惱害。見一
439c29 切佛剎清淨。道場莊嚴。見一切佛剎清淨。一
440a01 切眾生心常念佛。是為十。又見十種光明相。
440a02 何等為十。所謂見一切世界所有微塵。一一
440a03 塵中出一切世界微塵數佛光明網雲周遍照
440a04 [1]耀。一一塵中出一切世界微塵數佛光明輪
440a05 雲。種種色相周遍法界。一一塵中出一切世
440a06 界微塵數佛色像寶雲。周遍法界。一一塵中
440a07 出一切世界微塵數佛光焰輪雲。周遍法界。
440a08 一一塵中出一切世界微塵數眾妙香雲。周
440a09 遍十方。稱讚普賢一切行願大功德海。一
440a10 一塵中出一切世界微塵數日月星宿雲。皆
440a11 放普賢菩薩光明遍照法界。一一塵中出一
440a12 切世界微塵數一切眾生身色像雲。放佛光
440a13 明遍照法界。

简体字

见一切佛刹清净，一切众生身心清净；见一切佛刹清净，种种众宝之所庄严；见一切佛刹清净，一切众生诸相严身；见一切佛刹清净，诸庄严云以覆其上；见一切佛刹清净，一切众生互起慈心，递相利益，不为恼害；见一切佛刹清净，道场庄严；见一切佛刹清净，一切众生心常念佛。是为十。

又见十种光明相。何等为十？所谓：见一切世界所有微尘，一一尘中，出一切世界微尘数佛光明网云，周遍照耀；一一尘中，出一切世界微尘数佛光明轮云，种种色相周遍法界；一一尘中，出一切世界微尘数佛色像宝云，周遍法界；一一尘中，出一切世界微尘数佛光焰轮云，周遍法界；一一尘中，出一切世界微尘数众妙香云，周遍十方，称赞普贤一切行愿大功德海；一一尘中，出一切世界微尘数日月星宿云，皆放普贤菩萨光明，遍照法界；一一尘中，出一切世界微尘数一切众生身色像云，放佛光明，遍照法界；

He beheld the purity of all buddha *kṣetras* in which all beings are pure in body and mind;
He beheld the purity of all buddha *kṣetras* adorned with the many different kinds of jewels;
He beheld the purity of all buddha *kṣetras* in which the bodies of all beings are adorned with all the auspicious signs;
He beheld the purity of all buddha *kṣetras* covered with all kinds of clouds of adornments;
He beheld the purity of all buddha *kṣetras* in which all beings raise up thoughts of loving-kindness toward each other, bestow benefit on each other, and refrain from harming one another;
He beheld the purity of all buddha *kṣetras* in which their sites of enlightenment are graced with adornments; and
He beheld the purity of all buddha *kṣetras* in which all beings' minds are always devoted to mindfulness of the Buddha.

These are the ten. He also witnessed ten kinds of light signs. What are those ten? In all atoms in all world systems:

He saw emerging from each atom the emanation of clouds of buddha light nets as numerous as the atoms in all world systems, clouds that shone forth with universally pervasive brilliant radiance;
He saw emerging from each atom the emanation throughout the Dharma realm of buddha halo clouds as numerous as the atoms in all world systems, clouds that shone forth with many different colors and signs;
He saw emerging from each atom the emanation throughout the Dharma realm of jeweled buddha image clouds as numerous as the atoms in all world systems;
He saw emerging from each atom the emanation throughout the Dharma realm of clouds of spheres of buddhas' flaming radiance;
He saw emerging from each atom the emanation throughout the ten directions of clouds of many marvelous fragrances, clouds as numerous as the atoms in all world systems from which there resounded the praises of Samantabhadra's ocean of great meritorious qualities arising from his practices and vows;
He saw emerging from each atom the emanation of sun, moon, and constellation clouds as numerous as the atoms in all world systems, clouds that each streamed forth Samantabhadra Bodhisattva's radiance, everywhere illuminating the Dharma realm;
He saw emerging from each atom the emanation of clouds of images of all beings' bodies, clouds as numerous as the atoms in all world systems that streamed forth the buddhas' radiance, everywhere illuminating the Dharma realm;

正體字

一一塵中出一切世界微塵數
440a14‖ 一切佛色像摩尼雲周遍法界。一一塵中出
440a15‖ 一切世界微塵數菩薩身色像雲。充滿法界
440a16‖ 令一切眾生皆得出離所願滿足。一一塵中
440a17‖ 出一切世界微塵數如來身色像雲。說一切
440a18‖ 佛廣大誓願。周遍法界。是為十。時善財童
440a19‖ 子。見此十種光明相已。即作是念。我今必見
440a20‖ 普賢菩薩。增益善根。見一切佛。於諸菩薩
440a21‖ 廣大境界。生決定解得一切智。於時善財。普
440a22‖ 攝諸根。一心求見普賢菩薩起大精進心無
440a23‖ 退轉。即以普眼。觀察十方一切諸佛諸菩薩
440a24‖ 眾所見境界。皆作得見普賢之想。以智慧眼
440a25‖ 觀普賢道。其心廣大猶如虛空。大悲堅固猶
440a26‖ 如金剛。願盡未來。常得隨逐普賢菩薩。念
440a27‖ 念隨順。修普賢行。成就智慧。入如來境住普
440a28‖ 賢地。時善財童子。即見普賢菩薩。在如來
440a29‖ 前眾會之中。坐寶蓮華師子之座。諸菩薩眾。
440b01‖ 所共圍遶。最為殊特。世無與等。智慧境界
440b02‖ 無量無邊。難測難思。等三世佛。一切菩薩。無
440b03‖ 能觀察。[2]見普賢身一一毛孔。出一切世界
440b04‖ 微塵數光明雲。

简体字

一一尘中，出一切世界微尘数一切佛色像摩尼云，周遍法界；一一尘中，出一切世界微尘数菩萨身色像云，充满法界，令一切众生皆得出离、所愿满足；一一尘中，出一切世界微尘数如来身色像云，说一切佛广大誓愿，周遍法界。是为十。

时，善财童子见此十种光明相已，即作是念：“我今必见普贤菩萨，增益善根，见一切佛；于诸菩萨广大境界，生决定解，得一切智。”

于时，善财普摄诸根，一心求见普贤菩萨，起大精进，心无退转。即以普眼观察十方一切诸佛、诸菩萨众所见境界，皆作得见普贤之想；以智慧眼观普贤道，其心广大犹如虚空，大悲坚固犹如金刚，愿尽未来常得随逐普贤菩萨，念念随顺，修普贤行，成就智慧，入如来境，住普贤地。

时，善财童子即见普贤菩萨，在如来前众会之中，坐宝莲华师子之座，诸菩萨众所共围绕，最为殊特，世无与等；智慧境界无量无边，难测难思，等三世佛，一切菩萨无能观察。见普贤身一一毛孔，出一切世界微尘数光明云，

He saw emerging from each atom the emanation of buddha image *maṇi* jewel clouds as numerous as the atoms in all world systems, clouds that appeared everywhere throughout the Dharma realm;

He saw emerging from each atom the emanation of clouds of bodhisattva images as numerous as the atoms in all world systems, clouds that completely filled the Dharma realm and enabled all beings to succeed in gaining emancipation and completely fulfilling their vows; and

He saw emerging from each atom the emanation of clouds of *tathāgata* images as numerous as the atoms in all world systems, clouds that appeared everywhere throughout the Dharma realm proclaiming the vast vows of all buddhas.

These are the ten. Having seen these ten kinds of light signs, Sudhana the Youth then thought, "I must now see Samantabhadra Bodhisattva, increase my roots of goodness, see all buddhas, develop a definite understanding of the vast realms of all bodhisattvas, and attain all-knowledge."

Sudhana then focused all his faculties on single-mindedly seeking to see Samantabhadra Bodhisattva. He aroused great vigor and irreversible resolve and then used the universal eye to contemplate the realms seen by all buddhas and bodhisattvas of the ten directions and envisioned himself seeing Samantabhadra in all these phenomena. With his wisdom eye, he contemplated the path of Samantabhadra and, with a mind as vast as empty space and great compassion as solid as vajra, he vowed that, to the very end of future time, he would always be able to follow Samantabhadra Bodhisattva and pursue the cultivation of Samantabhadra's practices in each successive mind-moment, doing so with the aim of perfecting great wisdom, entering the realm of the Tathāgata, and dwelling on the ground of Samantabhadra.

At that very time, Sudhana the Youth immediately saw Samantabhadra Bodhisattva in the midst of the congregation and directly in front of the Tathāgata where he was seated on a jeweled lotus flower lion throne surrounded by a congregation of bodhisattvas, presenting the most splendidly extraordinary appearance without peer anywhere in the world. His realm of wisdom was measureless, boundless, unfathomable, inconceivable, equal to that of all buddhas of the three periods of time, and such that no other bodhisattva could even be able to contemplate.

He saw emerging from every pore of Samantabhadra's body the emanation of light clouds as numerous as the atoms in all world systems,

正體字

遍法界虛空界一切世界。除
440b05║ 滅一切眾生苦患。[3]令諸菩薩生大歡喜。見
440b06║ 一一毛孔。出一切佛刹微塵數種種色香焰
440b07║ 雲。遍法界虛空界一切諸佛眾會道場。而以
440b08║ 普[4]熏。見一一毛孔。出一切佛刹微塵數雜
440b09║ 華雲。遍法界虛空界一切諸佛眾會道場。雨
440b10║ 眾妙華。見一一毛孔出一切佛刹微塵數香
440b11║ 樹雲。遍法界虛空界一切諸佛眾會道場。雨
440b12║ 眾妙香。見一一毛孔。出一切佛刹微塵數妙
440b13║ 衣雲。遍法界虛空界一切諸佛眾會道場。
440b14║ 雨眾妙衣。見一一毛孔。出一切佛刹微塵
440b15║ 數寶樹雲。遍法界虛空界一切諸佛眾會道
440b16║ 場。雨摩尼寶。見一一毛孔。出一切佛刹
440b17║ 微塵數色界天身雲。充滿法界歎菩提心。
440b18║ 見一一毛孔。出一切佛刹微塵數梵天身雲。
440b19║ 勸諸如來轉妙法輪見一一毛孔。出一切佛
440b20║ 刹微塵數欲界天[5]主身雲。護持一切如來法
440b21║ 輪見。一一毛孔。念念中出一切佛刹微塵數
440b22║ 三世佛刹雲。

简体字

遍法界、虚空界、一切世界，除灭一切众生苦患，令诸菩萨生大欢喜；见一一毛孔，出一切佛刹微尘数种种色香焰云，遍法界、虚空界一切诸佛众会道场，而以普熏；见一一毛孔，出一切佛刹微尘数杂华云，遍法界、虚空界一切诸佛众会道场，雨众妙华；见一一毛孔，出一切佛刹微尘数香树云，遍法界、虚空界一切诸佛众会道场，雨众妙香；见一一毛孔，出一切佛刹微尘数妙衣云，遍法界、虚空界一切诸佛众会道场，雨众妙衣；见一一毛孔，出一切佛刹微尘数宝树云，遍法界、虚空界一切诸佛众会道场，雨摩尼宝；见一一毛孔，出一切佛刹微尘数色界天身云，充满法界，叹菩提心；见一一毛孔，出一切佛刹微尘数梵天身云，劝诸如来转妙法轮；见一一毛孔，出一切佛刹微尘数欲界天王身云，护持一切如来法轮；见一一毛孔，念念中出一切佛刹微尘数三世佛刹云，

clouds that appeared everywhere in all world systems throughout the Dharma realm and the realm of empty space, extinguishing the sufferings and troubles of all beings and causing all bodhisattvas to be filled with great happiness;

He saw emerging from each pore the emanation of multicolored clouds of many different kinds of incense and flaming radiance, clouds as numerous as the atoms in all buddha *kṣetras* that appeared everywhere in the congregations of all buddhas, completely imbuing them with their fragrances;

He saw emerging from each pore the emanation of clouds of various flowers as numerous as the atoms in all buddha *kṣetras*, clouds that appeared everywhere in the congregations of all buddhas throughout the Dharma realm and the realm of empty space, raining down many kinds of marvelous flowers;

He saw emerging from each pore the emanation of clouds of incense fragrance trees, clouds as numerous as the atoms in all buddha *kṣetras* that appeared everywhere in the congregations of all buddhas throughout the Dharma realm and the realm of empty space, raining down the many kinds of marvelous incense fragrances;

He saw emerging from each pore the emanation of clouds of marvelous raiment, clouds as numerous as the atoms in all buddha *kṣetras* that appeared everywhere in the congregations of all buddhas throughout the Dharma realm and the realm of empty space, raining down all kinds of marvelous raiment;

He saw emerging from each pore the emanation of clouds of jewel trees, clouds as numerous as the atoms in all buddha *kṣetras* that appeared everywhere in the congregations of all buddhas throughout the Dharma realm and the realm of empty space, raining down all varieties of *maṇi* jewels;

He saw emerging from each pore the emanation of clouds of form realm devas' congregations,[54] clouds as numerous as the atoms in all buddha *kṣetras* that filled the Dharma realm with their praises of the resolve to attain bodhi;

He saw emerging from each pore the emanation of clouds of Brahma Heaven deva congregations, clouds as numerous as the atoms in all buddha *kṣetras* in which those devas were requesting all *tathāgatas* to turn the wheel of the wondrous Dharma;

He saw emerging from each pore the emanation of clouds of desire realm deva rulers' congregations, clouds as numerous as the atoms in all buddha *kṣetras* in which they guarded and sustained all *tathāgatas'* turning of the Dharma wheel;

He saw emerging from each pore in each successive mind-moment the emanation of clouds of buddha *kṣetras* of the three periods of time,

正體字

遍法界虛空界。為諸眾生無歸
440b23‖ 趣者為作歸趣。無覆護者為作覆護。無依止
440b24‖ 者為作依止。見一一毛孔。念念中出一切佛
440b25‖ 剎微塵數清淨佛剎雲。遍法界虛空界一切
440b26‖ 諸佛。於中出世菩薩眾會。悉皆充滿。見一
440b27‖ 一毛孔。念念中出一切佛剎微塵數淨不淨
440b28‖ 佛剎雲。遍法界虛空界。令雜染眾生皆得清
440b29‖ 淨。見一一毛孔。念念中出一切佛剎微塵數
440c01‖ 不淨淨佛剎雲。遍法界虛空界。令雜染眾生
440c02‖ 皆得清淨。見一一毛孔。念念中出一切佛剎
440c03‖ 微塵數不淨佛剎雲。遍法界虛空界。令純染
440c04‖ 眾生皆得清淨。見一一毛孔。念念中。出一
440c05‖ 切佛剎微塵數眾生身雲。遍法界虛空界。隨
440c06‖ 其所應教化眾生。皆令發阿耨多羅三藐三
440c07‖ 菩提心。見一一毛孔。念念中出一切佛剎微
440c08‖ 塵數菩薩身雲。遍法界虛空界。稱揚種種諸
440c09‖ 佛名號。令諸眾生增長善根。

简体字

遍法界、虚空界，为诸众生，无归趣者为作归趣，无覆护者为作覆护，无依止者为作依止；见一一毛孔，念念中出一切佛刹微尘数清净佛刹云，遍法界、虚空界，一切诸佛于中出世，菩萨众会悉皆充满；见一一毛孔，念念中出一切佛刹微尘数净不净佛刹云，遍法界、虚空界，令杂染众生皆得清净；见一一毛孔，念念中出一切佛刹微尘数不净净佛刹云，遍法界、虚空界，令杂染众生皆得清净；见一一毛孔，念念中出一切佛刹微尘数不净佛刹云，遍法界、虚空界，令纯染众生皆得清净；见一一毛孔，念念中出一切佛刹微尘数众生身云，遍法界、虚空界，随其所应，教化众生，皆令发阿耨多罗三藐三菩提心；见一一毛孔，念念中出一切佛刹微尘数菩萨身云，遍法界、虚空界，称扬种种诸佛名号，令诸众生增长善根。

clouds as numerous as the atoms in all buddha *kṣetras* that appeared everywhere throughout the Dharma realm and the realm of empty space, serving for all beings as a refuge for those with no refuge, serving as a shelter for those with no shelter, and serving as a reliable support for those with no reliable support;

He saw emerging from each pore in each successive mind-moment the emanation of clouds of pure buddha *kṣetras* as numerous as the atoms in all buddha *kṣetras*, clouds that appeared everywhere throughout the Dharma realm and the realm of empty space in which all buddhas came forth into the worlds and those worlds were all filled with bodhisattva congregations;

He saw emerging from each pore in each successive mind-moment the emanation of clouds of relatively pure impure buddha *kṣetras*[55] as numerous as the atoms in all buddha *kṣetras*, clouds of *kṣetras* that appeared everywhere throughout the Dharma realm and the realm of empty space in which defiled beings might all be enabled to attain a state of purity;

He saw emerging from each pore in each successive mind-moment the emanation of clouds of relatively impure pure buddha *kṣetras*[56] as numerous as the atoms in all buddha *kṣetras*, clouds of *kṣetras* that appeared everywhere throughout the Dharma realm and the realm of empty space in which defiled beings might all be enabled to attain a state of purity;

He saw emerging from each pore in each successive mind-moment the emanation of clouds of impure buddha *kṣetras* as numerous as the atoms in all buddha *kṣetras*, clouds of *kṣetras* that appeared everywhere throughout the Dharma realm and the realm of empty space in which completely defiled beings might all be enabled to attain a state of purity;

He saw emerging from each pore in each successive mind-moment the emanation of clouds of congregations of beings as numerous as the atoms in all buddha *kṣetras* that appeared everywhere throughout the Dharma realm and the realm of empty space, adapting to the beings who should be taught, thereby enabling them all to resolve to attain *anuttara-samyak-saṃbodhi*;

He saw emerging from each pore in each successive mind-moment the emanation of clouds of bodhisattva congregations as numerous as the atoms in all buddha *kṣetras* that appeared everywhere throughout the Dharma realm and the realm of empty space, clouds of congregations in which they praised the many different names of the buddhas, thereby enabling all beings to increase their roots of goodness;

正體字

見一一毛孔。念
440c10‖ 念中出一切佛刹微塵數菩薩身雲。遍法界
440c11‖ 虛空界一切佛刹。宣揚一切諸佛菩薩從初
440c12‖ 發意所生善根。見一一毛孔。念念中出一切
440c13‖ 佛刹微塵數菩薩身雲。遍法界虛空界。於一
440c14‖ 切佛刹。一一刹中。宣揚一切菩薩願海。及
440c15‖ 普賢菩薩清淨妙行。見一一毛孔。念念中出
440c16‖ 普賢菩薩行雲。令一切眾生心得滿足。具足
440c17‖ 修集一切智道。見一一毛孔。出一切佛刹微
440c18‖ 塵數正覺身雲。於一切佛刹。現成正覺。令
440c19‖ 諸菩薩增長大法成一切智。爾時善財童子。
440c20‖ 見普賢菩薩如是自在神通境界。身心遍喜。
440c21‖ 踊躍無量。重觀普賢一一身分。一一毛孔。悉
440c22‖ 有三千大千世界。風輪水輪。地輪火輪。大
440c23‖ 海江河。及諸寶山。須彌鐵圍。村營城邑。宮殿
440c24‖ 園苑。一切地獄餓鬼畜生。閻羅王界。天龍
440c25‖ 八部。人與非人。欲界色界。無色界處。

简体字

见一一毛孔，念念中出一切佛刹微尘数菩萨身云，遍法界、虚空界一切佛刹，宣扬一切诸佛菩萨从初发意所生善根；见一一毛孔，念念中出一切佛刹微尘数菩萨身云，遍法界、虚空界，于一切佛刹一一刹中，宣扬一切菩萨愿海及普贤菩萨清净妙行；见一一毛孔，念念中出普贤菩萨行云，令一切众生心得满足，具足修习一切智道；见一一毛孔，出一切佛刹微尘数正觉身云，于一切佛刹，现成正觉，令诸菩萨增长大法、成一切智。

尔时，善财童子见普贤菩萨如是自在神通境界，身心遍喜，踊跃无量；重观普贤一一身分、一一毛孔，悉有三千大千世界。风轮、水轮、地轮、火轮，大海、江河及诸宝山、须弥、铁围，村营、城邑、宫殿、园苑，一切地狱、饿鬼、畜生、阎罗王界，天龙八部、人与非人，欲界、色界、无色界处，

He saw emerging from each pore in each successive mind-moment the emanation of clouds of bodhisattva congregations as numerous as the atoms in all buddha *kṣetras* that appeared everywhere throughout the Dharma realm and the realm of empty space, clouds of congregations in which they propagated the knowledge of all buddhas' and bodhisattvas' roots of goodness produced from the time when they made their initial resolve on up to the present;

He saw emerging from each pore in each successive mind-moment the emanation of clouds of bodhisattva congregations as numerous as the atoms in all buddha *kṣetras* that appeared everywhere throughout the Dharma realm and the realm of empty space in which, in all buddha *kṣetras* and in each single *kṣetra,* they made widely known all bodhisattvas' oceans of vows and the marvelous practices of Samantabhadra;

He saw emerging from each pore in each successive mind-moment the emanation of clouds of Samantabhadra Bodhisattva's practices as numerous as the atoms in all buddha *kṣetras* that caused all beings' minds to feel pleased and motivated to completely cultivate and accumulate the means for pursuing the path to all-knowledge; and

He saw emerging from each pore the emanation of clouds of congregations of rightly enlightened ones as numerous as the atoms in all buddha *kṣetras,* congregations that manifested the attainment of right enlightenment in all buddha *kṣetras* and motivated all bodhisattvas to increase their cultivation of great dharmas and attain all-knowledge.

Then, having witnessed Samantabhadra Bodhisattva's domain of experience in which he demonstrated such masterful command of the spiritual superknowledges, Sudhana the Youth's body and mind became suffused with joy and feelings of measureless rapture. He once again contemplated each part of Samantabhadra's body and saw that, completely contained within each of his pores was the entire great trichiliocosm, including:

All of its wind spheres, water spheres, earth spheres, and fire spheres;

All of its great oceans and rivers, jewel mountains, Sumeru mountains, and Iron Ring mountains;

All of its villages, towns, cities, palaces, parks and gardens;

All of its hells, hungry ghost realms, animal realms, and realms of King Yama;

All of its devas, dragons, the rest of the eight classes of spiritual beings,[57] and its humans and non-humans;

All of the stations of existence within the desire realms, form realms, and formless realms;

正體字

日月星
440c26‖ 宿。風雲雷電。晝夜月時。及以年劫。諸佛出
440c27‖ 世。菩薩眾會。道場莊嚴。如是等事悉皆明
440c28‖ 見。如見此世界。十方所有一切世界。悉如
440c29‖ 是見。如見現在十方世界。前際[6]後際一切
441a01‖ 世界。[1]亦如是見。各各差別不相雜亂。如於
441a02‖ 此毘盧遮那如來所。示現如是神通之力。於
441a03‖ 東方蓮華德世界賢首佛所。現神通力。亦復
441a04‖ 如是。如賢首佛所。如是東方一切世界。如
441a05‖ 東方。南西北方。四維上下。一切世界諸如
441a06‖ 來所。現神通力。當知悉爾。如十方一切世
441a07‖ 界。如是十方一切佛剎。一一塵中。皆有法
441a08‖ 界諸佛眾會。一一佛所。普賢菩薩。坐寶蓮
441a09‖ 華師子座上。現神通力。悉亦如是。彼一一
441a10‖ 普賢身中。皆現三世一切境界。一切佛剎。一
441a11‖ 切眾生。一切佛出現。一切菩薩眾。

简体字

日月星宿、风云雷电、昼夜月时及以年劫、诸佛出世、菩萨众会、道场庄严；如是等事，悉皆明见。如见此世界，十方所有一切世界悉如是见；如见现在十方世界，前际、后际一切世界亦如是见，各各差别，不相杂乱。如于此毗卢遮那如来所，示现如是神通之力；于东方莲华德世界贤首佛所，现神通力亦复如是。如贤首佛所；如是东方一切世界。如东方，南、西、北方，四维、上、下，一切世界诸如来所，现神通力当知悉尔。如十方一切世界；如是十方一切佛刹，一一尘中皆有法界诸佛众会，一一佛所普贤菩萨坐宝莲华师子座上现神通力悉亦如是。彼一一普贤身中，皆现三世一切境界、一切佛刹、一切众生、一切佛出现、一切菩萨众，

All of its suns, moons, stars, and constellations;
All of its wind, clouds, thunder, and lightning;
All of its periods of days, nights, months, years, and kalpas; and
All of its instances of buddhas appearing in the world together with their bodhisattva congregations and the adornments of their sites of enlightenment.

He clearly saw all the phenomena such as these. And just as he observed them in this world, so too did he see them all in all world systems throughout the ten directions. And just as he saw them throughout the world systems of the ten directions as they appeared in the present era, so too did he see them in this same way in all world systems in both the past and the future with none of their distinguishing aspects ever being mixed up.

Just as powers of the spiritual superknowledges such as these were then revealed within this abode of Vairocana Tathāgata, so too were such powers of the spiritual superknowledges also revealed in these same ways in the eastern region's Padmaśrī world system in the abode of Bhadraśrī Buddha.

And just as these circumstances were revealed in this way in the abode of Bhadraśrī Buddha, so too were they also revealed in all world systems to the east. One should realize that, just as they were revealed in this way in regions to the east, so too were such manifestations of the power of the spiritual superknowledges all also revealed in the same way in the abodes of all *tathāgatas* in all world systems in the south, the west, the north, the four midpoints, the zenith, and the nadir.

And just as this was so in all world systems throughout the ten directions, so too was this also so within each atom in all buddha *kṣetras* throughout the ten directions. In every case, there were the Dharma realm's buddhas and their congregations in which, in the presence of each buddha, Samantabhadra Bodhisattva sat on a lotus flower lion throne manifesting the power of the spiritual superknowledges.

Within each one of those bodies of Samantabhadra, there appeared as they existed in relation to all three periods of time:

All spheres of experience;
All buddha *kṣetras;*
All beings;
The arising of all buddhas;
All the congregations of bodhisattvas;

正體字

及聞一切
441a12║ 眾生言音。一切佛言音。一切如來所轉法輪。
441a13║ 一切菩薩所成諸行。一切如來遊戲神通。善
441a14║ 財童子。見普賢菩薩如是無量不可思議大
441a15║ 神通力。即得十種智波羅蜜。[2]何等為十。所
441a16║ 謂於念念中。悉能周遍一切佛剎智波羅蜜。
441a17║ 於念念中。悉能往詣一切佛所智波羅蜜。於
441a18║ 念念中。悉能供養一切如來智波羅蜜。於念
441a19║ 念中。普於一切諸如來所。聞法受持智波羅
441a20║ 蜜。於念念中。思惟一切如來法輪智波羅蜜。
441a21║ 於念念中。知一切佛不可思議。[3]太神通事智
441a22║ 波羅蜜。於念念中。說一句法盡未來際。辯
441a23║ 才無盡智波羅蜜。於念念中。以深般若觀一
441a24║ 切法智波羅蜜。於念念中。入一切法界實相
441a25║ 海智波羅蜜。於念念中。知一切眾生心智波
441a26║ 羅蜜。於念念中。普賢慧行。皆現在前智波
441a27║ 羅蜜。善財童子。既得是已。普賢菩薩。即伸
441a28║ 右手。摩觸其頂。既摩頂已。善財即得一切
441a29║ 佛剎微塵數三昧門。

简体字

及闻一切众生言音、一切佛言音、一切如来所转法轮、一切菩萨所成诸行、一切如来游戏神通。

善财童子见普贤菩萨如是无量不可思议大神通力，即得十种智波罗蜜。何等为十？所谓：于念念中，悉能周遍一切佛刹智波罗蜜；于念念中，悉能往诣一切佛所智波罗蜜；于念念中，悉能供养一切如来智波罗蜜；于念念中，普于一切诸如来所闻法受持智波罗蜜；于念念中，思惟一切如来法轮智波罗蜜；于念念中，知一切佛不可思议大神通事智波罗蜜；于念念中，说一句法尽未来际辩才无尽智波罗蜜；于念念中，以深般若观一切法智波罗蜜；于念念中，入一切法界实相海智波罗蜜；于念念中，知一切众生心智波罗蜜；于念念中，普贤慧行皆现在前智波罗蜜。

善财童子既得是已，普贤菩萨即伸右手摩触其顶。既摩顶已，善财即得一切佛刹微尘数三昧门，

The sounds of all beings' voices;
The sounds of all buddhas' voices;
The turnings of the Dharma wheel as initiated by all *tathāgatas;*
The practices perfected by all bodhisattvas; and
All *tathāgatas'* easeful mastery of the spiritual superknowledges.

Having seen Samantabhadra Bodhisattva's countless uses of inconceivably great spiritual powers such as these, Sudhana the Youth then immediately acquired ten[58] types of knowledge *pāramitās.* What then are those ten? They are as follows:

- The knowledge *pāramitā* that, in each successive mind-moment, is ever able to everywhere pervade all buddha *kṣetras;*
- The knowledge *pāramitā* that, in each successive mind-moment, is ever able to go forth and pay respects to all buddhas;
- The knowledge *pāramitā* that, in each successive mind-moment, is ever able to make offerings to all *tathāgatas;*
- The knowledge *pāramitā* that, in each successive mind-moment, everywhere listens to the teaching of the Dharma in the presence of all *tathāgatas,* absorbs it, and retains it;
- The knowledge *pāramitā* that, in each successive mind-moment, meditates on all *tathāgatas'* turnings of the Dharma wheel;
- The knowledge *pāramitā* that, in each successive mind-moment, knows the inconceivable great phenomena created by all buddhas' great spiritual superknowledges;[59]
- The knowledge *pāramitā* that, in each successive mind-moment, may expound with inexhaustible eloquence on but one sentence of Dharma, doing so on to the very end of future time;
- The knowledge *pāramitā* that, in each successive mind-moment, contemplates all dharmas with profound *prajñā pāramitā;*
- The knowledge *pāramitā* that, in each successive mind-moment, enters the ocean of the true character of the entire Dharma realm;
- The knowledge *pāramitā* that, in each successive mind-moment, knows the thoughts in the minds of all beings; and
- The knowledge *pāramitā* that, in each successive mind-moment, causes the wise practices of Samantabhadra to become directly and presently manifest.

Once Sudhana the Youth had acquired these *pāramitās,* Samantabhadra Bodhisattva then extended his right hand and rubbed the crown of his head. After he had rubbed the crown of Sudhana's head, Sudhana the Youth then immediately acquired an array of samādhi gateways as numerous as the atoms in all buddha *kṣetras,* each of which was in turn attended by a retinue of additional samādhis as numerous as

正體字

各以一切佛剎微塵數
441b01‖ 三昧。而為眷屬。[4]一一三昧。悉見昔所未見
441b02‖ 一切佛剎微塵數佛大海。集一切佛剎微塵
441b03‖ 數一切智助道具。生一切佛剎微塵數一切
441b04‖ 智上妙法。發一切佛剎微塵數一切智大誓
441b05‖ 願。入一切佛剎微塵數大願海。住一切佛剎
441b06‖ 微塵數一切智出要道。修一切佛剎微塵數
441b07‖ 諸菩薩所修行。起一切佛剎微塵數一切智
441b08‖ 大精進。得一切佛剎微塵數一切智淨光明。
441b09‖ 如此娑婆世界毘盧遮那佛所。普賢菩薩。摩
441b10‖ 善財頂。如是十方所有世界。及彼世界一一
441b11‖ 塵中。一切世界一切佛所。普賢菩薩。悉亦
441b12‖ 如是摩善財頂。所得法門亦皆同等。爾時普
441b13‖ 賢菩薩摩訶薩。告善財言。善男子汝見我此
441b14‖ 神通力不。唯然已見。大聖。此不思議大神通
441b15‖ 事。唯是如來之所能知。普賢告言。善男子。
441b16‖ 我於過去不可說不可說佛剎微塵數劫。行
441b17‖ 菩薩行。求一切智。一一劫中。為欲清淨菩
441b18‖ 提心故。承事不可說不可說佛剎微塵數佛。

简体字

各以一切佛刹微尘数三昧而为眷属；一一三昧，悉见昔所未见一切佛刹微尘数佛大海，集一切佛刹微尘数一切智助道具，生一切佛刹微尘数一切智上妙法，发一切佛刹微尘数一切智大誓愿，入一切佛刹微尘数大愿海，住一切佛刹微尘数一切智出要道，修一切佛刹微尘数诸菩萨所修行，起一切佛刹微尘数一切智大精进，得一切佛刹微尘数一切智净光明。如此娑婆世界毗卢遮那佛所，普贤菩萨摩善财顶；如是十方所有世界，及彼世界一一尘中一切世界一切佛所，普贤菩萨悉亦如是摩善财顶，所得法门亦皆同等。

尔时，普贤菩萨摩诃萨告善财言：“善男子，汝见我此神通力不？”

“唯然！已见。大圣，此不思议大神通事，唯是如来之所能知。”

普贤告言：“善男子，我于过去不可说不可说佛刹微尘数劫，行菩萨行，求一切智；一一劫中，为欲清净菩提心故，承事不可说不可说佛刹微尘数佛；

the atoms in all buddha *kṣetras*. In each one of those samādhis, the following events occurred:

He saw in its entirety what he had never seen before, namely the immense ocean of buddhas as numerous as the atoms in all buddha *kṣetras*.

He accumulated provisions for the path to all-knowledge that were as numerous as the atoms in all buddha *kṣetras*.

He produced supremely marvelous dharmas of all-knowledge that were as numerous as the atoms in all buddha *kṣetras*.

He made great vows regarding all-knowledge that were as numerous as the atoms in all buddha *kṣetras*.

He entered an ocean of great vows as numerous as the atoms in all buddha *kṣetras*.

He came to abide in emancipating paths to omniscience as numerous as the atoms in all buddha *kṣetras*.

He cultivated practices cultivated by all bodhisattvas, practices that were as numerous as the atoms in all buddha *kṣetras*.

He produced instances of great vigor in the pursuit of all-knowledge that were as numerous as the atoms in all buddha *kṣetras*.

He acquired pure lights of all-knowledge as numerous as the atoms in all buddha *kṣetras*.

Just as Samantabhadra Bodhisattva rubbed Sudhana's crown in the presence of Vairocana Buddha here in this Sahā World System, so too did Samantabhadra Bodhisattva also rub the crown of Sudhana's head in the presence of all buddhas in all world systems throughout the ten directions while also doing so in all world systems within every atom of those world systems. All those dharma gateways that he acquired in those instances were also identical to those acquired here.

Samantabhadra Bodhisattva-mahāsattva then spoke to Sudhana, asking, "Son of Good Family, did you or did you not see these spiritual powers of mine?"

Sudhana replied, "I did indeed see them. O Great Ārya, such inconceivable feats of spiritual powers could only be known by a *tathāgata*."

Samantabhadra replied:

Son of Good Family, in the quest for all-knowledge, I have practiced the bodhisattva practices for past kalpas as numerous as the atoms in an ineffable-ineffable number of buddha *kṣetras*.

In each of those kalpas, in order to purify the resolve to attain bodhi, I have served buddhas as numerous as the atoms in an ineffable-ineffable number of buddha *kṣetras*.

正體字

441b19 一一劫中。[5]為集一切智福德具故。設不可
441b20 說不可說佛剎微塵數廣大施會。一切世間。
441b21 咸使聞知。凡有所求悉令滿足。一一劫中。為
441b22 求一切智法故。以不可說不可說佛剎微塵
441b23 數財物布施。一一劫中。為求佛智故。以不
441b24 可說不可說佛剎微塵數城邑聚落。國土王
441b25 位。妻子眷屬。眼耳鼻舌。身肉手足乃至身命。
441b26 而為布施。一一劫中。為求一切智首故。以不
441b27 可說不可說佛剎微塵數頭。而為布施。一一
441b28 劫中。為求一切智故。於不可說不可說佛剎
441b29 微塵數諸如來所。恭敬尊重承事供養。衣服
441c01 臥具飲食湯藥。一切所須悉皆奉施。於其法
441c02 中出家學道。修行佛法護持正教。[6]善男子。
441c03 我於爾所劫海中。自憶未曾於一念間不順
441c04 佛教。於一念間。生瞋害心我我所心。自他
441c05 差別心。遠離菩提心。於生死中起疲厭心。懶
441c06 惰心。障礙心。迷惑心。唯住無上不可沮壞
441c07 集一切智助道之法大菩提心。善男子。我莊
441c08 嚴佛土。以大悲心。救護眾生。教化成就。

简体字

一一劫中，为集一切智福德具故，设不可说不可说佛刹微尘数广大施会，一切世间咸使闻知，凡有所求悉令满足；一一劫中，为求一切智法故，以不可说不可说佛刹微尘数财物布施；一一劫中，为求佛智故，以不可说不可说佛刹微尘数城邑、聚落、国土、王位、妻子、眷属、眼、耳、鼻、舌、身、肉、手、足乃至身命而为布施；一一劫中，为求一切智首故，以不可说不可说佛刹微尘数头而为布施；一一劫中，为求一切智故，于不可说不可说佛刹微尘数诸如来所，恭敬尊重，承事供养，衣服、卧具、饮食、汤药，一切所须悉皆奉施，于其法中出家学道，修行佛法，护持正教。

“善男子，我于尔所劫海中，自忆未曾于一念间不顺佛教，于一念间生瞋害心、我我所心、自他差别心、远离菩提心、于生死中起疲厌心、懒惰心、障碍心、迷惑心，唯住无上不可沮坏集一切智助道之法大菩提心。

“善男子，我庄严佛土，以大悲心，救护众生，教化成就，

In each of those kalpas, in order to accumulate the merit necessary for the realization of all-knowledge, I established great assemblies dedicated to giving, assemblies that were as numerous as the atoms in an ineffable-ineffable number of buddha *kṣetras*, assemblies in which everyone in the world was able to learn of them so that they could then all be completely satisfied with whatever it was they sought to acquire.

In each of those kalpas, in my quest to acquire the dharmas of all-knowledge, I engaged in acts of giving wealth that were as numerous as the atoms in an ineffable-ineffable number of buddha *kṣetras*.

In each of those kalpas, in my quest to acquire the Buddha's knowledge, I made gifts of cities, towns, villages, countries, the royal throne, wives, sons, retinues, eyes, ears, noses, tongues, bodily flesh, hands, feet, and even my own life, doing so in instances as numerous as the atoms in an ineffable-ineffable number of buddha *kṣetras*.

In each of those kalpas, in my quest to acquire the head endowed with all-knowledge, I made gifts of even my own head that were as numerous as the atoms in an ineffable-ineffable number of buddha *kṣetras*.

And, in each of those kalpas, in my quest to attain all-knowledge, I personally revered, honored, served, and made offerings to *tathāgatas* as numerous as the atoms in an ineffable-ineffable number of buddha *kṣetras*, making offerings to them of robes, bedding, drink, food, medicines, and whatever was needed, in every case making offerings of all those things. During the reign of their Dharma, I left the householder's life, trained in the path, cultivated the Buddha's Dharma, and preserved their right teaching.

Son of Good Family, I remember that, even in so very many oceans of kalpas, there has not been even one mind-moment in which I have failed to comply with the Buddha's teachings nor has there been even one mind-moment in which I have produced hate-filled or malicious thoughts, thoughts conceiving of a self or possessions of a self, thoughts of distinctions between self and other, thoughts of abandoning the resolve to attain bodhi, thoughts of weariness over continuing in *saṃsāra*, indolent thoughts, obstructive thoughts, or deluded thoughts. Rather, I have only dwelt in the unexcelled and invincible great resolve to attain bodhi that accumulates the dharmas essential to all-knowledge.

Son of Good Family, as for the efforts I have made in adorning buddha lands, in relying on great compassion to rescue and protect beings, in teaching beings and promoting their development, in

正體字

供養
441c09‖ 諸佛。事善知識。為求正法。弘宣護持。一切內
441c10‖ 外。悉皆能捨。乃至身命亦無所吝。一切劫海
441c11‖ 說其因緣。劫海可盡此無有盡。善男子。我法
441c12‖ 海中。無有一文。無有一句。非是捨施轉輪
441c13‖ 王位而求得者。非是捨施一切所有而求得
441c14‖ 者。善男子。我所求法。皆為救護一切眾生。一
441c15‖ 心思惟。願諸眾生得聞是法。願以智光普照
441c16‖ 世間。願為開示出世間智。願令眾生悉得安
441c17‖ 樂。願普稱讚一切諸佛所有功德。我如是等
441c18‖ 往昔因緣。於不可說不可說佛剎微塵數劫
441c19‖ 海。說不可盡。是故善男子。我以如是助道
441c20‖ 法力。諸善根力。大志樂力。修功德力。如實思
441c21‖ 惟一切法力。智慧眼力。佛威神力。大慈悲力。
441c22‖ 淨神通力。善知識力故。得此究竟三世平等
441c23‖ 清淨法身。復得清淨無上色身。超諸世間。隨
441c24‖ 諸眾生心之所樂。而為現形。入一切剎。遍
441c25‖ 一切處。於諸世界。廣現神通。令其見者靡不
441c26‖ 欣樂。

简体字

供养诸佛，事善知识；为求正法，弘宣护持，一切内外悉皆能舍，乃至身命亦无所吝。一切劫海说其因缘，劫海可尽，此无有尽。

“善男子，我法海中，无有一文，无有一句，非是舍施转轮王位而求得者，非是舍施一切所有而求得者。善男子，我所求法，皆为救护一切众生，一心思惟：‘愿诸众生得闻是法，愿以智光普照世间，愿为开示出世间智，愿令众生悉得安乐，愿普称赞一切诸佛所有功德。’我如是等往昔因缘，于不可说不可说佛刹微尘数劫海，说不可尽。

“是故，善男子，我以如是助道法力、诸善根力、大志乐力、修功德力、如实思惟一切法力、智慧眼力、佛威神力、大慈悲力、净神通力、善知识力故，得此究竟三世平等清净法身，复得清净无上色身，超诸世间，随诸众生心之所乐而为现形，入一切刹，遍一切处，于诸世界广现神通，令其见者靡不欣乐。

making offerings to the buddhas, in serving good spiritual guides, in my quest for right Dharma in which I have extensively propagated, protected, and preserved it, and in my being able to relinquish everything, whether inward or outward, even to the point of unstintingly sacrificing my own life—even if one attempted for an ocean of kalpas to describe all the causes and conditions involved in these efforts, that ocean of kalpas might come to an end, but one's description of these matters would still never come to an end.

Son of Good Family, in this entire ocean of Dharma of mine, there is not so much as one word or one sentence the acquisition of which has not involved giving up the wheel-turning king's throne or which has not involved giving up everything I possessed.

Son of Good Family, all the Dharma that I have sought has always been used for the sake of rescuing and protecting all beings and it has all been attended by single-minded meditative reflection in which I have wished to cause all beings to succeed in hearing this Dharma, in which I have wished to use the light of wisdom to everywhere illuminate the world, in which I have wished to instruct beings in world-transcending wisdom, in which I have wished to cause all beings to succeed in finding happiness, and in which I have wished to everywhere proclaim the praises of all buddhas' meritorious qualities.

The causes and conditions involved in such past efforts of mine are such that, even if one spoke of them for an ocean of kalpas as numerous as the atoms in an ineffable-ineffable number of buddha *kṣetras,* one would still never finish describing them even then.

Therefore, Son of Good Family, it is through the power of such path-assisting dharmas, the power of such roots of goodness, the power of such great determination, the power of such cultivation of meritorious qualities, the power of such reality-accordant contemplation of all dharmas, the power of such a wisdom eye, the power of such awesome spiritual powers of the Buddha, the power of such great kindness and compassion, the power of such purified spiritual superknowledges, and the power of such good spiritual guides—it is because of all these powers that I have acquired this ultimately pure Dharma body that is the same in all three periods of time and that I have also acquired this pure and unexcelled form body that surpasses all others in the world, that, adapting to whatever pleases beings' minds, manifests forms for their sakes, that enters all *kṣetras* and appears everywhere, and that extensively manifests spiritual superknowledges in all world systems, causing all who witness them to be delighted.

正體字

善男子。汝且觀我如是色身。我此色
441c27║ 身。無邊劫海之所成就。無量千億那由他劫。
441c28║ 難見難聞。善男子。若有眾生。未種善根。及種
441c29║ 少善根聲聞菩薩。猶尚不得聞我名字。況見
442a01║ 我身。善男子。若有眾生。得聞我名。於阿耨多
442a02║ 羅三藐三菩提。不復退轉。若見若觸。若迎
442a03║ 若送。若暫隨逐。乃至夢中。見聞我者。皆亦如
442a04║ 是。或有眾生。一日一夜。憶念於我。即得成
442a05║ 熟。或七日七夜。半月一月。半年一年。百年千
442a06║ 年。一劫百劫。乃至不可說不可說佛剎微塵
442a07║ 數劫。憶念於我而成熟者。或一生或百生。乃
442a08║ 至不可說不可說佛剎微塵數生。憶念於我
442a09║ 而成熟者。或[是>見]我放大光明。或見我[1]震動
442a10║ 佛剎。或生怖畏。或生歡喜。皆得成熟。善男
442a11║ 子。我以如是等佛剎微塵數方便門。令諸眾
442a12║ 生。於阿耨多羅三藐三菩提。得不退轉。善
442a13║ 男子。若有眾生。見聞於我清淨剎者。必得
442a14║ 生此清淨剎中。若有眾生。見聞於我清淨身
442a15║ 者。必得生我清淨身中。善男子。汝應觀我此
442a16║ 清淨身。[2]爾時善財童子。觀普賢菩薩身。相
442a17║ 好[3]肢節。一一毛孔中。

简体字

善男子，汝且观我如是色身；我此色身，无边劫海之所成就，无量千亿那由他劫难见难闻。

“善男子，若有众生未种善根，及种少善根声闻、菩萨，犹尚不得闻我名字，况见我身！善男子，若有众生得闻我名，于阿耨多罗三藐三菩提不复退转；若见若触，若迎若送，若暂随逐，乃至梦中见闻我者，皆亦如是。或有众生，一日一夜忆念于我即得成熟；或七日七夜、半月一月、半年一年、百年千年、一劫百劫，乃至不可说不可说佛刹微尘数劫，忆念于我而成熟者；或一生、或百生，乃至不可说不可说佛刹微尘数生，忆念于我而成熟者；或见我放大光明，或见我震动佛刹，或生怖畏，或生欢喜，皆得成熟。善男子，我以如是等佛刹微尘数方便门，令诸众生于阿耨多罗三藐三菩提得不退转。

“善男子，若有众生见闻于我清净刹者，必得生此清净刹中；若有众生见闻于我清净身者，必得生我清净身中。善男子，汝应观我此清净身。”

尔时，善财童子观普贤菩萨身，相好肢节，一一毛孔中，

Son of Good Family, now contemplate a form body such as mine. This form body of mine has been perfected over an ocean of boundlessly many kalpas of practice. It is rarely ever seen or heard of even in countless thousands of *koṭīs* of *nayutas* of kalpas.

Son of Good Family, if there are beings who have not yet planted roots of goodness, or if there are *śrāvaka* disciples or bodhisattvas who have planted only a minor measure of roots of goodness, they would not even be able to hear my name, how much the less would they be able to see my body.

Son of Good Family, there are some beings who, by being able to hear my name, then become irreversible in progressing toward *anuttara-samyak-saṃbodhi.* So too are there those who accomplish this by merely seeing me, touching me, welcoming me, escorting me off, briefly following along after me, or merely seeing or hearing me in a dream.

Some beings are able to become fully ripened by remaining mindful of me for but one day or one night. Others are able to become fully ripened by remaining mindful of me for seven days and seven nights, for a half month, for a month, for a half year, for a year, for a hundred years, a thousand years, a kalpa, a hundred kalpas, or for kalpas as numerous as the atoms in an ineffable-ineffable number of buddha *kṣetras.*

Others may require one lifetime or a hundred lifetimes, or even up to lifetimes as numerous as the atoms in an ineffable-ineffable number of buddha *kṣetras* before they will become fully ripened. Still others will become fully ripened by seeing me emanating brilliant light, by seeing me cause a buddha *kṣetra* to shake or move, or by being frightened or filled with joyous delight by such phenomena.

Son of Good Family, I use skillful means such as these that are as numerous as the atoms in a buddha *kṣetra* to enable beings to become irreversible in progressing toward *anuttara-samyak-saṃbodhi.*

Son of Good Family, if any being sees or hears of my pure *kṣetra,* he will certainly be able to be reborn in this pure *kṣetra.* If any being sees or hears of my pure body, he will certainly be able to be reborn within my pure body.

Son of Good Family, you should contemplate this pure body of mine.

Sudhana the Youth then contemplated the body of Samantabhadra Bodhisattva, its major marks and secondary signs, and its limbs. He saw that, within each pore, there were an ineffable-ineffable number

正體字

皆有不可說不可說佛
442a18 剎海。一一剎海。皆有諸佛。出興于世。大菩薩
442a19 眾。所共圍遶。又復見彼一切剎海。種種建立。
442a20 種種形狀。種種莊嚴。種種大山。周匝圍遶。種
442a21 種色雲彌覆虛空。種種佛興。演種種法。如是
442a22 等事。各各不同。又見普賢於一一世界海中。
442a23 出一切佛剎微塵數佛化身雲。周遍十方一
442a24 切世界。教化眾生。令向阿耨多羅三藐三菩
442a25 提。時善財童子。又見自身。在普賢身內。十方
442a26 一切諸世界中。教化眾生。又善財童子。親近
442a27 佛剎微塵數諸善知識。所得善根。智慧光明。
442a28 比見普賢菩薩所得善根。百分不及一。千分
442a29 不及一。百千分不及一。百千億分。乃至算
442b01 數譬[4]諭。亦不能[5]及是。善財童子。從初發心。
442b02 乃至得見普賢菩薩。於其中間。所入一切諸
442b03 佛剎海。今於普賢一毛孔中。一念所入諸佛
442b04 剎海。過前不可說不可說佛剎微塵數倍。如
442b05 一毛孔。一切毛孔。悉亦如是。善財童子。於普
442b06 賢菩薩毛孔剎中。行一步。

简体字

皆有不可说不可说佛刹海；一一刹海，皆有诸佛出兴于世，大菩萨众所共围绕。又复见彼一切刹海，种种建立、种种形状、种种庄严、种种大山周匝围绕，种种色云弥覆虚空，种种佛兴演种种法；如是等事，各各不同。又见普贤于一一世界海中，出一切佛刹微尘数佛化身云，周遍十方一切世界，教化众生，令向阿耨多罗三藐三菩提。时，善财童子又见自身在普贤身内，十方一切诸世界中教化众生。

又，善财童子亲近佛刹微尘数诸善知识所得善根、智慧光明，比见普贤菩萨所得善根，百分不及一，千分不及一，百千分不及一，百千亿分乃至算数譬喻亦不能及是。善财童子从初发心，乃至得见普贤菩萨，于其中间所入一切诸佛刹海，今于普贤一毛孔中一念所入诸佛刹海，过前不可说不可说佛刹微尘数倍；如一毛孔，一切毛孔悉亦如是。

善财童子于普贤菩萨毛孔刹中，行一步，

of oceans of buddha *kṣetras* and, in each *kṣetra* ocean, there were buddhas appearing in the world, each of whom was surrounded by an immense congregation of bodhisattvas.

He then also saw that all those oceans of *kṣetras* had many different kinds of foundations, many different shapes, many different adornments, many different great surrounding mountains, many different kinds of colored clouds spread across their skies, many different circumstances in which buddhas appear, and many different types of dharmas that were expounded. Each of the various phenomena such as these were distinctly different.

He also saw that, in each of those oceans of world systems, Samantabhadra emanated clouds of transformation-body buddhas as numerous as the atoms in all buddha *kṣetras* that appeared everywhere in all world systems throughout the ten directions, teaching beings and enabling them to progress toward *anuttara-samyaksaṃbodhi.*

Sudhana the Youth then also saw his own body within Samantabhadra's body, teaching beings in all world systems throughout the ten directions. Moreover, Sudhana observed that, if the roots of goodness and light of wisdom he acquired by drawing near to good spiritual guides as numerous as the atoms in a buddha *kṣetra* were compared to the roots of goodness he acquired by seeing Samantabhadra Bodhisattva, they still could not match even a hundredth part of these, a thousandth part of these, a hundred-thousandth part of these, one part in a hundred thousand *koṭīs* of parts of these, or even the tiniest fraction of these deducible by mathematical calculation or describable by analogy.

If one were to compare the number of all of the oceans of buddha *kṣetras* that Sudhana the Youth had entered from the time he made his initial resolve to the time he was able to see Samantabhadra Bodhisattva, comparing it with the number of all of the oceans of buddha *kṣetras* he now entered in one mind-moment in but one of Samantabhadra's pores, this latter number would exceed that former number by a multiplier equal to the number of atoms in an ineffable-ineffable number of world systems. And just as this was the case for but one pore, so too was it also the case for all of Samantabhadra's pores.

As Sudhana the Youth walked but one step in those *kṣetras* within Samantabhadra Bodhisattva's pores, he thereby passed through a number of world systems equal to that of all the atoms in an

正體字

過不可說不可說
442b07║ 佛剎微塵數世界。如是而行。盡未來劫。猶不
442b08║ 能知一毛孔中剎海次第。剎海藏。剎海差別。
442b09║ 剎海普入。剎海成。剎海壞。剎海莊嚴。所有邊
442b10║ 際。亦不能知佛海次第。佛海藏。佛海差別。佛
442b11║ 海普入。佛海生。佛海滅。所有邊際。亦不能知
442b12║ 菩薩眾海次第。菩薩眾海藏。菩薩眾海差別。
442b13║ 菩薩眾海普入。菩薩眾海集。菩薩眾海散。所
442b14║ 有邊際。亦不能知入眾生界。知眾生根。教化
442b15║ 調伏諸眾生智。菩薩所住甚深自在。菩薩所
442b16║ 入諸地諸道。如是等海所有邊際。善財童子。
442b17║ 於普賢菩薩毛孔剎中。或於一剎經於一劫。
442b18║ 如是而行。乃至或有經不可說不可說佛剎
442b19║ 微塵數劫。如是而行。亦不於此剎沒。於彼剎
442b20║ 現。念念周遍無邊剎海。教化眾生。令向阿
442b21║ 耨多羅三藐三菩提。當是之時。善財童子。則
442b22║ 次第得普賢菩薩諸行願海。與普賢等。與諸
442b23║ 佛等。

简体字

过不可说不可说佛刹微尘数世界；如是而行，尽未来劫，犹不能知一毛孔中刹海次第、刹海藏、刹海差别、刹海普入、刹海成、刹海坏、刹海庄严所有边际；亦不能知佛海次第、佛海藏、佛海差别、佛海普入、佛海生、佛海灭所有边际；亦不能知菩萨众海次第、菩萨众海藏、菩萨众海差别、菩萨众海普入、菩萨众海集、菩萨众海散所有边际；亦不能知入众生界、知众生根、教化调伏诸众生智、菩萨所住甚深自在、菩萨所入诸地诸道，如是等海所有边际。

善财童子于普贤菩萨毛孔刹中，或于一刹经于一劫如是而行，乃至或有经不可说不可说佛刹微尘数劫如是而行，亦不于此刹没、于彼刹现，念念周遍无边刹海，教化众生，令向阿耨多罗三藐三菩提。

当是之时，善财童子则次第得普贤菩萨诸行愿海，与普贤等，与诸佛等，

ineffable-ineffable number of buddha *kṣetras*. If he continued to walk in this way until he came to the end of all kalpas of the future, he would still have been unable to discover the bounds of all the phenomena contained in but one pore, including the sequential order of those oceans of *kṣetras*, the matrices of those oceans of *kṣetras*, the differences in those oceans of *kṣetras*, the instances of universal interpenetration in those oceans of *kṣetras*, the formation of those oceans of *kṣetras*, the destruction of those oceans of *kṣetras*, or the adornments of those oceans of *kṣetras*.

Nor would he have been able to discover the bounds of all those buddha oceans' sequential orders, the matrices of those buddha oceans, the differences in those buddha oceans, the universal interpenetration of those buddha oceans, the arising of those buddha oceans, or the destruction of those buddha oceans.

Nor would he have been able to discover the bounds of those bodhisattva congregations' sequential orders, those bodhisattva congregations' matrices, those bodhisattva congregations' differences, those bodhisattva congregations' universal interpenetration, those bodhisattva congregations' gathering together, or those bodhisattva congregations' dispersion.

Nor would he have been able to know the bounds of other such phenomena associated with oceans such as these, including the entry into the realms of beings, the cognition of beings' faculties, the knowledge involved in teaching and training beings, the extremely profound types of miraculous powers[60] in which those bodhisattvas dwelt, or the grounds and paths entered by those bodhisattvas.

In some cases, while within the *kṣetras* in Samantabhadra Bodhisattva's pores, Sudhana the Youth would pass through one kalpa within one *kṣetra* and then, continuing to travel along in this way, he might even pass through kalpas as numerous as the atoms in an ineffable-ineffable number of buddha *kṣetras*. Though he continued to travel along in this way, he still did not disappear from this *kṣetra* and then appear in that *kṣetra*. As in each successive mind-moment he went everywhere throughout an ocean of boundlessly many kalpas, he taught beings and caused them to progress toward *anuttara-samyak-saṃbodhi*.

It was at this time that Sudhana the Youth then gradually acquired the ocean of all practices and vows of Samantabhadra Bodhisattva-mahāsattva to a degree [bound before long to] equal that of Samantabhadra himself as he also [became bound to] attain equality with all buddhas in all the following things:[61]

正體字

一身充滿一切世界。剎等行等正覺等
442b24‖ 神通等。法輪等辯才等。言辭等音聲等。力無
442b25‖ 畏等。佛所住等。大慈悲等。不可思議。解脫自
442b26‖ 在。悉皆同等。爾時普賢菩薩摩訶薩。即說頌
442b27‖ 言
442b28‖ 汝等應除諸惑垢　一心不亂而諦聽
442b29‖ 我說如來具諸度　一切解脫真實道
442c01‖ 出世調[6]柔勝丈夫　其心清淨如虛空
442c02‖ 恒放智日大光明　普使群生滅癡暗
442c03‖ 如來難可得見聞　無量億劫今乃值
442c04‖ 如優曇華時一現　是故應聽佛功德
442c05‖ 隨順世間諸所作　譬如幻士現眾業
442c06‖ 但為悅可眾生心　未曾分別起想念
442c07‖ 爾時諸菩薩。聞此說已。一心渴仰。唯願得聞
442c08‖ 如來世尊真實功德。咸作是念。普賢菩薩。具
442c09‖ 修諸行。體性清淨。所有言說。皆悉不虛。一切
442c10‖ 如來。共所稱歎。作是念已。深生渴仰。爾時普
442c11‖ 賢菩薩。功德智慧。具足莊嚴。

简体字

一身充满一切世界，刹等、行等、正觉等、神通等、法轮等、辩才等、言辞等、音声等、力无畏等、佛所住等、大慈悲等、不可思议解脱自在悉皆同等。

尔时，普贤菩萨摩诃萨即说颂言：

“汝等应除诸惑垢，一心不乱而谛听；
我说如来具诸度，一切解脱真实道。
出世调柔胜丈夫，其心清净如虚空，
恒放智日大光明，普使群生灭痴暗。
如来难可得见闻，无量亿劫今乃值，
如优昙华时一现，是故应听佛功德。
随顺世间诸所作，譬如幻士现众业，
但为悦可众生心，未曾分别起想念。”

尔时，诸菩萨闻此说已，一心渴仰，唯愿得闻如来世尊真实功德，咸作是念：“普贤菩萨具修诸行，体性清净，所有言说皆悉不虚，一切如来共所称叹。”作是念已，深生渴仰。

尔时，普贤菩萨功德智慧具足庄严，

Equality in filling all worlds and *kṣetras* with a single body;
Equality in practices:
Equality in right enlightenment;
Equality in spiritual superknowledges;
Equality in turning the Dharma wheel;
Equality in eloquence;
Equality in the use of language;
Equality in the use of voices;
Equality in the powers and fearlessnesses;
Equality in the stations dwelt in by the buddhas;
Equality in the great kindness and compassion; and
Equality in the inconceivable liberations and sovereign masteries.

Samantabhadra Bodhisattva-mahāsattva then spoke the following verses:

You should all rid yourselves of the afflictions' defilements
and listen closely and single-mindedly, without distraction,
as I speak about the perfections that the Tathāgata possesses
and the genuine path leading to all the liberations.

As for that supreme world-transcending trainer of beings,
his mind is as pure as empty space.
He forever emanates the brilliant light of the sun of wisdom and
everywhere causes the many beings to dispel the darkness of delusion.

The Tathāgata is one who is difficult to ever see or hear,
yet, after countless *koṭīs* of kalpas, now one encounters him.
This is like the *uḍumbara* blossom's appearing but once in an eon.[62]
Therefore, you should listen to this account of the Buddha's qualities.

He adapts to everything those in the world do,
and, like a master conjurer, manifests the many kinds of actions,
doing so solely to please the minds of beings,
this even as he never discriminates or produces any thoughts.

Having heard what was spoken, those bodhisattvas then gazed up in single-minded anticipation, wishing only to be able to hear about the genuine meritorious qualities of the Bhagavat. They all then had this thought: "Samantabhadra Bodhisattva is one who completely cultivates all the practices, one whose essential nature is pure, one whose every pronouncement is never false, and one whom all *tathāgatas* join in praising." Having had this thought, they were then filled with deeply felt anticipation.

Samantabhadra Bodhisattva, completely adorned with meritorious qualities and wisdom and like a lotus flower in his freedom from the

正體字

猶如蓮華。不著
442c12| 三界一切塵垢。告諸菩薩言。汝等諦聽。我今
442c13| 欲說佛功德海一滴之相。即說頌言
442c14| 佛智廣大同虛空　普遍一切眾生心
442c15| 悉了世間諸妄想　不起種種異分別
442c16| 一念悉知三世法　亦了一切眾生根
442c17| 譬如善巧大幻師　念念示現無邊事
442c18| 隨眾生心種種行　往昔諸業誓願力
442c19| 令其所見各不同　而佛本來無動念
442c20| 或有處處見佛坐　充滿十方諸世界
442c21| 或有其心不清淨　無量劫中不見佛
442c22| 或有信解離憍慢　發意即得見如來
442c23| 或有諂誑不淨心　億劫尋求莫值遇
442c24| 或一切處聞佛音　其音美妙令心悅
442c25| 或有百千萬億劫　心不淨故不聞者
442c26| 或見清淨大菩薩　充滿三千大千界
442c27| 皆已具足普賢行　如來於中儼然坐
442c28| 或見此界妙無比　佛無量劫所嚴淨
442c29| 毘盧遮那最勝尊　於中覺悟成菩提
443a01| 或見蓮華勝妙剎　賢首如來住在中
443a02| 無量菩薩眾圍遶　皆悉勤修普賢行

简体字

犹如莲华不著三界一切尘垢，告诸菩萨言：“汝等谛听，我今欲说佛功德海一滴之相。”即说颂言：

“佛智广大同虚空，普遍一切众生心，
悉了世间诸妄想，不起种种异分别。
一念悉知三世法，亦了一切众生根，
譬如善巧大幻师，念念示现无边事。
随众生心种种行，往昔诸业誓愿力，
令其所见各不同，而佛本来无动念。
或有处处见佛坐，充满十方诸世界，
或有其心不清净，无量劫中不见佛。
或有信解离憍慢，发意即得见如来；
或有谄诳不净心，亿劫寻求莫值遇。
或一切处闻佛音，其音美妙令心悦；
或有百千万亿劫，心不净故不闻者。
或见清净大菩萨，充满三千大千界，
皆已具足普贤行，如来于中俨然坐。
或见此界妙无比，佛无量劫所严净；
毗卢遮那最胜尊，于中觉悟成菩提。
或见莲华胜妙刹，贤首如来住在中，
无量菩萨众围绕，皆悉勤修普贤行。

three realms' defilements, then spoke to those bodhisattvas, saying, "You should all listen closely, for I now wish to describe the characteristics of but a single drop of the Buddha's ocean of meritorious qualities." He then spoke the following verses:

The reach of the Buddha's wisdom is as vast as space,
for it extends everywhere to the minds of all beings.
It completely knows all the discursive thoughts of those in the world,
but never gives rise to the many kinds of different discriminations.

In but one mind-moment, he knows all dharmas of the three times
and also completely knows the faculties of all beings.
He is like a great and skillful master conjurer
manifesting boundless phenomena in each ensuing moment.

He adapts to beings' minds and many different practices
as well as to the power of all of their past karma and aspirations,
thereby causing what each of them sees to differ,
and yet the Buddha never has any movement of thought.

Some beings see the Buddha seated everywhere,
completely filling up all world systems throughout the ten directions,
whereas other beings whose minds are impure,
will pass through countless kalpas and never see the Buddha.

Some beings with resolute faith who have abandoned arrogance,
upon forming the intention, are immediately able to see the Tathāgata,
whereas others with impure minds prone to flattery and deception
may search for him for a *koṭī* of kalpas and still never encounter him.

Some beings hear the voice of the buddha in all places,
his voice exquisite, sublime, and causing their minds to be delighted,
even as others go for a hundred thousand myriads of *koṭīs* of kalpas,
and, because their minds are impure, never hear it at all.

Some beings see pure and great bodhisattvas
completely filling up the world systems of the great trichiliocosm
who have already completely fulfilled Samantabhadra's practices
and in whose midst the Tathāgata sits in majestic splendor.

Some beings see this realm as incomparably marvelous,
as adorned and purified by the Buddha for countless kalpas,
and see Vairocana, the Most Supremely Revered One,
awakening there and realizing bodhi.

Some beings see the supremely marvelous lotus flower *kṣetra*
in which Bhadraśrī Tathāgata abides,
surrounded by a congregation of countless bodhisattvas,
all of whom have diligently cultivated Samantabhadra's practices.

正體字

443a03	或有見佛無量壽	觀自在等所圍遶
443a04	悉已住於灌頂地	充滿十方諸世界
443a05	或有見此三千界	種種莊嚴如妙喜
443a06	阿閦如來住在中	及如香象諸菩薩
443a07	或見月覺大名稱	與金剛幢菩薩等
443a08	住如圓鏡妙莊嚴	普遍十方清淨剎
443a09	或見日藏世所尊	住善光明清淨土
443a10	及與灌頂諸菩薩	充遍十方而說法
443a11	或見金剛大焰佛	而與智幢菩薩俱
443a12	周行一切廣大剎	說法除滅眾生翳
443a13	一一毛端不可說	諸佛具相三十二
443a14	菩薩眷屬共圍遶	種種說法度眾生
443a15	或有觀見一毛孔	具足莊嚴廣大剎
443a16	無量如來悉在中	清淨佛子皆充滿
443a17	或有見一微塵內	具有恒沙佛國土
443a18	無量菩薩悉充滿	不可說劫修諸行
443a19	或有見一毛端處	無量塵沙諸剎海
443a20	種種業起各差別	毘盧遮那轉法輪
443a21	或見世界不清淨	或見清淨寶所成
443a22	如來住壽無量時	乃至涅槃諸所現

简体字

或有见佛无量寿，观自在等所围绕，
悉已住于灌顶地，充满十方诸世界。
或有见此三千界，种种庄严如妙喜，
阿閦如来住在中，及如香象诸菩萨。
或见月觉大名称，与金刚幢菩萨等，
住如圆镜妙庄严，普遍十方清净刹。
或见日藏世所尊，住善光明清净土，
及与灌顶诸菩萨，充遍十方而说法。
或见金刚大焰佛，而与智幢菩萨俱，
周行一切广大刹，说法除灭众生翳。
一一毛端不可说，诸佛具相三十二，
菩萨眷属共围绕，种种说法度众生。
或有观见一毛孔，具足庄严广大刹，
无量如来悉在中，清净佛子皆充满。
或有见一微尘内，具有恒沙佛国土，
无量菩萨悉充满，不可说劫修诸行。
或有见一毛端处，无量尘沙诸刹海，
种种业起各差别，毗卢遮那转法轮。
或见世界不清净，或见清净宝所成，
如来住寿无量时，乃至涅槃诸所现。

Some beings see the Buddha Amitāyus,
surrounded by Avalokiteśvara and others
who all already dwell on the crown-anointing consecration ground
and who completely fill up all world systems in the ten directions.

Some beings see this trichiliocosm
with the many kinds of adornments like those of Abhirati
in which Akṣobhya Buddha dwells,
attended by bodhisattvas such as Gandhahastin.

Some beings see the bodhisattvas Candrabodhi, Mahāyaśa,
and Vajra Banner as well as others who,
abiding like marvelous adornments reflected in a mirror,
everywhere pervade the pure *kṣetras* throughout the ten directions.

Some beings see Sūryagarbha, revered by the entire world,
dwelling in his Fine Radiance Pure Land
together with bodhisattvas at the crown-anointing consecration stage
who everywhere fill the ten directions and expound on the Dharma.

Some beings see Vajra's Great Flaming Radiance Buddha
together with Wisdom Banner Bodhisattva
who travel everywhere to all the vast *kṣetras* and,
by teaching the Dharma, extinguish beings' obscurations.

On the tip of every hair, there are an ineffable number
of buddhas perfectly endowed with the thirty-two major marks
who are all surrounded by a retinue of bodhisattvas
and who, in many different ways, teach the Dharma to liberate beings.

Some beings contemplate one pore and see
vast *kṣetras* graced with perfectly complete adornments
in which countless Tathāgatas all reside
and pure sons of the Buddha fill them all.

Some beings see within but a single atom
a Ganges sands' of buddha lands completely present therein,
all of which are filled with countless bodhisattvas
who cultivate all the practices for an ineffable number of kalpas.

Some beings see on the tip of a single hair
countless oceans of *kṣetras* as numerous as dust and sands,
all arising from the many kinds of karma, each individually distinct,
in which Vairocana Buddha resides, turning the wheel of the Dharma.

Some beings see world systems that are impure
whereas yet others see worlds composed of pure jewels
where *tathāgatas* abide for life spans of limitless duration
in which they display many appearances up until they enter *nirvāṇa*.

正體字

443a23 普遍十方諸世界　種種示現不思議
443a24 隨諸眾生心智業　靡不化度令清淨
443a25 如是無上大導師　充滿十方諸國土
443a26 示現種種神通力　我說少分汝當聽
443a27 或見釋迦成佛道　已經不可思議劫
443a28 或見今始為菩薩　十方利益諸眾生
443a29 或有見此釋師子　供養諸佛修行道
443b01 或見人中最勝尊　現種種力神通事
443b02 或見布施或持戒　或忍或進或諸禪
443b03 般若方便願力智　隨眾生心皆示現
443b04 或見究竟波羅蜜　或見安住於諸地
443b05 總持三昧神通智　如是悉現無不盡
443b06 或現修行無量劫　住於菩薩堪忍位
443b07 或現住於不退地　或現法水灌其頂
443b08 或現梵釋護世身　或現剎利婆羅門
443b09 種種色相所莊嚴　猶如幻師現眾像
443b10 或現兜率始降神　或見宮中受嬪御
443b11 或見棄捨諸榮樂　出家離俗行學道
443b12 或見始生或見滅　或見出家學異行
443b13 或見坐於菩提樹　降伏魔軍成正覺

简体字

普遍十方诸世界，种种示现不思议，
随诸众生心智业，靡不化度令清净。
如是无上大导师，充满十方诸国土，
示现种种神通力，我说少分汝当听。
或见释迦成佛道，已经不可思议劫；
或见今始为菩萨，十方利益诸众生。
或有见此释师子，供养诸佛修行道；
或见人中最胜尊，现种种力神通事。
或见布施或持戒，或忍或进或诸禅，
般若方便愿力智，随众生心皆示现。
或见究竟波罗蜜，或见安住于诸地，
总持三昧神通智，如是悉现无不尽。
或现修行无量劫，住于菩萨堪忍位；
或现住于不退地，或现法水灌其顶。
或现梵释护世身，或现刹利婆罗门，
种种色相所庄严，犹如幻师现众像。
或现兜率始降神，或见宫中受嫔御，
或见弃舍诸荣乐，出家离俗行学道。
或见始生或见灭，或见出家学异行，
或见坐于菩提树，降伏魔军成正觉。

They everywhere pervade all worlds of the ten directions
and present many different kinds of inconceivable manifestations
adapted to all beings' minds, knowledge, and karmic circumstances,
having no one they fail to teach, liberate, and enable to attain purity.

It is in this way that the unexcelled great guides
fill all lands throughout the ten directions
and manifest many different powers of the spiritual superknowledges.
As I describe only a small fraction of them, you should listen closely.

Some beings see Śākyamuni realizing buddhahood,
but as having gone an inconceivable number of kalpas since doing so.
Other beings see him as just now beginning as a bodhisattva
who is benefiting all beings throughout the ten directions.

Some beings see this lion of the Śākya clan
making offerings to all buddhas and cultivating the path
while yet others see this most supremely honored one among all men
manifesting many different powers and feats of the superknowledges.

Some beings see him practicing giving, some as observing precepts,
some as practicing patience, some as cultivating vigor or the *dhyānas,*
prajñā, skillful means, vows, the powers, or the types of knowledge,
as they manifest all of these while adapting to the minds of beings.

Some beings see him as perfecting the *pāramitās*
whereas others see him as securely abiding on the grounds,
or as bringing forth *dhāraṇīs,* the samādhis, the superknowledges,
or wisdom, endlessly appearing in all ways such as these.

For some, he appears as cultivating for countless kalpas
and as abiding in the bodhisattva's stage of patience.
For some, he appears as abiding on the ground of irreversibility and
for others, as with the waters of the Dharma anointing his crown.

For some, he appears in a body of Brahmā, Śakra, or a world protector,
while for others he appears as a *kṣatriya* or a brahman.
Manifesting thus, adorned with many different forms and features,
he is like a master conjurer manifesting a multitude of appearances.

For some, he appears in Tuṣita, about to descend and take birth.
For others, he is seen in the palace, with a retinue of consorts.
For yet others, he is seen renouncing all glory and pleasure,
leaving home, abandoning the mundane, and training in the path.

For some, he is seen just born, for others, he is seen entering nirvāṇa.
For others, he is seen leaving home to train in heterodox practices.
For yet others, he is seen as sitting beneath the bodhi tree,
as vanquishing Māra's armies, and as gaining right enlightenment.

正體字

443b14 或有見佛始涅槃　或見起塔遍世間
443b15 或見塔中立佛像　以知時故如是現
443b16 或見如來無量壽　與諸菩薩授尊記
443b17 而成無上大導師　次補住於安樂剎
443b18 或見無量億千劫　作佛事已入涅槃
443b19 或見今始成菩提　或見正修諸妙行
443b20 或見如來清淨月　在於梵世及魔宮
443b21 自在天宮化樂宮　示現種種諸神變
443b22 或見在於兜率宮　無量諸天共圍遶
443b23 為彼說法令歡喜　悉共發心供養佛
443b24 或見住在夜摩天　忉利護世龍神處
443b25 如是一切諸宮殿　莫不於中現其像
443b26 於彼然燈世尊所　散華布髮為供養
443b27 從是了知深妙法　恒以此道化群生
443b28 或有見佛久涅槃　或見初始成菩提
443b29 或[1]有住於無量劫　或見須臾即滅度
443c01 身相光明與壽命　智慧菩提及涅槃
443c02 眾會所化威儀聲　如是一一皆無數
443c03 或現其身極廣大　譬如須彌大寶山
443c04 或見[2]跏趺不動搖　充滿無邊諸世界

简体字

或有见佛始涅槃，或见起塔遍世间，
或见塔中立佛像，以知时故如是现。
或见如来无量寿，与诸菩萨授尊记，
而成无上大导师，次补住于安乐刹。
或见无量亿千劫，作佛事已入涅槃；
或见今始成菩提，或见正修诸妙行。
或见如来清净月，在于梵世及魔宫，
自在天宫化乐宫，示现种种诸神变。
或见在于兜率宫，无量诸天共围绕，
为彼说法令欢喜，悉共发心供养佛。
或见住在夜摩天，忉利护世龙神处，
如是一切诸宫殿，莫不于中现其像。
于彼燃灯世尊所，散华布发为供养，
从是了知深妙法，恒以此道化群生。
或有见佛久涅槃，或见初始成菩提；
或见住于无量劫，或见须臾即灭度。
身相光明与寿命，智慧菩提及涅槃，
众会所化威仪声，如是一一皆无数。
或现其身极广大，譬如须弥大宝山；
或见跏趺不动摇，充满无边诸世界。

For some, they see the Buddha just then entering nirvāṇa
while, for others, they see the building of stupas all over the world.
For yet others, they see the erecting of buddha images in the stupas.
It is through knowing the right time that he appears in these ways.

Some see him as a *tathāgata* possessed of limitless life
who bestows on bodhisattvas the *bhagavat*'s prediction
that they will become unexcelled great guides who,
while still next to fill that position, will dwell in the Land of Bliss.[63]

Some beings see him as entering nirvāṇa after having accomplished
the works of a buddha for countless *koṭīs* of thousands of kalpas,
whereas others see him as just now having realized bodhi.
For still others, he is seen as rightly cultivating wondrous practices.

Some beings see the pure moon of the Tathāgata abiding
in the Brahma World, in Māra's palace,
in the Vaśavartin Heaven Palace, or in the Nirmāṇarati Heaven Palace,
manifesting there many different kinds of spiritual transformations.

For some beings, he may be seen in the Tuṣita Heaven Palace,
surrounded by an audience of countless devas,
teaching the Dharma for them, causing them to feel joyous delight,
and inspiring them all to resolve to make offerings to the Buddha.

For yet others, he may be seen as abiding in the Suyāma Heaven,
the Trāyastriṃśa, or abodes of world-protectors, dragons, or spirits.
Thus, in this very manner, of all those palaces,
there are none in which he does not manifest his appearance.

In the presence of Dīpaṃkara Tathāgata,
he scattered flowers and spread out his hair as he made offerings.
Thenceforth, he completely understood the deep and sublime Dharma
and always used this path to teach the many kinds of beings.

Some observe the Buddha as having long ago entered nirvāṇa
and others see him at the beginning as he is first realizing bodhi.
Some see[64] him as remaining for countless kalpas
while others see him stay only a short time and then enter nirvāṇa.

His body's signs, his radiance, and his life span,
his wisdom, his bodhi, and his nirvāṇa—
the congregations he teaches, his awesome comportment, and voice—
The manifestations of every one of these are countless.

For some, he manifests his body as so extremely vast
that it resembles Sumeru or an immense mountain of jewels.
For others, he is seen as sitting, motionless, in the lotus posture,
completely filling all the boundlessly many worlds.

正體字

443c05 | 或見圓光一尋量　或見千萬億由旬
443c06 | 或見照於無量土　或見充滿一切剎
443c07 | 或見佛壽八十年　或壽百千萬億歲
443c08 | 或住不可思議劫　如是展轉倍過此
443c09 | 佛智通達淨無礙　一念普知三世法
443c10 | 皆從心識因緣起　生滅無常無自性
443c11 | 於一剎中成正覺　一切剎處悉亦成
443c12 | 一切入一一亦爾　隨眾生心皆示現
443c13 | 如來住於無上道　成就十力四無畏
443c14 | 具足智慧無所礙　轉於十二行法輪
443c15 | 了知苦集及滅道　分別十二因緣法
443c16 | 法義樂說[3]辭無礙　以是四辯廣開演
443c17 | 諸法無我無有相　業性不起亦無失
443c18 | 一切遠離如虛空　佛以方便而分別
443c19 | 如來如是轉法輪　普震十方諸國土
443c20 | 宮殿山河悉搖動　不使眾生有驚怖
443c21 | 如來普演廣大音　隨其根欲皆令解
443c22 | 悉使發心除惑垢　而佛未始生心念
443c23 | 或聞施戒忍精進　禪定般若方便智
443c24 | 或聞慈悲及喜捨　種種音辭各差別

简体字

或见圆光一寻量，或见千万亿由旬，
或见照于无量土，或见充满一切刹。
或见佛寿八十年，或寿百千万亿岁，
或住不可思议劫，如是展转倍过此。
佛智通达净无碍，一念普知三世法，
皆从心识因缘起，生灭无常无自性。
于一刹中成正觉，一切刹处悉亦成，
一切入一一亦尔，随众生心皆示现。
如来住于无上道，成就十力四无畏；
具足智慧无所碍，转于十二行法轮。
了知苦集及灭道，分别十二因缘法；
法义乐说辞无碍，以是四辩广开演。
诸法无我无有相，业性不起亦无失，
一切远离如虚空，佛以方便而分别。
如来如是转法轮，普震十方诸国土，
宫殿山河悉摇动，不使众生有惊怖。
如来普演广大音，随其根欲皆令解，
悉使发心除惑垢，而佛未始生心念。
或闻施戒忍精进，禅定般若方便智，
或闻慈悲及喜舍，种种音辞各差别。

For some, he is seen with a halo of light several yards in diameter.
For some, it is seen as spanning a thousand myriads of *koṭīs* of *yojanas*.
For others, he is seen as illuminating countless lands.
For still others, his radiance completely fills all *kṣetras*.

Some witness the Buddha's life span as lasting eighty years.
For others, that life span is a hundred thousand myriad *koṭīs* of years.
For yet others, he is seen as staying for inconceivably many kalpas.
In this way, [for still others, these perceptions] redouble even more.

The comprehension of Buddha's wisdom is pure and unimpeded, for,
in but an instant, he knows all dharmas of the three times and knows
they all arise from the mind consciousness's causes and conditions
and are created, destroyed, transient, and devoid of inherent nature.

Though it is in one *kṣetra* that he achieves the right enlightenment,
he also achieves that realization in all places in all *kṣetras*.
They all enter into but a single one and any single one also enters all.
Adapting to beings' minds, he manifests for them all.

The Tathāgata abides in the unexcelled path,
perfects the ten powers and the four fearlessnesses,
and is completely possessed of unimpeded wisdom
as he turns the Dharma wheel through its twelve-phase course.[65]

He completely understands suffering, origination, cessation, and path,
and distinguishes the dharmas of the twelve causes and conditions.
In dharmas, meanings, delight in speech, and unimpeded phrasings,
he uses these four aspects of eloquence to give extensive discourses.[66]

All dharmas are selfless and signless.
Karmic actions' nature is unproduced, yet they are still never lost.
Everything is utterly transcendent and comparable to empty space.
Using expedient means, the Buddha distinguishes all these matters.

It is in ways such as these that the Tathāgata turns the Dharma wheel,
thus everywhere causing the lands of the ten directions to quake
and causing all the palaces, mountains, and rivers to shake,
yet he never causes beings to be frightened by this.

The Tathāgata everywhere expounds with his vastly resonant voice
adapted to their faculties and desires, enabling them all to understand
and enabling all to resolve to rid themselves of afflictions' defilements,
this even as the Buddha has never had any thoughts arise.

Some beings hear teachings on giving, moral virtue, patience, vigor,
dhyāna, *prajñā*, skillful means, [vows, powers], and knowledge[67]
while others hear teachings on kindness, compassion, sympathetic joy,
and equanimity[68] in many different languages specific to each being.

正體字

443c25 | 或聞四念四正勤　神足根力及覺道
443c26 | 諸念神通止觀等　無量方便諸法門
443c27 | 龍神八部人非人　梵釋護世諸天眾
443c28 | 佛以一音為說法　隨其品類皆令解
443c29 | 若有貪欲瞋恚癡　忿覆慳嫉及憍諂
444a01 | 八萬四千煩惱異　皆令聞說彼治法
444a02 | 若未具修白淨法　令其聞說十戒行
444a03 | 已能布施調伏人　令聞寂滅涅槃音
444a04 | 若人志劣無慈愍　厭惡生死自求離
444a05 | 令其聞說三脫門　使得出苦涅槃樂
444a06 | 若有自性少諸欲　厭背三有求寂靜
444a07 | 令其聞說諸緣起　依獨覺乘而出離
444a08 | 若有清淨廣大心　具足施戒諸功德
444a09 | 親近如來具慈愍　令其聞說大乘音
444a10 | 或有國土聞一乘　或二或三或四五
444a11 | 如是乃至無有量　悉是如來方便力
444a12 | 涅槃寂靜未曾異　智行勝劣有差別
444a13 | 譬如虛空體性一　鳥飛遠近各不同
444a14 | 佛體音聲亦如是　普遍一切虛空界
444a15 | 隨諸眾生心智殊　所聞所見各差別

简体字

或闻四念四正勤，神足根力及觉道，
诸念神通止观等，无量方便诸法门。
龙神八部人非人，梵释护世诸天众，
佛以一音为说法，随其品类皆令解。
若有贪欲瞋恚痴，忿覆悭嫉及憍谄，
八万四千烦恼异，皆令闻说彼治法。
若未具修白净法，令其闻说十戒行；
已能布施调伏人，令闻寂灭涅槃音。
若人志劣无慈愍，厌恶生死自求离；
令其闻说三脱门，使得出苦涅槃乐。
若有自性少诸欲，厌背三有求寂静；
令其闻说诸缘起，依独觉乘而出离。
若有清净广大心，具足施戒诸功德，
亲近如来具慈愍，令其闻说大乘音。
或有国土闻一乘，或二或三或四五，
如是乃至无有量，悉是如来方便力。
涅槃寂静未曾异，智行胜劣有差别；
譬如虚空体性一，鸟飞远近各不同。
佛体音声亦如是，普遍一切虚空界，
随诸众生心智殊，所闻所见各差别。

Some hear the four foundations of mindfulness, four right efforts,
psychic power bases, faculties, powers, limbs of bodhi, eightfold path,
the types of mindfulness, spiritual powers, calming, contemplation,
and countless other kinds of expedients and Dharma gateways.

For the eight divisions[69] of dragons and spirits, humans, nonhumans,
Brahma Heaven lords, Indras, world-protectors, and groups of devas,
the Buddha uses but one voice to speak the Dharma for them all that,
adapted to their individual type, enables them all to understand.

Wherever there are any beings beset with desire, hatred, delusion,
anger, concealment, miserliness, jealousy, arrogance, flattery,
or any of the other eighty-four thousand variants of the afflictions,
he enables them all to hear his teachings on their antidotal dharmas.

For those not yet perfectly cultivating the white dharmas of purity,
he enables them to hear teachings on practicing ten moral precepts.[70]
For those already able to practice giving and personal discipline,
he enables them to hear a voice teaching about quiescent *nirvāṇa*.

If there are those of inferior resolve bereft of kindness or compassion
who, detesting *saṃsāra*, seek their own emancipation,
he enables them to hear teachings on the three gates to liberation,[71]
thereby enabling them to escape suffering and reach nirvāṇa's bliss.

For those who by nature have but few desires,
renounce the three realms of existence, and seek quiescence,
he enables them to hear teachings on conditioned arising
and gain emancipation in reliance on the *pratyekabuddha* vehicle.

Wherever there are those with a pure and vast resolve
who have completely fulfilled the qualities of giving and moral virtue,
who draw near to the Tathāgata, and who possess kindly sympathy,
he enables them to hear teachings on the Great Vehicle.

In some cases, lands hear the teaching of the One Vehicle,
or perhaps the teaching of two, three, four, or five,
and so forth in this way on up to their hearing of countlessly many.
These are all due to the Tathāgata's powers in using skillful means.

Though the quiescence of nirvāṇa has never varied,
Supremacy or inferiority in wisdom and practice still differ.
This is just as when, though the empty sky has one essential nature,
each bird's capacity for long or short flight differs from the others.

So too it is with the Buddha's body and the sounds of his voice
that everywhere pervade all realms of empty space,
adapting to distinctions in beings' minds and wisdom.
Thus, what is heard and what is seen differ in every instance.

正體字

444a16 佛以過去修諸行　能隨所樂演妙音
444a17 無心計念此與彼　我為誰說誰不說
444a18 如來面門放大光　具足八萬四千數
444a19 所說法門亦如是　普照世界除煩惱
444a20 具足清淨功德智　而常隨順三世[1]間
444a21 譬如虛空無染著　為眾生故而出現
444a22 示有生老病死苦　亦示住壽處於世
444a23 雖順世間如是現　體性清淨同虛空
444a24 一切國土無有邊　眾生根欲亦無量
444a25 如來智眼皆明見　隨所應化示佛道
444a26 究竟虛空十方界　所有人天大眾中
444a27 隨其形相各不同　佛現其身亦如是
444a28 若[2]在沙門大眾會　剃除鬚髮服袈裟
444a29 執持衣鉢護諸根　令其歡喜息煩惱
444b01 若時親近婆羅門　即為示現羸瘦身
444b02 執杖持瓶恒潔淨　具足智慧巧談說
444b03 吐故納新自充飽　吸風飲露無異食
444b04 若坐若立不動搖　現斯苦行摧異道
444b05 或持彼戒為世師　善達醫方等諸論
444b06 書數天文地眾相　及身休咎無不了

简体字

佛以过去修诸行，能随所乐演妙音，
无心计念此与彼，我为谁说谁不说。
如来面门放大光，具足八万四千数；
所说法门亦如是，普照世界除烦恼。
具足清净功德智，而常随顺三世间，
譬如虚空无染著，为众生故而出现。
示有生老病死苦，亦示住寿处于世；
虽顺世间如是现，体性清净同虚空。
一切国土无有边，众生根欲亦无量；
如来智眼皆明见，随所应化示佛道。
究竟虚空十方界，所有人天大众中，
随其形相各不同，佛现其身亦如是。
若在沙门大众会，剃除须发服袈裟，
执持衣钵护诸根，令其欢喜息烦恼。
若时亲近婆罗门，即为示现羸瘦身，
执杖持瓶恒洁净，具足智慧巧谈说。
吐故纳新自充饱，吸风饮露无异食，
若坐若立不动摇，现斯苦行摧异道。
或持彼戒为世师，善达医方等诸论，
书数天文地众相，及身休咎无不了。

Due to his past cultivation of all the practices, the Buddha
is able to adapt to what is pleasing as he expounds in a sublime voice,
doing so without mental planning or thinking of this one or that one:
"For whom should I speak?" or "For whom should I not speak?"

The Tathāgata's countenance emits a great radiance
that contains eighty-four thousand light rays.
So too it is with the Dharma gateways on which he expounds
that everywhere illuminate the worlds, doing away with afflictions.

He is completely possessed of pure meritorious qualities and wisdom
and yet always adapts to those throughout the three periods of time.
Like space, he is free of any defiling attachment,
and yet he manifests for the sake of beings.

He appears as having the suffering of birth, aging, sickness, and death
and also appears as abiding for a life span and residing in the world.
Although he accords with the world in presenting such appearances,
his essential nature is pure and the same as empty space.

All lands are boundless in number
and the sum of beings' faculties and desires is also measureless.
The Tathāgata's wisdom eye clearly sees them all
and adapts to what is fitting in teaching and revealing Buddha's path.

He goes to the very ends of space and the realms of the ten directions
and, in the midst of immense congregations of humans and devas,
he adapts to their forms and characteristics, each of which differ.
The Buddha's manifestation of his bodies occurs in just this way.

When residing in a great congregation of *śramaṇas,*
he cuts off his beard and hair, dons the *kaṣāya* robe,
firmly holds his robes and bowl, guards all his faculties,
and enables them to feel delighted and extinguish their afflictions.

If there are times when he draws near to brahmans,
he then manifests for them an emaciated body
and grasps a staff, holds a vase, and is constantly perfectly pure
as, fully possessed of wisdom, he engages them in skillful discussions.

By expelling the old and inhaling the fresh, he is able to become full.
Inhaling the wind and drinking the dew, he has no other food.
Whether sitting or standing, he remains unmoving, and,
by manifesting such austerities, subdues the heterodox traditions.

He may appear upholding their morality, as a teacher of the world,
as skillful in knowing medical decoctions and all the other treatises,
writing, mathematics, astronomy, geography, physiognomy, and
personal fortune and misfortune, having none he has not fathomed.

正體字

444b07 | 深入諸禪及解脫　三昧神通智慧行
444b08 | 言談諷詠共嬉戲　方便皆令住佛道
444b09 | 或現上服以嚴身　首戴華冠蔭高蓋
444b10 | 四兵前後共圍遶　[3]誓眾宣威伏小王
444b11 | 或為聽訟斷獄官　善解世間諸法務
444b12 | 所有與奪皆明審　令其一切悉欣伏
444b13 | 或作大臣[4]事弼輔　善用諸王治政法
444b14 | 十方利益皆周遍　一切眾生莫了知
444b15 | 或為粟散諸小王　或作飛行轉輪帝
444b16 | 令諸王子采女眾　悉皆[5]授化無能測
444b17 | 或作護世四天王　統領諸龍夜叉等
444b18 | 為其眾會而說法　一切皆令大欣慶
444b19 | 或為忉利大天王　住善法堂歡喜園
444b20 | 首戴華冠說妙法　諸天覲仰莫能測
444b21 | 或住夜摩兜率天　化樂自在魔王所
444b22 | 居處摩尼寶宮殿　說真實行令調伏
444b23 | 或至梵天眾會中　說四無量諸禪道
444b24 | 普令歡喜便捨去　而莫知其往來相
444b25 | 或至阿迦尼吒天　為說覺分諸寶華
444b26 | 及餘無量聖功德　然後捨去無知者

简体字

深入诸禅及解脱，三昧神通智慧行，
言谈讽咏共嬉戏，方便皆令住佛道。
或现上服以严身，首戴华冠荫高盖，
四兵前后共围绕，警众宣威伏小王。
或为听讼断狱官，善解世间诸法务，
所有与夺皆明审，令其一切悉欣伏。
或作大臣专弼辅，善用诸王治政法，
十方利益皆周遍，一切众生莫了知。
或为粟散诸小王，或作飞行转轮帝，
令诸王子采女众，悉皆受化无能测。
或作护世四天王，统领诸龙夜叉等，
为其众会而说法，一切皆令大欣庆。
或为忉利大天王，住善法堂欢喜园，
首戴华冠说妙法，诸天觐仰莫能测。
或住夜摩兜率天，化乐自在魔王所，
居处摩尼宝宫殿，说真实行令调伏。
或至梵天众会中，说四无量诸禅道，
普令欢喜便舍去，而莫知其往来相。
或至阿迦尼吒天，为说觉分诸宝华，
及余无量圣功德，然后舍去无知者。

He may appear deeply entering the practice of the *dhyānas*, liberations,
samādhis, spiritual superknowledges, and wisdom,
participating in discussions, chanting, singing, or humorous repartee,
using expedients to enable everyone to abide in the Buddha's path.

He may appear with supremely fine robes adorning his body,
wearing a floral crown on his head, and shaded by a high canopy,
with his fourfold army preceding, following, and surrounding him,
warning all, extending awesome power, and subduing lesser kings.

For others, he acts as a judge, hearing and adjudicating their disputes,
skillful in understanding all of the world's laws and responsibilities,
clearly assessing all cases where assets are awarded or confiscated,
thereby causing everyone involved to happily submit to his decisions.

In some cases, he serves as a great official serving the chief minister,
skillfully using the kings' methods of governance,
bringing about pervasive benefit to everyone in the ten directions
even as none of those beings completely understand his actions.

Sometimes he is one of the lesser kings as numerous as scattered millet
and sometimes he serves as a flying wheel-turning emperor.
He causes the princes and the groups of female retainers
to all accept[72] teachings, doing so in ways none of them can fathom.

In some cases, he serves as one of four world-protecting deva kings
who commands and leads all the dragons, *yakṣas*, and others,
teaching the Dharma for their congregations,
thereby causing them all to feel great joyous happiness.

Sometimes he serves as a great Trāyastriṃśa deva king
abiding in the Hall of Good Dharma and the Garden of Delights
who wears a floral crown and speaks on the sublime Dharma.
The devas come to pay their respects even as none can fathom him.

In some cases, he abides in the Suyāma or Tuṣita Heaven,
the Nirmāṇarati Heaven, or the abode of the Vaśavartin *māra* king
where he resides in a palace made of *maṇi* jewels and
speaks on genuine practice, causing his listeners to accept the training.

Sometimes he goes among a congregation of Brahma Heaven devas,
speaks on the four immeasurables and the path of the *dhyānas,*
causes them all to feel joyous delight, and then disappears,
all with none of them perceiving any signs of his going or coming.

In some cases, he goes to the Akaniṣṭha Heaven,
speaks for them about the precious flowers of the limbs of bodhi
or on the other measureless qualities of the *āryas,*
after which he then disappears without anyone knowing it at all.

正體字

444b27	如來無礙智所見	其中一切諸眾生
444b28	悉以無邊方便門	種種教化令成[6]熟
444b29	譬如幻師善幻術	現作種種諸幻事
444c01	佛化眾生亦如是	為其示現種種身
444c02	譬如淨月在虛空	令世眾生見增減
444c03	一切河池現影像	所有星宿奪光色
444c04	如來智月出世間	亦以方便示增減
444c05	菩薩心水現其影	聲聞星宿無光色
444c06	譬如大海寶充滿	清淨無濁無有量
444c07	四洲所有諸眾生	一切於中現其像
444c08	佛身功德海亦爾	無垢無濁無邊際
444c09	乃至法界諸眾生	靡不於中現其影
444c10	譬如淨日放千光	不動本處照十方
444c11	佛日光明亦如是	無去無來除世暗
444c12	譬如龍王降大雨	不從身出及心出
444c13	而能霑洽悉周遍	滌除炎熱使清涼
444c14	如來法雨亦復然	不從於佛身心出
444c15	而能開悟一切眾	普使滅除三毒火
444c16	如來清淨妙法身	一切三界無倫匹
444c17	以出世間言語道	其性非有非無故

简体字

如来无碍智所见，其中一切诸众生，
悉以无边方便门，种种教化令成就。
譬如幻师善幻术，现作种种诸幻事；
佛化众生亦如是，为其示现种种身。
譬如净月在虚空，令世众生见增减，
一切河池现影像，所有星宿夺光色。
如来智月出世间，亦以方便示增减，
菩萨心水现其影，声闻星宿无光色。
譬如大海宝充满，清净无浊无有量；
四洲所有诸众生，一切于中现其像。
佛身功德海亦尔，无垢无浊无边际；
乃至法界诸众生，靡不于中现其影。
譬如净日放千光，不动本处照十方；
佛日光明亦如是，无去无来除世暗。
譬如龙王降大雨，不从身出及心出，
而能沾洽悉周遍，涤除炎热使清凉。
如来法雨亦复然，不从于佛身心出，
而能开悟一切众，普使灭除三毒火。
如来清净妙法身，一切三界无伦匹；
以出世间言语道，其性非有非无故。

For all of those beings
seen by the Tathāgata's unimpeded wisdom,
he employs boundlessly many approaches to the use of skillful means
and thus gives many different teachings to bring about their ripening.

In this, he is like a master conjurer skilled in the art of casting illusions
who manifests appearances of all kinds of illusory phenomena.
In his teaching of beings, the Buddha is also just like this
as he manifests many different bodies for their sakes.

Just as the clearly shining moon up in the sky
causes the beings in the world to see its waxings and wanings
as its image is reflected in all the rivers and ponds
and it outshines the radiance from all the stars and constellations,

so too, the moon of the Tathāgata's wisdom comes forth into the world
and also, through skillful means, manifests waxings and wanings.
Its reflections appear in the waters of the bodhisattvas' minds as
the *śrāvakas'* stars and constellations then lose their bright appearance.

Just as the great ocean is full of precious jewels,
pristinely pure, free of turbidity, and measureless,
and just as the images of all beings of the four continents
all appear as reflected in it,

so too it is with the ocean of meritorious qualities of Buddha's body
that is free of defilement, free of turbidity, boundless,
and such that, of all beings within the Dharma realm,
there are none of them whose images do not appear reflected in it.

Just as the clearly shining sun emanates a thousand rays of light and,
without moving from its original place, illuminates the ten directions,
so too it is with the light of the Buddha sun that,
even without ever going or coming, still rids the world of its darkness.

Just as the dragon king sends down the great rains
that come forth neither from his body or his mind,
and yet they are still able to drench everything everywhere,
rinsing away the burning heat and causing clarity and coolness,

so too it is with the Tathāgata's Dharma rain
that does not come forth from either the Buddha's body or his mind,
and yet it is still able to awaken all beings,
and everywhere extinguish the fires of the three poisons.

The Tathāgata's pure and wondrous Dharma body
has no peer anywhere in the three realms
because it transcends the path of worldly discourse
and because its nature is neither existent nor nonexistent.

正體字

444c18 雖無所依無不住　雖無不至而不去
444c19 如空中畫夢所見　當於佛體如是觀
444c20 三界有無一切法　不能與佛為譬[7]諭
444c21 譬如山林鳥獸等　無有依空而住者
444c22 大海摩尼無量色　佛身差別亦復然
444c23 如來非色非非色　隨應而現無所住
444c24 虛空真如及實際　涅槃法性寂滅等
444c25 唯有如是真實法　可以顯示於如來
444c26 剎塵心念可數知　大海中水可飲盡
444c27 虛空可量風可繫　無能盡說佛功德
444c28 若有聞斯功德海　而生歡喜信解心
444c29 如所稱揚悉當獲　慎勿於此懷疑念

简体字

虽无所依无不住，虽无不至而不去；
如空中画梦所见，当于佛体如是观。
三界有无一切法，不能与佛为譬喻；
譬如山林鸟兽等，无有依空而住者。
大海摩尼无量色，佛身差别亦复然；
如来非色非非色，随应而现无所住。
虚空真如及实际，涅槃法性寂灭等；
唯有如是真实法，可以显示于如来。
刹尘心念可数知，大海中水可饮尽，
虚空可量风可系，无能尽说佛功德。
若有闻斯功德海，而生欢喜信解心，
如所称扬悉当获，慎勿于此怀疑念。”

Though it has no place it depends on, it has no place it does not abide.
Though it has no place it fails to reach, still, it does not go anywhere.
It is like a painting made in space and like what is seen in a dream.
Just so should one contemplate the body of the Buddha.

Of all dharmas in the three realms, whether existent or nonexistent,
there are none of them that can be compared to the Buddha,
just as, of all birds, beasts, or other creatures in the mountains' forests,
there are none of them that can dwell solely in the sky.

Just as the great ocean's *maṇi* jewels are found in countless colors,
so too it is with the differences existing in the Buddha's bodies.
The Tathāgata is neither form nor formless.
He appears in response to what is fitting, yet has no place he dwells.

Empty space, true suchness, as well as the apex of reality,
nirvāṇa, the nature of dharmas, quiescent cessation, and such—
it is only by resort to such genuine dharmas as these
that one might be able to reveal the Tathāgata.

Perhaps one could count all *kṣetras'* dusts and all minds' thoughts
or drink up all the waters of the great ocean.
And perhaps one could measure empty space and tie up all the winds.
Still, no one can fully describe the Buddha's meritorious qualities.

Whosoever hears of this ocean of meritorious qualities and
experiences joyous delight and thoughts of resolute faith
will thereby be bound to acquire them all as here proclaimed.
Be careful not to harbor any doubting thoughts about this.

The End of the Śikṣānanda Translation's Chapter Thirty-Nine

Chapter 39 Conclusion:

The Conduct and Vows of Samantabhadra

(Taisho T10, no. 293, Fascicle 40)

Translated under Imperial Auspices by the Tang Dynasty Tripiṭaka Master Prajñā from the State of Kashmir

English Translation by Bhikshu Dharmamitra

正體字

844b16‖ [2]大方廣佛華嚴經卷[3]第四十
844b18‖ [4]罽賓國三藏般若奉　詔譯
844b19‖ [5]入不思議解脫境界普賢行願品[6]
844b20‖ 爾時普賢菩薩摩訶薩。稱歎如來勝功德已。
844b21‖ 告諸菩薩及[7]善財言。善男子。如來功德。假
844b22‖ 使十方一切諸佛經不可說[8]不可說佛剎極
844b23‖ 微塵數劫。相續演說不可窮盡。若欲成就此
844b24‖ 功德門。應修十種廣大行願。何等為十。[9]一
844b25‖ 者禮敬諸佛。二者稱讚如來。三者廣修供養。
844b26‖ 四者懺悔業障。五者隨喜功德。六者請轉法
844b27‖ 輪。七者請佛住世。八者常隨佛學。九者恒順
844b28‖ 眾生。十者普皆迴向
844b29‖ 善財白言。大聖。云何禮敬乃至迴向。普賢菩
844c01‖ 薩。告善財言。善男子。言禮敬諸佛者。所有盡
844c02‖ 法界。虛空界。十方三世一切佛剎極微塵數
844c03‖ 諸佛世尊。我以普賢行願力故。[10]起深信解。
844c04‖ 如對目前。悉以清淨身語意業。常修禮敬。一
844c05‖ 一佛所。皆現不可說不可說佛剎極微塵數
844c06‖ 身。

简体字

大方广佛华严经普贤菩萨行愿品卷第四十

唐罽宾三藏般若奉诏译

入不思议解脱境界普贤行愿品

尔时普贤菩萨摩诃萨。称叹如来胜功德已。告诸菩萨及善财言。善男子。如来功德。假使十方一切诸佛经不可说不可说佛刹极微尘数劫。相续演说不可穷尽。若欲成就此功德门。应修十种广大行愿。何等为十。一者礼敬诸佛。二者称赞如来。三者广修供养。四者忏悔业障。五者随喜功德。六者请转法轮。七者请佛住世。八者常随佛学。九者恒顺众生。十者普皆回向。

善财白言。大圣。云何礼敬乃至回向。普贤菩萨。告善财言。善男子。言礼敬诸佛者。所有尽法界。虚空界。十方三世一切佛刹极微尘数诸佛世尊。我以普贤行愿力故。起深信解。如对目前。悉以清净身语意业。常修礼敬。一一佛所。皆现不可说不可说佛刹极微尘数身。

Chapter 39 Conclusion

The Conduct and Vows of Samantabhadra

At that time, after Samantabhadra Bodhisattva-mahāsattva had praised the supreme qualities of the Tathāgata, he spoke to the bodhisattvas and Sudhana, saying:

Son of Good Family, if all buddhas of the ten directions were to continuously expound upon the meritorious qualities of the Tathāgata, doing so for kalpas as numerous as the atoms in an ineffable-ineffable[73] number of buddha *kṣetras*, they would still be unable to come to the end of them. If one wishes to perfect these gateways to the meritorious qualities, then one should cultivate ten kinds of vast practices and vows. What then are those ten? They are as follows:

The first is to revere all buddhas;
The second is to proclaim the praises of the Tathāgata;
The third is to extensively cultivate the making of offerings;
The fourth is to repent of karmic obstacles;
The fifth is to rejoice in others' merit;
The sixth is to request the turning of the Dharma wheel;
The seventh is to request the buddhas to remain in the world;
The eighth is to always follow the buddhas' course of training;
The ninth is to constantly accord with beings; and
The tenth is to universally dedicate all merit.

Sudhana then addressed him, asking, "O Great Ārya, what is meant by 'revering all buddhas' and so forth, up to and including 'universally dedicating all merit'"?

Samantabhadra Bodhisattva addressed Sudhana, saying:

Son of Good Family, as for what is meant by "revering all buddhas," through the power of Samantabhadra's practices and vows, I arouse deeply resolute faith[74] in all the buddhas, all the *bhagavats*, as numerous as the atoms in all buddha *kṣetras* of the ten directions and three periods of time throughout the Dharma realm and the realms of space, and then, as if they were right before my very eyes, with pure actions of body, speech, and mind, I always cultivate bowing down in reverence to them all.

Manifesting before every one of those buddhas' bodies as numerous as the atoms in an ineffable-ineffable number of buddha *kṣetras*,

正體字

一一身遍禮不可說不可說佛剎極微塵
844c07║ 數佛。虛空界盡。我禮乃盡。[11]而虛空界不可
844c08║ 盡故。我此禮敬無有窮盡。如是乃至眾生界
844c09║ 盡。眾生業盡。眾生煩惱盡。我禮乃盡。[12]而眾
844c10║ 生界。乃至煩惱無有盡故。我此禮敬無有窮
844c11║ 盡。念念相續。無有間斷。身語意業無有疲厭
844c12║ 復次善男子。言稱讚如來者。所有盡法界。虛
844c13║ 空界。十方三世一切剎土。所有極微。一一塵
844c14║ 中。皆有一切世[13]界極微塵數佛。一一佛所。
844c15║ 皆有菩薩海會圍遶。我當悉以甚深勝解。現
844c16║ 前知見。各以出過辯才天女微妙舌根。一一
844c17║ 舌根。出無盡音聲海。一一音聲。出一切言
844c18║ [14]辭海。稱揚讚歎一切如來諸功德海。窮未來
844c19║ 際。相續不斷。盡於法界。無不周遍。如是虛空
844c20║ 界盡。眾生界盡。眾生業盡。眾生煩惱盡。我讚
844c21║ 乃盡。[*]而虛空界乃至煩惱。無有盡故。我此
844c22║ 讚歎無有窮盡。念念相續。無有間斷。身語意
844c23║ 業無有疲厭
844c24║ 復次善男子。言廣修供養者。

简体字

一一身遍礼不可说不可说佛刹极微尘数佛。虚空界尽。我礼乃尽。而虚空界不可尽故。我此礼敬无有穷尽。如是乃至众生界尽。众生业尽。众生烦恼尽。我礼乃尽。而众生界。乃至烦恼无有尽故。我此礼敬无有穷尽。念念相续。无有间断。身语意业无有疲厌复次善男子。言称赞如来者。所有尽法界。虚空界。十方三世一切刹土。所有极微。一一尘中。皆有一切世界极微尘数佛。一一佛所。皆有菩萨海会围绕。我当悉以甚深胜解。现前知见。各以出过辩才天女微妙舌根。一一舌根。出无尽音声海。一一音声。出一切言辞海。称扬赞叹一切如来诸功德海。穷未来际。相续不断。尽于法界。无不周遍。如是虚空界尽。众生界尽。众生业尽。众生烦恼尽。我赞乃尽。而虚空界乃至烦恼。无有尽故。我此赞叹无有穷尽。念念相续。无有间断。身语意业无有疲厌复次善男子。言广修供养者。

with each of those bodies, I shall everywhere bow down in reverence to buddhas as numerous as the atoms in an ineffable-ineffable number of buddha *kṣetras*. Only when the realms of space come to an end will my bowing in reverence to them then come to an end. However, because the realms of space can never end, my bowing in reverence to them has no end.

I shall continue in this way until the realms of beings come to an end, until beings' karmic actions come to an end, and until beings' afflictions come to an end. Only then will my bowing in reverence to them come to an end. However, because the realms of beings and so forth up to and including their afflictions are all endless, my bowing down in reverence to them will have no end. It continues on in each successive mind-moment, without interruption, free of any weariness in the actions of body, speech, or mind.

Again, Son of Good Family, as for what is meant by "proclaiming the praises of the Tathāgata," in every one of the atoms throughout all buddha *kṣetras* of the ten directions and the three periods of time to the very end of the Dharma realm and the realms of space, there are buddhas as numerous as the atoms in all worlds. In every place where there are buddhas, they are all surrounded by an oceanic congregation of bodhisattvas.

With extremely deep conviction[75] and directly manifest knowledge and vision, in the presence of each of them, I shall bring forth faculties of the tongue surpassing even those of the Goddess Sarasvatī's[76] marvelous tongue. Each one of those tongues shall send forth an inexhaustible ocean of voices and each one of those voices shall send forth an ocean of all words and phrases proclaiming the praises of all *tathāgatas'* oceans of meritorious qualities. They shall do so until the very exhaustion of the bounds of future time, doing so continuously and without interruption throughout the Dharma realm, having no place they do not pervade. I shall continue in this way until the realms of space come to an end, until the realms of beings come to an end, until beings' karmic actions come to an end, and until beings' afflictions come to an end. Only then will my praises come to an end. However, because the realms of space and so forth up to and including beings' afflictions are all endless, these praises of mine will have no end. They continue on in each successive mind-moment, without interruption, free of any weariness in the actions of body, speech, or mind.

Again, Son of Good Family, as for what is meant by "extensively cultivating the making of offerings," in each of the atoms

正體字

所有盡法界。虛
844c25‖ 空界。十方三世一切佛剎極微塵中。一一各
844c26‖ 有一切世界極微塵數佛。一一佛所。種種菩
844c27‖ 薩海會圍遶。我以普賢行願力故。起深信解。
844c28‖ 現前知見。悉以上妙諸供養具。而為供養。所
844c29‖ 謂[15]華雲鬘雲。天音樂雲。天傘蓋雲。天衣服
845a01‖ 雲。天種種香塗香燒香末香。如是等雲。一一
845a02‖ 量如須彌山王。然種種燈。[1]酥燈油燈諸香油
845a03‖ 燈。一一燈炷。如須彌山。一一燈油。如大海
845a04‖ 水。以如是等諸供養具。常為供養。善男子。諸
845a05‖ 供養中。法供養最。所謂如說修行供養。利益
845a06‖ 眾生供養。攝受眾生供養。代眾生苦供養。勤
845a07‖ 修善根供養。不捨菩薩業供養。不離菩提心
845a08‖ 供養。善男子。如前供養無量功德。比法供養。
845a09‖ 一念功德。百分不及一。千分不及一。百千俱
845a10‖ 胝那由他分。迦羅分。算分。數分。[2]諭分。優
845a11‖ [3]婆尼沙陀分。亦不及一。何以故。以諸如來
845a12‖ 尊重法故。以如說[4]修行出生諸佛故。若諸菩
845a13‖ 薩。行法供養。則得成就供養如來。如是修行。
845a14‖ 是真供養故。

简体字

所有尽法界。虚空界。十方三世一切佛刹极微尘中。一一各有一切世界极微尘数佛。一一佛所。种种菩萨海会围绕。我以普贤行愿力故。起深信解。现前知见。悉以上妙诸供养具。而为供养。所谓华云鬘云。天音乐云。天伞盖云。天衣服云。天种种香涂香烧香末香。如是等云。一一量如须弥山王。然种种灯。酥灯油灯诸香油灯。一一灯炷。如须弥山。一一灯油。如大海水。以如是等诸供养具。常为供养。善男子。诸供养中。法供养最。所谓如说修行供养。利益众生供养。摄受众生供养。代众生苦供养。勤修善根供养。不舍菩萨业供养。不离菩提心供养。善男子。如前供养无量功德。比法供养。一念功德。百分不及一。千分不及一。百千俱胝那由他分。迦罗分。算分。数分。谕分。优婆尼沙陀分。亦不及一。何以故。以诸如来尊重法故。以如说修行出生诸佛故。若诸菩萨。行法供养。则得成就供养如来。如是修行。是真供养故。

throughout all buddha *kṣetras* of the ten directions and three periods of time to the very end of the Dharma realm and realms of space, there are buddhas as numerous as the atoms in all worlds. In every place where there are buddhas, they are surrounded by an oceanic congregation of many different kinds of bodhisattvas. Through the power of the practices and vows of Samantabhadra, I arouse deep resolute faith and directly manifest knowledge and vision with which I make offerings to all of them of supremely marvelous offering gifts, namely flower clouds, garland clouds, heavenly music clouds, heavenly canopy clouds, heavenly apparel clouds, and clouds of various kinds of heavenly scents, including perfumes, burning incenses, and powdered incenses with each of the clouds such as these being the size of Sumeru, the king of mountains.

I light many different kinds of lamps, including butter lamps, oil lamps, and all kinds of fragrant oil lamps. The wick of each of these lamps is as large as Mount Sumeru and the oil of each of these lamps is like the waters of a great ocean. Using all kinds of offering gifts such as these, I constantly make offerings.

Son of Good Family, among all the kinds of offerings, the offering of Dharma is supreme, including for instance the offering of cultivating in accordance with what was taught, the offering of benefiting beings, the offering of gathering in beings, the offering of substituting for beings in taking on their sufferings, the offering of diligently cultivating roots of goodness, the offering of never forsaking the bodhisattva's works, and the offering of never abandoning the bodhi resolve.

Son of Good Family, when compared with the merit of but a single mind-moment of Dharma giving, the measureless merit from making all the aforementioned kinds of offerings would not amount to even a hundredth part, a thousandth part, a single part in a hundred thousand *koṭīs* of *nayutas* of parts, a single part in a *kalā* of parts, a single part in the greatest amount reached through calculation, enumeration, or analogy, or to even a single part in an *upaniṣad* of parts.

And why is this so? This is because all *tathāgatas* venerate the Dharma, because cultivating in accordance with what was taught gives birth to all buddhas, because, if bodhisattvas practice making offerings of Dharma, they thereby succeed in making offerings to the Tathāgata, and because cultivating in this manner is what constitutes the true making of offerings.

正體字

此廣大最勝供養。虛空界盡。
845a15║ 眾生界盡。眾生業盡。眾生煩惱盡。我供乃盡。
845a16║ 而虛空界。乃至煩惱。不可盡故。我此供養。亦
845a17║ 無有盡。念念相續無有間斷。身語意業無有
845a18║ 疲厭
845a19║ 復次善男子。言懺除業障者。菩薩自念。我於
845a20║ 過去無始劫中。由貪瞋癡。發身口意。作諸惡
845a21║ 業。無量無邊。若此惡業。有體相者。盡虛空
845a22║ 界不能容受。我今悉以清淨三業。遍於法界
845a23║ 極微塵剎一切諸佛菩薩眾前。誠心懺悔。後
845a24║ 不復造。恒住淨戒。一切功德。如是虛空界盡。
845a25║ 眾生界盡。眾生業盡。眾生煩惱盡。我懺乃盡。
845a26║ 而虛空界。乃至眾生煩惱。不可盡故。我此懺
845a27║ 悔無有窮盡。念念相續無有間斷。身語意業
845a28║ 無有疲厭
845a29║ 復次善男子。言隨喜功德者。所有盡法界。虛
845b01║ 空界。十方三世一切佛剎極微塵數諸佛如
845b02║ 來。從初發心。為一切智。勤修福聚。不惜身
845b03║ 命。經不可說不可說佛剎極微塵數劫。一一
845b04║ 劫中。捨不可說不可說佛剎極微塵數頭目
845b05║ 手足。

简体字

此广大最胜供养。虚空界尽。众生界尽。众生业尽。众生烦恼尽。我供乃尽。而虚空界。乃至烦恼。不可尽故。我此供养。亦无有尽。念念相续无有间断。身语意业无有疲厌。

复次善男子。言忏除业障者。菩萨自念。我于过去无始劫中。由贪嗔痴。发身口意。作诸恶业。无量无边。若此恶业。有体相者。尽虚空界不能容受。我今悉以清净三业。遍于法界极微尘刹一切诸佛菩萨众前。诚心忏悔。后不复造。恒住净戒。一切功德。如是虚空界尽。众生界尽。众生业尽。众生烦恼尽。我忏乃尽。而虚空界。乃至众生烦恼。不可尽故。我此忏悔无有穷尽。念念相续无有间断。身语意业无有疲厌。

复次善男子。言随喜功德者。所有尽法界。虚空界。十方三世一切佛刹极微尘数诸佛如来。从初发心。为一切智。勤修福聚。不惜身命。经不可说不可说佛刹极微尘数劫。一一劫中。舍不可说不可说佛刹极微尘数头目手足。

I continue this vast practice of making the most excellent kinds of offerings until the realms of space come to an end, until the realms of beings come to an end, until beings' karmic actions come to an end, and until beings' afflictions come to an end. Only then will my making of offerings come to an end. However, because the realms of space and so forth up to and including beings' afflictions can never end, these offerings of mine are also endless. They continue on in each successive mind-moment, uninterrupted and free of any weariness in the actions of body, speech, or mind.

Again, Son of Good Family, as for what is meant by "repenting of karmic obstacles," the bodhisattva thinks to himself, "Throughout the beginningless kalpas of the past, due to greed, hatred, and delusion manifesting in body, speech, and mind, I have committed measurelessly and boundlessly many bad karmic actions. If these bad karmic actions had substance and signs, even all the realms of space would be unable to contain them. Now, with purity in the three types of karmic actions, directly before all buddhas and bodhisattva congregations everywhere in all *kṣetras* as numerous as the atoms in the entire Dharma realm, I sincerely repent [of these bad karmic actions], resolving to never commit them again and resolving to always abide in all the meritorious qualities of the pure moral precepts. I continue in this way until the realms of space come to an end, until the realms of beings come to an end, until beings' karmic actions come to an end, and until beings' afflictions come to an end. Only then will my repentance come to an end. However, because the realms of space and so forth up to and including beings' afflictions can never end, this repentance of mine is endless. It continues on in each successive mind-moment, uninterrupted and free of any weariness in the actions of body, speech, or mind."

Again, Son of Good Family, as for what is meant by "rejoicing in others' merit," this refers to [the merit created by] all buddhas, the *tathāgatas*, throughout the Dharma realm and the realms of space who are as numerous as the atoms in all buddha *kṣetras* in the ten directions and three periods of time. From the time when they first aroused the resolve to attain all-knowledge, they diligently cultivated a mass of merit, never stinting in sacrificing their own bodies and lives, doing so for kalpas as numerous as the atoms in an ineffable-ineffable number of buddha *kṣetras*. During every one of those kalpas, they sacrificed heads, eyes, hands, and feet as numerous as the atoms in an ineffable-ineffable number of buddha *kṣetras* as they practiced all the difficult-to-practice austerities

正體字

如是一切難行苦行。圓滿種種波羅蜜
845b06║ 門。證入種種菩薩智地。成就諸佛無上菩提。
845b07║ 及般涅槃。分布舍利。所有善根。我皆隨喜。及
845b08║ 彼十方一切世界。六趣四生。一切種類。所有
845b09║ 功德。乃至一塵。我皆隨喜。十方三世一切
845b10║ 聲聞。及辟支佛。有學無學。所有功德。我皆隨
845b11║ 喜。一切菩薩所修無量難行苦行。志求無上
845b12║ 正等菩提。廣大功德。我皆隨喜。如是虛空界
845b13║ 盡。眾生界盡。眾生業盡。眾生煩惱盡。我此隨
845b14║ 喜。無有窮盡。念念相續無有間斷。身語意業
845b15║ 無有疲厭
845b16║ 復次善男子。言請轉法輪者。所有盡法界。虛
845b17║ 空界。十方三世一切佛剎極微塵中。一一各
845b18║ 有不可說不可說佛剎極微塵數廣大佛剎。
845b19║ 一一剎中。念念有不可說不可說。佛剎極微
845b20║ 塵數一切諸佛成等正覺。一切菩薩海會圍
845b21║ 遶。而我悉以身口意業。種種方便。慇懃勸請。
845b22║ 轉妙法輪。如是虛空界盡。眾生界盡。眾生業
845b23║ 盡。眾生煩惱盡。我常勸請一切[5]諸佛。轉正
845b24║ 法輪。無有窮盡。念念相續無有間斷。身語意
845b25║ 業無有疲厭

简体字

如是一切难行苦行。圆满种种波罗蜜门。证入种种菩萨智地。成就诸佛无上菩提。及般涅槃。分布舍利。所有善根。我皆随喜。及彼十方一切世界。六趣四生。一切种类。所有功德。乃至一尘。我皆随喜。十方三世一切声闻。及辟支佛。有学无学。所有功德。我皆随喜。一切菩萨所修无量难行苦行。志求无上正等菩提。广大功德。我皆随喜。如是虚空界尽。众生界尽。众生业尽。众生烦恼尽。我此随喜。无有穷尽。念念相续无有间断。身语意业无有疲厌。

复次善男子。言请转法轮者。所有尽法界。虚空界。十方三世一切佛刹极微尘中。一一各有不可说不可说佛刹极微尘数广大佛刹。一一刹中。念念有不可说不可说。佛刹极微尘数一切诸佛成等正觉。一切菩萨海会围绕。而我悉以身口意业。种种方便。殷勤劝请。转妙法轮。如是虚空界尽。众生界尽。众生业尽。众生烦恼尽。我常劝请一切诸佛。转正法轮。无有穷尽。念念相续无有间断。身语意业无有疲厌。

such as these, perfected the many different kinds of *pāramitā* gateways, realized and entered the many different kinds of bodhisattva wisdom grounds, perfected the unexcelled bodhi of all buddhas, and then reached *parinirvāṇa* after which their *śarīra* relics were distributed. I rejoice in all their roots of goodness and rejoice as well in all the merit produced by all the different kinds of beings of the six rebirth destinies and the four types of birth in all worlds of the ten directions, doing so even where their merit is only as small as a mote of dust.

I rejoice in all the merit produced by all *śrāvaka* disciples and *pratyekabuddhas* throughout the ten directions and three periods of time, whether still at the stage of training or beyond further training, and I rejoice in all the vast merit of the measureless difficult-to-practice austerities cultivated by all bodhisattvas in their resolute quest to reach the utmost right and perfect bodhi. I continue [to rejoice] in this way until the realms of space come to an end, until the realms of beings come to an end, until beings' karmic actions come to an end, and until beings' afflictions come to an end. This rejoicing of mine is endless. It continues on in each successive mind-moment, uninterrupted and free of any weariness in the actions of body, speech, or mind.

Again, Son of Good Family, as for what is meant by "requesting the turning of the Dharma wheel," in every one of the atoms throughout all buddha *kṣetras* of the ten directions and three periods of time to the very end of the Dharma realm and realms of space, there are vast buddha *kṣetras* as numerous as the atoms in an ineffable-ineffable number of buddha *kṣetras*. In every one of those *kṣetras*, there are all those buddhas as numerous as the atoms in an ineffable-ineffable number of buddha *kṣetras* who, in each successive mind-moment, are attaining the universal and right enlightenment surrounded by an oceanic congregation of all bodhisattvas. In all of them, using many different kinds of skillful means in the actions of body, speech, and mind, I earnestly request them to turn the wheel of the sublime Dharma.

I continue in this way until the realms of space come to an end, until the realms of beings come to an end, until beings' karmic actions come to an end, and until beings' afflictions come to an end. My always requesting all buddhas to turn the wheel of right Dharma is endless. It continues on in each successive mind-moment, uninterrupted and free of any weariness in the actions of body, speech, or mind.

正體字

845b26‖ 復次善男子。言請佛住世者。所有盡法界。虛
845b27‖ 空界。十方三世一切佛剎極微塵數諸佛如
845b28‖ 來。將欲示現般涅槃者。及諸菩薩。聲聞[6]緣
845b29‖ 覺。有學無學。乃至一切諸善知識。我悉勸請。
845c01‖ 莫入涅槃。經於一切佛剎極微塵數劫。為欲
845c02‖ 利樂一切眾生。如是虛空界盡。眾生界盡。眾
845c03‖ 生業盡。眾生煩惱盡。我此勸請無有窮盡。念
845c04‖ 念相續無有間斷。身語意業無有疲厭
845c05‖ 復次善男子。言常隨佛學者。如此娑婆世界。
845c06‖ 毘盧遮那如來。從初發心。精進不退。以不可
845c07‖ 說不可說身命而為布施。剝皮為紙。[7]折骨為
845c08‖ 筆。[8]刺血為墨。書寫經典。積如須彌。為重法
845c09‖ 故。不惜身命。何況王位。城邑聚落。宮殿園
845c10‖ 林。一切所有。及餘種種難行苦行。乃至樹下
845c11‖ 成大菩提。示種種神通起種種變化。現種種
845c12‖ 佛身。處種種眾會。或處一切諸大菩薩眾會
845c13‖ 道場。或處聲聞及辟支佛眾會道場。或處轉
845c14‖ 輪聖王小王眷屬眾會道場。

简体字

复次善男子。言请佛住世者。所有尽法界。虚空界。十方三世一切佛刹极微尘数诸佛如来。将欲示现般涅槃者。及诸菩萨。声闻缘觉。有学无学。乃至一切诸善知识。我悉劝请。莫入涅槃。经于一切佛刹极微尘数劫。为欲利乐一切众生。如是虚空界尽。众生界尽。众生业尽。众生烦恼尽。我此劝请无有穷尽。念念相续无有间断。身语意业无有疲厌复次善男子。言常随佛学者。如此娑婆世界。毗卢遮那如来。从初发心。精进不退。以不可说不可说身命而为布施。剥皮为纸。折骨为笔。刺血为墨。书写经典。积如须弥。为重法故。不惜身命。何况王位。城邑聚落。宫殿园林。一切所有。及余种种难行苦行。乃至树下成大菩提。示种种神通起种种变化。现种种佛身。处种种众会。或处一切诸大菩萨众会道场。或处声闻及辟支佛众会道场。或处转轮圣王小王眷属众会道场。

Again, Son of Good Family, as for what is meant by "requesting the buddhas to remain in the world," whenever anywhere to the very end of the Dharma realm and the realms of space throughout the ten directions and three periods of time, there are any of the buddhas, the *tathāgatas,* as numerous as the atoms in all buddha *kṣetras* who are about to enter *parinirvāṇa,* including any such bodhisattvas, *śrāvaka* disciples, *pratyekabuddhas,* those in training, those beyond training, and all good spiritual guides, I then beseech them all to refrain from entering nirvāṇa and to remain for kalpas as numerous as the atoms in all buddha *kṣetras,* doing so in order to benefit and gladden all beings.

I continue in this way until the realms of space come to an end, until the realms of beings come to an end, until beings' karmic actions come to an end, and until beings' afflictions come to an end. These entreaties of mine are endless. They continue on in each successive mind-moment, uninterrupted and free of any weariness in the actions of body, speech, or mind.

Again, Son of Good Family, as for what is meant by "always following the buddhas' course of training," this refers to [the practices of] those such as this Sahā World's Vairocana Tathāgata who, from the time when he first resolved [to attain bodhi], continued with nonretreating vigor to make gifts of an ineffable-ineffable number of his bodies and lives, peeling off his own skin to serve as paper, breaking his own bones to serve as pens, and drawing his own blood to serve as ink, doing so in order to write out copies of the scriptures that, if gathered together, would reach as high as Mount Sumeru.

Because of his profound esteem for the Dharma, he was never stinting even in sacrificing his own bodies and lives, how much the less in sacrificing the royal throne, cities, towns, and villages, palaces, parks, and groves, or all of his other possessions. He also practiced many other different kinds of difficult-to-practice austerities until finally, beneath the tree, he attained the great bodhi, displayed the many different kinds of spiritual superknowledges, manifested many different kinds of spiritual transformations, manifested many different kinds of buddha bodies, and dwelt in many different kinds of congregations.

Sometimes he dwelt in a congregation[77] of all the great bodhisattvas. Sometimes he dwelt in a congregation of *śrāvaka* disciples or *pratyekabuddhas.* Sometimes he dwelt in congregations of wheel-turning sage kings[78] or lesser kings and their retinues. Sometimes he dwelt in congregations of *kṣatriyas,* brahman elders, or householders, and

正體字

或處刹利及婆羅
845c15‖ 門長者[9]居士眾會道場。乃至或處天龍八部
845c16‖ 人非人等眾會道場。[10]處於如是種種眾會。以
845c17‖ 圓滿音。如大雷震。隨其樂欲成熟眾生。乃至
845c18‖ 示現入於涅槃。如是一切我皆隨學。如今世
845c19‖ 尊毘盧遮那。如是盡法界。虛空界。十方三世
845c20‖ 一切佛刹所有塵中。一切如來皆亦如是。於
845c21‖ 念念中。我皆隨學。如是虛空界盡眾生界盡。
845c22‖ 眾生業盡。眾生煩惱盡。我此隨學無有窮盡。
845c23‖ 念念相續無有間斷身語意業無有疲厭
845c24‖ 復次善男子。言恒順眾生者。謂盡法界。虛空
845c25‖ 界。十方刹海。所有眾生種種差別。所謂卵生。
845c26‖ 胎生。濕生。化生。或有依於地水火風而生住
845c27‖ 者。或有依空及諸卉木而生住者。種種生類。
845c28‖ 種種色身。種種形狀。種種相貌。種種壽量。種
845c29‖ 種族類。種種名號。種種心性。種種知見。種種
846a01‖ 欲樂。種種意行。種種威儀。種種衣服。種種飲
846a02‖ 食。處於種種村營聚落城邑宮殿。乃至一切
846a03‖ 天龍八部人非人等。無足二足。四足多足。有
846a04‖ 色無色。有想無想。非有想。非無想。

简体字

或处刹利及婆罗门长者居士众会道场。乃至或处天龙八部人非人等众会道场。处于如是种种众会。以圆满音。如大雷震。随其乐欲成熟众生。乃至示现入于涅槃。如是一切我皆随学。如今世尊毗卢遮那。如是尽法界。虚空界。十方三世一切佛刹所有尘中。一切如来皆亦如是。于念念中。我皆随学。如是虚空界尽众生界尽。众生业尽。众生烦恼尽。我此随学无有穷尽。念念相续无有间断身语意业无有疲厌复次善男子。言恒顺众生者。谓尽法界。虚空界。十方刹海。所有众生种种差别。所谓卵生。胎生。湿生。化生。或有依于地水火风而生住者。或有依空及诸卉木而生住者。种种生类。种种色身。种种形状。种种相貌。种种寿量。种种族类。种种名号。种种心性。种种知见。种种欲乐。种种意行。种种威仪。种种衣服。种种饮食。处于种种村营聚落城邑宫殿。乃至一切天龙八部人非人等。无足二足。四足多足。有色无色。有想无想。非有想。非无想。

so forth until we come to his dwelling in congregations of devas, dragons, others among the eight types of spiritual beings, humans, non-humans, or others. Abiding in many different kinds of congregations such as these, with his perfectly full voice like the quaking of thunder, adapting to their particular aspirations, he enabled the ripening of beings and continued on in this manner until he manifested entry into nirvāṇa.

I follow all such ways of training as these. And just as I do so with respect to the *bhagavat* of this present era, Vairocana, so too do I also follow in this manner in each successive mind-moment the training of all the *tathāgatas* in all the atoms in all the buddha *kṣetras* to the very end of the Dharma realm and the realms of space everywhere throughout the ten directions and the three periods of time.

I continue in this way until the realms of space come to an end, until the realms of beings come to an end, until beings' karmic actions come to an end, and until beings' afflictions come to an end. My following their course of training is endless. It continues on in each successive mind-moment, uninterrupted and free of any weariness in the actions of body, speech, or mind.

Again, Son of Good Family, as for what is meant by "constantly according with beings," this refers to [according with] all the many different kinds of beings in the oceans of *kṣetras* throughout the ten directions of the Dharma realm and the realms of space, including those who are egg-born, womb-born, moisture-born, or transformationally-born, those who are born in and live in reliance on earth, water, fire, or wind, and those who are born in and live in reliance on the air or the plants and trees.

These include the many different kinds of sentient beings with their various physical bodies, their various forms, their various appearances, their various lifespans, their various species, their various names, their various mental natures, their various kinds of knowledge and vision, their various aspirations, their various volitions, their various kinds of behavior, their various kinds of clothing, and their various kinds of food and drink, including those who dwell in many different kinds of settlements, villages, cities, towns, or palaces, and including even all the devas, dragons, and others among the eight kinds of spiritual beings as well as humans, nonhumans, and so forth, including those without feet, those with two feet, four feet, or many feet, those with physical forms, those without physical forms, those with perception, those without perception, and those with neither perception nor non-perception.

正體字

如是等
846a05 類。我皆於彼。隨順而轉。種種承事。種種供
846a06 養。如敬父母。如奉師長。及阿羅漢。乃至如
846a07 來。等無有異。於諸病苦。為作良醫。於失道
846a08 者。示其正路。於闇夜中。為作光明。於貧窮
846a09 者。令得伏藏。菩薩如是平等饒益一切眾生。
846a10 何以故。菩薩若能隨順眾生。則為隨順供養
846a11 諸佛。若於眾生。尊重承事。則為尊重承事如
846a12 來。若令眾生生歡喜者。則令一切如來歡喜。
846a13 何以故。諸佛如來。以大悲心而為體故。因於
846a14 眾生。而起大悲。因於大悲。生菩提心。因菩
846a15 提心。成等正覺。譬如曠野沙磧之中。有大樹
846a16 王。若根得水。枝葉華果悉皆繁茂。生死曠
846a17 野菩提樹王。亦復如是。一切眾生而為樹根。
846a18 諸佛菩薩而為華果。以大悲水。饒益眾生。則
846a19 能成就諸佛菩薩智慧華果。何以故。若諸菩
846a20 薩。以大悲水。饒益眾生。則能成就阿耨多羅
846a21 三藐三菩提故。是故菩提。屬於眾生。若無眾
846a22 生。一切菩薩。終不能成無上正覺。善男子。汝
846a23 於此義。應如是解。以於眾生心平等故。則能
846a24 成就圓滿大悲。以大悲心。隨眾生故。則能成
846a25 就供養如來。

简体字

如是等类。我皆于彼。随顺而转。种种承事。种种供养。如敬父母。如奉师长。及阿罗汉。乃至如来。等无有异。于诸病苦。为作良医。于失道者。示其正路。于闇夜中。为作光明。于贫穷者。令得伏藏。菩萨如是平等饶益一切众生。何以故。菩萨若能随顺众生。则为随顺供养诸佛。若于众生。尊重承事。则为尊重承事如来。若令众生生欢喜者。则令一切如来欢喜。何以故。诸佛如来。以大悲心而为体故。因于众生。而起大悲。因于大悲。生菩提心。因菩提心。成等正觉。譬如旷野沙碛之中。有大树王。若根得水。枝叶华果悉皆繁茂。生死旷野菩提树王。亦复如是。一切众生而为树根。诸佛菩萨而为华果。以大悲水。饶益众生。则能成就诸佛菩萨智慧华果。何以故。若诸菩萨。以大悲水。饶益众生。则能成就阿耨多罗三藐三菩提故。是故菩提。属于众生。若无众生。一切菩萨。终不能成无上正觉。善男子。汝于此义。应如是解。以于众生心平等故。则能成就圆满大悲。以大悲心。随众生故。则能成就供养如来。

I accord with all the different kinds of beings such as these by transforming my appearance in a manner that is appropriate to them. I then serve them in many different ways and present them with many different kinds of offerings, just the same as and no differently than if I was revering my parents or serving teachers, elders, arhats, or others up to and including the Tathāgata.

For those suffering from any of the many kinds of illnesses, I serve as an especially good physician. For those who have lost the path, I show them the right road. For those who are in the dark of night, I produce illumination. And for those who are poor, I enable them to find hidden treasure. In this way, the bodhisattva benefits all beings equally.

And why [does he do this]? This is because, if the bodhisattva is able to accord with beings, then this is to accord with and make offerings to all buddhas. If he reveres and serves beings, then this is to revere and serve the Tathāgata. If he causes beings to feel pleased, then this is to please all *tathāgatas*.

How is this so? This is because the buddhas, the *tathāgatas*, take the mind of great compassion as their very essence. It is because of beings that they then produce the great compassion. It is because of the great compassion that they produce the resolve to attain bodhi. And it is because of their resolve to attain bodhi that they then realize the universal and right enlightenment.

It is just as if there was a great king of trees in a wilderness desert that, so long as its roots find water, its branches, leaves, blossoms, and fruit all flourish luxuriantly. So too it is with the king of bodhi trees that grows in the wilderness of *saṃsāra*. It is all beings who form the roots of this tree and it is all buddhas and bodhisattvas who form its blossoms and fruit. So long as the waters of the great compassion benefit beings, then it is able to produce the fully developed blossoms and fruit of all buddhas' and bodhisattvas' wisdom.

Why is this? This is because, if bodhisattvas use the water of the great compassion to benefit beings, then they are able to gain *anuttarā-samyak-saṃbodhi*. Therefore bodhi itself depends on beings. If there were no beings, then none of the bodhisattvas would ever become able to gain the utmost right enlightenment.

Son of Good Family, you should understand the meaning of this in this way. It is because one has a mind of equal regard for all beings that one is able to develop perfectly complete great compassion. It is due to using the mind of great compassion to accord with beings that one is able to perfect one's offerings to the Tathāgata.

正體字

菩薩如是隨順眾生。虛空界盡。
846a26 眾生界盡。眾生業盡。眾生煩惱盡。我此隨順
846a27 無有窮盡。念念相續無有間斷。身語意業無
846a28 有疲厭
846a29 復次善男子。言普皆迴向者。從初禮拜。乃至
846b01 隨順。所有功德。皆悉迴向。盡法界。虛空界
846b02 一切眾生。願令眾生常得安樂。無諸病苦。欲
846b03 行惡法皆悉不成。所修善業。皆速成就。關閉
846b04 一切諸惡趣門。開示人天涅槃正路。若諸眾
846b05 生。因其積集諸惡業故。所感一切極重苦果。
846b06 我皆代受。令彼眾生悉得解脫。究竟成就無
846b07 上菩提。菩薩如是所修迴向。虛空界盡。眾生
846b08 界盡。眾生業盡。眾生煩惱盡。我此迴向無有
846b09 窮盡。念念相續無有間斷。身語意業無有疲
846b10 厭。善男子。是為菩薩摩訶薩十種大願具足
846b11 圓滿。若諸菩薩。於此大願。隨順趣入。則能成
846b12 熟一切眾生。則能隨順阿耨多羅三藐三菩
846b13 提。則能成滿普賢菩薩諸行願海。是故善男
846b14 子。汝於此義。應如是知。若有善男子善女人。
846b15 以滿十方無量無邊不可說不可說佛剎極微
846b16 塵數一切世界。

简体字

菩萨如是随顺众生。虚空界尽。众生界尽。众生业尽。众生烦恼尽。我此随顺无有穷尽。念念相续无有间断。身语意业无有疲厌。

复次善男子。言普皆回向者。从初礼拜。乃至随顺。所有功德。皆悉回向。尽法界。虚空界一切众生。愿令众生常得安乐。无诸病苦。欲行恶法皆悉不成。所修善业。皆速成就。关闭一切诸恶趣门。开示人天涅槃正路。若诸众生。因其积集诸恶业故。所感一切极重苦果。我皆代受。令彼众生悉得解脱。究竟成就无上菩提。菩萨如是所修回向。虚空界尽。众生界尽。众生业尽。众生烦恼尽。我此回向无有穷尽。念念相续无有间断。身语意业无有疲厌。善男子。是为菩萨摩诃萨十种大愿具足圆满。若诸菩萨。于此大愿。随顺趣入。则能成熟一切众生。则能随顺阿耨多罗三藐三菩提。则能成满普贤菩萨诸行愿海。是故善男子。汝于此义。应如是知。若有善男子善女人。以满十方无量无边不可说不可说佛刹极微尘数一切世界。

The bodhisattva continues to accord with beings in this way until the realms of space come to an end, until the realms of beings come to an end, until beings' karmic actions come to an end, and until beings' afflictions come to an end. This according with beings of mine is endless. It continues on in each successive mind-moment, uninterrupted and free of any weariness in the actions of body, speech, or mind.

Again, Son of Good Family, as for what is meant by "universally dedicating all merit," this refers to dedicating all the merit produced by all these vows, from the first, "revering all buddhas," up to and including "constantly according with beings," dedicating it to all beings throughout the Dharma realms and the realms of space, wishing thereby to enable beings to always gain peace and happiness and remain free of the sufferings of sickness, wishing that, whenever they want to practice evil dharmas, they will not succeed, wishing that the good karmic actions they cultivate will swiftly succeed, wishing that the gates to the wretched rebirth destinies will become closed to them, wishing that the right road leading to human rebirth, deva rebirth, and nirvāṇa will be revealed to them, wishing that, wherever beings bring on themselves extremely severe sufferings due to having accumulated all kinds of bad karma, I may then substitute for them in experiencing those sufferings, and wishing thereby to enable all those beings to attain liberation and ultimately realize unexcelled bodhi.

Such dedication of merit cultivated by the bodhisattva continues until the realms of space come to an end, until the realms of beings come to an end, until beings' karmic actions come to an end, and until beings' afflictions come to an end. These dedications of mine are endless. They continue on in each successive mind-moment, uninterrupted and free of any weariness in the actions of body, speech, or mind.

Son of Good Family, this is what constitutes the complete fulfillment of the bodhisattva-mahāsattva's ten kinds of great vows. If bodhisattvas accord with and enter into these great vows, then they are able to ripen all beings, they are able to accord with *anuttarā-samyak-saṃbodhi,* and they are able to completely fulfill Samantabhadra Bodhisattva's ocean of practices and vows. Therefore, Son of Good Family, you should understand the meaning of these in this way.

Suppose that there was a son or daughter of good family who filled all the measureless and boundless worlds of the ten directions as numerous as the atoms in an ineffable-ineffable number of buddha *kṣetras* with the supremely marvelous seven precious things

正體字

上妙七寶及諸人天最勝安
846b17‖ 樂。布施爾所一切世界所有眾生。供養爾所
846b18‖ 一切世界諸佛菩薩。經爾所佛剎極微塵數
846b19‖ 劫。相續不斷。所得功德。若復有人。聞此願
846b20‖ 王。一經於耳。所有功德。比前功德。百分不
846b21‖ 及一。千分不及[1]一。乃至優波尼沙陀分。亦
846b22‖ 不及一。或復有人。以深信心。於此大願。受持
846b23‖ 讀誦。乃至書寫一四句偈。速能除滅五無間
846b24‖ 業。所有世間身心等病。種種苦惱。乃至佛剎
846b25‖ 極微塵數一切惡業。皆得[2]銷除。一切魔軍。
846b26‖ 夜叉羅剎。若鳩槃[3]茶若毘舍闍。若部多等。
846b27‖ 飲血噉肉諸惡鬼神。皆悉遠離。或時發心。
846b28‖ 親近守護。是故若人誦此願者。行於世間。無
846b29‖ 有障礙。如空中月出於雲翳。諸佛菩薩之所
846c01‖ 稱讚。一切人天皆應禮敬。一切眾生悉應供
846c02‖ 養。此善男子。善得人身。圓滿普賢所[4]有功
846c03‖ 德。不久當如普賢菩薩速得成就微妙色身。
846c04‖ 具三十二大丈夫相。若生人天。所在之處。常
846c05‖ 居勝族。悉能破壞一切惡趣。悉能遠離一切
846c06‖ 惡友。悉能制伏一切外道。悉能解脫一切煩
846c07‖ 惱。如師子王摧伏群獸。堪受一切眾生供養。

简体字

上妙七宝及诸人天最胜安乐。布施尔所一切世界所有众生。供养尔所一切世界诸佛菩萨。经尔所佛刹极微尘数劫。相续不断。所得功德。若复有人。闻此愿王。一经于耳。所有功德。比前功德。百分不及一。千分不及一。乃至优波尼沙陀分。亦不及一。或复有人。以深信心。于此大愿。受持读诵。乃至书写一四句偈。速能除灭五无间业。所有世间身心等病。种种苦恼。乃至佛刹极微尘数一切恶业。皆得销除。一切魔军。夜叉罗刹。若鸠槃荼若毗舍阇。若部多等。饮血啖肉诸恶鬼神。皆悉远离。或时发心。亲近守护。是故若人诵此愿者。行于世间。无有障碍。如空中月出于云翳。诸佛菩萨之所称赞。一切人天皆应礼敬。一切众生悉应供养。此善男子。善得人身。圆满普贤所有功德。不久当如普贤菩萨速得成就微妙色身。具三十二大丈夫相。若生人天。所在之处。常居胜族。悉能破坏一切恶趣。悉能远离一切恶友。悉能制伏一切外道。悉能解脱一切烦恼。如师子王摧伏群兽。堪受一切众生供养。

and the most superior peace and happiness of humans and devas after which they then gave these as gifts to all the beings in all those worlds and also made offerings to all the buddhas and bodhisattvas in all those worlds, doing so continuously and without interruption for kalpas as numerous as the atoms in just so very many buddha *kṣetras.* As for the merit acquired by that person from doing this, if it were then compared to the merit acquired by some other person who merely heard these kings of vows pass through their ears but once, all of that former person's merit would not amount to a hundredth part, would not amount to a thousandth part, and would not amount to even a single part in an *upaniṣad* of parts of this latter person's merit.

Suppose that there was yet another person who, with a mind of deep faith, accepted, upheld, read, and recited these great vows, or merely wrote out but one of its four-line verses. This person would quickly be able to extinguish even the karma of the five deeds entailing immediate retribution.[79] He would be able to melt away all the many kinds of suffering and torment from the world's illnesses of body and mind as well as from all his evil deeds as numerous as the atoms in a buddha *kṣetra.* All the armies of Māra, the *yakṣas, rākṣasas, kumbhāṇḍas, piśācas, bhūtas,* and others—all the evil ghosts and spirits that drink blood and eat flesh—they would all stay far away from him or sometimes they would even resolve to remain close by and protect him.

Therefore, if there is any person who recites these vows, wherever he goes in the world, he becomes as unimpeded as the moon in space escaping from a veil of clouds. He is one who is praised by all buddhas and bodhisattvas, one who should be revered by all humans and devas, and one to whom all beings should make offerings.

Such a son of good family as this becomes well able to acquire rebirths in a human body in which he fulfills all the meritorious qualities of Samantabhadra. Before long, like Samantabhadra Bodhisattva, he will succeed in swiftly perfecting a marvelous form body replete with the thirty-two marks of a great man. Wherever he is born among humans or devas, he will always reside in a superior clan. He will be able to do away with all rebirths in any of the wretched destinies, will be able to separate from all bad friends, will be able to subdue all adherents of non-Buddhist paths, and will be able to gain liberation from all afflictions. In this, he is like the king of lions who overwhelmingly defeats the many other kinds of beasts. He is one who is worthy to receive the offerings of all beings.

正體字

846c08‖ 又復是人。臨命終時。最後剎那。一切諸根悉
846c09‖ 皆散壞。一切親屬悉皆捨離。一切威勢悉皆
846c10‖ 退失。輔相大臣。宮城內外象馬車乘。珍寶伏
846c11‖ 藏。如是一切無復相隨。唯此願王不相捨離。
846c12‖ 於一切時。引導其前。一剎那中。即得往生極
846c13‖ 樂世界。到已即見阿彌陀佛。文殊師利菩薩。
846c14‖ 普賢菩薩。觀自在菩薩。彌勒菩薩等。此諸菩
846c15‖ 薩色相端嚴。功德具足。所共圍遶。其人自見。
846c16‖ 生蓮華中。蒙佛授記。得授記已。經於無數百
846c17‖ 千萬億那由他劫。普於十方不可說不可說
846c18‖ 世界。以智慧力。隨眾生心。而為利益。不久當
846c19‖ 坐菩提道場。降伏魔軍。成等正覺。轉妙法輪。
846c20‖ 能令佛剎極微塵數世界眾生。發菩提心。隨
846c21‖ 其根性。教化成熟。乃至盡於未來劫海。廣能
846c22‖ 利益一切眾生。善男子。彼諸眾生。若聞若信
846c23‖ [5]此大願王。受持讀誦。廣為人說。所有功德。
846c24‖ 除佛世尊餘無知者。是故汝等。聞此願王。莫
846c25‖ 生疑念。應當諦受。受已能讀。讀已能誦。誦已
846c26‖ 能持。乃至書寫。廣為人說。是諸人等。於一念
846c27‖ 中。所有行願。皆得成就。

简体字

又复是人。临命终时。最后刹那。一切诸根悉皆散坏。一切亲属悉皆舍离。一切威势悉皆退失。辅相大臣。宫城内外象马车乘。珍宝伏藏。如是一切无复相随。唯此愿王不相舍离。于一切时。引导其前。一刹那中。即得往生极乐世界。到已即见阿弥陀佛。文殊师利菩萨。普贤菩萨。观自在菩萨。弥勒菩萨等。此诸菩萨色相端严。功德具足。所共围绕。其人自见。生莲华中。蒙佛授记。得授记已。经于无数百千万亿那由他劫。普于十方不可说不可说世界。以智慧力。随众生心。而为利益。不久当坐菩提道场。降伏魔军。成等正觉。转妙法轮。能令佛刹极微尘数世界众生。发菩提心。随其根性。教化成熟。乃至尽于未来劫海。广能利益一切众生。善男子。彼诸众生。若闻若信此大愿王。受持读诵。广为人说。所有功德。除佛世尊余无知者。是故汝等。闻此愿王。莫生疑念。应当谛受。受已能读。读已能诵。诵已能持。乃至书写。广为人说。是诸人等。于一念中。所有行愿。皆得成就。

Moreover, when this person draws near to the end of his life and reaches that very last *kṣaṇa* in which all his faculties fade, in which all of his relatives and retinue leave him, in which all his awesome power disappears, and in which none of his ministers, great officials, palaces, cities, inner and outer palace possessions, elephants, horses, carriages, precious jewels, or treasuries follow along with him, it is only these kings of vows that do not abandon him. They always lead him forth so that, in but a single *kṣaṇa,* he is immediately reborn in the Land of Ultimate Bliss. Having arrived there, he immediately sees Amitābha Buddha surrounded by Mañjuśrī Bodhisattva, Samantabhadra Bodhisattva, Avalokiteśvara Bodhisattva, Maitreya Bodhisattva, and other bodhisattvas, all of whom are possessed of the majestic physical marks and are replete with the meritorious qualities.

This person then sees himself born in a lotus flower, receiving the Buddha's bestowal of his prediction. Having received that prediction, he then passes through countless hundreds of thousands of myriads of *koṭīs* of *nayutas* of kalpas during which, in an ineffable-ineffable number of worlds throughout the ten directions, he uses the power of wisdom to adapt to beings' minds and thereby benefit them. Before long, he will sit at a site of enlightenment, vanquish the armies of Māra, attain the universal and right enlightenment, and turn the wheel of the sublime Dharma. He will then be able to cause beings in worlds as numerous as the atoms in a buddha *kṣetra* to arouse the resolve to attain bodhi. Adapting to their faculties and natures, he will teach and ripen them until, having exhausted an ocean of future kalpas, he will have been able to extensively benefit all beings.

Son of Good Family, all those beings who have either heard or have faith in these great kings of vows, who accept and retain them, who read or recite them, or who extensively explain them for others, the merit they thereby acquire is such that, aside from the Buddha, the Bhagavat, there is no one else who could know its full extent. Therefore, all of you who hear these kings of vows must not have any doubts about them. Rather, you should truly accept them and, having accepted them, you should be able to read them aloud. Having become able to read them aloud, you should be able to recite them. And, having recited them, you should be able to retain them, and so forth up to and including being able to write them out and extensively explain them for others.

In but a single mind-moment, all persons such as these will be able to achieve success in all their practices and vows. The accumulation

正體字

所獲福聚無量無邊。
846c28║ 能於煩惱大苦海中。拔濟眾生。令其出離。皆
846c29║ 得往生阿彌陀佛極樂世界。爾時普賢菩薩
847a01║ 摩訶薩。欲重宣此義。普觀十方。而說偈言
847a02║ 所有十方世界中　三世一切人師子
847a03║ 我以清淨身語意　一切遍禮盡無餘
847a04║ 普賢行願威神力　普現一切如來前
847a05║ 一身復現剎塵身　一一遍禮剎塵佛
847a06║ 於一塵中塵數佛　各處菩薩眾會中
847a07║ 無盡法界塵亦然　深信諸佛皆充滿
847a08║ 各以一切音聲海　普出無盡妙言辭
847a09║ 盡於未來一切劫　讚佛甚深功德海
847a10║ 以諸最勝妙華鬘　妓樂塗香及傘蓋
847a11║ 如是最勝莊嚴具　我以供養諸如來
847a12║ 最勝衣服最勝香　末香燒香與燈燭
847a13║ 一一皆如妙高聚　我悉供養諸如來
847a14║ 我以廣大勝解心　深信一切三世佛
847a15║ 悉以普賢行願力　普遍供養諸如來
847a16║ 我昔所造諸惡業　皆由無始貪[1]恚癡
847a17║ 從身語意之所生　一切我今皆懺悔

简体字

所获福聚无量无边。能于烦恼大苦海中。拔济众生。令其出离。皆得往生阿弥陀佛极乐世界。尔时普贤菩萨摩诃萨。欲重宣此义。普观十方。而说偈言。

所有十方世界中　三世一切人师子
我以清净身语意　一切遍礼尽无余
普贤行愿威神力　普现一切如来前
一身复现刹尘身　一一遍礼刹尘佛
于一尘中尘数佛　各处菩萨众会中
无尽法界尘亦然　深信诸佛皆充满
各以一切音声海　普出无尽妙言辞
尽于未来一切劫　赞佛甚深功德海
以诸最胜妙华鬘　妓乐涂香及伞盖
如是最胜庄严具　我以供养诸如来
最胜衣服最胜香　末香烧香与灯烛
一一皆如妙高聚　我悉供养诸如来
我以广大胜解心　深信一切三世佛
悉以普贤行愿力　普遍供养诸如来
我昔所造诸恶业　皆由无始贪恚痴
从身语意之所生　一切我今皆忏悔

of merit that they thereby acquire shall be measureless and boundless. They will be able to rescue beings from the afflictions and the great ocean of sufferings. Having enabled them to escape, they will all be able to be reborn in Amitābha Buddha's Land of Ultimate Bliss.

Then, wishing to once again proclaim the meaning of this, Samantabhadra Bodhisattva-mahāsattva surveyed the ten directions and then spoke these verses:[80]

Before all the lions among men of the three periods of time
in all of the worlds throughout the ten directions—
with pure body, speech, and mind,
I bow down in reverence to them all without exception. {1}

By the awesome power of Samantabhadra's practices and vows,
I appear everywhere before all *tathāgatas*, with this one body
in turn manifesting bodies as many as a *kṣetra*'s atoms
which each everywhere revere buddhas as many as a *kṣetra*'s atoms. {2}

In each atom there are buddhas as numerous as all atoms,
each of whom abides within a congregation of bodhisattvas.
So too it is in all atoms throughout the endless Dharma realm.
I deeply believe that all of them are full of buddhas. {3}

With an ocean of all kinds of voices, each of them
everywhere sends forth endless marvelous phrases
that, to the very end of all kalpas of future time,
praise the buddhas' extremely deep ocean of meritorious qualities. {4}

With all kinds of the most excellent marvelous flower garlands,
as well as music, perfumes, and canopies,
and other of the most excellent kinds of adornments such as these,
I make offerings to all *tathāgatas*. {5}

With the most excellent robes and the most excellent incenses,
powdered incense, burning incense, lamps, and candles,
each collection of which is as high as the wonderfully tall[81] mountain,
I make offerings of all such things to all *tathāgatas*. {6}

With a mind imbued with vast conviction,[82]
I deeply believe in all buddhas of the three periods of time and,
by the power of Samantabhadra's practices and vows,
I everywhere make offerings to all the *tathāgatas*. {7}

All the bad karmic actions that I have committed throughout the past
have arisen because of beginningless greed, hatred, and delusion
which have then manifested through body, speech, and mind.
Of them all I do now repent. {8}

正體字

847a18 十方一切諸眾生　二乘有學及無學
847a19 一切如來與菩薩　所有功德皆隨喜
847a20 十方所有世間燈　最初成就菩提者
847a21 我今一切皆勸請　轉於無上妙法輪
847a22 諸佛若欲示涅槃　我悉至誠而勸請
847a23 唯願久住刹塵劫　利樂一切諸眾生
847a24 所有禮讚供養[2]福　請佛住世轉法輪
847a25 隨喜懺悔諸善根　迴向眾生及佛道
847a26 我隨一切如來學　修習普賢圓滿行
847a27 供養過去諸如來　及與現在十方佛
847a28 未來一切天人師　一切意樂皆圓滿
847a29 我願普隨三世學　速得成就大菩提
847b01 所有十方一切刹　廣大清淨妙莊嚴
847b02 眾會圍遶諸如來　悉在菩提樹王下
847b03 十方所有諸眾生　願離憂患常安樂
847b04 獲得甚深正法利　滅除煩惱盡無餘
847b05 我為菩提修行時　一切趣中成宿命
847b06 常得出家修淨戒　無垢無破無穿漏
847b07 天龍夜叉鳩槃荼　乃至人與非人等
847b08 所有一切眾生語　悉以諸音而說法

简体字

十方一切诸众生　二乘有学及无学
一切如来与菩萨　所有功德皆随喜
十方所有世间灯　最初成就菩提者
我今一切皆劝请　转于无上妙法轮
诸佛若欲示涅槃　我悉至诚而劝请
唯愿久住刹尘劫　利乐一切诸众生
所有礼赞供养佛　请佛住世转法轮
随喜忏悔诸善根　回向众生及佛道
我随一切如来学　修习普贤圆满行
供养过去诸如来　及与现在十方佛
未来一切天人师　一切意乐皆圆满
我愿普随三世学　速得成就大菩提
所有十方一切刹　广大清净妙庄严
众会围绕诸如来　悉在菩提树王下
十方所有诸众生　愿离忧患常安乐
获得甚深正法利　灭除烦恼尽无余
我为菩提修行时　一切趣中成宿命
常得出家修净戒　无垢无破无穿漏
天龙夜叉鸠槃荼　乃至人与非人等
所有一切众生语　悉以诸音而说法

I rejoice in all merit that has been created
by all beings throughout the ten directions,
by disciples of the two vehicles still in or beyond training,
and by all *tathāgatas* and bodhisattvas. {9}

All those lamps of the world[83] throughout the ten directions
who were the very first to succeed in realizing bodhi—
I now entreat all of them
to turn the unexcelled wheel of the sublime Dharma. {10}

Whenever buddhas are about to manifest entry into nirvāṇa,
with utmost sincerity, I entreat them all to stay, only wishing
they will long remain for kalpas as numerous as a *kṣetra*'s atoms,
in order to benefit and bring happiness to all beings. {11}

All merit from revering, praising, making offerings,
requesting buddhas to stay in the world and turn the Dharma wheel,
and all roots of goodness from rejoicing and repentance—
I dedicate this all to beings and to the realization of buddhahood. {12}

I follow all *tathāgatas'* course of training,
cultivate Samantabhadra's perfectly fulfilled practices,
and make offerings to all *tathāgatas* of the past
as well as to all buddhas of the present throughout the ten directions.

May[84] all future teachers of gods and men[85]
achieve the perfect fulfillment of all their aspirations. {13}
I vow to fully follow the training [of all buddhas] of the three times
and quickly succeed in realizing the great bodhi.

May all the *kṣetras* throughout the ten directions
become vast, purified, and wonderfully adorned
and have *tathāgatas* surrounded by congregations
all of whom reside beneath a bodhi tree, the king of trees. {14}

May all beings throughout the ten directions
become free of sorrows and illness and always be happy.
May they acquire the extremely profound benefit of right Dharma
and completely extinguish all the afflictions without exception. {15}

As I cultivate for the sake of attaining bodhi,
may I acquire recall of past lives in all the destinies of rebirth and
always be able to leave the home life {16} and cultivate pure precepts,
upholding them with no defilement, no breakage, and no defects. {17}

May I use the languages of all the various kinds of beings,
including those of the gods, the dragons, the *yakṣas,* and *kumbhāṇḍas,*
as well as those of humans, non-humans, and others,
using all their different voices to thus teach them all the Dharma. {18}

正體字

正體字	847b09	勤修清淨波羅蜜	恒不忘失菩提心
	847b10	滅除障垢無有餘	一切妙行皆成就
	847b11	於諸惑業及魔境	世間道中得解脫
	847b12	猶如蓮華不著水	亦如日月不住空
	847b13	悉除一切惡道苦	等與一切群生樂
	847b14	如是經於剎塵劫	十方利益恒無盡
	847b15	我常隨順諸眾生	盡於未來一切劫
	847b16	恒修普賢廣大行	圓滿無上大菩提
	847b17	所有與我同行者	於一切處同集會
	847b18	身口意業皆同等	一切行願同修學
	847b19	所有益我善知識	為我顯示普賢行
	847b20	常願與我同集會	於我常生歡喜心
	847b21	願常面見諸如來	及諸佛子眾圍遶
	847b22	於彼皆興廣大供	盡未來劫無疲厭
	847b23	願持諸佛微妙法	光顯一切菩提行
	847b24	究竟清淨普賢道	盡未來劫常修習
	847b25	我於一切諸有中	所修福智恒無盡
	847b26	定慧方便及解脫	獲諸無盡功德藏
	847b27	一塵中有塵數剎	一一剎有難思佛
	847b28	一一佛處眾會中	我見恒演菩提行

简体字

简体字	勤修清净波罗蜜	恒不忘失菩提心
	灭除障垢无有余	一切妙行皆成就
	于诸惑业及魔境	世间道中得解脱
	犹如莲华不着水	亦如日月不住空
	悉除一切恶道苦	等与一切群生乐
	如是经于刹尘劫	十方利益恒无尽
	我常随顺诸众生	尽于未来一切劫
	恒修普贤广大行	圆满无上大菩提
	所有与我同行者	于一切处同集会
	身口意业皆同等	一切行愿同修学
	所有益我善知识	为我显示普贤行
	常愿与我同集会	于我常生欢喜心
	愿常面见诸如来	及诸佛子众围绕
	于彼皆兴广大供	尽未来劫无疲厌
	愿持诸佛微妙法	光显一切菩提行
	究竟清净普贤道	尽未来劫常修习
	我于一切诸有中	所修福智恒无尽
	定慧方便及解脱	获诸无尽功德藏
	一尘中有尘数刹	一一刹有难思佛
	一一佛处众会中	我见恒演菩提行

May I diligently cultivate the pure *pāramitās,*
never forget the resolve to attain bodhi,
extinguish all obstacles and defilements without exception,
and completely perfect all the marvelous practices. {19}

Even when in the midst of the worldly paths, may I become free of
the karma of the afflictions[86] and the realms of the *māras*
just as a lotus flower does not adhere to its waters
and just as the sun and moon do not remain fixed in the sky. {20}

May I do away with all the sufferings of the wretched destinies
and bestow happiness equally on all the many kinds of beings,
continuing on in this way for kalpas as numerous as a *kṣetra*'s atoms,
constantly and endlessly benefiting all in the ten directions. {21}

May I always accord with all beings,
doing so to the very end of all kalpas of the future,
and may I constantly cultivate Samantabhadra's vast practices
and reach the perfect fulfillment of unexcelled bodhi. {22}

May I gather together in all places
with all who cultivate the same practices as I do,
engaging in actions of body, speech, and mind that are all the same,
cultivating and training together in all of these practices and vows. {23}

As for all those good spiritual guides who have benefited me
and who have revealed to me the practices of Samantabhadra,
may they always gather together with me
and always feel pleased with me. {24}

May I always meet all *tathāgatas* in person
together with the congregations of Buddha's sons who surround them
and then offer up vast offerings to all of them,
tirelessly continuing to do so until the end of all future kalpas. {25}

May I uphold the sublime Dharma of all buddhas,
illuminate all the practices leading to bodhi,
and purify to the utmost the path of Samantabhadra,
always cultivating it to the very end of all future kalpas, {26}

In all the stations of existence,
the merit and wisdom I cultivate shall always be endless.
Through absorptions, wisdom, skillful means, and liberations,
may I acquire an inexhaustible treasury of meritorious qualities. {27}

Within a single atom, there are *kṣetras* as numerous as all atoms
and in each *kṣetra* there are an inconceivable number of buddhas.
Each of those buddhas abides amidst a congregation.
May I see them there constantly expounding on the bodhi practices. {28}

正體字

847b29	普盡十方諸剎海	一一毛端三世海
847c01	佛海及與國土海	我遍修行經劫海
847c02	一切如來語清淨	一[3]言具眾音聲海
847c03	隨諸眾生意樂音	一一流佛辯才海
847c04	三世一切諸如來	於彼無盡語言海
847c05	恒轉理趣妙法輪	我深智力普能入
847c06	我能深入於未來	盡一切劫為一念
847c07	三世所有一切劫	為一念際我皆入
847c08	我於一念見三世	所有一切人師子
847c09	亦常入佛境界中	如幻解脫及威力
847c10	於一毛端極微中	出現三世莊嚴剎
847c11	十方塵剎諸毛端	我皆深入而嚴淨
847c12	所有未來照世燈	成道轉法悟群有
847c13	究竟佛事示涅槃	我皆往詣而親近
847c14	速疾周遍神通力	普門遍入大乘力
847c15	智行普修功德力	威神普覆大慈力
847c16	遍淨莊嚴勝福力	無著無依智慧力
847c17	定慧方便[4]諸威力	普能積集菩提力
847c18	清淨一切善業力	摧滅一切煩惱力
847c19	降伏一切諸魔力	圓滿普賢諸行力

简体字

普尽十方诸刹海	一一毛端三世海
佛海及与国土海	我遍修行经劫海
一切如来语清净	一言具众音声海
随诸众生意乐音	一一流佛辩才海
三世一切诸如来	于彼无尽语言海
恒转理趣妙法轮	我深智力普能入
我能深入于未来	尽一切劫为一念
三世所有一切劫	为一念际我皆入
我于一念见三世	所有一切人师子
亦常入佛境界中	如幻解脱及威力
于一毛端极微中	出现三世庄严刹
十方尘刹诸毛端	我皆深入而严净
所有未来照世灯	成道转法悟群有
究竟佛事示涅槃	我皆往诣而亲近
速疾周遍神通力	普门遍入大乘力
智行普修功德力	威神普覆大慈力
遍净庄严胜福力	无著无依智慧力
定慧方便诸威力	普能积集菩提力
清净一切善业力	摧灭一切烦恼力
降伏一切诸魔力	圆满普贤诸行力

Everywhere in the oceans of *kṣetras* throughout the ten directions,
throughout the ocean of the three times on the tip of every hair,
with the oceans of buddhas, and in the oceans of their lands,
may I everywhere cultivate these practices for oceans of kalpas. {29}

May I understand the pure speech of all *tathāgatas*,
in which but one word embodies an ocean of the many sounds
with voices adapted to all beings' mental dispositions,
each one streaming forth the ocean of the Buddha's eloquence. {30}

In that endless ocean of their speech,
all *tathāgatas* of the three periods of time
ever turn the wheel of the sublime Dharma's principles and purport.
By the power of deep wisdom, may I be able to everywhere enter it. {31}

May I be able to deeply enter the future
and exhaustively subsume all kalpas in but a single mind-moment.
And may all kalpas of the three times become a single mind-moment
so that then I may be able to enter them all. {32}

In but a single mind-moment, may I see
all the lions among men of the three periods of time,
and may I also always penetrate the realms of the buddhas,
including their illusion-like liberations and awesome powers. {33}

Amidst the extreme subtleties found on the tip of but a single hair,
there appear the adorned *kṣetras* of the three periods of time.
On the tips of all hairs, in *kṣetras* as many as the ten directions' atoms,
may I deeply enter them all and thus purify them. {34}

When all the world-illuminating lamps[87] of the future
gain enlightenment, turn the Dharma wheel, awaken the many beings,
finish their buddha works, and manifest the appearance of nirvāṇa,
may I go there, pay respects to them all, and then draw near to them. {35}

By[88] the swift and all-pervasive power of the superknowledges,
by the universal gate's power to everywhere enter the Great Vehicle,
by the power of knowledge and practice to cultivate the qualities,
by the power of all-embracing spiritual powers and great kindness, {36}

by the power of supreme merit to everywhere purify and adorn,
by the power of unattached and independent wisdom,
and by the awesome powers of samādhi, wisdom, and skillful means,
being everywhere able to accumulate the power of bodhi, {37}

purifying the power of all good karmic deeds,
vanquishing the power of all afflictions,
and subduing the power of all *māras*,
may I completely fulfill the power of Samantabhadra's practices, {38}

正體字

847c20	普能嚴淨諸剎海	解脫一切眾生海
847c21	善能分別諸法海	能甚深入智慧海
847c22	普能清淨諸行海	圓滿一切諸願海
847c23	親近供養諸佛海	修行無倦經劫海
847c24	三世一切諸如來	最勝菩提諸行願
847c25	我皆供養圓滿修	以普賢行悟菩提
847c26	一切如來有長子	彼名號曰普賢尊
847c27	我今迴向諸善根	願諸智[5]行悉同彼
847c28	願身口意恒清淨	諸行剎土亦復然
847c29	如是智慧號普賢	願我與彼皆同等
848a01	我為遍淨普賢行	文殊師利諸大願
848a02	滿彼事業盡無餘	未來際劫恒無倦
848a03	我所修行無有量	獲得無量諸功德
848a04	安住無量諸行中	了達一切神通力
848a05	文殊師利勇猛智	普賢慧行亦復然
848a06	我今迴向諸善根	隨彼一切常修學
848a07	三世諸佛所稱歎	如是最勝諸大願
848a08	我今迴向諸善根	為得普賢殊勝行
848a09	願我臨欲命終時	盡除一切諸障礙
848a10	面見彼佛阿彌陀	即得往生安樂剎

简体字

普能严净诸刹海	解脱一切众生海
善能分别诸法海	能甚深入智慧海
普能清净诸行海	圆满一切诸愿海
亲近供养诸佛海	修行无倦经劫海
三世一切诸如来	最胜菩提诸行愿
我皆供养圆满修	以普贤行悟菩提
一切如来有长子	彼名号曰普贤尊
我今回向诸善根	愿诸智行悉同彼
愿身口意恒清净	诸行刹土亦复然
如是智慧号普贤	愿我与彼皆同等
我为遍净普贤行	文殊师利诸大愿
满彼事业尽无余	未来际劫恒无倦
我所修行无有量	获得无量诸功德
安住无量诸行中	了达一切神通力
文殊师利勇猛智	普贤慧行亦复然
我今回向诸善根	随彼一切常修学
三世诸佛所称叹	如是最胜诸大愿
我今回向诸善根	为得普贤殊胜行
愿我临欲命终时	尽除一切诸障碍
面见彼佛阿弥陀	即得往生安乐刹

being everywhere able to purify the ocean of all *kṣetras*
and liberate the ocean of all beings,
being well able to distinguish the ocean of all dharmas,
being able to deeply enter the ocean of wisdom, {39}

being everywhere able to purify the ocean of all practices,
perfectly fulfilling the ocean of all vows,
and drawing near to and making offerings to the ocean of all buddhas.
May I thus cultivate tirelessly for an ocean of kalpas. {40}

Regarding the most excellent practices and vows leading to bodhi
as made by all *tathāgatas* of the three periods of time—
May I make offerings to them all and fulfill their cultivation
by relying on Samantabhadra's practices in awakening to bodhi. {41}

All *tathāgatas* have a senior son
who is known as the Venerable Samantabhadra.
I now dedicate all of my roots of goodness,
wishing that all my wisdom and practices may be the same as his. {42}

May I become forever pure in body, speech, and mind,
and may all my practices and *kṣetras* become so as well.
Wisdom such as this is called "Universally Worthy."[89]
May I be able to become the same as him in all respects. {43}

In order to everywhere purify the practices of Samantabhadra
as well as all the great vows of Mañjuśrī,
may I fulfill the practice of all their works without exception
and stay forever tireless in doing so to the end of all future kalpas. {44}

May whatever I cultivate be measureless
and may I acquire measureless meritorious qualities.
May I abide securely in the measureless practices
and completely penetrate all their spiritual powers. {45}

Just as it is with Mañjuśri's courageous wisdom,
so too it is with Samantabhadra's wisdom and practice.
I now dedicate all of my roots of goodness
to always cultivating and training in accord with all that they do. {46/55}[90]

What is praised by all buddhas of the three periods of time
are just such supremely great vows as these.
I now dedicate all of my roots of goodness to acquiring
these especially supreme practices of Samantabhadra. {47/56}

As I draw near to the end of this life,
may I completely get rid of all obstacles,
personally see that Buddha, Amitābha, and then be able
to immediately go forth to rebirth in his land of peace and bliss.[91] {48/57}

正體字	848a11	我既往生彼國已	現前成就此大願
	848a12	一切圓滿盡無餘	利樂一切眾生界
	848a13	彼佛眾會咸清淨	我時於勝蓮華生
	848a14	親覩如來無量光	現前授我菩提記
	848a15	蒙彼如來授記已	化身無數百俱胝
	848a16	智力廣大遍十方	普利一切眾生界
	848a17	乃至虛空世界盡	眾生及業煩惱盡
	848a18	如是一切無盡時	我願究竟恒無盡
	848a19	十方所有無邊剎	莊嚴眾寶供如來
	848a20	最勝安樂施天人	經一切剎微塵劫
	848a21	若人於此勝願王	一經於耳能生信
	848a22	求勝菩提心渴仰	獲勝功德過於彼
	848a23	即常遠離惡知識	永離一切諸惡道
	848a24	速見如來無量光	具此普賢最勝願
	848a25	此人善得勝壽命	此人善來人中[1]生
	848a26	此人不久當成就	如彼普賢菩薩行
	848a27	往昔由無智慧力	所造極惡五無間
	848a28	誦此普賢大願王	一念速疾皆[2]銷滅
	848a29	族姓種類及容色	相好智慧咸圓滿
简体字		我既往生彼国已	现前成就此大愿
		一切圆满尽无余	利乐一切众生界
		彼佛众会咸清净	我时于胜莲华生
		亲睹如来无量光	现前授我菩提记
		蒙彼如来授记已	化身无数百俱胝
		智力广大遍十方	普利一切众生界
		乃至虚空世界尽	众生及业烦恼尽
		如是一切无尽时	我愿究竟恒无尽
		十方所有无边刹	庄严众宝供如来
		最胜安乐施天人	经一切刹微尘劫
		若人于此胜愿王	一经于耳能生信
		求胜菩提心渴仰	获胜功德过于彼
		即常远离恶知识	永离一切诸恶道
		速见如来无量光	具此普贤最胜愿
		此人善得胜寿命	此人善来人中生
		此人不久当成就	如彼普贤菩萨行
		往昔由无智慧力	所造极恶五无间
		诵此普贤大愿王	一念速疾皆销灭
		族姓种类及容色	相好智慧咸圆满

Then, having achieved rebirth in that land,
may I directly manifest the completion of these great vows,
perfectly fulfilling all of them without exception
while benefitting and bringing happiness to all realms of beings. {49/58}

In that buddha's congregation which is entirely pure,
May I then be reborn in a supreme lotus flower
and personally see Measureless Light Tathāgata
who will then directly bestow on me the prediction of bodhi. {50/59}

Then, having received that *tathāgata's* bestowal of the prediction,
may I issue countless hundreds of *koṭīs* of transformation bodies and,
with wisdom power so vast as to pervade the ten directions,
may I everywhere benefit all realms of beings. {51/60}

May I continue on in this until the realms of space and worlds end,
and till the realms of beings, their karma, and their afflictions all end.
Since all such things as these have no time when they will ever end,
so too my vows shall ultimately never come to an end. {52/46}

Suppose someone adorned the boundless *kṣetras* of the ten directions
with the many kinds of jewels, offered them all to the Tathāgata,
then gave supreme peace and happiness to the devas and humans,
continuing all of this for kalpas as many as the atoms in all *kṣetras* — {53/47}

If someone else heard but once these supreme kings of vows
and was then able to develop faith in them by which
he sought supreme bodhi with a thirsting and admiring resolve,
he would thereby gain supreme merit surpassing that of the former. {54/48}

He would then always avoid bad spiritual guides,
would forever abandon all the wretched destinies,
would soon see the Tathāgata, Measureless Light,
and would then perfect these supreme vows of Samantabhadra. {55/49}

This person is well able to obtain a supremely fine life span,
this person is well able to gain rebirths in the human realm,
and this person becomes bound before long to perfect
practices like those of Samantabhadra Bodhisattva. {56/50}

The five extremely evil actions that entail immediate retribution
that he has committed in the past due to having no wisdom powers—
If he but recites these great kings of vows of Samantabhadra,
in but a single mind-moment, they will all be quickly melted away. {57/51}

His clan and class as well as his countenance and physical form—
his major marks, signs, and wisdom—all become perfectly fulfilled.

正體字

848b01 ‖ 諸魔外道不能摧　堪為三界所應供
848b02 ‖ 速詣菩提大樹王　坐已降伏諸魔眾
848b03 ‖ 成等正覺轉法輪　普利一切諸含識
848b04 ‖ 若人於此普賢願　讀誦受持及演說
848b05 ‖ 果報唯佛能證知　決定獲勝菩提道
848b06 ‖ 若人誦此普賢願　我說少分之善根
848b07 ‖ 一念一切悉皆圓　成就眾生清淨願
848b08 ‖ 我此普賢殊勝行　無邊勝福皆迴向
848b09 ‖ 普願沈溺諸眾生　速往無量光佛剎
848b10 ‖ 爾時普賢菩薩摩訶薩。於如來前。說此普賢
848b11 ‖ 廣大願王清淨偈已。善財童子。踊躍無量。一
848b12 ‖ 切菩薩皆大歡喜。如來讚言。善哉善哉。
848b13 ‖ 爾時世尊。與諸聖者菩薩摩訶薩。演說如是
848b14 ‖ 不可思議解脫境界勝法門時。文殊師利菩
848b15 ‖ 薩而為上首。諸大菩薩。及所成熟。六千比丘。
848b16 ‖ 彌勒菩薩而為上首。賢劫一切諸大菩薩。無
848b17 ‖ 垢普賢菩薩而為上首。一生補處住灌頂位
848b18 ‖ 諸大菩薩。及餘十方種種世界。普來集會。一
848b19 ‖ 切剎海極微塵數諸菩薩摩訶薩眾。大智舍
848b20 ‖ 利弗。摩訶目犍連等。而為上首。諸大聲聞。

简体字

诸魔外道不能摧　堪为三界所应供
速诣菩提大树王　坐已降伏诸魔众
成等正觉转法轮　普利一切诸含识
若人于此普贤愿　读诵受持及演说
果报唯佛能证知　决定获胜菩提道
若人诵此普贤愿　我说少分之善根
一念一切悉皆圆　成就众生清净愿
我此普贤殊胜行　无边胜福皆回向
普愿沉溺诸众生　速往无量光佛刹

尔时普贤菩萨摩诃萨。于如来前。说此普贤广大愿王清净偈已。善财童子。踊跃无量。一切菩萨皆大欢喜。如来赞言。善哉善哉。尔时世尊。与诸圣者菩萨摩诃萨。演说如是不可思议解脱境界胜法门时。文殊师利菩萨而为上首。诸大菩萨。及所成熟。六千比丘。弥勒菩萨而为上首。贤劫一切诸大菩萨。无垢普贤菩萨而为上首。一生补处住灌顶位诸大菩萨。及余十方种种世界。普来集会。一切刹海极微尘数诸菩萨摩诃萨众。大智舍利弗。摩诃目犍连等。而为上首。诸大声闻。

All the *māras* and non-Buddhists will remain unable to vanquish him
and he can become one worthy of offerings for all in the three realms. {58/52}

He will quickly proceed to the bodhi tree, the great king of trees,
and having sat there, he will subdue all of Māra's hordes,
reach the universal and right enlightenment, turn the Dharma wheel,
and everywhere benefit all sentient beings. {59/53}

If anyone reads, recites, accepts and retains,
or expounds upon these vows of Samantabhadra,
only the Buddha can realize and know his karmic rewards.
He is then definitely bound to gain the path to supreme bodhi. {60/54}

I have described here only a small part of the roots of goodness
acquired by one who recites these vows of Samantabhadra.
In but a single mind-moment, all [he strives for] is perfectly realized,
and he enables the success of all the pure vows of beings. {61}

I dedicate all the boundless supreme merit gained by my practice
of these especially supreme and "Universally Worthy"[92] practices,
wishing that all beings who have become sunken in the floods[93]
may swiftly go forth to the land of the Buddha of Measureless Light. {62}

At that time, after, in the presence of the Tathāgata, Samantabhadra Bodhisattva-mahāsattva had finished speaking these pure verses on Samantabhadra's vast kings of vows, the youth Sudhana was filled with measureless exultation and all the bodhisattvas felt great joy. The Tathāgata then praised him, saying, "This is good indeed, good indeed."

At that time when the Bhagavat together with the *ārya* bodhisattva-mahāsattvas expounded on such supreme Dharma gateways of the inconceivable realm of liberation, they were headed by Mañjuśrī Bodhisattva. The great bodhisattvas and the six thousand bhikshus whose practice had become fully developed were headed by Maitreya Bodhisattva. All the great bodhisattvas of the Worthy Kalpa were headed by the Immaculate One, Samantabhadra Bodhisattva. [Present too were] the great bodhisattvas at the consecration stage with but one more birth [before buddhahood] as well as the congregations of other bodhisattva-mahāsattvas who, as numerous as the atoms in the ocean of all *kṣetras,* had all come and assembled there from the many different worlds of the ten directions. The great *śrāvaka* disciples were headed by the greatly wise Śāriputra, Mahāmaudgalyāyana, and others. Together with all the great congregations of world leaders among humans and devas as well as the devas, dragons, *yakṣas, gandharvas,*

正體字

并

848b21‖ 諸人天一切世主。天龍夜叉乾闥婆阿脩羅

848b22‖ 迦樓羅緊那羅摩睺羅伽人非人等一切大

848b23‖ 眾。聞佛所說。皆大歡喜。信受奉行

简体字

并诸人天一切世主。天龙夜叉乾闼婆阿修罗迦楼罗紧那罗摩睺罗伽人非人等一切大众。闻佛所说。皆大欢喜。信受奉行。

asuras, garuḍas, kiṃnaras, mahoragas, humans, non-humans, and others, having heard what the Buddha had proclaimed, everyone in that great assembly was filled with immense joy, accepted these teachings with faith, and upheld them in practice.

The End of the Flower Adornment Sutra

Volume Six Endnotes

1. What I translate here as "purified earnest resolve" (深淨心) is reflected in DSBC as *"ādhyāśayaviśuddhi."*

2. With regard to "the stage of the pure youth" (童真位), or "the stage of the *kumāra-bhūta*," QL says, "It is because he is going from the eighth ground to enter the ninth ground that it speaks here of 'dwelling at the stage of the pure youth.'" (從第八地入第九地故云住童真位 / L130n1557_0707a12).

3. I emend the reading here (substituting 辨 for Taisho's 辯) in accordance with two other editions of the text and the passage's sensibility requirements, this as a correction of a fairly obvious graphic-similarity induced scribal error.

4. This is a reference to "the three groups of beings." The "three groups [of beings]" (三聚, *tri-skandha*): 1) those who are fixed in what is right; 2) those who are not fixed [in either what is right or what is wrong], i.e., those who are as yet "unfixed" with regard to their inclinations toward doing what is right or doing what is wrong; and 3) those who are fixed in what is wrong. Although the order differs, this is a list common to nearly all traditions and schools.

5. Regarding the first of these last two listed circumstances, QL says, "As for 'roots of unwholesomeness gathered through roots of goodness,' take for example upholding the moral precepts with a mind of hatred, and so forth. Understand the next clause similarly." (如瞋心持戒等下句類知 / L130n1557_725a07). Perhaps an example of the last circumstance ("roots of goodness gathered through roots of unwholesomeness") might be "telling a lie to save someone's life" where "telling a lie" is classified under "roots of unwholesomeness" but "saving someone's life" is classified under "roots of goodness."

6. As VB clarifies in his review notes, "The *xing* ( ) here merely establishes that this is an abstract noun." Hence there is no intention to include the concept of "the nature" of all-knowledge here. The somewhat more elaborate analogue passage in the Sanskrit edition supports this interpretation (*sarvajñātādhigamāvatāranayasamudrānapyavatarāmi*).

7. Here, where SA has "all the *beings* in all his congregations" (其所有道場眾會。其眾會中一切眾生。), the Prajñā translation specifies "all the *bodhisattvas* in all his congregations" (所有一切道場眾會。其眾會中。一切菩薩。).

8. As explained by HH, "The difficulties" is a reference to the eight difficulties.

9. Both HH and QL note that this refers to the Dharma body held in common by all buddhas.

10. I go ahead and translate here as "the perfection of giving" what SA retains in Chinese transliteration as *dāna pāramitā.*
11. In this long list of nearly two hundred buddha names, even though neither the Sanskrit nor the Chinese inserts any breaks into the list, I deliberately do so after every ten names to make recitation of the text easier.
12. I deliberately prefer a synonym here for this nineteenth name to distinguish it from the otherwise identical Chinese rendering of the twelfth name.
13. I deliberately prefer a synonym here for this twenty-first name to distinguish it from the otherwise identical Chinese rendering of the thirteenth name.
14. As pointed out by VB in his review notes, "Note that *daoyan* (道眼) is an inversion of the Sanskrit compound *cakṣuṣpatha,* which is not "eye of the path" but "pathway of the eyes," that is, 'range of vision.'"
15. The Chinese that I render here as "monastic dwellings" is 僧伽藍, a transliteration of the slightly euphemistic Sanskrit *saṃghārāmā* which would more literally mean, "a pleasure garden for the monastic sangha."
16. I follow HH here in interpreting Taisho's 辨 as 辦, this to correct a fairly obvious scribal error based on graphic similarity. True, Taisho records the use of 辯 in four other editions of this text, but that too appears to be a scribal error based on graphic similarity. More recent editions of Cbeta go ahead and incorporate this emendation.
17. Although the surviving DSBC Sanskrit manuscript gives the name as "Muktāsāra," that is fairly obviously a later corruption, for both the much earlier BB and SA translations translate the name as "Solid Liberation" (堅固解脫), which corresponds exactly to "Muktisāra."
18. Both the BB translation and the Sanskrit refer not to what SA translates as "the three periods of time" (三世), but rather to "the three realms of existence" (三界 / *sarvatraidhātukaṃ*). This appears then to be an error on the part of the SA translation team.
19. The bracketed emendation follows the Prajñā translation's inclusion here of "to benevolently give it to beings" (惠施眾生) in its otherwise identically phrased analogue passage found at T10n0293_p809c02–3. Absent this emendation the clause could sound as if the bodhisattva was accumulating all the world's wealth for no particular reason or to benefit himself.
20. The Sanskrit here is *apramāṇam adhimuktibalaṃ dṛḍhīkartavyam.*
21. In accordance with five alternative editions of the text, I emend Taisho's reading here by substituting 辦 for 辨, this to remedy an obvious scribal error generated by graphic similarity and demanded by sensibility.

More recent editions of Cbeta go ahead and incorporate this emendation.

22. "Difficulties" refers to the eight difficulties. The Sanskrit here is *akṣaṇāpāyapathāḥ* for which VB suggests "the pathways of the inopportune conditions and the wretched destinies."
23. Per the Sanskrit, "dharmas of verbal expression" (言辭法) is an indirect reference to mantras (*apramāṇā mantravibhaktiḥ parijñātavyā*). VB suggests this translation of the Sanskrit: "He should know the countless divisions among mantras."
24. VB points out that here we have *gocara* rather than *viṣayo* and that the BB translation supports this with "countless actions" (無量諸行). Hence this refers to "spheres of action" rather than to "spheres of cognition (or experience)."
25. VB points out that here we have *bodhisattva-viṣayo* rather than *bodhisattva-gocaro,* hence my translation here as "spheres of cognition."
26. "Right and definite position" (正位 or perhaps more commonly 正定位 / *samyaktva-niyata*) refers to the stage of definite irreversibility where eventual complete enlightenment is assured.
27. What I translate here as "wrong thinking" (妄想) is more complex in the Sanskrit (*abhūtaparikalpasamutthitavitathasaṃkalpa*) for which VB suggests "he had aroused distorted thoughts through false mental constructions."
28. DSBC Sanskrit: *ucchedasaṃjñāvigatena pariṇāmanājñānena.* Although at first glance, this line would appear to be referring to "dedication" as in "dedication of merit," that would make no sense in this context. However, per BHSD, definition numbers two and three, *pariṇāmana* refers to "ripening," as of a seed, etc. This points directly to the biggest problem of those who cling to an annihilationist view: They do not understand how karma "ripens."
29. In commenting on this line, QL says, "As for the view that takes Mahesvara [to be the creator], this refers to thinking that [one's circumstances] are a result of the god Maheśvara being able to create the myriad things. Because one realizes that they arise from one's own karma, [one realizes] they are not due to anyone else." (自在見者謂自在天能生萬物故知由自業故不由他.)
30. The DSBC Sanskrit has *sarvasaṃjñācittamanoviviktavihāravihāriṇāṃ.*
31. The DSBC Sanskrit here is *sarvabodhisattvasamādhigocara,* hence my translation of *jingjie* (境界) as "sphere of action" rather than "sphere of cognition," "sphere of experience," etc.
32. As VB points out in his review notes, "The Sanskrit '*buddhasaṃjñābhi niveśavigatāśca*' means "they are devoid of **attachment** to any idea of a buddha."

33. "The nine sequential meditative absorptions" refers to the four *dhyānas*, the four formless absorptions, and the meditative concentration in which the activity of both the feeling and the perception aggregates are extinguished. This last one is also referred to as "the complete cessation absorption."
34. According to DZDL (T25n1509_p0503c25–6), the four *māras* are: the five aggregates, afflictions, death, and "the devas' sons of the Paranirmita Vaśavartin Heaven" (per DSBC = *"iśvara-devaputra-māra*"*), this last of which refers most especially to Pāpīyān, the king of the *māras.*
35. The Sanskrit here is *"ye ekacittaprasareṇa vibuddha bodhiṃ."* This is yet another illustration of "path" (道) being used in many cases as a translation for "enlightenment."
36. "…gain, loss, disrepute, fame, and such…" is clearly a reference to the eight worldly dharmas.
37. What I translate here as "what should be known" is a Chinese transliteration of the Sanskrit *jñeya* (爾焰) which, per MW (Page 426, Column 3), means, "To be known; to be learnt or understood or ascertained or investigated or perceived or inquired about."
38. Referring to this line of the verse as preserved in the Sanskrit edition *"karmakleśadukhayantravartaniṃ,"* VB notes that this is a triadic compound referring to the three divisions of the twelve links of conditioned arising where "afflictions" refers to ignorance, craving, and grasping, "karma" refers to volitional factors (*saṃskārās*) and becoming, and "suffering" refers to the rest of the twelve links. Hence the sense of these last two lines of the verse may be understood as: "…and before long, you will shed the entire cycle of conditioned arising."
39. "Places beset by the difficulties" is another reference to the eight difficulties.
40. The Sanskrit has *"so'vakrānto bodhisattvaniyāmam"* or "One has entered the bodhisattva's stage of certainty."
41. VB points out that, although both the SA and BB translations refer to the burning up of all conditioned dharmas (一切有為法), the DSBC text instead speaks of the burning up of all "misdeeds" or "misdemeanors" (*kalpoddāhāgnibhūtaṃ sarva**duṣkṛta**nirdahanatayā*), hence the "all conditioned dharmas" reading versus the "all misdeeds" reading could have resulted from the corruption or misreading of but a single syllable (***saṃ**skṛta* versus ***duṣ**kṛta*). Fortunately, deeply contemplated, they both make good sense.
42. The SA translation gives the name of this medicine tree as "non-growing roots," but that appears to be with reference to the condition that its medicine treats.

43. *Añjana* is a kind of eye medicine or cosmetic.
44. A *danavat* is a type of *asura* that does not harm beings and which has the quality of generosity.
45. "Universal bases" (遍處 or 一切處 / *kṛtsnāyatana*) are better known by the Pali spelling (*kasiṇa*) in association with the Theravada tradition's meditation on the various "*kasiṇa*" objects for each of the colors, etc. For a better understanding, VB recommends reading about the meditation on the earth *kasiṇa* in Chapter Four of the *Visuddhimagga* or "The Path of Purification" by Buddhaghosa.
46. Per MW, p. 452, *tuṣāra* means "frost, cold, snow, mist, dew, thin rain."
47. The eight [intermittently observed] lay abstinence precepts (八齋戒) are the first eight of the ten precepts. These eight precepts are observed by pious lay practitioners wishing to undertake this special practice protocol on six days, namely on the eighth, fourteenth, fifteenth, twenty-third, twenty-ninth, and thirtieth of each lunar month. They consist of: not killing; not taking what is not given; observing celibacy; not lying; not consuming intoxicants; not using cosmetics, perfumes, or jewelry while also not dancing or singing or watching or listening to such performances; not sleeping on high or wide beds; and not eating after noon.
48. Again, "universal bases" (遍處 or 一切處 / *kṛtsnāyatana*) is a reference to what is referred to in Theravada Buddhism as meditation on *kasiṇa* objects (Sanskrit: *kṛtsna*).
49. In both the BB and Sanskrit editions, these statements are presented in the form of a question posed to Sudhana by Maitreya along the lines of, "Did you see this? Did you see that?" to which, as here, Sudhana replies in the affirmative. It could be that an interrogative marker or short phrase such as, "Did you see these things?" was accidentally lost from the SA translation.
50. Because the SA translation is so vague here as to be difficult to understand, it helps to consult the Sanskrit which, per VB's review notes translation, has, "In order to recite together with [other] bodhisattvas who have one more birth with the Dharma gateway of great knowledge called 'the mode of passing away.'" (*cyavanākāraṃ nāma mahājñānadharmamukham ekajātibaddhairbodhisattvaiḥ sārdhaṃ saṃgāyanāya.* / DSBC)
51. Both the BB translation (普門城) and DSBC Sanskrit specify "the city of Sumanāmukha" and do not mention any country name.
52. VB provides this translation of the corresponding Sanskrit passage: "For those who lack the faculty of faith, who are weary in mind, lax in mind, who do not make exertions, who easily give up diligence,

who are content with minor virtues, who possess just one wholesome root, who are not skilled in undertaking the conduct and vows, who are not supported by good spiritual guides, who are not attended to by the buddhas, this dharma nature cannot be understood. This method, this sphere, this abode, cannot be understood, grasped, entered upon, resolved upon, conceived, comprehended, or obtained."

53. HH explains this as meaning that Sudhana was thereby enabled to dwell in the wisdom of Mañjuśrī.

54. The Chinese for "congregations" here (and seven more times in this list) is "bodies" (身) which would usually seem to refer to beings' physical bodies, however, as VB notes, "The Sanskrit here is *rūpadhātudevanikāya*. *Nikāya* is, of course, based on *kāya*, but it refers not to a physical body but to a group, company, or multitude, as in 'a body of people,' 'this august body of men,' etc."

55. DSBC: *"viśuddhasaṃkliṣṭakṣetramegha."*

56. DSBC: *"saṃkliṣṭacittaviśuddhakṣetramegha."*

57. The eight classes of spiritual beings (八部衆, *aṣṭa-gatyaḥ*) consist of: devas, *nāgas, yakṣas, gandharvas, asuras, garuḍas, kiṃnaras,* and *mahoragas.*

58. The DSBC Sanskrit, the BB translation, and the SA translation all list eleven knowledge perfections here, not merely the "ten" stipulated here.

59. I emend the text here by substituting 大 for Taisho's 太 in accordance with two alternative editions of the text, this to correct an obvious scribal error arising due to graphic similarity.

60. Although, if one referred only to the Chinese text here, one might first suppose that this is referring to the ten types of sovereign mastery listed in Chapter 26, the Ten Grounds Chapter, the Sanskrit makes it quite clear that, yet again, "the extremely profound types of 'sovereign mastery' in which those bodhisattvas dwelt" (菩薩所住甚深自在) is a reference to bodhisattvas' miraculous powers (*gambhīra-bodhisattva-vikurvita-vihārāṇāṃ*).

61. The bracketed phrases here reflect important gradualistic elements evident in the Sanskrit and very explicit in the BB translation's "before long bound to become the same as all buddhas" (不久當與一切佛等 / T09n0278_p0785c29–86a01), but only vague in the SA translation which otherwise might be construed to mean that Sudhana was attaining complete equivalence with the buddhas right then and there, a meaning which is obviously not intended, for Sudhana is still a seeker whereas the buddhas are already buddhas.

62. The *uḍumbara* is a tree that supposedly flowers but once every one thousand or several thousand years.

63. HH notes that "Land of Bliss" (安樂剎) here is referring to [Amitābha Buddha's] "Land of Ultimate Bliss" or Sukhāvatī.

64. I follow S,Y,M, and G editions here in emending the text by preferring *jian* (見), "see," to *you* (有), "have," this to correct an apparent graphic-similarity scribal error.

65. HH points out that this line is referring to the three turnings of the four truths. (也就是三轉四諦法。 / HYQS)

66. The last two lines of this quatrain are referring to the four types of unimpeded knowledge (四無礙智 / *catuṣpratisaṃvid*).

67. Because it is clear here that the text intends to refer here to all of the ten *pāramitās*, but only had room for eight of them in the seven-character per line verse format, I add the two missing *pāramitās* in brackets.

68. The verse is referring here to the four immeasurable minds.

69. Here, "eight divisions" (八部) refers to "the eight classes of spiritual beings" (八部衆, *aṣṭa-gatyaḥ*) consisting of: devas, *nāgas, yakṣas, gandharvas, asuras, garuḍas, kiṃnaras,* and *mahoragas*.

70. Per HH and the passage from Chapter Thirty-Eight of this sutra which he cites, "practicing the ten moral precepts" refers to the ten precepts contained in the following passage:

> Sons of the Buddha, the bodhisattva-mahāsattva has ten kinds of moral precepts. What then are those ten? They are as follows:
>
> The moral precept requiring that one never relinquish the bodhi resolve;
>
> The moral precept requiring that one leave the grounds of the two vehicles far behind;
>
> The moral precept requiring one to contemplate and benefit all beings;
>
> The moral precept requiring one to enable all beings to abide in the Buddha's Dharma;
>
> The moral precept requiring one to cultivate everything in which all bodhisattvas train;
>
> The moral precept requiring that one find nothing attainable in any dharma;
>
> The moral precept requiring that one engage in the transference of all roots of goodness;
>
> The moral precept requiring that one refrain from becoming attached to the body of any of the *tathāgatas;*
>
> The moral precept that requires one to meditate on all dharmas and abandon any attachment to them; and

The moral precept requiring that one observe right regulation of all of one's faculties.

These are the ten. If bodhisattvas abide in these dharmas, then they will acquire the Tathāgata's unexcelled and vast moral virtue *pāramitā*. (T10n0279_p0281a09–16)

71. The three gates to liberation (*vimokṣamukha*) are emptiness, signlessness, and wishlessness.
72. I emend the text here, following the Song, Yuan, Ming, and Gong editions in preferring *shou* (受), "to receive or accept" to the Taisho edition's *shou* (授), "to transmit or pass on," this to correct a fairly obvious scribal error.
73. An "ineffable-ineffable" (不可說不可說 / *anabhilāpya-anabhilāpya*) is an inconceivably large number, the next-to-highest (the 122nd level) numerical denomination described in the SA translation of the Avataṃsaka Sutra, Chapter 30 ("Asaṃkhyeya").
74. Prajña's *xinjie* (信解) is a sino-Buddhist rendering of a meaning of the Sanskrit *adhimukti* usually equivalent to "resolute faith."
75. Per BCSD (p. 208), *shengjie* (勝解) is a Sino-Buddhist rendering of various forms of the Sanskrit *adhimukti*. Here it is equivalent to the sort of "strong conviction" that prevents the mind from wavering from the object of its attention.
76. Sarasvatī is the goddess of eloquence.
77. Although the Chinese here (眾會道場) and in four more instances which follow would appear to mean "congregation at a site of enlightenment" or "enlightenment-site congregation," the antecedent Sanskrit in these Huayan Sūtra texts is usually instead simply *parṣan-maṇḍala* which really just means "congregation," hence I translate it as such here and hereafter.
78. "Wheel-turning sage king" (轉輪聖王) translates the Sanskrit *cakravartin* which is otherwise often translated as "universal monarch," "wheel-turning monarch," etc.
79. "The five deeds entailing immediate retribution" (五無間業 / *pañcānantariyakarman*) are usually listed as patricide, matricide, killing an arhat, spilling the blood of a buddha, or causing a schism in the monastic Sangha. They are referred to as "immediate" (lit. "uninterrupted") because, with no intervening interval, one is bound to fall directly into the Avīci (lit. "uninterrupted") Hells immediately upon dying.
80. Note: In the following verses, the end of each of the corresponding Sanskrit verses is marked by its verse number embedded in the English translation in bold small-font curly braces: **{1}**, **{2}**, **{3}**, etc.

81. "Wonderfully tall" is a reference to Mount Sumeru.

82. Again, *shengjie* (勝解) is a Sino-Buddhist rendering of various forms of the Sanskrit *adhimukti*. Here it is equivalent to "strong conviction," *not* the "supreme comprehension" or "supreme understanding" that a straightforward translation of the Chinese characters would otherwise imply.

83. "Lamps of the world" is a metaphoric reference to the buddhas.

84. Those only following the Chinese may notice that, beginning with this Sanskrit verse number thirteen, I often use the optative mood ("May I…" etc.) where its presence in the Chinese text does not seem to be particularly obvious. For the most part, I do this only where the presence of the optative mood is explicit in the grammar of the Sanskrit.

    Once one has noticed that the Sanskrit edition contains the optative mood throughout so many of these verses, on rereading the Chinese text, one notices that even though Chinese optative markers are only occasionally present in the Chinese text, the optative mood *really is* implicit throughout those verses where it is not so explicitly marked in the grammar of the Chinese.

    The sparseness of concretely specified optative mood markers in the Chinese is due to the fact that the Chinese translators were very often unable to include such markers of the optative such as *yuan* (願) because of the requirement to limit the verse lines to only seven characters.

    Together with the obvious sensibility to the intended meaning of including the optative mood here, I feel that its explicit presence in the Sanskrit grammar definitely justifies this "optative tuning" of so many of these Chinese verses that fail to otherwise specifically include it. That said, there are exceptions (such as Sanskrit verse number thirty) where I decline to mirror the Sanskrit text's optative mood because the meaning of the Chinese text does not really seem to call for it.

85. "Teacher of Gods and Men" is one of the standard list of ten names of all buddhas.

86. Even though this *huo* (惑) is often rightly rendered as "delusion," comparison with the Sanskrit shows it is very often a translation of *kleśa,* i.e., "afflictions." And so it is in this case as revealed by this line in the P. L. Vaidya Sanskrit of this verse: *"karmatu kleśatu mārapathāto."*

87. Again, "world-illuminating lamps" is a metaphoric reference to the buddhas.

88. The Sanskrit text indicates the use of the instrumental case for the ensuing clauses related to these powers, etc., hence the meaning of "by," "with," or "through" is clearly intended. This holds from this

point through the third line of Sanskrit verse number thirty-seven. The use of this instrumental case is barely even implicit in the Chinese text, hence the wide-ranging renderings of this entire section as found in other English translations.

89. This is a deliberate reference to the name of this great bodhisattva. (The Chinese translation of the Sanskrit name, "Samantabhadra," means "Universally Worthy.")

90. Starting with this verse, the Sanskrit text varies from the sequence of these sixty-two verses as they appear in Tripiṭaka Master Prajñā's translation. Hence Prajñā's vv. 46-51 correspond to the Sanskrit vv. 55-60 and his vv. 52-60 correspond to the Sanskrit vv. 46-54.

91. I prefer here to go ahead and translate Prajñā's *kṣetra* as "land."

92. Here again, this is a deliberate reference to the name of this great bodhisattva for which the Chinese translation of his Sanskrit name, "Samantabhadra," means "Universally Worthy."

93. This is clearly a reference to the "floods" which, either three-fold or four-fold, consist of: 1) sensual desire; 2) desire for continued existence; 3) ignorance; and, as the sometimes missing fourth component, "views."

Variant Readings from Other Chinese Editions

Fascicle 1 Variant Readings (p01a01–05b17)

[0001001] 〔大周新譯〕－【明】
[0001002] 明註曰天冊金輪聖神皇帝製北藏作唐武則天製
[0001003] 冊＝策【宮】
[0001004] 仙＝山【宋】，＝僊【元】
[0001005] 牒＝葉【明】
[0001006] 辭＝詞【宋】＊【元】＊【明】＊
[0001007] 然＋（圓）【明】【宮】
[0001008] 筌＝詮【明】
[0001009] 然＋（而）【明】
[0001010] （唐）＋于【明】＊
[0001011] 藏＋（沙門）【宋】＊【元】＊【明】＊，
（法師）【宮】＊
[0001012] 〔奉制〕－【宋】【元】【明】【宮】＊
[0001013] 輝＝暉【宋】【元】【明】【宮】
[0001014] 圓＝圍【宮】
[0001015] 玉＝王【宋】【元】【明】【宮】
[0002001] 齎＝臍【宋】【元】【明】【宮】＊［＊ 1］
[0002002] 眾神＝神眾【宮】
[0003001] 芽＝牙【宋】【元】【明】
[0003002] 耀＝曜【宋】【元】【明】【宮】混用
[0003003] 遠塵離垢＝遠離塵垢【宋】【明】【宮】
[0003004] 聲＝音【元】【明】
[0003005] 漩＝旋【宮】
[0004001] 善＝普【元】【明】
[0004002] 癡＝愛【宮】
[0004003] 荼＝茶【宋】【元】【明】【宮】
＊［＊ 1 2 3 4 5 6 7 8 9 10］
[0005001] 法＋（門）【宋】【元】【明】【宮】

Fascicle 2 Variant Readings (p05b18–10b28)

[0006001] 〔靜〕－【宋】
[0006002] 土＝上【宋】
[0006003] 門＋（星宿音妙莊嚴天王得放光現佛三輪攝化解脫門）
【元】【明】【宮】
[0006004] 消＝銷【明】【宮】＊
[0007001] 耀＝曜【宮】＊［＊ 1 2 3］

[0007002] 神＝威【宋】【元】【明】
[0007003] 威神遍＝威力普【宋】【元】【明】
[0008001] 大＝天【宋】【元】【明】【宮】
[0008002] 主＝妙【明】
[0009001] 臍＝齊【宋】【元】【明】【宮】＊
[0009002] 熟＝就【宮】
[0009003] 如＝大【元】【明】
[0009004] 明註曰南藏俾作解
[0009005] 纓＝瓔【宮】＊
[0009006] 遍＝普【宋】【元】【明】【宮】
[0010001] 神＝威【宋】【元】【明】
[0010002] 曰＝言【宋】【元】【明】
[0010003] 明註曰目南藏作月

Fascicle 3 Variant Readings (p10c01–15c21)

[0010004] 見＝現【宮】
[0010005] 消＝銷【宮】＊ [＊ 1]
[0010006] 耀＝曜【宋】
[0010007] 光＝華【宋】【元】【明】【宮】
[0011001] 妙音如是觀於佛＝普放寶光如是見【明】
[0011002] 荼＝茶【宋】＊【元】＊【明】＊
[＊ 1 2 3 4 5 6 7 8 9 10]
[0011003] 門＋（焰龍王得一切眾生瞋癡蓋纏如來慈愍令除滅解脫門）【元】【明】【宮】
[0011004] 即＝而【明】
[0011005] 滅除＝除滅【宋】【元】【明】【宮】
[0012001] 塗＝途【宮】
[0012002] 主＝王【宋】【元】【明】
[0012003] 明註曰力北藏作方
[0012004] 憶＝億【宮】
[0012005] 言＝曰【宮】
[0013001] 門＋（大海處攝持力迦樓羅王得能竭眾生煩惱海解脫門）二十一字【元】，明註曰南藏亦同，（大海處攝持力迦樓羅王得入佛行廣大智慧海解脫門）二十二字【明】【宮】
[0014001] 耀＝曜【宋】【元】【明】【宮】＊
[0014002] 怨＝冤【宋】【元】【明】
[0014003] 辨＝辦【明】
[0014004] 往＝住【宋】【元】【明】
[0015001] 悉＝昔【明】
[0015002] 境＝道【宮】

Fascicle 4 Variant Readings (p15c22–21b24)

[0016001] 門＋（眾妙宮殿主火神得大慈悲廣蔭眾生解脫門）十八字【元】，明註曰南藏亦同，（眾妙宮殿主火神得觀如來神通力示現無邊際解脫門）二十二字【明】【宮】

[0016002] 耀＝曜【宋】【元】【明】【宮】＊ [＊ 1 2 3 4 5]

[0016003] 遍＝普【宋】＊【元】＊【明】＊ [＊ 1 2 3 4 5]

[0016004] 旋＝漩【宋】【元】【明】【宮】

[0016005] 悟＋（一切世間眾導師法雲大雨不可測消竭無窮諸苦海此離垢塵入法門）四句【元】【明】【宮】

[0017001] 攝＋（取）【宮】

[0018001] 悉＝昔【元】【明】【宮】

[0018002] 芽＝牙【宮】

[0018003] 習＝集【宋】

[0018004] 迷＝業【宮】

[0018005] 言＝曰【明】

[0019001] 消＝銷【宮】

[0019002] 門＋（香幢莊嚴髻主城神得破一切煩惱臭氣出生一切智性香氣解脫門）【元】明註曰南藏亦同，（香幢莊嚴主城神得觀如來自在力普遍世間調伏眾生解脫門）【明】，（香髻莊嚴主城神得觀如來自在力普遍世間調伏眾生解脫門）【宮】

[0019003] 目＝城【宮】

[0020001] 纓＝瓔【宋】【元】【明】【宮】＊ [＊ 1]

[0020002] 辭＝訶【宮】

[0020003] 神＝威【宋】【元】【明】

[0020004] 覩＝觀【宮】

[0020005] 矚＝囑【宮】

[0021001] 攝＝護【宋】【元】【明】

[0021002] 現＝見【宮】

Fascicle 5 Variant Readings (p21c01–26a13)

[0021003] 遍＝滿【宮】

[0022001] 門＋（普覺悅意聲菩薩摩訶薩得親近承事一切諸佛供養藏解脫門）二十五字【元】【明】【宮】，但元本無諸之字，明註曰南藏無諸之字

[0022002] 薩＋（得出世一切神變廣大加持解脫門普寶髻華幢菩薩摩訶薩）【元】【明】，＋（得出世一切神變廣大加持解脫門普寶髻菩薩摩訶薩）【宮】

[0022003] 消＝銷【宮】

[0022004] 齎＝齊【宋】【元】【明】【宮】

[0023001] （如）＋是【宮】

[0023002] 纓＝瓔【宮】＊

[0023003] 耀＝曜【宮】＊
[0023004] 即＝而【宮】＊［＊ 1 2 3 4 5］
[0023005] 踊＝涌【宮】
[0024001] 明註曰睟南藏作眸
[0024002] 王＝玉【宮】
[0024003] 覩＝現【宋】【元】【明】【宮】
[0024004] 輝＝暉【宋】【元】【明】【宮】
[0025001] 深＝心【宋】【元】【明】
[0025002] 〔會〕－【宋】【元】【明】【宮】
[0025003] 〔已〕－【元】【明】【宮】
[0025004] 返＝反【宋】【元】【明】【宮】
[0025005] 令＝今【宋】【元】【明】【宮】
[0025006] 威神＝威力【宮】
[0025007] （（觀察十方））四字＝（（普觀一切道場眾海））八字【宮】
[0025008] 涌＝踊【宋】＊【元】＊【明】＊【宮】［＊ 1 2］

Fascicle 6 Variant Readings (p26a14–32c19)

[0026001] 昧＋（云何是諸佛神通云何是諸佛自在）【明】
[0026002] 海＋（法海安立海）【明】
[0027001] 瓔珞＝纓絡【宋】【元】
[0027002] 十種＋（眾寶）【宮】
[0028001] 跏＝加【宋】
[0029001] 辭＝詞【宋】＊【元】＊【明】＊［＊ 1］
[0029002] 雲＝雨【宮】
[0029003] 色＝光【宮】
[0029004] 震＝振【宮】
[0029005] 瑩＝嚴【宋】【明】
[0029006] 住＝坐【明】【宮】
[0029007] 凝＝疑【宋】【元】【明】【宮】
[0030001] 立＝坐【宋】【元】【明】【宮】
[0030002] 充遍＝充滿【宮】
[0030003] 明註曰智南藏作知
[0031001] 游＝遊【元】【明】【宮】
[0031002] 威力＝威神【宋】＊【元】＊【明】＊
[0032001] 曰＝言【宮】＊［＊ 1］
[0032002] 威神＝威力【宮】

Fascicle 7 Variant Readings (p32c20–39a08)

[0033001] 漩＝旋【宋】【宮】
[0033002] 現＝見【明】
[0033003] 辭＝詞【宋】【元】【明】

[0033004] 〔而〕－【宋】【元】【明】【宮】
[0033005] 耀＝曜【宋】【元】【明】【宮】
[0034001] 〔大方廣佛華嚴經〕－【明】
[0035001] 〔觀察十方〕－【宮】
[0035002] 通＝變【宋】【明】【宮】
[0036001] 漩＝旋【宋】【元】【明】【宮】
[0036002] 纏＝擁【宮】
[0036003] 主＝住【宋】【元】【明】【宮】
[0037001] 觀察＝普觀【宮】
[0038001] 住＋（或有不可說不可說劫住）【明】
[0038002] 見＝者【元】【明】
[0038003] 數＋（無差別）【元】【明】【宮】
[0038004] 威力＝威神【宮】

Fascicle 8 Variant Readings (p39a09–44a02)

[0040001] 神力＝威力【宮】
[0040002] 有＋（十）【明】
[0040003] 漩＝旋【宋】【元】【明】【宮】＊［＊ 1］
[0040004] 神力＝威神【宮】
[0040005] 而說＝說此【宮】
[0041001] 洄澓＝迴復【宋】【宮】
[0041002] 一切＝一一【宮】
[0041003] 華＝萃【明】【宮】
[0041004] 剎＝別【宋】
[0041005] 此＋（十）【明】
[0041006] 有＋（十）【明】
[0042001] 漩＝旋【宋】【宮】＊［＊ 1］
[0042002] 此＋（十）【明】
[0043001] 空＋（雲）【元】【明】
[0043002] 卍＝卍【宋】【元】【明】【宮】

Fascicle 9 Variant Readings (p44a03–48c17)

[0044001] 離塵＝離苦【宮】
[0044002] 明註曰喜南藏作廣
[0044003] 〔雲〕－【宋】【元】【明】【宮】
[0044004] 卍＝卍【宋】【元】【明】【宮】＊［＊ 1 2］
[0044005] 漩＝旋【宋】【元】【明】【宮】＊［＊ 1 2］
[0044006] 彌＝而【元】【明】【宮】＊
[0045001] 普光寶＝普光明【明】，＝普光明寶【宮】
[0045002] 王＝人【宋】
[0045003] （以）＋無【明】

[0046001] 彌＝而【宋】【元】【明】【宮】＊ [＊ 1 2 3]
[0046002] 〔實〕－【宋】【元】【明】【宮】
[0047001] 此＝世【明】
[0047002] 而＝彌【宮】
[0047003] 瓔珞＝纓珞【宋】
[0047004] 耀＝曜【宋】
[0048001] 昇＝升【宋】＊【元】＊【明】＊

Fascicle 10 Variant Readings (p48c18–53c14)

[0049001] 〔明〕－【宋】【元】【明】【宮】
[0051001] 輪圓＝輪圍【宮】
[0052001] 嚴飾＝莊嚴【宮】
[0052002] 鞕＝硬【宋】【元】【明】【宮】
[0053001] 能＝佛【明】【宮】
[0053002] 嘷＝號【宮】

Fascicle 11 Variant Readings (p53c15–57c16)

[0053003] 〔第〕－【聖】＊
[0053004a] （于闐國三藏實叉難陀奉制譯）十二字＝（新譯）二字【聖】＊
[0053004b] （唐）＋于【明】
[0053005] 藏＋（沙門）【宋】＊【元】＊【明】＊
[0053006] 〔奉制〕－【宋】＊【元】＊【明】＊
[0053007] 耀＝曜【宋】【元】【明】【宮】＊ [＊ 1 2]
[0054001] 大＋（蓮）【明】【宮】
[0054002] 普＝昔【宮】
[0054003] 莊嚴＋（次有緊那羅城名遊戲快樂次有摩睺羅城名金剛幢）【明】【宮】
[0054004] 万＝方【宋】【元】【明】【宮】
[0054005] 言辭＝言詞【宮】
[0054006] 雲＝音【聖】
[0054007] 法＝世【宋】【宮】，明註曰法南藏作世
[0054008] 采女＝婇女【宮】＊ [＊ 1]
[0054009] 〔別本…人〕八字－【宋】【元】【明】
[0056001] 〔王〕－【宋】
[0057001] 實＝寶【聖】

Fascicle 12 Variant Readings (p57c17–62b09)

[0058001] 結跏＝結加【宮】下同
[0058002] 薝＝瞻【宋】【宮】【聖】下同
[0058003] 〔曰〕－【宋】【宮】，明註曰無南藏曰字

[0058004] 玻瓈＝頗梨【宋】【聖】下同
[0058005] 雲＝聖【聖】
[0059001] 王＝主【聖】
[0059002] 意＋（或名聞慧）【明】【宮】
[0059003] 意＋（或名無上尊或名大智炬或名無所依或名光明藏或名智慧藏或名福德藏或名天中天或名大自在）四十字【元】【明】【宮】
[0059004] 言辭＝言詞【宮】
[0059005] 辭＝詞【聖】【宮】
[0060001] 〔大方…經〕七字－【明】
[0060002] 躁＝燥【宮】
[0060003] 處＝趣【明】【宮】
[0060004] 怨＝冤【明】＊［＊ 1］
[0060005] 印＝卵【明】
[0060006] 毀＋（呰）【明】【宮】
[0061001] 揀＝簡【宋】【元】【明】【宮】
[0061002] 生＋（或名失利）【明】【宮】
[0061003] 〔諸佛子〕－【聖】
[0062001] 駛＝駃【宮】

Fascicle 13 Variant Readings (p62b10–69b11)

[0062002] 天＝大【宮】
[0062003] 薝＝瞻【宮】
[0062004] 玻瓈＝頗梨【宮】
[0063001] 寤＝悟【宋】【元】【明】【宮】＊
[0064001] 此神通智力＝神通大智力【明】【宮】
[0064002] 言說＝言語【宮】
[0064003] 言＝曰【宮】
[0065001] 十＝七【聖】
[0066001] 聽＝諦【元】【明】
[0067001] 震＝振【宮】＊［＊ 1］
[0067002] 曜＝耀【宋】【元】【明】
[0068001] 餧＝餒【宋】【元】【明】【宮】
[0068002] 度＝受【明】
[0068003] 明註曰怒南藏作好，怒＝好【宮】
[0069001] 世間＝世界【明】【宮】

Fascicle 14 Variant Readings (p69b12–75b17)

[0070001] 怨＝冤【明】
[0070002] 妓＝伎【宮】＊［＊ 1］
[0070003] 和尚＝和上【宮】

[0070004] 結跏=結加【宮】
[0070005] 帬=裙【宋】【元】【明】【宮】
[0072001] 具神足力=具足神力【宋】
[0072002] 〔大方…經〕七字－【明】【CB】
[0072003] 集=習【宋】【元】【明】【宮】* [* 1]
[0073001] 為=得【宋】
[0073002] 獲=得【宋】【元】【明】【宮】
[0074001] 言辭=言詞【宮】* [* 1]
[0074002] 鐘=鍾【宮】
[0074003] 蓮=華【宮】
[0074004] 隨樂=隨業【宮】
[0074005] 受=愛【明】【宮】
[0075001] 技=妓【宮】
[0075002] 醫=毉【宋】【元】【明】
[0075003] 五熱=三熱【宮】

Fascicle 15 Variant Readings (p75b18–80c01)

[0075004] 二=下【宋】【元】【宮】，下+（新）【聖】
[0075005] 光=先【宋】【元】【明】
[0075006] 耀=曜【宋】【元】【明】【宮】* [* 1]
[0075007] 酥=蘇【聖】
[0076001] 決了=便了【宮】
[0076002] 沒=歿【宮】
[0076003] 主=王【宋】【元】【明】
[0077001] 瑩=鎣【明】
[0077002] 切德=功德【宋】【元】【明】【宮】【CB】
[0078001] 諭=喻【宮】* [* 1 2 3 4]
[0078002] 亦=自【宮】
[0078003] 淨=海【聖】
[0079001] 三=三【元】【明】
[0079002] 作=化【宋】【元】【明】
[0079003] 悴=怖【聖】
[0079004] 昇=升【宋】下同【元】下同【明】下同
[0079005] 如=妙【聖】
[0079006] 辨=辯【宋】【元】【明】【宮】【聖】
[0079007] 碼碯=瑪瑙【宮】*，=馬碯【聖】
[0079008] 玻瓈=頗梨【宮】*
[0080001] 大=天【宮】
[0080002] 妓=伎【宮】【聖】
[0080003] 注=霔【宋】【元】【明】
[0080004] 瓔珞=纓絡【聖】

[0080005] 返＝反【宋】【元】【明】

Fascicle 16 Variant Readings (p80c02–88a27)

[0080006] 耀＝曜【宋】【元】【明】【宮】＊ [＊ 1 2]
[0081001] 〔大廣佛華嚴經〕七字－【明】＊【CB】＊ [＊ 1]
[0081002] 結跏＝結加【宮】
[0081003] 天王＝天主【宮】
[0082001] 翳＝瞖【宋】【元】【明】
[0082002] 辭＝詞【宋】【元】【明】【宮】
[0083001] 一＝二【宋】【元】【明】【宮】【CB】
[0083002] 得＝說【明】
[0083003] 言語＝語言【宮】
[0083004] 過＝遍【宮】
[0083005] 明註曰眾南藏作諸
[0084001] 住＋（法）【明】【宮】
[0084002] 集＝習【元】【明】
[0085001] 聞＋（有）【元】【明】【宮】【CB】
[0085002] （法）＋王子【元】【明】【宮】
[0085003] 震＝振【宮】＊ [＊ 1]
[0085004] 涌＝踊【宋】【元】【明】【宮】＊ [＊ 1 2]
[0085005] 大＝天【宋】【元】【明】【宮】
[0086001] 抹＝末【宮】
[0087001] 轉＝動【宋】【元】【明】【宮】
[0088001] 抹＝末【宮】

Fascicle 17 Variant Readings (p88b01–95a15)

[0088002] 〔第〕－【聖】＊
[0088003] （（于闐…譯））十二字＝（（新譯））二字【聖】＊
[0088004] 胸＝脣【明】【宮】
[0088005] 諭＝喻【宮】
[0088006] 耶＋（不隨順是法耶無所得是法耶）【明】
[0088007] 和尚＝和上【聖】下同
[0088008] 鬚＝剃【宮】
[0089001] 〔大方…經〕七字－【明】
[0089002] 諭＝喻【宋】【元】【明】【宮】＊
[＊ 1 2 3 4 5 6 7 8 9 10 11 12 13]
[0091001] 〔復〕－【宋】
[0091002] 是＋（說）【宋】【元】【明】
[0091003] 當＝即【宮】
[0091004] 震＝振【聖】
[0092001] 涌＝踊【宋】＊【元】＊【明】＊ [＊ 1 2]

[0092002] 妓＝伎【宮】
[0092003] 慈＝悉【宮】
[0093001] 眾＝趣【宋】【元】【明】【宮】【聖】
[0094001] 耀＝明【聖】
[0094002] 功＝福【宋】【聖】，明註曰功南藏作福
[0095001] 身＝心【宋】【元】【明】【宮】

Fascicle 18 Variant Readings (p95a16–99a13)

[0095002] 明註曰常南藏作當
[0095003] 怨＝冤【明】
[0095004] 王＋（龍王）【宋】【元】【明】【宮】
[0095005] 乘＝業【宮】
[0095006] 惠＝慧【宮】
[0096001] 和尚＝和上【宮】＊［＊ 1］
[0096002] 有＝所【宋】【元】【明】【宮】
[0097001] 諭＝喻【宋】【元】【明】
[0098001] 修習＝修集【宋】【宮】
[0098002] 諭＝喻【宮】
[0099001] 所＝一【聖】

Fascicle 19 Variant Readings (p99a14–105c12)

[0099002] 交＝絞【宮】
[0099003] 耀＝曜【宋】【元】【明】【宮】＊
[0099004] 神力＝威神【宋】【宮】，＝威力【元】【明】
[0099005] 十萬＝十方【宮】
[0100001] 求＝於【宮】
[0100002] 暉＝輝【宮】
[0101001] 法＝佛【宮】
[0101002] 住＝在【明】
[0101003] 主＝住【明】
[0102001] 異相＝異色【宮】
[0102002] 一＝上【宋】【元】【宮】
[0102003] 橈＝撓【宮】＊［＊ 1 2］
[0103001] 唯＝惟【宮】
[0103002] 補＋（特）【宮】
[0103003] 脆＝脃【宋】【元】【明】【宮】
[0104001] 辭＝詞【宋】【元】【明】
[0104002] 諂＝諂【宋】
[0104003] 抹＝末【宮】
[0105001] 示現＝現示【宮】

Fascicle 20 Variant Readings (p105c13–111a21)

[0105002] 二＝下【宋】【元】
[0106001] （若）＋有【明】
[0106002] 成熟＝成就【宋】【元】【明】【宮】
[0107001] 雙＝雙【宋】【元】【明】【宮】
[0107002] 辭＝詞【宋】【元】【明】【宮】＊［＊ 1］
[0107003] 〔此〕－【宋】
[0107004] 辭＝詞【宋】＊【元】＊【明】＊［＊ 1 2］
[0107005] 世間＝世門【宮】
[0108001] 涌＝踊【宋】【元】【明】【宮】＊［＊ 1 2］
[0108002] 辭＝詞【宋】【元】【明】【宮】＊［＊ 1］
[0108003] 根＋（故）【元】【明】【宮】
[0108004] 曰＝言【宮】
[0108005] 者＝有【明】
[0109001] 諭＝喻【宋】【宮】
[0109002] 勤修＝勤求【宮】
[0110001] 決＝抉【明】
[0110002] 了＝示【明】
[0110003] 其＝於【宋】【元】【明】

Fascicle 21 Variant Readings (p111a22–115a07)

[0111001] 〔第〕－【聖】＊
[0111002a] （于闐國三藏實叉難陀奉制譯）十二字＝（新譯）二字【聖】＊
[0111002b] （唐）＋于【明】＊
[0111003] 三藏＋（沙門）【宋】＊【元】＊【明】＊，三藏＋（法師）【宮】＊
[0111004] 〔奉制〕－【宋】【元】【明】【宮】＊
[0112001] 欲＝慾【宋】【元】【明】
[0113001] 唯＝惟【宋】＊【元】＊【明】＊
[0113002] 味＝求【宮】
[0113003] 祜＝祐【宮】
[0114001] 教化＝故化【宮】
[0114002] 無數無量＝無量無數【宋】【元】【明】
[0114003] 〔不可說〕－【宋】【元】，明註曰南藏無不可說三字
[0114004] 他＝陀【元】【明】【宮】
[0114005] 諭＝喻【宋】【元】【明】【宮】
[0114006] 耀＝曜【宮】
[0114007] 有十種無盡＝十有種無盡【宋】，＝有十種無盡法【明】

Fascicle 22 Variant Readings (p115a08–121a06)

[0115001] 所＝有【宋】【元】【明】
[0115002] 越＝起【宮】
[0116001] 〔寶〕－【宋】【元】【明】【宮】
[0116002] 耀＝曜【宮】＊［＊ 1］
[0117001] 〔香〕－【宮】
[0118001] 盡＝邊【宋】
[0118002] 〔諸〕－【宮】
[0118003] 根＝恨【宮】
[0118004] 辭＝詞【宋】【元】【明】【宮】＊［＊ 1］
[0119001] 芽＝牙【宋】
[0119002] 于＝於【宋】【元】【明】
[0120001] 諭＝喻【宋】【元】【明】【宮】
[0120002] 辨＝辦【宋】【元】【明】【宮】
[0120003] 跏＝加【宋】【元】

Fascicle 23 Variant Readings (p121a07–127b11)

[0121001] 跏＝加【宋】【元】【明】
[0121002] 眼＝願【宋】【元】【明】【宮】【聖】
[0121003] 言＝曰【宮】
[0121004] 法＝身【聖】
[0122001] 勝＝最【聖】
[0122002] 示＝不【聖】
[0123001] 取＝收【宮】
[0124001] 登＝證【明】【聖】
[0124002] 〔大方廣佛華嚴經〕－【明】
[0124003] 辨＝辦【宋】【元】【明】【宮】＊［＊ 1］
[0124004] 〔等〕－【宮】
[0124005] 生＋（善根）【宮】
[0125001] 誤＝設【聖】
[0126001] 己＝已【聖】

Fascicle 24 Variant Readings (p127b12–132c23)

[0127001] 待＝侍【元】【明】【宮】
[0128001] 觀察十方承佛神力＝承佛神力普觀十方【明】
[0129001] 善＋（根）【明】【宮】
[0129002] 噉＝敢【宮】
[0130001] 今＝令【明】
[0131001] 競＝竟【宮】
[0131002] 明註曰南藏無處字
[0132001] 相＝性【元】，明註曰相南藏作性

[0132002] 熟＝就【宋】【元】【明】【宮】
[0132003] 明註曰常南藏作當

Fascicle 25 Variant Readings (p133a01–138a25)

[0133001] 都＝覩【宮】
[0135001] 肢＝支【宮】
[0136001] 惠＝慧【宮】
[0136002] 嚥＝咽【宋】【元】【明】【宮】【聖】
[0137001] 住＋（處）【明】
[0137002] 酥＝蘇【宋】【元】
[0137003] 璨＝璃【宮】下同

Fascicle 26 Variant Readings (p139a01–144a24)

[0139001] 采＝婇【宋】【元】【明】【宮】＊
[0140001] 宗＝崇【宮】
[0140002] 辨＝辦【明】
[0140003] （思）＋議【明】
[0141001] 主＝王【宮】
[0142001] 廕＝蔭【宮】
[0142002] 皦＝皎【宮】
[0142003] 幢幡＝幔幡【明】
[0143001] 主＝王【明】【宮】
[0143002] 槍＝鏘【宮】【聖】
[0144001] 記別＝記莂【宋】【元】【明】【宮】

Fascicle 27 Variant Readings (p144b01–150a13)

[0144002] 卍＝卍【宋】＊【元】＊【明】＊，＝萬【宮】＊［＊ 1］
[0144003] 瞖＝翳【宋】【元】【明】【宮】
[0145001] 免＝勉【宋】【元】【明】
[0145002] 壅＝擁【宋】【元】
[0145003] 瞶＝聵【宮】
[0145004] 入＝八【宮】
[0145005] 耀＝曜【宮】
[0146001] 返＝反【宋】【元】【明】【宮】
[0146002] 明註曰常南藏作當
[0146003] 行＝切【宮】
[0147001] 卍＝卍【元】【明】＊，＝萬【宮】＊［＊ 1］
[0147002] 惠＝慧【宮】＊［＊ 1］
[0147003] 任＝住【宋】
[0147004] 肢＝支【宋】【元】【明】【宮】＊［＊ 1 2 3］
[0148001] 盡＋（意）【宮】

[0148002] 阬=坑【宮】＊［＊ 1 2 3 4 5］
[0149001] 普=苦【宮】
[0149002] 栽=災【宋】【元】【明】【宮】

Fascicle 28 Variant Readings (p150a14–156c21)

[0150001] 辨=辦【宋】【元】【明】【宮】＊［＊ 1 2 3］
[0150002] 辭=詞【宋】【元】【明】
[0151001] 達=遠【宋】【元】【明】
[0151002] 耀=曜【宮】
[0151003] 任=住【宮】
[0152001] 王=主【宮】
[0152002] 栽=災【宋】【元】【明】【宮】
[0152003] 才=材【聖】
[0153001] 繼=繫【宋】【元】【明】
[0154001] 免=勉【宋】【元】【明】【宮】
[0154002] （世）+界【宋】【元】【明】
[0155001] 癈=廢【宋】【元】【明】【宮】
[0156001] 求=乞【宮】
[0156002] 如=知【宋】【元】【明】【宮】
[0156003] 解悟=悟解【宋】【元】【明】【宮】

Fascicle 29 Variant Readings (p156c22–160c18)

[0157001] 辨=辦【宋】【元】【明】【宮】
[0157002] 施+（住一切智智心）【明】
[0158001] 尸=口【宮】
[0159001] 生=樂【明】
[0159002] 集=習【宮】
[0159003] 住=往【宮】
[0159004] 剎=利【宮】＊［＊ 1］
[0159005] 辭=詞【宋】【元】【明】【宮】【聖】＊［＊ 1］
[0160001] 遍=滿【宮】
[0160002] 廢=癈【宮】

Fascicle 30 Variant Readings (p160c19–165a29)

[0160003] 〔于闐國三藏實叉難陀奉制譯〕－【福】，（唐）+于【明】＊
[0161001] 集=習【明】【宮】
[0161002] 辨=辦【宋】【元】【明】【宮】
[0163001] 普=善【宮】
[0163002] 行=徧【明】
[0164001] 辭=詞【宋】【元】【明】【宮】
[0164002] 希=布【福】

Fascicle 31 Variant Readings (p165b01–170c27)

[0165001] （唐）＋于【明】＊
[0165002] 三藏＋（沙門）【宋】＊【元】＊【明】＊，三藏＋（法師）【宮】＊
[0165003] 〔奉制〕－【宋】【元】【明】【宮】＊
[0165004] 如＝亦如【宮】
[0166001] 辭＝詞【宋】【元】【明】【宮】＊ [＊ 1 2]
[0166002] 得＝行【聖】
[0167001] 一＋（切）【宋】【元】【明】
[0170001] 震＝振【宮】【聖】
[0170002] 使＝悉【宮】
[0170003] 采＝婇【宋】【元】【明】
[0170004] 知＝相【宮】

Fascicle 32 Variant Readings (p171a01–174b26)

[0171001] 辨＝辯【宮】
[0172001] 覵＝覩【聖】
[0173001] （為）＋欲【宋】【元】【明】【宮】
[0174001] 耀＝曜【宮】下同

Fascicle 33 Variant Readings (p174c01–178b22)

[0175001] 綵＝采【宋】
[0175002] 彩＝采【宋】
[0175003] 跏＝加【宋】【元】【宮】＊ [＊ 1]
[0176001] 皆＋（得）【宋】【元】【明】【宮】
[0177001] 涌＝踊【宋】【元】【明】【宮】【聖】＊ [＊ 1 2]
[0177002] 妓＝伎【宋】【宮】
[0177003] 辭＝詞【宮】
[0178001] 諭＝喻【宋】【元】【明】【宮】Fascicle 34 Variant Readings (p178b23 - 184c27)
[0179001] 揀＝簡【宋】【元】【明】【宮】【聖】
[0179002] 彩＝采【宋】
[0180001] 惟＝唯【宮】
[0180002] 曰＝言【宮】
[0181001] 諭＝喻【宋】【元】【明】【宮】
[0181002] 方＝力【宋】【元】【明】【宮】
[0181003] 寶＝實【宮】
[0182001] 任＝住【宮】
[0183001] 生＝人【宮】
[0183002] 取＝諸【宮】
[0184001] 玷＝點【宋】【元】【明】【聖】

[0184002] 愍＝悲【宮】
[0184003] 滿＝遍【宋】【元】【明】【宮】【聖】
[0184004] 震＝振【聖】

Fascicle 35 Variant Readings (p185a01–189b14)

[0185001] 無誑無諂＝無諂無誑【宮】
[0185002] 斃＝弊【宮】
[0186001] 洄澓＝迴復【宮】【聖】
[0186002] 利行＝利益【宋】【宮】
[0187001] 如＝燒【宮】
[0187002] 〔第三地〕－【宋】【元】【明】【宮】【聖】
[0188001] 阬＝坑【宮】下同
[0188002] 跏＝加【宋】【明】
[0188003] 稱＝秤【宋】【元】【明】【宮】
[0188004] 譣＝險【宮】
[0189001] 鍊＝練【宮】

Fascicle 36 Variant Readings (p189b15–193b11)

[0189002] 西福寺本卷首缺
[0189003] 地＝法【宋】【元】【明】【宮】【福】
[0189004] 踊＝勇【宋】【元】【明】【宮】【聖】【福】
[0189005] 〔皆震動〕－【福】
[0189006] 〔自在…言佛〕十七字－【福】
[0189007] 循＝脩【聖】下同
[0190001] 習＝集【宋】【元】【宮】
[0190002] 熟＝就【福】
[0190003] 鍊＝練【宮】【聖】
[0190004] 治＝冶【福】
[0191001] 〔第五地〕－【宋】【元】【明】【宮】【聖】【福】
[0191002] 采＝婇【宋】【元】【明】
[0191003] 受＝愛【福】
[0191004] 明註曰行南藏作無
[0192001] 魅＝鬼【福】
[0192002] 妓＝技【宋】，＝伎【宮】
[0193001] 胥＝[冰-水+胥]【宋】【元】【宮】【福】
[0193002] 詞＝辭【宋】【元】【明】

Fascicle 37 Variant Readings (p193b12–198b26)

[0193003] 瓔珞＝纓絡【宋】【元】
[0193004] 成＝滅【明】
[0193005] 漏＝滿【宋】

[0194001] 恚＝惡【宋】【元】【明】【宮】
[0195001] 成＝滅【宋】【元】【明】【宮】
[0195002] 若＝苦【宋】
[0195003] 〔第七地〕－【宋】【元】【明】【宮】【聖】
[0195004] 王＝主【聖】
[0196001] 比＝上【宮】
[0196002] 闡＝間【聖】
[0196003] 〔地〕－【宋】【元】【明】【宮】
[0197001] 習＝集【宋】【元】【宮】
[0197002] 明註曰超南藏作起
[0198001] 行＝修【宋】【元】【明】【宮】
[0198002] 明註曰令北藏作今
[0198003] 此＝其【宋】【元】【明】
[0198004] 逾＝踰【宋】【元】【明】【宮】
[0198005] 詞＝辭【宋】【元】【明】
[0198006] 故＝成【宋】【元】【明】【宮】

Fascicle 38 Variant Readings (p198c01–204c01)

[0198007] 〔大…佛〕西福寺本卷首缺
[0198008] 瓔珞＝纓絡【宋】【元】【宮】
[0198009] 說＝法【宋】【宮】
[0199001] 自＝目【宮】
[0199002] 渡＝度【宋】【元】【明】【宮】【福】＊［＊ 1］
[0199003] 覺＝寤【宮】【福】＊
[0199004] （此）＋不【宋】【元】【明】
[0199005] 諭＝喻【宋】【元】【明】【宮】
[0200001] 熟＝就【福】
[0200002] 魔邪＝邪魔【宮】
[0201001] 其＝此【宮】
[0201002] 甚＝其【福】
[0201003] 住＝任【聖】
[0201004] 因＝曰【福】
[0201005] 明註曰知北藏作智
[0201006] 〔第九地〕－【宋】【元】【明】【宮】【聖】【福】
[0201007] 震＝振【聖】【福】
[0201008] 耀＝曜【宮】＊［＊ 1］
[0201009] 供＝共【宋】
[0201010] 詣＝諸【福】
[0202001] 相＝想【福】
[0202002] 芽＝牙【福】

[0202003] 聚＝趣【明】【宮】
[0202004] 辭＝詞【宮】【聖】【福】＊［＊ 1 2 3 4 5 6 7 8 9］
[0203001] 王＝三【宋】
[0204001] 知＝加【宋】
[0204002] 芽＝牙【福】
[0204003] 是＝見【福】
[0204004] 此下西福寺本有孝謙天皇願文

Fascicle 39 Variant Readings (p204c11–210c25)

[0205001] 諭＝喻【宋】【元】【明】【宮】＊［＊ 1 2］
[0206001] 震＝振【聖】
[0206002] 各＝名【宮】
[0206003] 〔解脫〕－【明】
[0207001] 返＝反【宮】
[0209001] 如＝知【宮】
[0209002] 涌＝踊【宋】【元】【明】【宮】＊［＊ 1 2］
[0209003] 妓＝技【宋】，＝伎【明】【宮】
[0210001] 鞞＝毘【宋】【元】【宮】【聖】，明註曰鞞南藏作毘

Fascicle 40 Variant Readings (p211a01–214c28)

[0211001] 聖本首缺
[0211002] 通＝踊【宋】【元】【明】【宮】
[0212001] 綵＝采【宋】
[0212002] 〔不〕－【聖】＊［＊ 1］
[0213001] 幢＝憧【聖】
[0213002] 辯＝辨【聖】＊［＊ 1］
[0213003] 跏＝加【聖】
[0213004] 西福寺本住以下缺損
[0214001] 顯＝影【宋】【元】
[0214002] 界＝間【宋】【元】【明】
[0214003] 〔龍宮〕－【聖】
[0214004] 補＋（特）【宮】

Fascicle 41 Variant Readings (p215a01–218c20)

[0215001] （唐）＋于【明】＊
[0215002] 三藏＋（沙門）【宋】【元】【明】【宮】
[0215003] 〔奉制〕－【宋】【元】【明】【宮】
[0216001] 辭＝詞【宋】【元】【明】【宮】
[0218001] 耀＝曜【宮】

Fascicle 42 Variant Readings (p218c21–223b29)

[0218002] 〔第〕－【聖】＊

[0218003] （于闐國三藏實叉難陀奉制譯）十二字＝（新譯）二字【聖】＊，（唐）＋于【明】＊
[0219001] 辨＝辦【明】【宮】＊ [＊ 1]
[0219002] 耀＝曜【宮】
[0220001] 肢＝支【宋】【元】【明】【宮】【聖】
[0220002] 度＝土【明】
[0222001] （流）＋出【明】【宮】
[0222002] 蘂＝葉【宋】
[0222003] 辭＝詞【宋】【元】【明】【宮】【聖】
[0222004] 惱＝惚【聖】
[0223001] 十＝四【宋】【元】【明】【宮】

Fascicle 43 Variant Readings (p223c01–229c10)

[0224001] 不＝無【元】【明】
[0224002] 諭＝喻【宋】【元】【明】【宮】
[0224003] 辭＝詞【宮】＊ [＊ 1]
[0226001] 昧＝時【聖】
[0226002] 明註曰雲北藏作雨，雲＝雨【宮】
[0226003] 時＋（劫）【明】
[0227001] 〔王〕－【聖】
[0228001] 相＝切【宮】
[0229001] 肢＝支【宋】【元】【明】【宮】
[0229002] 六＝七【宋】
[0229003] 采＝婇【宋】【元】【宮】＊

Fascicle 44 Variant Readings (p229c11–237b01)

[0231001] 〔佛〕－【宋】【元】【明】【宮】【聖】
[0231002] 明註曰固下北藏有色字
[0231003] 諭＝喻【宮】
[0231004] 耀＝曜【宮】
[0232001] 辨＝辦【明】【宮】＊ [＊ 1]
[0232002] 住＝位【宋】【元】【明】【宮】
[0233001] 各＝名【宋】【元】【明】【宮】
[0233002] 沒＝歿【宮】
[0233003] 芽＝牙【宮】
[0234001] 歿＝沒【宮】
[0235001] 故＝道【明】
[0236001] 悉＝忘【聖】

Fascicle 45 Variant Readings (p237b02–241c26)

[0237001] 〔呼〕－【明】
[0237002] 上＋（聲）夾註【明】＊

[0237003] 〔上〕－【明】
[0238001] 擢＝櫂【宮】＊［＊ 1 2 3 4 5］
[0238002] 曰＝言【宋】【元】【明】
[0239001] 辨＝辯【宮】
[0239002] 歷＝塵【聖】
[0239003] 昇＝升【宋】【元】【明】
[0240001] 恒＝性【宋】
[0240002] 來入＝入來【明】，明註曰入來南藏作來入
[0241001] 羅＝眾【宮】

Fascicle 46 Variant Readings (p242a01–246b11)

[0242001] 一＝上【宋】【元】【宮】
[0242002] 曜＝耀【宋】【元】【明】【聖】
[0242003] 跏＝加【宋】【元】【明】【宮】【聖】
[0243001] 辨＝辦【宋】【明】【宮】，＝辯【聖】
[0244001] 一切＝一一【聖】
[0244002] 寞＝漠【聖】
[0244003] 一＋（切）【宮】
[0244004] （皆能於一切世界演說正法無障礙住一切諸佛）十九字∞（皆能於一切世界住兜率天宮無障礙住一切諸佛）二十字【宮】
[0244005] （皆能於一切世界演說正法無障礙住一切諸佛）十九字∞（皆能於一切世界住兜率天宮無障礙住一切諸佛）二十字【宮】
[0244006] 明註曰等下北藏無為十二字【宮】
[0244007] （所謂）＋一【明】，明註曰南藏無所謂二字
[0245001] 迫＝追【宮】

Fascicle 47 Variant Readings (p246b12–251b18)

[0246001] 卷首缺【聖】
[0246002] 二＝下【宋】【元】【宮】
[0246003] 旋＝族【宮】
[0247001] 昔＝普【明】【宮】
[0248001] 辨＝辦【宋】【元】【明】【宮】
[0248002] 辭＝詞【宮】
[0248003] 一＝二【宋】【元】【明】【宮】【聖】
[0248004] 種＋（力何等為十所謂）【明】【宮】
[0248005] 力＋（是為十佛子諸佛世尊有種）【明】【宮】
[0249001] 跏＝加【宋】【元】【聖】＊［＊ 1］
[0249002] 昇＝升【宋】【元】【明】
[0249003] 諭＝喻【宋】【元】【明】【宮】
[0249004] 豎＝竪【宮】
[0250001] 別＝蒴【宋】【明】

[0250002] 〔常〕－【聖】
[0251001] 令＝念【聖】
[0251002] 授＝受【宮】【聖】

Fascicle 48 Variant Readings (p251b19–257c03)

[0251003] 〔第〕－【聖】
[0251004] （于闐國三藏實叉難陀奉制譯）十二字＝（新譯）二字【聖】，（唐）＋于【明】
[0252001] 曜＝耀【宋】【元】【明】
[0252002] 跏＝加【宋】【元】【聖】＊ [＊ 1 2 3]
[0253001] 舌＋（掌）【宮】
[0253002] 耀＝曜【宮】＊ [＊ 1 2 3]
[0253003] 于＝於【明】【聖】＊ [＊ 1]
[0253004] 卍＝卍【宋】【元】【明】【宮】
[0253005] 輪＝論【聖】
[0253006] 卍＝卍【宋】【元】【明】，＝[乏-之+(屯-一)]【宮】
[0254001] 震＝振【宮】【聖】
[0254002] 腨＝膊【宮】
[0255001] 卍＝卍【元】【明】
[0255002] 善＝菩【宮】
[0256001] 玻瓈＝頗梨【宋】＊【元】＊【明】＊ [＊ 1]
[0256002] 業＝善【宋】【聖】
[0257001] 銷＝消【宋】【元】【明】
[0257002] 諸＝許【宋】【元】【明】【宮】
[0257003] 諭＝喻【宋】【元】【明】【宮】＊ [＊ 1 2]

Fascicle 49 Variant Readings (p257c04–262a09)

[0257004] 卷首少缺【聖】
[0257005] （唐）＋于【明】
[0257006] 于＝於【明】
[0258001] 啞＝瘂【宮】
[0258002] 辭＝詞【宮】【聖】
[0259001] 耀＝躍【宮】
[0259002] 乎＝于【明】
[0259003] 是＝見【聖】
[0259004] 于＝於【明】＊ [＊ 1]

Fascicle 50 Variant Readings (p262a10–268a17)

[0262001] 〔第〕－【聖】
[0262002] （（于闐…譯））十二字＝（（新譯））二字【聖】
[0262003] 〔一〕－【宮】

[0262004] 震=振【聖】
[0262005] 昇=升【宋】【元】【明】
[0262006] 礙=破【聖】
[0262007] 法+（輪）【明】【宮】
[0263001] 諭=喻【宋】【元】【明】【宮】* [* 1]
[0263002] 謂=說【聖】
[0263003] 句=向【聖】
[0264001] 于=於【明】
[0264002] 〔大〕－【聖】
[0265001] 相=際【宮】
[0265002] 蒙=家【聖】
[0266001] 辨=辦【宋】【元】【明】【宮】
[0266002] 耀=曜【宮】
[0267001] 鍊=練【宮】【聖】

Fascicle 51 Variant Readings (p268a18–273b23)

[0268001] 〔卷第〕－【聖】*
[0268002] （于闐國三藏實叉難陀奉制譯）
十二字=（新譯）二字【聖】*，（唐）+于【明】
[0268003] 戀=變【聖】
[0268004] 憂=優【聖】
[0269001] 采=婇【元】【明】【宮】
[0269002] 明註曰與南藏作為
[0269003] 玻瓈=頗梨【宋】下同【元】下同【明】下同
[0269004] 電=雲【聖】
[0269005] 妓=技【宋】【聖】
[0269006] 至=王【聖】
[0270001] 耀=曜【宋】【元】【明】【宮】
[0270002] 明盛=熾然【明】
[0270003] 怨=冤【明】
[0271001] 習=集【宮】
[0272001] 葉=棄【聖】
[0272002] 大經=經卷【明】，明註曰經卷宋南藏作大經

Fascicle 52 Variant Readings (p273c01–278c23)

[0274001] 霔=澍【宋】【元】【明】【宮】【聖】* [* 1 2]
[0274002] 震=覆【聖】
[0274003] 出=山【宋】
[0274004] 入=八【聖】
[0274005] 諭=喻【宋】【元】【明】【宮】* [* 1 2 3 4]
[0274006] 如來=如是【聖】

[0274007] 起＝現【聖】
[0275001] 性＝恒【宮】
[0275002] 〔見〕－【聖】
[0275003] （以）＋一【明】
[0276001] 覺＝學【聖】
[0276002] 跏＝加【宋】【元】【宮】【聖】
[0277001] 照＝明【聖】
[0277002] 消＝銷【宮】【聖】＊［＊ 1 2 3］
[0277003] 纏＝經【聖】
[0277004] 餘＝除【聖】
[0277005] 趣＝起【聖】
[0278001] 涌＝踊【宋】下同【元】下同【明】下同，【宮】
[0278002] 威＝滅【聖】
[0278003] 越＝起【宮】
[0278004] 減＝滅【聖】
[0278005] 諭＝喻【宋】【元】【明】【宮】【聖】＊［＊ 1］

Fascicle 53 Variant Readings (p279a01–283c24)

[0279001] 聖本卷首缺
[0279002] （唐）＋于【明】
[0279003] 〔業〕－【聖】
[0279004] 辨＝辦【明】【宮】
[0280001] 集＝習【明】
[0280002] 故＋（一切神通行變化自在故）【明】
[0281001] 讃＝讚【明】
[0281002] 辯＝辨【宮】
[0282001] 本來＝未來【聖】
[0282002] 明註曰令南藏作戒
[0282003] 惱＝惚【聖】＊
[0283001] 諭＝喻【宋】【元】【明】【宮】

Fascicle 54 Variant Readings (p284a01–288c16)

[0284001] 于＝於【明】＊［＊ 1］
[0284002] 震＝振【聖】＊［＊ 1］
[0284003] 曜＝耀【宋】【元】【明】【聖】
[0284004] 惑＝或【聖】
[0285001] 〔往〕－【宋】【元】，明註曰南藏無往字
[0285002] 集＝習【明】
[0286001] 渡＝度【宮】
[0287001] 受＝授【宋】【宮】【聖】
[0287002] 揀＝簡【宮】【聖】

Fascicle 55 Variant Readings (p288c17–293c04)

[0288001] 諭＝喻【宋】【宮】【聖】*
[0289001] 明註曰成北藏作我
[0289002] 切＝相【聖】
[0289003] 〔界〕－【宋】【元】【明】【宮】
[0290001] 于＝於【明】
[0290002] 諸劫數＝微塵數【聖】
[0291001] 曜＝耀【宋】【元】【明】
[0291002] 有＝被【宋】【元】【明】【宮】
[0292001] 令＝今【宋】【明】【宮】
[0292002] 明註曰南藏無隨字

Fascicle 56 Variant Readings (p293c05–299b05)

[0293001] 跏＝加【宋】【元】【宮】【聖】
[0294001] 耀＝曜【宮】
[0294002] 子＝二【宮】
[0294003] 諸＝說【聖】
[0294004] 用＋（一微塵出現廣大佛剎無量莊嚴無礙用）【明】
[0295001] 酬＝訓【宋】*【元】*【明】*［* 1］
[0296001] 作是念言＝作如是念【明】【聖】
[0296002] 及＝天【聖】
[0296003] 問＝聞【宮】
[0296004] 采＝婇【明】【宮】
[0297001] 耽＝耽【聖】
[0297002] 潦＝潦【宋】【元】【明】【宮】【聖】
[0297003] 跏＝加【宋】【元】【宮】
[0298001] 〔佛子〕－【宋】【元】【明】【宮】
[0298002] 徒＝從【聖】
[0298003] 辨＝辦【宋】【元】【明】【宮】
[0298004] 擊＝繫【聖】
[0298005] 二＝三【宮】

Fascicle 57 Variant Readings (p299b06–304c15)

[0300001] 與世共＝世與共【聖】
[0300002] 善知＝菩薩知【聖】
[0301001] 〔界〕－【聖】
[0301002] 采＝婇【明】【宮】
[0301003] 尚＝上【聖】
[0301004] 弛＝絕【聖】
[0302001] 樂＝藥【宮】
[0302002] 卍＝卍【宮】

[0303001] 肢＝支【宋】【元】【明】【宮】【聖】
[0303002] 辨＝辯【宋】【宮】【聖】
[0303003] 歎＝歡【宋】【元】【明】【宮】【聖】
[0303004] 辨＝辯【宋】【元】【明】【宮】
[0303005] 別＝莂【宋】【明】
[0304001] 耀＝曜【宮】
[0304002] [穀-禾+卵]＝聲【聖】
[0304003] 怨＝冤【明】＊ [＊ 1]

Fascicle 58 Variant Readings (p304c16–310c20)

[0304004] 揀＝簡【宮】
[0305001] 善＝菩【聖】
[0305002] 師＝佛【聖】
[0305003] 心＝一【聖】
[0305004] 禪＝離【聖】
[0305005] 法＝清【聖】
[0305006] 揀＝簡【宮】【聖】
[0306001] 獷＝曠【宮】
[0307001] 霓＝蜺【宮】
[0307002] 大＝天【宋】【元】【明】
[0307003] 吝＝悕【聖】
[0307004] 使＋（使）【聖】
[0308001] 術＝述【宋】【元】【明】【宮】【聖】
[0308002] 顰＝嚬【宮】【聖】
[0309001] 宮本魔波乃至一切一千二百二十三字斷缺 p. 310 C段第二行參照
[0309002] 明註曰流通本他下有眾字
[0310001] 間＝聞【聖】
[0310002] 于＝於【明】
[0310003] 徙＝從【聖】
[0310004] 妓＝伎【聖】
[0310005] 卍＝卍【宋】【元】【明】
[0310006] 曰眼＝日眼【元】，＝曰月【明】

Fascicle 59 Variant Readings (p310c21–318c21)

[0311001] 免＝勉【宋】【元】【明】
[0311002] 同共＝共同【宋】【元】【明】【宮】
[0312001] 妓＝伎【聖】
[0312002] 行＋（為令眾生樂寂靜法增長善根故示行苦行）【明】
[0312003] 耀＝曜【宮】＊ [＊ 1]
[0312004] （時）＋有【宮】

[0312005] 謂＝詣【聖】
[0312006] 震＝振【聖】
[0312007] 以下聖語藏副本校合
[0312008] 觀＝現【明】，明註曰現北藏作觀
[0313001] 〔業〕－【聖】
[0313002] 別＝蔛【明】，＝[竺-二+別]【宮】
[0313003] 洎于＝洎於【明】，＝暨于【聖乙】
[0314001] 吝＝悋【聖】
[0314002] 諭＝喻【宋】【元】【明】【宮】【聖】
[0314003] 無＝不【宋】【元】【明】【宮】【聖】
[0314004] 鳥＝蔦【明】
[0314005] 授＝受【宋】【元】【明】【宮】
[0314006] 王＝正【聖】【聖乙】
[0314007] 間＝問【宮】
[0315001] 澣＝浣【宋】【元】【明】【宮】
[0315002] 降＝除【聖乙】
[0315003] 妓＝技【聖】
[0316001] 苦＝善【宋】【元】，明註曰苦宋南藏作善
[0316002] 采＝婇【宋】【元】【明】【宮】
[0316003] 間＝門【聖乙】
[0316004] 想＝視【聖】
[0316005] 著＝者【宮】
[0317001] 其＝真【宮】
[0317002] 想＝相【聖】
[0317003] 隱＝慰【宮】【聖】
[0317004] 辨＝辦【宮】
[0317005] 初發＝發心【宋】【元】【聖】【聖乙】，明註曰初發北藏作發心
[0317006] 甲＝中【聖】
[0317007] 貪＝會【聖】
[0318001] 納＝綱【聖乙】
[0318002] 菩薩＝善禮【宮】
[0318003] 未＝去【宮】【聖】【聖乙】
[0318004] 梵釋＝釋梵【宋】【元】【明】【宮】
[0318005] 行＝得【明】
[0318006] 昇＝升【宋】【元】【明】
[0318007] 采＝婇【明】【宮】＊
[0318008] 臣＝神【宋】【元】【明】【宮】【聖】

Fascicle 60 Variant Readings (p319a101–326c15)

[0319001] （唐）＋于【明】

[0319002] 〔一切〕－【宋】【元】【明】【宮】
[0319003] 明註曰音南藏作智
[0320001] 頻＝顰【明】＊［＊ 1］
[0320002] 迴＝廻【明】
[0320003] 氛＝氣【宮】
[0320004] 跏＝加【宮】
[0321001] 跏＝加【宋】【元】【宮】下同
[0322001] 肢＝支【宋】【元】【明】【宮】＊［＊ 1］
[0322002] 熟＝就【宋】【元】【明】【宮】
[0323001] 瞖＝翳【宮】
[0323002] 采＝綵【明】【宮】

Fascicle 61 Variant Readings (p326c16–331c21)

[0326001] 三藏＋（沙門）【宋】＊【元】＊【明】＊，（法師）【宮】＊
[0326002] 〔奉制〕－【宋】【元】【明】【聖乙】＊
[0326003] 頻＝嚬【明】＊［＊ 1］
[0326004] 申＝由【宮】
[0327001] 具＝是【宮】
[0328001] 迹＝跡【宮】
[0328002] 想＝相【宋】【元】【明】【宮】
[0328003] 日＝念【宮】
[0328004] 辭＝詞【宮】
[0329001] 諭＝喻【宮】
[0329002] 中＝界【明】
[0330001] 肢＝支【宋】【元】【明】
[0330002] 妓＝伎【宮】
[0330003] 技＝伎【宮】
[0330004] 耀＝曜【宮】
[0331001] 蜜＝密【宮】
[0331002] 熟＝就【宋】【元】【明】【宮】
[0331003] 一＝十【宋】【元】【明】【宮】
[0331004] 姓＝性【宋】【元】【明】【宮】

Fascicle 62 Variant Readings (p331c22–331b16)

[0332001] 芽＝牙【宋】【元】【明】【宮】
[0332002] 玻[黎>瓈]＝頗梨【宋】【元】【宮】＊［＊ 1 2］
[0332003] 肢＝支【宋】【元】【明】【宮】
[0332004] 涌＝踊【宮】
[0332005] 耀＝曜【宮】＊［＊ 1 2 3 4］
[0332006] 諭＝喻【宋】【元】【明】【宮】＊［＊ 1］
[0333001] 鎋＝轄【宋】【元】【明】【宮】

[0333002] 震=振【宮】＊［＊ 1］
[0333003] 箱=廂【宋】
[0333004] 類=願【宋】【元】【明】
[0333005] 城=位【宋】【元】【明】【宮】
[0333006] 能=垂【宮】
[0333007] 哉=財【元】，明註曰哉作財
[0334001] 于=於【明】
[0334002] 日=念【明】【宮】
[0335001] 〔已〕－【宋】【元】【明】【宮】
[0335002] 天=大【元】【明】
[0335003] 吠=大【宋】【宮】
[0335004] 藏=華【明】
[0335005] 濩=護【宮】
[0335006] 銜=銜【宋】
[0335007] 跏=加【宋】【元】【明】【宮】
[0336001] 辨=辯【宮】
[0336002] 時=隨【明】
[0336003] 漩=旋【宮】
[0336004] 治=持【宋】【元】【明】【宮】
[0336005] 翳=瞖【宋】【元】
[0336006] 道＋（邊）【宋】【元】【明】【宮】
[0337001] 婆=娑【宮】
[0337002] 跏=加【宋】【元】【明】【宮】

Fascicle 63 Variant Readings (p337b17–343a02)

[0338001] 一＋（切）【元】【明】
[0338002] 住=任【元】【明】
[0339001] 澣=浣【宋】【元】【明】【宮】
[0339002] 涼=淨【宋】【元】【明】
[0340001] 彼=復【宮】
[0340002] 跏=加【宋】【元】【明】【宮】
[0340003] 與=無【宮】
[0341001] 離=難【宋】
[0341002] 翳=瞖【宋】【元】
[0341003] 玻瓈=頗梨【宋】【元】【宮】＊［＊ 1］
[0341004] 辨=辦【宋】【元】【明】【宮】＊［＊ 1 2］
[0341005] 諍=靜【宮】
[0342001] 〔礙見…障〕四十四字－【宋】
[0342002] 辨=辯【宋】【元】【明】【宮】

Fascicle 64 Variant Readings (p343a03–348a19)

[0343001] 耀＝曜【宮】
[0344001] 齎＝齊【宮】
[0345001] 吒＝咤【明】
[0345002] 興＝與【宋】【明】【宮】
[0346001] 勝＝務【宋】
[0347001] （諸）＋莊【宮】
[0347002] 明註曰時下有令
[0347003] 荼＝茶【宋】【宮】＊［＊ 1］
[0347004] 唱＝作【宮】

Fascicle 65 Variant Readings (p348a20–353b23)

[0348001] 〔于闐國三藏〕－【宮】
[0348002] 玻瓈＝頗梨【宋】【元】
[0348003] 圓＝園【宮】
[0349001] 瞖＝翳【宮】
[0350001] 土＝上【宮】
[0350002] 如＝知【宮】
[0350003] 鍊＝練【宮】
[0350004] 諭＝喻【宋】【元】【明】【宮】＊［＊ 1 2］
[0351001] （云）＋何【宮】
[0351002] 辨＝辯【宋】【元】【明】【宮】
[0351003] 如＋（是）【宮】
[0352001] 以＝已【明】
[0352002] 明註曰長者流布本作居士

Fascicle 66 Variant Readings (p353c01–359c25)

[0353001] 遊＝游【宮】
[0353002] 玻瓈＝頗梨【宋】【元】【宮】＊［＊ 1 2］
[0353003] 碼＝馬【宋】＊
[0354001] ［山/陵］＝峻【宮】
[0354002] 痰＝淡【宋】
[0355001] 銷＝消【宋】【元】【明】
[0355002] 詣＝諸【宮】
[0356001] 跏＝加【宋】【元】【明】【宮】
[0356002] 象＝像【宮】
[0356003] 妓＝伎【宮】＊［＊ 1］
[0358001] 芽＝牙【宮】
[0358002] 耀＝曜【宮】
[0358003] 消＝銷【宮】
[0359001] 辭＝詞【宮】

[0359002] 技＝伎【宮】
[0359003] 撓＝托【宋】【元】【明】【宮】

Fascicle 67 Variant Readings (p360a01–365a21)

[0360001] 德＝得【宋】【宮】
[0360002] 耀＝曜【宮】＊［＊ 1 2］
[0360003] 技＝伎【宮】＊［＊ 1］
[0361001] 明註曰王南北藏俱作三
[0361002] （云）＋何【宮】
[0361003] 堅＝豎【宮】
[0362001] 漩＝旋【宮】
[0362002] 消＝銷【宮】
[0362003] 垢＝姤【明】
[0362004] 茶＝荼【宮】
[0363001] 頻＝嚬【明】＊［＊ 1 2 3 4 5］
[0365001] 詣＝諸【宮】

Fascicle 68 Variant Readings (p365a22–372a03)

[0365002] 芬＝分【宮】
[0365003] 申＝伸【宮】
[0366001] 縈＝瑩【宮】
[0366002] 跏＝加【宋】【元】【明】【宮】
[0367001] 耀＝曜【宮】
[0368001] 〔提〕－【宮】
[0368002] 薩＝提【宮】
[0368003] 踊＝涌【宋】＊【元】＊【明】＊［＊ 1］
[0368004] 授＝受【宋】【元】【明】【宮】
[0369001] 藏＝慧【宋】
[0369002] 久＝定【宮】
[0369003] 頻＝嚬【明】
[0369004] 申＝呻【宮】
[0369005] 晨＝辰【宮】
[0370001] 曰＝言【宋】【元】【宮】
[0370002] 像＝象【宋】【元】【明】
[0371001] 〔華〕－【宮】
[0371002] 諭＝喻【宮】
[0371003] （云）＋何【宮】

Fascicle 69 Variant Readings (p372a04–378a18)

[0372001] 十＝智【宋】【元】【明】【宮】
[0373001] 辨＝辦【宋】【元】【明】【宮】

[0373002] 〔又〕－【宋】【元】【明】【宮】
[0374001] 辭＝詞【宮】
[0374002] 與＝興【明】【宮】
[0374003] 茶＝荼【宮】＊ [＊ 1 2]
[0374004] 主＝王【明】【宮】
[0375001] 蜜＝密【宮】＊ [＊ 1 2 3 4 5 6 7]
[0375002] 揀＝簡【明】【宮】＊ [＊ 1]
[0376001] 寤＝悟【宋】【元】【明】【宮】
[0376002] 月＝日【宮】
[0377001] 明註曰主[王>]南藏作[>王]

Fascicle 70 Variant Readings (p378a19–384a12)

[0378001] 言辭＝言詞【宮】
[0379001] 采女＝婇女【宮】
[0380001] 跏＝加【宋】【元】【明】【宮】
[0382001] 妓＝伎【宮】
[0383001] 娑＝婆【元】【明】
[0383002] 眾妙音＝眾妙香【宮】

Fascicle 71 Variant Readings (p384a15–390c29)

[0384001] 〔第〕－【聖】
[0384002] （（于闐…譯））十二字＝（（新譯））二字【聖】
[0384003] 三藏＋（沙門）【宋】【元】【明】，（法師）【宮】
[0384004] 〔奉制〕－【宋】【元】【明】【宮】
[0384005] 怨＝寃【明】
[0384006] 采＝婇【宮】
[0385001] 生＝人【聖】
[0386001] 諭＝喻【宋】【元】【明】【宮】
[0386002] 〔諸〕－【宋】【元】【明】【宮】【聖】
[0386003] 瓔珞＝纓絡【聖】
[0386004] 耀＝曜【宮】
[0386005] [馱>駄]＝馱【宋】【元】【明】【宮】＊ [＊ 1]
[0387001] （出）＋生【宋】
[0389001] 異＋（眾）【元】【明】【宮】
[0390001] 辭＝詞【宮】
[0390002] 辨＝辯【宋】【元】【明】【宮】
[0390003] 量與＝無量【明】
[0390004] 先＝光【聖】
[0390005] 王＝土【宮】，明註曰王流通本作土

Fascicle 72 Variant Readings (p391a01–396b06)

[0391001] （大方廣佛華嚴經卷第七十二）十二字＝（大方廣佛華嚴經入法界品第三十九之十三，卷七十二）二十二字【聖乙】
[0391002] 〔第〕－【聖】
[0391003] （（于闐…譯））十二字＝（（新譯））二字【聖】，〔于闐…譯〕十二字－【聖乙】
[0391004] 三藏＋（沙門）【宋】【元】【明】，（法師）【宮】
[0391005] 〔奉制〕－【宋】【元】【明】【宮】
[0391006] 〔入法…三〕十一字－【聖乙】
[0391007] 蜜＝密【宮】＊［＊ 1 2 3 4］
[0391008] 闇＝瞑【聖乙】
[0391009] 〔出〕－【聖乙】
[0391010] 〔學如…故〕五十三字－【聖乙】
[0391011] 〔出〕－【聖】【聖乙】
[0391012] 縛＝纏【聖乙】
[0391013] 乏＝之【聖乙】
[0391014] 〔於一…見〕五百七十二字－【聖乙】
[0391015] 漩＝旋【聖】
[0391016] 悲＝慈【宮】
[0391017] 悉皆＝皆悉【宋】【元】【明】【宮】【聖】
[0391018] 位＝住【聖】
[0391019] 現＝見【宮】
[0392001] 〔又為…慧〕百[十>]字－【聖乙】
[0392002] 〔無雜…生〕百八十三字－【聖乙】
[0392003] 〔親近…淨〕三百六十四字－【聖乙】
[0392004] 大＝太【宋】【元】【明】【宮】【聖】
[0392005] 〔一一…生〕六十九字－【聖乙】
[0392006] 〔此世…中〕百十四字－【聖乙】
[0393001] 采＝婇【宮】＊
[0393002] 咸＝感【聖乙】
[0393003] 踊＝涌【宮】
[0393004] 〔得所…想〕四十字－【聖乙】
[0393005] 彊＝強【宮】
[0393006] 瓔珞＝纓絡【聖】＊［＊ 1］
[0393007] 〔十寶…業〕百三十二字－【聖乙】
[0393008] 肢＝支【宮】【聖】【聖乙】
[0394001] 〔捨離…生〕二百八十字－【聖乙】
[0394002] 揀＝簡【宋】【元】【明】【宮】【聖】
[0394003] 瓔珞＝纓絡【宋】【元】【聖】＊［＊ 1］
[0394004] 姝＝殊【元】【明】

[0394005] 〔如彼…生〕五十二字－【聖乙】
[0394006] 本＝木【宮】【聖乙】
[0394007] 秔＝粳【宮】
[0394008] 陵＝凌【宮】
[0395001] 成＝化【聖】
[0395002] 美水＝米水【宮】
[0395003] 慶喜＝多喜【宮】
[0395004] 宵＝有【聖乙】
[0395005] 跏＝加【宋】【元】【明】【宮】【聖】
[0395006] 掬＝鞠【宋】【元】【明】【宮】【聖】
[0395007] 涌＝踊【聖】
[0395008] 閉＝門【聖乙】
[0395009] 〔具種…殿〕四十二字－【聖乙】
[0396001] 闐＝間【聖】
[0396002] 〔憶知…海〕百八十三字－【聖乙】
[0396003] 〔大方…二〕十二字－【聖乙】

Fascicle 73 Variant Readings (p396b07–401c09)

[0396004] （大方…三）十二字＝（大方廣佛華嚴經入法界品第三十九之十四，卷七十三）二十二字【聖乙】
[0396005] 〔第〕－【聖】[【聖乙】>]
[0396006] （于闐國三藏實叉難陀奉制譯）十二字＝（新譯）二字【聖】，〔于闐國三藏實叉難陀奉制譯〕十二字－【聖乙】
[0396007] 三藏＋（沙門）【宋】【元】【明】，（法師）【宮】
[0396008] 〔奉制〕－【宋】【元】【明】【宮】
[0396009] 〔入法…四〕十一字－【聖乙】
[0396010] 〔現隨…身〕百四十字－【聖乙】
[0396011] 辨＝辯【聖】＊［＊ 1］
[0396012] 〔於善…故〕千二百[四>五]字－【聖乙】
[0396013] 間＝門【宮】
[0397001] 住處＝處住【聖】
[0397002] 震＝振【聖】＊［＊ 1］
[0397003] 〔我念…恩〕百四十字－【聖乙】
[0397004] 〔證無…行〕八百八十五字－【聖乙】
[0398001] 奪奪＝映奪【明】【宮】
[0398002] 耀＝曜【宮】
[0398003] 〔一一…轉〕九十三字－【聖乙】
[0398004] 〔汝說…故〕七十字－【聖乙】
[0398005] 〔亦無…劫〕二十字－【聖乙】
[0398006] 〔諸想…伏〕五十六字－【聖乙】
[0398007] 大＝太【宋】【元】【明】

[0398008] 〔善男…力〕百三十四字－【聖乙】
[0398009] 肢＝支【宋】【元】【明】【宮】
[0399001] 語＝言【明】【宮】
[0399002] 瓔珞＝纓絡【宋】【元】【聖】
[0399003] 銷＝消【宋】【元】【明】
[0399004] 法眼淨＝淨法眼【宋】【元】【明】【宮】【聖】【聖乙】
[0400001] 菩薩＝菩提【聖】
[0400002] 〔百萬…了〕百六十六字－【聖乙】
[0400003] 荼＝茶【宋】【元】【明】
[0400004] 〔種種…便〕百二十六字－【聖乙】
[0401001] 〔於中…力〕六百五十三字－【聖乙】
[0401002] 令＝今【宮】
[0401003] 〔大方…三〕十二字－【聖乙】

Fascicle 74 Variant Readings (p401c10–405b23)

[0401004] （大方廣佛華嚴經卷第七十四）十二字＝（大方廣佛華嚴經入法界品第三十九之十五卷，七十四）二十二字【聖乙】
[0401005] 〔第〕－【聖】
[0401006] （（于闐…譯））十二字＝（（新譯））二字【聖】，〔于闐…譯〕十二字－【聖乙】
[0401007] 三藏＋（沙門）【宋】【元】【明】，（法師）【宮】
[0401008] 〔奉制〕－【宋】【元】【明】【宮】
[0401009] 〔入法…五〕十一字－【聖乙】
[0401010] 〔不疲…境〕[八十一>七十六]字－【聖乙】
[0402001] 藏＋（生藏）【聖】
[0402002] 〔是為…藏〕三百五十六字－【聖乙】
[0402003] 吝＝怯【宮】
[0402004] （破）＋礙【聖乙】
[0402005] 〔云何…間〕八百八十八字－【聖乙】
[0402006] 習＝集【宋】【宮】
[0402007] 〔佛〕－【聖】
[0403001] 〔一切…門〕三百三十字－【聖乙】
[0403002] 芽＝牙【宮】【聖】
[0403003] 涌＝踊【宮】
[0403004] 齎＝齊【宮】【聖】
[0403005] 〔何等…心〕百二十字－【聖乙】
[0403006] 智＝知【聖】
[0404001] 普＝著【聖】
[0404002] 辯＝辨【宋】【元】

[0404003] 肉＝脈【宮】
[0404004] 妓＝伎【宮】【聖】
[0404005] 〔屬〕－【聖】
[0404006] 〔昔〕－【聖】
[0404007] 耀＝曜【宮】
[0404008] 大＝火【宮】
[0404009] 〔亦見…是〕三百九十七字－【聖乙】
[0405001] 〔專求…行〕五百[八十八>七十九]字－【聖乙】
[0405002] 〔大方…四〕十二字－【宋】【聖乙】

Fascicle 75 Variant Readings (p405c01–413c02)

[0405003] （大方廣佛華嚴經卷第七十五）十二字＝（大方廣佛華嚴經入法界品第三十九之十六，
卷七十五）廿二字【聖乙】
[0405004] 〔第〕－【聖】
[0405005] （于闐國三藏實叉難陀奉制譯）十二字＝（新譯）二字【聖】，〔于闐國三藏實叉難陀奉制譯〕十二字－【聖乙】
[0405006] 藏＋（沙門）【宋】【元】【明】，（法師）【宮】
[0405007] 〔奉制〕－【宋】【元】【明】【宮】
[0405008] 普＝著【聖】
[0405009] 見＝現【宋】
[0405010] 〔不久…樂〕十六字－【聖乙】
[0406001] 肢＝支【宋】【元】【明】【宮】【聖】
[0406002] 〔何以…樂〕三百七十字－【聖乙】
[0406003] 船＝紅【宮】
[0406004] 放＝故【宮】
[0406005] 昇＝升【宋】【元】【明】
[0406006] 闇＝間【聖】
[0406007] 〔汝於…識〕百二十字－【聖乙】
[0406008] 〔雖行…力〕四十字－【聖乙】
[0406009] 其＝具【宮】
[0406010] 先＝元【宮】
[0406011] 〔超過…息〕九十二字－【聖乙】
[0406012] 〔佛子…逆〕百四十一字－【聖乙】
[0407001] 〔志樂…道〕二百八十字－【聖乙】
[0407002] 〔正定…故〕八百五十五字－【聖乙】
[0408001] 〔陰藏…服〕二百八十六字－【聖乙】
[0408002] 具＝口【宮】
[0408003] 芽＝牙【宋】【元】【明】【宮】＊ [＊ 1 2 3]
[0408004] 妓＝伎【宮】，＝技【聖】
[0408005] 母＝女【宮】

[0408006] 采＝妹【宮】
[0408007] 辭＝詞【宮】
[0408008] 明註曰其流通本作彼，其＝彼【宮】
[0408009] 若＝如【宮】
[0409001] 誨＝誑【聖】
[0409002] 修＝脩【宮】＊［＊ 1］
[0409003] 肢＝支【聖】＊［＊ 1 2］
[0409004] 慶＝塵【聖乙】
[0409005] 日初＝初日【宮】
[0409006] 妓＝伎【宮】【聖】
[0409007] 〔當隨…當〕七十八字－【聖乙】
[0410001] 肢＝支【宮】【聖】
[0410002] 〔爾時…意〕二百十二字－【聖乙】
[0410003] 或＝勿【宮】
[0410004] 〔紺青…來〕百四十字－【聖乙】
[0410005] 冠＝髻【聖】
[0410006] 〔身色…佛〕百字－【聖乙】
[0411001] 〔所謂…昧〕九十六字－【聖乙】
[0411002] 〔未久…是〕十七字－【聖】
[0411003] 〔人耶〕－【聖乙】
[0411004] 授＝受【宮】
[0411005] （可）＋思【宮】＊
[0411006] 萬＝方【宮】
[0411007] 〔復以…法〕四十四字－【聖乙】
[0411008] 〔入城…願〕百二十字－【聖乙】
[0411009] 〔以等…願〕七十六字－【聖乙】
[0412001] 〔次名…華〕二百八十四字－【聖乙】
[0412002] 〔於其…界〕百二十六字－【聖乙】
[0412003] 〔轉佛…行〕六百四十五字－【聖乙】
[0413001] 瓔珞＝纓絡【宋】【聖】
[0413002] 〔於彼…五〕二百七十字－【聖乙】

Fascicle 76 Variant Readings (p413c03–419c07)

[0413003] （大方廣佛華嚴經卷第七十六）十二字＝（大方廣佛華嚴經入法界品第三十九之十七，七十六）二十一字【聖乙】
[0413004] 〔第〕－【聖】
[0413005] （（于闐…譯））十二字＝（（新譯））二字【聖】，〔于闐…譯〕十二字－【聖乙】
[0413006] 三藏＋（沙門）【宋】【元】【明】，（法師）【宮】
[0413007] 〔奉制〕－【宋】【元】【明】【宮】
[0413008] 〔入法…七〕十一字－【聖乙】

[0413009] 〔無起…言〕百十六字－【聖乙】
[0413010] 〔應淨…法〕四十二字－【聖乙】
[0413011] 辨＝辯【聖】＊
[0414001] 耀＝曜【宮】
[0414002] 〔法應…佛〕四百五十八字－【聖乙】
[0414003] 實＝貴【明】
[0414004] 〔得淨…故〕九十九字－【聖乙】
[0414005] 〔知諸…識〕二百五十九字－【聖乙】
[0414006] 視＝觀【宮】
[0414007] 涌＝踊【宋】【聖】
[0414008] 〔金剛…網〕百二十八字－【聖乙】
[0414009] 臺＝喜【宮】
[0414010] 納＝網【聖】
[0414011] 瓔珞＝纓絡【聖】＊［＊ 1］
[0415001] 〔隨心…故〕四百八十八字－【聖乙】
[0415002] 想＝患【宮】
[0415003] 身＝一【宮】
[0415004] 〔修習…薩〕三百二十八字－【聖乙】
[0415005] 之＝法【宮】
[0415006] 〔一一…飾〕五百八十二字－【聖乙】
[0416001] 破＝邊【宮】
[0416002] 〔法幢…界〕七百五十九字－【聖乙】
[0416003] 炬＝明【明】
[0416004] 薝＝瞻【明】
[0417001] 〔當成…界〕十七字－【聖乙】
[0417002] 兵＝其【宮】
[0417003] 齎＝臍【宮】，＝齊【聖】
[0417004] 〔我唯…子〕六十三字－【聖乙】
[0417005] 辨＝辯【宋】【元】【明】【宮】
[0417006] 〔又過…來〕百六十九字－【聖乙】
[0417007] 〔如是…生〕百五字－【聖乙】
[0418001] 〔唱波…藏〕八百十一字－【聖乙】
[0418002] 柂＝施【聖乙】
[0418003] （音）＋輕呼【宋】【元】【宮】【聖】
[0418004] （音）＋蒲【宋】【元】【宮】【聖】
[0418005] 切＝反【宮】【聖】＊［＊ 1 2 3 4 5 6 7］
[0418006] （音）＋徒【宋】【元】【聖】
[0418007] （音）＋史【宋】【元】【聖】
[0418008] （音）＋房【宋】【元】【聖】
[0418009] （音）＋都【宋】【元】【聖】

[0418010] （音）＋以【宋】【元】【聖】
[0418011] （音）＋蘇【宋】【元】【聖】
[0418012] 霔＝霔【宋】【元】【明】【宮】【聖】
[0418013] （音）＋上聲【宋】【元】【宮】【聖】
[0418014] （音）＋他可【宋】【元】【聖】
[0418015] 切＝反【宋】【宮】【聖】
[0418016] 揀＝簡【宋】【元】【明】【宮】
[0418017] （音）＋尸苛【宋】【元】【宮】【聖】
[0418018] 切＝反【宮】＊［＊ 1]
[0418019] （音）＋上聲【宮】
[0418020] 〔呼〕－【宮】【聖】＊［＊ 1 2]
[0418021] 上聲＋（呼）【宋】【元】【明】，（音）＋上聲【宮】
[0418022] 切＝反【宮】【聖】＊［＊ 1 2 3 4 5 6 7]
[0418023] 二字皆上聲呼＝訶婆字並上聲呼之【聖】，
（訶婆）＋二【宋】【元】【明】，皆＝並【宮】
[0418024] 波＝婆【宮】
[0418025] 舸＝可【宮】
[0418026] 〔善知…此〕五百六十一字－【聖乙】
[0418027] 技＝伎【宮】
[0418028] 該＝揀【聖】
[0418029] 辨＝辯【宮】
[0419001] 沃＝泼【聖】
[0419002] 〔我唯…子〕五十字－【聖乙】
[0419003] 〔善男…行〕三十八字－【聖乙】
[0419004] 〔我以…行〕五十五字－【聖乙】
[0419005] 〔無已…說〕七十八字－【聖乙】
[0419006] 〔大方…六〕十二字－【聖乙】

Fascicle 77 Variant Readings (p419c08–428a25)

[0419007] （大方廣佛華嚴經卷第七十七）十二字＝（大方廣佛華嚴經入法界品第三十九之十八，
卷七十七）二十二字【聖乙】
[0419008] 〔第〕－【聖】
[0419009] （（于闐…譯））十二字＝（（新譯））二字【聖】，〔于闐…譯〕十二字－【聖乙】
[0419010] 藏＋（沙門）【宋】【元】【明】，（法師）【宮】
[0419011] 〔奉制〕－【宋】【元】【明】【宮】
[0419012] 〔入法…八〕十一字－【聖乙】
[0419013] 〔一切…議〕百六十五字－【聖乙】
[0419014] 明註曰老下南藏無病，〔病〕－【宮】
[0420001] 〔又欲…故〕百三十五字－【聖乙】

[0420002]〔已證…力〕三十五字－【聖乙】
[0420003]〔善男…心〕百五十六字－【聖乙】
[0420004]〔應消…事〕千五十六字－【聖乙】
[0420005] 消＝銷【宮】【聖】
[0420006] 辨＝辦【宋】【元】【明】【宮】，＝辯【聖】
[0420007] 別＝莂【明】
[0421001]〔順〕－【明】
[0421002] 芽＝牙【聖】
[0421003] 密＝蜜【聖】
[0421004]〔由善…故〕八十字－【聖乙】
[0421005] 道＝導【聖】
[0421006]〔能令…門〕百五字－【聖乙】
[0421007] 辦＝辯【聖】
[0421008] 耀＝曜【宮】
[0421009] 消＝銷【宮】
[0421010]〔如良…故〕四十字－【聖乙】
[0421011] 鋹＝長【聖】
[0421012]〔復次…想〕四百二字－【聖乙】
[0421013] 檝＝艥【宮】【聖】
[0421014] 身生＝生身【明】
[0422001]〔又應…想〕六十六字－【聖乙】
[0422002]〔又應…淨〕八十二字－【聖乙】
[0422003] 鍊＝練【聖】
[0422004]〔善男…起〕百十五字－【聖乙】
[0422005]（聞）＋善【明】
[0422006]〔復憶…觀〕百七十字－【聖乙】
[0422007]〔即於…界〕二百十四字－【聖乙】
[0422008]〔等實…起〕百二十四字－【聖乙】
[0423001] 芽＝牙【聖】
[0423002]〔知質…故〕五十[六>五]字－【聖乙】
[0423003] 明註曰澤流通本作懌
[0423004]〔是知…處〕千二百五十二字－【聖乙】
[0423005] 明＝解【宮】
[0424001]〔智慧…處〕二百八十字－【聖乙】
[0424002] 人＝生【聖】
[0424003]〔修行…處〕八十四字－【聖乙】
[0424004]〔成就…處〕二百五十二字－【聖乙】
[0425001]〔佛子…中〕百字－【聖乙】
[0425002] 跏＝加【宋】【元】【明】【聖】
[0425003]〔佛子…盡〕百四十字－【聖乙】

[0425004] 〔善來…別〕四十字－【聖乙】
[0425005] 〔汝觀…行〕百字－【聖乙】
[0426001] 〔善財…洲〕二十字－【聖乙】
[0426002] 〔善財…寶〕二十字－【聖乙】
[0426003] 昇＝升【宋】*【元】*【明】*［* 1］
[0426004] 〔善財…提〕二百八十字－【聖乙】
[0426005] 肢＝支【宮】【聖】
[0426006] 〔一切…界〕八十字－【聖乙】
[0426007] 〔當示…海〕六十字－【聖乙】
[0427001] 〔汝當…界〕八十字－【聖乙】
[0427002] 〔所行…道〕百二十字－【聖乙】
[0427003] 諸＝詣【聖】
[0427004] 〔菩薩…受〕六十字－【聖乙】
[0427005] 〔信樂…習〕四十字－【聖乙】
[0427006] 〔若有…善〕四十字－【聖乙】
[0427007] 〔若於…法〕二十字－【聖乙】
[0427008] 〔若入…會〕百二十字－【聖乙】
[0428001] 薩＋（摩訶薩）【聖】
[0428002] 〔大方…七〕十二字－【聖乙】

Fascicle 78 Variant Readings (p428b01–434c22)

[0428003] （大方廣佛華嚴經卷第七十八）十二字＝（大方廣佛華嚴經入法界品第三十九之十九，
七十八）二十一字【聖乙】
[0428004] 〔第〕－【聖】
[0428005] （（于闐…譯））十二字＝（（新譯））二字【聖】，〔于闐…譯〕十二字－【聖乙】
[0428006] 三藏＋（沙門）【宋】【元】【明】，（法師）【宮】
[0428007] 〔奉制〕－【宋】【元】【明】【宮】
[0428008] 〔入法…九〕十一字－【聖乙】
[0428009] 〔界〕－【明】
[0428010] 〔則已…提〕百四十一字－【聖乙】
[0428011] 〔則已…身〕二百九十八字－【聖乙】
[0428012] 往＝生【宮】
[0429001] 〔為嬰…城〕百六十五字－【聖乙】
[0429002] 諭＝喻【宋】【元】【明】【宮】
[0429003] 〔恒勤…逆〕六十四字－【聖乙】
[0429004] 〔又能…得〕百三十二字－【聖乙】
[0429005] 〔汝身…受〕四十五字－【聖乙】
[0429006] 〔菩提…故〕二百八字－【聖乙】
[0429007] 〔菩提…故〕四十八字－【聖乙】

[0429008] 〔菩提…故〕九十六字－【聖乙】
[0429009] 戾＝[仁-二+戾]【宋】【元】【明】【宮】
[0430001] 〔菩提…故〕百十四字－【聖乙】
[0430002] 〔菩提…故〕四十八字－【聖乙】
[0430003] 〔菩提…故〕四十八字－【聖乙】
[0430004] 任＝住【宮】
[0430005] 病＝疾【聖】
[0430006] 消＝銷【宮】【聖】
[0430007] 〔菩提…故〕三百二十一字－【聖乙】
[0431001] 〔善男…病〕百三十七字－【聖乙】
[0431002] 〔善男…失〕九十二字－【聖乙】
[0431003] 〔善男…濁〕百八十九字－【聖乙】
[0431004] 瓔珞＝纓絡【聖】
[0431005] 彩＝采【宋】【元】【明】
[0431006] 〔善男…生〕四十四字－【聖乙】
[0431007] 〔善男…滅〕百五十六字－【聖乙】
[0431008] 〔善男…冥〕八十四字－【聖乙】
[0431009] 採＝采【宋】【元】【明】
[0431010] 船＝舡【宮】
[0432001] 〔善男…及〕八十字－【聖乙】
[0432002] 〔善男…在〕百字－【聖乙】
[0432003] 降＝除【聖乙】
[0432004] 仗＝伏【聖乙】＊
[0432005] 〔善男…涼〕六十四字－【聖乙】
[0432006] 薝＝瞻【明】【聖】
[0432007] 〔善男…處〕六十四字－【聖乙】
[0432008] 〔善男…心〕七十六字－【聖乙】
[0432009] 〔善男…及〕百二十四字－【聖乙】
[0432010] 〔善男…脫〕百五十四字－【聖乙】
[0433001] 〔善男…嚴〕三百六十六字－【聖乙】
[0433002] 技＝伎【聖】
[0433003] 〔善男…故〕二百三十二字－【聖乙】
[0433004] 磁＝慈【宮】＊［＊ 1］
[0433005] 〔善男…德〕百七十六字－【聖乙】
[0433006] 〔善男…滅〕三百三十六字－【聖乙】
[0434001] 〔善男…生〕六十六字－【聖乙】
[0434002] 〔善男…德〕百八十五字－【聖乙】
[0434003] 〔善男…得〕六十六字－【聖乙】
[0434004] 小＝少【宋】【元】【明】
[0434005] 〔善男…界〕二百八十五字－【聖乙】

[0434006] 〔善男…持〕百三十四字－【聖乙】
[0434007] 集＝習【宋】【元】【明】【宮】
[0434008] 〔大方…八〕十二字－【聖乙】

Fascicle 79 Variant Readings (p434c23–439a26)

[0434009] （大方廣佛華嚴經卷第七十九）十二字＝（大方廣佛華嚴經入法界品第三十九之二十，卷七十九）二十二字【聖乙】
[0434010] 〔第〕－【聖】
[0434011] 〔于闐…譯〕十二字－【聖】【聖乙】
[0434012] 三藏＋（沙門）【宋】【元】【明】，（法師）【宮】
[0434013] 〔奉制〕－【宋】【元】【明】【宮】
[0434014] 〔入法…十〕十一字－【聖乙】
[0435001] 〔闥阿…帳〕百五十九字－【聖乙】
[0435002] 瓔珞＝纓絡【聖】＊［＊ 1 2］
[0435003] 爐＝鑪【宋】【元】【明】
[0435004] 〔又見…見〕五十七字－【聖乙】
[0435005] 〔令其…見〕六十字－【聖乙】
[0435006] 諸＝請【宮】
[0435007] 〔或為…傲〕百三十二字－【聖乙】
[0435008] 阿＝訶【宮】
[0435009] 〔或復…法〕百三十字－【聖乙】
[0435010] 〔或見…門〕百二十字－【聖乙】
[0435011] 〔或入…雲〕百十一字－【聖乙】
[0435012] 〔所謂…吼〕二百四十一字－【聖乙】
[0436001] 昇＝升【宋】【元】【明】
[0436002] 〔所修…同〕二十四字－【聖乙】
[0436003] 〔所謂…蜜〕二百二十三字－【聖乙】
[0436004] 螺＝蠡【宋】【元】【明】【聖】
[0436005] 〔或聞…事〕千三百二十五字－【聖乙】
[0436006] 澤＝懌【明】
[0436007] 玻瓈＝頗梨【宋】【元】
[0436008] 挂＝掛【聖】
[0436009] 瓔珞＝纓絡【宋】
[0436010] 耀＝曜【宮】
[0436011] 跏＝加【宋】【元】【明】【宮】【聖】
[0437001] 護＝諸【宮】【聖】
[0437002] 齋＝齊【聖】
[0437003] 入＝人【宮】
[0437004] 〔或見…事〕八十八字－【聖乙】

[0437005] 〔滅諸…界〕四十字－【聖乙】
[0437006] 者＝復【宮】
[0437007] 名＝若【宮】
[0437008] 〔復如…業〕百五十字－【聖乙】
[0437009] 〔此是…願〕百十一字－【聖乙】
[0437010] 〔善男…得〕二十六字－【聖乙】
[0438001] 〔善男…來〕百四十七字－【聖乙】
[0438002] 〔從無…故〕五十八字－【聖乙】
[0438003] 蜜＝密【宮】＊［＊ 1 2 3 4 5 6］
[0438004] 澣＝浣【宋】【元】【明】【宮】【聖】
[0438005] 〔於諸…界〕二百五十七字－【聖乙】
[0438006] 憂＝疲【元】【明】
[0438007] 〔為欲…天〕五十七字－【聖乙】
[0439001] 〔云何…子〕二十三字－【聖乙】
[0439002] 熟＝就【宋】【元】【明】【宮】【聖】
[0439003] 〔能如…子〕百十四字－【聖乙】
[0439004] 〔大方…九〕十二字－【聖乙】

Fascicle 80 Variant Readings (p439b01–444c30)

[0439005] 聖本缺卷首，
（大方廣佛華嚴經卷第八十）十一字＝
（大方廣佛華嚴經入法界品第三十九之二十一，
卷八十）二十二字【聖乙】
[0439006] 〔于闐…譯〕十二字－【聖乙】
[0439007] 三藏＋（沙門）【宋】【元】【明】，（法師）【宮】
[0439008] 〔奉制〕－【宋】【元】【明】【宮】
[0439009] 〔入法…一〕十二字－【聖乙】
[0439010] 由＝遊【宮】
[0439011] 〔蘇摩…財〕二百六十二字－【聖乙】
[0439012] 以＝已【宋】【元】【明】
[0439013] 〔增長…心〕三百六十二字－【聖乙】
[0439014] 智＝剎【宮】
[0439015] 〔故見…地〕六百十三字－【聖乙】
[0439016] 惡＝悉【宮】
[0440001] 耀＝曜【宮】
[0440002] 〔見普…智〕七百六十一字－【聖乙】
[0440003] 令＝今【宮】
[0440004] 熏＝重【宮】
[0440005] 主＝王【明】
[0440006] 〔後際〕－【聖乙】

[0441001] 〔亦如…通〕二百十一字－【聖乙】
[0441002] 〔何等…子〕百九十六字－【聖乙】
[0441003] 太＝大【明】【宮】
[0441004] 〔一一…明〕百二十九字－【聖乙】
[0441005] 〔為集…中〕百二十一字－【聖乙】
[0441006] 〔善男…故〕三百三十一字－【聖乙】
[0442001] 震＝振【聖】
[0442002] 〔爾時…生〕百七十六字－【聖乙】
[0442003] 肢＝支【宮】【聖】
[0442004] 諭＝喻【宮】
[0442005] 聖本別寫以下斷缺
[0442006] 明註曰柔流通本作御
[0443001] 有＝見【宋】【元】【明】【宮】
[0443002] 跏＝加【宋】【元】【明】【聖】
[0443003] 辭＝詞【宮】【聖】
[0444001] 間＝佛【宋】【元】【宮】
[0444002] 在＝有【聖】
[0444003] 誓＝警【明】【宮】
[0444004] 事＝專【宮】
[0444005] 授＝受【宋】【元】【明】【宮】
[0444006] 熟＝就【宋】【元】【明】【宮】
[0444007] 諭＝喻【宮】

T10n0293, Fascicle 40 Variant Readings (p844b14–848b24)

[0844002] 四十華嚴中宋元二本唯有此一卷
[0844003] 第四十＝入不思議解脫境界普賢行願品【宋】【元】
[0844004] （（罽賓國三藏））五字＝（（唐貞元年罽賓三藏法師））十字【元】，（唐）＋罽【明】
[0844005] 〔入不…品〕十三字－【宋】【元】
[0844006] ＋（此經凡四十卷今將末卷權續大部）十四字【元】，＋（之四十）【明】
[0844007] 〔善財言〕－【和】
[0844008] 〔不可說〕－【元】
[0844009] 一者乃至迴向六十字元本作六字十句
[0844010] 起深＝深心【宋】【元】【明】
[0844011] 而＝以【宋】【元】【明】
[0844012] 而＝以【和】＊［＊ 1］
[0844013] 界＝間【宋】【明】
[0844014] 辭＝詞【宋】【元】【和】下同
[0844015] 華雲＝天花【和】
[0845001] 酥＝蘇【和】

[0845002] 諭＝喻【宋】【元】【明】【和】
[0845003] 婆＝波【宋】【元】【明】
[0845004] 〔修〕－【宋】【元】【明】【和】
[0845005] 〔諸〕－【和】
[0845006] 緣＝獨【和】
[0845007] 折＝析【宋】【元】【明】
[0845008] 刺＝剌【宋】【元】
[0845009] 居＝處【和】
[0845010] 〔處〕－【和】
[0846001] 〔一〕－【和】
[0846002] 銷＝消【宋】【元】
[0846003] 荼＝茶【元】【明】
[0846004] 有＝得【和】
[0846005] 此＝信【和】
[0847001] 恚＝瞋【明】
[0847002] 明註曰福流通本作佛
[0847003] 言＝切【和】
[0847004] 諸威力＝威神力【明】
[0847005] 明註曰行流通本作慧
[0848001] 生＝王【和】
[0848002] 銷＝消【宋】【元】【明】
[0848003] （（卷第四十））四字＝（（入不思議解脫境界普賢行願品））十三字【宋】，
＝（（普賢行願品））五字【元】
[0848004] 麗本無此譯經因緣并譯場列位依宋元二本對校明本，（南天竺王進奉梵本經願文）＋南【和】
[0848005] 荼＝茶【宋】【和】
[0848006] 子＋（王）【宋】【元】【和】
[0848007] 〔可〕－【宋】【元】【和】
[0848008] 以下仁和寺本缺
[0848009] （（進奉…日））十一字＝（（南天竺國王進奉梵夾十二年六月十日））十六字【宋】，
＝（（沙門釋蓮華等奉進梵夾十二年六月十日））十七字【元】
[0848010] 〔進上〕－【元】
[0848011] 柔＋（智通）【宋】
[0848012] 〔保壽…綴〕九字－【宋】
[0848013] 軍＋（臣）【元】

Bibliography

Bodhi. The Numerical Discourses of the Buddha: A Translation of the Aṅguttara Nikāya (Teachings of the Buddha). Boston: Wisdom Publications, 2012.

Bodhiruci (*c.* 508–511 CE). *Shidi jing lun* (十地經論). T26, no. 1522.

Buddhabhadra (*c.* 418–20 CE). *Dafangguang fo huayan jing* (大方廣佛華嚴經). T10, no. 278.

Cheng Guan. *Dafangguang fo huayan jing shuchao hui ben.* (大方廣佛華嚴經疏鈔會本) L130n1557.

Cleary, T. *The Flower Ornament Scripture: A Translation of the Avatamsaka Sutra*. Boulder: [New York]: Shambhala Publications, 1984. Distributed in the U.S. by Random House.

Conze, E. and Suzuki Gakujutsu Zaidan. *Materials for a Dictionary of the Prajñāpāramitā Literature*. Tokyo: Suzuki Research Foundation, 1967.

Dharmarakṣa (*c.* 297 CE). *Pusa shizhu xingdao pin* (菩薩十住行道品). T10, no. 283.

Edgerton, F. (1953). *Buddhist Hybrid Sanskrit Grammar and Dictionary*. (William Dwight Whitney linguistic series). New Haven: Yale University Press, 1953.

Hamar, Imre. "*The History of the Buddhāvataṃsaka-sūtra*: Shorter and Larger Texts" in *Reflecting Mirrors: Perspectives on Huayan Buddhism*. Wiesbaden: Harrassowitz Verlag, 2007

Hsuan Hua. *Dafangguang fo huayan jing qian shi* (大方廣佛華嚴經淺釋) online digital edition at Dharma Realm Buddhist Association, http://www.drbachinese.org/online_reading/sutra_explanation/Ava/contents.htm

Kumārajīva and Buddhayaśas (*c.* 408 CE). *Shizhu jing* (十住經). T10, no. 286.

Li Tongxuan. *Huayan jing he lun*. (X04n0223 華嚴經合論).

----------. *Xin huayen jing lun* (新華嚴經論). T 1739, vol. 36.

Ñāṇamoli and Bodhi. *The Middle Length Discourses of the Buddha: A New Translation of the Majjhima Nikāya* (Teachings of the Buddha). Boston: Wisdom Publications in association with the Barre Center for Buddhist Studies, 1995.

Nattier, Jan. "Indian Antecedents of Huayan Thought: New Light from Chinese Sources" in *Reflecting Mirrors: Perspectives on Huayan Buddhism*. Wiesbaden: Harrassowitz Verlag, 2007

----------. "The Proto-History of the *Buddhāvataṃsaka*: The *Pusa benye jing* 菩薩本業經 and the *Dousha jing* 兜沙經" in Annual Report of the International Research Institute for Advanced Buddhology at Soka University for the Academic Year 2004 [ARIRIAB] (2005) 8: 323–360.

Prajñā, trans. *Dafangguang fo huayen jing*. T 293, vol. 10.

Rahder, J. *Glossary of the Sanskrit, Tibetan, Mongolian, and Chinese Versions of the Daśabhūmika-Sūtra*. Compiled by J. Rahder. (Buddhica, Documents et Travaux pour l'Étude du Bouddhisme publiés sous la direction de J. Przyluski; Deuxième Série; Documents—Tome I). Paris: Librarie Orientaliste Paul Geuthner, 1928.

Rahder, J. and Vasubandhu. *Daśabhumikasutra*. Leuven: J.B. Istas, 1926.

Ruegg, D. *The Literature of the Madhyamaka school of Philosophy in India* (History of Indian Literature ; vol. 7, fasc. 1). Wiesbaden: Harrassowitz, 1981.

Śikṣānanda (*c.* 695–699 CE). *Dafangguang fo huayan jing* (大方廣佛華嚴經). T10, no. 279.

Śīladharma (*c.* 790 CE). T 287. *Foshuo shidi jing* (佛說十地經). T10, no. 287.

Sinor, D., Raghu Vira, Megumu Honda and Permanent International Altaistic Conference. *Studies in South, East, and Central Asia: Presented as a memorial volume to the late Professor Raghu Vira* (Śata-piṭaka series; vol. 74). New Delhi: International Academy of Indian Culture, 1968.

Takakusu, J. and Watanabe, Kaigyoku. *Taishō shinshū Daizōkyō*. Tōkyō; 東京 :: Taishō Issaikyō Kankōkai; 大正一切經刊行會, 1924

Vaidya, P. L., ed. *Daśabhūmikasūtram*. Darbhanga: The Mithila Institute of Post-Graduate Studies and Research in Sanskrit Learning, 1969.

Walshe, M. *The Long Discourses of the Buddha: A Translation of the Dīgha Nikāya* (Teachings of the Buddha). Boston: Wisdom Publications, 2012.

Williams, M. Monier, Sir. (n.d.). *A Sanskrit-English Dictionary*. Delhi: Sri Satguru.

Yongguang. *Dafangguang fo huayan jing gang mu guan she* (大方廣佛華嚴經綱目貫攝) X09, no. 241, 301a16–c02.

Zhonghua dian zi fo dian xie hui. CBETA *dian zi fo dian ji cheng* = CBETA *Chinese Electronic Tripitaka Collection* (Version 2004. ed.). Taibei; 台北 :: Zhonghua dian zi fo dian xie hui; 中華電子佛典協會. 2004

Glossary

A.

ācārya – An *ācārya,* generally speaking, is a senior teacher of monastics. More specifically, he is the senior instructor of the precepts in the context of a formal monastic ordination.

afflictions – "Afflictions" (煩惱 / *kleśa*) are unwholesome states of mind conducing to unenlightened thoughts, words, and deeds. Generally speaking this refers to greed, hatred, and delusion and all of their permutations. More specifically, they consist of six fundamental afflictions and twenty secondary afflictions. The six fundamental afflictions are: greed, hatred, delusion, pride, skeptical doubtfulness, and wrong views. The twenty secondary afflictions are: anger, enmity, tormenting others, concealment, deception, flattery, arrogance, harming, jealousy / envy, absence of a sense of shame, absence of a dread of blame, absence of faith, neglectfulness, dullness / drowsiness (as an impediment to clarity in meditation, etc.), restlessness, loss of mindfulness, wrong cognition, and mental scatteredness.

agada medicine – The *agada* medicine (阿伽陀藥) is a panacea that cures all ills.

aggregates – See "five aggregates."

all-knowledge – "All-knowledge" (一切智 / *sarvajña*) or "omniscience" is a quality acquired only by fully enlightened buddhas upon realizing the utmost, right, and perfect enlightenment (*anuttara-samyak-saṃbodhi*).

Ambulation spirits – See "foot-travel spirits."

anāgāmin – An *anāgāmin* (阿那含), the so-called "nonreturner" or "never returner," is one who has gained the third of the four fruits on the path of the individual liberation vehicle. This involves doing away with the first five of the ten fetters and weakening the last five of the ten fetters which bind beings to cyclic existence in *saṃsāra.*

añjana – *Añjana* is a kind of eye medicine or cosmetic.

anuttara-samyak-saṃbodhi – *anuttara-samyak-saṃbodhi* (阿耨多羅三藐三菩提) is the utmost, right, and perfect enlightenment realized only by fully enlightened buddhas.

apex of reality – The "apex of reality" or "ultimate reality" (實際 / *bhūta-koṭi*) is a synonym for "ultimate truth" (*paramārtha-satya*).

araṇya – An *araṇya* (阿練若) is an isolated forest dwelling usually associated with solitary cultivation of *dhyāna* samādhi.

arhat – An arhat (阿羅漢) is one who has gained the fourth of the four fruits on the path of the individual liberation vehicle. This involves doing away with all ten of the fetters which bind beings to cyclic existence in *saṃsāra*.

ārya – An *ārya* is any being who has realized one of the fruits of the path. For the individual-liberation path of the *śrāvaka* disciple, this refers to having become a stream-winner, once-returner, never-returner, or arhat. For the universal liberation path of the bodhisattva, this refers to having reached an equivalent level of realization to at least that of the stream-winner who has cut off the first three of the ten fetters. Although commonly rendered in Theravada translations as "noble ones" or more generally as "sages," etc., those renderings don't really work as accurate translations of what is actually a technical term. Although arhats, highly realized bodhisattvas, and buddhas are all of course "noble," this has nothing to do with the achievement by which they are referred to as *āryas*.

asaṃkhyeya – An *asaṃkhyeya* (阿僧祇) is a huge number which also describes an indescribably large kalpa.

asura – An *asura* is a demigod or "titan" with sufficient karma to be born in celestial realms but otherwise bereft of the levels of karmic merit typical of even the lower desire realm devas. They are often characterized as possessed of anger, arrogance, and jealousy and are often portrayed as engaged in battle with the lower-level devas, in particular the devas of the Trāyastriṃśa Heaven or "Heaven of the Thirty-three."

avaivartika – An "*avaivartika*" (不退轉) is one who has become irreversible on the bodhisattva path to buddhahood.

B.

bases of psychic powers – The four bases of psychic power (*catvāra ṛddhi-pāda*) are: zeal (*chanda*); vigor (*vīrya*); [concentration of] mind/thought (*citta*); and reflective or investigative consideration, examination, or imagination (*mīmāṃsā*).

bhadra kalpa – See "worthy kalpa" (a.k.a. "good kalpa").

Bhagavat, *bhagavats* – "The Bhagavat" is one of the ten standard names of every buddha. The Chinese translators attempted to capture the meaning of this honorific epithet by rendering it as "the World Honored One" (世尊). Because "World Honored One" is both unwieldy and only partially accurate and also because "*bhagavat*" is defined in many English dictionaries, I have chosen to simply reconstruct the Sanskrit honorific "*bhagavat*" throughout this translation. As an indication of its no longer rare occurrence in English these days, even per the Merriam-Webster online dictionary, "*bhagavat*" means: "blessed one" or "lord" – used chiefly as an epithet of deities in Hinduism and Buddhism. MW (p. 743, Column 3) gives (among other things): "possessing fortune, fortunate, prosperous, happy…glorious, illustrious, divine, adorable, venerable…holy (applied to gods, demigods, and saints as a term of address….) Under "*bhagavant*," BHSD says: "as in Pali, a standard designation of the Buddha."

bhikshu – A bhikshu (比丘 / *bhikṣu*) is a fully ordained Buddhist monk.

bhikshuni – A bhikshuni (比丘尼 / *bhikṣuṇī*) is a fully ordained Buddhist nun.

bhūta – According to DCBT (digital), a *bhūta* (部多) is "a kind of demon produced by metamorphosis." Per MW (p. 761, Column 3), a *bhūta* is: "a spirit (good or evil), the ghost of a deceased person, a demon, imp, goblin." PDB: "A class of harm-inflicting and formless obstructing spirits (i.e., 'elemental spirits') …"; "… sometimes equivalent to *preta* (hungry ghosts)…."; "Because they obstruct rainfall, the *bhūta* are propitiated by rituals to cause precipitation."

bodhi – "*Bodhi*" (菩提) is the Sanskrit word for "awakening" or "enlightenment." In its most exalted form this refers exclusively to the utmost, right, and perfect enlightenment (*anuttara-samyak-saṃbodhi*) of a buddha.

bodhimaṇḍa – A *bodhimaṇḍa* (道場 or 菩提場), often reconstructed (perhaps erroneously) as "*bodhimaṇḍala*," is "a circle or terrace of enlightenment." This originally referred specifically to the site in which a buddha achieves the complete realization of the utmost, right, and perfect enlightenment, or *anuttara-samyak-saṃbodhi*. Even more specifically, it referred to the site beneath the bodhi tree in Bodhgaya in the state of Bihar where Śākyamuni Buddha attained buddhahood. This term subsequently came to be applied more generally to any site of Buddhist spiritual cultivation such as a Buddhist temple or monastery.

bodhimaṇḍa spirit – A *bodhimaṇḍa* spirit (道場神) is a spirit who serves as a protector of a site of enlightenment.

bodhi resolve – The bodhi resolve (菩提心 / *bodhicitta*) is the resolve to attain the utmost right and perfect enlightenment (*anuttara-samyak-saṃbodhi*) of a fully realized buddha.

bodhisaṃbhāra – The *bodhisaṃbhāra* (菩提資糧) are the "provisions for enlightenment." Consisting of merit and wisdom (*puṇya* and *jñāna*), they are essential for completing the path to the attainment of buddhahood.

bodhisattva – A bodhisattva is a being who has resolved to attain the utmost, right, and perfect enlightenment of buddhahood while also working forever to facilitate that same awakening in all beings.

bodhisattva-mahāsattva – A bodhisattva-mahāsattva (菩薩摩訶薩) is a bodhisattva who is a "great being" (mahāsattva / 摩訶薩) by virtue of having practiced and perfected the bodhisattva path for an immensely long period of many eons. Per DCBT (digital): "The mahāsattva is sufficiently advanced to become a Buddha and enter nirvāṇa, but according to his vow he remains in the realm of incarnation to save all conscious beings."

bodhi tree – The "bodhi tree" (菩提樹 / *bodhi-druma, bodhivṛkṣa*) is the tree in Bodhgaya in the Indian state of Bihar under which the Buddha reached enlightenment approximately 2600 years ago.

Brahmā – "Brahmā" (大梵天王) is the king of the eighteen Brahma worlds who, manifesting in one of his forms as Sahāṃpati ("Master of the Sahā World"), first requested the Buddha to teach the Dharma just after the Buddha had attained enlightenment beneath the bodhi tree in Bodhigaya. According to PDB, Brahmā is: "An Indian divinity who was adopted into the Buddhist pantheon as a protector of the teachings and king of the Brahmaloka ["Brahma world"] (in the narrow sense of that term)." "Brahmaloka" here refers to the first three heavens of the form realm.

brahmacārin – A *brahmacārin* (梵志) is a practitioner of *brahmacarya,* which is most easily defined as the cultivation of pure spiritual practices in which celibacy is strictly observed. More specifically, per MW (p. 738, Column 2), this refers to: "a young Brāhman who is a student of the Veda (under a preceptor) or who practises chastity."

brahmacarya (梵行) – *Brahmacarya* (梵行) refers to pure spiritual practice in which celibacy is strictly observed.

brahman – A brahman (婆羅門) is a member of the Hindu clerical caste.

brahma vihāras – The "four *brahma vihāras*" (四梵住) are "the four immeasurable minds" (四無量心) consisting of loving-kindness, compassion, sympathetic joy, and equanimity.

Buddha / buddha – A "buddha" (佛) is one who has attained the utmost, right, and perfect enlightenment (*anuttara-samyak-saṃbodhi*), whether we speak of the Buddha of the present era in this world, Shakyamuni Buddha, any of the seven buddhas of antiquity, or, in Mahāyāna cosmology, any of the countless buddhas of the ten directions and three periods of time.

buddha *kṣetra* – A "buddha *kṣetra*" (佛刹, 佛土 / buddha-*kṣetra*), otherwise known as a "buddha land," per BHSD (p. 401, Column 1), means: "*Buddha-field, region or* (usually) *world* or *world-system* in which a particular Buddha lives and operates…. buddhakṣetra is clearly equated with *lokadhātu*, meaning merely *world-system*, presumably as *potential field for a Buddha*, but not necessarily containing one."

C.

campaka flowers – Per MW, this refers to the flowers of the *campaka* tree (*Michelia Campaka*) which produces fragrant yellow flowers.

chiliocosm – A chiliocosm (千世界 / *sāhasra-lokadhātu*) corresponds to what we would ordinarily refer to as a "universe."

clarities – See "three clarities."

"complete-retention" or "comprehensive-retention" formula (總持 or 陀羅尼/ *dhāraṇī*) – See *dhāraṇī*.

conceptual proliferation – Conceptual proliferation (戲論 / *prapañca*), sometimes translated as "conceptual speculation" or "metaphysical speculation," refers to intellectual speculation or doctrinal speculation, whether thought-based, spoken, or written, which finally only serves to complicate and obscure truth rather than reveal it.

contaminants – The "contaminants" (漏 , 有漏 / *sāsrava, āsrava*) are usually defined as either threefold or fourfold: 1) sensual desire (*kāma*); 2) [craving for] becoming (*bhāva*), i.e., the craving for continued existence; 3) ignorance (*avidyā*), i.e., delusion; and 4) [wrong] views (*dṛṣṭi*). This fourth type is not included in some listings. Often-encountered alternative translations include "taints" and "outflows" and, less commonly, "influxes" and "fluxes."

crown-anointing consecration stage – The stage of the crown-anointing consecration (灌頂位 / *abhiṣekabhūmi, abhiṣekāvasthā*) corresponds to the tenth of the ten bodhisattva grounds.

D.

dāna pāramitā – "*Dāna pāramitā*" (檀波羅蜜, 施波羅蜜) is the perfection of giving, the first of "the six *pāramitās*" or "six perfections."

dānavat – A *dānavat* is a type of *asura* that does not harm beings and has the quality of generosity.

desire realm – The "desire realm" (欲界 / *kāma-dhātu*) is the lowest of the three realms. It consists of the rebirth realms of the hells, the hungry ghosts (*pretas*), the animals, humans, *asuras*, and the six desire-realm heavens, in all of which the predominant obsession of all these beings is the satisfaction of desires and the avoidance of suffering.

deva – The "devas" (天) are divinities residing in the heavens who collectively constitute the highest of the six rebirth destinies within the realm of *saṃsāra*. There are twenty-seven categories of devas and their heavens in the desire realm, form realm, and formless realm. Although the lifespans of the devas in these various heavens may be immensely long, when their karmic merit runs out, they are all still destined to eventually fall back into the other five paths of rebirth wherein they are reborn in accordance with their residual karma from previous lifetimes..

deva-*māras* – "Deva-*māras*" (天魔 / *deva-māra, deva-putra-māra*) are the "demons" who dwell in the Paranirmita-vaśavartin Heaven, the sixth of the heavens in the desire realm.

devaputra – *Devaputras* are the young devas dwelling in the Paranirmita-vaśavartin Heaven, the sixth of the heavens in the desire realm.

dhāraṇī – A *dhāraṇī* (總持 or 陀羅尼) is a formula of spiritually potent sacred syllables (usually in Sanskrit) which may constitute either a protective or power-invoking mantra affording protection from negative spiritual forces such as ghosts and demons or a magically efficacious set of Sanskrit phrases bestowing the power of "complete retention" by which one never forgets any Dharma teachings one receives, this even after the passage of countless ensuing lifetimes. Although the significance of each Sanskrit phrase within these mantra formulae may indeed be explained, they are nonetheless never actually translated, for to recite a translation of a mantra would destroy all of the spiritually potent resonances inherent in the particular Sanskrit syllables and phrases, whereupon the desired effect would therefore not occur at all. In addition, there are particular *devanāgarī* or *siddham* syllabary *dhāraṇī* glyphs the spiritual activation of which occurs through being visualized in the mind's eye of the yogin as objects of meditation.

Dharma – By convention, when capitalized, "Dharma" (法) refers to the teachings of the Buddha.

dharmas – By convention, when not capitalized, "dharmas" (法) has two primary meanings: 1) Fundamental constituent aspects, elements, or factors of mental and physical existence, as for instance, "the hundred dharmas" with which Vasubandhu analytically catalogued all that exists. In this sense, dharmas are somewhat analogous to the elements of the periodic table in chemistry; 2) Any individual teaching, as for instance in "the dharma of conditioned origination."

Dharma body – The "Dharma body" (法身 / *dharma-kāya*) is one of the "three bodies of the Buddha" (the Dharma body, the reward body, and the transformation bodies). In the most cosmically and metaphysically vast sense, the "Dharma body," like the "Dharma realm," refers in aggregate to all conventionally-existent phenomena and the universally pervasive noumenal "true suchness" (*tathatā*) that underlies and characterizes all of those phenomena.

Dharma gateway – A "Dharma gateway" (法門 / *dharma-mukha, dharma-dvāra, dharma-paryāya*) or "gateway into the Dharma" is a term of reference for a spiritual cultivation technique by which one gains access to Dharma cultivation techniques. Examples of Dharma gateways are pure land practice, secret school practice, *dhyāna* meditation practice, practice of *śīla* (moral virtue), practice of scriptural study in order to attain wisdom realizations, etc.

Dharma Master or "Dharma teacher" (法師 / *dharma-bhānaka*) – One who is learned in the Dharma and who teaches the Dharma to others. Usually, but not necessarily, a monk or nun. In Chinese Buddhism, this term became a standard title and term of address for all fully ordained monastics, regardless of their level of advancement in study of the scriptures and regardless of whether or not they specialize in teaching the Dharma to others.

Dharma-nature body – The Dharma-nature body (**dharmatā-kāya, *dharma-dhātu-kāya* [BCSD, p. 715]) is synonymous with "the Dharma body" and also, per DDB, is an abbreviation for "Dharma nature Dharma body" the Sanskrit for which would likely be *dharmatā-kāya dharmakāya*.

Dharma realm: As a Buddhist technical term, "Dharma realm" or "dharma realm," *dharma-dhātu*, has at least several levels of meaning:

1) At the most granular level, "dharma realm" refers to one of the eighteen sense realms, dharmas as "objects of mind" (*dharma-āyatana*);

2) In the most cosmically and metaphysically vast sense, "Dharma realm" refers in aggregate to all conventionally-existent phenomena and the universally pervasive noumenal "true suchness" (*tathatā*) that underlies and characterizes all of those phenomena. In this sense, it is identical with the "Dharma body" (*dharma-kāya*);

3) As a classifying term, "dharma realm" is used to distinguish realms of existence (as in the ten dharma realms consisting of the realms of buddhas, bodhisattvas, *śrāvaka* disciples, *pratyekabuddhas*, devas, *asuras*, humans, animals, hungry ghosts, hell-dwellers) or metaphysical modes of existence (as in the "four dharma realms" of the Huayan hermeneutic tradition that speaks of: a] the dharma realm of the "noumenal" [synonymous with emptiness or *śūnyatā*]; b] the dharma realm of the "phenomenal"; c] the dharma realm of the unimpeded interpenetration of the phenomenal and the noumenal; and d] the dharma realm of the unimpeded interpenetration of all phenomena with all other phenomena in a manner that resonates somewhat with quantum entanglement and non-locality).

dharmas patience – "Dharma patience" or "dharmas patience" (法忍 / *dharma-kṣānti*) refers either to "unproduced dharmas patience" (無生法忍 / *anutpattika-dharma-kṣānti*) for which this is usually an abbreviation or otherwise to a moment of doctrinal knowledge that occurs in the realization of each of the four truths.

Dharma wheel – The "Dharma wheel" (法輪 / *dharma-cakra*) is a term derived by comparing the Buddha's teaching to a wheel which is "turned" whenever and wherever someone teaches the Dharma. Visually, this appears in the form of an eight-spoked wheel representing the eightfold path taught by all buddhas. It is also compared to a wheel in three senses: 1) Its ability to roll on and crush all that lies before it, specifically its ability to crush all of the karmic offenses that beings commit; 2) Its quality of perpetually turning, specifically the Dharma's constant rolling on in the world, irrespective of any single individual or any single place in which it is being taught; and 3) Its quality of perfect completeness as represented by the wholeness of the circle emblematically shown in the round shape of a wheel.

dhūta austerities – "*Dhūta* austerities" (頭陀行 / *dhūta-guṇa, dhutaṇga*) is a reference to a set of usually twelve beneficial austerities (十二頭陀行

/ *dvādaśa dhūta-guṇa*) recommended by the Buddha for monastics as means for deepening practice of the path. These include such practices as wearing rag robes from a charnel ground, wearing only the three robes, dwelling in a forest hermitage, always living only on alms food, going strictly in accordance with all the houses one encounters on the alms round (not selecting those houses preferentially based on prior knowledge that the inhabitants are rich and generous, etc.), eating only one meal each day, not eating after midday, eating only a fixed amount, always sitting and living beneath a tree, dwelling out in the open without shelter, dwelling in a cemetery or charnel ground, and only sitting and never lying down. In contrast to the non-beneficial ascetic practices of some non-Buddhist traditions (such as lying on a bed of nails, etc.), these are austerities beneficial to progress on the path to liberation from cyclic existence in *saṃsāra*.

dhyāna – "*Dhyāna*" is a general term broadly corresponding to all forms of Buddhist meditative skill. The Chinese "*ch'an*" or "*chan*" (禪) and the Japanese term "*zen*" are transliterations of the same Sanskrit word "*dhyāna*." All forms of Buddhist "calming" and "insight" meditation are subcategories of "*dhyāna*."

dhyānas – The "*dhyānas*" is usually a reference to the first four levels of meditation known as "the four *dhyānas*."

dhyāna pāramitā – The perfection of meditative discipline.

Difficulties – See "eight difficulties."

E.

easeful mastery – "Easeful mastery" (遊戲 / *vikrīḍita*), at least in its Chinese translation from Sanskrit, literally means "sporting," whereas the Sanskrit from which it translates refers to miracles, exhibitions of supernatural powers, etc. BHSD definition two, however, claims: "oftener, fig., something like *easy mastery*."

eight classes of spiritual beings – The "eight classes of spiritual beings" (八部衆, *aṣṭa-gatyaḥ*) consist of: devas, *nāgas, yakṣas, gandharvas, asuras, garuḍas, kiṃnaras,* and *mahoragas*.

eight difficulties – The "eight difficulties" or "eight difficult circumstances" (八難 / *aṣṭa akṣaṇa*) consist of: rebirths in the hells; rebirths among hungry ghosts, rebirths among animals; rebirths in the long-life heavens (where bliss is so overwhelming there is no motivation to cultivate the path); rebirths on the continent of Uttarakuru (where, again, life is so pleasant there is no motivation to cultivate the path); rebirths as deaf, dumb, or blind; rebirths as someone possessed of merely worldly knowledge and eloquence (who is thus inclined to be a spiritual philistine insensitive to the preciousness of the Dharma); and rebirths either before or after a buddha appears in the world (which prevent one from encountering the Dharma).

eighteen dharmas exclusive to the buddhas – The "eighteen dharmas exclusive to the buddhas" (十八不共法 / *aṣṭa-daśa-aveṇika-buddha-dharma*) are eighteen qualities possessed only by buddhas. These consist of: faultless physical actions, faultless speech, faultless mindfulness, absence of notions of differences (between beings, etc.), never not maintaining mental focus, having no dharma toward which one is equanimous that one has not first known, undiminished zeal, undiminished vigor, undiminished mindfulness, undiminished wisdom, undiminished liberation, undiminished knowledge and vision arising from liberation, all physical actions according with wisdom, all verbal actions according with wisdom, all mental actions according with wisdom, unimpeded wisdom-based knowledge of the past, unimpeded wisdom-based knowledge of the future, and unimpeded wisdom-based knowledge of the present.

eighteen sense realms – The "eighteen sense realms" (十八界 / *aṣṭādaśa-dhātu*) consist of: the six sense faculties (eye, ear, nose, tongue, body, and mind), the six sense objects (visual forms, sounds, smells, tastes, touchables, and ideas, etc. as objects of mind), and the six sense consciousnesses (visual, auditory, olfactory, gustatory, tactile, and mental).

eightfold path – The "eightfold path" otherwise known as "the eightfold right path" (八正道 / *aṣṭa-aṅga-mārga*) or "the eightfold path of the *āryas*" (八聖道 / *ārya-aṣṭa-aṅga-mārga*) consists of: right view, right intention (or thought), right speech, right action, right livelihood, right effort, right mindfulness, and right meditative concentration.

eight precepts, a.k.a. "lay abstinence precepts" – The "eight lay abstinence precepts" (八齋戒 / *aṣta-aṅga-samanvāgataṃ upavāsaṃ*) are intermittently observed lay precepts consisting of the first eight of the ten precepts. These eight precepts are observed by pious lay practitioners wishing to undertake this special practice protocol on six days, namely on the eighth, fourteenth, fifteenth, twenty-third, twenty-ninth, and thirtieth of each lunar month. They consist of: not killing; not taking what is not given; observing celibacy; not lying;

not consuming intoxicants; not using cosmetics, perfumes, or jewelry while also not dancing or singing or watching or listening to such performances; not sleeping on high or wide beds; and not eating after noon.

eight worldly dharmas – The "eight worldly dharmas" (八世法 / *aṣṭa-loka-dharma*), otherwise known as the "eight winds" (八風) are: gain and loss, fame and disrepute, praise and blame, pleasure and pain.

elephant treasure – The "elephant treasure" (象寶 / *hasti-ratna*) is one of the seven treasures of a wheel-turning sage king.

elixir of immortality – The "elixir of immortality" or "celestial ambrosia" (甘露 / *amṛta*) is often used as metaphor for the Dharma of the Buddha which liberates from *saṃsāra* and bestows nirvāṇa.

emptiness – "Emptiness" (空 / *śūnyatā*) is a Buddhist concept referring in ultimate reality terms to the absence of any inherently or permanently existent reality in anything whatsoever. In particular, this refers to the merely imputed idea of a real "self" or "other" which, upon examination, is found to be empty of inherent existence. Thus all phenomena are "empty" of any enduringly real entity, are but temporary effects produced through a series of causal processes, are but transiently-existent conventionalities, are only temporary conjunctions of impermanent subcomponent conditions, and are, in fact, mere "names."

extreme views – "Extreme views" (邊見 / *anta-grāha-dṛṣṭi*) refers to views such as eternalism versus annihilationism, existence versus nonexistence, etc.

F.

far shore / to reach the far shore – "To reach the far shore" (到彼岸 / *pāramitā*) is synonymous with the attainment of liberation by reaching the far shore of the ocean of suffering. This also means to achieve perfection in the cultivation of any particular dharma as in "the perfection of wisdom," etc.

fetters – The "fetters" (結 / *saṃyojana*) are ten mental characteristics of unenlightened existence that bind beings to uncontrolled rebirths in the six destinies of rebirth. They are: 1) "the view of a truly existent self," the wrong view that believes in the existence of an eternally existent self in association with the five aggregates; 2) "skeptical doubt" about the truth of the Dharma and the path to enlightenment; 3) "clinging to [the observance of] rules and rituals" in and of themselves as constituting the path to spiritual liberation; 4) sensual desire; 5) ill will; 6) desire for rebirth in the form realm [heavens]; 7) desire for rebirth in the formless realm [heavens]; 8) "conceit," i.e., the belief that "I" exist; 9) "agitation" or "restlessness" that prevents deep concentration; and 10) "ignorance."

field of merit – A "field of merit" (福田 / *puṇya-kṣetra*) refers to any worthy recipient of gifts or support of any kind, the support of whom produces karmic merit for the benefactor. Examples would include the Buddha, the Dharma, the members of the *ārya* sangha and monastic sangha, one's parents, spiritual mentors, those who are hungry or otherwise in need, and even contributing to works for the welfare of everyone such as fixing bridges and roads, and so forth. Just as planting seeds in a fertile field produces abundant crops, so too, supporting these fields of merit plants the seeds for future good fortune for the benefactor.

five aggregates – The "five aggregates" (五蘊 / *pañca-skandha*) upon which the foolish common person imputes self-hood which consist of: 1) physical form; 2) feelings (i.e., sensations as received through eye, ear, nose, tongue, body, or mind); 3) perceptions; 4) karmic formative factors (such as volitions); and 5) consciousness (visual, auditory, olfactory, gustatory, tactile, and mental).

five desires – The "five desires" (五欲 / *pañca-kāma, pañca-kāma-guṇa*) or "five types of desires" or "five objects of desire" are: wealth, sex, fame, fine food, and leisure (literally "sleep") or the objects of the five sense faculties, namely visual forms, sounds, smells, tastes, and touchables.

five destinies – The "five destinies" (五道, 五趣 / *pañca-gati*) or "five destinies of rebirth" are: rebirth in the hells, among the hungry ghosts, as an animal, as a human, or as a deva (a "god"). "Asuras" is often added to this list which is then called "the six destinies" or "six destinies of rebirth."

five faculties – See "five roots."

five hindrances – The five hindrances (五蓋 / *pañca-nīvaraṇa*) that block the development of *dhyāna* meditation are: sensual desire, ill-will, dullness and drowsiness, restlessness and regretfulness; and afflicted doubtfulness.

five nefarious karmic offenses – The five "nefarious karmic offenses" (五逆罪, *pañca-anantarya*) are: matricide, patricide, killing an arhat, drawing the blood of a buddha, and creating a schism in the [monastic] Sangha. This same list is referred to in Chinese translation from an only slightly different Sanskrit name as "the five deeds involving immediate retribution" (五無間業 / *pañcānantariyakarman*). In this sense, they are referred to as "immediate" (lit. "uninterrupted") because, with no intervening interval, one is bound to fall directly into the Avīci (lit. "uninterrupted") Hells immediately upon dying.

five powers – The "five powers" (五力 / *pañca-bala*) are: faith, vigor, mindfulness, concentration, and wisdom. They arise through the strengthening of the five roots.

five precepts – The "five precepts" (五戒, *pañca-śīla*) prohibit killing, stealing, sexual misconduct, false speech, and intoxicants. Observance of the five precepts in this life ensures that one will gain at least a human rebirth in the next life.

five roots – The "five roots" (五根 / *pañca-indriya*) otherwise known as "the five faculties" are: faith, vigor, mindfulness, concentration, and wisdom.

five turbidities – The "five turbidities" (五濁 / *pañca-kaṣāya*) are five kinds of deterioration occurring as each kalpa progresses past the point when beings' life spans begin to decrease. This refers then to the deterioration that takes place in the quality of the kalpa, views, afflictions, beings, and life spans.

foot-travel spirits – "Foot-travel spirits" (足行神 / *pāda-kāyikābhir devatābhiḥ*) are a kind of protector spirit. Noting that these are simply "road spirits," QL notes that these "foot-travel" spirits exist in relationship to those who travel on foot, serving them as their protectors. One example of this is those who support each footstep of buddhas and other holy beings with a "stepping-stone" consisting of an immense flower blossom.

form realm – The "form realm" (色界 / *rūpa-dhātu*) is the middle realm of the three realms. There, the beings have become free from the afflictions dominating the minds of beings in the desire realm. Inhabiting bodies of subtle form, based on the level of their mental purification and karmic merit, they reside in one or another of the seventeen *dhyāna* heavens of the form realm. There are three heavens corresponding to each of the first, second, and third *dhyānas* and seven heavens corresponding to the fourth *dhyāna*.

formless realm – The "formless realm" (無色界 / *ārūpya-dhātu*) is the highest of the three realms of existence. It consists of four progressively more subtle stations of formless existence in which one has no body, namely: the station of limitless space, the station of limitless consciousness, the station of nothing whatsoever, and the station of neither perception nor nonperception.

four abodes of Brahma – The "four abodes of Brahma" or "four pure abodes" (四梵住 / *catvāro brahma-vihāra*) are identical to the four immeasurable minds (四無量心 / *catvāri-apramāṇa-citta*), namely: loving-kindness, compassion, sympathetic joy, and equanimity.

four bases of psychic power – the "four bases of psychic power" (四如意足, 四神足) *catvāra ṛddhi-pāda*) consist of zeal (*chanda*), vigor (*vīrya*), concentration (*citta*), and investigation (*mīmāṃsa*).

four dharma realms – "The four Dharma realms" (四法界) consist of: 1) the dharma realm of the phenomenal (事法界); 2) the dharma realm of the "noumenal" (理法界) which corresponds to the metaphysical emptiness of inherent existence of all phenomena; 3) the dharma realm of the unimpeded relationship between the noumenal and the phenomenal (理事無礙法界); and 4) the dharma realm of the unimpeded relationship between any phenomenon with all other phenomena (事事無礙法界).

four *dhyānas* – The "four *dhyānas*" (四禪 / *catur-dhyāna*) are the first four of eight increasingly deep and progressively more subtle *dhyāna* meditation stages. These first four levels of meditation corresponding to the mind states of formless realm heavens, whereas the highest four *dhyāna* meditation states correspond to the mind states of the formless realm heavens. In the first *dhyāna,* one experiences the joy and bliss which arise as a result of abandoning the mind states of the desire realm. In the second *dhyāna,* one experiences the joy and bliss produced by meditative absorption. In the third *dhyāna,* one experiences the sublime bliss born of abandoning joyfulness. And in the fourth *dhyāna,* having left behind both joy and bliss, one's existence is characterized by four factors: 1) neither joy nor bliss; 2) equanimity; 3) mindfulness; and 4) single-mindedness.

four equalities – The "four equalities" (四等) are four qualities that the buddha and great bodhisattvas hold in equal measure toward all beings, namely: loving-kindness, compassion, sympathetic joy, and equanimity. This is an abbreviation for "the four equal minds" (四等心) which are identical to the "four immeasurable minds" (四無量心 / *apramāṇa-citta*).

four floods – The four floods (四暴流 / *catur-ogha*) are: desire, existence, ignorance, and [wrong] views.

four formless absorptions – The "four formless absorptions" (四無色定 / *catvāra-arūpya-samāpatti*) are: the station of limitless space, the station of limitless consciousness, the station of nothing whatsoever, and the station of neither perception nor nonperception.

four great elements – the "four great elements" (四大 / *catur-mahā-bhūta*) are: earth, water, fire, and wind. One might think of these as the phases of all elements: solidity, liquidity, ignition, and vaporization. It seems most all of the elements of western science can exist in all these phases, depending on the temperature to which they are exposed.

four immeasurable minds – The "four immeasurable minds" (四無量心 / *catvāri-apramāṇa-citta*), identical to "the four abodes of Brahma" (四梵住 / *catvāro brahma-vihāra*), are: loving-kindness, compassion, sympathetic joy, and equanimity.

four lineage bases of the *ārya* – The "four lineage bases of the *ārya*" (四聖種 / *catur-ārya-vaṃśa*) are being pleased with mere sufficiency in robes, food and drink, and bedding, while delighting in severance and cultivation.

four *māras* – The "four māras" (四魔 / *catur-māra*) are: the *māras* of the afflictions, the *māras* of the aggregates, the *māras* of death, and the *deva-putra māras* of the Sixth Desire Heaven.

four means of attraction – The "four means of attraction" (四攝法 / *catur-saṃgraha-vastu*) are giving, pleasing words, beneficial actions, and joint endeavors.

four speech transgressions – The "four transgressions in speech" (語四過) are lying, harsh speech, divisive speech, and frivolous or lewd speech. These are the four verbal transgressions against the ten courses of good karmic action.

four stations of mindfulness – The "four stations of mindfulness" (四念處 / *catur-smṛti-upasthāna*) are: mindfulness of the body as unlovely; mindfulness of feelings or sensations (experienced via the eye, ear, nose, tongue, body, and mind consciousnesses) as ultimately finally conducing to suffering; mindfulness of one's mind as impermanent, i.e., as constantly changing; and mindfulness of dharmas devoid of any inherent existence of their own, literally "as devoid of self."

four truths of the *āryas* – The "four truths of the *āryas*" (四聖諦 / *catur-ārya-satya*) otherwise known simply as "the four truths" (四諦 / *ārya-satya*) were the topic of the Buddha's first teaching which was given in Vārāṇasī shortly after he attained enlightenment in Bodhgaya. Although their name is sometimes translated as "holy truths," this is wrong. Rather they are truths for the *āryas,* those enlightened beings who have actually directly realized them, hence their name as "the four truths of the *āryas*." They are:

1) The truth of suffering (苦 / *duḥkha*). This simply means that unenlightened existence inevitably conduces to suffering, the condition of all beings in the six rebirth destinies;

2) The truth of the "origination" or "accumulation" of suffering (集 / *samudaya*);

3) The truth of the "cessation" of suffering (滅 / *nirodha*); and

4) The "path" to the cessation of suffering (道 / *mārga*). The "path" here is the eightfold path.

four unimpeded knowledges – The "four unimpeded knowledges" (四無礙智 / *catur-pratisaṃvid*) are: unimpeded knowledge with respect to Dharma, meanings, language, and eloquence.

G.

gandharva – A "*gandharva*" (乾闥婆 / *gandharva*), one of the eight classes of spiritual beings, is a type of musical spirit who is said to live on fine scents.

garuḍa – A "*garuḍa*" (迦樓羅), one of the eight classes of spiritual beings, is a type of immense bird that pounces on and eats serpents and dragons.

gates to liberation – The "gates to liberation" (解脫門 / *vimokṣa-mukha, vimokṣa-dvāra*) usually refers to "the three gates to liberation" (三解脫門) consisting of emptiness (*śūnyatā*), signlessness (*animitta*), and wishlessness (*apraṇihita*).

gateways – See "Dharma gateways."

good spiritual guide – "Good spiritual guide" (善知識 / *kalyāṇamitra*) or "good spiritual friend" translates the Sanskrit *kalyāṇamitra,* which is a term used in the prior case to refer to one who is senior in the spiritual path and who serves as one's primary spiritual guide, teacher, or advisor. In the latter case, this is a term of reference for one's peers in the cultivation of the path to liberation from karma-bound suffering in *saṃsāra*.

Great Assembly – "Great Assembly" (大眾 / *mahāsaṃgha*) is a translation into Chinese of the Sanskrit *mahāsaṃgha* which means "the Great Sangha." It is a term with two slightly different uses: a) Everyone in any given monastic community; and b) All the monks, nuns, laymen, and laywomen in any given Buddhist community, meeting, or religious ceremony.

great compassion – The "great compassion" (大悲 / *mahā-karuṇā*) is a term used to describe the most ultimate and grand implementation of "compassion" (悲 / *karuṇā*) which has as its purpose to accomplish the aim of liberating all beings from karma-bound suffering in *saṃsāra*. This refers to compassion as practiced by the buddhas and great bodhisattvas who are willing to remain forever in conditioned existence to strive toward this aim. Compassion is the first of "the four immeasurable minds."

great kindness – The "great kindness" (大慈 / *mahā-maitrī*) is a term used to describe the most ultimate and grand implementation of "loving-kindness" (慈 / *maitrī*)) which has as its altruistic aim to bestow true spiritual happiness on all beings. This refers to loving-kindness as practiced by the buddhas and great bodhisattvas who are willing to remain forever in conditioned existence to strive toward this aim. "Loving-kindness" is the second of "the four immeasurable minds."

great vehicle – The "great vehicle" (大乘 / *mahāyāna*) is the term used by practitioners of the bodhisattva path to describe the bodhisattva path to buddhahood.

ground – "Ground" (地 / *bhūmi*) generally refers to levels or stages of spiritual cultivation or realization or, alternatively, to planes of existence or stations of rebirth such as the six destinies of rebirth (devas, *asuras*, humans, hungry ghosts, animals, and hells).

H.

habitual karmic propensities – "Habitual karmic propensities" (習氣 / *vāsanā*) are latent tendencies present in the karmic continua of all beings except buddhas. They are the product of countless lifetimes of both afflicted and unafflicted thoughts, words, deeds, and experiences.

hindrances – See "five hindrances."

hindrances and entanglements – "Hindrances and entanglements" (蓋纏) is a reference to the five hindrances and the ten entanglements. The "five hindrances" (五蓋 / *pañca-nivaraṇa*) are: desire, ill-will, dullness and drowsiness, restlessness and regretfulness, and skeptical doubt. The "ten entanglements" (十纏 / *daśa-paryavasthānāni*) are: lack of sense of shame, lack of dread of blame, envy, miserliness, drowsiness, restlessness, dullness, anger, and concealment.

Honored One among the Great Āryas – The "Honored One among the Great Āryas" (大聖尊 / *maharṣi*) is another honorific epithet for the Buddha.

horse treasure – The "horse treasure" (馬寶 / *aśva-ratna*) is one of the seven treasures of a wheel-turning sage king.

I.

immeasurable minds – See "four immeasurable minds."

impurity contemplation – See "meditation on impurity / unloveliness."

inapprehensible, inapprehensibility – "Inapprehensibility" (不可得 / *anupalabdha*) or "imperceptibility" is a reference to the inability to perceive any inherent existence in any and all phenomena, this because they are mere names, mere false conceptions, and mere conjunctions of subsidiary conditions that are devoid of any ultimate reality of their own. Hence, no matter how hard one might try, one still can never find anything truly real in any phenomena.

indranīla jewels (帝青寶) – According to MW (p. 168, Column 3), an *indranīla* is a sapphire.

Indra's net – "Indra's net" (因陀羅網, 帝網 / *indra-jāla*) is an immense curtain net in the Heaven of the Thirty-three (the Trāyastriṃśa Heaven) in which the jewels set in each of the countless interstices of the net endlessly reflect and re-reflect the light from all the other jewels. This phenomenon is used in the Chinese Huayan teaching tradition as an analogy for the interpenetration of all phenomena with all other phenomena.

ineffable – As a number, an "ineffable" (不可說 / *anabhilāpya*) is an inexpressibly large number, the 121st highest level of 123 levels of Sanskrit denominational numbers described in the "Asaṃkhyeyas" chapter of the Avataṃsaka Sutra (Chapter Thirty). In this numbering schema, each level of denomination is the square of the immediately previous denominational number. (The first and lowest of those 123 levels is a *lakṣa* [100,000].)

ineffable-ineffable – An "ineffable-ineffable" (不可說不可說 / *anabhilāpya-anabhilāpya*) is the next-to-highest number of one hundred and twenty-four numbers in this sutra's numbering schema, each number of which is the result of the successive squaring of the immediately previous number. The first and smallest of these numbers known as a *lakṣa* is 100,000. These numbers are all defined in Chapter Thirty, "Asaṃkhyeyas."

in or beyond training – "In or beyond training" (學無學 / *śaikṣa-aśaikṣa*) is a reference to those on the various levels of attainment of the four fruits of the arhat's individual liberation path with the first three levels being those who are still "in training" and the fourth level being the arhat who is "beyond training."

inverted views – The "inverted views" (or "perceptions") (顛倒 / *viparyāsa*) is usually a reference to "the four inverted views" (*catur-viparyāsa*) which are:

1) imputing permanence to the impermanent, namely to the mind or states of mind;

2) imputing pleasurability to what cannot deliver it, namely to feelings or sensations associated with the six sense objects;

3) imputing "inherent existence" or "self-hood" to what is devoid of any inherently existence or self-hood, namely to dharmas or elements of existence; and

4) imputing loveliness or "purity" to what does not actually possess that quality, namely to the body (of those one might think of as desirable."

irreversible, irreversibility – "Irreversibility" (不退 / *avaivartya*, etc.) is a reference to having reached a point on one's chosen path of liberation in which one can no longer fall back into the state of a foolish common person who wanders endlessly in karma-bound suffering in *saṃsāra*.

K.

kalala – A "*kalala*" (歌羅邏) is the first stage in the growth of an embryo.

kalaviṅka bird – A "*kalaviṅka*" (迦陵頻伽) is a kind of Himalyan cuckoo bird that starts to sing a lovely and mesmerizing sound even before it breaks out of its shell. In the pure land of Amitābha Buddha, it appears as a magical and beautiful bird with a human head who constantly sings the sounds of the Dharma.

kalpa – A "kalpa" (劫) is roughly equivalent to the western concept of and "eon." There are different categories of these kalpas, all of which are nearly inconceivably long, ranging from millions to billions of years in duration.

kalpas of existence – "Kalpas of existence" (住劫 / *vivarta-siddha-kalpa*) is usually defined as a period of twenty small or middle-size kalpas in the lifespan of a world system during which beings exist, this occurring between the equally long periods of the formation of the kalpa and the destruction of the kalpa. Before and after each of these three phases of formation, existence, and destruction, there is an equally long twenty-kalpa period of complete nonexistence of anything at all.

kalyāṇamitra – See "good spiritual guide."

karmadāna – A "*karmadāna*" (羯磨陀那, 羯磨) is a "director of monks" in a monastery and is also one of the essential officiants in ordination ceremonies.

karmic formative factors – "Karmic formative factors" (行 / *saṃskāra*), otherwise known as "volitional factors," are the constituents of the fourth of the five skandhas, the *saṃskāra* skandha (行蘊 / *saṃskāra-skandha*). Per BHSD (p. 542, Column 2), they are "*predisposition(s)*, the effect of past deeds and experience as conditioning a new state."

karmic inaction – Where "karmic inaction" (無作 / *anabhisaṃskāra, apraṇihita*) is translating *anabhisaṃskāra,* it refers to refraining from the creation of any *saṃskāras* or karmic formative factors. Per BHSD's definition number one (p. 20, Column 2), among other closely related ideas, this can mean "*non-accumulation* (of *karman*)" or "*having or characterized by no accumulation* (of *karman*)." Where it is translating *apraṇihita,* it refers to "wishlessness," the third of the three gates to liberation, otherwise known as the "three samādhis."

karmic obstacles – "Karmic obstacles" (業障 / *karma-āvaraṇa*) are unfortunate occurrences that arise and create difficulties in a being's life because of bad actions committed in the past. See the "two obstacles" or the "three obstacles."

kāṣāya robe – The "*kāṣāya* robe" (袈裟 / *kāṣāya*) is the ochre-colored robes worn by fully ordained monks and nuns. Traditionally, it consists of three robes; an under robe, an upper robe, and an outer robe that is worn draped over the left shoulder.

kasiṇa / *kṛtsnāyatana* – See the "ten universal objects."

kiṃnara or *kinnara* – A "*kiṃnara*" (緊那羅 / *kiṃnara* or *kinnara* [Pali]) is one of the eight classes of spiritual beings, one who is devoted to making music and dancing along with it. They are sometimes described as having a horn and/or as having a human body.

King Yama – "King Yama" (閻羅王 / *yama*) is reputed according to various iterations of Indian or Buddhist mythology to be the king of the world of the dead who passes judgment on beings when they die and determines where they will be reborn. "The place of King Yama" (閻羅王處) or "realm of King Yama" (閻羅王界) is a euphemist term for the underworld, i.e., the hells.

kleṣa – The *"kleṣas"* (煩惱 / *kleṣa*) are the afflictions consisting primarily of the "three poisons" of greed, hatred, and delusion. See "afflictions."

knowledge of all modes – The "knowledge of all modes" (一切種智 / *sarvākāra-jñatā*), otherwise known as the "knowledge of all aspects," per DCBT is: "Buddha-knowledge, or perfect knowledge of all things in their every aspect and relationship past, present, and future."

koṭī – A *"koṭī"* (億 / *koṭī*) is a large number for which MW, p. 312, gives "the highest number in the older system of numbers (viz. a Krore or ten millions)." DDB reports that the Buddhist definitions vary between "one million" and "a hundred million."

krośa – A *"krośa"* (俱盧舍 / *krośa*) is a measure of distance that is more or less the equivalent of a mile. According to MW, p. 322, a *krośa* is "a cry, yell, shriek, shout, the range of the voice in calling or hallooing, a measure of distance (an Indian league)."

kṣaṇa – A *"kṣaṇa"* (刹那, 一念 / *kṣaṇa, eka-kṣaṇika*) is an especially small fraction of a second perhaps translatable as a "micro-moment" or "instant" in very non-technical passages. It is supposedly the shortest of all measures of time. A commonly cited definition says there are 4,500 *kṣaṇas* in a minute which would mean there are seventy-five *kṣaṇas* in every second.

kṣaṇas, lavas, and *muhūrtas* – *"Kṣaṇas, lavas,* and *muhūrtas"* (刹那 translates *"kṣaṇa."* / 羅婆, 羅預, 臘縛, and 頃刻 are the various sino-translations for *"lava."* / 須臾 translates *"muhūrta."*) *Kṣaṇa, lava,* and *muhūrta* are short increments of time measurement in ancient Indic time enumeration somewhat analogous to modern "milliseconds," "seconds," and "hours" respectively.

kṣānti pāramitā – *"Kṣānti pāramitā"* (羼提波羅蜜 / *kṣānti pāramitā*) is the third of the six perfections, the perfection of patience.

kṣetra – A *"kṣetra"* (刹, 土, 國土 / *kṣetra*) is a "land" or "field" but, by implication, the term may very often instead mean "buddha land" or "buddha field." See "buddha *kṣetra*."

kumbhāṇḍa – A *"kumbhāṇḍa"* (鳩槃荼 / *kumbhāṇḍa*), according to MW (p. 293, Column 2): "Having testicles shaped like a *kumbha* [a winter melon]," a class of demons (at whose head stands Rudra). Per PDB: "In Sanskrit, a type of evil spirit, and typically listed along with especially *rākṣasa*, but also *piśāca, yakṣa,* and *bhūta* spirits. Virūḍhaka, one of the four world-guardians, who protects the southern cardinal direction, is usually said to be their overlord, although some texts give Rudra this role instead. The *kumbhāṇḍa* are also sometimes listed among the minions of Māra, evil personified."

L.

latent tendencies – The "latent tendencies" (隨眠 / *anuśaya*), six or seven in number, per PDB are: "…sensual passion, hostility, pride, ignorance, views, and skeptical doubt; sometimes passion for existence is added as a seventh."

lion's sprint samādhi – The "lion's sprint samādhi" (師子奮迅三昧 / *siṃha-vijṛmbhita samādhi*) is the Buddha's samādhi with which he is able to quickly enter the first *dhyāna* and ascend through all eight *dhyānas* to the cessation of the feeling and perception absorption and then come back down through all of these absorptions in sequence to then emerge again from the first *dhyāna*.

M.

mahāparinirvāṇa – The "*mahāparinirvāṇa*" (摩訶般涅槃, 大般涅槃 / *mahāparinirvāṇa*) is the final nirvāṇa of a buddha at the very end of his teaching career.

mahāsattva – A mahāsattva (摩訶薩) is a "great being," a great bodhisattva who has been cultivating the bodhisattva path for an immensely long period of time. Per DCBT (digital): "The mahāsattva is sufficiently advanced to become a Buddha and enter nirvāṇa, but according to his vow he remains in the realm of incarnation to save all conscious beings."

Mahāyāna – The Mahāyāna or "Great Vehicle" (大乘) is the "universal liberation" vehicle in which the practitioner is equally devoted to attaining buddhahood for himself and facilitating the achievement of buddhahood for all other beings. The "Mahāyāna" is synonymous with the "bodhisattva vehicle" (菩薩乘 / *bodhisattva-yāna*) and the "buddha vehicle" (佛乘 / *buddha-yāna*) and it stands in contrast to the individual liberation vehicles of *śrāvakas* and *pratyekabuddhas* sometimes referred to as belonging to the Hīnayāna or "Small Vehicle" (小乘) because they are primarily concerned with gaining spiritual liberation for themselves and only secondarily concerned with aiding the liberation of other beings. Because "Hīnayāna" is regarded as a pejorative term by Theravada practitioners, "*śrāvaka-yāna*" is probably a preferable term for the path of individual liberation.

mahoraga – A mahoraga is one of the eight classes of spiritual beings, one that is shaped like a large-bellied serpent.

maṇi jewel – A *maṇi* jewel (摩尼珠 / *maṇī-ratna*) is a kind of jewel usually held to be a kind of wish-fulfilling jewel.

many-bodied spirits – "Many-bodied spirits" (身眾神 / *śarīra-kāyika-devatā, śarīra-kāyika*) are spirits who are able to transformationally produce many bodies to act as Dharma protectors and serve buddhas and bodhisattvas.

māra – The *māras* are the "demons" or minions of Māra, the demon king in the sixth of the desire realm heavens.

Māra – Māra is the king of the *māras* or "the demon king" of the sixth desire realm heaven.

Master Guide – The "Master Guide" (導師, *nāyaka*) is another of the many honorific names for the Buddha.

meditation on impurity / unloveliness – "Meditation on impurity" or, more literally, "meditation on the unlovely" (不淨觀, *asubha-bhāvanā*) is a reference to the various meditations on the inherently unattractive or impure nature of the bodies of those to whom one might otherwise be sexually attracted. These include meditations on the 32 (or 36) parts of the body, the white-boned skeleton contemplation, the contemplation of the stages in the decomposition of a rotting corpse, etc.

merit – "Merit" (福德, 福, and sometimes, depending on the Chinese translator, 功德 / *puṇya*) is the karmically accumulated stock of potential good fortune produced by all of one's good thoughts, words, and deeds throughout all of one's lifetimes. "Merit" is one of the two provisions for enlightenment, the other being "wisdom."

meritorious qualities – "Meritorious qualities" (功德, *guṇa*) are good qualities, personal attributes, or virtues developed through spiritual goodness and cultivation over time and throughout lifetimes.

mind-moment – A "mind-moment" (一念 / *eka-kṣaṇika, citta-kṣaṇa*) is "A *kṣaṇa*, the shortest space of time, a moment, the 90th part of a thought and 4,500th part of a minute, during which 90 or 100 are born and as many die." (DCBT, digital)

Most Honored One among All Bipeds – "The Most Honored One among all bipeds" (兩足尊 / *dvipada uttama*) is an honorific epithet referring to the Buddha's supremacy among all humans and devas. This also refers to the Buddha's two-fold repletion in merit and wisdom.

muni – A *"muni"* (牟尼 / *muni*), per MW, p 823, column 1, is: "a saint, sage, seer, ascetic, monk, devotee, hermit (esp. one who has taken the vow of silence)." This is also an abbreviation for the name of Śākyamuni Buddha. It is also synonymous with the word "buddha."

N.

nāga – A *"nāga"* (龍, 那伽 / *nāga*) is one of the eight types of spiritual beings, one that may manifest in human form, dragon form, serpent form or elephant form and which is characterized as having spiritual powers and the ability to bring the rains.

namo – "Namo" (南無 / *namas, namaḥ, namo*) is an expression of homage, obeisance, reverential salutation, or adoration, from the Sanskrit *namas*, which, per MW, p. 528, means: *"namas n. bow, obeisance, reverential salutation, adoration (by gesture or word)…."*

nārāyaṇa – "A *"nārāyaṇa"* (那羅延, *nārāyaṇa*) is generally portrayed in Mahāyāna texts as a vajra-bearing Dharma protector spirit or deva. This word also commonly occurs as an adjective referring to the possession of great strength and powers. Also supposed to be an emanation of Brahmā or Viṣṇu.

nayuta – A *"nayuta"* (那由他 / *nayuta*) is a large number for which definitions vary. BHSD, p. 291, Column 1 mentions values as low as one million, but says that it is "generally 100,000,000,000," i.e., a hundred billion. MW mentions the absurdly low and implausible "1,000."

nine sequential meditative absorptions – The "nine sequential meditative absorptions" (九次第定 / *nava-anupūrva-samāpattayaḥ, anupūrva-vihāra-samāpatti*) refers to the four *dhyānas*, the four formless absorptions, and the meditative concentration in which the activity of both the feeling and the perception aggregates are extinguished. This last one is also referred to as the complete cessation absorption.

nirvāṇa – "Nirvāṇa" (涅槃 / *nirvāṇa*) is the ultimate goal of the path of Buddhist spiritual cultivation that corresponds to the elimination of the three poisons (covetousness, aversion, delusion) and the ending of compulsory and random rebirth in *saṃsāra*, the cycle of existences in the deva realm, the demigod realm, the human realm, the animal realm, the hungry ghost realm, and the hell realms.

In the case of the individual liberation path practitioner exemplified by arhats and *pratyekabuddhas*, all future existence ends for them with the acquisition of nirvāṇa.

In the case of the universal liberation practitioners exemplified by bodhisattvas and buddhas, they achieve the direct cognition of the emptiness of all beings and phenomena and realize an ongoing realization of a nirvana-like state even as, by force of vow, they continue to take on intentional rebirths within *saṃsāra* in order to facilitate the spiritual liberation of all beings.

nirvāṇa without residue – The "nirvāṇa without residue" (無餘涅槃 / *anupadhi-śeṣa-nirvāṇa*) is the final nirvāṇa realized at death by fully awakened beings whether they be arhats, *pratyekabuddhas*, or buddhas.

O.

obstacles – See the "two obstacles" and the "three obstacles."

oceanic imprint samādhi – The "oceanic imprint samādhi" (海印三昧 / *sāgara-mudrā-samādhi*) is the samādhi entered by the Buddha when teaching the Avataṃsaka Sutra.

P.

Pāpīyān – Pāpīyān is another name for Māra, the king of the *māras* or demons of the sixth desire realm heaven, the Parinirmita Vaśavartin Heaven.

pāramitā – "*Pāramitā*" (波羅蜜, 度 / *pāramitā*) or "perfection" which means "reaching the far shore" (到彼岸) is a reference to one of the six or ten *pāramitās*. The six perfections are: giving, moral virtue, patience, vigor, *dhyāna* (meditative skill), and *prajñā* (world-transcending wisdom). To these, the ten perfections add: skillful means, vows, powers, and knowledges.

Paranirmita Vaśavartin Heaven – The "Paranirmita Vaśavartin Heaven" (他化自在天 / *para-nirmita-vaśa-vartino devāḥ*) is the sixth of the six desire realm heavens. Per PDB, it is "The heaven of the gods who have power over the creations of others, or [in the case of the devas who dwell there], the gods who partake of the pleasures created in other heavens." Per DDB, it is "The abode of Maheśvara (i.e., Śiva), and of Māra … where Pāpīyān, the King of the Māras, resides."

parinirvāṇa – "*Parinirvāṇa*" (般涅槃, 般泥洹 / *parinirvāṇa*) is the final and complete nirvāṇa of a Buddha at the end of his last life.

personality view – "Personality view" (身見, 有身見 / *satkāya-dṛṣṭi, ātma-dṛṣṭi*) or "identity view" is the mistaken view that one has an inherently existent "self," a truly existent person in association with the five aggregates.

prajñā-pāramitā – "*Prajñā-pāramitā*" (般若波羅蜜 / *prajñā-pāramitā*) is the perfection of world-transcending wisdom. It is the sixth of the six perfections and is also the sixth of the ten perfections.

pratyekabuddha – A *"pratyekabuddha"* (辟支佛 / *pratyekabuddha*) is one who attains an enlightenment comparable to that of an arhat when no buddha is in the world, doing so on his own by contemplating dependent arising (*pratītyasamutpāda*) and the twelve links of conditioned co-production. Mahāyāna literature attributes this ability to awaken in the absence of a buddha or his Dharma to direct exposure to the Dharma in previous lives, the seeds of which enable enlightenment in the present life.

provisions for enlightenment – The "provisions for enlightenment" (菩提資糧 / *bodhisaṃbhāra*) consisting of merit and wisdom (*puṇya* and *jñāna*) are the necessary prerequisites for bodhisattvas to be able to complete the path to the attainment of buddhahood.

psycho-physical spiritual power – The "psycho-physical spiritual power" (神足通 / *ṛddhi-pratihārya*) is the power of unimpeded physical action by which one can manifest one's body anywhere.

pudgala – The *"pudgala"* (補伽羅 / *pudgala*) is a supposedly permanent personal soul wrongly conceived of as being inherently existent and hence actually "real."

pure youth – A "pure youth" (童子/ *kumāra*) is a chaste young man.

R.

rākṣasa – A *"rākṣasa"* (羅剎 / *rākṣasa*) is a swift flying malignant flesh-eating demon that changes its form to seduce humans and eat them. According to DCBT: "Malignant spirits, demons; sometimes considered inferior to *yakṣa*s, sometimes similar. Their place of abode was Laṅkā in Ceylon, where they are described as the original inhabitants, anthropophagi, once the terror of shipwrecked mariners; also described as the barbarian races of ancient India. As demons they are described as terrifying, with black bodies, red hair, green eyes, devourers of men."

right and definite position – "Right and definite position" (正位 / *samyaktva-niyama, samyaktva-niyāma,* or just *niyāma*) or "right and fixed position" refers to the position of irreversibility on the bodhisattva path from which one can never fall back or retreat. It also has a similar meaning of "stage of irreversibility" for those on the individual-liberation path to arhatship.

S.

Sahā World – The "Sahā World" (娑婆世界 / *sahā-loka-dhātu*) is the name of the world in which we live that is so full of so many kinds of evil and afflictions. *"Sahā"* means "to be endured."

sakṛdāgāmin – The *"sakṛdāgāmin"* (斯陀含, 一來 / *sakṛdāgāmin*) or "once-returner" is one who has gained the third of the four fruits on the individual-liberation path of the *śrāvaka* disciple.

samādhi – "Samādhi" (三昧, 定 / *samādhi*) is a state of solidly established meditative concentration. It refers both to any single instance of one-pointed concentration and also, more usually, to enduring states of persistently maintained one-pointed concentration.

samāpatti – The *samāpattis* (三摩鉢底), 三摩鉢提 / *samāpatti*) are usually interpreted as referring to the four *dhyānas*, the four formless absorptions, and the complete cessation absorption. In fact *"samāpatti"* is synonymous with *"samādhi."* According to BHSD (p. 569, Column 2): "The fact seems to be that these two words are fundamentally and substantially identical in mg., and that the attempts to differentiate are scholastic pedantry."

śamatha – *"Śamatha"* (奢摩他 / *śamatha*) is "calm abiding" meditation in which one develops stillness of mind and the cessation of discursive thinking.

saṃghārama – A *"saṃghārama"* (伽藍, 僧伽藍, 僧院 / *saṃghārama*) is a monastic residence and/or monastery.

saṃghāṭī – The *"saṃghāṭī"* (僧伽梨 / *saṃghāṭī*) is the fully ordained monastic's outer robe.

saṃsāra – *"Saṃsāra"* (生死 / *saṃsāra*) is the endless cycle of deaths and rebirths in the six realms of cyclic existence consisting of: devas (gods), *asuras* ("demigods" or "titans"), humans, animals, hungry ghosts (*pretas*), and hell-dwellers.

sangha – Broadly defined, a "sangha" (僧, 僧伽, 衆 / *saṃgha* [Skt.], *sangha* [Pali]) is a community of fully ordained Buddhist monks (*bhikshus*). *Saṃgha* is the Sanskrit spelling of the more commonly encountered and already anglicized Pali word *"sangha."* In the more traditional and formal sense as one of the three objects of refuge, i.e., "the Sangha Jewel," this does *not* refer to anyone who happens to self-identify as "Buddhist." Rather, it refers exclusively to those persons who have already acquired one of the fruits of the path from which one can then never fall away, whether on the individual-liberation paths of the arhats or *pratyekabuddhas*, or on the bodhisattva path.

śarīra – *"Śarīra"* (舍利 / *śarīra*) are the remains or "relics" of eminent members of the Sangha, bodhisattvas, or buddhas that are left over in the ashes of the funeral pyre. Sutras are also considered to be "relics" and hence "Dharma *śarīra*."

seven kinds of wealth – Lists of "the seven kinds of wealth" (七財, 七聖財 / *sapta-dhana, sapta-ārya-dhana*) or "seven kinds of wealth of *āryas*" vary slightly, depending on the source. In his Treatise on the Ten Bodhisattva Grounds, Nāgārjuna lists: faith, moral virtue, a sense of shame, a dread of blame, relinquishing (i.e., "giving"), learning, and wisdom (信戒慚愧捨聞慧 / SZPPS_ T26n1521_p0091c01–02).

seven jewels – The "seven jewels" (七寶 / *sapta-ratna*), otherwise known as "the seven precious things," vary slightly from list to list. Probably the most common list is exemplified by one of the lists found in the Lotus Sutra where they are listed as being: gold, silver, lapis lazuli, crystal, carnelian, emerald, coral, and amber (金, 銀, 琉璃, 車璩, 馬腦, 珊瑚, 虎珀).

signlessness – "Signlessness" (無相 / *animitta*) is the second of the "three gates to liberation" (the others being emptiness [*śūnyatā*] and wishlessness [*apraṇihita*]). It refers to the ultimate absence of inherent existence, inapprehensibility, and unreality of all characteristics such as, for instance (per the Nirvāṇa Sūtra): forms, sounds, smells, tastes, touchables, arising, abiding, destruction, male, and female.

śīla pāramitā – "*Śīla pāramitā*" (尸羅波羅蜜 / *śīla pāramitā*) is the second of the six perfections, the perfection of moral virtue.

six destinies – The "six destinies" (六道, 六趣 / *ṣaḍ-gati*) or "six rebirth destinies" are: rebirth in the hells, among the hungry ghosts, as an animal, as a human, as an *asura* (a "titan" or "demigod"), or as a deva (a "god").

six dharmas of harmony and respect – The "six dharmas of harmony and respect" (六和敬法 / *sad-saṃrañjanīyaṃ dharmam*) are six ways in which monastics live in harmony. These refer to harmony in body, mouth, mind, precepts, views, and benefits.

six dharmas of solidity – The "six dharmas of solidity" (六堅固法), per QLSCHB (p. 222a09ff), refer to solidity in faith, Dharma, cultivation, virtue, supremacy, and awakening.

six kinds of mindfulness – The "six kinds of mindfulness" (六念 / *ṣaḍ anusmṛtayaḥ*) are: mindfulness of the Buddha, mindfulness of the Dharma, mindfulness of the Sangha, mindfulness of the precepts, mindfulness of giving, and mindfulness of the heavens.

six kinds of shaking and moving – The "six kinds of shaking and moving" (六種震動 / *ṣaḍ-vikārāḥ prakampāḥ*) are movement, universal movement, equal-and-universal movement; rising, universal rising, equal-and-universal rising; upward thrusting, universal upward thrusting, equal-and-universal upward thrusting; shaking, universal shaking, equal-and-universal shaking; roaring, universal roaring, equal-and-universal roaring; and striking, universal striking, and equal-and-universal striking.

six *pāramitās* – The "six *pāramitās*" (六波羅蜜, 六度 / *ṣaṭ-pāramitā*), also known as the six "perfections," are: giving, moral virtue, patience, vigor, *dhyāna* (meditative skill), and *prajñā* (world-transcending wisdom).

solid incense – "Solid incense" (堅固香 / *kālānusāri-gandha*) per BCSD (p. 298) and BHSD (p. 180, Column 2) seems most likely to be "some kind of sandalwood."

son of good family – "Son of good family" (善男子 / *kula-putra*) is a polite form of address for Buddhist laymen similar to "gentleman."

sovereign mastery – See "ten kinds of sovereign mastery" and "three kinds of sovereign mastery."

spiritual superknowledges – The "six spiritual superknowledges" (六神通, 六通 / *ṣaḍ-abhijña*) are: unimpeded physical action, the heavenly eye, the heavenly ear, the cognition of others' thoughts, the cognition of one's own and others' past lives, and the cessation of all contaminants.

śramaṇa – "*Śramaṇa*" (沙門 / *śramaṇa*) is a specific term of reference for a Buddhist monk and is also a general term of reference for renunciants in general, including Jains.

śrāvaka – A "*śrāvaka*" (聲聞 / *śrāvaka*), otherwise translated as "*śrāvaka* disciple," literally means "voice-hearer." It was originally a general term of reference for monastic disciples of the Buddha who had personally heard him teach them the Dharma. Later, especially in Mahāyāna literature, it came to refer to monastic adherents of the teachings of the individual-liberation vehicle who sought to realize the final nirvāṇa of the arhat.

srota-āpanna – A "*srota-āpanna*" (須陀洹, 預流, 入流 / *srota-āpanna*) is a "stream-winner" or "stream-enterer," one who has gained the first fruit of the four fruits on the individual-liberation path of the arhat that culminates in final nirvāṇa from which one is never again subject to rebirth in the cyclic existence of *saṃsāra*.

stream-enterer – See "*srota-āpanna*."

suchness – See "true suchness."

superknowledges – See "spiritual superknowledges."

T.

Tamer of Men to be Tamed – "Tamer of Men to Be Tamed" (調御士, *puruṣa-damya-sārathi*) is one of the ten standard honorific titles for all buddhas.

tāla tree – Of the approximately forty species of palm trees, the "*tāla* tree" (多羅樹 / *tāla*) is the *Borassus*, a genus consisting of five species of fan palms.

tathāgata – "*Tathāgata*" (如來 / *tathāgata*) is one of the ten standard honorific titles for all buddhas. It means "Thus Come One."

tathāgata-garbha – The "*tathāgata-garbha*" (如來藏 / *tathāgata-garbha*) is the so-called "womb of the Tathāgatha" or "matrix of the Tathāgata" which refers to the idea that the potential for the complete realization of buddhahood is present in all sentient beings.

ten courses of good karmic action – The "ten courses of good karmic action" (十善業道 / *daśa-kuśala-karma-patha*) are refraining from: killing, stealing, sexual misconduct, lying, harsh speech, divisive speech, frivolous or lewd speech, covetousness, ill will, and wrong views.

ten directions – The "ten directions" (十方 / *daśa-diś*) are the four cardinal directions of north, south, east, and west, their four midpoints of northeast, southeast, northwest, southwest, and the zenith and the nadir.

ten kinds of sovereign mastery – The "ten kinds of sovereign mastery" (十自在 / *daśa-vaśitā*) consist of sovereign mastery of: life span, mind, equipage, karma, birth, resolute faith, vows, spiritual superknowledges, Dharma, and knowledge or cognition.

ten *pāramitās* – The "ten *pāramitās*" (*daśa-pāramitā* / 十波羅蜜) consist of the "six *pāramitās*" (giving, moral virtue, patience, vigor, *dhyāna*, and *prajñā*) plus skillful means, vows, powers, and knowledge.

ten universal objects [of meditation] – The "ten universal objects [of meditation]" (十一切處, 十遍處 / kṛtsnāyatana, *kasiṇa*) are: earth, water, fire, wind, blue, yellow, red, white, space, and consciousness. These "universal objects" are better known by their Pali spelling (*kasiṇa*) in association with the Theravada tradition's meditation on the various "*kasiṇa*" objects for each of the colors, etc. For a better understanding, VB recommends reading about the meditation on the earth *kasiṇa* in Chapter Four of the *Visuddhimagga* or "The Path of Purification" by Buddhaghosa.

three clarities – The "three clarities" (三明 / *trividya*) are the heavenly eye, cognition of past lives, and cessation of the contaminants.

three classes of moral precepts – The "three classes of pure moral precepts" (三種淨戒 / *trividhāni śīlāni*), otherwise known as the "the three groups of moral precepts" (三聚戒) or "the three groups of pure moral precepts" (三聚淨戒) consist of: 1) "The moral precepts of the moral codes" which include the five precepts, the eight precepts, the ten precepts, the bodhisattva precepts, or the complete monastic precepts; 2) "The moral precepts of the good dharmas" which refers to the moral standard requiring the cultivation of goodness in all situations; and 3) "The moral precept of benefiting beings" which refers to cultivating goodness aimed at benefiting beings, especially by guiding beings to follow the moral precepts.

three gates to liberation – The "three gates to liberation" (三解脫門 / *vimokṣa-mukha, vimokṣa-dvāra*) consist of emptiness (*śūnyatā*), signlessness (*animitta*), and wishlessness (*apraṇihita*).

three groups [of beings] – The "three groups [of beings]" (三聚 / *tri-skandha*) are: 1) those who are fixed in what is right; 2) those who are not fixed [in either what is right or what is wrong], i.e., those who are as yet "unfixed" with regard to their inclinations toward doing what is right or what is wrong; and 3) those who are fixed in what is wrong. Although the order differs, this is a list common to nearly all traditions and schools.

three kinds of sovereign mastery – Both QL and HH interpret the "three kinds of sovereign mastery" (三種自在) as referring to sovereign mastery in the three types of karmic actions (physical, verbal, and mental).

three obstacles – The "three obstacles" (三障 / *āvaraṇa-traya*) are affliction obstacles, karmic obstacles, and retribution obstacles.

three periods of time – The "three periods of time" (三世 / *try-adhvan*) are the past, the present, and the future.

three poisons – The "three poisons" (三毒 / *tri-doṣa, tri-viṣa**) are greed, hatred, and delusion.

three realms – The "three realms" (三界 / *tri-dhātu*) which are also known as "three realms of existence" are: the desire realm, the subtle form realm, and the formless realm.

three spheres involved in giving – The "three spheres involved in giving" (三輪 / *trimaṇḍala*) are the benefactor, the recipient, and the gift.

three spheres of action – The "three spheres of action" (三種輪 or 三輪 / *trimaṇḍala*) refers to physical, verbal, and mental actions.

three sufferings – The "three sufferings" (三苦 / *tri-duḥkhatā*) are: the suffering of physical and mental pain (苦苦 / *duḥkha-duḥkha*), the suffering inherent in change (壞苦 / *vipariṇāma-duḥkha*); and the suffering inherent in the karmic formative factors of conditioned existence (行苦 / *saṃskāra-duḥka*).

three turnings of the Dharma wheel – The "three turnings of the Dharma wheel" (三轉法輪 / *tri-parivarta dharmacakra*) are: 1) The "expository" turning of the Dharma wheel in which the Buddha taught each of the four truths of the *āryas*; 2) The "exhortative" turning of the Dharma wheel in which the Buddha encouraged the disciples to cultivate and realize each of the four truths; and 3) The "realizational" turning of the Dharma wheel in which the Buddha declared that he had realized each of the four truths.

three types of moral precepts (三律儀) – The "three types of moral precepts" (三律儀) are the moral precepts of individual liberation (別解脫律儀), the moral precepts produced by *dhyāna* (靜慮律儀), and the moral precepts of the cessation of the contaminants (無漏律儀).

three vehicles – The three vehicles (三乘 / *triyāna*) are three kinds of vehicles for achieving liberation from endless cyclic existence in the sufferings of *saṃsāra*. These consist of two vehicles concerned with achieving individual liberation, namely the vehicle of the *śrāvaka* disciples and the vehicle of the *pratyekabuddhas* along with the vehicle concerned with universal liberation of all beings, namely the so-called "great vehicle" (大乘 / *mahāyāna*), the vehicle of the bodhisattvas and bodhisattvas.

three wretched destinies – "The three wretched destinies" (三惡道) consist of the three lowest rebirth destinies consisting of the hells, the "hungry ghosts" (*pretas*), and the animals.

trichiliocosm – A trichiliocosm (三千世界, a.k.a. 大千世界 or 三千大千世界 / *trisāhasra-mahāsāhasra lokadhātu*) is an Indian cosmic unit consisting of a billion worlds, each of which has its own Mt. Sumeru, surrounding continents, and various levels of heavens.

true suchness – "True suchness" (眞如, 如 / *bhūta-tathatā, tathatā*) otherwise known simply as "suchness," is the essential nature of all things or the true character of all dharmas in their emptiness of any inherent existence of their own.

two extreme views – The "two extreme views" (二邊見, *antagrāha-dṛṣṭi*) refers to the two opposite views of eternalism and annihilationism which hold either that one lives on forever, even after death, or that one lives only once and one's existence ends at the end of this one life.

two obstacles – The "two obstacles" (二障 / *āvaraṇa-dvaya*) are affliction obstacles and cognitive obstacles.

two types of actions – Per HH, the "two types of actions" (二行) are: actions dominated by views and actions dominated by craving. QL obliquely refers to another of the several standard lists for "two kinds of actions" consisting of actions reflective of the "two kinds of obstacles," the "affliction obstacles" and the "cognitive obstacles."

two vehicles – The "two vehicles" (二乘 / *dviyāna, yāna-dvaya*) are the two kinds of individual-liberation vehicles consisting of that of the *śrāvaka* disciples and that of the *pratyekabuddhas* in both of which the primary aim of practice is to quickly attain emancipation from cyclic existence in *saṃsāra* without delaying this quest with concerns for the universal liberation of all beings.

U.

uncontaminated – "Uncontaminated" (無漏 / *anāsrava*) refers to being free of the contaminants which consist of sensual desire; desire for continued existence, and ignorance. Sometimes a fourth category of "wrong views" is added.

unimpeded knowledges – See "four unimpeded knowledges."

universal bases – See "ten universal objects [of meditation]."

unloveliness contemplation – See "meditation on impurity / unloveliness."

unproduced dharmas patience – The unproduced dharmas patience (無生法忍 / *anutpattika-dharma-kṣānti*) may be described as the continuous directly realized knowledge of and acquiescence in all dharmas and all phenomena as empty of inherent existence and having no arising at all. This realization is synonymous with the attainment of "irreversibility" on one's chosen path of liberation, whether that be the individual-liberation path of the *śrāvaka*-vehicle practitioner or the universal-liberation path of the great-vehicle practitioner on the bodhisattva path to buddhahood. In the case of the *śrāvaka*-vehicle practitioner, this realization is synonymous with attainment of the path of seeing (*darśana-mārga*) and becoming a stream-winner (*srota-āppana*) who thereby cuts off the first three of the ten fetters. In the case of the bodhisattva-path practitioner, realizing the unproduced dharmas patience occurs either on the first or the eighth of the ten bodhisattva grounds (depending on which of the hermeneutic models one is referencing). For the bodhisattva, it is this very patience or "acquiescence" that allows him to happily continue on for countless kalpas striving to enable the spiritual liberation of other beings as he gradually makes his own way toward buddhahood, deeply understanding all along that there is neither any "self" who is liberating other beings nor are there even any "beings" who are being liberated.

upādhi nirvāṇa – The term "*upādhi* nirvāṇa" (烏波提涅槃 / *upādhi-nirvāṇa*) refers to all forms of mere semblance nirvāṇa clung to by non-Buddhist traditions that do not really constitute any form of genuine nirvāṇa as understood by Buddhists.

upādhyāya – An "*upādhyāya*" (和尙 , 和尚 / *upādhyāya*) is a very senior member of a monastic community, usually one serving as a preceptor or instructor of other monks. In the modern era, this has become a general term of reference for any fully ordained Buddhist monk.

upaniṣad – An "*upaniṣad*" (優波尼沙陀 / *upaniṣad*) is usually explained as the smallest particle of matter closest to being just empty space.

uṣṇīṣa – "Uṣṇīṣa" (肉髻 / *uṣṇīṣa*) is the Sanskrit term that refers either to the bulge on the top of the head of a Buddha (a fleshy lump on the top center of a buddha's head, one of the thirty-two marks of a buddha) or to the topknot of hair commonly seen on images of bodhisattvas. (More generally, it can refer to a turban, headband, or other form of headdress.)

utpala flower – The "*utpala* flower" (*utpala* / 優鉢羅華) is the flower of the blue lotus.

V.

vaiḍūrya – "*Vaiḍūrya*" (*vaidūrya* / 琉璃) is lapis lazuli, a deep blue gem.

vajra – "Vajra" (金剛 / *vajra*) is an indestructible substance that is usually equated with diamond. A symbol of indestructibility. Also, a pestle-shaped scepter or "thunderbolt" weapon held by Dharma protectors and deities.

vajra-bearing spirit – A "vajra-bearing spirit" (執金剛神 / *vajradhara, vajrapāṇi*) is: a) a type of vajra-wielding *yakṣa* who guards the gates of the palace of Indra; or b) one of a class of vajra-wielding Dharma protectors who guard the buddhas and their sites of enlightenment.

vinaya – The "*vinaya*" (比尼 / *vinaya*) is the code of moral discipline for monastics.

vipaśyanā – (觀) Contemplation; contemplative meditation; insight meditation.

volitional factors – See "*saṃskāras*."

W.

Wealth of the *āryas* – "Wealth of the *āryas*" (聖財, *ārya-dhāna*) or "the seven kinds of wealth of the *āryas*" (七聖財, *saptāryadhāna*) or "seven kinds of Dharma wealth" (七法財). These all refer to personal qualities of awakened beings. Lists vary somewhat. In his Treatise on the Ten Bodhisattva Grounds, Nāgārjuna lists: faith, moral virtue, a sense of shame, a dread of blame, relinquishing (i.e., "giving"), learning, and wisdom (信戒慚愧捨聞慧 / SZPPS_T26n1521_p0091c01–02).

Well Gone One – "Well Gone One" (善逝, *sugata*) is the fifth of the ten names of the Buddha.

wheel-turning king – In Buddhism, a "wheel-turning king" (轉輪王, 轉輪聖王 / *cakravartin*) is a universal monarch.

wishlessness – "Wishlessness" (無作, 無願 / *apraṇihita*) is the third of the three gates to liberation by which, through realizing that all dharmas are impermanent and conducive to suffering, one views all dharmas as empty of inherent existence without any aspirations for involvement with them.

world transformation – A "world transformation" (世界轉 / *lokadhātuparivarta*) is a nearly unimaginably large number. In his HYQS, HH explains that a "world transformation" is a number calculated from supposing that one ground a world to dust, then allowed each one of those motes of dust to represent a *kṣetra* (a "land") that one then in turn also ground to dust. The resulting number of dust motes produced from grinding up all those *kṣetras* equals this very large number known as a "world transformation."

worthy – In Mahāyāna literature, a "worthy" (賢 / *bhadra*) is a wise and morally pure practitioner of the bodhisattva path who has made the bodhisattva vow but who is still cultivating the preparatory stages and thus has not yet reached the ten bodhisattva grounds and has not yet become an *ārya*.

worthy kalpa –The "worthy kalpa" or "good kalpa" (賢劫 / *bhadrakalpa*) is this present kalpa into which it is usually said that a total of a thousand buddhas will be born. Among them, the buddha of the present era, Śākyamuni, is the fourth and Maitreya is the next, after which nine hundred and ninety-five other buddhas will follow.

wretched destinies – The "wretched destinies" (惡道) / *durgati*) are either the "three wretched destinies" (三惡道 / *trayo durgatayaḥ*) consisting of the hells, the "hungry ghosts" (*pretas*), and the animals, or "the four wretched rebirth destinies" (四惡趣) which also include the rebirth destiny of the *asuras* who are somewhat analogous to the "demigods" or "titans" of western mythology.

Y.

yakṣa – A "*yakṣa*" (夜叉 / *yakṣa*), one of the eight classes of spiritual beings, is a kind of either good or evil spirit possessed of supernatural powers that may manifest either as a malignant and demonic ghost that devours human flesh and possesses people or else, under certain circumstances, instead serves as a guardian spirit.

Yama – See "King Yama."

yojana – A "*yojana*" (由旬 / *yojana*) is measure of distance in ancient India usually defined as being the distance that an ox cart would travel in a day without unharnessing (somewhat less than ten miles).

About the Translator

Bhikshu Dharmamitra (ordination name "Heng Shou" – 釋恆授) is a Chinese-tradition translator-monk and one of the earliest American disciples (since 1968) of the late Guiyang Ch'an patriarch, Dharma teacher, and pioneer of Buddhism in the West, the Venerable Master Hsuan Hua (宣化上人). He has a total of 33 years in robes during two periods as a monastic (1969–1975 & 1991 to the present).

Dharmamitra's principal educational foundations as a translator of Sino-Buddhist Classical Chinese lie in four years of intensive monastic training and Chinese-language study of classic Mahāyāna texts in a small-group setting under Master Hsuan Hua (1968–1972), undergraduate Chinese language study at Portland State University, a year of intensive one-on-one Classical Chinese study at the Fu Jen University Language Center near Taipei, two years of course work at the University of Washington's Department of Asian Languages and Literature (1988–90), and an additional three years of auditing graduate courses and seminars in Classical Chinese readings, again at UW's Department of Asian Languages and Literature.

Since taking robes again under Master Hua in 1991, Dharmamitra has devoted his energies primarily to study and translation of classic Mahāyāna texts with a special interest in works by Ārya Nāgārjuna and related authors. To date, he has translated more than fifteen important texts comprising approximately 150 fascicles, including most recently the 80-fascicle *Avataṃsaka Sūtra* (the "Flower Adornment Sutra"), Nāgārjuna's 17-fascicle *Daśabhūmika Vibhāśa* ("Treatise on the Ten Grounds"), and the *Daśabhūmika Sūtra* (the "Ten Grounds Sutra"), all of which are current Kalavinka Press publications.

A Commentarial Synopsis Of The Flower Adornment Sutra

By Bhikshu Dharmamitra

Preface

The Flower Adornment Sutra's description of the cosmos as consisting of infinitely many quantumly entangled interpenetrating worlds populated by countless buddhas, bodhisattvas, and other beings playing out a grand scenario of karma and Dharma in all the realms of rebirth is so vast, so multi-leveled, so intricate, and so marvelous that it is nearly impossible for anyone to envision, grasp, and simultaneously hold all of its amazing teachings in mind without the aid of some sort of simplifying skillful means with which to keep track of this scripture's main story lines and ideas as they are set forth in its thirty-nine chapters and several thousand pages.

To that end, for the benefit of those readers who feel they might benefit from such an aid to reinforced understanding, in addition to the approximately thirteen hundred clarifying and commentarial endnotes provided for my translation of the Flower Adornment Sutra, I have also included here a general synopsis of the main events, primary teachings, and most important ideas contained in each of those thirty-nine chapters as well as in the traditionally appended conclusion, "The Conduct and Vows of Samantabhadra" with which this grand spiritual saga concludes.

For the most part, these synopses of the content of each of the sutra chapters are constructed from a series of quotations interspersed with my brief comments that together more or less reconstruct the narrative and most important ideas of the often rather long chapters that in a half dozen instances range between one hundred and seven hundred pages in length.

Hopefully this series of forty short chapter synopses with their commentarial observations will help the reader stay relatively well oriented to the grand design of all these interwoven bodhisattva path teachings unfolding across the course of the more than three thousand pages of this Greatly Expansive Buddha's Flower Adornment Sutra. These synopses may also serve the reader as a means to go back and review the general contents of particular chapters whenever one feels the need to refresh one's memory before continuing to read the rest of the scripture.

Chapter 1

The Wondrous Adornments of the Leaders of the Worlds

As the sutra begins, it describes the magnificently radiant and wondrously adorned scene unfolding in our own world in India, in the state of Magadha, in Bodhgaya, where the Buddha, having just attained the utmost, right and perfect enlightenment, is seated beneath the bodhi tree in majestic glory where he then becomes surrounded by countless groups of beings devoted to the bodhisattva path who have come to celebrate and praise the Buddha's attainment of highest enlightenment. The beings who assembled there included leaders and retinues of countless great bodhisattvas, Dharma-protecting spirits, *bodhimaṇḍa* spirits, city spirits, earth spirits, mountain spirits, forest spirits, herb spirits, crop spirits, river spirits, ocean spirits, water spirits, fire spirits, wind spirits, space spirits, direction spirits, night spirits, day spirits, *asura* kings, *garuḍa* kings, *kiṃnara* kings, *mahoraga* kings, *yakṣa* kings, dragon kings, *kumbhāṇḍa* kings, *gandharva* kings, and the leaders and retinues of all the various classes of devas from all the heavens.

Leaders of each of these groups then took turns uttering verses in praise of the Buddha in which they marveled at his enlightenment and recounted the role of his bodhisattva path teachings in bringing about advancement on the path for those in their retinues. At the conclusion of all these verses of praise, exaltation, and celebration, due to the spiritual powers of the Buddha, the entire Flower Treasury Ocean of Worlds quaked in six ways, whereupon all those classes of beings manifested countless clouds of offerings which they rained down as gifts to the Buddha, doing so not only here in this world's Bodhgaya, but also in all those other worlds of the Flower Treasury Ocean of Worlds where countless other simultaneously awakened emanation buddhas sitting beneath their bodhi trees were also surrounded by other groups of all these same classes of leaders of the worlds who had also come together just then to celebrate and praise the enlightenment of all those other emanation buddhas upon whom they also rained down clouds of offerings in appreciation of their bringing right Dharma into all those other worlds.

This chapter's title "Leaders of the Worlds" is multivalent in its connotations. Of course it most directly refers to the Buddha who is the foremost spiritual leader in the world. But it also refers to all the other buddhas throughout the Flower Treasury Ocean of Worlds as well as to the bodhisattva-*mahāsattvas* who are so devoted to propagating the Dharma and liberating beings, and also refers to the leaders of these other many classes of beings who serve as Dharma protectors striving to ensure that right Dharma endures forever in the world.

Throughout this chapter, the reader is provided with an indirect introduction to the most emblematic ideas for which the Flower Adornment Sutra is so well known, namely the so-called "four dharma realms" consisting of: 1) "the dharma realm of the noumenal" which refers to true suchness and absence of inherent existence; 2) "the dharma realm of the phenomenal" which refers to all phenomena, whether large or small, coarse, or subtle; 3) "the dharma realm of the unimpeded relationship between the noumenal and the phenomenal" which refers to the fact that all phenomena are but manifestations of true suchness which are themselves devoid of any inherent existence of their own; and 4) "the dharma realm of the unimpeded relationship between any given phenomenon and all other phenomena" which, after the manner of modern quantum theory, posits that all phenomena can be viewed within any and all other phenomena.

These four dharma realms are not ever explicitly and concisely described in so many words. Rather they appear as implicit within the text and the verses of praise uttered by the various world leaders. For example:

> "Delighting in Quiescence Deva King acquired the liberation gateway of manifesting an inconceivable number of buddha *kṣetras* in but a single pore without any mutual interference [between the large and the small]."

> "All the lands of the past
> appear in but a single pore.
> This is due to the great spiritual superknowledges of the buddhas.
> Delighting in Quiescence is able to expound on this."

> "The Buddha is able to manifest within but a single pore,
> all of the different aspects of creation and destruction as they occur
> in all the countless kalpas throughout the three periods of time.
> This is what Superior Cloud Sound Deva completely understood."

> "The bodhi practices of all sons of the Buddha
> are entirely manifested by the Tathāgata within a single pore.
> Even as countless as they are, they are all completely shown there.
> This is what Mindfulness Deva King has clearly seen."

> "The Buddha is able to cause to enter a single pore
> the populations of countless boundless lands
> even as the Tathāgata sits peacefully within their congregations.
> This is what Flaming Mouth Dragon saw."

These are just a few examples from the first of this sutra's thirty-nine chapters in which, all told, there are many thousands of examples of all four these "four dharma realms."

Chapter 2
The Manifest Appearances of the Tathāgatha

After the world had shaken in six ways and the clouds of offerings had all appeared, this next chapter opens with each of the bodhisattvas and other "leaders of the worlds" in the vast congregation simultaneously having the same inquiring thoughts which they each mentally posed as questions to the Buddha, thoughts in which they wondered about the buddhas' qualities and aspects of body and mind, the buddhas' grounds, spheres of action, empowerments, actions, powers, fearlessnesses, samādhis, superknowledges, sovereign masteries, and types of invincibility. They also wondered about the buddhas' eyes, ears, nose, tongue, body, mind, aura, radiance, voice, and wisdom as well as all the other things explained by all buddhas, concluding with: "We wish that, in the same way, the Buddha, the Bhagavat, will also explain these matters for us."

Then, through the spiritual powers of the great bodhisattvas, a voice suddenly manifested from within the clouds which spoke aloud their request for the Buddha to teach the Dharma, expressing in verse the topics they hoped the Buddha would now teach them.

Then, knowing the thoughts in the bodhisattvas' minds, from between his teeth, the Bhagavat emanated countless rays of light of ten different kinds which appeared before all congregations of bodhisattvas throughout the ocean of Flower Treasury Adornment Worlds, telling them all to go and pay their respects before all the buddhas beneath all the bodhi trees so that then they could hear the Buddha teach the Dharma.

Then, in succession, the bodhisattvas from each of the ten directions came, made offerings, and paid their respects to the Buddha. The Bhagavat then emanated rays of light from between his brows which revealed the sites of enlightenment of Samantabhadra Bodhisattva, circumambulated the Buddha, and then returned, entering the bottom of his feet.

An immense lotus suddenly rose up in front of the Buddha whereupon, from between his brows, a great bodhisattva named "Supreme Sound of All Dharmas" appeared, followed by a retinue of bodhisattvas. They all circumambulated the Buddha, bowed down in reverence before him, and then sat down on that lotus after which, empowered by the Buddha, that bodhisattva and ten of his followers each took turns in uttering verses speaking to the questions with which the chapter began. Beginning with these verses, there is the mention of the interpenetration of large and small and the presence of countless worlds in even the smallest phenomena.

The chapter then ends with the advice that this very scene simultaneously also took place in all the sites of enlightenment in all of the lands in all the oceans of worlds.

Chapter 3
The Samādhis of Samantabhadra

Then Samantabhadra Bodhisattva sat down on a lotus flower dais lion throne in front of the Tathāgata where, aided by the Buddha's spiritual powers, he entered the "Vairocana *tathāgatagarbha* body of all buddhas samādhi" which enters the nature of all buddhas and reveals all their reflected images throughout the Dharma realm. As he did so, so too did all the other Samantabhadra Bodhisattvas do so before all the other buddhas throughout the Dharma realm. All those Tathāgatas then praised all those Samantabhadra Bodhisattvas and explained the reasons for their ability to enter this samādhi. All the buddhas of the ten directions then bestowed ten kinds of knowledge on all those Samantabhadra Bodhisattvas and extended their right hands to rub the crown of all those Samantabhadras, whereupon all those Samantabhadras arose from this samādhi and also arose from an ocean of other samādhi gateways at which point they each acquired clouds of oceans of samādhis, *dhāraṇīs,* and other such phenomena.

Then, due to the awesome spiritual power of all those buddhas and due to the power of Samantabhadra Bodhisattva's samādhis, a subtle trembling occurred in all those worlds as they all also became adorned with precious jewels and emanated marvelous voices which expounded on all dharmas. Then, at all those sites of enlightenment, there rained down ten kinds of clouds of *maṇi* jewels. Then, from within all the pores of all those *tathāgatas,* there streamed forth rays of light and, from within all those rays of light, a voice uttered ten verses in praise of Samantabhadra. At that time, all those in that congregation of bodhisattvas faced Samantabhadra, placed their palms together, and, aided by the Buddha's spiritual powers, they joined their voices in uttering ten verses in praise of Samantabhadra. In the next to last quatrain, they request that Samantabhadra teach the Dharma to them, asking him the questions that he next answers in Chapter Four, "The Formation of the Worlds":

> "How is it that these lands are established?
> How is it that the buddhas come forth and appear?
> And also, those matters having to do with the ocean of all beings—
> Please explain their meaning in accordance with reality."

There are many examples in this chapter of the four dharma realms, especially as demonstrated in mirror-like simultaneity of any given action everywhere at once throughout the Dharma realm, as for instance when all buddhas simultaneously rub the crowns of the heads of all Samantabhadra Bodhisattvas:

"And just as in this world Samantabhadra Bodhisattva was rubbed on the crown of the head by the buddhas of the ten directions, so too was this also so in all the oceans of worlds and in every atom in those oceans of worlds where all of those other Samantabhadras were all also rubbed on the crown of the head by the buddhas of the ten directions."

Chapter 4
The Formation of the Worlds

This chapter begins immediately after the point at the end of the previous chapter where, at the very end of a series of verses in praise of Samantabhadra Bodhisattva, the bodhisattvas had asked Samantabhadra the following question about the formation of worlds, the arising of buddhas, and "matters having to do with the ocean of all beings":

> "How is it that these lands are established?
> How is it that the buddhas come forth and appear?
> And also, those matters having to do with the ocean of all beings—
> Please explain their meaning in accordance with reality."

Then, aided by the Buddhas spiritual powers, Samantabhadra Bodhisattva contemplated the oceans of all worlds, beings, and buddhas, the ocean of the Dharma realm, the oceans of beings' karma, faculties, and aspirations, and the oceans of many other phenomena. Having contemplated them, he then described some thirty aspects of the buddhas, all of which he characterized as "inconceivable," after which he said, with the aid of the Buddha's powers, he would explain all dharmas such as these, doing so for ten reasons, all of which had to do with enabling ten kinds of salutary effects. He then described ten matters regarding the oceans of worlds which all buddhas speak. He next listed ten types of causes and conditions through which all oceans of worlds have become established after which he listed ten kinds of bases upon which all oceans of worlds abide. Then he listed the various sorts of shapes and appearances of these worlds followed by his listing of twenty kinds of substances of which these oceans of worlds are formed, ranging from substances such as jewels, the Buddha's powers, and incense to the stamens of flowers and the voice of the Buddha.

Samantabhadra next listed ten kinds of things which serve as the adornments of oceans of worlds, then listed ten kinds of skillful means by which they become purified, then listed ten differences in the ways that buddhas manifest within them, then listed the various kinds of durations for which these oceans of worlds last, then listed ten kinds of "kalpa transformations" which occur in all these oceans of worlds. Samantabhadra concludes this chapter by describing ten ways in which all these oceans of worlds do not differ from each other.

Chapter 5
The Flower Treasury [Ocean of] World[s]

Samantabhadra Bodhisattva again addressed that immense congregation saying that this Flower Treasury Adornment Ocean of Worlds was purified by Vairocana Tathāgata for countless kalpas during which he drew near to countless buddhas and cultivated countless vows. He then proceeded to describe the structure of this ocean of worlds, beginning by describing ten of the innumerably many "wind spheres" that support this ocean of worlds, noting that the highest level of wind spheres supports a fragrant ocean on top of which there is an immense lotus flower in the middle of which rests the Flower Treasury Adornment Ocean of worlds. He describes its surrounding mountains as made of various kinds of jewels, notes that all the ground surrounded by those mountains is made of vajra inlaid with various jewels, and states that the great earth in this ocean of world contains countless fragrant oceans with ocean floors made of jewels and jeweled flowers twirling about on their surfaces. He goes on to describe marvelously adorned cities, groves of jewels, and gems that glow with flaming radiance and emanate the sounds of the Buddha's voice.

Samantabhadra goes on to describe the rivers flowing into the oceans, saying that they have banks of vajra inlaid with jewels, whirlpools showing images of the causal practices cultivated by all buddhas, and clouds of jewels hanging over them revealing the appearance of Vairocana Buddha's transformation buddhas. He says that the groves of jeweled trees on the ground between these rivers emanate voices describing the vows of all *tathāgatas* and send down radiant jewels showing many phenomena including the ocean of all beings' karmic retributions.

Samantabhadra next describes the kinds of world systems within these fragrant oceans, saying that each world system contains countless worlds with various bases for their existence. Of the examples he lists, some take a great ocean of lotus flowers as the basis of their existence, some take infinitely colored oceans of jeweled flowers as the basis for their existence, and some take an ocean of jewels emanating the voices of all buddhas as the basis of their existence. Describing the forms these worlds take, he mentions many examples among which are some that take the form of Mount Sumeru, some that take the form of a river, some that take the form of a vortex, and some that take the form of beings' bodies.

In the next of many sets of verses in this chapter, Samantabhadra says that, "Within all the atoms contained in all lands, one everywhere sees the Tathāgata," and then says, "The body of the Buddha pervades all the *kṣetras.*" After this, he mentions that, "these fragrant oceans as numerous as the atoms in an ineffable number of buddha *kṣetras* are arrayed throughout the Flower Treasury Adornment Ocean of Worlds like [the jewels in] Indra's net."

Samantabhadra next describes some twenty levels of worlds, mentioning their different types of physical bases, their shapes, their different types of bejeweled clouds and nets, and the names of the buddhas who reign in each one of them. He tells us that there are worlds such as these as numerous as the atoms in an ineffable number of buddha *kṣetras,* each one of which is surrounded by vast worlds as numerous as the atoms in ten buddha *kṣetras,* and then says that every one of these worlds also has a retinue of worlds as numerous as the atoms in the previously described worlds.

Samantabhadra then describes the next fragrant ocean to the east and then proceeds to describe twenty more levels of worlds that rise above it. He then describes the next fragrant ocean to the south and some twenty levels of worlds above it, in each case mentioning the name of the buddha who reigns there. He then continues to repeat this same type of description of some twenty levels of worlds in place after place, explaining that all of these fragrant oceans and levels of world systems are each interconnected with all the others. Samantabhadra then concludes this chapter with one hundred and one verses in which he reiterates the structure of the Flower Treasury Adornment Ocean of Worlds.

Chapter 6
Vairocana

Samantabhadra then addressed that immense congregation, telling them that, in the ancient past, there was an ocean of worlds known as Pure Light of the Universal Gateway in which there was a marvelously adorned spherical world known as Supreme Sound that was surrounded by rings of mountains forested with jeweled trees, covered with clouds of jewels, illuminated with pure light, and possessed of cities and palaces resembling Mount Sumeru where food and drink spontaneously arrived in response to one's wishes. Within that world was a fragrant ocean known as Pure Light from which emerged an immense floral Mount Sumeru on which there was a great forest in which there were countless flower towers and jeweled viewing terraces. Within that forest was a site of enlightenment in front of which was a great ocean from which there emerged an immense lotus flower. At that time, a Buddha appeared who was named Supreme Cloud on the Sumeru Mountain of All Meritorious Qualities. That buddha emanated countless transformation buddhas and emanated light from between his brows that dispelled the delusions and obstacles of all the beings it touched, inspiring them to develop deep faith, to wish to see the buddha, and to cultivate the path to buddhahood.

In the city called Flaming Radiance, the king's foremost prince known as Prince Light of Great Power had been touched by the light from the Buddha's brow. This led him to attain ten Dharma gateways that included samādhi, *dhāraṇī* power, wise skillful means, the four immeasurable minds consisting of kindness, compassion, sympathetic joy, and equanimity, as well as spiritual superknowledges, great vows, and eloquence. Having attained these great spiritual benefits, he was inspired to utter verses that, due to the power of the Buddha, resounded throughout that Supreme Sound World where the power of those verses caused the king to be so impressed that he immediately ordered his retinue to prepare to go and see the Buddha. They all then went with the king to bow in reverence to the Buddha where they then sat off to one side along with the kings of devas, dragons, *yakṣas, gandharvas, asuras, garuḍas, kiṃnaras,* and *mahoragas,* the Brahma Heaven king, and many other human kings.

That buddha then taught a sutra for the training of beings by which all who had come to his site of enlightenment were enabled to progress on the path while that bodhisattva prince, Light of Great Power, acquired wisdom light of many kinds from the Buddha and then became greatly awakened.

The Buddha then spoke verses for the benefit of Great Power Bodhisattva in which he praised him, revealed the causes and conditions in the past that enabled him to attain such a great awakening in the present, and informed him that the great bodhisattvas who cultivate Samantabhadra's practices and adorn an ocean of buddha lands exist everywhere throughout the Dharma realm.

Samantabhadra then went on to say that, after that Buddha passed into nirvāṇa, another buddha achieved right enlightenment in that same site of enlightenment there within that very forest, whereupon that prince, Light of Great Power, attained another ten realizations analogous to those he had originally acquired when touched by the light of the previous buddha, this time acquiring yet another ten thousand Dharma gateways. Having attained all these Dharma gateways, that prince uttered verses for his retinue in which he urged them to resolve to attain buddhahood. Due to the power of that buddha, the sound of the prince's verses resounded everywhere, thereby inspiring countless beings to arouse the resolve to attain highest bodhi. That prince then went with his retinue to see that buddha, whereupon that buddha taught a sutra for their sakes that enabled them all to attain ten kinds of spiritual benefits, practices, realizations, and wisdom. This buddha then spoke verses for Light of Power Bodhisattva in which he assured him that he was bound for the realization of buddhahood.

After that buddha entered nirvāṇa, the prince ascended to the position of wheel-turning king. Shortly afterward, yet a third buddha gained enlightenment in that forest in that same site of enlightenment, whereupon this newly crowned wheel-turning king went with his retinue to visit that buddha who taught a sutra for their sakes that led this wheel-turning king to acquire a samādhi that enabled him to know the ocean of meritorious qualities of all bodhisattvas and all beings. That buddha then spoke verses for Light of Great Power Bodhisattva in which he praised him and foretold that everyone in that congregation would be so inspired by this bodhisattva king's vows that they would all enter the vehicle of Samantabhadra, resolve to attain bodhi, and progress toward buddhahood.

Then, later on, yet another buddha attained enlightenment in that very forest. During the era that followed, the bodhisattva prince passed away and was reborn atop Mount Sumeru where he became a great heavenly king known as Banner of Stainless Merit who went with a congregation of devas to see that buddha who spoke a sutra for them that caused them all to acquire a samādhi by which they were all able to penetrate the suchness of all dharmas. Having acquired this benefit, they returned to their original place.

By relating the events in the life of this prince from the ancient past, this chapter serves to assure the reader that the path to buddhahood is inconceivably ancient and bound to continue throughout all eons of the future.

Chapter 7
The Names of the Tathāgata

This next chapter is the first of six chapters in the second assembly that took place in the Hall of Universal Radiance where the Buddha dwelt together with countless bodhisattvas who had but one more birth prior to attaining buddhahood. These bodhisattvas had all come from other worlds to gather around the Buddha after his enlightenment.

At that time, those bodhisattvas all had thoughts in which they wished that the Buddha would teach them the dharmas of buddhahood, the stages on the path to buddhahood, and the many different realizations, qualities, and capacities of a *tathāgata.*

Knowing the thoughts in the minds of all these bodhisattvas, the Buddha then manifested spiritual superknowledges suited to each type of being, whereupon bodhisattvas and their retinues came there from each of the ten directions to pay their respects to the Buddha. After they had all arrived, Mañjuśrī Bodhisattva, chief among all the bodhisattvas who had come there from the east, commenced to speak, informing everyone in that immense congregation of how all things having to do with the buddha are inconceivable, for they are all adapted by the Buddha to suit the various differences in the beings who are the recipients of his teachings. He explained how the Buddha uses many different bodies with many different appearances and characteristics to enable all beings to acquire knowledge and vision. He then proceeded to list the names by which the Buddha is known within this Sahā world, in the worlds of each of the ten directions, starting with a world to the east called "Well Protected" where the Buddha may be known by any of ten names that he lists, beginning with "Vajra," "Sovereign Mastery," and "Wise," and concluding with "Mind's Delight," "Incomparable," and "Beyond Discourse."

Having listed these names by which the Buddha is known in ten of the worlds of the ten directions among the hundred *koṭīs* of lands within this Sahā world, Mañjuśrī proceeds then to list names by which the Buddha is known in the next world to the east of this Sahā world, the next world to the south of this Sahā world, the next world to the west of this Sahā world, and so on, telling of the names by which the Buddha is known in the next world off to each of the ten directions from this Sahā world.

Mañjuśrī concludes by stating that this is also true for all the countless worlds off in each of the ten directions from this Sahā world where, when the Buddha was a bodhisattva, just as he used many different discussions, languages, voices, deeds, karmic effects, situations, skillful means, faculties, beliefs, and stations on the path to become ripened himself, so too did he do so in this very same way in order to enable beings to acquire the knowledge and vision of buddhahood.

Chapter 8
The Four Truths of the Āryas

Chapter Eight begins with Mañjuśrī telling the bodhisattvas that, in this Sahā World, the truth of suffering is synonymous with karmic offense, coercion, and so forth, up to and including the actions of the foolish common person. He tells them that, in this Sahā World, the truth of the accumulation of suffering is synonymous with the fetters, destruction, cravings-based attachment, and so forth, up to and including conceptual proliferation, subsequent actions, or being based on inverted views. He then tells the bodhisattvas that, in this Sahā World, the truth of the cessation of suffering may be synonymous with noncontention, separation from defilement, and so forth, up to and including cessation, comprehending reality, or abiding in the actual nature [of dharmas]. He then says that, in this Sahā World, the path to the cessation of suffering may be synonymous with the One Vehicle, progression toward quiescence, and so forth, up to and including having nothing one pursues, according with the *āryas*, according with the practice of the rishis, or with the ten treasures (which is a reference to faith, moral virtue, a sense of shame, a dread of blame, learning, giving, wisdom, recollection, retention, and eloquence). He then concludes this section in relation to the Sahā World by saying that these are but a few of countless such designations.

Mañjuśrī goes on to list terms synonymous with the four truths in the Secret Training World, in the Most Victorious World, in the Immaculate World, in the Overflowing Abundance World, in the Attraction World, in the Beneficence World, in the Rarity World, in the Joyous Delight World, in the Gate Key World, and in the tenth of these worlds, the Shaking Sound World. He then concludes by saying that, just is this is true that there are so very many different synonymous terms for each of the four truths in all these worlds, so too is this true throughout all the worlds of the ten directions in which there are countless different designations synonymous with the four truths, all of which are adapted to the beings in each of these places, and all of which serve to enable their training.

It is clear here that, although the four truths are fundamentally the same, the buddhas must adapt the terminology with which they teach them to the different mentalities of beings everywhere in all worlds in order for the four truths to become most powerfully effective in facilitating the spiritual liberation of all those different types of beings in each of their different sorts of circumstances.

Chapter 9
The Radiant Enlightenment

Next, the Buddha emitted countless light rays from the bottoms of his two feet which then illuminated this great trichiliocosm, including all of its countless continents, its great seas, its encircling mountains, its countless bodhisattvas taking birth, leaving the home life, realizing right enlightenment, turning the wheel of Dharma, and entering nirvāṇa, its Mount Sumerus, all of its various heavens, and its countless buddhas sitting on lotus flower dais lion thrones.

Then, due to the Buddha's spiritual powers, a great bodhisattva came from each of the ten directions to where the Buddha was, each of them followed by a retinue of countless bodhisattvas. Then, in the presence of all those buddhas, each of those Mañjuśrī Bodhisattvas spoke a series of verses after which those light rays went beyond this world and illuminated ten buddha lands in all the ten directions, illuminating all of their continents all the way up to all of their Ultimate Form Heavens.

Then again, these light rays went farther and illuminated ten worlds to the east after which another ten great bodhisattvas came with their retinues and spoke a series of verses.

Then again, these light rays went farther and illuminated a hundred worlds to the east after which another ten great bodhisattvas came with their retinues and spoke a series of verses.

Then these light rays illuminated a thousand worlds to the east, followed by the arrival of ten more bodhisattvas, one from each of the ten directions. Then these light rays illuminated ten thousand worlds to the east, followed by the arrival of ten more directional bodhisattvas. This occurred again, except with the illumination of a hundred thousand worlds to the east, followed by the arrival of more bodhisattvas, and then again, except with a hundred myriads of worlds to the east, followed by the arrival of more bodhisattvas. And so this happened up until those light rays illuminated ten *koṭīs* of worlds to the east followed by the arrival of bodhisattvas led by another Mañjuśrī Bodhisattva who again spoke more verses in praise of the Buddha and his enlightenment.

Chapter 10
A Bodhisattva Asks For Clarification

For the benefit of all who were listening, Mañjuśrī Bodhisattva then asked Foremost Enlightenment Bodhisattva why, even though the nature of mind is singular, there are still many different distinctions involving going forth to either good or wretched destinies, coming to have complete or deficient faculties, becoming handsome or ugly, and experiencing suffering or happiness, and why does action not know mind, mind not know action, feeling not know retribution, and so forth until we come to cognition not know objects and objects not know conditions. Foremost Enlightenment Bodhisattva explains why these things are so by replying in verses which explain that none of these phenomena or concepts have any inherent existence and hence they are all really only artificial designations which do not reflect ultimate reality.

Mañjuśrī then asked Foremost Wealth Bodhisattva why, if all beings are but non-beings, the Buddha nonetheless adapts to their times, their life spans, their bodies, their actions, their understandings and so forth, manifesting for their sakes to teach and train them. Foremost Wealth replied in verse, explaining that, because of the absence of inherent existence of all these phenomena, all such aspects of existence are like dreams, impermanent, and unreal. Though he does not directly answer why the Buddha adapts to all these phenomena, we can deduce that it is necessary to adapt to the different perceptions of each being in selecting which skillful means are most appropriate to use in training them to follow the path to liberation.

Mañjuśrī then asked Foremost Jewel Bodhisattva why it is that, although beings are alike in having no inherent self or possessions of a self, some suffer and some are happy, some are handsome, some are ugly, some are inwardly good, some are outwardly good, some experience privation, some experience abundance, some undergo retribution in this life, and some undergo retribution in future lives, all of this even though, in the Dharma realm, there is no such thing as either "beauty" or "ugliness." Foremost Jewel responds in verse, explaining that karmic retributions arise even though there is no agent of actions who truly exists. He then offers a series of analogies to explain the nature of karmic actions and their effects, using comparisons to a mirror and images reflected in it, a field and seeds, a conjurer, a marionette, the various kinds of birds and the fact that they all lay eggs, a womb and the physical features of the infant, and the eventual burning up of all worlds.

For the benefit of all who were listening, Mañjuśrī Bodhisattva went on to ask other important Dharma questions of Foremost Qualities Bodhisattva, Foremost Eyes Bodhisattva, Foremost Diligence Bodhisattva, Foremost Dharma Bodhisattva, Foremost Wisdom Bodhisattva, and Foremost Worthy Bodhisattva, each of whom responded to the questions in verse. Then they all asked Mañjuśrī many questions about the Buddha's sphere of action to which he too replied in verse, stating that the Buddha's sphere of action is equal to the realm of empty space, that it could not be described even in countless kalpas, that it is a function of adapting to beings in how he responds with teaching, that his wisdom body is formless and invisible, that it is unimpeded in reaching throughout all three periods of time, that it is impartial, that it adapts to all ways of speaking, that it is unfathomable, that it amounts to the complete knowing of everything, that it is free of discriminations, that it is apart from karma or afflictions, and that it completely comprehends the minds of all beings in but an instant.

Then, throughout the Sahā World, due to the powers of the Buddha, the many sorts of differences in all beings, karmic actions, worlds, bodies, faculties, births, and karmic fruits became clearly revealed to everyone. So, too, they became clearly revealed in all worlds throughout the ten directions.

Chapter 11
Pure Conduct

Foremost Wisdom Bodhisattva opens the chapter by asking Mañjuśrī Bodhisattva ten questions about how a bodhisattva attains physical, verbal, and mental karma that is faultless, harmless, blameless, indestructible, irreversible, unshakable, extraordinarily superior, pure, undefiled, and guided by wisdom, after which he asks about how the bodhisattva attains ten kinds of fulfillment, how he attains ten kinds of wisdom, how he attains ten kinds of power, how he attains ten kinds of skillful means, how he attains skillful cultivation of the seven enlightenment factors and three gates to liberation, how he attains perfect fulfillment of the six perfections and the four immeasurable minds, how he acquires the ten wisdom powers, how he acquires the protection, reverence and offerings of the kings of the eight kinds of spiritual beings, human kings, and the Brahma Heaven kings, how he becomes a refuge, rescuer, and guide for all beings, and how in ten ways he becomes the most superior among all beings.

Mañjuśrī replied by praising Foremost Wisdom Bodhisattva for his questions and for his motivation in asking them, whereupon he stated that, if bodhisattvas use their minds skillfully, they will acquire all meritorious qualities, will become unimpeded in the dharmas of all buddhas, will abide in the path of all buddhas, will accord with beings and never forsake them, will comprehend all things in accordance with the true character of all dharmas, will cut off all evil and fulfill all goodness, will become like Samantabhadra and be foremost in physical appearance, will fulfill all practices and vows, will attain sovereign mastery in all dharmas, and will become a second guide for all beings. He then concluded by saying that the bodhisattva will be able to acquire every kind of supremely marvelous meritorious quality by according with some one hundred and forty reflections in just so very many stanzas, each of which is appropriate to doing just such a number of things that the bodhisattva will find himself doing in the course of his daily life, beginning with: "When the bodhisattva abides in the home life, / he should vow: 'May all beings / realize the home is inherently empty / and avoid being subjected to its pressures.'"

Mañjuśrī then finished the chapter by saying that, if bodhisattvas use their minds in this way, they will attain every kind of supremely meritorious quality and have minds that cannot be shaken by any deva, *māra*, brahman, *gandharva*, *asura*, or any other such being up to and including any *śrāvaka* disciple or *pratyekabuddha*.

So it was that, in response to so many seemingly complex and metaphysically difficult questions, Mañjuśrī responded with these most simple and practical kinds of skillful means.

Chapter 12
Foremost Worthy

Having already spoken of the merit of the pure conduct, Mañjuśrī began this chapter by asking Foremost Worthy Bodhisattva to expound on the meritorious qualities associated with making and cultivating the resolve to attain bodhi, whereupon Foremost Worthy replied with three hundred and seventy-two verses in which he made it clear that the meritorious qualities flowing from this are measureless, how much the more so when the bodhisattva then fully cultivates the grounds and perfections.

Foremost Worthy then observed that, when the bodhisattva arouses the resolve to attain highest bodhi, this is a result of causes and conditions of which the first and foremost is faith in the Buddha, the Dharma, and bodhi. Having generated such faith, he then does not seek worldly aims such as the five objects of desire, kingship, wealth, personal pleasure, or great fame. Rather, he makes this resolve with the aim of extinguishing the suffering of beings and enabling them to attain the highest happiness.

Foremost Worthy then pointed out that it is due to this faith that the bodhisattva is then able to uphold the precepts, cultivate the bases of training, and fulfill all the meritorious qualities. Foremost Worthy then embarked on a long series of some forty-five "if this, then that" verses by which he described how it is that each of the subsequent developments based on faith and cultivation result in the highest levels of accomplishment on the path to buddhahood.

Foremost Worthy then proceeded to describe how the bodhisattva then uses the skillful means of appearing in the forms of all different kinds of beings in order to successfully teach right Dharma to all beings, thus carrying out the Dharma works of all the great bodhisattvas and buddhas, sometimes using song, dance, discussions, and worldly arts and skills to spread the Dharma, sometimes becoming village elders, caravan guides, kings, great officials, or physicians, and sometimes becoming even large trees on a vast plain, medicine, a trove of jewels, sometimes becoming renunciates from other religious traditions, manifesting in all these different ways for the sake of turning beings to the path of right Dharma.

Foremost Worthy next described in some eighty stanzas a supreme "happiness" samādhi developed by the bodhisattva by which he is able to liberate the many kinds of beings, emanating many different kinds of inconceivable radiance that enable all who see these lights to take up the training. He then described this bodhisattva's amazing uses of right concentration by which he may enter concentration in a single pore and emerge in any manner of different phenomena, summarizing this very long section by saying, "This is what is meant by the inconceivable sovereign mastery of samādhi of those of countless meritorious qualities."

Foremost Worthy continued on to the end of the chapter rhapsodizing on the qualities and capacities that ultimately develop from the momentous act of long ago having made the resolve to attain the highest enlightenment, the resolve that finally, after the passage of countless lifetimes of using innumerably many different skillful means to bestow every kind of marvelous benefit on every sort of being then ultimately culminates in the realization of buddhahood. When Foremost Worthy came to the end of his verses, the lands of the ten directions shook and moved in six ways, the light of Māra's palaces became obscured, the wretched destinies came to a standstill, and the buddhas of the ten directions all appeared directly before him, touched the top of his head with their right hands, and said in unison, "It is good indeed, good indeed that you so quickly proclaim this Dharma. We all rejoice in accord with this." It was at this point that the second of this sutra's eight assemblies came to an end.

Chapter 13
Ascent to the Summit of Mount Sumeru

At that time, due to the Buddha's spiritual powers, everyone on all those Jambudvīpa continents saw the Tathāgata seated beneath the bodhi tree where bodhisattvas in all those places were expounding on the Dharma. Everyone thought they were constantly facing the Buddha. Then, without even leaving the bodhi tree, the Buddha ascended Mount Sumeru and headed for the palace of Lord Śakra who just then saw him coming from afar, whereupon he used his own spiritual powers to decorate his palace and prepare a lion throne made entirely of wondrous jewels that everywhere emanated light. He then respectfully welcomed the Buddha and invited him to stay in his palace, whereupon the Buddha accepted his invitation. As this occurred there in Lord Śakra's Palace in this world, this same scene unfolded in the very same way in all those other worlds throughout the ten directions. Śakra then caused the welcoming music to come to a natural pause, and, recalling the buddhas of the past, he spoke verses recounting the visits to his palace in the distant past by Kāśyapa Buddha, Kanakamuni Buddha, Krakucchanda Buddha, Viśvabhū Buddha, Śikhin Buddha, Vipaśyin Buddha, Puṣya Buddha Tiṣya Buddha, Padma Buddha, and Burning Lamp Buddha.

Just as at this time this Lord Śakra in this Trāyastriṃśa Heaven praised those ten buddhas, so too did all the other Śakras do so in the very same way in all the Trāyastriṃśa heavens throughout all the other worlds of the ten directions. When the Buddha entered that Marvelous Excellence Palace and took his seat on the lion throne in the lotus posture, that palace suddenly expanded to become as vast as that entire celestial congregation. As it did so in this world, so too did this occur in the very same way in all those other palaces in all the worlds of the ten directions.

Chapter 14

The Praise Verses on the Summit of Mount Sumeru

At that time, due to the Buddha's spiritual powers, great bodhisattvas came from distant worlds off in each of the ten directions. Each of them was attended by a retinue of countless bodhisattvas. Their names were Dharma Wisdom Bodhisattva, Comprehensive Wisdom Bodhisattva, Supreme Wisdom Bodhisattva, Meritorious Qualities Wisdom Bodhisattva, Vigorous Wisdom Bodhisattva, Fine Wisdom Bodhisattva, Knowing Wisdom Bodhisattva, Genuine Wisdom Bodhisattva, Unsurpassable Wisdom Bodhisattva, and Solid Wisdom Bodhisattva. They each bowed down in reverence to the Buddha and then each of them conjured a lion throne off in the direction from which they came, whereupon they each sat down there in the lotus posture. As this occurred in this way in this world, so too did this very same thing occur in the very same way in all the worlds of the ten directions.

The Buddha then emanated countless light rays from the toes of his two feet that everywhere illuminated the summits of all the Mount Sumerus in the worlds of the ten directions and illuminated the buddhas in the palaces of all those Indras.

At that time, both in this world and in a mirror-like fashion in all those other worlds, assisted by the Buddha's spiritual powers, each of those ten bodhisattvas took turns in speaking a series of ten verses praising the Tathāgata.

Chapter 15
The Ten Abodes

At that time, assisted by the Buddha's powers, Dharma Wisdom Bodhisattva entered "the bodhisattva's countless expedients samādhi," whereupon, by the power of that samādhi, countless buddhas, all named "Dharma Wisdom," came from far off worlds of the ten directions and spoke to Dharma Wisdom Bodhisattva, praising him for being able to enter this samādhi and informing him that the reason this occurred is so that he could now bring about the arising of the ten abodes by proceeding now to expound on those dharmas. Then, as a function of the power of this samādhi, they joined in bestowing ten kinds of knowledge on Dharma Wisdom Bodhisattva, after which they each extended their right hand and touched the top of his head, after which he arose from meditative absorption, addressed the congregation of bodhisattvas, and began to expound on the ten bodhisattva abodes, beginning by listing them as: the abode of initial generation of the resolve; the abode of preparation of the ground; the abode of cultivation of the practices; the abode of acquiring noble birth; the abode of complete fulfillment of skillful means; the abode of right mindedness; the abode of irreversibility; the abode of the pure youth; the abode of the prince; and the abode of the crown-anointing consecration.

Then, one by one, Dharma Wisdom Bodhisattva proceeded to explain these ten bodhisattva abodes, listing for each of them ten dharmas in which the bodhisattva dwelling there should encourage training while also explaining which bodhisattva purposes are served by his proceeding to encourage these different sets of ten trainings for each of the ten abodes.

After Dharma wisdom had finished expounding on all ten of these bodhisattva abodes, countless worlds in each of the ten directions moved and shook in six ways, and their rained down marvelous heavenly flowers, heavenly incenses, heavenly flower chaplets, heavenly perfumes, celestial robes, and celestial adornments accompanied by clouds of jewels, heavenly music, and the emanation of light.

Just as this proclamation of the ten abodes occurred there in the palace of Indra at the top of Mount Sumeru in this world, so too did this also occur in all worlds throughout the ten directions.

Then, by the spiritual powers of the Buddha, countless bodhisattvas came from each of the ten directions and praised Dharma Wisdom Bodhisattva, telling him that they too were all named "Dharma Wisdom" and that they had come there to bear witness to his teaching of the ten abodes.

Dharma Wisdom Bodhisattva then concluded the chapter with some one hundred reiterative stanzas on the bodhisattva's ten abodes.

Chapter 16
The Brahman Conduct

At that time, Right Mindfulness Devaputra asked Dharma Wisdom Bodhisattva how it is that monastic bodhisattvas attain purity in brahman conduct and proceed from the position of a bodhisattva to the attainment of highest enlightenment. (Here, "brahman conduct" or "*brahmacarya*" refers to pure spiritual practice that is inclusive of celibacy.) Dharma Wisdom replied by telling him that the bodhisattva should meditate on ten objects of contemplation: the body, physical actions, the mouth, verbal actions, the mind, mental actions, the Buddha, the Dharma, the Sangha, and the moral precepts, asking himself in each case whether each of these are synonymous with brahman conduct. Once the bodhisattva realizes that none of them are synonymous with brahman conduct, he becomes free of any seizing on any of these ten objects of contemplation and carries on these contemplations because: the dharma of the brahman conduct is inapprehensible; the dharmas of the three times are all empty and quiescent; the mind has nothing to which it attaches; the mind has no obstacles; one's practice is non-dual; one acquires sovereign mastery of skillful means; one accepts the dharma of signlessness; one contemplates the dharma of signlessness; one realizes the equality of all Buddha dharmas; and one is fulfilling all dharmas of the Buddha.

Dharma Wisdom Bodhisattva said that this is what is synonymous with the brahman conduct, after which he said that the bodhisattva should then cultivate ten dharmas, the ten powers of the Buddha, the contemplation of which will lead the bodhisattva to understand that each of these powers contains countless meanings into which the bodhisattva should inquire. He says that, in doing so, the bodhisattva should arouse great kindness and compassion to contemplate beings and never abandon them. He then says that the bodhisattva "should reflect on all dharmas incessantly, should engage in unexcelled karmic deeds but not seek any karmic reward, and should completely realize that objective spheres are like conjurations, like dreams, like reflections, like echoes, and also like spiritual transformations." He further says that this will lead to his no longer entertaining dualistic understandings of any dharma and to all the dharmas of buddhahood manifesting directly before him. He then says in essence that the bodhisattva's arousing of the initial resolve guarantees his eventual realization of highest enlightenment. He concludes the chapter by saying of such bodhisattvas that, "They will realize that all dharmas are identical to the very nature of the mind, they will perfect the wisdom body, and their own awakening will not arise in dependence on others."

Chapter 17
The Merit of the Initial Resolve

The chapter begins with Śakra Devānām Indra asking Dharma Wisdom Bodhisattva how much merit is acquired by the bodhisattva when he first makes the resolve to attain bodhi, after which Dharma Wisdom replies that, although this matter is extremely profound and difficult to describe, with the assistance of the Buddha, he will nonetheless explain it. He then says, "Suppose there was someone who made offerings of all kinds of pleasing things to all beings in an *asaṃkhyeya* of worlds to the east for an entire kalpa and afterward instructed and enabled them to purely observe the five moral precepts, whereupon he did this in the same way in the south, west, north, the four midpoints, the zenith, and the nadir. Son of the Buddha, what do you think? Would this person's merit be abundant, or not?" After acknowledging Śakra's assessment that such merit would be so great that only a buddha could know it, he said that, compared to the merit of the bodhisattva's initial resolve, "it would not amount to a hundredth part, would not amount to a thousandth part, would not amount to a hundred-thousandth part. In this same way, it would not be equal to even one part in a *koṭī* of parts, one part in a hundred *koṭīs* of parts, one part in a thousand *koṭīs* of parts, one part in a hundred thousand *koṭīs* of parts, one part in a *nayuta* of *koṭīs* of parts, one part in a hundred *nayutas* of *koṭīs* of parts, one part in a thousand *nayutas* of *koṭīs* of parts, one part in a hundred thousand *nayutas* of *koṭīs* of parts, one part in the largest numerable number of parts, one part in a *kalā* of parts, one part in the largest calculable number of parts, one part in the highest number of parts demonstrable by analogy, and it would not amount to even a single part in an *upaniṣad* of parts."

Dharma Wisdom then presented more than a dozen more analogies, each of which supposed deeds of astronomically greater merit than the previous one, in each case noting that such merit still could not even approach the merit of the bodhisattva's initial resolve. In each instance he listed yet more reasons why the bodhisattva's merit is so much greater than even the most spectacularly meritorious deeds he has just described.

When he had finished presenting all these analogies and had reiterated why this bodhisattva's merit is so great, by the power of the Buddha, the worlds of the ten directions moved and shook in six ways, whereupon, accompanied by heavenly light and music celestial flowers, chaplets, robes, jewels, and adornments rained down, after which countless buddhas, all named "Dharma Wisdom" came from the ten directions and praised Dharma Wisdom Bodhisattva.

Those buddhas then told him that he had proclaimed this Dharma just as all buddhas do, and also said to him, "When you proclaimed this Dharma, bodhisattvas as numerous as the atoms in a myriad buddha *kṣetras* all resolved to attain bodhi. We all now bestow a prediction on them that in a future age, beyond a thousand ineffable numbers of boundless kalpas, they will all succeed in attaining buddhahood." They then informed him that, just as he had just now proclaimed this teaching in this Sahā World, so too was this Dharma simultaneously taught in all worlds of the ten directions by countless other bodhisattvas who were all also named "Dharma Wisdom," each of whom proclaimed this Dharma teaching:

Due to the Buddha's spiritual powers;
Due to the power of the Bhagavat's original vows;
Due to a wish to reveal the Dharma of the Buddha;
To use the light of wisdom to produce universal illumination;
Due to a wish to explain the genuine meaning;
To enable beings to realize the nature of dharmas;
To enable the congregations to be filled with joyous delight;
Due to a wish to reveal the Buddha Dharma's causality;
To realize the equality of all buddhas; and
To comprehend the non-duality of the Dharma realm.

Dharma Wisdom Bodhisattva then surveyed all the congregations in the ten directions and, aided by the Buddha's powers, ended the chapter by speaking a series of one hundred and twenty-one reiterative verses describing, praising, and celebrating the merit of the bodhisattva when he makes his initial resolve to ultimately reach the utmost, right, and perfect enlightenment of a buddha.

Chapter 18
Clarifying the Dharma

The chapter begins with Vigorous Wisdom Bodhisattva asking Dharma Wisdom Bodhisattva how these bodhisattvas who have aroused the initial resolve to attain bodhi should cultivate the Buddha's teachings so that: they cause all *tathāgatas* to be delighted; they enter the stations in which bodhisattvas dwell; they accomplish the purification of all the great practices; they cause all the great vows to be fulfilled; they acquire the vast treasury of all bodhisattvas; they adapt to the beings they should teach and always speak Dharma for them; they never abandon the *pāramitā* practices; they enable the liberation of all beings of whom they are mindful; they continue the lineage of the Three Jewels and ensure that it is never cut off; and they ensure that their skillful means and roots of goodness are not implemented in vain. He then immediately asked a list of twenty more questions beginning with, "By using which skillful means will those bodhisattvas be able to cause this Dharma to become completely fulfilled?" and ending with, "How can they acquire the power of roots of goodness, increase the dharmas of pristine purity, expound on the Tathāgata's extremely profound Dharma treasury, and adopt and retain right Dharma as their adornment?" Then, wishing to restate his meaning, he summed up all these questions with ten complex questions embedded in eleven stanzas.

Dharma Wisdom Bodhisattva began his reply to all these questions by praising Vigorous Wisdom's abilities to ask these questions as equivalent even to that of the Buddha himself. He then proceeded to answer, beginning with the cautionary note that the bodhisattva who has aroused the bodhi resolve must diligently guard his resolve and refrain from becoming negligent, after which he listed seven ways in which the bodhisattva qualifies as avoiding negligence, beginning with guarding and upholding the moral precepts and ending with cultivating every kind of goodness and constantly contemplating the power of perseverance.

Dharma Wisdom then listed ten kinds of purity acquired through avoiding negligence in these ways, beginning with practicing in accordance with his own words and perfecting mindfulness and wisdom and concluding with feeling deep reverential esteem for precept-transmitting teachers, bodhisattvas, good spiritual guides, and masters of the Dharma. He next listed ten ways in which this bodhisattva is then able to delight all buddhas and then listed ten additional dharmas by which he is able to delight all buddhas, after which he spoke of ten dharmas that enable bodhisattvas to swiftly enter the [bodhisattva] grounds, beginning with the skillful and perfect fulfillment of the two practices of merit and wisdom and concluding with having roots of goodness and skillful means that are of the same essential nature as those of all buddhas of the three periods of time. Dharma Wisdom then recommended that, once bodhisattvas first dwell on the grounds, they should skillfully engage in a series of individually suited contemplations that will lead them to understand that all dharmas are just their own mind, thereby freeing them from any attachment to them and ensuring that they will become well established in the bodhisattva grounds.

Dharma Wisdom next listed ten types of dharmas that enable whatever the bodhisattvas practice to be pure, beginning with relinquishing all possessions to fulfill beings' wishes and ending with realizing that all beings are of the same single essential nature as all *tathāgatas*. This leads the bodhisattva to acquire ten especially supreme dharmas, beginning with being regarded with protective mindfulness by all buddhas of other regions and ending with becoming able to understand the power of the Tathāgata's skillful means.

Dharma Wisdom then listed the bodhisattva's ten types of pure vows, beginning with vowing to be tireless in ripening beings and ending with vowing to fulfill the conduct of Samantabhadra and purify the gateways to the knowledge of all modes. He next listed ten kinds of dharmas by which the bodhisattva enables all his great vows to become completely fulfilled, beginning with having a tireless mind, fulfilling the great adornments, and bearing in mind the vow power of all bodhisattvas and ending with always diligently preserving and protecting the unsurpassed gateways to the Dharma.

Dharma wisdom next listed ten kinds of inexhaustible treasuries immediately acquired by the bodhisattva who fulfills such vows, beginning with the inexhaustible treasury of everywhere seeing all buddhas and ending with the inexhaustible treasury of entering boundlessly many worlds. He then noted that, once the bodhisattva has acquired these ten kinds of treasuries, he then teaches the Dharma for all beings in accordance with what is fitting for each of them, doing so in ten ways, beginning with teaching the unloveliness contemplation for those beset by much desire and teaching great kindness for those beset by much hatred and ending with providing extensive Dharma teachings to ensure the complete development of those bodhisattvas who delight in quiescence. He then listed ten factors that mark the bodhisattva's teaching right Dharma to beings and then explains how the bodhisattva approaches purification of the ten perfections, how the bodhisattva uses wisdom to tailor his teachings to beings' individually dominant afflictions, how the bodhisattva's teachings prevent the lineage of the Three Jewels from ever being cut off, and how this leads to his fulfillment of ten kinds of adornments, beginning with the adornments of body, mouth, and mind and ending with the adornments of right teaching, the ground of nirvāṇa, and skillful speech that teaches the Dharma in a manner adapted to the individual capacities of the beings receiving his Dharma teaching. He then noted that, by perfecting adornments such as these, the bodhisattva never does anything in vain and dedicates everything to the realization of all-knowledge.

After Dharma Wisdom finished his answers to the questions asked him by Vigorous Wisdom bodhisattva at the beginning of the chapter, he finishing the chapter with a set of ten reiterative verses that end as follows:

> Cultivating in this manner, he acquires the wisdom of the Buddha,
> deeply enters the right Dharma treasury of the Tathāgata,
> and becomes a great Dharma master, expounding on sublime Dharma,
> like a rain of the elixir of immortality bestowing its moisture on all.
>
> His kindness, compassion, and deep sympathy extend to everyone.
> Of beings' thoughts and actions, there are none he does not know.
> He provides explanations for them, suited to their dispositions,
> of all the countlessly and boundlessly many dharmas of the Buddha.
>
> Going and stopping, he is as calm and unhurried as the elephant king
> while also being as courageous and fearless as a lion.
> He is as unshakeable as a mountain, possesses wisdom like an ocean,
> and is also like the great rains in dispelling the heat of the multitude.

Chapter 19

Ascent to the Suyāma Heaven Palace

In this chapter which begins the fourth of the Dharma assemblies, even without leaving the bodhi tree or the summit of Mount Sumeru, the Tathāgata next traveled toward the Hall of Jewel Adornments of the Suyāma Heaven Palace in which, having seen that the Buddha was coming, the Suyāma Heaven king used his spiritual powers to create a marvelously adorned lotus flower dais lion throne for the Buddha.

When the Buddha arrived, the king reverently welcomed him and requested him to stay, after which he spoke ten verses that praised and recalled ten buddhas of the past he had previously welcomed to this very palace.

Just as this scene was unfolding in the Suyāma Heaven king's palace in this world, so too was this same scene manifesting throughout the worlds of the ten directions.

When the Buddha entered this Hall of Jewel Adornments and sat down in the lotus posture on that lotus flower dais lion throne, that hall suddenly and miraculously expanded to become so vast that it was then able to contain that entire celestial congregation. And just as this occurred here in this Hall of Jewel Adornments, so too did this also occur in in all those other places throughout the ten directions.

Chapter 20

Praise Verses in the Suyāma Heaven Palace

Next, due to the power of the Buddha, a great bodhisattva came from distant worlds in each of the ten directions, each followed by a retinue of countless other bodhisattvas. After they had all arrived and bowed down in reverence to the Buddha, each of those great bodhisattvas transformationally created lotus dais lion thrones off in each of the ten directions where they sat down in the lotus posture. Just as this occurred here in this world, so too did this also occur in all those other worlds where the names of their bodhisattvas, their worlds, and their *tathāgatas* were all the same.

Then, the Bhagavat emanated from the top of his two feet a hundred thousand *koṭīs* of colored light rays that, in all those worlds of the ten directions, everywhere illuminated the buddhas and their assemblies in each of the Suyāma Heaven Palaces, causing them all to be fully revealed.

After the Buddha had emanated these light rays illuminating the worlds of the ten directions, assisted by the power of the Buddha, each of those ten great bodhisattvas from each of the ten directions took turns in speaking ten stanzas of verse describing the miraculous nature of this marvelously interpenetrating mirror-like scene transpiring in all the Suyāma Heaven palaces throughout the ten directions, commenting as well on the deeply abstruse and inconceivable nature of the Dharma, of metaphysical emptiness, and the miraculous way in which all buddhas manifest in the world to carry on the liberation of beings.

Chapter 21
The Ten Practices

Then, assisted by the power of the Buddha, Forest of Meritorious Qualities Bodhisattva entered "the bodhisattva's skillful reflection samādhi," whereupon countless buddhas from each of the ten directions, all of them named "Forest of Meritorious Qualities," manifested before him, joined in praising him for entering this samādhi, and requested him to expound on the ten practices. Each of those buddhas then extended his right hand and touched the crown of Forest of Meritorious Qualities Bodhisattva, whereupon he arose from samādhi, and began to speak of the ten practices, namely: joyful practice; beneficial practice; non-opposing practice; indomitable practice; unconfused practice; well-manifested practice; unattached practice; difficult-to-attain practice; the practice of good dharmas; and genuine practice.

Having listed the ten practices, Forest of Meritorious Qualities Bodhisattva then began to speak in detail on each of the ten practices, beginning with the first practice, "joyful practice," by which the bodhisattva acts with universal kindness and generosity toward beings, thus enabling them all to be filled with joy by his selfless beneficence in which he has no perception of a self, of a being, of a person, or of any inherently existent dharmas at all.

This bodhisattva next expounded on the second practice, "beneficial practice," which, for him, is characterized by careful observance of the moral precepts and a complete absence of attachment to the sense objects, to power or influence, to wealth, to fine appearance, or kingship. He does not raise even a single thought of desire and would rather give up his own life than ever produce afflictions toward any being due to attachment to any of the objects of desire. His sole aim with regard to others is to establish all beings in moral virtue and the resolve to gain highest enlightenment, thereby affording them access to the highest of all benefits any being could ever hope to enjoy.

Forest of Meritorious Qualities Bodhisattva then taught the third practice, "non-opposing practice," in which the bodhisattva always cultivates the dharma of patience by which he is humbly deferential and reverentially respectful, by which he refrains from harming anyone or encouraging anyone else to do so, refrains from taking what is not given or encouraging anyone else to do so, refrains from becoming attached to either self or others, and refrains from seeking fame or offerings, all the while reflecting that he should always teach Dharma for beings and enable them to abandon all evil and become established in patience and gentleness.

He next taught the fourth practice, "indomitable practice," by which the bodhisattva is so dedicated to the practice of vigor in the bodhisattva path that he is not the least bit discouraged at the prospect of working for the liberation and nirvāṇa of all beings before being able to attain the highest enlightenment himself.

Forest of Meritorious Qualities Bodhisattva then spoke about the fifth practice, "unconfused practice," in which the bodhisattva perfects right mindfulness in which his mind is not scattered and confused, and in which it remains steadfastly unmoving, is the most supremely pure, is measurelessly vast, and remains free of confusion or delusion even as he dies here and is reborn there, continuing to cultivate the bodhisattva practices even throughout an ineffable number of kalpas without his mind ever again becoming confused and without ever forgetting any of the Dharma that he has learned across the course of countless lifetimes of cultivating the bodhisattva path.

He next expounded on the sixth practice, "well manifested practice," in which the bodhisattva maintains purity of physical, verbal, and mental actions, abides in the inapprehensibility of all dharmas, always realizes the emptiness of inherent existence of all phenomena, "everywhere enters the three periods of time, never abandons the great resolve to attain bodhi, never retreats from his resolve to teach beings, ever increases his mind of great kindness and compassion, and serves as a refuge for all beings."

Forest of Meritorious Qualities Bodhisattva next taught the seventh practice, "unattached practice," in which he not only has no attachment to objects of the senses and such, but also has no attachment even to any being, any rebirth destinies, any samādhis, or any practices of the buddhas, for he contemplates the entire Dharma realm as like a magical conjuration, all buddhas as like shadows, all bodhisattva practices as like a dream, and the dharmas spoken by the Buddha as like echoes.

He next explained the eighth practice, the "difficult-to-attain practice," the ninth practice, "practice of good dharmas," and the tenth practice, "genuine practice," by which he is able to act in accordance with his speech, is able to speak in accordance with his actions, and is able to become perfectly developed in his wisdom.

When Forest of Meritorious Qualities Bodhisattva had finished expounding on these ten practices, due to the Buddha's spiritual powers, the worlds of the ten directions moved and shook in six ways and it rained down marvelous heavenly flowers, celestial perfumes and incense, heavenly flower garlands, heavenly jewels, and heavenly adornments as celestial music resounded and celestial radiance shone everywhere. Bodhisattvas arrived and praised him and he then finished the chapter with a verse of one hundred and one stanzas with which he summed up his teaching.

Chapter 22
The Ten Inexhaustible Treasuries

Forest of Meritorious Qualities again addressed that immense congregation of bodhisattvas, telling them that the bodhisattva-*mahāsattva* has ten kinds of treasuries of which all buddhas of the past, future, and present have spoken, will speak, and do now speak, namely the treasuries of: faith; moral precepts; a sense of shame; a dread of blame; learning; giving; wisdom; recollection; retention; and eloquence. After listing them, he proceeded to discuss the treasury of faith, listing ten kinds of faith by which his mind is never intimidated by the inconceivability of the Dharma, the buddhas, the realms of beings, the Dharma realm, empty space, nirvāṇa, the past, the future, the present, or entry into all kalpas.

He next explained the second inexhaustible treasury, the treasury of moral precepts, specifically listing and explaining ten kinds of precepts, namely the moral precepts of: universal benefit; not adopting wrong prohibitions; not dwelling; not having regrets; noncontentiousness; nonharming; nondefilement; noncovetousness; faultlessness; and nontransgression.

Forest of Meritorious Qualities next explained the treasury of a sense of shame and how it leads the bodhisattva to resolve to cut off shameless actions, pursue highest enlightenment, and teach true Dharma to beings.

He next spoke of the bodhisattva's treasury of a dread of blame and how it motivates the bodhisattva to resolve to refrain from ever again being affected by any of the afflictions and to again resolve to attain highest enlightenment and teach true Dharma to beings.

Forest of Meritorious Qualities next taught the fifth of these inexhaustible treasuries, the treasury of learning and the ten categories of dharmas to which it primarily refers beginning with dharmas of causality and concluding with conditioned dharmas, unconditioned dharmas, morally determinate dharmas, and indeterminate dharmas, each of which he then proceeds to explain.

He next taught the bodhisattva's inexhaustible treasury of giving, specifically mentioning ten kinds of giving, namely: shared giving, exhaustive giving, inward giving, outward giving, inward and outward giving, all-inclusive giving, past giving, future giving, present giving, and ultimate giving, each of which he then individually explained in great detail.

The next treasury he explained is the inexhaustible treasury of wisdom and the various categories of knowledge to which it refers by which the bodhisattva knows in accordance with reality and in relation to the four truths, the aggregates, *śrāvaka* disciples, *pratyekabuddhas*, bodhisattvas, and other dharmas.

Forest of Meritorious Qualities next explained the eighth of the inexhaustible treasuries, the inexhaustible treasury of recollection by which the bodhisattva recalls even countless hundred of thousands of past lives, an inconceivable number of kalpas, the names of countless buddhas, the ten kinds of canonical text of all those buddhas, those buddhas' congregations, and other such phenomena associated with all those buddhas. He also spoke of ten kinds of recollection and the benefits the bodhisattva receives from such recollection.

He then spoke of the ninth of the inexhaustible treasuries, the treasury of retention by which the bodhisattva retains the sutras spoken by all buddhas, including the meanings and principles of their texts and sentences, remembering all of this for even up to an ineffable-ineffable number of lifetimes. He also remembers the names of even up to an ineffable-ineffable number of buddhas' names, buddhas' bestowals of predictions, buddhas' sutras, and buddhas' discourses on an ineffable number of dharmas, maintaining this capacity of retention with measureless power and capacity generally only otherwise within the sphere of cognition of a buddha.

Forest of Meritorious Qualities Bodhisattva next spoke of the tenth and final bodhisattva's inexhaustible treasury, the inexhaustible treasury of eloquence by which the bodhisattva possessed of deep wisdom who completely knows the true character of phenomena extensively expounds on all dharmas for the sake of beings, never contradicting the scriptures as he does so. He may expound on but a single dharma or countless kinds of dharmas, may explain a single buddha's name or countless buddhas' names, may discourse on a single world, a single buddha's bestowal of predictions, a single sutra, or on countless numbers of all of these, doing so for a single day or for countless kalpas, in the latter case even then not necessarily reaching the end of the meanings and principles associated with any one of these topics to which he devotes his inexhaustible eloquence. His inexhaustible eloquence arises from his having completely perfected these ten inexhaustible treasuries which lead him then to acquire "the *dhāraṇī* gateway that subsumes all dharmas" with which, drawing on the light of Dharma, he extensively expounds on the Dharma for the sake of beings, adapting in every case to each being's particular faculty and nature, thus enabling each being to extinguish the defilement created by the afflictions that entangle him. Thus this bodhisattva can enable all beings to carry forth the lineage of the Buddha without interruption and with a continuously pure mind as he also uses the light of Dharma to expound on the Dharma endlessly and tirelessly.

These are the ten kinds of inexhaustible dharmas by which they are able to cause everything they do in the world to become an ultimate and inexhaustible great treasury.

Chapter 23
The Ascent to the Tuṣita Heaven Palace

At that time, due to the Buddha's spiritual powers, in all those worlds throughout the ten directions, everyone saw the Tathāgata seated beneath the tree where there were bodhisattvas who, assisted by the Buddha's spiritual powers, expounded on the Dharma. There was no one there who did not believe himself to be constantly in the direct presence of the Buddha.

At that time, again due to his spiritual powers, without leaving the bodhi tree, the summit of Mount Sumeru, or the Suyāma Heaven palace, the Bhagavat then went to the Tuṣita Heaven's Palace of Marvelous Jewel Adornments.

Seeing the Buddha coming from afar, the Tuṣita Heaven king prepared for him an inconceivably marvelous adorned and bejeweled throne that seemed to constitute a brilliantly radiant world of its own attended by every level of spiritual and celestial being who came together there with countless bodhisattvas to pay reverence to the Buddha.

Just as in this world the Tuṣita Heaven King offered up for the Tathāgata this high throne he had arranged, so too did all the Tuṣita Heaven kings in all worlds also arrange thrones such as these with adornments such as these, ceremonial propriety such as this, faithful devotion such as this, purity of mind such as this, delight such as this, joyfulness such as this, reverential esteem such as this, thoughts of appreciation of its rarity such as these, joyous exultation such as this, and thirst-like anticipation such as this. In each case, all of these circumstances were the same.

At that time, after the Tuṣita Heaven king had arranged this throne for the Tathāgata, his thoughts became imbued with deep reverential esteem, whereupon, together with ten myriads of *koṭīs* of *asaṃkhyeyas* of Tuṣita Heaven devas' sons, and all the other types of heavenly beings and bodhisattvas, he respectfully welcomed the Tathāgata there, and, with purified minds, they then rained down *asaṃkhyeyas* of clouds of colored flowers, colored incense clouds, colored garland clouds, pure sandalwood clouds, clouds of all different kinds of canopies, clouds of marvelously fine heavenly robes, and many other kinds of clouds including clouds of many kinds of marvelous jewels.

The anonymous narrator of the chapter then embarks on a very long eulogizing description of the qualities, capacities, and actions of the Tathāgata who carries forth the inconceivably vast and wondrous works of the buddhas devoted to the spiritual liberation of beings, adapting to all their different karmic retributions, mental dispositions, and faculties as he manifests in all worlds throughout all three periods of time, teaching the Dharma with infinite skillful means by which all living beings are led along on the path from immersion in cyclic existence to the highest enlightenment of all buddhas.

At that time, those in that great congregation saw the body of the Tathāgata emanating from every one of its pores hundreds of thousands of *koṭīs* of *nayutas* of *asaṃkhyeyas* of light rays that caused all the beings they illuminated to contemplate, to be filled with joyous delight, to increase their deep faith, to develop purified aspirations, to experience clarity and coolness in all their faculties, and to develop deep reverential esteem.

Because of the Buddha's spiritual powers, there emerged an immense and marvelous voice. That voice then proclaimed a hundred thousand *koṭīs* of *nayutas* of inconceivable praise verses that were transcendently superior to any expressed in worldly language and that were produced through world-transcending roots of goodness.

The Tuṣita Heaven king and his retinue of countless devas' sons then welcomed the Buddha, inviting him to reside in the Tuṣita Heaven palace. The Bhagavat accepted their invitation. And just as this was so in this world, so too did this also occur in all worlds throughout the ten directions. Then, assisted by the awesome power of the Buddha, the Tuṣita Heaven King uttered a verse in ten stanzas in which he recalled his having previously welcomed ten buddhas of the past to that very palace. Just as, assisted by the Buddha's spiritual powers, this world's Tuṣita Heaven king used verses to praise buddhas of the past, so too did the Tuṣita Heaven kings in all the worlds of the ten directions also then praise the meritorious qualities of the buddhas in this same way.

The Bhagavat then sat in the lotus posture on the *maṇi* jewel dais lion throne in the Palace of Every Jewel and, through the marvelous and masterful functions of the pure Dharma body, he dwelt in the same realm with all buddhas of the three periods of time. Abiding in all-knowledge, together with all buddhas, he entered the one nature. With the complete clarity of the buddha eye, he was unimpeded in his perception of all dharmas. Possessed of great awesome powers, he roamed everywhere throughout the Dharma realm, never resting. Equipped with the great spiritual superknowledges, wherever there were beings amenable to being taught, he was able to go everywhere to all of those places. Adorned with the unimpeded adornments of all buddhas and knowing well the appropriate time, he taught the Dharma for the multitudes.

Multitudes of bodhisattvas then arrived from the many different countries of other regions, assembled there, and presented marvelously fine offerings to the Buddha. Just as this happened here, so too was this also so in all Tuṣita Heavens throughout the ten directions.

Chapter 24
The Tuṣita Heaven Palace Praise Verses

At that time, because of the Buddha's spiritual powers, from each of the ten directions, beyond a number of lands as numerous as the atoms in a myriad buddha *kṣetras*, great bodhisattvas came to pay their respects to the Buddha, each of whom was attended by bodhisattvas as numerous as the atoms in a myriad buddha *kṣetras*. Their names were Vajra Banner Bodhisattva, Solid Banner Bodhisattva, Courage Banner Bodhisattva, Radiance Banner Bodhisattva, Wisdom Banner Bodhisattva, Jeweled Banner Bodhisattva, Vigor Banner Bodhisattva, Stainlessness Banner Bodhisattva, Constellation Banner Bodhisattva, and Dharma Banner Bodhisattva.

After those bodhisattvas had arrived in the presence of the Buddha, they bowed down in reverence at the feet of the Buddha. With the assistance of the Buddha's spiritual powers, they each conjured a marvelous jeweled dais lion throne covered by a jeweled net that encircled and completely filled the area. Then, off in each of the directions from which they came, each of those bodhisattvas' congregations sat down on their seats in the lotus posture.

Then their bodies all emanated a hundred thousand *koṭīs* of *nayutas* of *asaṃkhyeyas* of pure light rays. These rays of light all arose from these bodhisattvas' jewel of the pure mind and from their great vows by which they abandoned all faults. They revealed the pure dharmas of all buddhas' sovereign masteries. Through the power of their impartial vows, those bodhisattvas were everywhere able to rescue and protect all beings. They were those whom everyone in the world delighted in seeing and those who saw them did not do so in vain, for all who saw them acquired the training and discipline. Those multitudes of bodhisattvas had already perfected countless meritorious qualities, for example: they roam, unimpeded, to the lands of all buddhas; they see the non-dependent pure Dharma body; they use the wisdom body to manifest countless bodies that go throughout the ten directions, serving the buddhas; they enter all buddhas' measureless, boundless, and inconceivable dharmas of sovereign mastery; they dwell in the countless gateways of all-knowledge using the light of wisdom to thoroughly understand all dharmas; they attain fearlessness with respect to all dharmas by which, whatever they expound upon, they may do so with inexhaustible eloquence to the very end of future time; with great wisdom, they open the gateway to the complete-retention [*dhāraṇīs*]; with the purified wisdom eye, they enter the deep Dharma realm; their wisdom's sphere of cognition is boundless; and their ultimate purity is space-like.

Just as the multitudes of bodhisattvas gathered together there in this world's Tuṣita Heaven palace, so too did bodhisattvas of these very same names gather together in all the other Tuṣita Heaven Palaces throughout the ten directions in which the names of the countries from which they came and the buddhas with which they were associated were all identical and no different.

At that time, the Bhagavat emanated from his two kneecaps hundreds of thousands of *koṭīs* of *nayutas* of light rays that everywhere illuminated all worlds throughout the Dharma realm and the realm of empty space. All of those other bodhisattvas were able to see the appearance of this buddha's spiritual transformations and all of these bodhisattvas were able to see the appearance of all those other *tathāgatas'* spiritual transformations.

In the past, all of these bodhisattvas had planted roots of goodness and cultivated the bodhisattva practices together with Vairocana Tathāgata. They had all already awakened to and entered all buddhas' sovereign masteries and extremely deep liberations, had already acquired the body of the undifferentiated Dharma realm, had entered all lands and yet had no place where they dwelt, had already seen countless buddhas whom they had visited and served, and had in a single mind-moment traveled freely and unimpededly throughout the Dharma realm. Their minds were pure, like priceless jewels. They were aided by the constant protective mindfulness of measurelessly and countlessly many buddhas.

Then, assisted by the Buddha's spiritual powers, Vajra Banner Bodhisattva surveyed the ten directions and then uttered ten stanzas of verse in praise of the Buddha. Then, in turn, so too did those other nine great bodhisattvas do the same, finishing with the verses spoken by Dharma Banner Bodhisattva in praise of the Tathāgata and his Dharma, concluding with these three stanzas:

Even if one were to exhaust the bounds of future time,
roaming everywhere to all the buddha *kṣetras,*
so long as one does not seek this wondrous Dharma,
one would still never realize bodhi.

From the beginningless past on forward to the present,
beings have long drifted along and turned about in *saṃsāra,*
and yet still have not fully understood the genuine Dharma.
It is because of this that the buddhas have appeared in the world.

All of these dharmas are indestructible,
nor does there exist anyone capable of destroying them.
The great light of those with the sovereign masteries
is everywhere revealed throughout the world.

Chapter 25
The Ten Dedications

At that time, aided by the Buddha's spiritual powers, Vajra Banner Bodhisattva entered the "bodhisattva wisdom light samādhi." Having entered this samādhi, from each of the ten directions, beyond worlds as numerous as the atoms in ten myriads of buddha *kṣetras*, buddhas as numerous as the atoms in ten myriads of buddha *kṣetras*, all of whom were identically named "Vajra Banner," then appeared directly before him, whereupon they all praised him, saying: "It is good indeed, good indeed, Son of Good Family, that you have been able to enter this bodhisattva wisdom light samādhi. Son of Good Family, it is because of the joint assistance provided to you by the spiritual powers of buddhas from each of the ten directions as numerous as the atoms in ten buddha *kṣetras*, is also because of the awesome spiritual powers arising from the power of Vairocana Tathāgata's past vows, is also because of the purity of your wisdom, and is also because of the especially excellent roots of goodness of the bodhisattvas that you have been enabled to enter this samādhi and expound on the Dharma to enable all bodhisattvas:

To acquire pure fearlessness;
To possess unimpeded eloquence;
To enter the ground of unimpeded wisdom;
To dwell in the great mind of all-knowledge;
To fully develop inexhaustible roots of goodness;
To completely fulfill the dharmas of unimpeded purity;
To enter the Dharma realm of the universal gateways;
To manifest the spiritual powers of all buddhas;
To ensure the continuity of past mindfulness and wisdom;
To acquire all buddhas' protection of all their faculties;
To use countless gateways to extensively explain the many dharmas;
To completely understand, absorb, uphold, and never forget all the teachings that have been heard;
To accumulate all the roots of goodness of bodhisattvas;
To become fully accomplished in the world-transcending provisions for the path;
To prevent the severance of the wisdom of all-knowledge;
To instigate the generation of the great vows;
To explain the genuine meaning;

To completely know the Dharma realm;
To gladden all bodhisattvas;
To cultivate the same roots of goodness of all buddhas; and
To protect and preserve the lineage of all *tathāgatas*.

That is to say, [they have enabled you in this way] so that you will expound on the ten dedications of all bodhisattvas. Son of the Buddha, assisted by the awesome spiritual powers of the Buddha, you should expound on these dharmas, doing so:

To acquire the protective mindfulness of the Buddha;
To dwell in the family of the buddhas;
To increase world-transcending meritorious qualities;
To acquire the light of the *dhāraṇīs*;
To enter the unimpeded Dharma of the Buddha;
To everywhere illuminate the Dharma realm with great light;
To accumulate the pure dharmas free of all faults;
To abide in the realm of vast wisdom; and
To acquire the unimpeded light of the Dharma."

Then the buddhas bestowed on Vajra Banner Bodhisattva: measureless wisdom; unimpeded eloquence; skillful means for distinguishing statements and meanings; unimpeded Dharma light; a body the same as that of the Tathāgata; a pure voice possessed of countless different tones; the bodhisattvas' inconceivable samādhi of skillful contemplation; the wisdom that dedicates all indestructible roots of goodness; the perfection of skillful means in contemplating all dharmas; and uninterrupted eloquence in explaining all dharmas in all places.

Vajra Banner Bodhisattva then explained the ten kinds of dedications expounded on by all buddhas of the three periods of time, namely:

First, the dedication that saves all beings in the absence of any conception of a being;
Second, the indestructible dedication;
Third, the dedication that is the same as that of all buddhas;
Fourth, the dedication that reaches everywhere;
Fifth, the dedication of an inexhaustible treasury of meritorious qualities;
Sixth, the dedication of roots of goodness that penetrates the equality of everyone;
Seventh, the dedication that equally accords with all beings;
Eighth, the dedication that has the character of true suchness;
Ninth, the dedication of the unbound and unattached liberation; and
Tenth, the dedication that penetrates the measurelessness of the Dharma realm.

As for the first of these ten dedications, "the dedication that saves all beings in the absence of any conception of a being," Vajra Banner explains that, when this bodhisattva practices the six perfections and the four immeasurable minds, he dedicates his roots of goodness from such practice to benefiting all beings in such a way that they are able to attain purity and remain forever apart from the sufferings of the three wretched destinies. He also dedicates them wishing that he may become for them a shelter, a protector, a refuge, a path, a source of peace, a light, a torch, a lamp, a guide, and a great guide who provides them with great wisdom. In doing so, he dedicates his roots of goodness to all beings equally, even to those who might be hostile or wish him harm. And of course, although Vajra Banner does not say so here in so many words, due to his great wisdom, this bodhisattva all the while understands that there is no such thing as an inherently existent "being" anywhere in any world who is the beneficiary of his dedications, for the conception of a "being" is just a false imputation on what is really only a momentary conjunction of the five aggregates.

With regard to the second of these ten dedications, "the indestructible dedication," Vajra Banner begins by noting that this bodhisattva attains indestructible faith in all *tathāgatas,* in all bodhisattvas, in all dharmas of the Buddha, in all teachings of the Buddha, in all beings, in all dharmas of purity, in the path of all bodhisattvas' dedications, in all bodhisattva masters of the Dharma, in all buddhas' sovereign mastery of the superknowledges, and in all bodhisattvas' practice of skillful means. When the bodhisattva dedicates all roots of goodness, although he adapts to beings' circumstances in *saṃsāra,* he still does not change. In seeking all-knowledge, he never retreats. None of the dharmas of the world are able to either change him or cause him to be moved. Because this bodhisattva's resolve is indestructible, his dedications are indestructible.

In discussing the third of these ten dedications, "the dedication that is the same as that of all buddhas," Vajra Banner Bodhisattva begins by saying that this bodhisattva-*mahāsattva* accords with all buddhas, the *bhagavats,* of the past, future, and present in his cultivation and training in the path of dedications. Later on, he says that this bodhisattva has this thought: "Just as, when all buddhas of the past cultivated the bodhisattva practices, they dedicated all their roots of goodness in this way, and just as those of the future shall do so and those of the present now also do so, so too should I now also resolve, in the same way as all those buddhas, to dedicate all roots of goodness."

As for the fourth of these ten dedications, "the dedication that reaches everywhere," Vajra Banner says that this bodhisattva reflects in this manner: "May the power of the meritorious qualities associated with these roots of goodness reach everywhere. Just as the apex of reality has no place it does not reach as it reaches all things, reaches all worlds, reaches all beings, reaches all lands, reaches all dharmas, reaches all of empty space, reaches all three periods of time, reaches all that is either conditioned or unconditioned, and reaches the sounds of all speech, may it be that these roots of goodness also in this same way everywhere reach the places in which the *tathāgatas* dwell to serve as an offering to all buddhas of the three periods of time, facilitating the complete fulfillment of what was vowed by the buddhas of the past, facilitating the perfectly replete adornments of all buddhas of the future, and enabling all buddhas of the present as well as their lands and congregations at their sites of enlightenment to everywhere fill empty space and the Dharma realm." Later on, Vajra Banner said, "When the bodhisattva-*mahāsattva* abides in this dedication:

He acquires physical actions that reach everywhere by which he is everywhere able to respond by appearing in all worlds;

He acquires verbal actions that reach everywhere by which he expounds the Dharma in all worlds;

He acquires mental actions that reach everywhere by which he absorbs and upholds the Dharma proclaimed by all buddhas;

He acquires the spiritual superknowledge of psycho-physical travel that reaches everywhere by which he adapts to beings' minds and goes forth in response to them all;

He acquires wisdom concordant with realizations that reaches everywhere by which he is everywhere able to fully comprehend all dharmas;

He acquires complete-retention [*dhāraṇī* formulae] and eloquence that reaches everywhere by which he adapts to beings' minds and causes them to feel happy;

He acquires entry into the Dharma realm that reaches everywhere by which he everywhere enters all worlds even within a single pore;

He acquires a pervasively penetrating body that reaches everywhere by which he everywhere enters the bodies of all beings through entering the body of but a single being;

He acquires universal vision of kalpas that reaches everywhere by which he always sees all *tathāgatas* in every kalpa; and

He acquires all-seeing mindfulness that reaches everywhere by which, even in each successive mind-moment, all buddhas appear directly before him."

In discussing the fifth of these ten dedications, "the dedication of an inexhaustible treasury of meritorious qualities," Vajra Banner says that this bodhisattva acquires ten inexhaustible treasuries consisting of: the inexhaustible treasury of seeing the buddhas; the inexhaustible treasury of penetrating dharmas; the inexhaustible treasury of remembrance; the inexhaustible treasury of definite wisdom; the inexhaustible treasury of understanding meanings and their import; the inexhaustible treasury of boundless awakened understanding; the inexhaustible treasury of merit; the inexhaustible treasury of courageous wisdom; the inexhaustible treasury of definite eloquence; and the inexhaustible treasury of the ten powers and the fearlessnesses.

Regarding the sixth of these ten dedications which is first listed as "the dedication of roots of goodness that penetrates the equality of everyone," but which is later called "the dedication to strengthening everyone's roots of goodness," in one of many illustrations of this, Vajra Banner Bodhisattva says that this bodhisattva dedicates all of his roots goodness from his practice of giving as follows:

May all beings become trained in purity;
May all beings extinguish the afflictions and purify all buddha *kṣetras*;
May all beings, with a pure mind, pervade the Dharma realm in but a single mind-moment;
May all beings have wisdom that completely fills empty space and the Dharma realm;
May all beings attain all-knowledge, everywhere penetrate the three periods of time, and train beings, in all times forever turning the irreversible wheel of the pure Dharma;
May all beings perfect all-knowledge and become well able to manifest spiritual superknowledges and skillful means to benefit beings;
May all beings become able to awaken to and enter the bodhi of the buddhas and always incessantly expound on right Dharma in all worlds of the ten directions, doing so until the very end of future kalpas, thereby enabling all beings everywhere to hear and understand it;
May all beings cultivate the bodhisattva practices for countless kalpas and completely fulfill them all;
May all beings cultivate the bodhisattva practices for countless kalpas in all worlds that can be described among all types of worlds, having none in which they do not become pervasively present, whether those worlds be defiled or immaculate, small or immense, coarse or subtle, inverted or upward-facing, or adorned in but one way or adorned in many different ways; and
May all beings always perform the works of all buddhas of the three periods of time, doing so in every successive mind-moment as they teach beings and continue to progress toward all-knowledge.

In discussing the seventh of these ten dedications, "the dedication that equally accords with all beings," Vajra Banner Bodhisattva said that this bodhisattva "accords with whatever roots of goodness have been accumulated, namely: small roots of goodness, great roots of goodness, vast roots of goodness, abundant roots of goodness, measureless roots of goodness, various roots of goodness, roots of goodness as numerous as atoms, *asaṃkhyeyas* of roots of goodness, boundlessly many roots of goodness, inconceivably many roots of goodness, immeasurably many roots of goodness, roots of goodness related to the sphere of the buddhas, roots of goodness related to the sphere of the Dharma, roots of goodness related to the sphere of the Sangha, roots of goodness related to the sphere of good spiritual guides, roots of goodness related to the sphere of all beings, roots of goodness related to the sphere of skillful means, roots of goodness related to cultivating all good thoughts, roots of goodness related to inward objects, roots of goodness related to outward objects, roots of goodness related to the sphere of the boundlessly many aids to enlightenment, roots of goodness related to diligently cultivating giving away everything, roots of goodness related to the supreme resolve to maintain ultimate purity in observing the moral precepts, roots of goodness related to patience in which one maintains equanimity in all things and has nothing one cannot endure, roots of goodness related to always being vigorous and maintaining irreversible resolve, roots of goodness related to using great skillful means to enter countless samādhis, roots of goodness related to using wisdom in skillful contemplations, roots of goodness related to knowing the differences in all beings' mental behavior, roots of goodness related to accumulating boundless meritorious qualities, roots of goodness related to diligently cultivating the bodhisattva's actions and practices, and roots of goodness related to protecting and nurturing those in all worlds."

As for the eighth of these ten dedications, "the dedication that has the character of true suchness," Vajra Banner Bodhisattva described one hundred ways in which the bodhisattva's dedications of roots of goodness have the character of true suchness, beginning with "Just as true suchness is boundlessly pervasive, so too it is with [the bodhisattva's] dedications of roots of goodness, for they are boundlessly pervasive," and ending with, "Just as true suchness is ultimately pure and does not coexist with any afflictions, so too it is with the bodhisattva's dedications of roots of goodness, for they are able to extinguish all beings' afflictions and bring about the perfect fulfillment of all forms of pure wisdom."

In speaking of the ninth of these ten dedications, "the dedication of the unbound and unattached liberation," after describing some sixty-one ways in which the bodhisattva carries out the dedication of the unbound and unattached liberation, Vajra Banner Bodhisattva said that "the bodhisattva-*mahāsattva* dedicates his roots of goodness in these ways, namely with unattached and unbound liberation of mind, with unattached and unbound liberation of the body, with unattached and unbound liberation of the mouth, with unattached and unbound liberation of actions, with unattached and unbound liberation of karmic rewards, with unattached and unbound liberation in relation to worlds, with unattached and unbound liberation in relation to buddha *kṣetras*, with unattached and unbound liberation in relation to beings, with unattached and unbound liberation in relation to dharmas; and with unattached and unbound liberation in relation to knowledge."

In describing the tenth of these ten dedications which is first referred to as "the dedication that penetrates the measurelessness of the Dharma realm" and later referred to as "the dedication that is as measureless as the Dharma realm," Vajra Banner Bodhisattva said that the bodhisattva "also dedicates roots of goodness in these ways, namely: wishing to see countless buddhas commensurate with the Dharma realm, wishing to train countless beings commensurate with the Dharma realm, wishing to support and sustain countless buddha *kṣetras* commensurate with the Dharma realm, wishing to realize countless types of bodhisattva knowledge commensurate with the Dharma realm, wishing to acquire countless fearlessnesses commensurate with the Dharma realm, wishing to perfect countless bodhisattva *dhāraṇī* formulae commensurate with the Dharma realm, wishing to acquire countless inconceivable bodhisattva abodes commensurate with the Dharma realm, wishing to possess countless meritorious qualities commensurate with the Dharma realm, and wishing to fulfill countless roots of goodness from benefiting beings commensurate with the Dharma realm."

Dharma Banner later concluded his discussion of this tenth dedication by saying: "Sons of the Buddha, the bodhisattva-*mahāsattva* also dedicates these roots of goodness in these ways: dedicating them to abiding in the abodes as measureless as the Dharma realm; dedicating them to abiding in the physical karma as measureless as the Dharma realm; dedicating them to abiding in the verbal karma as measureless as the Dharma realm; dedicating them to abiding in the mental karma as measureless as the Dharma realm; dedicating them to abiding in the form as measureless as the Dharma realm; dedicating them to abiding in the feelings, perceptions, karmic formative factors, and consciousnesses as measureless as the Dharma realm; dedicating them to abiding in the aggregates as measureless as the Dharma realm; dedicating them to abiding in the sense realms as measureless as the Dharma realm; dedicating them to abiding in the sense bases as measureless as the Dharma realm; dedicating them to abiding in the inwardly associated dharmas as measureless as the Dharma realm; dedicating them to abiding in the outwardly associated dharmas as measureless as the Dharma realm; dedicating them to abiding in the [instances of the] initial setting forth as measureless as the Dharma realm; dedicating them to abiding in the profound thought as measureless as the Dharma realm; dedicating them to abiding in the skillful means as measureless as the Dharma realm; dedicating them to abiding in the resolute faith as measureless as the Dharma realm; dedicating them to abiding in the faculties as measureless as the Dharma realm; dedicating them to abiding in the past, present, and future periods of time as measureless as the Dharma realm; dedicating them to abiding in the karmic retributions as measureless as the Dharma realm; dedicating them to abiding in the defilement and purity as measureless as the Dharma realm; dedicating them to abiding in the beings as measureless as the Dharma realm; dedicating them to abiding in the buddha *kṣetras* as measureless as the Dharma realm; dedicating them to abiding in the dharmas as measureless as the Dharma realm; dedicating them to abiding in the light of the world as measureless as the Dharma realm; dedicating them to abiding in the buddhas and bodhisattvas as measureless as the Dharma realm; dedicating them to abiding in the bodhisattva conduct and vows as measureless as the Dharma realm; dedicating them to abiding in the emancipation as measureless as the Dharma realm; dedicating them to abiding in the bodhisattva teaching and training as measureless as the Dharma realm; dedicating them to abiding in the non-duality as measureless as the Dharma realm; and dedicating them to abiding in the congregations and sites of enlightenment as measureless as the Dharma realm.

Sons of the Buddha, when the bodhisattva-*mahāsattva* makes dedications in ways such as these: he abides in pure bodies as measureless as the Dharma realm; he abides in pure speech as measureless as the Dharma realm; he abides in pure minds as measureless as the Dharma realm; he abides in all bodhisattvas' pure conduct and vows as measureless as the Dharma realm; he abides in pure congregations and sites of enlightenment as measureless as the Dharma realm; he abides in pure wisdom as measureless as the Dharma realm with which he extensively explains all dharmas for all bodhisattvas; he abides in bodies as measureless as the Dharma realm that are able to enter all worlds throughout the Dharma realm; and he abides in pure fearlessness arising from the light of all dharmas that is as measureless as the Dharma realm. Thus he is able with but a single voice to completely cut away all beings' nets of doubt and then, by adapting to their faculties and inclinations, he enables them to be happy and come to dwell in the unexcelled knowledge of all modes, the fearlessnesses, the masterful spiritual superknowledges, and the dharmas of emancipation."

When Vajra Banner finished discussing this last one of the ten dedications, due to the Buddha's powers, the worlds of the ten directions moved and shook in six ways, whereupon, again due to the Buddha's powers, it rained down many kinds of celestial flowers, garlands, incense, fragrances, raiment, jewels, and other such things, whereupon the devas all exclaimed, "Good indeed!" bowed down in reverence, and offered music and songs of praise to the Tathāgata. Countless devas emanated great light that everywhere illuminated all the buddha lands throughout all of empty space.

Just as this Dharma was proclaimed within the Tuṣita Heaven palace in this world, so too did this also occur in the same manner in all the Tuṣita Heaven palaces in all worlds throughout the ten directions.

At that time, again due to the spiritual powers of the Buddha, from beyond a number of worlds off in each of the ten directions as numerous as the atoms in a hundred myriads of buddha *kṣetras,* there came bodhisattvas as numerous as the atoms in a hundred myriads of buddha *kṣetras.* Filling up the ten directions, they then spoke these words in unison:

"It is good indeed, good indeed, O Son of the Buddha, that you have now been able to expound on these great dedications. O Son of the Buddha, we all have the same name, 'Vajra Banner,' and we have all come to visit this land from the abode of Vajra Banner Buddha in the Vajra Light World. Due to the Buddha's spiritual powers, this Dharma is also being spoken in all those worlds where the congregations, retinues, language, and meanings of the sentences spoken are all just as set forth here, without anything being added or removed. We have all received the aid of the Buddha's spiritual powers in coming here from those lands to serve as witnesses. And just as we have come to this assembly to serve as witnesses for you, so too, in this same way, groups of bodhisattvas come to serve as witnesses in all the jewel-adorned palaces of the Tuṣita Heavens in all worlds throughout the ten directions."

Vajra Banner then finished this chapter on the ten dedications with a verse of fifty-one summarizing stanzas.

Chapter 26
The Ten Grounds

This chapter on the ten bodhisattva grounds begins when the Bhagavat was residing in the Maṇi Jewel Treasury Palace of the Paranirmita Vaśavartin Heaven King, together with an assembly of great bodhisattvas headed by Vajragarbha Bodhisattva. All of those bodhisattvas had already achieved irreversibility in their progression toward *anuttara-samyak-saṃbodhi*. They had all come to assemble there from the worlds of other regions.

Aided by the Buddha's spiritual powers, Vajragarbha Bodhisattva entered "the bodhisattva's great wisdom light samādhi." After he entered this samādhi, from beyond a number of worlds in each of the ten directions as numerous as the atoms in ten *koṭis* of buddha lands, buddhas as numerous as the atoms in ten *koṭis* of buddha lands, all of them identically named "Vajragarbha," immediately appeared directly before him, praised him, and bestowed qualities, capacities, and powers on him enabling him to hold forth on the bodhisattva grounds transited by the great bodhisattvas as they proceed from the time of their initial resolve to attain highest bodhi to the highest level of bodhisattva path attainment, the realization of buddhahood.

Those buddhas then each extended their right hands and touched the crown of Vajragarbha Bodhisattva's head after which Vajragarbha bodhisattva emerged from samādhi and began to expound on the ten bodhisattva grounds, beginning by listing them as follows:

First, the Ground of Joyfulness;
Second, the Ground of Stainlessness;
Third, the Ground of Shining Light;
Fourth, the Ground of Blazing Brilliance;
Fifth, the Difficult-to-Conquer Ground;
Sixth, the Ground of Direct Presence;
Seventh, the Far-Reaching Ground;
Eighth, the Ground of Immovability;
Ninth, the Ground of Excellent Intelligence;
Tenth, the Ground of the Dharma Cloud.

Having listed the names of the ten bodhisattva grounds, Vajragarbha Bodhisattva suddenly fell silent, still not beginning to teach them even after three requests to do so by Liberation Moon Bodhisattva followed by a request to do so made by that entire congregation of bodhisattvas.

The Buddha then emanated light from between his brows and all buddhas of the ten directions also emanated light from between their brows. From the midst of this light, there then resounded five stanzas of verse requesting Vajragarbha to teach this dharma of the ten bodhisattva grounds. Only then did Vajragarbha begin to teach this dharma, beginning with his explanation of the first ground, the joyfulness ground.

In teaching the first bodhisattva ground, Vajragarbha spoke of the qualifications of the bodhisattva cultivating this ground, the motivations of this bodhisattva, the characteristics of this bodhisattva's resolve to attain bodhi, the consequences of his generating his bodhisattva vow, the endowment of this bodhisattva with abundant joy, faith, delight, happiness, exultation, ebullience, fortitude, noncontentiousness, harmlessness, and avoidance of anger, and ten bases for this bodhisattva's joyfulness. He then spoke of this bodhisattva's ten reflections on why he feels joyful.

Vajragarbha then spoke of five kinds of fearfulness from which this first-ground bodhisattva is forever freed, thirty of this bodhisattva's grounds-purifying practices, this bodhisattva's ten great vows, this bodhisattva's mental qualities and faith, this bodhisattva's reflections on the Dharma and beings, this first-ground bodhisattva's ensuing resolve, renunciation, and purification of the ground, this bodhisattva's seeing and serving of countless buddhas, this bodhisattva's practice of the means of attraction and *pāramitās*, and this bodhisattva's acquisition of further knowledge about the grounds. After further comments about this first-ground bodhisattva's position as a member of royalty or nobility, his use of the four means of attraction, his mindfulness, his aspiration to serve beings, and the results of this bodhisattva's leaving the home life, he then finished his teaching on the first ground with some forty-five stanzas of summarizing verse.

After the bodhisattvas attending this teaching celebrated Vajragarbha's teaching of the ground of joyfulness, Liberation Moon requested that Vajragarbha Bodhisattva continue with the teaching of the second ground, the ground of stainlessness.

Vajragarbha began by speaking of the second-ground bodhisattva's ten resolute intentions. He then continued by speaking of this bodhisattva's observance of the ten courses of good karmic action and the karmic fruits of observing them, this bodhisattva's reflection on the karmic retributions arising from indulgence in the ten courses of unwholesome karmic action, his renunciation of the ten bad actions and his arousing of ten kinds of altruistic motivation, this bodhisattva's reflections on the plight of beings and his resolve to rescue them, this bodhisattva's seeing and serving countless buddhas, his purification of this bodhisattva ground, his practice of the "pleasing words" means of attraction and *pāramitās*, this bodhisattva's position as a wheel-turning sage king who enables beings to do away with miserliness and karmic transgressions, his mindfulness, his aspiration to serve beings, the results of his leaving the home life, his attainment of samādhis, his ability to manifest a thousand bodies and his ability to manifest a thousand bodhisattvas to serve in the retinue of each of those bodies.

Vajragarbha then concluded his teachings on the ground of stainlessness with fifteen summarizing stanzas.

Vajragarbha then launched into his teaching of the third ground, the ground of shining light, beginning with listing ten resolute intentions that serve as bases for entering the third ground. He then spoke of this bodhisattva's contemplation of all conditioned dharmas, his renunciation and quest to attain the knowledge of a buddha, this bodhisattva's ten sympathetic mental intentions toward beings, his generation and practice of great vigor, his conquest of the meditative absorptions, his development of the four immeasurable minds of loving kindness, compassion, sympathetic joy, and equanimity, his development of the superknowledges, this bodhisattva's acquisition of the heavenly ear, his knowledge of others' thoughts, his recall of past lives, his attainment of the heavenly eye, and his vow-determined rebirth independent of the *dhyāna* heavens. He then spoke of this bodhisattva's seeing and serving of countless buddhas, his karmic purification, and his practice of the "beneficial actions" means of attraction and the perfection of patience.

Vajragarbha then spoke of this bodhisattva's station as a king of the Heaven of the Thirty-three who uses skillful means to enable beings to abandon desire, his practice of mindfulness, his aspiration to serve beings, and the consequences of this third-ground bodhisattva's application of vigor and vows, after which he concluded his teachings on the third ground with a verse of eighteen summarizing stanzas.

Vajragarbha began his discussion of the fourth bodhisattva ground by speaking of the ten gateways to Dharma Light as bases for entering the fourth ground, the ground of blazing brilliance. He then spoke of this bodhisattva's ten knowledge-maturing dharmas as means to birth into the clan of the buddhas after which he spoke of this bodhisattva's practice of the thirty-seven enlightenment factors consisting of the four stations of mindfulness, the four right efforts, the four bases of psychic power, the five roots, the five powers, the seven limbs of enlightenment, and the eight-fold path. He next spoke of this bodhisattva's ten aims in practicing the thirty-seven enlightenment factors, his abandonment of wrong views, attachments, and defiled actions, and his mental and personal qualities gained in the bodhisattva's cultivation of the path.

Vajragarbha then spoke of this fourth-ground bodhisattva's acquisition of ten kinds of vigor and the other qualities developed in the course of his cultivation of the fourth ground, after which he spoke of this bodhisattva's seeing and serving countless buddhas, his purification of resolute intentions and faith, the radiance of his roots of goodness, his practice of the "joint endeavors" means of attraction, and his practice of the perfection of vigor.

Vajragarbha then spoke of this fourth-ground bodhisattva's station as a Suyāma Heaven king who uses skillful means to enable beings to rid themselves of personality view and other such delusions, after which he spoke of this bodhisattva's mindfulness in using the four means of attraction, this bodhisattva's aspiration to serve beings, and the consequences of this bodhisattva's application of vigor and vows, whereupon Vajragarbha finished his discussion of the fourth ground with a verse consisting of seventeen summarizing stanzas.

Vajragarbha Bodhisattva began his discussion of the fifth bodhisattva ground, the "difficult-to-conquer" ground, by speaking of ten impartial pure resolute intentions that a candidate for cultivation of this ground should practice. He next spoke of the bodhisattva's bases for generating the irreversible bodhi resolve, the bodhisattva's knowledge of the four truths, the bodhisattva's resultant generation of compassion and kindness, and the bodhisattva's contemplation of causality in the plight of beings as they flow along, trapped in the sufferings of *saṃsāra,* due to which he resolves to cultivate merit and wisdom, the provisions for the path to buddhahood, as he strives endlessly to lead beings to acquire the ten powers of a fully enlightened buddha.

Vajragarbha next spoke of this bodhisattva's compassionate dedication of his roots of goodness, this bodhisattva's qualities and their bases, the methods this bodhisattva uses in teaching beings, this bodhisattva's adoption of a wide array of means to benefit beings, the bodhisattva's seeing and serving of countless buddhas, his purification of his roots of goodness, and his practice of the *pāramitās.*

He next spoke of the fifth-ground bodhisattva's station as a Tuṣita Heaven king, his skill in refuting the wrong views of non-Buddhist religious traditions, his ability to enable other beings to abide in genuine truth, his aspiration to serve beings, and the consequences of the Bodhisattva's application of vigor and vows, after which Vajragarbha concluded his discussion of this fifth bodhisattva ground with a verse consisting of twenty-two summarizing stanzas.

In commencing his discussion of the sixth bodhisattva ground, the ground of direct presence, Vajragarbha first spoke of ten dharmas of identity enabling access to the sixth ground, then spoke of entry into the sixth ground, the development of acquiescent patience, and the primacy for this bodhisattva of the great compassion, after which he discussed this bodhisattva's close contemplation of causality in cyclic existence, this bodhisattva's contemplation of mind as the basis of all existence, his contemplation of the two functions of each link of the causal chain, his contemplation of production and destruction of the causal chain, his contemplation of the inseparability in the functions of adjacent links of the causal chain, and his contemplation of the twelve links as constituents of three paths (afflictions, karmic actions, and suffering). He then spoke of the twelve links' correlation with the three periods of time and with the three kinds of suffering, after which he spoke of his contemplation of the twelve links' arising and ceasing via causes and conditions. He next spoke of how ignorance and volitional actions conduce to karmic bondage and how, if they are extinguished, karmic bondage then ceases, after which he spoke of contemplation of the links in terms of "utter nonexistence" and "utter cessation." He then finished this discussion of causality with a summary listing of ten contemplations of the twelve causal factors, after which he discussed the bodhisattva's acquisition of the three gates to liberation (emptiness, signlessness, and wishlessness), his compassionate reluctance to proceed to final nirvāṇa, and the bodhisattva's samādhis in relation to the three gates to liberation.

Vajragarbha Bodhisattva next listed this bodhisattva's ten types of resolute intentions and their consequences, this bodhisattva's *prajñāpāramitā* practice and acquisition of patience, his seeing and serving of countless buddhas, his purifying good roots, his specialization in the perfection of wisdom, the bodhisattva's station as a Skillful Transformations Heaven king who enables beings to relinquish arrogance and deeply comprehend conditioned origination. After next speaking of this bodhisattva's mindfulness in the means of attraction, his aspiration to serve beings, and the consequences of the bodhisattva's application of vigor and vows, Vajragarbha concluded his discussion of the sixth bodhisattva ground with a verse consisting of twenty-two summarizing stanzas.

In commencing his discussion of the seventh bodhisattva ground, the far-reaching ground, Vajragarbha Bodhisattva first spoke of the ten types of skillful means and wisdom enabling access to the seventh bodhisattva ground, after which he listed this bodhisattva's twenty kinds of penetrating comprehension. He then spoke of this bodhisattva's adoption of effortlessness, nondiscrimination, and meditative practice and his practice of the ten *pāramitās* and all the other dharmas leading to bodhi.

After Liberation Moon asked about this bodhisattva's practice of the enlightenment factors, Vajragarbha replied that, although this practice is fulfilled on all ten grounds, it is especially on the seventh ground that the bodhisattva's vigorous cultivation of the enlightenment factors becomes most completely fulfilled.

Liberation Moon then asked about this seventh-ground bodhisattva's transcendence of the afflictions. Vajragarbha replied by confirming that the seventh-ground bodhisattva has stepped beyond the many sorts of afflictions and succeeds in perfecting his physical, verbal, and mental actions.

Vajragarbha next discussed this bodhisattva's conquest of samādhis and the unproduced-dharmas patience and noted that it is on this ground that the bodhisattva finally steps beyond the grounds of the practitioners of the two vehicles. Replying to Liberation Moon's question about the cessation concentration, Vajragarbha explains that, beginning with the seventh ground, the bodhisattva can freely enter and emerge from the cessation samādhi.

Vajragarbha next explained ten paradoxical aspects of this seventh-ground bodhisattva, beginning with the fact that, although this bodhisattva continues to manifest within *saṃsāra,* he still constantly abides in nirvāṇa. Vajragarbha then spoke of this bodhisattva's seeing and serving of countless buddhas, his purification of roots of goodness, his focus on the skillful means *pāramitā,* his station as a Vaśavartin Heaven king who uses skillful means to draw others into the realization of knowledge and hence to advancement on the path.

Then, after speaking of this bodhisattva's mindfulness in the four means of attraction and in his quest to gain all-knowledge, and after speaking of the consequences of this bodhisattva's application of vigor and vows, Vajragarbha concluded the discussion of the seventh bodhisattva ground with a verse consisting of twenty-one summarizing stanzas.

In commencing his discussion of the eighth bodhisattva ground, the ground of immovability, Vajragarbha Bodhisattva spoke of ten accomplishments associated with entering the eighth ground, ten types of penetrating comprehension acquired when entering the eighth ground, and the unproduced-dharmas patience as the basis for this bodhisattva's "profound practice" which he likened to that of a bhikshu who has perfected the superknowledges and absorptions to the point where all movement of the mind, all recollective thought, and all discriminations have entirely ceased. He then likened eighth-ground practice to someone awakening from a river-fording dream who then immediately ceases all deliberately effortful action.

Vajragarbha then spoke of all buddhas appearing directly before the eighth-ground bodhisattva, the importance of this, the reasons for this, and the reasons why this bodhisattva's practices are so measureless. He next spoke of this bodhisattva's contemplation of the realm of all-knowledge, his knowledge of the arising and destruction of worlds, his knowledge of the four elements, his knowledge of atoms' manifestations in worlds and beings, his knowledge of the three realms of existence, his application of knowledge in taking on adaptive births to teach beings, his transcendence of discriminations and knowledge of ten kinds of bodies, his manifestation of different types of bodies for beings, his knowledge of beings' bodies, his knowledge of the bodies of lands, his knowledge of retribution and names associated with the bodies of *śrāvaka* disciples, *pratyekabuddhas,* and bodhisattvas, his knowledge of *tathāgata* bodies, his knowledge of the knowledge body, his knowledge of the Dharma body, and his knowledge of the empty space body.

Vajragarbha then spoke of the ten characteristic aspects of this eighth-ground bodhisattva, his ten types of power, his ten names, and his other additional qualities and practice aspects. He next speaks of this bodhisattva's seeing and serving of countless buddhas, his receiving of Dharma light from the buddhas, the radiance of his roots of goodness, his emanation of light, his focus on the skillful means *pāramitā,* his station as a king of the Great Brahma Heaven who bestows the path of the *pāramitās* on *śrāvaka* disciples, *pratyekabuddhas,* and bodhisattvas, and his mindfulness in the practice of the four means of attraction. After speaking of the eighth-ground bodhisattva's aspiration to serve beings and the consequences of his application of vigor and vows, Vajragarbha Bodhisattva concluded his discussion of the eighth-ground bodhisattva with a verse consisting of twenty-two summarizing stanzas.

In beginning his explanation of the ninth bodhisattva ground, the excellent intelligence ground, Vajragarbha Bodhisattva spoke of ten earnestly pursued endeavors enabling this bodhisattva to enter the ninth ground, his ten types of reality-based knowledge of karmic effects, his reality-based knowledge of beings' entangling thickets or difficulties, his ten types of reality-based knowledge of the characteristics of beings' minds, his types of reality-based knowledge of the afflictions' characteristics, his ten types of reality-based knowledge of the characteristics of karmic actions, his ten types of reality-based knowledge of beings' faculties, his knowledge of resolute beliefs, sense realms, and resolute intentions, his knowledge of the characteristics associated with the latent tendencies, his knowledge of the characteristics associated with births, his knowledge of the characteristics of the habitual karmic propensities, and his knowledge of those who are fixed in what is right, fixed in what is wrong, or not yet fixed in either respect.

Vajragarbha then continued by discussing this bodhisattva's command of the four types of unimpeded knowledge, including the ten permutations of his expertise in those four unimpeded knowledges. He next spoke of this bodhisattva's acquisition of *dhāraṇīs,* his additional receipt of Dharma from all buddhas, his expounding on Dharma throughout a great trichiliocosm, his ten types of voice-like expression in teaching beings, his independent command of countless simultaneous voices, and his redoubled vigor in quest of the light of knowledge. He then spoke of this bodhisattva's seeing and serving of countless buddhas, the purity of his roots of goodness, his focus on the powers *pāramitā,* this bodhisattva's station as a king of the Great Brahma Heaven who is able to expound on the *pāramitās* for both two-vehicles practitioners and bodhisattvas, his mindfulness in practicing the four means of attraction, his aspiration to serve beings and the consequences of the bodhisattva's application of vigor and vows. Vajragarbha Bodhisattva then concluded his discussion of the ninth-ground bodhisattva with a verse consisting of twenty-four summarizing stanzas.

Vajragarbha Bodhisattva then began his explanation of the tenth bodhisattva ground, the Dharma cloud ground, by telling Liberation Moon Bodhisattva of ten categories of practice preliminary to entering this tenth ground. He then spoke of this bodhisattva's subsequent acquisition of ten samādhis, followed by his access to countless other samādhis among which the last one manifests an immense radiant lotus blossom atop which this bodhisattva sits encircled by his retinue of bodhisattvas. Vajragarbha then tells of this bodhisattva's body emanating light rays that illuminate ten realms of beings and then form a canopy that presents offerings to all buddhas and then circle around all buddhas and enter their feet, whereupon the bodhisattvas from each of the ten directions arrive, make offerings, and enter samādhi. Those bodhisattvas then emanate light from their chests that enter this bodhisattva's chest, whereupon all buddhas send forth light that enters the crown of this bodhisattva's head. This bodhisattva acquires samādhis and receives the consecration from all buddhas in a manner similar to the manner in which the wheel-turning sage king receives his consecration.

Vajragarbha Bodhisattva then spoke of the capacities that arise from this bodhisattva's consecration of his attainment of the Dharma cloud ground including his knowing in accordance with reality attainment as it takes place in ten realms and in many other circumstances, his knowledge of ten types of transformation, his knowledge of sustaining bases, his knowledge of subtleties of practice, his knowledge of the Tathāgata's secrets, his knowledge of the interpenetration of kalpas, his knowing of the Tathāgata's types of penetrating knowledge, his acquisition of countless liberations, his countless samādhis, *dhāraṇīs,* and superknowledges, and his limitless memory power.

Liberation Moon Bodhisattva then asked about the limits of this bodhisatva's memory, after which Vajragarbha Bodhisattva replied that the capacity of this bodhisattva's memory is so great that it cannot be grasped by numerical calculation and can only be understood by resort to analogies.

Vajragarbha Bodhisattva then spoke of this Dharma cloud ground bodhisattva's great Dharma rain that he lets fall in countless lands, after which he speaks of this bodhisattva's use of spiritual powers in the transformation of worlds. After he expounds at length on this, the assembled congregants then wonder, "What more could even a Buddha do?" Vajragarbha then entered "the nature of the physical form of all buddha lands samādhi" to provide the congregants with a direct metaphysical understanding of this matter.

Vajragarbha then spoke of the nature of this bodhisattva's practice and insuperable wisdom light and compared this bodhisattva's wisdom light to that of real gold and to that of the Maheśvara Heaven king. He next spoke of the buddhas' ongoing teaching of this bodhisattva, this tenth-ground bodhisattva's focus on the knowledges *pāramitā,* his station as a Maheśvara Heaven king with great command of Dharma, this bodhisattva's mindfulness in the practice of the four means of attraction, his aspiration to serve beings, and the consequences of this bodhisattva's application of vigor and vows.

Having explained all ten of the bodhisattva grounds, Vajragarbha Bodhisattva then set forth analogies by which he compared the ten grounds to ten kings of mountains among which the tenth ground is compared to Mount Sumeru, the king of all mountains. He then compared the ten grounds to ten aspects of the great ocean and to a large *maṅi* jewel.

Vajragarbha then spoke of the prerequisite conditions for even being able to hear the ten grounds teachings after which Liberation Moon Bodhisattva asked how much merit is gained by hearing this teaching. Vajragarbha replied that this merit is of the same sort as the merit of all-knowledge.

After this, because of the spiritual powers of the Buddha and because of the very nature of the Dharma, countless lands in all ten directions underwent six types and eighteen varieties of movement.

The bodhisattvas of the ten directions then attested to the universality of this teaching, after which, augmented by the Buddha's supporting powers, Vajragarbha Bodhisattva presented forty-two stanzas of verses summarizing the tenth ground and the ten grounds chapter.

Chapter 27
The Ten Samādhis

The seventh assembly and this "ten samādhis" chapter begins with the Buddha again in the state of Magadha at the site of his enlightenment, in the Hall of Universal Radiance, together with bodhisattva-*mahāsattvas* as numerous as the atoms in ten buddha *kṣetras*, all of whom had already entered the crown-anointing stage of consecration. After the listing of the names of one hundred of these marvelously accomplished bodhisattva-*mahāsattvas*, aided by the Buddha's spiritual powers, Universal Eye Bodhisattva asked the Buddha how many samādhis and liberations have been perfected by Samantabhadra Bodhisattva and the multitudes of bodhisattvas who abide in all the practices and vows of Samantabhadra that they are able to ceaselessly exercise sovereign mastery in the spiritual superknowledges and transformations.

After praising Universal Eye for asking this question, the Buddha praised Samantabhadra Bodhisattva as one who has perfected inconceivably many spiritual superknowledges to a degree that surpasses all other bodhisattvas. After praising more of Samantabhadra's qualities and accomplishments, the Buddha told Universal Eye that, given that Samantabhadra is now present, he should ask Samantabhadra this question directly as he will surely tell Universal Eye about his samādhis, sovereign masteries, and liberations.

On hearing the name of Samantabhadra, the multitude of bodhisattvas in that congregation immediately acquired an inconceivable and measureless samādhi in which they saw all buddhas manifest directly before them and acquired the powers of the Tathāgata. Those bodhisattvas looked everywhere for Samantabhadra, but were unable to see him. Universal Eye asked the Buddha where Samantabhadra was then located and the Buddha replied that Samantabhadra was indeed there and that he had not moved at all. After all the bodhisattvas bowed in reverence to Samantabhadra, praying to be able to see him, Samantabhadra's form body appeared sitting next to the Buddha on a lotus flower throne, myriad kinds of clouds rained down flowers, garlands, fragrances, incense, canopies, and other such adorning phenomena, an ineffable number of worlds moved and shook in six ways, great light was emanated in an ineffable number of worlds, the wretched destinies disappeared, countless worlds were purified, and an ineffable number of bodhisattvas entered the practices of Samantabhadra, perfected the practices of Samantabhadra, fulfilled the conduct and vows of Samantabhadra, and attained highest enlightenment.

The Tathāgata then told Samantabhadra that he should explain the ten samādhis for the benefit of Universal Eye and the multitudes of other bodhisattvas in the assembly. The Buddha then praised these ten samādhis and listed them as: the great samādhi of universal light; the great samādhi of sublime light; the great samādhi of sequential visitation of all buddha lands everywhere; the great samādhi of pure and deep-minded practice; the great samādhi of the knowledge of the treasury of past adornments; the great samādhi of a treasury of wisdom light; the great samādhi of the complete knowledge of all worlds' buddha adornments; the great samādhi of all beings' different bodies; the great samādhi of sovereign mastery throughout the Dharma realm; and the great samādhi of the unimpeded wheel.

After observing that all great bodhisattvas become able to skillfully enter these ten great samādhis, the Buddha listed ten ways in which those proficient in these samādhis are known, ten universal capacities of such bodhisattvas, ten respects in which these samādhis are gateways, and twenty circumstances typical of bodhisattvas with these samādhis. He then told Samantabhadra that he should clearly distinguish and extensively explain these ten great samādhis of all bodhisattvas, for everyone in the congregation wishes to hear this.

In response to the Buddha's instructions, Samantabhadra Bodhisattva began by explaining the first of the ten samādhis, "the samādhi of universal light," in the course of which he first listed ten kinds of inexhaustible dharmas that a bodhisattva in this samādhi possesses, after which he listed ten kinds of boundless resolve he makes, ten kinds of knowledge he has of different ways of entering samādhi, and ten kinds of knowledge he has of skillful means in entering samādhi.

Samantabhadra next described the second of these samādhis, "the great samādhi of sublime light," in which this bodhisattva is able to enter great trichiliocosms as numerous as the atoms in a great trichiliocosm and in which he is able to manifest in every one of those worlds bodies as numerous as the atoms in a great trichiliocosm, causing every one of those bodies to emanate light rays as numerous as the atoms in a great trichiliocosm.

Samantabhadra then explained the third of these samādhis, "the great samādhi of sequential visitation of all buddha lands everywhere," in which the bodhisattva enters it for as briefly as an instant or for as long as countless kalpas during which the bodhisattva makes no discriminations, his mind remains free of any defiling attachment, and, although he abandons these kinds of discriminations, he still uses skillful means involving the spiritual superknowledges so that, when he emerges from this samādhi, he does not ever forget or lose any of its dharmas.

Samantabhadra next described the fourth of these samādhis, "the great samādhi of pure and deep-minded practice," in which this bodhisattva sees countless buddhas more numerous than the atoms in an *asaṃkhyeya* of worlds, makes offerings to them, poses questions to them, praises their qualities, praises their impartiality, extols their meritorious qualities, enters their great compassion, acquires their powers, and becomes completely endowed with fearlessness and inexhaustible eloquence with which he explains and expounds on the extremely deep treasury of Dharma.

Samantabhadra then explained the fifth of these samādhis, "the samādhi of the knowledge of the treasury of past adornments," in which the bodhisattva is able to know the appearance in the world of the buddhas of the past and acquires knowledge of the buddhas of the past, the *kṣetras* of the past, the Dharma gateways of the past, the kalpas of the past, the dharmas of the past, the minds of the past, the understandings of the past, the beings of the past, the afflictions of the past, the ceremonial protocols of the past, and the purity of the past while also entering up to an ineffable-ineffable number of kalpas. When he emerges from this samādhi, he receives ten kinds of crown-anointing consecration dharmas from the Tathāgata with which he speaks with eloquence that does not contradict its meaning, he is inexhaustible in teaching the Dharma, his teachings are impeccable, he is incessantly eloquent, his mind is free of fear, his speech is definitely truthful, he is relied on by beings, he rescues and liberates the beings in the three realms of existence, he possesses the most supreme roots of goodness, and he provides training and guidance in the sublime Dharma.

Samantabhadra next described the sixth of these samādhis, "the samādhi of a treasury of wisdom light," in which the bodhisattva knows everything about all buddhas in all kalpas of the future, he enters countless kalpas in but a single mind-moment, he is able to enter ten kinds of gateways of retention, he skillfully abides in an ineffable-ineffable number of kalpas and *kṣetras* and knows an ineffable-ineffable number of beings' characteristics, retributions, practices, and defiled and pure ways of thinking, he enables beings to acquire ten kinds of fruitfulness, and he is revered by the kings of the eight kinds of spiritual beings as well as by human kings.

He then explained the seventh of these samādhis, "the samādhi of the complete knowledge of all worlds' buddha adornments," in which the bodhisattva is able to successively enter the worlds in each of the ten directions where he sees all buddhas appear in the world, sees their powers, their feats of easeful mastery, their awesome virtue, their sovereign masteries, their lion's roar, their practices, their adornments, their spiritual powers and transformations, and their congregations while also being able to go to countless congregations. This bodhisattva perfects ten kinds of swiftness dharmas, acquires ten kinds of Dharma seals, acquires ten kinds of treasuries of vast knowledge, and acquires a body possessed of ten kinds of supreme purity and awesome virtue. He can enable beings to acquire ten kinds of complete fulfillment and he accomplishes ten kinds of buddha works for the sake of beings.

Samantabhadra then described the eighth of these samādhis, "the samādhi of all beings' different bodies," in which the bodhisattva acquires ten kinds of nonattachment. He then narrated how this bodhisattva enters and emerges from this samādhi in many different kinds of bodies, in many different realms, in many different populations of beings, in each of the four elements, in different mountains, in different grains, trees, and forests, in any of the different kinds of adornments, in each of the different sense bases, in the atoms of different worlds, in different periods of time, and finally may even enter in speech and emerge in true suchness. He described how this bodhisattva acquires ten kinds of praiseworthy dharmas, how he acquires ten kinds of illumination, how he acquires ten kinds of effortlessness, and how he attains perfection in ten kinds of spiritual superknowledges.

Samantabhadra next explained the ninth of these samādhis, "the samādhi of sovereign mastery throughout the Dharma realm," in which this bodhisattva enters this samādhi on each of his sense bases and in every pore of his own body and is then spontaneously able to know the entire world, to know all worldly dharmas, and to know worlds as numerous as the atoms in an ineffable number of buddha *kṣetras*. In this samādhi, this bodhisattva possesses countless meritorious qualities and he is taken into the care of the buddhas of the ten directions, he acquires ten kinds of oceans, he acquires ten kinds of extraordinary supremacy, and he acquires ten kinds of powers.

Samantabhadra then described the tenth of these samādhis, "the samādhi of the unimpeded wheel," in which the bodhisattva abides in unimpeded actions of body, mouth, and mind, in which he contemplates all-knowledge, in which he never interrupts his cultivation of Samantabhadra's vast vows, resolve, practices, or other such practice aspects, and in which this bodhisattva has a lotus flower that is so vast that it extends to the very boundaries of the ten directions and that is produced by his roots of goodness. When this bodhisattva sits on that lotus, his body grows to match the dimensions of the lotus. In this samādhi, this bodhisattva manifests countless transformations with his spiritual superknowledges and is praised by all buddhas of the three periods of time. His practice is vast, signless, unimpeded, and commensurate in scope with the immeasurability and boundlessness of the Dharma realm itself. The bodhi that he has realized is as boundless as empty space and he is entirely free of bonds or attachments. He takes the Dharma realm as his own body and remains free of discriminations. The sphere of his wisdom is inexhaustible, his determination is always intrepid, and his mind is constantly equanimous. He contemplates the ground of the ten powers and uses wisdom in cultivation and training. He takes wisdom as the bridge to all-knowledge, uses the wisdom eye to remain unimpeded in seeing the Dharma, and skillfully enters all the grounds. He knows the many different kinds of meanings, is able to completely understand every one of all the Dharma gateways, and, of all the great vows, there are none that he does not completely fulfill.

The bodhisattva who enters this tenth great samādhi manifests the realization of the utmost right enlightenment, manifests an ineffable-ineffable number of gateways to realization of right enlightenment, manifests an ineffable-ineffable number of gateways to the turning of the Dharma wheel, manifests an ineffable-ineffable number of gateways to dwelling in the profound mind, manifests the gateways to the transformation of nirvāṇa in an ineffable-ineffable number of vast lands, manifests taking rebirth and cultivating Samantabhadra's practices in an ineffable-ineffable number of different worlds, and manifests an ineffable-ineffable number of *tathāgatas* realizing the utmost right enlightenment beneath the bodhi tree in an ineffable-ineffable number of vast lands, closely surrounded by a congregation consisting of an ineffable-ineffable number of bodhisattvas.

It may be that he cultivates Samantabhadra's practices for a mind-moment and then attains right enlightenment, or does so for an instant, for an hour, for a day, for a half-month, for a month, for a year, for countless years, for a kalpa, or even for an ineffable-ineffable number of kalpas during which he cultivates Samantabhadra's practices and then attains right enlightenment.

He also serves as the leader among those in all buddha *kṣetras* who draws near to the buddhas, bows down to them in reverence, makes offerings to them, poses questions to them, contemplates the spheres of experience as like illusions, purifies and cultivates the bodhisattva's countless practices, countless types of knowledge, various spiritual transformations, various forms of awesome virtue, various types of wisdom, various spheres of cognition, various spiritual superknowledges, various types of sovereign mastery, various liberations, various types of Dharma light, and various types dharmas used in teaching and training.

This is what constitutes the vast knowledge of the extraordinarily superior mind in the bodhisattva-*mahāsattva*'s tenth great samādhi, "the great samādhi of the unimpeded wheel."

Chapter 28
The Ten Superknowledges

Samantabhadra Bodhisattva began this chapter by addressing all the bodhisattvas and telling them about the bodhisattva's ten superknowledges, starting with the superknowledge that knows the minds of others by which he knows the thoughts in the minds of all beings in a great trichiliocosm, knowing their good thoughts, bad thoughts, vast thoughts, narrow thoughts, great thoughts, and small thoughts, knowing too the thoughts of all beings in all the realms of existence.

He next tells them how, using the superknowledge of the unimpeded heavenly eye, the bodhisattva sees how beings die here and are reborn there, being born in either a fortunate rebirth destiny or in one of the wretched destinies, in each case being possessed of the signs of merit or the signs of karmic offenses, being either fine-looking or homely, knowing this of all kinds of beings, including devas, dragons, and rest of the various types of spiritual beings, whether possessed of tiny bodies or immense bodies. With this superknowledge, he is able to completely and clearly see whatever karma these beings have accumulated and whatever suffering or happiness they have experienced.

Samantabhadra then described how, using the superknowledge that knows past lives at will, the bodhisattva knows matters associated with his own past lives as well as those of all the beings in worlds as numerous as the atoms in countless buddha *kṣetras*, knowing these with regard to all the lifetimes throughout kalpas as numerous as the atoms in countless buddha *kṣetras*.

He next told these bodhisattvas about the fourth of the bodhisattva's superknowledges, the superknowledge that knows the kalpas of the future even to the end of future time, after which he then described for them the fifth of the superknowledges, the superknowledge of the heavenly ear with which the bodhisattva is able to hear and always remember all sounds, including even whatever all buddhas everywhere proclaim, reveal, explain or expound.

Samantabhadra next described the superknowledge in which the bodhisattva hears the names of all buddhas even in the most extremely distant worlds, in a number of worlds as numerous as the atoms in an ineffable-ineffable number of worlds and then, having heard their names, he immediately sees himself in the presence of those buddhas. This is what is known as the sixth of the bodhisattva-*mahāsattva's* superknowledges, the spiritual superknowledge in which he abides in the absence of any substantial nature, remains motionless, and does nothing whatsoever even as he travels to all the buddha *kṣetras*.

Samantabhadra next described the seventh superknowledge, the spiritual superknowledge that skillfully distinguishes all languages in which the bodhisattva distinguishes the languages of all beings as numerous as the atoms in countless buddha *kṣetras*, in particular knowing the languages of *āryas*, the languages of non-*āryas*, the languages of devas, the languages of dragons, the languages of *yakṣas*, the languages of *gandharvas, asuras, garuḍas, kiṃnaras, mahoragas*, humans, and nonhumans and so forth until we come to his knowing all the languages of an ineffable-ineffable number of beings in all the different ways each of them manifests. Knowing the individual natures and propensities of all the beings in all the worlds he enters, the bodhisattva speaks the words by which those beings are all enabled to achieve complete understanding of whichever teachings this bodhisattva deems would be most beneficial to their progress on the path to liberation from *saṃsāra* and to their realization of highest enlightenment.

Samantabhadra then described the eighth of the superknowledges, the spiritual superknowledge of the countless form bodies which he diligently cultivates and perfects for the sake of liberating all beings. Using this superknowledge, the bodhisattva manifests every possible sort of form body, from that of ordinary beings to that of a sun or moon or cloud or flower, all of which he may enable to speak in any of an ineffable number of different voices with which he teaches dharmas to beings perfectly well adapted to those beings' propensities, karmic circumstances, and capacities.

Samantabhadra next described the ninth of the superknowledges, the spiritual superknowledge that knows all dharmas with which the bodhisattva knows all dharmas as neither dual nor non-dual, as devoid of a self, as neither produced nor destroyed, as neither conditioned nor unconditioned, and as neither ultimate truth nor not ultimate truth. This bodhisattva does not seize on mundane conventional truth, nor does he abide in ultimate truth, yet he still uses skillful means and inexhaustible eloquence guided by wisdom, loving kindness, and compassion with which he spreads forth the Dharma cloud and sends down the Dharma rains to attract all the many different kinds of beings to the Dharma and enable their escape from cyclic existence and their ascent to highest enlightenment.

Samantabhadra then explained the tenth of the superknowledges, the spiritual superknowledge of the complete cessation of all dharmas samādhi by which the bodhisattva-*mahāsattva* is able in every successive mind-moment to enter the samādhi of the complete cessation of all dharmas but still does not retreat from the bodhisattva path, does not abandon the bodhisattva works, and does not relinquish the mind of great kindness and great compassion. Although the bodhisattva may enter this samādhi of the complete cessation of all dharmas and remain in it for even a hundred thousand *nayutas* of *koṭīs* of kalpas, his body still never disintegrates, never atrophies, and never changes. Even though he does not engage in any endeavors at all in any sphere of existence or nonexistence, he is still able to continue accomplishing all kinds of bodhisattva works. That is to say, he never abandons all beings, but rather constantly teaches and trains them, never missing the appropriate time in doing so. Thus he enables them to grow in all dharmas of the Buddha and enables them to achieve complete fulfillment of all the bodhisattva practices. Because he wishes to benefit all beings, he never desists from using his spiritual superknowledges and transformations for their sake. These manifest like reflected images that appear everywhere for everyone even as he all the while remains quiescent and unmoving in this samādhi. This is what is known as the tenth of the bodhisattva-*mahāsattva's* superknowledges, the spiritual superknowledge of entering the samādhi of the complete cessation of all dharmas.

Samantabhadra Bodhisattva tells the assembled bodhisattvas that this bodhisattva-*mahāsattva's* abiding in these ten kinds of superknowledges is inconceivable to all devas and humans, is inconceivable to all beings, and is inconceivable to all *śrāvaka* disciples, to all *pratyekabuddhas,* and to all the other members of the bodhisattva sangha. He goes on to say that, aside from the buddhas and the bodhisattvas who have acquired these spiritual superknowledges, there is no one else even able to adequately describe and proclaim the praises of the meritorious qualities of a person such as this. He closes by saying that, if bodhisattva-*mahāsattvas* abide in these spiritual superknowledges, they all acquire all the spiritual superknowledges of unimpeded knowledge throughout all three periods of time.

Chapter 29
The Ten Patiences

This chapter begins with Samantabhadra Bodhisattva telling the bodhisattvas in that great assembly that the bodhisattva has ten kinds of patience which, if one acquires them, he will succeed in reaching the ground of all bodhisattvas' unimpeded patience and he will become endlessly unimpeded in all dharmas of the Buddha. He then listed those kinds of patience as:

Patience with the sounds [of the teachings];
Acquiescent patience;
Unproduced-dharmas patience;
Patience [due to seeing all as] like a conjured illusion;
Patience [due to seeing all as] like a mirage;
Patience [due to seeing all as] like a dream;
Patience [due to seeing all as] like echoes;
Patience [due to seeing all as] like reflections;
Patience [due to seeing all as] like supernatural transformations; and
Patience [due to seeing all as] like space.

Samantabhadra then explained "patience with the sounds[of the teachings]" as meaning that, when one hears the Dharma proclaimed by all buddhas, one is not alarmed, not frightened, and not intimidated. On the contrary, one responds to those teachings with deep faith, awakened understanding, delight, attraction, attentiveness, recollection, cultivation, and secure establishment in them.

He then explained "acquiescent patience" as referring to "reflecting upon and contemplating all dharmas equally and without opposition, acquiescing in and completely understanding them, enabling one's mind to remain in a state of purity, rightly abiding in cultivating them, entering them, and perfecting them."

Samantabhadra next explained the unproduced-dharmas patience as referring to when the bodhisattva "does not perceive that there is even the most minor dharma that is ever produced and also does not perceive that there is even the most minor dharma that is destroyed."

He then explained "the patience [due to seeing all as] like a conjured illusion" as developing once the bodhisattva realizes "that all dharmas are like conjured illusions and that they arise through causes and conditions."

Samantabhadra next explained the fifth of these kinds of patience, "the patience [due to seeing all as] like a mirage," as referring to when the bodhisattva realizes and sees that the world and all dharmas, like mirages, have no actual place, are neither inwardly existing nor outwardly existing, are neither existent nor nonexistent, are neither instantaneous nor eternal, are not of only a single form, are not of multiple forms, and are not formless, but rather are things manifested solely based on conventional worldly discourse.

He then explained the sixth kind of patience, "patience [due to seeing all as] like a dream" as referring to when the bodhisattva "realizes that that the entire world is the same as a dream: because of the absence of change; because its inherent nature is dreamlike; because attachment to it is like attaching to something in a dream; because, like a dream, it is by nature disconnected; because its original nature is like that of a dream; because all that appears in it is dreamlike; because, as in a dream, it is has no differentiating aspects; because all discriminations in one's perceptions are like those in a dream; and because, when one awakens, it is as if one were awakening from a dream."

Samantabhadra next explained the seventh kind of patience, "the patience [due to seeing all as] like echoes" as referring to when the bodhisattva "hears the Buddha teaching the Dharma, he contemplates the nature of all dharmas, cultivates the training to the far shore of perfection, and realizes that all sounds are like echoes in that, although they have neither any coming nor any going, they still manifest in this way."

He then explained "the patience [due to seeing all as] like reflections" as referring to when the bodhisattva realizes that "Just as the sun, moon, men, women, houses, mountains, forests, rivers, springs, and all other such things have their images reflected by the surfaces of oil, water, beings' bodies, jewelry, bright mirrors, and other such immaculate things—

And just as those reflections are neither one with nor different from and neither apart from nor united with those surfaces of the oil and other such things—

And just as they do not float along in the current of the river and do not sink down into and disappear within those ponds and wells—

And just as, although those reflections appear within them, they do not become attached to them or sullied by them—

And just as beings know that as these images appear in this place even as they realize that none of those things, whether far away or near, actually exist within these reflections—

And just as, although all of these things appear in these reflections, the appearances portrayed by the reflections do not correspond to the actual proximity or distance of the reflected phenomena—

So too it is with the bodhisattva-*mahāsattva,* for he is able to realize that his own physical being and the physical beings of others in all cases are simply spheres of cognition."

Samantabhadra Bodhisattva next explained "the patience [due to seeing all as] like transformations" as referring to when the bodhisattva realizes that "the entire world is comparable to [supernaturally produced] transformations. That is to say: all beings are transformations of mental deeds produced because of ideation and perceptions; all worlds are transformations of actions produced because of discriminations; all pain and pleasure are transformations of inverted views produced because of erroneous grasping; all worlds are transformations of unreal dharmas appearing as conventions based on language; and all afflictions are transformations of discriminations produced because of perceptions and thoughts."

Samantabhadra explained the tenth and final kind of patience, "the patience [that sees all as] like space" as referring to when the bodhisattva "understands the entire Dharma realm as like space because of its signlessness, understands all worlds as like space because of their non-arising, understands all dharmas as like space because of their non-duality, understands the actions of all beings as like space because they have nothing they enact, understands all buddhas as like space because they are free of discriminations, understands the powers of all buddhas as like space because they are no different, understands all *dhyāna* absorptions as like space because they are the same throughout all three periods of time, understands all dharmas that have been spoken as like space because they cannot be described in words, and understands the bodies of all buddhas as like space because they are free of attachments and are unimpeded."

Having explained all ten kinds of patience, Samantabhadra Bodhisattva concluded the chapter with a reiterative verse consisting of one hundred and seven summarizing stanzas.

Chapter 30
Asaṃkhyeyas

Mind King Bodhisattva began this chapter by asking the Buddha, "O Bhagavat, when expounding on the Dharma, the buddhas, the *tathāgatas*, use such numbers as *'asaṃkhyeya,'* 'measureless,' 'boundless,' 'incomparable,' 'innumerable,' 'indescribable,' 'inconceivable,' 'incalculable,' 'ineffable,' and 'ineffable-ineffable.' O Bhagavat, what is meant by *'asaṃkhyeya'* and so forth until we come to 'ineffable-ineffable'?"

The Buddha replied by saying, "It is good indeed, good indeed, O Son of Good Family, that, wishing to enable all those in the world to penetrate the meaning of these denominations of measurement known by the Buddha, you then now ask the Tathāgata, the Arhat, the One of Right and Universal Enlightenment, about this matter. Son of Good Family, listen carefully, listen carefully, and thoroughly ponder this as I now explain this for you."

The Buddha then listed in order all the numerical designations in these denominations of measurement known by the buddhas in which each of the one hundred and twenty-two successive designations after a *lakṣa* and a *koṭī* are the square of the immediately previous designation. Replying to Mind King Bodhisattva, the Buddha said:

A hundred *lakṣas* equals a *koṭī*.
A *koṭī* times a *koṭī* equals an *ayuta*.
An *ayuta* times an *ayuta* equals a *nayuta*.
A *nayuta* times a *nayuta* equals a *viṃvara*.
A *viṃvara* times a *viṃvara* equals a *kaṅkara*.
A *kaṅkara* times a *kaṅkara* equals an *agāra*.
An *agāra* times an *agāra* equals a *pravara*.
A *pravara* times a *pravara* equals a *mavara*.
A *mavara* times a *mavara* equals an *avara*.
An *avara* times an *avara* equals a *tavara*.
A *tavara* times a *tavara* equals a *sīmā*.
A *sīmā* times a *sīmā* equals a *hūma*.
A *hūma* times a *hūma* equals a *nema*.
A *nema* times a *nema* equals an *avaga*.
An *avaga* times an *avaga* equals a *mīgava*.
A *mīgava* times a *mīgava* equals a *viraga*.
A *viraga* times a *viraga* equals a *vigava*.
A *vigava* times a *vigava* equals a *saṃkrama*.

A *saṃkrama* times a *saṃkrama* equals a *visara.*
A *visara* times a *visara* equals a *vijambha.*
A *vijambha* times a *vijambha* equals a *vijāga.*
A *vijāga* times a *vijāga* equals a *visota.*
A *visota* times a *visota* equals a *vivāha.*
A *vivāha* times a *vivāha* equals a *vibhakti.*
A *vibhakti* times a *vibhakti* equals a *vikhyāta.*
A *vikhyāta* times a *vikhyāta* equals a *tulana.*
A *tulana* times a *tulana* equals a *dharaṇa.*
A *dharaṇa* times a *dharaṇa* equals a *vipatha.*
A *vipatha* times a *vipatha* equals a *viparya.*
A *viparya* times a *viparya* equals a *samarya.*
A *samarya* times a *samarya* equals a *viturṇa.*
A *viturṇa* times a *viturṇa* equals a *hevara.*
A *hevara* times a *hevara* equals a *vicāra.*
A *vicāra* times a *vicāra* equals a *vicasta.*
A *vicasta* times a *vicasta* equals an *atyudgata.*
An *atyudgata* times an *atyudgata* equals a *viśiṣṭa.*
A *viśiṣṭa* times a *viśiṣṭa* equals a *nevala.*
A *nevala* times a *nevala* equals a *hariva.*
A *hariva* times a *hariva* equals a *vikṣobha.*
A *vikṣobha* times a *vikṣobha* equals a *halibhu.*
A *halibhu* times a *halibhu* equals a *harisa.*
A *harisa* times a *harisa* equals a *heluga.*
A *heluga* times a *heluga* equals a *drabuddha.*
A *drabuddha* times a *drabuddha* equals a *haruṇa.*
A *haruṇa* times a *haruṇa* equals a *maluda.*
A *maluda* times a *maluda* equals a *kṣamuda.*
A *kṣamuda* times a *kṣamuda* equals an *elada.*
An *elada* times an *elada* equals a *maluma.*
A *maluma* times a *maluma* equals a *sadama.*
A *sadama* times a *sadama* equals a *vimuda.*
A *vimuda* times a *vimuda* equals a *vaimātra.*
A *vaimātra* times a *vaimātra* equals a *pramātra.*
A *pramātra* times a *pramātra* equals an *amātra.*
An *amātra* times an *amātra* equals a *bhramātra.*
A *bhramātra* times a *bhramātra* equals a *gamātra.*
A *gamātra* times a *gamātra* equals a *namātra.*
A *namātra* times a *namātra* equals a *hemātra.*
A *hemātra* times a *hemātra* equals a *vemātra.*

A *vemātra* times a *vemātra* equals a *paramātra*.
A *paramātra* times a *paramātra* equals a *śivamātra*.
A *śivamātra* times a *śivamātra* equals an *ela*.
An *ela* times an *ela* equals a *vela*.
A *vela* times a *vela* equals a *tela*.
A *tela* times a *tela* equals a *gela*.
A *gela* times a *gela* equals a *svela*.
A *svela* times a *svela* equals a *nela*.
A *nela* times a *nela* equals a *kela*.
A *kela* times a *kela* equals a *sela*.
A *sela* times a *sela* equals a *phela*.
A *phela* times a *phela* equals a *mela*.
A *mela* times a *mela* equals a *saraṭa*.
A *saraṭa* times a *saraṭa* equals a *meruda*.
A *meruda* times a *meruda* equals a *kheluda*.
A *kheluda* times a *kheluda* equals a *mātula*.
A *mātula* times a *mātula* equals a *samula*.
A *samula* times a *samula* equals an *ayava*.
An *ayava* times an *ayava* equals a *kamala*.
A *kamala* times a *kamala* equals a *magava*.
A *magava* times a *magava* equals an *atara*.
An *atara* times an *atara* equals a *heluya*.
A *heluya* times a *heluya* equals a *veluva*.
A *veluva* times a *veluva* equals a *kalāpa*.
A *kalāpa* times a *kalāpa* equals a *havava*.
A *havava* times a *havava* equals a *vivara*.
A *vivara* times a *vivara* equals a *navara*.
A *navara* times a *navara* equals a *malara*.
A *malara* times a *malara* equals a *savara*.
A *savara* times a *savara* equals a *meruṭu*.
A *meruṭu* times a *meruṭu* equals a *camara*.
A *camara* times a *camara* equals a *dhamara*.
A *dhamara* times a *dhamara* equals a *pramāda*.
A *pramāda* times a *pramāda* equals a *vigama*.
A *vigama* times a *vigama* equals an *upavarta*.
An *upavarta* times an *upavarta* equals a *nirdeśa*.
A *nirdeśa* times a *nirdeśa* equals an *akṣaya*.
An *akṣaya* times an *akṣaya* equals a *sambhūta*.
A *sambhūta* times a *sambhūta* equals an *amama*.
An *amama* times an *amama* equals an *avānta*.

An *avānta* times an *avānta* equals an *utpala*.
An *utpala* times an *utpala* equals a *padma*.
A *padma* times a *padma* equals a *saṃkhyā*.
A *saṃkhyā* times a *saṃkhyā* equals a *gati*.
A *gati* times a *gati* equals an *upagama*.
An *upagama* times an *upagama* equals an *asaṃkhyeya*.
An *asaṃkhyeya* times an *asaṃkhyeya* equals an *asaṃkhyeya-parivarta*.
An *asaṃkhyeya-parivarta* times an *asaṃkhyeya-parivarta* equals an *aparimāṇa*.
An *aparimāṇa* times an *aparimāṇa* equals an *aparimāṇa-parivarta*.
An *aparimāṇa-parivarta* times an *aparimāṇa-parivarta* equals an *aparyanta*.
An *aparyanta* times an *aparyanta* equals an *aparyanta-parivarta*.
An *aparyanta-parivarta* times an *aparyanta-parivarta* equals an *asamanta*.
An *asamanta* times an *asamanta* equals an *asamanta-parivarta*.
An *asamanta-parivarta* times an *asamanta-parivarta* equals an *agaṇeya*.
An *agaṇeya* times an *agaṇeya* equals an *agaṇeya-parivarta*.
An *agaṇeya-parivarta* times an *agaṇeya-parivarta* equals an *atulya*.
An *atulya* times an *atulya* equals an *atulya-parivarta*.
An *atulya-parivarta* times an *atulya-parivarta* equals an *acintya*.
An *acintya* times an *acintya* equals an *acintya-parivarta*.
An *acintya-parivarta* times an *acintya-parivarta* equals an *ameya*.
An *ameya* times an *ameya* equals an *ameya-parivarta*.
An *ameya-parivarta* times an *ameya-parivarta* equals an *anabhilāpya*.
An *anabhilāpya* times an *anabhilāpya* equals an *anabhilāpya-parivarta*.
An *anabhilāpya-parivarta* times an *anabhilāpya-parivarta* equals an *anabhilāpyānabhilāpya*.
This *anabhilāpyānabhilāpya*, times an *anabhilāpyānabhilāpya* equals an *anabhilāpyānabhilāpya-parivarta*.

The Buddha then concluded the chapter with a verse of one hundred and twenty stanzas repeatedly illustrating in many different ways the infinity of the inconceivably and infinitely large and vast and the inconceivably and infinitely tiny and microscopic and the pervasive interpenetration of them all in which inconceivably large numbers of infinitely vast cosmic terrains are found even in a single hair pore or on the tip of a single hair.

With regard to these verses, National Master Qingliang says: "The following one hundred and twenty verses consist of two major parts: The first six verses explain that Samantabhadra's meritorious qualities are so vast that one could never finish describing them. The remaining verses explain that the qualities of the Buddha are deep and vast and Samantabhadra exhaustively fathoms them all. Those first [six verses] are divided into two parts, of which the first four and a half verses clarify that the bases by which one is able to count them are numerous, whereas the last one and a half verses reveal that what is to be counted is vast." (百二十偈大分為二前六明普賢德廣說不可盡餘偈明佛德深廣普賢窮究前中分二前四偈半明能數多後一偈半顯所數廣 / L130n1557_0687b06)

Qingliang next mentions that there are ten levels to the description of the phenomena constituting the bases for enumerating the innumerable meritorious qualities of Samantabhadra. Obviously, this entire description is rooted in the Avataṃsaka Sutra's distinctive principle of "the interpenetration of all phenomena (large and small) with all other phenomena" which is one of the most outstanding and pervasive ideas in the entire sutra.

For those wishing to put a western style number on a few of these Sanskrit numerical designations, Upāsaka Ling Feng calculated the twenty highest levels of designations as follows:

asaṃkhyeya (阿僧祇) 10^7.09884336127809E+031
asaṃkhyeya-parivarta (阿僧祇轉) 10^1.41976867225562E+032
aparimāṇa (無量) 10^2.83953734451123E+032
aparimāṇa-parivarta (無量轉) 10^5.67907468902247E+032
aparyanta (無邊) 10^1.13581493780449E+033
aparyanta-parivarta (無邊轉) 10^2.27162987560899E+033
asamanta (無等) 10^4.54325975121797E+033
asamanta-parivarta (無等轉) 10^9.08651950243595E+033
agaṇeya (不可數) 10^1.81730390048719E+034
agaṇeya-parivarta (不可數轉) 10^3.63460780097438E+034
atulya (不可稱) 10^7.26921560194876E+034
atulya-parivarta (不可稱轉) 10^1.45384312038975E+035
acintya (不可思) 10^2.9076862407795E+035
acintya-parivarta (不可思轉) 10^5.81537248155901E+035
ameya (不可量) 10^1.1630744963118E+036
ameya-parivarta (不可量轉) 10^2.3261489926236E+036
anabhilāpya (不可說) 10^4.65229798524721E+036
anabhilāpya-parivarta (不可說轉) 10^9.30459597049441E+036
anabhilāpyānabhilāpya (不可說不可說) 10^1.86091919409888E+037
anabhilāpyānabhilāpya-parivarta (不可說不可說轉)
= 10^3.72183838819776E+037

Chapter 31
Life Spans

In this very short one-page chapter, Mind King Bodhisattva told the bodhisattvas in that congregation:

"Sons of the Buddha, a single kalpa in Śākyamuni Buddha's buddha *kṣetra* equals a single day and a single night in Amitābha Buddha's buddha *kṣetra* known as the World of Ultimate Bliss. A single kalpa in the World of Ultimate Bliss equals a single day and a single night in Vajra Solidity Buddha's buddha *kṣetra* known as Kaṣāya Banner World. A single kalpa in the Kaṣāya Banner World equals a single day and a single night in Lotus Blooming in Excellent Light Buddha's buddha *kṣetra* known as Voice of the Irreversible Wheel."

Mind King Bodhisattvas continued in this manner six more times, in each case saying that a single kalpa in a particular world is equal to but a day and a night in the next world, after which he said:

"Sons of the Buddha, following an orderly sequence such as this on through beyond a hundred myriads of *asaṃkhyeyas* of worlds, a kalpa in the very last of those worlds is equal to a day and a night in Worthy Supremacy Buddha's buddha *kṣetra* known as the Supreme Lotus World. It is completely filled with bodhisattvas such as Samantabhadra Bodhisattva and other such bodhisattvas who cultivate the same practices."

Apparently, the point of this would be to inform us that the unreality, mere relativity, and complete strangeness of time is so strange that a life of a hundred years here in this world probably takes no longer than the time that it would take to drink a cup of tea in some more refined world. So too, it is probably the case that all the time that has elapsed since the age of the dinosaurs in this world probably only equals the time of a sneeze in some other even more refined world than this.

Chapter 32

The Bodhisattva Abodes

In this chapter, Mind King Bodhisattva told the congregation of bodhisattvas of twenty-two places where, from the distant past until now, there have been congregations of bodhisattvas each headed by a great bodhisattva, with one of these groups of bodhisattvas off in each of the four directions, on Vajra Mountain off in the ocean, in places off toward the four midpoints of the northeast, southeast, southwest, northwest, in a place called Adorned Cave out in the ocean, in a place south of Vaiśālī, in the city of Mathurā, in the city of Kuṇḍina, in the city of Pure Perfection, in the state of Marūndha, in the state of Kamboja, in China, in Kashgar, in Kashmir, in the city of Increasing Delight, in the state of Ambulima, and in Gandhara. Thus he made it known to them that great bodhisattvas have all along been dwelling in all these places all over the world for an immensely long time, beginning well before Śākyamuni Buddha descended to take birth in Lumbini. The implication here would seem to be that great bodhisattvas are always present in the world, even between those times when the buddhas come forth to make their ever-so-rare appearances to make right Dharma well known in the world.

Chapter 33
The Inconceivable Dharmas of the Buddhas

This chapter begins with bodhisattvas in that great congregation spontaneously and simultaneously giving rise to ten questions in their minds, all of them wondering how the following matters related to the buddhas are inconceivable, namely: the lands of the buddhas, the original vows of the buddhas, the lineage of the buddhas, the buddhas' appearances in the world, the bodies of the buddhas, the voices of the buddhas, the wisdom of the buddhas, the sovereign powers of the buddhas, the unimpeded qualities of the buddhas, and the liberations of the buddhas.

Aware of the thoughts in the minds of those bodhisattvas, the Buddha enabled Blue Lotus Treasury Bodhisattva to gain a penetrating comprehension of all these matters, after which, aided by the Buddha's spiritual powers, this Blue Lotus Treasury Bodhisattva spoke to Lotus Treasury Bodhisattva and proceeded to describe the following aspects, qualities, and capacities of all buddhas:

Their countless abodes (of which he describes eight abodes);
Their ten kinds of dharmas by which they go everywhere throughout the Dharma realm;
Their ten kinds of knowledge they produce in every mind-moment;
Their ten ways in which they never miss the right time;
Their ten kinds of inconceivable spheres of action;
Their ten kinds of wisdom;
Their ten kinds of dharmas of pervasive entry;
Their ten kinds of vast dharmas;
Their ten kinds of great meritorious qualities;
Their ten kinds of ultimate purity;
Their ten kinds of buddha works;
Their ten kinds of dharmas associated with their ocean of wisdom;
Their ten kinds of dharmas which they always manifest;
Their ten kinds of discourse on all buddhas' countless Dharma gates;
Their ten ways in which they do buddha works for beings;
Their ten kinds of supreme dharmas;
Their ten kinds of unimpeded abiding;
Their ten kinds of supreme and unsurpassable adornments;
Their ten kinds of dharmas of sovereign mastery;
Their ten kinds of measureless and inconceivable perfectly fulfilled buddha dharmas;

Their ten kinds of skillful means;
Their ten kinds of vast buddha works;
Their ten kinds of masterful actions that could not be otherwise;
Their ten kinds of abiding in which they abide in all dharmas;
Their ten kinds of knowing of all dharmas without exception;
Their ten kinds of powers;
Their ten kinds of *nārāyaṇa* banner dharmas of bravery and strength;
Their ten kinds of definite dharmas;
Their ten kinds of swiftness dharmas;
Their ten kinds of pure dharmas that one should always bear in mind;
Their ten kinds of omniscient abiding;
Their ten kinds of measureless and inconceivable buddha samādhis;
Their ten kinds of unimpeded liberation.

It is Blue Lotus Treasury Bodhisattva's narration of these lists of all buddhas' inconceivable matters that constitutes the entirety of this chapter.

Chapter 34

The Ocean of Major Marks of the Tathāgata's Ten Bodies

Samantabhadra Bodhisattva told that great congregation of bodhisattvas, "I shall now explain for you the ocean of the Tathāgata's marks," whereupon he spoke of the marks on the body of the Buddha, beginning with the following thirty-two marks on the top of the buddha's head:

The light that illuminates all regions, everywhere emanating an immeasurably vast net of light rays;
The cloud of light of the buddha eye;
The cloud that fills the Dharma realm;
The cloud that manifests pervasive illumination;
The cloud that emanates the light of jewels;
The cloud that reveals the great sovereign mastery of the Tathāgata throughout the Dharma realm;
The Tathāgata's cloud of universally pervasive lamplight;
The vast cloud that everywhere illuminates all buddhas;
The cloud of light spheres;
The light cloud that everywhere illuminates the treasury of all bodhisattvas' practices;
The universally illuminating cloud of dazzling light;
The cloud of the right enlightenment;
The cloud of dazzling light;
The cloud of universally illuminating adornments;
The cloud revealing the practice of the Buddha's ocean of samādhis;
The universally illuminating cloud of the ocean of transformations;
The cloud of all *tathāgatas'* liberations;
The universally illuminating cloud of freely implemented expedient means;
The cloud instigating awakening to the lineage of the buddhas;
The cloud of sovereign powers revealing the marks of all *tathāgatas;*
The cloud that everywhere illuminates the entire Dharma realm;
The cloud of Vairocana Tathāgata's marks;
The light cloud that everywhere illuminates all buddhas;
The cloud that everywhere reveals all adornments;
The cloud that emanates all sounds of the Dharma realm;
The cloud that everywhere illuminates the sphere of all buddhas' spiritual transformations.

The cloud whose light illuminates the ocean of buddhas;
The cloud of bejeweled lamps;
The cloud of the undifferentiated Dharma realm;
The pervasively illuminating cloud that abides in the ocean of all worlds;
The cloud of all jewels' pure flaming radiance; and
The cloud that everywhere illuminates the entire Dharma realm's adornments.

Having spoken of these thirty-two marks on the top of the Buddha's head, for the remainder of the chapter, Samantabhadra Bodhisattva spoke of:

The thirty-third mark, a light cloud between the Buddha's eyebrows that is known as "the light cloud that pervades the Dharma realm";
The thirty-fourth mark, a mark of the Tathāgata's eyes that is known as "the cloud of independent pervasive vision";
The thirty-fifth mark, a mark of the Tathāgata's nose that is known as "the cloud of all spiritual superknowledges and wisdom";
The thirty-sixth mark, a mark of the Tathāgata's tongue that is known as "the cloud that manifests sounds and reflected images";
The thirty-seventh mark, a mark of the Tathāgata's tongue that is known as "the Dharma realm cloud";
The thirty-eighth mark, a mark of the Tathāgata's tongue that is known as "the light cloud that illuminates the Dharma realm";
The thirty-ninth mark, a mark of the Tathāgata's tongue that is known as "the cloud that illuminates the Dharma realm with dazzling radiance";
The fortieth mark, a mark of the Tathāgata's upper palate that is known as "the cloud that reveals the inconceivable Dharma realm";
The forty-first mark, a mark of the Tathāgata's lower right front teeth that is known as "the buddha tooth cloud";
The forty-second mark, a mark of the Tathāgata's upper right front teeth that is known as "the cloud of flaming jewel light Sumeru treasuries";
The forty-third mark, a mark of the Tathāgata's lower left front teeth that is known as "the universally illuminating cloud of jewel lamplight";
The forty-fourth mark, a mark of the Tathāgata's upper left front teeth that is known as "the cloud that illuminates the *tathāgatas*";
The forty-fifth mark, a mark of the Tathāgata's teeth that is known as "the cloud that manifests light everywhere";
The forty-sixth mark, a mark of the Tathāgata's lips that is known as "the cloud that reflects the light of all jewels";

The forty-seventh mark, a mark of the Tathāgata's neck that is known as "the cloud that everywhere illuminates all worlds";
The forty-eighth mark, a mark of the Tathāgata's right shoulder that is known as "the Buddha's vast cloud of every kind of jewel";
The forty-ninth mark, another mark of the Tathāgata's right shoulder that is known as "the cloud of supreme jewels' universal illumination";
The fiftieth mark, a mark of the Tathāgata's left shoulder that is known as "the cloud of supreme light that illuminates the Dharma realm";
The fifty-first mark, another mark of the Tathāgata's left shoulder that is known as "the cloud of universally illuminating light";
The fifty-second mark, another mark of the Tathāgata's left shoulder that is known as "the cloud of universally illuminating dazzling light";
The fifty-third mark, a mark of the Tathāgata's chest shaped like a *svastika* emblem that is known as "the cloud of the ocean of auspiciousness";
The fifty-fourth mark, a mark just to the right of the *svastika* emblem of auspiciousness that is known as "the cloud that manifests radiant illumination";
The fifty-fifth mark, a mark also just to the right of the *svastika* emblem of auspiciousness that is known as "the cloud that everywhere reveals the *tathāgatas*";
The fifty-sixth mark, another mark to the right of the *svastika* emblem of auspiciousness that is known as "the cloud of blooming flowers";
The fifty-seventh mark, another mark to the right of the *svastika* emblem of auspiciousness that is known as "the delightful golden cloud";
The fifty-eighth mark, another mark to the right of the *svastika* emblem of auspiciousness that is known as "the cloud of the ocean of buddhas";
The fifty-ninth mark, a mark to the left of the *svastika* emblem of auspiciousness that is known as "the cloud that manifests light";
The sixtieth mark, a mark just to the left of the *svastika* emblem of auspiciousness that is known as "the cloud that manifests light throughout the Dharma realm";
The sixty-first mark, a mark also just to the left of the *svastika* emblem of auspiciousness that is known as "the cloud of universal supremacy";

The sixty-second mark, another mark to the left of the *svastika* emblem of auspiciousness that is known as "the cloud of the marvelous sounds of turning the Dharma wheel";

The sixty-third mark, another mark to the left of the *svastika* emblem of auspiciousness that is known as "the cloud of adornments";

The sixty-fourth mark, a mark of the Tathāgata's right hand that is known as "the cloud of oceanic illumination";

The sixty-fifth mark, another mark of the Tathāgata's right hand that is known as "the cloud that reflects dazzling illumination";

The sixty-sixth mark, another mark of the Tathāgata's right hand that is known as "the universally purifying cloud of flaming lamplight and garlands";

The sixty-seventh mark, another mark of the Tathāgata's right hand that is known as "the cloud that everywhere reveals all *maṇi* jewels";

The sixty-eighth mark, another mark of the Tathāgata's right hand that is known as "the cloud of radiance";

The sixty-ninth mark, a mark of the Tathāgata's left hand that is known as "the cloud of pure *vaiḍūrya* lamplight";

The seventieth mark, another mark of the Tathāgata's left hand that is known as "the cloud of voices of the lamps of wisdom throughout all *kṣetras*";

The seventy-first mark, another mark of the Tathāgata's left hand that is known as "the cloud of light dwelling in a jeweled lotus";

The seventy-second mark, another mark of the Tathāgata's left hand that is known as "the cloud that everywhere illuminates the Dharma realm";

The seventy-third mark, a mark of the fingers of the Tathāgata's right hand that is known as "the swirling cloud revealing the ocean of all kalpas and *kṣetras*";

The seventy-fourth mark, a mark of the fingers of the Tathāgata's left hand that is known as "the cloud that rests on all kinds of jewels";

The seventy-fifth mark, a mark of the Tathāgata's right palm that is known as "the cloud of dazzling illumination";

The seventy-sixth mark, a mark of the Tathāgata's left palm that is known as "the cloud of flaming light spheres that everywhere increase the transformationally manifested sites of enlightenment throughout the Dharma realm";

The seventy-seventh mark, a mark of the Tathāgata's genital ensheathment that is known as "the cloud that everywhere streams forth the voice of the Buddha";

The seventy-eighth mark, a mark of the Tathāgata's right hip that is known as "the universally illuminating cloud of bejeweled lamps and garlands";

The seventy-ninth mark, a mark of the Tathāgata's left hip that is known as "the cloud that reveals the light of the ocean of the entire Dharma realm and blankets empty space";

The eightieth mark, a mark of the Tathāgata's right thigh that is known as "the universally revealing cloud";

The eighty-first mark, a mark of the Tathāgata's left thigh that is known as "the cloud that reveals the ocean of the countless signs of all buddhas";

The eighty-second mark, a mark of the Tathāgata's right calf that is known as "the cloud of all of empty space and the Dharma realm";

The eighty-third mark, a mark of the Tathāgata's left calf that is known as "the cloud of an ocean of adornments";

The eighty-fourth mark, a mark of the hair on the Tathāgata's jewel-adorned calves that is known as "the cloud that everywhere reveals reflected images of the Dharma realm";

The eighty-fifth mark, a mark of the bottom of the Tathāgata's feet that is known as "the cloud in which the ocean of all bodhisattvas resides";

The eighty-sixth mark, a mark of the top of the Tathāgata's right foot that is known as ""the light cloud that everywhere illuminates everything;

The eighty-seventh mark, a mark of the top of the Tathāgata's left foot that is known as "the cloud that everywhere reveals all buddhas";

The eighty-eighth mark, a mark of the spaces between the toes of the Tathāgata's right foot that is known as "the cloud that brightly illuminates the ocean of the entire Dharma realm";

The eighty-ninth mark, a mark of the spaces between the toes of the Tathāgata's left foot that is known as "the cloud that reveals the ocean of all buddhas";

The ninetieth mark, a mark of the Tathāgata's right heel that is known as "the cloud of freely shining dazzling illumination";

The ninety-first mark, a mark of the Tathāgata's left heel that is known as "the cloud that reveals the marvelous voice expounding on the ocean of all dharmas";

The ninety-second mark, a mark of the Tathāgata's right ankle that is known as "the light cloud that reveals all adornments";

The ninety-third mark, a mark of the Tathāgata's left ankle that is known as "the cloud that reveals the many forms and appearances";

The ninety-fourth mark, a mark of the circumference of the Tathāgata's right foot that is known as "the cloud of the universal treasury";

The ninety-fifth mark, a mark of the circumference of the Tathāgata's left foot that is known as "the cloud whose light everywhere illuminates the Dharma realm";

The ninety-sixth mark, a mark of the tips of the Tathāgata's right toes that is known as "the cloud that reveals adornments"; and

The ninety-seventh mark, a mark of the tips of the Tathāgata's left toes that is known as "the cloud that reveals the spiritual transformations of all buddhas."

Having described these ninety-seven marks associated with parts of the Buddha's body, Samantabhadra Bodhisattva ended this chapter by saying: "Sons of the Buddha, Vairocana Tathāgata has marks of the great man such as these as numerous as the atoms in ten oceans of worlds such as the Flower Treasury World. Every one of the parts of his body is adorned with marvelous signs made of the many kinds of jewels."

CHAPTER 35
Qualities of the Light of the Tathāgata's Subsidiary Signs

The chapter opens with the Buddha telling Jewel Hand Bodhisattva that the Buddha has a subsidiary sign known as "the king of perfect fulfillment" from which there streams forth a great light known as "flourishing abundance" which has a retinue of countless light rays. He then told the bodhisattvas in that great assembly that, when he was a bodhisattva in the Tuṣita Heaven palace, he emanated a great light that illuminated countless worlds and caused all those worlds' hell-realm beings to have no more suffering, to have their six sense faculties purified, and then, once their lives had come to an end, to gain rebirth in the Tuṣita Heaven. Having been reborn there, a drum in that heaven called "Delightful" emanated a voice that told them all how it was that they were able to be reborn in the Tuṣita Heaven, that this was a function of a thousand-spoked wheel emblem on the bottom of the Bodhisattva's feet known as "the king of universally illuminating light" which has a subsidiary sign known as "the king of perfect fulfillment" that always emanates forty kinds of light, one of which is known as "pure meritorious qualities" which is able to illuminate countless worlds and which, adapting to beings' karma and aspirations, enables them to become fully ripened. When beings undergoing the most extreme sufferings in the Avīci Hells encounter this light, once they all reach the end of their lives there, they are born in the Tuṣita Heaven. Having been reborn in this heaven, they then hear the sound of the celestial drum telling them: "Good indeed. Good indeed. Sons of the Devas, Vairocana Bodhisattva has entered the stainless samādhi. You should go and bow in reverence to him."

Having heard these sounds, those beings who had become devas' sons in the Tuṣita Heaven prepared to make offerings to Vairocana Bodhisattva by transformationally creating myriads of clouds of flowers, incense, music, banners, canopies, and praise songs. Having done so, they found they were unable to see the bodhisattva, for, as they were told by a devas' son, that Vairocana Bodhisattva had already descended from the Tuṣita Heaven into the world where he now dwelt in the womb of the Lady Māyā.

Those devas' sons used their heavenly eyes to see the body of the Bodhisattva in the human realm in the household of the Pure Rice King and then felt motivated to descend to Jambudvīpa to pay their respects and express their gratitude to the Bodhisattva there. When they had this thought, the celestial drum emanated a voice which told them that, since the Bodhisattva's descent to take rebirth in the world was only an appearance produced by skillful means adapted to what is appropriate for the teaching of beings in the world, they should all instead "bring forth the resolve to attain *anuttara-samyak-saṃbodhi,* purify your minds, abide in the fine awesome deportment, repent of and rid yourselves of all karmic obstacles, all affliction obstacles, all retribution obstacles, and all obstacles arising from views. Using bodies as numerous as all beings throughout the Dharma realm, using heads as numerous as all beings throughout the Dharma realm, using tongues as numerous as all beings throughout the Dharma realm, and using good physical actions, good verbal actions, and good mental actions as numerous as all beings throughout the Dharma realm, you should repent of and rid yourselves of all obstacles and faults."

Those devas' sons then asked the celestial drum, "How then is it that the bodhisattva-*mahāsattva* repents of and rids himself of all faults?" The celestial drum told them that, as regards karmic deeds, "Although they are able to produce all kinds of karmic rewards and retributions, they have no place from whence they come and no place to which they go. Sons of the Devas, it is as if there were a master conjurer who used illusions to deceive people's vision. One should realize that all karmic deeds are just the same as this. If one knows them in this way, then this constitutes [the means of] genuine repentance by which all the evils of one's karmic offenses can be purified."

Having heard this teaching, those devas gained the unproduced dharmas patience and resolved to attain highest enlightenment. Then, "due to having reached the ten grounds by hearing the teaching of Samantabhadra's vast dedications, due to acquiring samādhis adorned with powers, and due to repenting and ridding themselves of all their heavy karmic obstacles by engaging in the three kinds of pure karmic actions as numerous as all beings, all those devas immediately saw seven-jeweled lotus flowers as numerous as the atoms in a hundred thousand *koṭīs* of *nayutas* of buddha *kṣetras.* Atop every one of those flowers, there was a bodhisattva seated in the lotus posture emanating a great light. Every one of the subsidiary signs of those bodhisattvas emanated light rays as numerous as all beings and, within those light rays, there were buddhas as numerous as all beings who were seated in the lotus posture, speaking the Dharma for beings in ways adapted to the minds of those beings, and yet they still had not yet manifested even a small amount of the powers of the samādhi of stainless purity."

Those devas then transformationally created clouds of fine flowers as offerings to Vairocana Tathāgata, "doing so by taking them up and scattering them down over the Buddha, where all those flowers then remained suspended in the air above the Buddha's body. All their clouds of fragrance then everywhere rained down their fragrances across a number of worlds as numerous as the atoms in countless buddha *kṣetras.* Wherever any being's body received this fragrance, his body felt peace and happiness comparable to that of a bhikshu who, on entering the fourth *dhyāna,* then experiences the complete melting away of all of his karmic obstacles."

Of those beings possessed of karmic obstacles who heard this teaching, those who smelled this fragrance realized their inherent unreality and then created fragrance banner clouds and spontaneously acquired radiant pure roots of goodness. Whenever any beings saw their canopy clouds, they planted roots of goodness equal to those of pure gold net wheel-turning kings as numerous as sands in the Ganges River.

There then followed a description of the vast teaching activities of the wheel-turning king whose teaching activities and powers are so marvelous that anyone who is touched by a ray of his light becomes bound to attain the position of a bodhisattva on the tenth bodhisattva ground due to the power of having previously cultivated roots of goodness. At the end of the chapter, the Buddha told Jewel Hand Bodhisattva that all such teaching activities and "all circumstances such as these are brought to perfect development through the extremely deep samādhi, merit, and roots of goodness of a pure gold net wheel-turning king."

Chapter 36
The Practices of Samantabhadra

The chapter begins with Samantabhadra Bodhisattva addressing that great assembly of bodhisattvas, telling them that all buddhas come into the world for beings because of beings' absence of wisdom on account of which they commit evil deeds, their conception of a self and its possessions, their attachment to the body, their inverted views and skeptical doubtfulness, their discriminations based on wrong views, their constant involvement with the fetters and bonds, their following along with the flow of *saṃsāra,* and their tendency to stray away from the path of the Tathāgata.

Samantabhadra next said that he sees no transgression greater than when a bodhisattva engenders thoughts of hatred toward other bodhisattvas, this because it creates a gateway to a million obstacles of which he then listed ninety-two of them, beginning with:

The obstacle of not perceiving bodhi;
The obstacle of not hearing right Dharma;
The obstacle of being reborn in an impure world;
The obstacle of being reborn in the wretched rebirth destinies;
The obstacle of being reborn into the [eight] difficult circumstances;
The obstacle of being much beset by illnesses;
The obstacle of being extensively slandered by others;
The obstacle of being reborn in destinies with unintelligent beings;
The obstacle of diminished right mindfulness; and
The obstacle of deficient wisdom.

The list ends with:

The obstacle of having cut oneself off from the bodhisattva's domain of objective experience;
The obstacle of having a mind that timidly retreats from the bodhisattva's heroically courageous dharmas;
The obstacle of having a mind that is indolent in its pursuit of the bodhisattva's path of emancipation;
The obstacle of having a mind that stops and rests at the gateway to the bodhisattva's light of wisdom;
The obstacle of having a mind that becomes inferior and weak in developing the bodhisattva's power of mindfulness;
The obstacle of being unable to maintain and preserve the Tathāgata's teaching dharmas;

The obstacle of being unable to draw near to the bodhisattva's path of transcending births in cyclic existence;

The obstacle of being unable to cultivate the uncorrupted path of the bodhisattva;

The obstacle of pursuing realization of the Two Vehicles' right and fixed position; and

The obstacle of distancing oneself from the lineage of all buddhas and bodhisattvas of the three periods of time.

Samantabhadra next said that, if a bodhisattva wishes to swiftly fulfill all the bodhisattva practices, he should cultivate ten dharmas, namely:

His mind never abandons any being;

He envisions all bodhisattvas as *tathāgatas;*

He never slanders any dharma of the Buddha;

He realizes that all lands are endless;

He feels deep faith and delight in the bodhisattva practices;

He never relinquishes a bodhi resolve that is commensurate with empty space and the Dharma realm;

He contemplates bodhi and enters the powers of the Tathāgata;

He is energetically diligent in cultivating unimpeded eloquence;

He is tireless in teaching beings; and

He abides in any world with a mind free of attachments.

Samantabhadra next said that, after the bodhisattva securely abides in these ten dharmas, he is then able to fulfill ten kinds of purity which in turn lead to his fulfillment of ten kinds of vast knowledge, after which he succeeds in entering ten kinds of universal penetration and then in abiding in ten kinds of supremely sublime mind.

Samantabhadra Bodhisattva next said that, after the bodhisattva comes to abide in these ten kinds of supremely sublime mind, he acquires ten kinds of skillful knowledge with regard to the Dharma of the Buddha. He next says that, once they have heard these dharmas, all bodhisattva-*mahāsattvas* who uphold these dharmas will be able to quickly reach highest enlightenment and fulfill all dharmas of the Buddha that are equal to those of all buddhas of the three periods of time.

Then, because of the Buddha's spiritual powers, the worlds of the ten directions shook and moved in six ways, after which the skies rained down clouds of flowers, incense, robes, canopies, banners, pennants, jewels, and other adornments. There were also clouds of music, clouds of bodhisattvas, clouds of *tathāgatas'* physical signs, clouds of praises of the Tathāgata, clouds of *tathāgatas'* voices, and other such clouds, including clouds of lights and clouds of proclamations of Dharma through the use of spiritual powers.

And just as, in this world with its four continents, beneath the bodhi tree, in the *bodhimaṇḍa,* within the bodhisattva's palace, one could see the Tathāgata realize the universal and right enlightenment and then proclaim this Dharma, so too could one see this in all worlds throughout the ten directions. Then, from each of the ten directions, beyond a number of worlds as numerous as the atoms in ten ineffable numbers of large buddha *kṣetras,* bodhisattva-*mahāsattvas* as numerous as the atoms in ten buddha *kṣetras* came forth to this land to pay their respects and, filling up the ten directions, they spoke words such as these: "It is good indeed, good indeed, O Son of the Buddha, that you have now been able to speak of the profound dharmas of the greatest vows and the prediction of buddhahood of all buddhas, all *tathāgatas.*

"O Son of the Buddha, all of us have the same name, 'Samantabhadra.' We have each come to pay our respects in this land, coming here from the abode of Universal Banner of Mastery Tathāgata in the Universal Supremacy World. Through the Buddha's spiritual powers, all of us proclaim this Dharma everywhere just as it is set forth in the midst of this congregation, doing so in a way that everything is the same, free of any additions or omissions. Through having received the aid of the Buddha's awesome spiritual power, we have all come to this *bodhimaṇḍa* to serve as certifying witnesses for you. And just as we bodhisattvas as numerous as the atoms in ten buddha *kṣetras* have come to this *bodhimaṇḍa* to serve here as certifying witnesses, so too is this also so in all other worlds throughout the ten directions."

Finally, aided by the Buddha's spiritual power and the power of his own roots of goodness, Samantabhadra Bodhisattva spoke a verse of one hundred and twenty-one stanzas that reiterated and expanded upon the aforementioned ideas while also clarifying the wisdom, vows, and powers integral to the practices of Samantabhadra.

Chapter 37
The Manifestation of the Tathāgata

This chapter begins with the Buddha emanating from the white hair mark between his brows a great light known as "the manifestation of the Tathāgata" that had a retinue of countless light rays. It illuminated all worlds throughout the ten directions after which it circumambulated him ten times while revealing his measureless works of miraculous spiritual powers and awakening countless bodhisattvas. It then caused shaking and movement in all worlds of the ten directions, extinguished the sufferings in the wretched destinies, and obscured the palaces of the *māras*, after which it revealed all buddhas and their congregations, circumambulated the congregation of bodhisattvas, and then entered the top of the head of Sublime Qualities of the Manifestations of the Tathāgata's Nature Bodhisattva. That bodhisattva then respectfully knelt on one knee before the Buddha and spoke ten verses in which he asked the Buddha, "Who is the Tathāgata's most senior Dharma son who is able to expound on the Buddhas sphere of actions?"

In response to this, the Tathāgata emanated a great light from his mouth which did all that the previous light from his forehead had done, after which it entered the mouth of Samantabhadra Bodhisattva and caused the light of that bodhisattva's body to become a hundred times brighter. Sublime Qualities Bodhisattva then asked Samantabhadra to explain this auspicious sign just then manifested by the Buddha, after which Samantabhadra replied that he had seen this same display of auspicious signs in the past which then was followed by those earlier buddhas proceeding to explain the Dharma gateway known as "the manifestation of the Tathāgata." Sublime Qualities then asked Samantabhadra how one should understand this dharma of the manifestation of the Tathāgata. Then, having declared that those in that assembly were well qualified to receive such a teaching and having stated that Samantabhadra was well qualified to expound on this matter, he spoke another series of verses by which he formally asked Samantabhadra to please proceed to explain this dharma of the manifestation of the Tathāgata.

Samantabhadra replied by saying that this circumstance is inconceivable and that it is because of countless dharmas that the Tathāgata's enlightenment is able to manifest. He then declared that it was due to ten measureless matters subsuming hundreds of thousands of *asaṃkhyeyas* of factors that the manifestation of the Tathāgata is able to be accomplished and that the manifestation of the Tathāgata is characterized by ten marks. He then said that there are ten marks of the Tathāgata's body.

Samantabhadra next spoke of ten marks of the voice of the Tathāgata. Then having spoken of the ten marks of the Tathāgata's voice, he expounded on the ten kinds of measurelessness of the Tathāgata's voice. Having spoken of the ten kinds of measurelessness of the Tathāgata's voice, he then expounded on the ten marks of the Tathāgata's mind. Having spoken of the marks of the Tathāgata's mind, he then discussed the objective realms of the Tathāgata. Having spoken of the objective realms of the Tathāgata, he then spoke of the actions of the Tathāgata.

Samantabhadra then spoke of the Tathāgata's attainment of right enlightenment, noting that the bodhisattva should know it:

As not requiring any contemplation of any meaning;
As regarding all dharmas equally;
As free of doubt;
As non-dual and signless;
As neither going nor stopping;
As measureless and boundless;
As having abandoned the two extremes;
As abiding in the Middle Way;
As having gone beyond all language and speech; and
As knowing the actions of all beings' thoughts, the nature of their faculties, their aspirations, their afflictions, and their defiled habitual tendencies.

Then, to sum it up, he said, "to state it in terms of what is most essential, he should understand it as knowing in a single mind-moment all dharmas of the three periods of time."

Samantabhadra then said with regard to the Buddha's attainment of right and universal enlightenment that:

He acquires bodies as measureless as all beings;
He acquires bodies as measureless as all dharmas;
He acquires bodies as measureless as all *kṣetras;*
He acquires bodies as measureless as the three periods of time;
He acquires bodies as measureless as all buddhas;
He acquires bodies as measureless as all languages;
He acquires bodies as measureless as true suchness;
He acquires bodies as measureless as the Dharma realm;
He acquires bodies as measureless as the realms of empty space;
He acquires bodies as measureless as the unimpeded realms;
He acquires bodies as measureless as all vows;
He acquires bodies as measureless as all practices; and
He acquires bodies as measureless as the realm of quiescent nirvāṇa.

He then said that, "just as it is with the bodies he acquires, so too it is with his speech and mind in which he also acquires just such measureless and innumerable endowments of all three of these pure spheres [of body, mouth, and mind]."

Samantabhadra concluded his discussion of the Buddha's attainment of right and universal enlightenment by saying: "Sons of the Buddha, the bodhisattva-*mahāsattva* should realize that, within one's own mind, in each successive mind-moment, buddhas are always attaining right enlightenment. How is this so? This is because, it is not apart from this very mind that all buddhas, the *tathāgatas,* attain right enlightenment. And just as it is with one's own mind, so too it is with the minds of all beings. In all of them, there are *tathāgatas* attaining the universal and right enlightenment which, vast and universally pervasive, has no place in which it is not present. It is never abandoned, never cut off, and never ceases. So it is that one enters the gateway of inconceivable skillful means.

Sons of the Buddha, it is in these ways that the bodhisattva-*mahāsattva* should know the Tathāgata's attainment of right enlightenment."

Then, wishing to reiterate and clarify the meaning of this, Samantabhadra spoke the following verses:

> The Rightly Enlightened One completely knows all dharmas
> as non-dual, apart from duality, as all of a uniform equality,
> as possessed of an essential nature of purity comparable to space,
> and as not involving discriminations regarding "self" or "not-self."
>
> Just as the ocean reflects the bodies of beings
> and because of this is said to be "the great ocean,"
> so too, bodhi everywhere reflects all thoughts and actions
> and is therefore described as "right enlightenment."
>
> Just as when the worlds undergo creation and destruction,
> empty space is still not thereby either increased or decreased,
> so too, when all buddhas appear in the world,
> bodhi still has but a single sign, that of being forever signless.
>
> If someone conjured minds and transformed them into buddhas—
> conjured and not-conjured, the nature of the matter would not differ.
> So too, even if all beings were to realize bodhi, both after realization
> and before realization, it would neither increase nor decrease.
>
> The Buddha has a samādhi called "thoroughly enlightened wisdom."
> It is beneath the bodhi tree that he enters this meditative absorption,
> emanates countless light rays as numerous as beings,
> and then awakens the many beings as if causing lotuses to bloom.
>
> It is because of the manifestation of bodies as numerous
> as the thoughts, faculties, and inclinations of all beings

throughout all the kalpas and *kṣetras* of the three periods of time that right enlightenment is therefore described as "measureless."

Samantabhadra next explained how it is that the Tathāgata turns the wheel of the Dharma, noting that the bodhisattva should known it in these ways:

Through the sovereign power of the mind and without any arising and without any turning, the Tathāgata turns the wheel of Dharma, for he knows all dharmas as forever unarisen;

Through three kinds of turning by which one cuts off what should be cut off he turns the wheel of Dharma, for he knows all dharmas transcend the extreme views;

Through transcendence of both the extreme of desire and the extreme of its negation, he turns the wheel of Dharma, for he has penetrated to the utmost that all dharmas are like space;

Without resort to speech, he turns the wheel of Dharma, for he knows all dharmas as ineffable;

Through ultimate quiescence, he turns the wheel of Dharma, for he knows all dharmas as having the nature of nirvāṇa;

Through all languages and through all forms of speech, he turns the wheel of Dharma, for there is no place the voice of the Tathāgata does not reach;

Through knowing all sounds as like echoes, he turns the wheel of Dharma, for he completely understands the true nature of all dharmas;

Through sending forth all voices from within a single voice, he turns the wheel of Dharma, for there is ultimately no subjective agent; and

Through doing so endlessly and without omission, he turns the wheel of Dharma, for he is free of any inward or outward attachment.

In concluding his discussion of the Tathāgata's turning of the Dharma Wheel, Samantabhadra Bodhisattva spoke these verses:

When the Tathāgata turns the Dharma wheel, nothing at all is turned,
In all three times, there is neither any arising nor any attainment.
Just as there will be no time when all written words are exhausted,
so too it is with the Dharma wheel as turned by the Ten-Powered One.

Just as words can enter all places and yet still never reach them,
so too it is with the Dharma wheel of the Rightly Enlightened One.
It enters all verbal expressions and yet has nothing at all it enters
even as it is still able to cause all beings to feel joyous delight.

The Buddha has a samādhi called "ultimate unimpeded fearlessness."
After he has entered this concentration, he then speaks the Dharma.
For all the countless beings, he everywhere speaks in their languages,
thereby causing them to awaken and thus then understand.

Every one of those voices in turn additionally expounds
in countlessly many languages, each of which are different,
with which he freely holds forth in the world without discrimination,
adapting to their individual dispositions, thus enabling all to hear.

Those words do not arise from within or from without,
are never lost, and are free of any accumulation,
yet he thereby turns the wheel of Dharma for the sake of beings
with just such sovereign mastery in his very extraordinary manner.

Samantabhadra next expounded on the Tathāgata's *parinirvāṇa,* saying of it that the bodhisattva who wishes to know it must know its fundamental and essential nature, as follows:

"Just as it is with the nirvāṇa of true suchness, so too it is with the Tathāgata's nirvāṇa;

Just as it is with the nirvāṇa of the apex of reality, so too it is with the Tathāgata's nirvāṇa;

Just as it is with the nirvāṇa of the Dharma realm, so too it is with the Tathāgata's nirvāṇa;

Just as it is with the nirvāṇa of empty space, so too it is with the Tathāgata's nirvāṇa;

Just as it is with the nirvāṇa of the nature of dharmas, so too it is with the Tathāgata's nirvāṇa;

Just as it is with the nirvāṇa of the apex of dispassion, so too it is with the Tathāgata's nirvāṇa;

Just as it is with the nirvāṇa of the apex of signlessness, so too it is with the Tathāgata's nirvāṇa;

Just as it is with the nirvāṇa of the apex of the nature of a self, so too it is with the Tathāgata's nirvāṇa;

Just as it is with the nirvāṇa of the apex of the nature of all dharmas, so too it is with the Tathāgata's nirvāṇa; and

Just as it is with the nirvāṇa of the apex of true suchness, so too it is with the Tathāgata's nirvāṇa.

And how is this so? This is because nirvāṇa has no arising and no manifestation. If a dharma has no arising and no manifestation, then it has no cessation.

Sons of the Buddha, the Tathāgata does not speak about the *tathāgatas'* ultimate nirvāṇa for the bodhisattvas, nor does he show that matter to them. Why not? He prefers to enable them to see all *tathāgatas* always abiding directly before them so that, in but a single mind-moment, they also see all buddhas of the past and future with their perfectly fulfilled physical marks just as if they were here now, doing so without raising any dual or non-dual perceptions. And why? Because the bodhisattva-*mahāsattvas* have forever abandoned all attachments to perceptions.

Sons of the Buddha, it is in order to enable beings to find happiness that all buddhas, *tathāgatas,* appear in the world and it is out of a wish to cause beings to develop a fond admiration for it that they manifest the appearance of nirvāṇa. However, in truth, the Tathāgata has no emergence into the world nor does he have any nirvāṇa. How is this so? The Tathāgata forever dwells in the pure Dharma realm. It is as an adaptation to the minds of beings that he manifests the appearance of entering nirvāṇa."

After finishing this discussion of the Buddha's nirvāṇa, Samantabhadra Bodhisattva next spoke of the roots of goodness which are planted through seeing, hearing, or drawing near to the Tathāgatha, saying of them that none of those roots of goodness are ever planted in vain:

Because they produce the inexhaustible wisdom of enlightenment;
Because they allow one to leave behind the difficulties of all obstacles;
Because they ensure one will definitely reach the ultimate;
Because they are free of any false or deceptive aspects;
Because they enable one to fulfill all vows;
Because they lead one to never end one's practices in the realm of the conditioned;
Because they accord with unconditioned wisdom;
Because they produce the wisdom of all buddhas;
Because they continue on to the end of future time;
Because they lead to perfecting all the many kinds of supreme practices; and
Because they allow one to reach the ground of effortless wisdom.

Continuing in this vein, Samantabhadra Bodhisattva then says a few paragraphs later that:

"If anyone is able to see the form body of the Tathāgata, his eyes will become purified; if anyone is able to hear the name of the Tathāgata, his ears will become purified; if anyone smells the fragrance of the Tathāgata's moral virtue, his nose will become purified; and if anyone is able to taste the flavor of the Tathāgata's Dharma, his tongue will become purified and he will possess the vast and long tongue and come to understand the dharma of languages. If anyone is able to be touched by the Tathāgata's light, his body will become purified and he will ultimately acquire the unexcelled Dharma body.

If anyone develops mindfulness of the Tathāgata, he will acquire the purification of the mindfulness-of-the-Buddha samādhi. If any being makes an offering to a spot of land the Tathāgata has passed through or makes an offering to one of his stupas or shrines, then he will acquire roots of goodness allowing him to extinguish all affliction-based troubles and he will also acquire the bliss of the worthies and the *āryas.*

Sons of the Buddha, I shall now tell you: Even if there is some being who sees or hears the Buddha, but then, due to being encumbered by karmic obstructions, fails to develop faith and feel happiness on this account, they still thereby plant roots of goodness which will not have been planted in vain, for even this will eventually culminate in his entering nirvāṇa.

Sons of the Buddha, it is in this way that the bodhisattva-*mahāsattva* should know the roots of goodness planted in the presence of the Tathāgata by seeing, hearing, or drawing near to him. This will in all cases lead to abandoning all bad dharmas and perfecting the good dharmas."

Later on, Samantabhadra Bodhisattva says:

"If one succeeds in hearing this Dharma gateway of the Tathāgata's incalculable, inconceivable, unobstructed, and unimpeded wisdom and then, having heard it, has faith in it, understands it, accords with it, awakens to it, and enters into it, one should know that this person:

Is one who has been born into the clan of the Tathāgata;

Is one who accords with the realm of all *tathāgatas;*

Is one who completely fulfills all the bodhisattva dharmas;

Is one who abides securely in the realm of the knowledge of all modes;

Is one who has left all worldly dharmas far behind;

Is one who has developed all of the Tathāgata's practices;

Is one who has a penetrating comprehension of the nature of all bodhisattva dharmas;

Is one whose mind is free of doubts about the Buddha's powers of transformation;

Is one who abides in the independently realized Dharma; and

Is one who has deeply entered the unimpeded realm of the Tathāgata.

Sons of the Buddha, after hearing this Dharma, the bodhisattva-*mahāsattva*:

Is able to use the knowledge of equality to know the immeasurable dharmas;

Is able to use the correct and straight mind to abandon all discriminations;

Is able through supreme aspiration to see all buddhas directly before him;

Is able through the power of mental engagement to enter a realm of uniform equality like empty space;

Is able through sovereign mastery of mindfulness to travel throughout the boundless Dharma realm;

Is able to use the power of wisdom to possess all the meritorious qualities;

Is able to use spontaneously arising wisdom to abandon all of the world's defilements;

Is able to use the bodhi resolve to enter the web of all the ten directions;

Is able to use great contemplation to know all buddhas of the three periods of time as of the same single essential nature; and

Is able to use the wisdom that dedicates one's roots of goodness to everywhere enter dharmas such as these, not entering them and yet entering them, not seizing on even a single dharma even as he constantly contemplates all dharmas through but a single dharma.

Sons of the Buddha, the bodhisattva-*mahāsattva* perfects meritorious qualities such as these and, with the power of but a minor effort, acquires the spontaneously arising wisdom realized without the assistance of a teacher."

As this chapter approaches its end, it says that, due to the Buddha's spiritual powers, countless worlds then moved and shook in six ways, rains of adornments descended, and countless *tathāgatas* came there, all of whom were named "Samantabhadra." They said:

"It is good indeed, good indeed, Son of the Buddha, that you have been able to receive the assistance of the Buddha's awesome powers and, according with the nature of dharmas, expound upon the inconceivable Dharma of the manifestation of the Tathāgata. Son of the Buddha, all of us identically named buddhas from each of the ten directions, in each case as numerous as the atoms in eighty ineffable numbers of hundreds of thousands of *koṭīs* of *nayutas* of buddha *kṣetras*—we all speak this very Dharma. And just as it is what is spoken by us, so too is it also what is spoken by all buddhas of the ten directions.

O Son of the Buddha, now, within this congregation, there are bodhisattva-*mahāsattvas* as numerous as the atoms in ten myriads of buddha *kṣetras* who have acquired the spiritual superknowledges and samādhis of all bodhisattvas. We now bestow upon them their predictions of being bound to realize *anuttara-samyak-saṃbodhi* in but one more lifetime."

Then, from each of the ten directions, countless bodhisattvas came to pay their respects. Aided by the Buddha's spiritual powers, they each proclaimed:

"It is good indeed, Son of the Buddha, that you have been able to speak about this indestructible Dharma of the Tathāgata. Son of the Buddha, we are all identically named "Samantabhadra" and we have all come here from the presence of the tathāgata named "Universal Banner of Sovereign Mastery" in worlds known as "Universal Light." In all those places, they also teach this very Dharma with just such phrasings as these, just such principles as these, just such explanations as these, and just such certitude as this. They are all the same as found here, neither more nor less.

It is due to the aid of the Buddha's spiritual powers and due to having acquired the Dharma of the Tathāgata that we have come here to pay our respects and bear witness for you. And just as we have come here for this purpose, so too is this also occurring in just this same way in all of the four-continent worlds throughout the ten directions of empty space everywhere throughout the Dharma realm."

The chapter then ended as follows:

"At that time, aided by the Buddha's spiritual powers, Samantabhadra Bodhisattva surveyed that entire great congregation of bodhisattvas, and, wishing to once again clarify:

The vast awesome virtue of the manifestation of the Tathāgata;
The indestructibility of the Tathāgata's right Dharma;
The non-futility of planting measureless roots of goodness;
The inevitability that, when all buddhas appear in the world, they will be completely possessed of all the most superior dharmas;
Their excellent ability to contemplate the minds of all beings;
Their adaptation to whatever is appropriate in speaking the Dharma without ever missing the right time;
Their production of all bodhisattvas' measureless light of Dharma;
The miraculous adornment of all buddhas;
All *tathāgatas'* sharing of a single body free of individual differences; and
Their arising from their great original practices—

He then spoke these verses:

All that is done by all the *tathāgatas* is so indescribable
that none of the worlds' analogies could even come close.
Still, to enable beings to awaken and understand,
in what is inaccessible to analogies, I make analogies to instruct.

Such subtle, secret, and extremely deep Dharma
could only rarely be heard in a hundred thousand myriads of kalpas.
It is only those who are vigorous, wise, and well trained
who are then able to hear these mysterious and abstruse meanings.

Whoever, on hearing this Dharma, is filled with rejoicing
is one who has already made offerings to incalculably many buddhas,
is one who is supported and drawn forth by the Buddha, and
is one to whom men and devas give praise and always make offerings.

This constitutes the foremost world-transcending wealth,
this is able to rescue and liberate all the many kinds of beings,
and this is able to bring forth the path of purity.
You should all uphold it and must never be neglectful in doing so."

Chapter 38
Transcending the World

The eighth assembly begins with the Buddha for the third time in the state of Magadha at the site of enlightenment in the Hall of Universal Light where:

His marvelous awakening was in all respects completely fulfilled;
He had forever cut off the two kinds of action;
He had acquired the penetrating comprehension of the dharma of signlessness;
He had come to dwell where buddhas dwell;
He had attained the equality of the buddhas;
He had reached the station free of obstacles;
He had attained the Dharma that cannot be overturned;
He had become unimpeded in his actions;
He had established what is inconceivable; and
He had attained the universal vision of the three periods of time.

His body pervaded all lands, his wisdom penetrated all dharmas, and he had completed all the practices. He dwelt together there with countless bodhisattvas who all had but one more life before highest enlightenment and who all possessed the bodhisattva's skillful means and wisdom.

At that time, Samantabhadra Bodhisattva-*mahāsattva* entered a vast samādhi known as "the flower adornment of the Buddha." When he entered this samādhi, all worlds of the ten directions shook in six ways, moved in eighteen ways, and produced a loud sound that no one did not hear. After this, he arose from his samādhi, whereupon Universal Wisdom Bodhisattva asked him to please answer two hundred and one questions of which the first two hundred were mostly with regard to many different qualities and practice aspects of the bodhisattva-*mahāsattva,* whereas the last one was, "Why does the Tathāgata, the Arhat, the One of Right and Perfect Enlightenment manifest *parinirvāṇa*?" Those questions were as follows:

What does the bodhisattva-*mahāsattva* rely on?
What constitutes his extraordinary kinds of thought?
What constitutes his practices?
What serves as his good spiritual guide?
What constitutes his diligent vigor?
What constitutes his bases for attaining peace of mind?
What constitutes his ways to develop beings?
What constitutes his moral precepts?

What constitutes his bases for realizing he is bound to receive his prediction?
What constitutes his entry among the bodhisattvas?
What constitutes his entry among the *tathāgatas*?
What constitutes his penetration of beings' mental actions?
What constitutes his entry into worlds?
What constitutes his entry into kalpas?
What constitutes his ways of speaking of the three periods of time?
What constitutes his penetrating knowledge of the three periods of time?
What constitutes his bringing forth of the tireless mind?
What constitutes his knowledge of differences?
What constitutes his *dhāraṇīs*?
What constitutes his proclamations regarding buddhas?
What constitutes his bringing forth of the universally worthy mind [of Samantabhadra]?
What constitutes his dharmas of universally worthy practice [of Samantabhadra]?
What constitutes his reasons for generating the great compassion?
What constitutes the causes and conditions for his arousing the bodhi resolve?
What are the types of mind he uses in revering the good spiritual guide?
What constitutes his purity?
What constitutes his *pāramitās*?
What constitutes his knowledge pursuant to awakening?
What constitutes his knowing based on realizations?
What constitutes his powers?
What constitutes his equal regard?
What constitutes his statements on the true meaning of the dharmas of the Buddha?
What constitutes his speaking about dharmas?
What constitutes what he preserves?
What constitutes his eloquence?
What constitutes his sovereign masteries?
What is the nature of his nonattachment?
What constitutes his types of impartial mind?
What constitutes his ways of developing wisdom?
What constitutes his transformations?
What constitutes his means of empowerment?
What constitutes the bases for great happiness and satisfaction?

What constitutes his deep penetration of the Buddha's Dharma?
What constitutes those things on which he is based?
What constitutes his ways of arousing fearless resolve?
What constitutes his ways of arousing doubt-free resolve?
What constitutes his inconceivability?
What constitutes his skillful and esoteric speech?
What constitutes his skillfully distinguishing wisdom?
What constitutes his kinds of entry into samādhi?
What constitutes his kinds of pervasive penetration?
What constitutes his gateways to liberation?
What constitutes his spiritual superknowledges?
What constitutes his clarities?
What constitutes his liberations?
What constitutes his gardens and groves?
What constitutes his palaces?
What constitutes his bases of delight?
What constitutes his kinds of adornments?
What constitutes his manifestations of the unshakable mind?
What constitutes his kinds of never-relinquished profound and great resolve?
What constitutes his kinds of [wise] contemplations?
What constitutes his explanations of dharmas?
What constitutes his [other] kinds of purity?
What constitutes his seals?
What constitutes his illumination with the light of wisdom?
What constitutes his peerless dwelling?
What constitutes his types of flawless resolve?
What constitutes his types of especially superior mountain-like mind?
What constitutes his oceanic wisdom by which he enters unexcelled bodhi?
What constitutes his jewel-like abiding?
What constitutes his generation of the vajra-like Great Vehicle resolve?
What constitutes his great undertakings?
What constitutes his ultimate and great endeavors?
What constitutes his indestructible faith?
What constitutes his ways of receiving the prediction [of future buddhahood]?
What constitutes his ways of dedicating roots of goodness?
What constitutes his ways of attaining wisdom?
What constitutes his ways of arousing boundlessly vast resolve?
What constitutes his hidden treasures?

What constitutes his types of moral standards?
What constitutes his sovereign masteries?
What constitutes his unimpeded functions?
What constitutes his unimpeded functions in relation to beings?
What constitutes his unimpeded functions in relation to *kṣetras*?
What constitutes his unimpeded functions in relation to dharmas?
What constitutes his unimpeded functions in relation to bodies?
What constitutes his unimpeded functions in relation to vows?
What constitutes his unimpeded functions in relation to realms?
What constitutes his unimpeded functions in relation to knowledge?
What constitutes his unimpeded functions in relation to the spiritual superknowledges?
What constitutes his unimpeded functions in relation to the spiritual powers?
What constitutes his unimpeded functions in relation to the powers?
What constitutes his easeful mastery?
What constitutes his spheres of action?
What constitutes his [other kinds of] powers?
What constitutes his kinds of fearlessness?
What constitutes his exclusive dharmas?
What constitutes his works?
What constitutes his bodies?
What constitutes his physical actions?
What constitutes his [other] bodies?
What constitutes his speech?
What constitutes his ways of purifying speech?
What constitutes his sources of protection?
What constitutes his accomplishment of great endeavors?
What constitutes his types of mind?
What constitutes his resolutions?
What constitutes his types of all-pervasive mind?
What constitutes his faculties?
What constitutes his deep mind?
What constitutes his kinds of especially superior deep mind?
What constitutes his diligent cultivation?
What constitutes his definite understanding?
What constitutes his definite understanding in entering worlds?
What constitutes his definite understanding in entering the realms of beings?
What constitutes his habitual karmic propensities?

What constitutes his grasping?
What constitutes his cultivation?
What constitutes his fulfillment of the dharmas of the Buddha?
What constitutes the ways of retreating from the path of the Buddha's Dharma?
What constitutes his paths for transcendence of rebirths?
What constitutes his definite dharmas?
What constitutes the paths by which he develops the dharmas of the Buddha?
What constitutes his names that are used for great men?
What constitutes his paths?
What constitutes his measureless paths?
What constitutes his provisions for enlightenment?
What constitutes his cultivation of the path?
What constitutes his adornments of the path?
What constitutes his feet?
What constitutes his hands?
What constitutes his stomach?
What constitutes his inner organs?
What constitutes his heart?
What constitutes his armor?
What constitutes his weapons?
What constitutes his head?
What constitutes his eyes?
What constitutes his ears?
What constitutes his nose?
What constitutes his tongue?
What constitutes his body?
What constitutes his mind?
What constitutes his practices?
What constitutes his abiding?
What constitutes his sitting?
What constitutes his recumbence?
What constitutes his abodes?
What constitutes his places of practice?
What constitutes his [other] contemplations?
What constitutes his universal contemplations?
What constitutes his swiftness?
What constitutes his lion's roar?
What constitutes his pure giving?
What constitutes his pure moral precepts?

What constitutes his pure patience?
What constitutes his pure vigor?
What constitutes his pure meditative concentration?
What constitutes his pure wisdom?
What constitutes his pure kindness?
What constitutes his pure compassion?
What constitutes his pure sympathetic joy?
What constitutes his pure equanimity?
What constitutes his meanings?
What constitutes his dharmas?
What constitutes his merit-based provisions for the enlightenment?
What constitutes his wisdom-based provisions for enlightenment?
What constitutes his completely developed clarities?
What constitutes his ways of seeking the Dharma?
What constitutes his dharmas for attaining complete understanding?
What constitutes his cultivation dharmas?
What constitutes the *māras*?
What constitutes the works of the *māras*?
What constitutes the ways of abandoning the works of the *māras*?
What constitutes the ways of seeing the Buddha?
What constitutes the buddha works?
What constitutes the arrogant actions?
What constitutes the wise actions?
What constitutes the ways of being possessed by Māra?
What constitutes the ways of being possessed by the Buddha?
What constitutes the ways of being possessed by the Dharma?
What constitutes the works accomplished while dwelling in the Tuṣita Heaven?
Why does he pass away from his dwelling in the Tuṣita Heaven?
Why does he manifest as dwelling within the womb?
What then constitutes his manifestation of subtle endeavors?
Why does he manifest as having just taken birth?
Why does he manifest a subtle smile?
Why does he manifest the walking seven steps?
Why does he manifest on the ground of the pure youth?
Why does he manifest abiding within the inner palace?
Why does he manifest as leaving the household life?
Why does he manifest as practicing the austerities?
Why does he then go to the site of enlightenment?
Why does he then sit at the site of enlightenment?

What constitutes the extraordinary signs that occur when he sits at the site of enlightenment?
Why does he manifest as conquering the *māras*?
What constitutes his realization of the Tathāgata's powers?
Why does he turn the wheel of the Dharma?
How is it that, because of turning the wheel of the Dharma, he acquires the dharmas of purity?
Why does the Tathāgata, the Arhat, the One of Right and Perfect Enlightenment manifest *parinirvāṇa*?

Samantabhadra Bodhisattva then proceeded to answer these questions, beginning by providing ten answers for each of them, starting with ten things on which the bodhisattva relies, ten kinds of extraordinary thought, ten kinds of practices, ten kinds of good spiritual guides, ten kinds of diligent vigor, and so forth, continuing all the way through this list of questions until he finished the entire list by providing ten meaningful considerations why the Tathāgata manifests entry into *parinirvāṇa*.

Having come to the end of providing ten-fold answers to all two hundred and one of these questions, doing so for approximately two hundred pages in the English translation, Samantabhadra Bodhisattva then spoke more generally about the importance of the Dharma gateway constituted by his aforementioned answers, saying:

"Sons of the Buddha, this gateway into the Dharma is known as 'the bodhisattva's vast pure practice' which countless buddhas all join in proclaiming. It enables the wise to completely comprehend countless meanings and become filled with joyous delight. It enables the great vows and great practices of all bodhisattvas to be continuously sustained.

Sons of the Buddha, if there are any beings who are able to hear this Dharma and, having heard it, then believe and understand it, and having understood it, then cultivate it—they will definitely be able to swiftly realize *anuttara-samyak-saṃbodhi*. And why is this? This is due to their having cultivated it in accordance with what has been taught.

Sons of the Buddha, if bodhisattvas do not practice in accordance with what has been taught, one should realize these people will forever remain apart from the bodhi of the Buddha. Therefore the bodhisattva should practice in accordance with what has been taught.

Sons of the Buddha, this 'Transcending the World' chapter is the basis for the practice of all bodhisattvas' meritorious qualities and is the flower of the definitive meaning which everywhere enters all dharmas, which everywhere produces all-knowledge, which steps beyond all worlds, which abandons the paths of the two vehicles, which is not held in common with any other class of being, which is able to completely illuminate all Dharma gateways, and which increases beings' world-transcending roots of goodness. One should revere it, listen to it, recite it, remember it, reflect on it, admire and delight in it, and cultivate it. If one is able to proceed in this manner, one should realize that such a person will swiftly gain *anuttara-samyak-saṃbodhi*."

When the proclamation of this chapter came to an end, due to the powers of the Buddha, all the worlds of the ten directions quaked and shook and bright light illuminated them all, whereupon the buddhas of the ten directions appeared before Samantabhadra Bodhisattva, praising him, rejoicing in accordance with his teaching, and swearing to preserve this scripture and enable it to be heard by all present and future bodhisattva congregations. Then, aided by the Buddha's spiritual powers, Samantabhadra Bodhisattva surveyed all the Dharma assemblies throughout the ten directions and then spoke a series of two hundred and twelve verses which expanded upon, summarized, and reiterated the teachings he had presented in his answers to those two hundred and one questions originally asked by Universal Wisdom Bodhisattva.

CHAPTER 39

Entering the Dharma Realm / The Gaṇḍavyūha Sūtra

The setting for this ninth assembly and final chapter of the Flower Adornment Sutra was the Jeta Grove in Śravāsti where, in the Garden of the Benefactor of Orphans and the Solitary, the Buddha was abiding in the multistory Great Adornment Pavilion together with a congregation of five hundred great bodhisattvas headed by Samantabhadra Bodhisattva and Mañjuśrī Bodhisattva.

All of these bodhisattvas had already perfected the conduct and vows of Samantabhadra and were possessed of marvelous qualities, capacities, and accomplishments among which the text lists the following:

Their spheres of cognition were unimpeded, for they pervaded the *kṣetras* of all buddhas;

They manifested countless bodies, for they drew near to all *tathāgatas;*

The vision of their purified eyes was unobstructed, for they observed all buddhas' spiritual transformations;

They were unlimited in the places to which they went, for they were forever traveling to pay their respects where all *tathāgatas* achieved the right enlightenment;

Their radiance was boundless, for their wisdom light everywhere illuminated the ocean of all true dharmas;

They were inexhaustible in speaking Dharma, for they could hold forth endlessly, doing so with pure eloquence throughout boundless kalpas;

They were commensurate with the realm of empty space, for their wisdom's actions were all completely purified;

There had no particular place in which they dwelt, for they adapted to the minds of beings in manifesting their form bodies;

They had extinguished the cataracts of the delusions, for they completely understood that the realms of beings contained no beings at all; and

They possessed wisdom commensurate with empty space, for they illuminated the Dharma realm with an immense net of light.

At this same time, the Buddha was also together with a congregation of five hundred *śrāvaka* disciples and countless world leaders. The bodhisattvas, *śrāvaka* disciples, and world leaders all had the thought that they wished that the Buddha would adapt to their capacities in revealing:

His past resolve to set out in the quest for all-knowledge;
His past generation of the bodhisattva's great vows;
His past purification of the *pāramitās*;
His past entry onto the bodhisattva grounds;
His past fulfillment of the bodhisattva practices;
His past perfection of expedient means;
His past cultivation of all paths;
His past acquisition of the dharmas of emancipation;
His past feats of the spiritual superknowledges; and
The causes and conditions of his previous lifetimes as well as:
His realization of the universal and right enlightenment;
His turning of the wheel of the sublime Dharma;
His purification of his buddha land;
His training of beings;
His opening of the Dharma city of all-knowledge;
His revealing of all beings' paths;
His entry into the places in which all beings dwell;
His acceptance of the gifts of all beings;
His instruction to all beings about the merit of giving; and
His displaying for all beings the appearance of all buddhas.

Then, aware of the thoughts in their minds, the Buddha entered the lion sprint samādhi through which the Greatly Adorned Pavilion suddenly became boundlessly vast and the Jeta Grove suddenly became so expansively vast as to equal in its dimensions buddha lands as numerous the atoms in countless buddha *kṣetras*.

Then, off in the easterly direction, beyond an ocean of worlds as numerous as the atoms in an ineffably great number of buddha *kṣetras*, there was a world known as Golden Lamp Cloud Banner with a buddha named Vairocana's Supreme Virtue King. Within that buddha's congregation, there was a bodhisattva named Light of Vairocana's Vows who, accompanied by bodhisattvas as numerous as the atoms in an ineffably great number of buddha *kṣetras*, came to where the Buddha dwelt.

After those bodhisattvas had all arrived in the presence of the Buddha, they bowed down in reverence at the Buddha's feet and then transformationally created off in the easterly direction a jewel-adorned tower with a jeweled lotus dais lion throne that everywhere illuminated the ten directions. Over it hung a net canopy made of wish-fulfilling jewels that spread forth and covered them all. Then, together with his entire retinue, that bodhisattva sat down there in the lotus posture.

Then this same thing occurred with bodhisattvas coming from the south, the west, the north, the northeast, the southeast, the southwest, the northwest, the nadir, and the zenith, with each of those groups of countless bodhisattvas bowing in reverence to the buddha and then ending up seated on lotuses off toward the direction from which they had come.

All of those bodhisattvas of the ten directions and their retinues were born from the conduct and vows of Samantabhadra Bodhisattva. That all of these bodhisattvas filled up the Jeta Grove in this way was entirely due to the awesome spiritual powers of the Tathāgata.

At that time, although the most senior *śrāvaka* disciples including Śāriputra, Mahāmaudgalyāyana, Mahākāśyapa, Revata, Subhuti, Aniruddha, Nanda, Kapphiṇa, Kātyāyana, Pūrṇa, and others were present there in the Jeta Grove, none of them saw the Buddha's powers, adornments, spheres of action, and such. Nor were they able to see all of the marvelous realms, actions, congregations, spiritual transformations and such of those great bodhisattvas. That those *śrāvaka* disciples were unable to see any of these phenomena was:

Because their roots of goodness were not of the same sort;

Because they did not previously cultivate the roots of goodness of the sovereign masteries that enable one to see the buddhas;

Because they did not previously praise the pure qualities of all buddha *kṣetras* among the worlds of the ten directions;

Because they did not previously praise the many different spiritual transformations of the buddhas, the *bhagavats*;

Because, while in the midst of transmigration in *saṃsāra*, they did not previously resolve to gain *anuttara-samyak-saṃbodhi*;

Because they did not previously influence others to abide in the resolve to realize bodhi;

Because they were previously incapable of preventing the lineage of the Tathāgata from being cut off;

Because they did not previously attract all beings;

Because they did not previously encourage others to cultivate the bodhisattva's *pāramitās*;

Because previously, when abiding in the midst of *saṃsāra's* births and deaths, they did not exhort beings to seek the Supremely Victorious One's eye of great wisdom;

Because they did not previously cultivate the roots of goodness that produce all-knowledge;

Because they did not previously perfect the Tathāgata's world-transcending roots of goodness;

Because they did not previously acquire knowledge of the spiritual superknowledges used in purifying buddha *kṣetras*;

Because they did not previously acquire the sphere of cognition known to the eyes of all bodhisattvas;

Because they did not previously seek the world-transcending roots of goodness conducive to exclusive realizations of bodhi;

Because they did not previously bring forth the great vows of all bodhisattvas;
Because they were not previously born through the aid of the Tathāgata's assistance;
Because they did not previously realize all dharmas are like an illusion and bodhisattvas are like a dream; and
Because they did not previously acquire the great bodhisattvas' vast joyous delight.

All of these phenomena are spheres of cognition perceived by Samantabhadra Bodhisattva's wisdom eye that are not held in common with any adherents of the two vehicles. It is for these reasons that the great *śrāvaka* disciples:

Were not able to see them;
Were not able to know them;
Were not able to hear them;
Were not able to enter into them;
Were not able to acquire them;
Were not able to bear them in mind;
Were not able to contemplate them;
Were not able to assess them;
Were not able to meditate on them; and
Were not able to distinguish them.

Consequently, although those *śrāvakas* did reside within the Jeta Grove, facing the Tathāgata, they still did not see such vast spiritual transformations as these that he manifested there.

At that time, Light of Vairocana's Vows Bodhisattva, aided by the Buddha's spiritual powers, surveyed the ten directions and then spoke a series of verses praising the Buddha and that assembly of bodhisattvas. In that same way, the other leaders of those groups of bodhisattvas from the other nine directions followed him in also speaking verses in praise of the Buddha and the bodhisattvas.

At that time, Samantabhadra Bodhisattva-*mahāsattva* surveyed this entire congregation of bodhisattvas and, adopting methods commensurate with the Dharma realm, methods commensurate with the realm of empty space, methods commensurate with the realms of beings, and methods commensurate with the three periods of time, commensurate with all kalpas, commensurate with all beings' karma, commensurate with all beings' aspirations, commensurate with all beings' convictions, commensurate with all beings' faculties, commensurate with all beings' time of maturation, and commensurate with the reflections of the light of all dharmas, he then used these methods to present for the bodhisattvas ten kinds of Dharma instructions with which to open, reveal, illuminate, and expound on this lion sprint samādhi. What then were those ten? They were as follows:

Dharma instructions in which he expounded on its capacity to reveal on a scale commensurate with the Dharma realm the sequence of all buddhas' emergence and the sequence of all *kṣetras'* creation and destruction as these phenomena occur within all buddha *kṣetras'* atoms.

Dharma instructions in which he expounded on its capacity to reveal on a scale commensurate with the realm of empty space, within all Buddha *kṣetras*, the sounds of praises of the Tathāgata's qualities that continue on to the end of all future kalpas;

Dharma instructions in which he expounded on its capacity to reveal on a scale commensurate with the realm of empty space the *tathāgatas'* emergence in the world within all buddha *kṣetras* and their teaching of measurelessly and boundlessly many gateways to right enlightenment;

Dharma instructions in which he expounded on its capacity to reveal on a scale commensurate with the realm of empty space the presence in all buddha *kṣetras* of buddhas sitting in their sites of enlightenment, surrounded by congregations of bodhisattvas;

Dharma instructions in which he expounded on the emanation of transformation bodies that stream forth from their pores in every mind-moment, filling the Dharma realm in numbers equal to that of all buddhas of the three periods of time;

Dharma instructions in which he expounded on its capacity to cause one body to fill up the ocean of all *kṣetras* of the ten directions, manifesting equally everywhere.

Dharma instructions in which he expounded on its capacity to cause the appearance of the spiritual transformations of all buddhas of the three periods of time to manifest everywhere in all spheres of cognition.

Dharma instructions in which he expounded on its capacity to cause the appearance within all buddha *kṣetras'* atoms of the various spiritual transformations performed for countless kalpas by all buddhas of the three periods of time who are as numerous as the atoms in all buddha *kṣetras*.

Dharma instructions in which he expounded on its capacity to cause all of their pores to send forth until the very end of all future kalpas the sound of the ocean of great vows made by all buddhas of the three periods of time which serves for all bodhisattvas as a means of initiation and transformative guidance; and

Dharma instructions in which he expounded on its capacity to cause the Buddha's lion throne to become equal in size to the Dharma realm, to cause the bodhisattva congregation and the adornments of the site of enlightenment to become equally large and no different, and to also cause the turning of the Dharma wheel and the exposition of the many different kinds of sublime teachings to continue on to the very end of all future kalpas.

Then, aided by the Buddha, Samantabhadra Bodhisattva spoke a series of verses in praise of the Buddha and the bodhisattvas.

Then, because the Bhagavat wished to enable the bodhisattvas to abide securely in the Tathāgata's vast lion sprint samādhi, he emanated an immense beam of light from the white hair mark between his brows. That light known as "universal illumination of the Dharma realm's gateways of the three periods of time" had a retinue of light rays as numerous as the atoms in an ineffable number of buddha *kṣetras*. It everywhere illuminated all buddha lands in the oceans of worlds throughout the ten directions.

At that time, that great assembly of bodhisattvas within the Jeta Grove all saw that, in every atom in all buddha *kṣetras* throughout the Dharma realm and the realm of empty space, there were buddha lands as numerous as the atoms in all buddha *kṣetras*, buddha lands that had many different names, many different physical forms, many different manifestations of purity, many different abodes, and many different shapes and characteristics.

In each one of all those lands such as these, there was a great bodhisattva within a site of enlightenment, seated on a lion throne, realizing the universal and right enlightenment, who was entirely surrounded by an immense congregation of bodhisattvas as the world's rulers then presented offerings to him.

All of those bodhisattvas had become completely endowed with acuity and sovereign mastery in great wisdom and the spiritual superknowledges. They dwelt on the grounds and used vast wisdom to everywhere contemplate everything. They were born from the lineage of wisdom. The wisdom of all-knowledge always manifested directly before them. They had acquired the purified wisdom eye that had left behind all the obscurations of delusion.

They served all beings as teachers who train them. They dwelt in the Buddha's uniform equality and remained free of any discriminations regarding any dharmas. They possessed a completely penetrating comprehension of the objective realms and knew the entire world to be quiescent by nature.

They had no place upon which they depended. They went forth everywhere to pay their respects in all buddha lands, and yet, in doing so, they remained free of any attachment. They were able to contemplate all dharmas and yet, in doing so, they had no place in which dwelt.

They everywhere entered the palace of all wondrous dharmas and yet they had no place from which they came. They taught and trained everyone in all worlds. They everywhere revealed for beings the station of peace and security. Wisdom and liberation constituted the bases of their practices.

They constantly relied on the wisdom body and dwelt at the very peak of the transcendence of desire. They stepped beyond the ocean of all stations of existence and unveiled the very apex of reality. The light of their wisdom was perfectly full. They everywhere perceived all dharmas and dwelt in solid and unshakable samādhi.

They constantly aroused the great compassion for all beings even as they realized all gateways into the Dharma were like illusions, realized all beings were like dreams, realized all *tathāgatas* were like reflections, realized all speech was like echoes, and realized all dharmas were like transformationally created phenomena.

All of those bodhisattvas possessed a treasury of boundlessly many qualities of merit and wisdom. They were always praised by all buddhas and were such that, even if one used many different kinds of phrasing to describe their meritorious qualities, one would never be able to finish doing so. None of them were not present there in the Jeta Grove where they deeply entered the great ocean of the Tathāgata's qualities and were all illuminated by the radiance of the Buddha.

At that time, as they attained the light of the inconceivable right Dharma, those bodhisattvas' minds became suffused with immense joyous delight whereupon they each transformationally manifested many different kinds of great adornment clouds. Those clouds streamed forth from their bodies, their towers, their adornments, the lion thrones on which they sat, and everything in the Jeta Grove and filled up the ten directions of the entire Dharma realm.

At that time, Mañjuśrī Bodhisattva, aided by the Buddha's spiritual powers and wishing to summarize the feats of spiritual transformation that had just occurred in this Jeta Grove, surveyed the ten directions and spoke these verses:

You should all contemplate this Jeta Grove that,
due to Buddha's awesome spiritual powers, is limitlessly vast.
Every sort of adornment has been manifested here
and it has filled all ten directions of the Dharma realm.

All the lands throughout the ten directions
have become arrayed with countless kinds of great adornment.
Within the scenes appearing in his throne and the other objects,
the physical appearances of those phenomena are all clearly shown.

There flow forth from the pores of all these sons of the Buddha
jeweled flaming-light clouds with their many different adornments
as well as resounding emanations of the Tathāgata's wondrous voice,
all of which everywhere pervade all *kṣetras* of the ten directions.

Within the jeweled trees' blossoms these marvelous bodies appear.
Their forms and features equal those of a Brahma Heaven king.
When they rise from *dhyāna* absorption and proceed to roam about,
their awesome deportment in going and stopping is forever serene.

Within every one of the pores of the Tathāgata,
there always appear inconceivably many transformation bodies,
all of which resemble that of Samantabhadra, the great bodhisattva,
in the ways they are adorned with the many different signs.

Up in the sky above the Jeta Grove,
all those adornments send forth wondrous voices
that everywhere speak of the bodhisattvas of the three periods of time
and their perfection of the ocean of all meritorious qualities.

All the jeweled trees within the Jeta Grove
also emanate the sounds of countless wondrous voices
expounding on each of the differences in the ocean of various deeds
as they are carried out by all the many types of beings.

In all the phenomena there within the Grove,
there appear every feat of great spiritual powers
as numerous as the atoms in the oceans of *kṣetras* in the ten directions
that ever were produced by all *tathāgatas* of the three periods of time.

All the lands throughout the ten directions,
as numerous as the atoms in the ocean of all *kṣetras,*
all enter into the pores of the Tathāgata
in which the sequences in their adornment are all shown and seen.

All of those adornments show the buddhas
as numerous as the beings throughout the world.
Every one of them emanates rays of bright light as, in various ways,
they adapt to what is fitting in teaching the many kinds of beings.

Of all those clouds of especially marvelous adornments, including
fragrances, flaming light, many kinds of flowers, and jewel treasuries,
there are none not so vast as to equal the expanse of empty space
as they everywhere pervade all the lands of the ten directions.

All of the adorned and marvelous sites of enlightenment
of all buddhas of the ten directions and three periods of time—
the images of every one of their forms are all clearly shown
in the scene arrayed here within this garden and grove.

All these sons of the Buddha of Samantabhadra
have adorned *kṣetras* for an ocean of hundreds of thousands of kalpas.
Their numbers are so measureless as to equal the number of all beings.
There are none of them not seen here within this grove.

Then, because they were illuminated by the light of the Buddha's samādhi, all those bodhisattvas entered samādhis by which they gained countless entryways into the great compassion with which they benefited and pleased all beings. From all the pores of their bodies, countless rays of light streamed forth which each manifested countless bodhisattvas who all adopted the appearance of world leaders who appeared directly before all beings everywhere throughout the ten directions where they used skillful means to teach and train all beings in all the paths of rebirth.

Mañjuśrī then emerged from his Tower of Skillful Abiding together with countless bodhisattvas and every kind of deva and spirit, all of whom were devoted to benefiting beings and revering the Buddha. Mañjuśrī and his retinue of devas and spirits came forth, circumambulated the Buddha countless times, and made offerings, after which they all headed south to travel among the people.

When the Venerable Śāriputra saw Mañjuśrī Bodhisattva and his bodhisattva retinue starting to head off to the south, he decided to follow along, accompanied by his own retinue of six thousand bhikshus. Śāriputra praised Mañjuśrī to those bhikshus who all then asked to be able to go pay their respects to him. Śāriputra then took them to see Mañjuśrī who taught them the ten dharmas by which they could all attain highest enlightenment, namely:

With tireless resolve, accumulate all roots of goodness;
With tireless resolve, see all buddhas, serve them, and make offerings to them;
With tireless resolve, seek to acquire all dharmas of the Buddha;
With tireless resolve, practice all the *pāramitās;*
With tireless resolve, perfect all the bodhisattva samādhis;
With tireless resolve, enter all three periods of time in succession;
With tireless resolve, everywhere accomplish the purification of buddha *kṣetras* throughout the ten directions;
With tireless resolve, teach and train all beings;
With tireless resolve, perfect the bodhisattva practices in all *kṣetras* and in all kalpas; and
With tireless resolve, for the sake of ripening one being, cultivate *pāramitās* as numerous as the atoms in all buddha *kṣetras,* perfect one of the Tathāgata's powers, and then, for the sake of ripening all realms of beings, sequentially perfect all of the other powers of the Tathāgata.

Then, having just listened to Mañjuśrī's teachings, those six thousand bhikshus all gained a marvelous samādhi and immediately perfected a myriad ways of invoking their bodhi resolve, a myriad samādhis, a myriad *pāramitās,* the light of great wisdom, and ten kinds of bodhisattva superknowledges whereby they dwelt in a solid and unshakable bodhi resolve.

Mañjuśrī then exhorted all those bhikshus, instructing them to abide in Samantabhadra's practices by which they could enter the ocean of great vows, perfect the ocean of great vows, gain purity of mind, acquire physical purity, acquire buoyant physical agility, acquire great spiritual superknowledges, manifest their bodies in the dwelling places of all buddhas everywhere throughout the ten directions, and perfect all dharmas of the Buddha.

Mañjuśrī then traveled on to a place to the east of Dhanyākara, or Merit City, where he then dwelt at the site of a great stupa temple in the Adornment Banner *Śāla* Tree Grove, a place in which buddhas of the past had dwelt as they taught beings. He then taught a scripture there called "the Universal Illumination of the Dharma Realm" which led countless dragons to renounce dragon rebirths and become devas and humans.

Among the inhabitants of Dhanyākara, there was the youth known as Sudhana or "Good Wealth" whom Mañjuśrī provided with kind and gentle instruction, including instruction on all dharmas of the buddhas. Having heard these teachings, Sudhana single-mindedly sought highest enlightenment and followed along after Mañjuśrī, intoning verses that greatly impressed Mañjuśrī who then praised him for having already aroused the resolve to attain highest bodhi and instructed him on the importance of always drawing near to a good spiritual guide. Sudhana then requested that Mañjuśrī explain for him:

How one should train in the bodhisattva practices;
How one should cultivate the bodhisattva practices;
How one should progress into the bodhisattva practices;
How one should carry out the bodhisattva practices;
How one should purify the bodhisattva practices;
How one should reach a penetrating comprehension of the bodhisattva practices;
How one should perfect the bodhisattva practices;
How one should comply with the bodhisattva practices;
How one should bear in mind the bodhisattva practices;
How one should broaden the bodhisattva practices; and
How one should bring about the swift fulfillment of Samantabhadra's practices?

Mañjuśrī then spoke a series of verses for Sudhana in which he praised him and revealed his past extensive cultivation of Samantabhadra's practices. He then instructed Sudhana that he should go and seek instruction in the bodhisattva practices from a bhikshu called Megaśrī in a country to south known as Rāmāvarānta, on a mountain called Sugrīvo. Sudhana then bowed to Mañjuśrī, circumambulated him countless times, and then respectfully withdrew and traveled south.

1: Meghaśrī

When Sudhana encountered Meghaśrī and asked him about how to train in and cultivate the bodhisattva practices, how to fulfill the practices of Samantabhadra, and how to attain highest bodhi, Meghaśrī taught him about his Dharma gateway of universal vision with which he bears in mind all buddhas' spheres of cognition and light of wisdom. Claiming that he only knew this much, he sent him off to see a bhikshu known as Sāgaramegha in the country of Sāgaramukha.

2: Sāgaramegha

When Sudhana met Sāgaramegha and asked him about the bodhisattva path to all-knowledge, Sāgaramegha taught him about his Dharma gateway of the universal eye. Claiming to know only this much, he sent Sudhana off to see a bhikshu known as Supratiṣṭhita who lived sixty *yojanas* off to the south in a village known as Sāgaratīra.

3: Supratiṣṭhita

Sudhana then went to see Supratiṣṭhita and asked him about the dharmas of a buddha, whereupon Supratiṣṭhita taught him about his gateway of a bodhisattva's unimpeded liberations. Claiming to know only this gateway of liberations, he sent Sudhana off to see a man known as Megha in a city named Vaśitā in the country known as Draviḍa.

4: Megha

Sudhana then gradually traveled south to the city of Vaśitā to pay his respects to Megha and ask him about training in the bodhisattva practices, cultivating the bodhisattva path, and other such topics, after which Megha taught him about his Dharma gateway of the light of the bodhisattva's sublime sounds *dhāraṇī*. Claiming then to know only this gateway, he then sent Sudhana off to the south to see an elder known as Muktaka in a village known as Vanavāsī.

5: Muktaka

Sudhana gradually traveled for twelve years until he reached the city of Vanavāsī where he searched all around for Muktaka the Elder and told him, "I hope, O Ārya, that you will explain for me how a bodhisattva should train in the bodhisattva practices, how he should cultivate the bodhisattva path, how he may accord with what is to be cultivated and then swiftly acquire purity, and how he may swiftly acquire complete clarity of understanding."

Muktaka then taught him about his liberation gateway of the Tathāgata's unimpeded adornments. Claiming to only known this liberation gateway of the Tathāgata's unimpeded adornments, Muktaka sent him of to the south to the very boundary of Jambudvīpa where there is a country known as Milaspharaṇa in which there is a bhikshu known as Sāgaradhvaja or "Ocean Banner." He said, "You should go there, pay your respects to him, and ask him how a bodhisattva should train in the bodhisattva practices and how he should cultivate the bodhisattva path."

6: Sāgaradhvaja

Sudhana then gradually traveled southward to the borderlands of Jambudvīpa, to the village of Mali where he searched all around for Sāgaradhvaja Bhikshu. He then saw him alongside his meditation walkway where, sitting in the lotus posture, he had entered samādhi. He had left behind outward and inward breathing, he had become free of discriminating thought and awareness, and his body remained calm and motionless.

Sudhana the Youth single-mindedly contemplated Sāgaradhvaja Bhikshu and felt deep admiration for him. In this way, he stood there, meditatively contemplating him for one day and one night, and then on through seven days and seven nights, a half month, a month, and then for six months in all. He then continued doing so for an additional six days, after which Sāgaradhvaja Bhikshu arose from samādhi. Sudhana then asked him about this samādhi which Sāgaradvaja then identified as "the universal eye acquired through equanimity," otherwise known as "the pure light of the realm of *prajñāpāramitā*" and as "the gateway of universal adornment and purification."

After providing Sudhana with instruction in this and explaining that he knew only this one "light of *prajñāpāramitā* samādhi," he recommended that Sudhana seek further instruction on the bodhisattva practices and cultivation by traveling south to pay his respects to an *upāsikā* known as Āśā.

7: Āśā

Sudhana next traveled south until he met and paid his respects to the *upāsikā* known as Āśā and asked her for instruction on training in and cultivation of the bodhisattva path. She taught him about this single bodhisattva liberation gateway by which all who succeed in seeing her become irreversible in their progress toward highest bodhi. She then told Sudhana that he should seek further instruction by traveling south to the country of Nālayus to pay his respects to a rishi known as Bhīṣmottaranirghoṣa.

8: Bhīṣmottaranirghoṣa

Sudhana then gradually traveled along until he reached the country of Nālayus where he searched around everywhere for Bhīsmottaranirghoṣa whom he eventually saw sitting beneath a sandalwood tree before a group of a myriad disciples. Sudhana went up to him, paid his respects, and asked for further instruction on training in and cultivation of the bodhisattva path. That rishi then taught him about his bodhisattva liberation known as "the banner of invincibility." After providing Sudhana with this teaching, he said that, given that he knows only this liberation, Sudhana should next seek further instruction by traveling to the south to a village known as Īṣāṇa in which there is a brahman named Jayoṣmāyatana or "Supreme Heat."

9: Jayoṣmāyatana

Sudhana gradually travel onward until he reached the village of Īśāna. There he saw Jayoṣmāyatana or "Supreme Heat" who was cultivating the austerities in quest of all-knowledge. After teaching Sudhana about his "bodhisattva's endless wheel liberation," he told Sudhana that he should next travel south to a city known as Siṃhavijṛmbhita or "Lion's Sprint" in which there is a young maiden named Maitrāyaṇī who would be able to provide him further instruction in training in and cultivating the bodhisattva path.

10: Maitrāyaṇī

Sudhana then gradually traveled south until he reached the city of Siṁhavijṛmbhita where he searched all around for Maitrāyaṇī, the young maiden, and heard that this maiden was the daughter of King Siṃhaketu or "Lion Banner," that she was attended by a group of five hundred young maidens who served in her retinue, and that she dwelt in the Vairocana Treasury Hall where she taught the sublime Dharma while sitting on a seat with dragon-supremacy sandalwood legs that was covered with celestial robes made of gold-thread lace. He then went there, paid his respects, and asked for instruction in the bodhisattva path. After receiving instruction from her on her specialty, the *prajñāpāramitā* universal adornment gateway, she recommended to him that he next travel south to a country known as Trinayana in which there is a bhikshu named Sudarśana from whom he could receive further training.

11: Sudarśana

Sudhana then traveled onward until he arrived in the country known as Trinayana where he searched all over in its cities, villages, hamlets, neighborhoods, markets, rivers, plateaus, mountains, and valleys, looking everywhere for Bhikshu Sudarśana. Finally, he saw him in a forest where he was engaged in back-and-forth walking meditation. Sudhana went up to him, bowed down in reverence, and requested to be provided with training in and cultivation of the bodhisattva path. After teaching Sudhana about his own practice and realizations, he told him that, since he knew only this "lamp of compliance" bodhisattva liberation gateway, Sudhana should next seek instruction from a bhikshu named Indriyeśvara in the country of Sumukha.

12: Indriyeśvara

Sudhana next went to the country of Sumukha where he met and paid his respects to the bhikshu known as Indriyeśvara from whom he requested instruction on training in and cultivation of the bodhisattva path after which Indriyeśvara taught him about his Dharma gateway into the light of knowledge of all skills, arts, and great spiritual superknowledges. He then recommended that Sudhana go south to the city of Samudrapratiṣṭhāna, pay his respects to an upāsikā known as Prabhūtā, and ask her for instruction on training in and cultivation of the bodhisattva path.

13: Prabhūtā

Sudhana then gradually traveled onward until he reached the city of Samudrapratiṣṭhāna where, after searching in place after place for Upāsikā Prabhūtā, he paid his respects to her and requested instruction on training in the bodhisattva practices and cultivation of the bodhisattva path. Having taught him about her specialty known as "the bodhisattva's liberation gateway of the treasury of endless merit," she then recommended that he travel south to a city known as Mahāsaṃbhava and seek further instruction from a householder there known as Vidvān or "Clear Knowledge."

14: Vidvān

Sudhana next gradually traveled on to that city of Mahāsaṃbhava in which he searched all around for that householder, Vidvān, whom he found on a seven-jeweled stage in the market at the city's crossroads where he was sitting on a throne adorned with countless jewels. Sudhana bowed in reverence to him and requested instruction in training in the bodhisattva practices and cultivating the bodhisattva path. Vidvān taught him about his "liberation gateway of producing at will a treasury of merit," after which he recommended that he seek further instruction in the bodhisattva path by traveling south to Siṃhapota or "Lion Temple" in which there is an elder known as Ratnacūḍa to whom he should pay his respects and seek further teachings in the bodhisattva path.

15: Ratnacūḍa

Sudhana then gradually traveled onward until he reached Siṃhapota or "Lion City" where he searched all around for Ratnacūda, the Elder, until he saw this elder in the marketplace. He then immediately went up to him paid his respects and requested that he teach him about training in the bodhisattva practices and cultivating the bodhisattva path.

After Ratnacūḍa taught him about his bodhisattva liberation gateway of the jewel treasury of measureless merit, he suggested that Sudhana next travel south to the land of Vetramūlaka where, in the city of Samantamukha, he should pay his respects to an elder known as Samantanetra and request further instruction in the bodhisattva path.

16: Samantanetra

Sudhana next gradually traveled onward until he reached the country of Vetramūlaka in which he searched for the city of Samantamukha where he found the elder known as Samantanetra to whom he paid his respects and from whom he sought further instruction in the bodhisattva path. After Samantanetra taught Sudhana about his Dharma gateway of delighting all beings by enabling them to everywhere see all buddhas, Sudhana was told by that elder that he should travel south to the city of Tāladhvaja, pay his respects to King Anala, and request further instruction from him in training in the bodhisattva practices and cultivating the bodhisattva path.

17: Anala

Sudhana then gradually traveled onward, passing through countries, villages, and towns until he reached the city of Tāladhvaja where he paid his respects to King Anala and sought further instruction in bodhisattva practices and cultivation of the bodhisattva path. After teaching Sudhana about his "bodhisattva's illusion-like liberation," King Anala recommended that Sudhana travel south to the city of Suprabha, pay his respects to King Mahśprabha, and ask him to provide him with further instruction in training in the bodhisattva practices and cultivating the bodhisattva path.

18: Mahāprabha

Sudhana then gradually traveled south to the city of Suprabha where he paid his respects to King Mahāprabha and requested his instructions in the bodhisattva path after which that king taught him about his bodhisattva's samādhi gateway known as "taking great kindness as foremost in adapting to the world," after which he recommended that Sudhana travel south to a city called Sthirā to seek further instruction in the bodhisattva path from an *upāsikā* known as Acalā.

19: Acalā

Sudhana next traveled on to the city of Sthirā where he searched about everywhere until he found that *upāsikā* known as Acalā to whom he paid his respects and from whom he sought further instruction in the bodhisattva practices and bodhisattva cultivation. After teaching him about her bodhisattva's adornment gateway called "the insatiable quest for all dharmas," she recommended that he seek further instruction in the bodhisattva practices and path cultivation by traveling south to the city of Amitatosala to pay his respects to a wandering ascetic called Sarvagāmin from whom he could receive instruction in training in the bodhisattva practices and cultivating the bodhisattva path.

20: Sarvagāmin

Sudhana then traveled south to the city of Tosala where he searched for Sarvagamin and eventually found him on a mountain called Sulabha where he paid his respects to him and requested further training in the bodhisattva practices and path cultivation. Sarvagāmin taught him about his bodhisattva practice of going everywhere, after which he suggested to Sudhana that, to receive further training in the bodhisattva practices and path cultivation, he should next travel south to the land of Pṛthurāṣtra where he should pay his respects to an elder, a fragrance seller called Utpalabhūti, and then request bodhisattva path training from him.

21: Utpalabhūti

Sudhana next traveled onward until he reached the country of Pṛthurāṣṭra where he paid his respects to the elder known as Utpalabhūti and requested his teachings on the bodhisattva practices and path cultivation, after which Utpalabhūti taught him about his dharma of fragrance blending and suggested to Sudhana that, to receive further instruction in the bodhisattva practices and path cultivation, he should next travel south to the city of Kūtāgāra where he could seek teachings there from a ship captain known as Vaira.

22: Vaira

Sudhana then traveled south to Kūtāgāra where he found Vaira teaching an immense congregation about the Buddha's ocean of meritorious qualities. After paying his respects to him, Sudhana then requested his instruction in the bodhisattva practices and cultivation of the bodhisattva path. Vaira then taught him about his practice of the banner of the great compassion, after which he suggested to Sudhana that he next travel south to the city of Nandihāram to pay his respects to an elder called Jayottama and seek his instruction in the bodhisattva practices and bodhisattva path cultivation.

23: Jayottama

Sudhana next traveled on to the city of Nandihāram where he looked for Jayottama whom he found east of that city in the Aśoka Forest where he paid his respects to him and then requested his teachings on the bodhisattva practices and cultivation of the bodhisattva path. Jayottama taught Sudhana about his perfection of the bodhisattva's practice gateway of going everywhere using the independent and effortless powers of the spiritual superknowledges, after which he recommended to Sudhana that he seek further training in the bodhisattva practices and path cultivation by traveling south to the city of Kaliṅgavana where he should look for and pay his respects to a bhikshuni known as Siṃhavijṛmbitā who should be able to help him with instruction in the bodhisattva practices and cultivation of the bodhisattva path.

24: Siṃhavijṛmbhitā

Sudhana then traveled south until he reached the city of Kaliṅgvana where he eventually was able to find the bhikshuni Siṃhavijṛmbhitā, pay his respects, and request instruction in training in the bodhisattva practices and cultivating the bodhisattva path. After teaching him about her "perfection of all-knowledge" liberation, she recommended that Sudhana travel to the south and seek further instruction in these matters from a woman named Vasumitrā in the city of Ratnavyūha.

25: Vasumitrā

Sudhana then gradually traveled onward until he reached the city of Ratnavyūha in the country of Durga in which he searched everywhere for Lady Vasumitrā. Once he found her, he paid his respects and requested her to provide him with guidance and instruction in the bodhisattva practices and cultivation of the bodhisattva path. After teaching him about her "pinnacle of dispassion" liberation, she told him that he should travel to the south and pay his respects to a layman named Vesṭhila in the city of Śubhpāraṃgama from whom he could receive further instruction in the bodhisattva practices and cultivation of the bodhisattva path.

26: Veṣṭhila

Sudhana next gradually traveled onward until he reached the city of Śubhapāraṃgama. When he arrived at that Veṣṭhila's household, he bowed down in reverence at his feet and requested instruction in the bodhisattva practices and cultivation of the bodhisattva path. After teaching him about his "endless lineage of the buddhas" samādhi and his bodhisattva liberation known as "nonentry into the apex of *parinirvāṇa*," Veṣṭhila told Sudhana that he should next travel to the south and receive further instruction in these matters from a bodhisattva known as Avalokiteśvara at a mountain known as Potalaka.

27: Avalokiteśvara

Sudhana then gradually traveled onward until he reached Potalaka mountain. He then searched about everywhere for this great bodhisattva until, on its western slope, he saw Avalokiteśvara Bodhisattva sitting there in the full lotus posture. Sudhana then paid his respects and requested further teachings on the bodhisattva practices and cultivation of the bodhisattva path. Avalokiteśvara Bodhisattva then taught him about his liberation gateway known as "the practice of the great compassion," after which he told Sudhana that he should seek further instruction in these matters from a bodhisattva named Ananyagāmin who dwelt on the peak of the Sahā World's Iron Ring Mountains.

28: Ananyagāmin

Sudhana next went, paid his respects, and asked for instruction in the bodhisattva path from Ananyagāmin Bodhisattva who taught him about his bodhisattva's liberation known as "swift travel through the universal gateway." After doing so, he told Sudhana, "I have acquired only this bodhisattva's liberation of universal and swift travel with which I am able to swiftly go to all places everywhere." He then told Sudhana that he should seek further instruction in these matters by heading south to a city known as Dvāratī in which there is a spirit known as Mahādeva to whom he should pay his respects and ask for teachings on training in the bodhisattva practices and cultivating the bodhisattva path.

29: Mahādeva

Sudhana then traveled south to the city of Dvāratī where he searched for and found Mahādeva to whom he paid his respects and from whom he requested teaching in the bodhisattva practices and cultivation of the bodhisattva path, whereupon Mahādeva taught him about the "net of clouds" liberation that he had perfected, after which he suggested that Sudhana travel to the site of enlightenment in the state of Magadha and seek further instruction in these matters from an earth spirit known as Sthāvarā.

30: Sthāvarā

Sudhana then gradually traveled onward until he arrived at the abode of the spirit Sthāvarā at the site of enlightenment in the state of Magadha. Having paid his respects to Sthāvarā and asked him for instruction in the bodhisattva practices and cultivation of the bodhisattva path, the earth spirit then taught Sudhana about his bodhisattva liberation known as "the indestructible treasury of wisdom" which he always uses to assist the development of beings. Sthāvarā then advised Sudhana that he should go to Kapilavastu and pay his respects to a night spirit by the name of Vāsantī from whom he could request further teachings in these matters.

31: Vāsantī

Sudhana gradually traveled onward until he reached Kapilavastu and entered its eastern gates. After he located Vāsantī, he paid his respects and requested instruction from her in the bodhisattva practices and cultivation of the bodhisattva path, after which she taught Sudhana about her bodhisattva liberation known as "the Dharma light that dispels the darkness of all beings' delusions," she told him to go to the site of enlightenment in Magadha and seek further instruction in these matters from a night spirit by the name of Samantagambhīraśrīvimalaprabhā.

32: Samantagambhīraśrīvimalaprabhā

Sudhana then gradually traveled along until he met that night spirit at the site of enlightenment in Magadha, Samantagambhīraśrīvimalaprabhā, to whom he paid his respects, after which he requested instruction from her in the bodhisattva practices and cultivation of the bodhisattva path. After she taught Sudhana about her bodhisattva liberation known as "roaming everywhere in the bliss of quiescent *dhyāna* absorption," she instructed him to go visit and pay his respects to another night spirit who went by the name of Pramuditanayanajagadvirocanā from whom he could receive further teachings on the bodhisattva practices and cultivation of the bodhisattva path.

33: Pramuditanayanajagadvirocanā

Sudhana searched for and met Pramuditanayanajagadvirocanā to whom he paid his respects and from whom he requested further teachings in training in the bodhisattva practices and cultivating the bodhisattva path. That night spirit then taught Sudhana about her liberation known as "the immensely powerful banner of universal joy" with which she is able to benefit all beings, after which she instructed him to next seek out and request further instructions in the bodhisattva path from a night spirit by the name of Samantasattvatrāṇojaḥśrī.

34: Samantasattvatrāṇojaḥśrī

Sudhana then went and paid his respects to the night spirit who was known as Samantasattvatrāṇojaḥśrī, after which he asked for further instruction in the bodhisattva training and cultivation of the bodhisattva path. After teaching Sudhana about her bodhisattva's liberation gateway called "appearing everywhere in all worlds to train beings," she told Sudhana that he should go and pay his respects to a night spirit by the name of Praśāntarutasāgaravatī from whom he could request further instructions in these matters of the bodhisattva training and the cultivation of the bodhisattva path.

35: Praśāntarutasāgaravatī

Sudhana next went and searched out and paid his respects to the night spirit known as Praśāntarutasāgaravatī from whom he requested further instructions in the bodhisattva training and cultivation of the bodhisattva path. After teaching him about her bodhisattva's "liberation that produces the adornment of vast joy in every mind-moment," she told Sudhana that he should next seek further training in these matters from a night spirit known as Sarvanagararaksāsambhavatejahśrī.

36: Sarvanagararaksāsambhavatejahśrī

Sudhana then went to visit and pay his respects to the night spirit known as Sarvanagararakṣāsaṁbhavatejaḥśrī. After bowing to her he requested further instruction in the bodhisattva training and cultivation of the bodhisattva path. After teaching Sudhana about her bodhisattva liberation known as "the extremely profound and miraculous sublime sound," she told Sudhana that he should next seek further training in these matters from a night spirit by the name of Sarvavṛkṣapraphullanasukhasaṃvāsā.

37: Sarvavṛkṣapraphullanasukhasaṃvāsā

Sudhana next went and paid his respects to the night spirit by the name of Sarvavṛkṣapraphullanasukhasaṁvāsā from whom he sought further instruction in training in the bodhisattva practices and cultivating the bodhisattva path. After teaching Sudhana about her liberation gateway of "the generation of the light of vast joy," she told him that he should next go and seek further teachings on these matters from a night spirit by the name of Sarvajagadrakṣāpraṇidhānavīryaprabhā.

38: Sarvajagadrakṣāpraṇidhānavīryaprabhā

Sudhana then left to go see and pay his respects to the night spirit known as Sarvajagadrakṣāpraṇidhānavīryaprabhā. After having met her and paid his respects, he asked her for further instruction in the bodhisattva training and the cultivation of the bodhisattva path. She then taught Sudhana about her gateway to liberation known as "teaching beings to produce roots of goodness," after which she instructed him to seek out further training in these matters from a spirit in Lumbinī known as Sutejomaṇḍalaratiśrī.

39: Sutejomaṇḍalaratiśrī

Sudhana next gradually traveled on to Lumbinī where he searched for the spirit known as Sutejomaṇḍalaratiśrī until he saw her in a tower beautified by trees adorned with all kinds of jewels. After paying his respects to her and requesting teachings from her in the bodhisattva practices and cultivation of the bodhisattva path, she taught him about her liberation gateway known as "the bodhisattva's sovereign mastery in manifesting the taking on of births in all places for countless kalpas," after which she told him that he should next travel to Kapilavastu and seek further instruction in these matters from a maiden in the lineage of the Śākya clan known as Gopā whom he should ask, "How should the bodhisattva teach beings in *saṃsāra*?"

40: Gopā

Sudhana then traveled to the city of Kapilavastu in search of that maiden from the Śākya clan, finally finding Gopā in a lecture hall known as Universally Manifesting the Light of the Dharma Realm where she was surrounded by countless female attendants. After paying his respects to her and requesting teachings from her in the bodhisattva practices and the cultivation of the bodhisattva path, Gopā taught Sudhana about her liberation known as "the sphere of contemplation of the ocean of all bodhisattvas' samādhis" and then told him that he should next seek instruction in these matters from the mother of the Buddha, the Lady Māyā.

41: Māyā

Sudhana then traveled to see the mother of the buddha, the Lady Māyā, whom he found seated on a throne, surrounded by a measurelessly large congregation. After Sudhana paid his respects to her and requested teachings in the bodhisattva practices and the attainment of highest enlightenment, the Lady Māyā taught him about the bodhisattva liberation she had perfected known as "the illusion-like manifestation of the knowledge of great vows," after which she recommended that he next seek further instruction in these matters from Surendrābhā, the daughter of the king of the Trāyastriṃśa Heaven.

42: Surendrābhā

Sudhana then traveled to that palace in the heavens where he saw that celestial maiden, paid his respects, and then requested instruction from her in the bodhisattva practices and cultivation of the bodhisattva path. After teaching Sudhana about her bodhisattva liberation known as "the purified adornment of unimpeded recollection," she told him that he should next seek further instruction in these matters by traveling to Kapilavastu to pay his respects to a teacher of youths known as Viśvāmitra who should be able to assist him with more teachings on the bodhisattva practices and cultivation of the bodhisattva path.

43: Viśvāmitra

Sudhana then descended from the Trāyastriṃśa Heaven and gradually traveled toward Kapilavastu where he paid his respects to Viśvāmitra and requested teachings in the bodhisattva practices and cultivation of the bodhisattva path. Viśvāmitra referred him to a youth known as Śilpābhijña for further instruction in these matters.

44: Śilpābhijña

Sudhana went directly to Śilpābhijña, paid his respects, and requested instruction in the bodhisattva practices and cultivation of the bodhisattva path. After teaching Sudhana about his bodhisattva liberation known as "skillful knowledge of the many arts," Śilpābhijña told Sudhana that he should seek further instruction in these matters by traveling to the city of Vartanaka to pay his respects to an *upāsikā* name Bhadrottamā from whom he should request more training in the bodhisattva practices and cultivation of the bodhisattva path.

45: Bhadrottamā

After traveling to Vartanaka and paying his respects to the *upāsikā* known as Bhadrottamā, Sudhana requested that she instruct him in the bodhisattva practices and cultivation of the bodhisattva path. After teaching him about her bodhisattva liberation known as "the *maṇḍala* of independence," she suggested that he seek further training in these matters by traveling to the south to a city called Bharukaccha where, after paying his respects to an elder known as Muktisāra, he should ask for instruction in the bodhisattva practices and the cultivation of the bodhisattva path.

46: Muktisāra

Sudhana then traveled to Vartanaka and paid his respects to the elder known as Muktisāra, after which he requested to receive instruction in the bodhisattva practices and cultivation of the bodhisattva path. After teaching Sudhana about his bodhisattva liberation known as "the pure adornment of unattached mindfulness," Muktisāra recommended that Sudhana next seek further instruction in these matters by paying his respects to an elder in the same city who went by the name Sucandra who should be able to assist him with teachings on the bodhisattva practices and cultivation of the bodhisattva path.

47: Sucandra

Sudhana then went to the abode of Sucandra, paid his respects to him, and requested instruction in the bodhisattva practices and cultivation of the bodhisattva path. After teaching Sudhana about his bodhisattva liberation known as "the light of pure wisdom," Sucandra then advised Sudhana to seek further instruction in these matters by traveling south to the city of Roruk, paying his respects to an elder known as Ajitasena, and then asking him for teachings on the bodhisattva practices and cultivation of the bodhisattva path.

48: Ajitasena

Sudhana next traveled gradually toward the city of Roruk and then went to the abode of Ajitasena to whom he paid his respects and from whom he requested teachings on the bodhisattva practices and cultivation of the bodhisattva path. After teaching Sudhana about his bodhisattva liberation known as "inexhaustible appearance, Ajitasena recommended that Sudhana seek further training in these matters by traveling south to the city of Dharma where he should pay his respects to a brahman known as Śivarāgra and ask for teachings on the bodhisattva practices and the cultivation of the bodhisattva path.

49: Śivarāgra

Sudhana then gradually traveled south to the village known as Dharma where he saw Śivarāgra, paid his respects to that elder, and then requested teachings on the bodhisattva practices and cultivation of the bodhisattva path. After teaching Sudhana about his bodhisattva liberation known as "speech arising from the vow to be truthful," Śivarāgra recommended that Sudhana seek further training in these matters by traveling south to the city of Sumanāmukha where he should pay his respects to a youth known as Śrīsaṃbhava and aske him for further instruction on the bodhisattva practices and cultivation of the bodhisattva path.

50: Śrīsambhava and Śrīmati

Sudhana next headed south and gradually made his way to the city of Sumanāmukha where he saw and paid his respects to the youth known as Śrīsaṃbhava and the maiden known as Śrīmati. He then requested their teachings on the bodhisattva practices and cultivation of the bodhisattva path, after which they taught him about their bodhisattva liberation known as "illusory existence" and then suggested he seek further training in these matters by traveling south to Great Adornment Park in the country of Samudrakaccho, paying respects to Maitreya Bodhisattva, and asking him for more instruction on the bodhisattva practices and cultivation of the bodhisattva path.

51: Maitreya Bodhisattva

Sudhana next traveled on to that Great Adornment Park in the country of Samudrakaccho where he paid his respects to Maitreya Bodhisattva at his tower known as "the Chamber of Vairocana's Adornments" and requested instruction from him in the bodhisattva practices and cultivation of the bodhisattva path. Maitreya Bodhisattva then taught him about his liberation gateway known as "the treasury of adornments associated with the unforgetting mindfulness that enters the knowledge of all objects in the three periods of time," after which he told Sudhana that he should go and see Mañjuśrī Bodhisattva and ask him how the bodhisattva should train in the bodhisattva practices and how he should enter, perfect, broaden, accord with, purify, and completely fulfill Samantabhadra's gateways of practice.

52: Mañjuśrī

Sudhana then followed Maitreya Bodhisattva's instructions by traveling on in search of Mañjuśrī, passing through more than a hundred and ten other cities before he finally reached the city of Sumana where Mañjuṣrī contacted him from afar and provided him with the spiritual instructions by which he enabled Sudhana to become accomplished in countless Dharma gateways, to become endowed with the light of measureless great wisdom, and to acquire the bodhisattva's boundless *dhāraṇīs,* boundless vows, boundless samādhis, boundless superknowledges, and boundless knowledge. Mañjuśrī also enabled Sudhana to enter the *maṇḍala* of Samantabhadra's practices and become established in the very place in which he himself dwelt, whereupon Mañjuśrī withdrew and disappeared.

53: Samantabhadra

After Mañjuśrī Bodhisattva withdrew and disappeared, Sudhana progressed in his development on the path to highest bodhi and then contemplated Samantabhadra's realm of liberation, whereupon he immediately heard the name of Samantabhadra, his practices and vows, his provisions for enlightenment, his right path, his grounds, his skillful means on the grounds, his entry into the grounds, his vigor on the grounds, his dwelling on the grounds, his cultivation of the grounds, his realms of experience on the grounds, his awesome power on the grounds, and his dwelling together with others on the grounds.

As he was eagerly yearning to see Samantabhadra Bodhisattva, he then immediately came to be sitting in this vajra treasury site of enlightenment on a lotus flower seat adorned with all kinds of jewels, directly in front of Vairocana Tathāgata's lion throne where he witnessed ten kinds of auspicious signs and ten kinds of light signs, after which he thought, "I must now see Samantabhadra Bodhisattva, increase my roots of goodness, see all buddhas, develop a definite understanding of the vast realms of all bodhisattvas, and attain all-knowledge."

Sudhana then saw Samantabhadra Bodhisattva in the midst of the congregation and directly in front of the Tathāgata where he was seated on a jeweled lotus flower lion throne surrounded by a congregation of bodhisattvas, presenting the most splendidly extraordinary appearance without peer anywhere in the world. His realm of wisdom was measureless, boundless, unfathomable, inconceivable, equal to that of all buddhas of the three periods of time, and such that no other bodhisattva could even be able to contemplate.

Sudhana then saw emerging from every pore of Samantabhadra's body the emanation of countless light clouds, the emanation of countless multi-colored clouds, the emanation of countless clouds of various flowers, the emanation of countless clouds of incense fragrance trees, the emanation of countless clouds of marvelous raiment, the emanation of countless clouds of jewel trees, the emanation of countless clouds of devas, the emanation of countless clouds of buddha *kṣetras* of the three periods of time, the emanation of countless buddha *kṣetras* of every level of purity and impurity, the emanation of countless clouds of congregations of beings, countless clouds of congregations of bodhisattvas, countless clouds of Samantabhadra Bodhisattva's practices, and countless clouds of congregations of rightly enlightened ones.

Contemplating each part of Samantabhadra's body, Sudhana saw that, completely contained within each of his pores was the entire great trichiliocosm. He clearly saw all the phenomena such as these. And just as he observed them in this world, so too did he see them all in all world systems throughout the ten directions. And just as he saw them throughout the world systems of the ten directions as they appeared in the present era, so too did he see them in this same way in all world systems in both the past and the future with none of their distinguishing aspects ever being mixed up.

Just as powers of the spiritual superknowledges such as these were then revealed within this abode of Vairocana Tathāgata, so too were such powers of the spiritual superknowledges also revealed in these same ways in the eastern region's Padmaśrī world system in the abode of Bhadraśrī Buddha.

And just as these circumstances were revealed in this way in the abode of Bhadraśrī Buddha, so too were they also revealed in all world systems to the east. One should realize that, just as they were revealed in this way in regions to the east, so too were such manifestations of the power of the spiritual superknowledges all also revealed in the same way in the abodes of all *tathāgatas* in all world systems in the south, the west, the north, the four midpoints, the zenith, and the nadir.

And just as this was so in all world systems throughout the ten directions, so too was this also so within each atom in all buddha *kṣetras* throughout the ten directions. In every case, there were the Dharma realm's buddhas and their congregations in which, in the presence of each buddha, Samantabhadra Bodhisattva sat on a lotus flower lion throne manifesting the power of the spiritual superknowledges.

Within each one of those bodies of Samantabhadra, there appeared as they existed in relation to all three periods of time:

All spheres of experience;
All buddha *kṣetras*;
All beings;

The arising of all buddhas;
All the congregations of bodhisattvas;
The sounds of all beings' voices;
The sounds of all buddhas' voices;
The turnings of the Dharma wheel as initiated by all *tathāgatas;*
The practices perfected by all bodhisattvas; and
All *tathāgatas'* easeful mastery of the spiritual superknowledges.

Having seen Samantabhadra Bodhisattva's countless uses of inconceivably great spiritual powers such as these, Sudhana the Youth then immediately acquired ten types of knowledge *pāramitās.*

Once Sudhana the Youth had acquired these *pāramitās,* Samantabhadra Bodhisattva then extended his right hand and rubbed the crown of his head. After he had rubbed the crown of Sudhana's head, Sudhana the Youth then immediately acquired an array of samādhi gateways as numerous as the atoms in all buddha *kṣetras,* each of which was in turn attended by a retinue of additional samādhis as numerous as the atoms in all buddha *kṣetras.*

Just as Samantabhadra Bodhisattva rubbed Sudhana's crown in the presence of Vairocana Buddha here in this Sahā World System, so too did Samantabhadra Bodhisattva also rub the crown of Sudhana's head in the presence of all buddhas in all world systems throughout the ten directions while also doing so in all world systems within every atom of those world systems. Samantabhadra Bodhisattva-*mahāsattva* then spoke to Sudhana, asking, "Son of Good Family, did you or did you not see these spiritual powers of mine?"

Sudhana replied, "I did indeed see them. O Great Ārya, such inconceivable feats of spiritual powers could only be known by a *tathāgata.*"

Samantabhadra then held forth at length on his practice of the bodhisattva practices for past kalpas a numerous as the atoms in an ineffable-ineffable number of buddha *kṣetras.* He then told Sudhana, "If there are beings who have not yet planted roots of goodness, or if there are *śrāvaka* disciples or bodhisattvas who have planted only a minor measure of roots of goodness, they would not even be able to hear my name, how much the less would they be able to see my body.

Son of Good Family, there are some beings who, by being able to hear my name, then become irreversible in progressing toward *anuttara-samyak-saṃbodhi.* So too are there those who accomplish this by merely seeing me, touching me, welcoming me, escorting me off, briefly following along after me, or merely seeing or hearing me in a dream.

Some beings are able to become fully ripened by remaining mindful of me for but one day or one night. Others are able to become fully ripened by remaining mindful of me for seven days and seven nights, for a half month, for a month, for a half year, for a year, for a hundred years, a thousand years, a kalpa, a hundred kalpas, or for kalpas as numerous as the atoms in an ineffable-ineffable number of buddha *kṣetras*.

Others may require one lifetime or a hundred lifetimes, or even up to lifetimes as numerous as the atoms in an ineffable-ineffable number of buddha *kṣetras* before they will become fully ripened. Still others will become fully ripened by seeing me emanating brilliant light, by seeing me cause a buddha *kṣetra* to shake or move, or by being frightened or filled with joyous delight by such phenomena.

Son of Good Family, I use skillful means such as these that are as numerous as the atoms in a buddha *kṣetra* to enable beings to become irreversible in progressing toward *anuttara-samyak-saṃbodhi*.

Son of Good Family, if any being sees or hears of my pure *kṣetra*, he will certainly be able to be reborn in this pure *kṣetra*. If any being sees or hears of my pure body, he will certainly be able to be reborn within my pure body.

Son of Good Family, you should contemplate this pure body of mine."

Sudhana the Youth then contemplated the body of Samantabhadra Bodhisattva, its major marks and secondary signs, and its limbs. He saw that, within each pore, there were an ineffable-ineffable number of oceans of buddha *kṣetras* and, in each *kṣetra* ocean, there were buddhas appearing in the world, each of whom was surrounded by an immense congregation of bodhisattvas.

He then also saw that all those oceans of *kṣetras* had many different kinds of foundations, many different shapes, many different adornments, many different great surrounding mountains, many different kinds of colored clouds spread across their skies, many different circumstances in which buddhas appear, and many different types of dharmas that were expounded. Each of the various phenomena such as these were distinctly different.

He also saw that, in each of those oceans of world systems, Samantabhadra emanated clouds of transformation-body buddhas as numerous as the atoms in all buddha *kṣetras* that appeared everywhere in all world systems throughout the ten directions, teaching beings and enabling them to progress toward *anuttara-samyak-saṃbodhi*.

Sudhana the Youth then also saw his own body within Samantabhadra's body, teaching beings in all world systems throughout the ten directions. Moreover, Sudhana observed that, if the roots of goodness and light of wisdom he acquired by drawing near to good spiritual guides as numerous as the atoms in a buddha *kṣetra* were compared to the roots of goodness he acquired by seeing Samantabhadra Bodhisattva, they still could not match even a hundredth part of these, a thousandth part of these, a hundred-thousandth part of these, one part in a hundred thousand *koṭīs* of parts of these, or even the tiniest fraction of these deducible by mathematical calculation or describable by analogy.

As Sudhana the Youth walked but one step in those *kṣetras* within Samantabhadra Bodhisattva's pores, he thereby passed through a number of world systems equal to that of all the atoms in an ineffable-ineffable number of buddha *kṣetras*. If he continued to walk in this way until he came to the end of all kalpas of the future, he would still have been unable to discover the bounds of all the phenomena contained in but one pore, including the sequential order of those oceans of *kṣetras*, the matrices of those oceans of *kṣetras*, the differences in those oceans of *kṣetras*, the instances of universal interpenetration in those oceans of *kṣetras*, the formation of those oceans of *kṣetras*, the destruction of those oceans of *kṣetras*, or the adornments of those oceans of *kṣetras*.

In some cases, while within the *kṣetras* in Samantabhadra Bodhisattva's pores, Sudhana the Youth would pass through one kalpa within one *kṣetra* and then, continuing to travel along in this way, he might even pass through kalpas as numerous as the atoms in an ineffable-ineffable number of buddha *kṣetras*. Though he continued to travel along in this way, he still did not disappear from this *kṣetra* and then appear in that *kṣetra*. As in each successive mind-moment he went everywhere throughout an ocean of boundlessly many kalpas, he taught beings and caused them to progress toward *anuttara-samyak-saṃbodhi*.

It was at this time that Sudhana the Youth then gradually acquired the ocean of all practices and vows of Samantabhadra Bodhisattva-*mahāsattva* to a degree [bound before long to] equal that of Samantabhadra himself.

Samantabhadra Bodhisattva-*mahāsattva* then spoke the following verses for all the bodhisattvas:

You should all rid yourselves of the afflictions' defilements
and listen closely and single-mindedly, without distraction,
as I speak about the perfections that the Tathāgata possesses
and the genuine path leading to all the liberations.

As for that supreme world-transcending trainer of beings,
his mind is as pure as empty space.
He forever emanates the brilliant light of the sun of wisdom and
everywhere causes the many beings to dispel the darkness of delusion.

The Tathāgata is one who is difficult to ever see or hear,
yet, after countless *koṭīs* of kalpas, now one encounters him.
This is like the *uḍumbara* blossom's appearing but once in an eon.
Therefore, you should listen to this account of the Buddha's qualities.

He adapts to everything those in the world do,
and, like a master conjurer, manifests the many kinds of actions,
doing so solely to please the minds of beings,
this even as he never discriminates or produces any thoughts.

Samantabhadra Bodhisattva, completely adorned with meritorious qualities and wisdom and like a lotus flower in his freedom from the three realms' defilements, then spoke to those bodhisattvas, saying, "You should all listen closely, for I now wish to describe the characteristics of but a single drop of the Buddha's ocean of meritorious qualities." He then spoke a series of ninety-five verses in which he described and praised the realms of practice, skillful means, and perfection of all bodhisattvas and buddhas in liberating countless beings in all worlds throughout the ten directions throughout all three periods of time.

Chapter 39 Conclusion

The Conduct and Vows of Samantabhadra

In this conclusion to the last chapter of the Flower Adornment Sutra as found in the Gaṇḍavyūhā translation by Tripiṭaka Master Prajñā, Samantabhadra Bodhisattva had just finished praising the supreme qualities of the Tathāgata when he then spoke to Sudhana, saying:

Son of Good Family, if all buddhas of the ten directions were to continuously expound on the meritorious qualities of the Tathāgata, doing so for kalpas as numerous as the atoms in an ineffable-ineffable number of buddha *kṣetras,* they would still be unable to come to the end of them. If one wishes to perfect these gateways to the meritorious qualities, then one should cultivate ten kinds of vast practices and vows. What then are those ten? They are as follows:

The first is to revere all buddhas;
The second is to proclaim the praises of the Tathāgata;
The third is to extensively cultivate the making of offerings;
The fourth is to repent of karmic obstacles;
The fifth is to rejoice in others' merit;
The sixth is to request the turning of the Dharma wheel;
The seventh is to request the buddhas to remain in the world;
The eighth is to always follow the buddhas' course of training;
The ninth is to constantly accord with beings; and
The tenth is to universally dedicate all merit.

Sudhana then asked Samantabhadra, "O Great Ārya, what is meant by 'revering all buddhas' and so forth, up to and including 'universally dedicating all merit'"?

Samantabhadra replied to Sudhana, saying: "Son of Good Family, as for what is meant by 'revering all buddhas,' through the power of Samantabhadra's practices and vows, I arouse deeply resolute faith in all the buddhas, all the *bhagavats,* as numerous as the atoms in all buddha *kṣetras* of the ten directions and three periods of time throughout the Dharma realm and the realms of space, and then, as if they were right before my very eyes, with pure actions of body, speech, and mind, I always cultivate bowing down in reverence to them all.

Manifesting before every one of those buddhas' bodies as numerous as the atoms in an ineffable-ineffable number of buddha *kṣetras,* with each of those bodies, I shall everywhere bow down in reverence to buddhas as numerous as the atoms in an ineffable-ineffable number of buddha *kṣetras.*

Only when the realms of space come to an end will my bowing in reverence to them then come to an end. However, because the realms of space can never end, my bowing in reverence to them has no end.

I shall continue in this way until the realms of beings come to an end, until beings' karmic actions come to an end, and until beings' afflictions come to an end. Only then will my bowing in reverence to them come to an end. However, because the realms of beings and so forth up to and including their afflictions are all endless, my bowing down in reverence to them will have no end. It continues on in each successive mind-moment, without interruption, free of any weariness in the actions of body, speech, or mind."

Samantabhadra continued, saying of the second of his vows, "Again, Son of Good Family, as for what is meant by 'proclaiming the praises of the Tathāgata,' in every one of the atoms throughout all buddha *kṣetras* of the ten directions and the three periods of time to the very end of the Dharma realm and the realms of space, there are buddhas as numerous as the atoms in all worlds. In every place where there are buddhas, they are all surrounded by an oceanic congregation of bodhisattvas. With extremely deep conviction and directly manifest knowledge and vision, in the presence of each of them, I shall bring forth faculties of the tongue surpassing even those of the Goddess Sarasvatī's marvelous tongue. Each one of those tongues shall send forth an inexhaustible ocean of voices and each one of those voices shall send forth an ocean of all words and phrases proclaiming the praises of all *tathāgatas'* oceans of meritorious qualities."

Next, speaking of the third of his vows, Samantabhadra said, "Again, Son of Good Family, as for what is meant by 'extensively cultivating the making of offerings,' in each of the atoms throughout all buddha *kṣetras* of the ten directions and three periods of time to the very end of the Dharma realm and realms of space, there are buddhas as numerous as the atoms in all worlds. In every place where there are buddhas, they are surrounded by an oceanic congregation of many different kinds of bodhisattvas. Through the power of the practices and vows of Samantabhadra, I arouse deep resolute faith and directly manifest knowledge and vision with which I make offerings to all of them of supremely marvelous offering gifts, namely flower clouds, garland clouds, heavenly music clouds, heavenly canopy clouds, heavenly apparel clouds, and clouds of various kinds of heavenly scents, including perfumes, burning incenses, and powdered incenses with each of the clouds such as these being the size of Sumeru, the king of mountains.

Son of Good Family, among all the kinds of offerings, the offering of Dharma is supreme, including for instance the offering of cultivating in accordance with what was taught, the offering of benefiting beings, the offering of gathering in beings, the offering of substituting for beings in taking on their sufferings, the offering of diligently cultivating roots of goodness, the offering of never forsaking the bodhisattva's works, and the offering of never abandoning the bodhi resolve."

Speaking of the fourth of his vows, Samantabhadra said, "Again, Son of Good Family, as for what is meant by 'repenting of karmic obstacles,' the bodhisattva thinks to himself, "Throughout the beginningless kalpas of the past, due to greed, hatred, and delusion manifesting in body, speech, and mind, I have committed measurelessly and boundlessly many bad karmic actions. If these bad karmic actions had substance and signs, even all the realms of space would be unable to contain them. Now, with purity in the three types of karmic actions, directly before all buddhas and bodhisattva congregations everywhere in all *kṣetras* as numerous as the atoms in the entire Dharma realm, I sincerely repent [of these bad karmic actions], resolving to never commit them again and resolving to always abide in all the meritorious qualities of the pure moral precepts."

Next, with regard to the fifth of his vows, Samantabhadra said, "Again, Son of Good Family, as for what is meant by 'rejoicing in others' merit,' this refers to [the merit created by] all buddhas, the *tathāgatas*, throughout the Dharma realm and the realms of space who are as numerous as the atoms in all buddha *kṣetras* in the ten directions and three periods of time. From the time when they first aroused the resolve to attain all-knowledge, they diligently cultivated a mass of merit, never stinting in sacrificing their own bodies and lives, doing so for kalpas as numerous as the atoms in an ineffable-ineffable number of buddha *kṣetras*. During every one of those kalpas, they sacrificed heads, eyes, hands, and feet as numerous as the atoms in an ineffable-ineffable number of buddha *kṣetras* as they practiced all the difficult-to-practice austerities such as these, perfected the many different kinds of *pāramitā* gateways, realized and entered the many different kinds of bodhisattva wisdom grounds, perfected the unexcelled bodhi of all buddhas, and then reached *parinirvāṇa* after which their *śarīra* relics were distributed. I rejoice in all their roots of goodness and rejoice as well in all the merit produced by all the different kinds of beings of the six rebirth destinies and the four types of birth in all worlds of the ten directions, doing so even where their merit is only as small as a mote of dust."

Speaking of the sixth of his vows, Samantabhadra said, "Again, Son of Good Family, as for what is meant by 'requesting the turning of the Dharma wheel,' in every one of the atoms throughout all buddha *kṣetras* of the ten directions and three periods of time to the very end of the Dharma realm and realms of space, there are vast buddha *kṣetras* as numerous as the atoms in an ineffable-ineffable number of buddha *kṣetras*. In every one of those *kṣetras*, there are all those buddhas as numerous as the atoms in an ineffable-ineffable number of buddha *kṣetras* who, in each successive mind-moment, are attaining the universal and right enlightenment surrounded by an oceanic congregation of all bodhisattvas. In all of them, using many different kinds of skillful means in the actions of body, speech, and mind, I earnestly request them to turn the wheel of the sublime Dharma."

Next, with regard to the seventh of his vows, Samantabhadra said, "Again, Son of Good Family, as for what is meant by 'requesting the buddhas to remain in the world,' whenever anywhere to the very end of the Dharma realm and the realms of space throughout the ten directions and three periods of time, there are any of the buddhas, the *tathāgatas*, as numerous as the atoms in all buddha *kṣetras* who are about to enter *parinirvāṇa*, including any such bodhisattvas, *śrāvaka* disciples, *pratyekabuddhas*, those in training, those beyond training, and all good spiritual guides, I then beseech them all to refrain from entering *nirvāṇa* and to remain for kalpas as numerous as the atoms in all buddha *kṣetras*, doing so in order to benefit and gladden all beings."

Speaking of the eighth of his vows, Samantabhadra said, "Again, Son of Good Family, as for what is meant by 'always following the buddhas' course of training,' this refers to [the practices of] those such as this Sahā World's Vairocana Tathāgata who, from the time when he first resolved [to attain bodhi], continued with nonretreating vigor to make gifts of an ineffable-ineffable number of his bodies and lives, peeling off his own skin to serve as paper, breaking his own bones to serve as pens, and drawing his own blood to serve as ink, doing so in order to write out copies of the scriptures that, if gathered together, would reach as high as Mount Sumeru. Because of his profound esteem for the Dharma, he was never stinting even in sacrificing his own bodies and lives, how much the less in sacrificing the royal throne, cities, towns, and villages, palaces, parks, and groves, or all of his other possessions. He also practiced many other different kinds of difficult-to-practice austerities until finally, beneath the tree, he attained the great bodhi, displayed the many different kinds of spiritual superknowledges, manifested many different kinds of spiritual transformations, manifested many different kinds of buddha bodies, and dwelt in many different kinds of congregations. I follow all such ways of training as these. And just as I do so with respect to the *bhagavat* of this present era, Vairocana, so too do I also follow in this manner in each successive mind-moment the training of all the *tathāgatas* in all the atoms in all the buddha *kṣetras* to the very end of the Dharma realm and the realms of space everywhere throughout the ten directions and the three periods of time."

Next with regard to the ninth of his vows, Samantabhadra said, "Again, Son of Good Family, as for what is meant by 'constantly according with beings,' this refers to [according with] all the many different kinds of beings in the oceans of *kṣetras* throughout the ten directions of the Dharma realm and the realms of space, including those who are egg-born, womb-born, moisture-born, or transformationally-born, those who are born in and live in reliance on earth, water, fire, or wind, and those who are born in and live in reliance on the air or the plants and trees. These include the many different kinds of sentient beings with their various physical bodies, their various forms, their various appearances, their various lifespans, their various species, their various names, their various mental natures, their various kinds of knowledge and vision, their various aspirations, their various volitions, their various kinds of behavior, their various kinds of clothing, and their various kinds of food and drink, including those who dwell in many different kinds of settlements, villages, cities, towns, or palaces, and including even all the devas, dragons, and others among the eight kinds of spiritual beings as well as humans, non-humans, and so forth, including those without feet, those with two feet, four feet, or many feet, those with physical forms, those without physical forms, those with perception, those without perception, and those with neither perception nor non-perception. I accord with all the different kinds of beings such as these by transforming my appearance in a manner that is appropriate to them. I then serve them in many different ways and present them with many different kinds of offerings, just the same as and no differently than if I was revering my parents or serving teachers, elders, arhats, or others up to and including the Tathāgata."

Finally, speaking of the tenth of his vows, Samantabhadra said, "Again, Son of Good Family, as for what is meant by 'universally dedicating all merit,' this refers to dedicating all the merit produced by all these vows, from the first, 'revering all buddhas,' up to and including 'constantly according with beings,' dedicating it to all beings throughout the Dharma realms and the realms of space, wishing thereby to enable beings to always gain peace and happiness and remain free of the sufferings of sickness, wishing that, whenever they want to practice evil dharmas, they will not succeed, wishing that the good karmic actions they cultivate will swiftly succeed, wishing that the gates to the wretched rebirth destinies will become closed to them, wishing that the right road leading to human rebirth, deva rebirth, and nirvāṇa will be revealed to them, wishing that, wherever beings bring on themselves extremely severe sufferings due to having accumulated all kinds of bad karma, I may then substitute for them in experiencing those sufferings, and wishing thereby to enable all those beings to attain liberation and ultimately realize unexcelled bodhi."

Concluding his explanation of his conduct and vows, Samantabhadra said, "Son of Good Family, this is what constitutes the complete fulfillment of the bodhisattva-*mahāsattva*'s ten kinds of great vows. If bodhisattvas accord with and enter into these great vows, then they are able to ripen all beings, they are able to accord with *anuttarā-samyak-saṃbodhi,* and they are able to completely fulfill Samantabhadra Bodhisattva's ocean of practices and vows. Therefore, Son of Good Family, you should understand the meaning of these in this way."

Later, Samantabhadra said, "Therefore, if there is any person who recites these vows, wherever he goes in the world, he becomes as unimpeded as the moon in space escaping from a veil of clouds. He is one who is praised by all buddhas and bodhisattvas, one who should be revered by all humans and devas, and one to whom all beings should make offerings.

Such a son of good family as this becomes well able to acquire rebirths in a human body in which he fulfills all the meritorious qualities of Samantabhadra. Before long, like Samantabhadra Bodhisattva, he will succeed in swiftly perfecting a marvelous form body replete with the thirty-two marks of a great man. Wherever he is born among humans or devas, he will always reside in a superior clan. He will be able to do away with all rebirths in any of the wretched destinies, will be able to separate from all bad friends, will be able to subdue all adherents of non-Buddhist paths, and will be able to gain liberation from all afflictions. In this, he is like the king of lions who overwhelmingly defeats the many other kinds of beasts. He is one who is worthy to receive the offerings of all beings.

Moreover, when this person draws near to the end of his life and reaches that very last *kṣaṇa* in which all his faculties fade, in which all of his relatives and retinue leave him, in which all his awesome power disappears, and in which none of his ministers, great officials, palaces, cities, inner and outer palace possessions, elephants, horses, carriages, precious jewels, or treasuries follow along with him, it is only these kings of vows that do not abandon him. They always lead him forth so that, in but a single *kṣaṇa*, he is immediately reborn in the Land of Ultimate Bliss. Having arrived there, he immediately sees Amitābha Buddha surrounded by Mañjuśrī Bodhisattva, Samantabhadra Bodhisattva, Avalokiteśvara Bodhisattva, Maitreya Bodhisattva, and other bodhisattvas, all of whom are possessed of the majestic physical marks and are replete with the meritorious qualities.

This person then sees himself born in a lotus flower, receiving the Buddha's bestowal of his prediction. Having received that prediction, he then passes through countless hundreds of thousands of myriads of *koṭīs* of *nayutas* of kalpas during which, in an ineffable-ineffable number of worlds throughout the ten directions, he uses the power of wisdom to adapt to beings' minds and thereby benefit them. Before long, he will sit at a site of enlightenment, vanquish the armies of Māra, attain the universal and right enlightenment, and turn the wheel of the sublime Dharma. He will then be able to cause beings in worlds as numerous as the atoms in a buddha *kṣetra* to arouse the resolve to attain bodhi. Adapting to their faculties and natures, he will teach and ripen them until, having exhausted an ocean of future kalpas, he will have been able to extensively benefit all beings."

Samantabhadra Bodhisattva then concluded his teaching on the conduct and vows of Samantabhadra with a series of sixty-two verses summarizing and expanding upon the teachings presented earlier in the body of the text.

At that time, after, in the presence of the Tathāgata, Samantabhadra Bodhisattva-*mahāsattva* had finished speaking these pure verses on Samantabhadra's vast kings of vows, the youth Sudhana was filled with measureless exultation and all the bodhisattvas felt great joy. The Tathāgata then praised him, saying, "This is good indeed, good indeed."

At that time when the Bhagavat together with the *ārya* bodhisattva-*mahāsattvas* expounded on such supreme Dharma gateways of the inconceivable realm of liberation, they were headed by Mañjuśrī Bodhisattva. The great bodhisattvas and the six thousand bhikshus whose practice had become fully developed were headed by Maitreya Bodhisattva. All the great bodhisattvas of the Worthy Kalpa were headed by the Immaculate One, Samantabhadra Bodhisattva. [Present too were] the great bodhisattvas at the consecration stage with but one more birth [before buddhahood] as well as the congregations of other bodhisattva-*mahāsattvas* who, as numerous as the atoms in the ocean of all *kṣetras,* had all come and assembled there from the many different worlds of the ten directions. The great *śrāvaka* disciples were headed by the greatly wise Śāriputra, Mahāmaudgalyāyana, and others. Together with all the great congregations of world leaders among humans and devas as well as the devas, dragons, *yakṣas, gandharvas, asuras, garuḍas, kiṃnaras, mahoragas,* humans, non-humans, and others, having heard what the Buddha had proclaimed, everyone in that great assembly was filled with immense joy, accepted these teachings with faith, and upheld them in practice.

Kalavinka Buddhist Classics

(http: www.kalavinka.org)

Fall, 2025 Title List

Meditation Instruction Texts

The Essentials of Buddhist Meditation

A marvelously complete classic *śamathā-vipaśyanā* (calming-and-insight) meditation manual. By Tiantai Śramaṇa Zhiyi (538–597 CE).

Six Gates to the Sublime

The early Indian Buddhist meditation method involving six practices used in calming-and-insight meditation. Also by Śramaṇa Zhiyi

Bodhisattva Path Texts

The Flower Adornment Sutra

Bhikshu Dharmamitra's English translation of *The Mahāvaipulya Buddha Avataṃsaka Sūtra* edition translated from Sanskrit in 699 CE by Tripiṭaka Master Śikṣānanda (T0279: 大方廣佛華嚴經)

On Generating the Resolve to Become a Buddha

On the Resolve to Become a Buddha by Ārya Nāgārjuna

Exhortation to Resolve on Buddhahood by Patriarch Sheng'an Shixian

Exhortation to Resolve on Buddhahood by the Tang Literatus, Peixiu

Letter from a Friend - The Three Earliest Editions

The earliest extant editions of Ārya Nāgārjuna's *Suhṛlekkha*:

Translated by Tripiṭaka Master Guṇavarman (*ca* 425 CE)

Translated by Tripiṭaka Master Saṇghavarman (*ca* 450 CE)

Translated by Tripiṭaka Master Yijing (*ca* 675 CE).

Marvelous Stories from the Perfection of Wisdom

130 Stories from Ārya Nāgārjuna's *Mahāprājñāpāramitā Upadeśa.*

Nāgārjuna's Guide to the Bodhisattva Path

The *Bodhisaṃbhāra Treatise* with abridged Vaśitva commentary.

The Bodhisaṃbhāra Treatise Commentary

The complete exegesis by the Indian Bhikshu Vaśitva (*ca* 300–500).

Nāgārjuna on Mindfulness of the Buddha

Ch. 9 and Chs. 20–25 of Nāgārjuna's *Daśabhūmika Vibhāṣā*

Ch. 1, Subchapter 36a of Nāgārjuna's *Mahāprājñāpāramitā Upadeśa.*

Nāgārjuna on the Six Perfections

Ch.1, Subchapters 17–30 of Nāgārjuna's *Mahāprājñāpāramitā Upadeśa.*

A Strand of Dharma Jewels (Ārya Nāgārjuna's *Ratnāvalī*)
The earliest extant edition, translated by Paramārtha: *ca* 550 CE

The Ten Bodhisattva Grounds
Śikṣānanda's translation of The Flower Adornment Sutra, Ch. 26

Nāgārjuna's Treatise on the Ten Bodhisattva Grounds
Nāgārjuna's 35-chapter *Daśabhūmika Vibhāṣā*

The Ten Grounds Sutra
Kumārajīva's translation of the *Daśabhūmika Sūtra*

Vasubandhu's Treatise on the Bodhisattva Vow
By Vasubandhu Bodhisattva (*ca* 300 CE)

Bodhisattva Moral Virtue (Śīla) Texts

The Bodhisattva's Practice of Moral Virtue
Part One: The Brahmā's Net Sutra Bodhisattva Precepts
Part One Supplement: The Semimonthly Bodhisattva Precepts Recitation Ceremony
Part Two: Nāgārjuna on the Perfection of Moral Virtue (from Ārya Nāgārjuna's *Mahāprajñāpāramitā Upadeśa*)

www.ingramcontent.com/pod-product-compliance
Lightning Source LLC
Chambersburg PA
CBHW031128160426
43193CB00008B/67
* 9 7 8 1 9 3 5 4 1 3 5 3 0 *